DICTIONARY OF MEXICAN AMERICAN HISTORY

DICTIONARY OF MEXICAN AMERICAN HISTORY

Matt S. Meier and Feliciano Rivera

GREENWOOD PRESS
Westport, Connecticut • London, England

Library of Congress Cataloging in Publication Data

Meier, Matt S
Dictionary of Mexican American history.

Bibliography: p.
Includes index.

1. Mexican Americans--History--Dictionaries.
I. Rivera, Feliciano, joint author. II. Title.
E184.M5M453 973'.046872 80-24750
ISBN 0-313-21203-1 (lib. bdg.)

Library of Congress Catalog Card Number: 80-24750
ISBN: 0-313-21203-1

First published in 1981

Greenwood Press
A division of Congressional Information Service, Inc.
88 Post Road West
Westport, Connecticut 06881

Printed in the United States of America

10 9 8 7 6 5 4 3 2 1

We dedicate this volume to the memory of Carey McWilliams,
the man who led the way *North from Mexico*.

CONTENTS

PREFACE

This historical dictionary has been organized and written to provide a useful, basic guide for a wide audience, which might include high school and college students, librarians, and scholars. Because the work is a single volume and comprehensive in scope, it treats numerous subjects rather briefly. In many instances, however, entries include information unavailable elsewhere in one source, and many include references for further reading.

The term *history* is used in a broad sense so that the range of items runs from Abelardo, border culture, and Brown Berets to urbanism, Viva Kennedy Clubs, and Emiliano Zapata. Chicano history is represented by a wide variety of entries, including institutions, developments, and organizations, as well as individual actors on the historical stage.

Debate as to when Mexican American history begins still goes on among Mexican Americanists, and in this debate we take a middle position. The chronology in the appendix begins 50,000 years ago, but the *Dictionary* begins, as befits a work about a mestizo people, with La Malinche and Hernán Cortés. In the years between 1519 and 1836 it concentrates on the principal individuals and events that led to the exploration, opening, and development of that area of northern New Spain (Mexico) which we know today as the Southwest—the homeland of the Mexican American. Some historical figures, like La Malinche, Cuauhtémoc, and Moctezuma II, are included because they are seen as culture heroes or villains by Mexican Americans today. The main body of the work covers the period from the Texas revolt against Mexico in 1835, which marked the birth of the "Mexican American," to the beginning of "the decade of the Hispanic" in 1980.

Arrangement of this *Dictionary* is alphabetical, using the word-by-word principle. Sets of initials are listed as if they were words. Phrases normally are listed under the first word of the phrase unless the first word is of lesser importance, in which case the phrase is inverted; for example, Virgin of Guadalupe is listed under Guadalupe, and Treaty of Velasco is listed under Velasco. Entries for organizations are listed under their full names, but those which are commonly referred to by their acronyms (for example, MAPA, CUOM, and MALDEF), are cross-referenced from the initials to the full title. When an organization is known by both its Spanish and English name, it is listed under its English name with suitable cross-reference from the Spanish. The Spanish articles *el*, *la*, *los*, and *las* are usually not used in alphabetizing; however, in a few instances where the article has come to be considered an integral part of the name, as in El Paso and Los Angeles, or is used in an acronym, as in, El Mexicano Preparado, Listo, Educado y Organizado (EMPLEO), the entry is listed under the article. Because of the extensive use of Spanish words, they are not italicized in the body of the work.

Many entries include the suggestion that readers should see or see also a related entry. An implicit suggestion to see also is indicated by an asterisk following a word or phrase. Sometimes the starred phrases are in forms slightly different from the entry. Although entries often relate to each other, we have used the asterisk only when we felt that the cross-reference would appreciably add to the entry in which it appears. At the end of many entries—most of the larger ones—there are suggestions for further reading. These are intended to help readers find more details on the entry should they wish to delve deeper into a specific topic.

The appendices include a chronology, the complete text of the Treaty of Guadalupe Hidalog, the Protocol of Querétaro, a glossary of frequently encountered Chicano terms, an annotated list of the more important Chicano journals, a briefly annotated list of general works, a number of historical maps, and some valuable statistical tables. We hope that the users of the *Dictionary* will find these useful.

For all and any shortcomings in the *Dictionary* we take full and complete responsibility. It is only a starting point; as Arnold Toynbee once suggested, if we were to wait until we were completely satisfied with the work, it would perhaps never see the typesetter. In this pioneering work we are certain to have overlooked some important aspect or item of Chicano history. For any gaps our sincere apologies.

Matt S. Meier
Feliciano Rivera

ACKNOWLEDGMENTS

Our goal has been to make the *Dictionary* accurate, balanced, and comprehensive. In seeking to meet these objectives we asked experts in many fields of Chicano studies to contribute their knowledge. With two principal authors and over thirty other contributors, inevitably there are occasional overlaps and differences of viewpoint. There has been no attempt to follow any single frame of historical interpretation, and the contributors were allowed complete freedom in developing their entries. We believe this helps rather than detracts from the effort. Differences illustrate the diversity and individualism that characterize Chicano culture.

We would like to thank our colleagues who were so generous as to contribute their time and expertise to this work. Many of their articles present a broad survey of topics important to Mexican American history. Their contributions have made the *Dictionary* more useful and valuable.

We also wish to thank Alice Whistler and the other librarians at the University of Santa Clara and librarians at San José State University and other universities in California, New Mexico, Texas, and Arizona who were gracious and tireless in their pursuit of obscure historical fact. In addition, our students over the years have helped us in a variety of ways in developing the *Dictionary*. And finally our special thanks to Linda Campbell who maintained her usual good humor in the face of the trying job of typing, retyping, and again retyping the bulk of the manuscript.

CONTRIBUTORS

Gilda M. Bloom, Stanford University
Y. Arturo Cabrera, San José State University, California
George Coalson, Texas Arts and Industries University
Chris García, University of New Mexico
Mario T. García, University of California, Santa Barbara
Sharon Girard, San Francisco State University
José Angel Gutiérrez, Crystal City, Texas
Abraham Hoffman, Reseda, California
Francisco Jiménez, University of Santa Clara
Oakah Jones, Purdue University
Jorge Klor de Alva, San José State University, California
Clark Knowlton, University of Utah
Manuel Machado, University of Montana
Gerald McKevitt, S.J., University of Santa Clara
Christine N. Marín, Arizona State University
Oscar Martínez, University of Texas at El Paso
Michael C. Meyer, University of Arizona
Richard Nostrand, University of Oklahoma
James Officer, University of Arizona
Raymund A. Paredes, University of California, Los Angeles
Jacinto Quirarte, University of Texas at San Antonio
Francisco Rosales, University of Houston, Texas
Stanley Ross, University of Texas at Austin
John Shockley, Western Illinois University
Antonio Soto, San José State University, California
Ellwyn Stoddard, University of Texas at El Paso
Henry Trueba, San Diego State University, California
Marta Weigle, University of New Mexico

THE DICTIONARY

A

ABELARDO. *See* DELGADO, ABELARDO BARRIENTOS.

ACADEMIA DE LA NUEVA RAZA. Founded in New Mexico in late 1969 as the Academia de Aztlán, the Academia is an institution responding to the confusion and alienation many young Chicanos experience in Anglo society. It argues that Chicano culture as maintained in the barrio (especially the small town barrio) is a viable alternative for young Mexican Americans. By rediscovering the culture and philosophy of the barrio, mainly through oral history projects with old barrio members, and by reflecting on, analyzing, and organizing this lore, the members of the Academia feel a body of knowledge can be developed to supplant the Anglo view of Mexican American culture. This knowledge, which the Academia diffuses through a journal and newsletters, may help Chicanos achieve greater cultural awareness. With its emphasis on the philosophical and literary rather than the political, the Academia has had only a limited following.

ACCPE. *See* AMERICAN COORDINATING COUNCIL OF POLITICAL EDUCATION.

ACCULTURATION, also called cultural assimilation or culture contact. The process by which members of one ethnic group adapt to the cultural patterns of another ethnic group, occurring where cultural systems are significantly diverse. Acculturation is also a process of social change arising from necessity or force and tends to be a gradual process rather than an abrupt one. Although cultural changes produced by the influence of another culture may be reciprocal, history indicates the phenomenon is overwhelmingly one way.

The rate and degree to which Mexican Americans acculturate varies widely and is affected by the following factors: whether they are native or foreign born, their degree of isolation and segregation, their educational level and achievement, their degree of English language dominance, and their type of employment.

Adoption of Anglo American cultural patterns by Mexican Americans is voluntary and is an individual action. They acculturate mainly for personal reasons, usually consistent with individual goals and aspirations.

FURTHER READING: Alan R. Beals et al., *Culture in Process*, New York: Holt Rinehart and Winston, Inc., 1967; A. L. Kroeber, *Anthropology*, New York: Harcourt, Brace and Co., 1948; Edward H. Spicer and Raymond H. Thompson eds., *Plural Society in the Southwest*, New York: Interbook, Inc., 1972.

G.M.B.

ACTIVE MEXICANOS (AM), founded in 1969 originally as a private social club in Seattle, Washington, is a nonprofit community organization that provides a wide variety of public services, from job placement to legal assistance, through federally funded programs.

ACUÑA, RODOLFO (1932-), author, critic, university professor, and political activist. Born and raised in Los Angeles, Acuña has been involved in the Chicano Movement* and community organizations and associated with the development of Chicano studies since the fall of 1966, when he taught a course at Mount Saint Mary's College in Los Angeles on the history of the Mexican American. Following his belief that an academic-activist approach to Chicano history and culture was a necessity, he founded the department of Chicano Studies at California State University at Northridge.

Acuña received his Ph.D. in Latin American History at the University of Southern California in 1967. He has authored four books and numerous articles on Mexican Americans. Presently he is Professor of Chicano Studies at California State University at Northridge. He is perhaps best known for *Occupied America: The Chicano's Struggle Toward Liberation* (1972) in which he explains the Mexican American experience within a framework of internal colonialism. A revised edition titled *Occupied America: A History of Chicanos* (1981) abandons the internal colonial model.

ADOBE, a clay from which sun-dried bricks are made. The clay is sometimes mixed with straw and used extensively for construction of buildings and walls in the low-rainfall Southwest where it was introduced by the early Spanish-Mexican settlers.

AGABACHADO. A Mexican American who is judged pro-Anglo but is not seen as a vendido* (one who has sold out La Raza). The term is derived from gabacho.*

AGRICULTURAL LABOR, SOUTHWESTERN, during the Spanish and Mexican eras in Mexico's northern frontier area consisted principally of local Indians and immigrants from central Mexico. In an essentially subsistence economy (except in the California missions), these sources of labor were sufficient to herd livestock, to cultivate orchards and gardens, and to raise corn and wheat. In the last quarter of the nineteenth century, after the United States takeover, this subsistence economy began to be replaced by a market economy of seasonal crops which required large numbers of workers for short time periods. The change took place first in California, where Chinese became available after the completion of the Central Pacific Railroad in 1869 and dominated the agricultural labor market until passage of the Chinese Exclusion Act in 1882. Then Japanese workers replaced the Chinese, although they quickly fell out of favor because of their interest in buying farm property of their own. The Gentlemen's Agreement of 1907, by which Japan consented to limit emigration of the coolie class, ended this source of labor and was followed by the use of Filipino and East Indian labor.

Before 1900 most agricultural labor in Texas and New Mexico was done by the farmer and his family, with only occasional outside help. However, toward the end of the last century expansion of cotton acreage, mechanization of much field preparation, and the beginning of vegetable, citrus, and other fruit production in the lower Rio Grande Valley* began to create an increasing demand for harvest workers. In Texas blacks at first supplied much of this labor, but by the 1890s Mexican nationals were regularly crossing the Rio Grande to follow the cotton harvest from Texas up into Arkansas.

The tripling of the amount of land under cultivation in the West between 1870 and 1900 created additional pressures for seasonal farm labor that were filled largely by Mexican American and Mexican workers. At the beginning of the twentieth century, completion of the Roosevelt and Elephant Butte dams led to further commercial agricultural expansion and a need for still more workers. This need in turn led to the establishment of labor colonias,* where agricultural workers were persuaded to winter over rather than return to the border areas or Mexico. After 1910 agricultural employers began to rely on the heavy influx of Mexican nationals for harvest labor.

Between 1900 and the thirties nearly half of the nation's fruit and truck garden crops were produced by a labor force that was at least two-thirds Mexican American and Mexican, mostly in California. In addition, this new work force was extremely important in such commercial crops as sugar beets and cotton. During World War I thousands of acres were converted from other crops to cotton as demand soared, and tenant farmers and sharecroppers were increasingly replaced with migrant Mexican emigrés and Mexican Americans, especially in Texas. In California growers began to seek Mexican workers for agriculture only when cotton culture hit the Imperial Valley* in the teens. By 1917 both Arizona cotton growers and the Colorado beet sugar industry were recruiting workers in Mexico, which had become the major agricultural labor source. The decade of the 1920s witnessed recruitment of thousands of Mexican nationals as agriculture boomed along with the rest of the economy; in California and the rest of the Southwest, Mexican and Mexican American agricultural labor was fundamental to the rapid development of commercial crops.

Then, in the 1930s, tens of thousands of Mexicans were repatriated as farm prices collapsed, crop surpluses glutted the market, and jobs disappeared. Displaced farm labor from Oklahoma and Arkansas replaced Mexican Americans in large numbers until the economy began recovering in the late 1930s. When World War II directly involved the United States after Pearl Harbor (1941), demand for agricultural labor led to the Bracero Program* by which thousands of Mexican workers were brought to western fields. At the end of the war the practice of importing large numbers of agricultural workers continued on a less formal basis, and the outbreak of the Korean conflict led to a renewal of the earlier government-to-government arrangements for bracero labor. Between 1950 and the end of the bracero legislation in 1964, approximately four and one half million Mexicans were brought in to help harvest America's crops. In the peak years between 1955 and 1959, an average 430,000 braceros were imported annually. By 1960 increasing mechanization* of important crops had begun to reduce the demand for harvest labor.

Since its post-World War II highs, the migrant labor force has declined considerably, but its numbers are difficult to ascertain due to the large percentage of undocumented* workers. The announcement in December 1979 by Secretary of Agriculture Robert Bergland that no more Department of Agriculture funds would be allocated to research on farm mechanization may mean a halt to this downward trend and a stabilizing of the farm labor force.

Acceleration of farm mechanization in the forties and the Bracero Program caused many Mexican Americans to turn from agriculture to more stable employment in industrial and service fields. Today less than 15 percent of the Mexican American work force is employed in agriculture, having been displaced by further mechanization and the use of commuter and undocumented Mexican labor.

FURTHER READING: Stuart Jamieson, *Labor Unionism in American Agriculture*, Washington, D.C.: U.S. Government Printing Office, 1945, reprint, 1976; Dick Meister and Ann Loftis, *A Long Time Coming: The Struggle to Unionize America's Farm Workers*, N.Y.: Macmillan, 1977; George O. Coalson, *The Development of the Migratory Farm Labor System in Texas, 1900-1954*, San Francisco: R & E Research Associates, 1977; Ernesto Galarza, *Farm Workers and Agri-business in California, 1947-1960*, Notre Dame, Indiana: University of Notre Dame Press, 1977.

AGRICULTURAL WORKERS FREEDOM TO WORK ASSOCIATION (California), a farm group organized in mid-1968 at Bakersfield, California, during the United Farm Workers'* strike against Giumarra Vineyards. Its chief officers were Mexican Americans (Gilberto Rubio was its first president), and it was organized with the help of some of the San Joaquin Valley grape growers. Officials of the association traveled to a number of larger cities in the United States speaking against the United Farm Workers' grape boycott and for right-to-work legislation.

AGRICULTURE, SOUTHWESTERN, begun before the time of Christ with the expansion of a corn-bean-squash culture from central Mexico to southern Arizona and later to the Pueblo groups of the upper Rio Grande Valley* and the Yuma and Mohave Indians on the lower Colorado River. To this base the Spaniards, and particularly missionaries, added wheat, barley, various beans and other vegetables, olives, grapes, apples, citrus, and other fruits and nuts. Cattle, sheep, hogs, horses, and mules were also introduced; sheep becoming especially important in the New Mexican economy by the late 1700s, and cattle forming the backbone of the California rancho* economy after the secularization and breakup of the missions* there in 1833.

The California gold rush created a tremendous demand for all kinds of foodstuffs. As a result, grain cultivation and cattle raising rapidly expanded. During the 1860s the Civil War interruption of transcontinental trade led to the planting of cotton and tobacco for local consumption. Citrus groves began to be planted in post-Civil War California and wine grape cultivation was both expanded and improved. Severe droughts in the 1860s and reduction of rangelands ended the premier position of her cattle industry, but sheep raising was less seriously affected by the dry years. Many rancho owners sold their lands in small lots, and truck gardening rapidly increased. The development of irrigation in the San Joaquin Valley opened up a vast new area to agriculture. By 1900 California was producing a wide variety of fruits and vegetables in commercial quantities. Especially notable were wine grapes, citrus, fruits, raisins, sugar beets, and melons.

In New Mexico subsistence farming and sheep raising continued to dominate agriculture after the Treaty of Guadalupe Hidalgo.* Although Indian difficulties, especially Apache raids, discouraged agricultural expansion, sheep raising increased rapidly, especially after the Civil War. With the end of Indian harassment and the arrival of railroads in the end of 1880s, Anglo farmers began moving into the eastern New Mexico grasslands, and by the end of the century dry-farming techniques were being used there. Along the upper Rio Grande and its tributaries Nuevo Mexicanos* continued their separate, subsistence village agriculture.

Since the 1820s Texas agriculture had been a mix of subsistence and market crops, with cotton dominating the market crops. In the aftermath of the Civil War a boom developed in both cattle raising and sheepherding but subsided after the mid-1880s, when an agricultural revolution began. As both the range cattle industry and border difficulties declined, cotton culture expanded rapidly, based on a steady stream of migrant Mexican labor which replaced earlier black tenant farmers. With improved transportation and dietary changes the end of the century saw the beginnings of truck gardening in the heavily Mexican lower Rio Grande Valley.

During the early part of the twentieth century changes that were just beginning to be seen at the end of the nineteenth century rapidly accelerated southwestern agriculture. One of the principal elements in this expansion was the widespread development of dams and irrigation systems from Texas to California. In the latter state new agricultural techniques opened up the Sacramento, San Joaquin, Imperial, and Coachella valleys to the raising of fruits, nuts, grapes, sugar beets, lettuce, tomatoes, and cotton on large-scale commercial farms.

After World War II a movement toward mechanization of agriculture developed, especially in the cotton and sugar beet industries. A drive to create farm labor unions gave added impetus to mechanization. By 1950 nearly 90 percent of the sugar beet crop and 20 percent of the cotton crop were machine-harvested. In turn, the economies of mechanization led to the considerable growth of large-scale farming, Carey McWilliams's "factories in the fields," and to a corresponding decline of so-called family farming.

Similar agricultural patterns were developing in Arizona, New Mexico, and Texas. In the Salt River Valley of Arizona irrigation opened vast areas to cotton, and later lettuce became an important crop. In the upper Rio Grande Valley in New Mexico the construction of Elephant Butte Dame paved the way for cotton expansion, and in the lower Rio Grande winter garden area of Texas irrigation led to domination by truck-garden crops. In all these areas Mexican Americans and Mexicans, provided the labor foundation on which rapid expansion was based.

Post-World War II agriculture has been much more important to California than to the other states of the Southwest. For example in New Mexico farm income in 1970 amounted to $460 million; in California, on the other hand, it reached $4,456 million. In California over 200 crops were being harvested on 36.8 million acres, making California the number one farming state. This development was possible, in large part, because of the availability of abundant cheap labor—mostly Mexican American and Mexican.

FURTHER READING: Claude B. Hutchinson, ed., *California Agriculture*, Berkeley: University of California, 1946.

AGRINGADO, progringo, pro-Anglo. A pejorative term for a Mexican or Mexican American who is viewed as being too favorably disposed toward Anglos or as having adopted (excessively) Anglo ways, attitudes, or ideas.

LAS ÁGUILAS NEGRAS, (The Black Eagles), a secret society founded in the midnineteenth century by Juan (Cheno) Cortina* to inform himself about his enemies along both sides of the Texas-Mexican border. Members, dressed in black hoods and robes, sometimes used their appearance as a scare tactic to frighten Cortina's opponents.

Also the name of a society in Cuernavaca, Morelos (Mexico), between 1900 and 1905. A patriotic and social organization, it endeavored to promote study of the Nahuatl language.

ALAMBRISTA, from alambre (wire), a fence climber, an illegal entrant into the United States from Mexico. *See* UNDOCUMENTED.

ALAMO, a later name for the mission of San Antonio Valero founded in May 1718 on the banks of the San Antonio River in south-central Texas by Spanish Franciscan missionaries. From the very beginning it flourished in terms of both its Indian population and its agriculture and cattle raising. Abandoned as a mission in 1793, its chapel seems to have been given the name Alamo by troops from San José y Santiago del Alamo de Parras in Chihuahua who were stationed there at the beginning of the nineteenth century. In 1813 the forces of the revolutionary, Bernardo Gutiérrez de Lara,* briefly occupied the Alamo but soon found it necessary to withdraw before Spanish loyalist attack.

During his efforts to suppress the Texas revolt against Mexican centralism in 1835, the Mexican general, Martín Perfecto de Cos,* was forced to surrender the Alamo and his army to Texas forces. In February of the following year a Texas troop of about 180 men, including 9 Tejanos,* under Colonel William Travis established itself at the Alamo. Armed with twenty-one cannons and under the flag of the 1824 federal Mexican republic, this group prepared to repel attacks from a Mexican-centralist army of about three thousand ill-trained conscripts led by President Antonio López de Santa Anna.* Refusing to surrender, the hard-pressed defenders of the Alamo resisted repeated attacks for two weeks and finally sent Captain Juan Seguín* through the enemy lines for help. Santa Anna, signaling a policy of no quarter to the defenders in the Alamo, began the final assault early on March 6, 1836, and, despite heavy losses (over four hundred), the Mexican forces ultimately carried the day because of their numbers. Most of the defenders of the Alamo were killed in the fighting, and those who surrendered were executed at Santa Anna's orders. As a result of this execution "Remember the Alamo" became a rallying cry for the Texas forces during the rest of the war, although militarily the building itself was quite unimportant.

In 1883 the state of Texas purchased the Alamo chapel from the Catholic church, and in 1905 the state bought the convent, scene of the siege of the

Alamo, and turned it over to the Daughters of the Republic of Texas as a historical site. The convent, the historically important part of the Alamo, was saved from razing largely through the efforts of Adina de Zavala,* who argued against the mistaken belief that it dated from after the siege. *See also* TEXAS REVOLT.

FURTHER READING: Walter Lord, *A Time to Stand*, New York: Harpers, 1961; Thomas L. Miller, "Mexican Texans in the Texas Revolution," *Journal of Mexican American History* 3 (1973): 105-130.

ALBUQUERQUE WALKOUT (1966), an important incident of the incipient Chicano movement. Early in 1966 fifty Chicano leaders made a dramatic exit from an Equal Employment Opportunity conference in Albuquerque alleging La Raza* needs were not being considered. They demanded that the Lyndon Johnson administration hold a White House conference on Mexican American problems. As a result, in May President Johnson met with a group of prominent Chicano leaders and a conference was set up in El Paso. Shortly before the conference César Chávez,* Corky Gonzales,* and Bert Corona* announced they would boycott the meeting because of its format and guidelines. Although this move did not result in a generaly boycott, it did lead to the organizing of a counter conference in El Paso's south barrio called La Raza Unida Conference,* which brought together for the first time many Chicano youth and student groups.

ALEMANY, JOSÉ SADOC (1814-1888), bishop and archbishop. A Catalan, Alemany entered the Dominican Order in Spain, completed his religious studies in Italy, and came to the United States in 1840. When the Mexican-U.S. War* ended he was named first bishop of the diocese of Monterey, California, with jurisdiction over Alta and Baja California. In 1853 he became the first archbishop of the new diocese of San Francisco, which included all of the new state of California. During his thirty years as archbishop he ably kept up with the rapid growth of the area and was successful in regaining church title to some mission property. At the end of 1884 he resigned and returned to Spain where he died a few years later.

ALIANCISTA, a member or supporter of the Alianza Federal de Pueblos Libres*.

ALIANZA FEDERAL DE MERCEDES. *See* ALIANZA FEDERAL DE PUEBLOS LIBRES.

ALIANZA FEDERAL DE PUEBLOS LIBRES (Federal Alliance of Free Towns). Formerly known as the Alianza Federal de Mercedes (The Federal

Alliance of Grants), the Alianza was founded by Reies López Tijerina* and a group of followers early in 1963 to implement his ideas about Spanish and Mexican land grants in New Mexico. In September 1963 people representing about fifty New Mexican grants held a meeting and drew up a constitution which then led to incorporation in New Mexico. Headquarters were established in Albuquerque.

The organization's ultimate goal was to regain for Nuevo Mexicanos the land grants* (especially pueblo* grants) given to them by Spain and Mexico —a goal with considerable appeal to the conservative rural poor of the Rio Arriba area of northwestern New Mexico and to young Chicano activists as well. Alleging that the problems of Mexican Americans derive from the loss of these lands, the Alianza argues that their recovery is basic to any improvement of the social and economic position of La Raza.*

In 1963 and 1964 Tijerina sought financial and political support for the Alianza among politicians and liberal groups, but he got little more than verbal expressions of support. The Alianza grew slowly in its first two years, but in the following year received an influx of small ranchers and farmers who joined largely because their use of national forest lands for grazing had been reduced. By 1965 the Alianza claimed a membership of twenty thousand, but the press claimed that the figure was closer to three thousand. Meanwhile the Alianza initiated a legal action fund and hired lawyers to process the land claims of its members. A series of public acts by Alianza members (for example, a march from Albuquerque to Santa Fe in July 1966 and the takeover of Echo Amphitheater in Kit Carson National Forest in October) focused public attention on the Alianza but in the process created much antagonism. Early in 1967 vandalism and arson attributed to Aliancistas (Alianza members) created further feelings of ill-will. In May, District Attorney Alfonso Sánchez got a federal court order demanding a list of Alianza members; Tijerina then resigned as head of the Alianza and disbanded the organization. A few days later he organized the Alianza de Pueblos Libres.

A June 3, 1967, meeting of the Alianza was broken up by Sánchez, and ten Aliancistas were arrested. Two days later the Alianza replied with a raid on the Tierra Amarilla courthouse. The Alianza planned to free its members and make a citizen's arrest of Sánchez. A massive manhunt that followed the raid was aided by helicopters, tanks, and Apache police. Again the Alianza received tremendous publicity—little of it favorable. In subsequent trials Tijerina was found not guilty of federal charges but guilty of state charges arising out of the raid and was sentenced to two years in prison. In October 1969 he resigned as president of the Alianza, partly because of a moderate-radical split in the organization. In January 1970 Tijerina was sentenced concurrently to 1-5 and 2-10 years in prison on charges arising out of the courthouse raid. A condition of his release from prison in 1971 was that he could not hold office in the Alianza. His position of leadership was taken by Santiago Tapia y Anaya. In 1976 when his five-year probation ended, Tijerina returned to the presidency of the Alianza. Meanwhile, under less dynamic leadership, the Alianza had largely limited itself to making statements, publishing pamphlets, and filing lawsuits. Since Tijerina's return to the presidency the Alianza has emphasized the lack of compliance with provisions of the Treaty of Guadalupe Hidalgo* and has tried to enlist the support of Mexican presidents Luis Echeverría and José López Portillo.

FURTHER READING: Patricia B. Blawis, *Tijerina and the Land Grants*, New York: International Publishers Co., 1971; Richard Gardner, *¡ Grito! Reies Tijerina and the New Mexico Land Grant War of 1967*, Indianapolis: Bobbs-Merrill, 1970; Peter Nabokov, *Tijerina and the Courthouse Raid*, Albuquerque: University of New Mexico, 1969; Frances L. Swadesh, "The Alianza Movement of New Mexico, The Interplay of Social Change and Public Commentary," in Henry J. Tobias and Charles E. Woodhouse (eds.), *Minorities and Politics*, Albuquerque: University of New Mexico Press, 1969, pp. 53-84.

ALIANZA HISPANO-AMERICANA, one of the earliest Mexican American "local" organizations, founded in Arizona in 1894 with its headquarters in Tucson. Originally largely mutualist in nature, the Alianza was organized along Masonic lines into lodges with considerable local autonomy. It promoted acculturation and civic virtues and provided low-cost sickness and death benefits as well as social activities for its members. The incorporation of the Alianza in 1907 emphasized the financial aspects of the organization. By 1930 it had spread all over the Southwest with more than ten thousand members in Arizona, California, Colorado, New Mexico, and Texas. During the thirties and forties the Alianza's conservative leadership was more involved with internal problems than with problems of La Raza.*

In the post-World War II period the Alianza developed a concern for civil liberties and the quality of education and of justice meted out to Mexican Americans. In 1955, after a number of legal victories, it organized a civil rights department headed by Ralph Guzmán. During the following year the Alianza developed a scholarship program for Chicano students needing financial help. With the rise of activism and multiplying new organizations, the Alianza suffered a decline in membership during the 1960s. Today it has over three hundred lodges in the Southwest and publishes a bulletin titled *Alianza*.

ALINSKY, SAUL (1909-1972), social activist. With an undergraduate degree in archeology and graduate training in criminology, Alinsky first worked with juvenile delinquents but in 1938 turned to community organizing, which was to occupy his energies for the rest of his life. In the following year he established the Industrial Areas Foundation to train leaders in his concepts and techniques. Along with many other projects he undertook among poor whites, blacks, and Chicanos, after World War II he organized some thirty Mexican American barrio communities in California. His ideas were the inspiration for both the regional Community Service Organization* and the Communities Organized for Public Service* of San Antonio, Texas. He also inspired many disciples who have worked with Chicanos.

ALTA CALIFORNIA, the approximate area of the present-day state of California. it was referred to as Alta (upper) or Nueva (new) California to distinguish it from the earlier settled area of the peninsula of California, which subsequently became known as Baja (lower) California. After its discovery and brief explorations from the sea which date to the 1530s, Alta California was finally settled, beginning in 1769 with the expedition of Gaspar de Portolá and Father Junípero Serra.* In 1804 California was divided into Baja or Antigua California and Alta or Nueva California.

ALURISTA (Alberto Urista) (1947-   ), poet, was born in Mexico City and has lived in the United States since 1959. Considered the leading Chicano poet of the 1960s, he actively participated in the Chicano movement* by helping to formulate the "Plan of Aztlán" and by using his poetry to awaken the public conscience. His early poetry published in the collection *Floricanto en Aztlán* became the point of departure for other Chicano poets.

Alurista's early poetry was seminal in both content and form. Thematically, he originated and explored the Amerindian ideology of Aztlán—an ideology which defines the Chicano in terms of his Mexican indigenous heritage and his experience living in the United States. Stylistically, he popularized the writing of poetry in bilingual form by using Spanish and English in one poem. In this respect, he was one of the first Chicano poets to create poetry by utilizing the language spoken in everyday conversation by many Chicanos. Presently, Alurista is the editor of *Maize*, a literary magazine.

FURTHER READING: Alurista, *Floricanto en Aztlán*, Los Angeles: Chicano Studies at UCLA, 1971; Alurista, *Nationchild Plumaroja*, San Diego: Centro Cultural de la Raza, 1972; Alurista, *Timespace Huracán*, Albuquerque: Pajarito Publications, 1976.

F.J.

ALVARADO, JUAN BAUTISTA (1800-1882), Californio* leader and governor. Born in Monterey, Alvarado was one of the few Californios who were truly literate, having been taught by Governor Pablo Vicente de Solá. His education and family helped make him a northern Californio leader, a position which he used to acquire for himself and his class both political power (in competition with the Carrillos and other southern leaders) and mission lands. Angered by the centralist government of Santa Anna and its governors in California, in 1836 he ousted the Mexican officials and established the sovereign state of California with himself as provisional governor until Mexico returned to her earlier federalist system. However, his bickering with his uncle, Mariano Vallejo, who was military commander, and poor health led Alvarado in 1842 to surrender his authority to the new Mexican governor, Manuel Micheltorena. In 1845 he was overwhelmingly elected Alta California's representative to the National Congress in Mexico City, but was unable to assume his duties.

During the American invasion of California in 1846 he did not participate in the fighting against the United States forces and withdrew from public life under parole. In the following year he sold the Mariposa land grant, which he had received from Micheltorena, to John Charles Frémont for $3,000, although Alvarado had never actually occupied or even seen the grant. He retired then to a large rancho on the east shore of San Francisco Bay which belonged to his wife, Martina Castro de Alvarado.

ÁLVAREZ, EVERETT, JR. (1937-), naval aviator. Born in Salinas, California, and educated there and at the University of Santa Clara, Everett graduated in 1960 as an electrical engineer. After college he studied naval aviation and was shot down over North Vietnam in 1964, becoming the first American taken prisoner in North Vietnam. When he returned early in 1973 after more than eight years imprisonment, he came back a national hero. He found a United States and a world that had undergone considerable change and slipped into grateful anonimity. Everett Álvarez still continues his naval career.

ÁLVAREZ, FRANCISCO S. (1928-1980), organic chemist. Born at Jalapa in the state of Veracruz, Mexico, Dr. Álvarez studied in the Faculty of Chemistry at the National University of Mexico. After completing his undergraduate work in 1953, he joined Syntex (Mexico) as a research assistant and two years later undertook graduate studies at Harvard University with Professor Louis Fieser. In 1957 he returned to Syntex as a development research chemist. He came to Syntex, Palo Alto, California, in 1964 as a department head in Development Research, and in 1973 he was appointed Principal Scientist. Dr. Álvarez' most notable achievements were his work on the development of processes for the production of Synalar, an important topical antiinflammatory drug, and Norethindrone, a principal component of many birth control pills. He also made major contributions to the development of basic methodology for the synthesis of prostaglandins and novel polyfluorinated corticoids. In addition to being the author of over fifteen scientific publications, Dr. Álvarez has been named as the inventor in over eighty U.S. and foreign patents.

ÁLVAREZ, MANUEL (1794-1856), mountain man and trader. Álvarez, a Spaniard, established himself in Santa Fe, New Mexico in the mid-1820s after a short sojourn in Missouri. In addition to being active in the Santa Fe trade,* he became an important fur trader in the Yellowstone and upper Missouri River areas. Returning to Santa Fe in 1834 he started a general store which he operated for two decades. Although he was not a U.S. citizen in 1839 he was appointed United States consul in Santa Fe, and served till 1846 when he helped in General Stephen Kearney's peaceful takeover of New Mexico. During the years immediately after annexation he led a move to admit New Mexico as a state of the Union. When that movement failed with the Compromise of 1850, New Mexico became a territory and Álvarez remained a minor official in the territorial government until his death in 1856.

FURTHER READING: David Weber, *The Taos Trappers*, Norman: University of Oklahoma Press, 1971.

AMERICAN COORDINATING COUNCIL OF POLITICAL EDUCATION (ACCPE), founded in Phoenix, Arizona, in the early 1960s as a result of efforts by the Political Association of Spanish-Speaking Organizations* to establish chapters in that state. Instead, ACCPE, tailored more to Arizona Chicano needs, was formed and within two years had a membership of twenty-five hundred in ten of Arizona's fourteen counties. It was quite successful at the municipal level, electing Chicanos to city councils and school boards in Arizona, especially in Miami, but was unable to repeat these successes at the county, state, and federal level.

AMERICAN COUNCIL OF SPANISH-SPEAKING PEOPLE, an alliance of Mexican Americans in the Southwest, formed in 1950 in response to civil rights demands of Chicanos and initially headed by Dr. George I. Sánchez.* With goals of eliminating ethnic discrimination in education, employment, and housing and of increasing Chicano political participation, it was particularly active in the school desegregation movement of the fifties.

AMERICAN G.I. FORUM (AGIF), one of a number of Mexican American organizations that developed out of La Raza's* World War II experiences; in this instance particularly out of the 1947 Longoria* case in Texas. It was founded primarily through the efforts of Dr. Héctor P. García,* a highly decorated combat surgeon. Its form was modeled somewhat after the American Legion. Despite the immediate specific reasons for its founding, it developed a broad and balanced program of goals for Mexican Americans and soon developed into one of the largest Chicano organizations, attracting its membership from all educational and economic levels. The G.I. Forum was active at every level of the U.S. political system and adopted a nonpartisan stance; however, it has been predominantly Democratic in sympathy. For example, a number of Forum leaders were prominent in organizing Viva Kennedy clubs* in 1960 to support the presidential ambitions of John F. Kennedy.

In the 1970s there was an influx of newly college-educated businessmen and professionals into the AGIF who served to modify and revitalize the group with their infusion of new blood. Although basically a Texas organization, it is strong throughout the Southwest and has over two hundred chapters in forty-three states. As befits an organization that strongly accents legal and political action, it maintains a fulltime lobbyist in Washington, D.C., and publishes a monthly bulletin, *The Forumeer*, which emphasizes information on federal and state social legislation of special interest to Mexican Americans.

AMERICANO, literally, American; a Latin American term used when referring to anyone from the United States.

Historically, Mexican Americans have used Americano to describe non-Raza* people (those with other than Hispanic cultural roots) who settled in the Southwest. It is also used by Europeans, especially Spaniards, to describe anyone residing in the Western Hemisphere.

ANAYA, RUDOLFO (1937-   ), novelist, was born in Pastura, New Mexico. In 1971 he was awarded the second Quinto Sol Prize for literature for *Bless Me, Ultima* which has become the best-selling Chicano novel. This work focuses on the struggle of a young Chicano to define the mysteries of life in an isolated area of New Mexico. The novelist makes use of myth, legends, and superstition to produce what is considered to be one of the best artistic achievements in the genre of the Chicano novel. Anaya is currently Professor of English at the University of New Mexico at Albuquerque.

more. By the early 1740s Spanish families were living at Tubac, Arivaca, and Sópori, as well as in the Guevavi area. A major revolt against the missionaries by Pima Indians in 1751 temporarily interrupted Spanish colonization, but the founding of a presidio at Tubac in the next year encouraged settlers. The establishment of the Tubac presidio is usually cited as the beginning of permanent Spanish settlement in southern Arizona.

In 1775-1776 the Tubac garrison was transferred to Tucson while its commander, Captain Juan Bautista de Anza*, left on his colonizing expedition to California. Thereafter Tucson became the principal Spanish settlement in the region. After Mexican independence in 1821, the Tucson presidio seldom had a full complement of soldiers, and southern Arizona settlers were hard put to survive in the face of repeated Apache attacks. By the late 1840s most ranches and mines were abandoned, their owners and laborers having fled south or moved into Tucson.

The part of Arizona north of the Gila River became a part of the United States in 1848 with the Treaty of Guadalupe Hidalgo* and the southern portion was purchased from Mexico in 1854 in accordance with the Gadsden Treaty* (1853), sometimes known in Mexico as the Treaty of La Mesilla. Until 1863 Arizona formed part of the Territory of New Mexico.

Apache raids continued and were intensified during the Civil War period and for more than a decade thereafter. Yet the presence of American soldiers in the territory made it seem safer than many parts of Sonora, and large numbers of Sonorans came to southern Arizona in the 1860s and 1870s in search of both security and employment. In spite of the Apache menace, ranching, farming, and mining expanded rapidly after 1870, and Mexican laborers contributed to these developments. The completion of large irrigation projects around the time Arizona achieved statehood in 1912 created new demands for Mexican workers. The demand for laborers, combined with the revolution in Mexico, led to continuing streams of immigrants into the state from the south.

The population of Arizona increased slowly between the two world wars, with Mexican Americans making up more than 20 percent of the state's total population. As a result of heavy Anglo immigration after World War II that percentage has declined somewhat, although the actual number of Spanish surnames has more than doubled. Today the largest concentrations of Mexican Americans are in Phoenix and Tucson; but the most Mexican of Arizona cities is Nogales, where almost all native Anglos grow up speaking Spanish as fluently as English, and where two border cities (known as Ambos Nogales or Both Nogales) function socially, culturally, and economically as a single community.

According to the 1970 census, there were 246,390 persons with Spanish surnames in Arizona, representing 13.9 percent of the state's total population.

FURTHER READING: Michael E. Parrish, *Mexican Workers, Progressives and*

Copper, La Jolla, Calif.: University of California, 1979; Marshall Trimble, *Arizona: A Panoramic History of a Frontier State*, Garden City, N.Y.: Doubleday, 1977; University of Arizona Faculty, *Arizona, Its People and Resources*, Tucson: University of Arizona Press, 1972; Rufus K. Wyllys, *Arizona: The History of a Frontier State*, Phoenix: Hobson & Herr, 1950; Griggs et al., *The Mexican Experience in Arizona*, New York: Arno Press, 1976.

J.E.O.

ARMIJO, MANUEL (1792-1853), frontier governor and businessman. Although born to a humble Nuevo Mexicano family near Albuquerque and having little formal education, Armijo taught himself to read and write as an adult and had become an influential and well-to-do citizen before he was thirty. In the early 1820s he became one of the Nuevo Mexicanos deeply involved in the Santa Fe trade.

Armijo served as territorial governor of New Mexico three times; from 1827 to 1829, from 1837 to 1844, and again from 1845 to 1846. His second term in office was largely the result of his suppression of the New Mexican revolt against President Santa Anna's centralist governor of New Mexico, Albino Pérez and was highlighted by his decisive action against the Texans' Santa Fe expedition* of 1841. As governor he augmented his business prominence by awarding to friends numerous large (and sometimes illegal) land grants in many of which he held an interest. He also continued to be active in the Santa Fe trade, where abuse of his powers as governor earned him an unsavory reputation among Anglos.

In 1846 when the American invasion of New Mexico under Colonel Stephen Kearny* began, Governor Armijo readied a force to resist it but then fled south to Chihuahua without engaging the enemy. This action has led to some suspicion of his selling out to the American forces, and indeed he was tried and acquitted of the charge of treason by the Mexican government.

After the Treaty of Guadalupe Hidalgo* Armijo returned to New Mexico and settled near Socorro, where he owned a ranch. He resumed his ranching and trading activities and even ran for election, but he was defeated. When he died in 1853, his will included a bequest of one thousand dollars to establish a public school.

ARRASTRE, an ore-grinding mill of circular shape with a horizontal pole pivoted at the center and several large rocks hanging from it by rawhide thongs. The pole was turned, usually by a horse or mule, and the rocks thus dragged over quartz ore, eventually pulverizing it so it could be treated with mercury and the gold amalgamated. The arrastre was one of many Mexican contributions to western mining. A variation of the arrastre, using heavy wheels in place of rocks, was sometimes referred to as a chili mill.

ART AND ARTISTS, The contemporary movement in Chicano art, while initially largely a form of aggressive social protest which criticized the ills of American society and exalted self-worth, has roots deep in tradition. It is related to Pre-Hispanic, Hispano (colonial), Mexican, and American art in content and form. Distinctions between Hispano (*See* HISPANO SUBCULTURE), Mexican American, and Chicano art are based primarily on the artist's own perception of the historical, cultural, and ethnic record of the Spanish-Mexican people in the Southwest. In spite of differences in perception, all three groups share a common language and basic culture which bind them together far more than is generally realized.

Labels used to encompass the arts of the Southwestern United States during the centuries of Spanish control have contributed to perpetuating the excessive distinctions mentioned above. Even today most New Mexicans continue to perceive themselves as Hispanic Americans rather than Mexican Americans, though they and other southwestern Hispanos derive from the same Spanish and indigenous cultural base, tempered by the American experience. The differences have been magnified unnecessarily and are due largely to the timing of settlements in each of the borderland provinces, and twentieth-century political and economic developments in Mexico and the United States.

The perception among Hispanos that Spanish as an identifying label has somehow been more legitimate and therefore preferable to Mexican, or more recently, to Chicano, has also contributed to the confusion. Attitudes of Anglo Americans, of course, have been and continue to be, a major factor in this matter. As Mexican Americans and Chicanos in the Southwest and Great Lakes region have developed pride in their backgrounds this defensive attitude has receded to insignificant proportions.

Essentially, Hispanic Americans emphasize the Spanish component in their artistic background while Mexican Americans tend to embrace the Mexican. Chicanos, on the other hand, discard both as totally inappropriate because they do not reflect the true reality of a people who are distinct from the Spanish, the Mexican, and the American. The result is a Chicano disdain for the dual names, Hispanic Americans and Mexican Americans. Chicano activists accept their antecedents who are traceable to Spain and Mexico, but they bridle at the most immediate component, those of the United States. They wish to embrace that part of their background which is traceable to the pre-Columbian Indians of Mesoamerica in much the same way that Mexicans did some fifty years ago after the Mexican revolution.

While Hispanos and Mexican Americans both create works of art that reflect their backgrounds, they do not consciously seek to identify these works with a specific Hispanic or Mexican American view of the world. Chicanos on the other hand do precisely that. Work by two Chicano artists, Willie Herron and Luis Jiménez, illustrate this point.

Willie Herron of Los Angeles is one of the most promising of the younger Chicano artists working in California. Herron has worked independently as well as with a group of artists known as ASCO. The group, comprised of Herron, Patssi Valdez, Gronk, and Harry Gamboa are also active in the publication *La Regeneración*.

Willie Herron's murals are painted on various buildings in the Los Angeles area. These include murals on the the buildings fronting an alley near East City Terrace and North Miller Avenue, cooperative murals painted on City Terrace Stairway located off North Eastern Avenue and Comly Drive (1972), and murals on the City Terrace Park Outdoor Pavilion at 1126 North Hazard Drive (1973). Herron and Gronk have also worked on the end wall of one of the buildings comprising Estrada Courts housing complex at Olympic Boulevard and Lorena Avenue (1972-1974).

Willie Herron's work can be viewed against the backdrop of other Chicano murals painted in San Diego, Los Angeles, Santa Barbara, Fresno, Sacramento, and San Francisco. Comparable murals are found in Santa Fe, and Las Vegas, New Mexico; San Antonio, and Houston, Texas; Denver, Colorado; Chicago, Illinois; and other cities in the Great Lakes Region. Most of these murals have pre-Columbian, colonial and contemporary Mexican themes. Examples from San Diego and Los Angeles painted on freeway and bridge surfaces and sides of buildings show in a very general way the Chicano artists' reliance on pre-Columbian motifs. Pryamids and contiunous scrolls are a favorite motif. Olmec colossal heads, the Aztec calendar stone, El Tajín ballcourt scenes, and Toltec Atlantean figures are several of many pre-Columbian motifs used by Chicano artists in their work.

Colonial references usually include Our Lady of Guadalupe, as in a number of murals in San Diego and East Los Angeles, in Santa Fe, New Mexico, and in Chicago, Illinois. This signals a strong religious and political tradition. Our Lady of Guadalupe has been a powerful symbol in Mexico since the wars of independence in that country. While more recently Our Lady of Guadalupe was used as a symbol by the farm workers led by César Chávez, she has been used repeatedly as a theme for Chicano muralists.

Specific Chicano concerns are demonstrated by the use of the huelga eagle,* Spanish phrases such as Viva La Raza, carnal,* and others on several Los Angeles murals and elsewhere. Far more elaborate themes dealing with the Chicano movement in California are shown in a Willie Herron mural in Estrada Courts entitled *Mi Mural es Suyo* (1972-1974). Gronk also worked on this painting, which has in a number of panels vivid black and white images chronicling and commenting on the violence which took place in East Los Angeles in 1971 during a Chicano demonstration. One of the central panels is based on a photograph of Los Angeles police moving in formation through the streets.

Luis Jiménez, born in El Paso in 1940, has introduced unique points of view into his sculptures made of fiberglass, epoxy, resin, and neon lights.

He has exhibited in New York, Houston, Santa Fe, New Orleans, and is presently residing in El Paso where he is working fulltime on a major project entitled *Progress*.

During the late sixties Jiménez dealt with themes that encompass those values that have a direct bearing on the lives of all Americans and Mexican Americans and Chicanos in particular. Among these themes were those in which the mass media is personified by a television screen just barely containing a woman with an outrageously oversized mouth and massive breasts bursting through the screen. The use of sex for merchandising is further personified in Jiménez's work by blonde blue-eyed females. Themes dealing with the meaning and influence of the machine have also been explored by the artist, particularly the automobile and the motorcycle. Jiménez has also had a strong sense of history, particularly that of Mexico, where he studied briefly in 1964 soon after his graduation from the University of Texas at Austin.

More recently Jiménez has become quite interested in creating images that deal with the Southwest and the West as seen through the movies, the rodeo, the demolition derby, and overly familiar western paintings and sculptures. Among the latter are the many murals which were painted in post offices during the depression. Southwesterners' views of progress inevitably showed up in many of these mural programs. Luis Jiménez has continued using these concepts in his work of the seventies and eighties.

His recent works, entitled *Progress I* and *Progress II*, are completed parts of a model presented in his one man show at the O. K. Harris Gallery in New York in 1972. The completed work, to be called *Progress*, is comprised of six units: 1) Indian with Buffalo, 2) Indian and Conquistador, 3) Longhorns and Vaquero, 4) Charro and Stage Coach, 5) Gunfighter, and 6) Machines. Jiménez has finished a very large sculpture (8′8″ x 5′5″) dealing with the first segment of this project and a plaster model of segment three.

Jiménez continues to move in directions that enable him to comment on American society by using cherished images of the American past or its present as themes for his sculptures.

Articles and books reflecting the distinctions and the contributions made to U.S. culture by Mexican Americans and Chicanos have appeared only during the last five to ten years. The literature on Hispano arts has been more extensive and of longer duration. As more and more Hispano artists identify themselves as such, whether Mexican Americans or Chicanos, there will be more attention paid to their work. This has been the case with Mexican American art and the Chicano murals painted in California, Colorado, New Mexico, Texas, Illinois, and other Great Lakes Region states.

FURTHER READING: Eva Cockcroft, John Weber, and James Cockcroft, *Toward a People's Art: The Contemporary Mural Movement*, New York: E. P. Dutton & Co., 1977; M. Rupert García, "A Historical Look at Raza Murals and Muralists," *El Tecolote* (San Francisco) (July 26, 1972), p. 14; Jacinto Quirarte, *Mexican American Artists*, Austin: University of Texas Press, 1973; Jacinto Quirarte, "Murals of el Barrio," *Exxon U.S.A.* 13, no. 4 (1974): 2-9; Willard Houghland, *American Primitive Art*, New York: Kleijkamp and Monroe, 1947. *J.Q.*

ASOCIACIÓN DE JORNALEROS, a union organized in Laredo, Texas, in 1933 largely in response to the labor section of the National Recovery Act (NRA) of the New Deal. This independent union included workers in construction, mining, and agriculture. In 1936, in an effort to expand its membership and area of influence, the association obtained an AFL charter as Agricultural Workers Labor Union No. 20212 and immediately undertook a statewide organizing drive. The association was absorbed into the Texas Agricultural Workers Organizing Committee during the following year and then became a part of the CIO's United Cannery, Agricultural, Packing and Allied Workers of America* (UCAPAWA). The member unions of the association were weakened by Mexican national and communist leadership, and most became inactive and disintegrated by the end of 1937.

FURTHER READING: Stuart M. Jamieson, *Labor Unionism in American Agriculture*, Washington, D.C.: Government Printing Office, 1945; reprint New York: Arno Press, 1976.

ASOCIACIÓN NACIONAL PRO PERSONAS MAYORES (NATIONAL ASSOCIATION FOR SPANISH SPEAKING ELDERLY), established in 1975 to voice the economic, cultural, and psychological needs of elderly persons of Spanish heritage. This organization works with federal, state, and private agencies to improve the quality of social services delivered to the Spanish-speaking aged. Partially funded through a variety of federal programs, it maintains offices in Los Angeles, Albuquerque, Miami, New York, and Washington, D.C., and publishes a bimonthly newsletter called *ANPPM* in which pending legislation about the elderly is reported.

ASSIMILATION, the process by which a minority ethnic group is accepted, absorbed, and incorporated into the life of the majority ethnic group or host society. Minority groups lose their original identity by discarding their distinct ethnic customs, values, norms, and language, becoming ethnically indistinguishable from the dominant majority group.

Assimilation suggests conformity and in the United States this means acceptance of white Anglo-Saxon Protestant mores and values. Generally these values affirm the superiority of all things English and imply a belief in white racial supremacy. Today English institutions, English language, and English-oriented cultural patterns continue to be the standards for admittance into the mainstream of American life.

In predominantly white America, Mexican Americans for the most part have been outsiders. Consequently, Mexican Americans' social, political, and economic status has been markedly different from that of other ethnic groups. Unlike other groups, Mexican Americans are not assimilated into American society. Linguistic, cultural, and historical factors have contributed to their rejection by the majority group.

FURTHER READING: Milton M. Gordon, *Assimilation in American Life*, New York: Oxford University Press, 1964; Edward Murguía, *Assimilation, Colonialism, and the Mexican American People*, Austin: University of Texas, 1975; Lloyd W. Warner and Leo Srole, *The Social Systems of American Ethnic Groups*, New Haven: Yale University Press, 1945. *G.M.B.*

ASSOCIATED FARMERS OF CALIFORNIA, an organization of California farmers and associated interest groups, arising out of the big 1933 San Joaquin cotton strike and a resulting meeting of the Agricultural Labor Subcommittee of the state Chamber of Commerce in Los Angeles during November of that year. The Associated Farmers was formally organized in May 1934 with business support and contributions to fight the organization of farm unions, especially the Cannery and Agricultural Workers Industrial Union,* affiliated with the Communist party. As the result of support from the Southern Pacific Railroad, the Atchison, Topeka and Santa Fe, Pacific Gas and Electric Company, the Canners' League, Holly Sugar Corporation, and other companies, the Associated Farmers was seen by many as merely a front organization for big business.

The Associated Farmers viewed the labor problem as paramount in the late thirties and opposed as a surrender of agribusiness's rights any unionization of farm labor, as well as the use of the closed shop, hiring hall, and picketing. Techniques used by the Associated Farmers varied with the occasion, running the gamut from lobbying in Sacramento and "educative" programs to the use of tear gas, axe handles, and accusation of communist affiliations. After the U.S. Senate's La Follette Committee* investigation in 1939 and 1940 and the development of World War II agricultural prosperity, the Associated Farmers declined in importance.

ASSOCIATION OF MEXICAN AMERICAN EDUCATORS (AMAE), Founded in 1965, the AMAE is an organization with headquarters in Redwood City, California. It is concerned with educational activities and programs affecting Chicano scholars and students and strongly supports bilingual and bicultural education. Although it is a national organization, a majority of its twelve hundred members are located in California. The AMAE publishes a monthly newsletter.

AUSTIN, MOSES (1761-1821), a yankee merchant who became interested in lead mining, in 1798 Austin obtained a mining grant in Missouri from the Spanish government. He was successful in his venture at Potosi until the post-War of 1812 depression ruined him. As a former Spanish subject, he then applied to the Spanish government for an empresario* grant in Texas. In March 1821 he was granted two hundred thousand acres on which to settle three hundred families. He died before he could complete the settlement, and his son, Stephen F. Austin,* took up the project.

AUSTIN, STEPHEN F. (1793-1836), Texas colonizer and leader, son of Moses Austin. Stephen F. Austin was educated at Transylvania and Yale universities, helped manage the family lead mine, and served in the Missouri territorial legislature from 1814 to 1820. Taking over his father's colonization project in Texas after the former's death in 1821, he brought the first Anglo American settlers into the colony on the lower Brazos River by the end of 1821. When Mexico achieved independence he renegotiated his agreement first with the Mexican Empire of 1822-1823 and then with the 1824 Republic. Austin worked hard both to make the colony a success and to fulfill his duties as an empresario* by seeing that his colonists carried out the terms of the grant. Of approximately twenty thousand colonists in Texas by the end of the eighteen-twenties, six thousand were his.

By the late twenties the Mexican government had become alarmed at the large number of Anglo settlers in Texas and by United States interest in acquiring the area. In 1830 Mexican legislation greatly limited Anglo immigration, encouraged European immigration, and provided for the establishment of border presidios and customs houses. In this atmosphere Austin traveled through Texas trying to get Tejano support for separate statehood within Mexico in order to avoid more radical action which might lead to complete separation. Anglo and Mexican Texans held conventions in 1832 and 1833 and decided to ask the Mexican government for separattion from the state of Coahuila-Texas and repeal of the 1830 laws. In mid-1833 Austin was sent to Mexico City to present the convention's views to Mexican officials, but because of political instability he had difficulty in getting Texas views heard. The restrictive colonization legislation was repealed in late 1833, but Austin's pleas for separate statehood fell on unresponsive ears. In January 1834, while on his way back to Texas, Austin was arrested on suspicion of inciting revolt as the result of intercepted correspondence from the San Antonio ayuntamiento (city council). Jailed for over a year, he was released, at first on parole, and in September 1835 finally returned to Texas where he was hailed as the only leader who could unite all Texans.

Meanwhile in Mexico City Antonio López de Santa Anna* had taken over the government from Vice President Valentín Gómez Farías and was on his way to converting Mexico from federalism to a centralist republic. Santa Anna also sent his brother-in-law, General Martín Perfecto de Cos* to Texas with a federal army. The imminent arrival of Cos convinced Austin that complete independence was the only possible ultimate solution for Texas; nevertheless, on November 7 the Texans declared conditional independence as Mexican federalists. Later that month Austin, who had been selected to head the Texas volunteer forces, was relieved of his army duties to head a mission to Washington D.C. in order to seek help. Though not particularly successful, Austin returned to Texas in June 1836 to find that Santa Anna's army had been defeated at San Jacinto and that the Treaty of Velasco* (May 14, 1836) gave promise that the struggle might be over.

In August Austin declared himself a candidate for the presidency of the new Texas republic but was defeated for that position a month later by Sam Houston. The new president selected Austin to head the Texas department of state, and Austin accepted, although hesitating because of ill health. Two days after Christmas, Stephen Austin died at age 43. A Texas leader of great integrity and honest intentions, he had tried to fulfill his obligations to Mexico and to make Texas a model Mexican state. He enjoyed the respect of most Texans, Tejanos, and Mexican government officials.

FURTHER READING: Eugene C. Barker, *The Life of Stephen F. Austin, 1793-1836*, Nashville, Tenn.: Cokesbury Press, 1925.

AWOC (AGRICULTURAL WORKERS ORGANIZING COMMITTEE). *See* UNITED FARM WORKERS and ITLIONG, LARRY.

AYRES, LT. EDWARD DURAN. *See* AYRES REPORT.

AYRES REPORT, a report read to the 1942 grand jury in Los Angeles by Edward Duran Ayres, chief of the Foreign Relations Bureau in the Los Angeles Sheriff's department at the time of the Sleepy Lagoon* affair. His report, based on pseudoanthropological and genetic ideas, argued that people of Mexican origin had inborn characteristics coming from their Indian ancestry and passed down through generations that caused them to be prone to violence and especially to bloodletting. Ayres' views, supported by Sheriff E. W. Biscailuz, influenced law enforcement attitudes in the Los Angeles area and added to existing anti-Mexican attitudes.

AZTLÁN, historical and mythical place of origin of the Aztecs. It was from Aztlán that the Aztecs claimed to have initiated their migration which began around 1111 A.D. and ended over two hundred years later in the Valley of Mexico where they founded Tenochtitlán, modern Mexico City. Sources vary as to Aztlán's location; and scholars have therefore identified it with such areas as the Valley of Mexico itself; Lake Chapala; the Bajío; the state of Sonora; Lower or Upper California; the state of New Mexico; the region encompassed by Oregon, Idaho, and Wyoming; Puget Sound in Washington; Asia; and some unspecified mythical region "somewhere to the north."

Today two opposing opinions predominate. One is that Aztlán is only a mythical region. The other says it is the island Metzcaltitán located on the lake of Aztatlán on the northern coast of the state of Nayarit, northwest of the present-day city of Santiago Ixcuintla. The archaeology of the region helps to confirm this area as the location of the Aztlán repeatedly mentioned by various sixteenth-century native and Spanish sources.

Both Aztecs and Spaniards sent expeditions to areas northwest of Mexico City in search of the legendary Aztlán. As the excursions of the Spaniards pushed farther north in the sixteenth and seventeenth centuries so also the elusive location of Aztlán was progressively moved northward by these disappointed explorers and their chroniclers.

In modern Mexico only ethnohistorians and archaeologists have been concerned with the idea and location of Aztlán. However, among Mexican Americans it has become a popular symbolic name for either the southwest of the United States, where most Mexican Americans live, or for the metaphorical space that exists wherever Chicano culture flourishes. For a minority of them Aztlán represents a territory whose autonomy under Chicano sovereignty should be sought by political or revolutionary action.

FURTHER READING: Wigberto Jiménez Moreno, "Nayarit: Etnohistoria y Arqueología," in *Historia y Sociedad en el mundo de habla española*, Bernardo García Martínez *et al.*, eds., Mexico, 1970; "El Plan Espiritual de Aztlán," *El Grito del Norte* 2 (1969).

J.J.K.A.

B

BACA, ELFEGO (1865-1945), New Mexican folk hero, lawyer, sheriff, and private detective. Growing up on the lawless post-Civil War frontier of Kansas and the Southwest, Baca quickly learned the lessons of survival. In 1884, when he was still a teenager, Baca volunteered to help the deputy sheriff, his brother-in-law, bring under control a group of wild-shooting Texas cowboys who, in their carousing enthusiasm, were using Mexican Americans and their animals for target practice. Baca's arrest of one of the cowboys brought eighty of them after him the next day. In the sensational shoot-out that followed, Baca took refuge in a hut, and after a siege of thirty-six hours and three or four thousand shots, he had wounded eight and killed four cowboys. Surrendering on the promise of a fair hearing, he was tried for murder in Albuquerque and found not guilty.

As a result of his exploits Baca became an overnight folk hero among Nuevo Mexicanos and was able to begin a long political career. Running for some elective office in nearly every election after he was twenty-one, Baca became successively deputy sheriff, county clerk, and county superintendent of schools. After reading for the law during this period, Baca was admitted to the bar in 1894 and practiced in Socorro, New Mexico. In 1911, having moved to Albuquerque, Elfego Baca became a Republican candidate for the house of representatives in New Mexico's first statehood election, but he lost.

During the Mexican Revolution of 1910 Baca had brief dreams of becoming an important figure in Mexican politics when he first was hired by the Victoriano Huerta government to defend one of its generals accused of violating U.S. neutrality. After Huerta's ouster from the Mexican presidency, Baca was appointed Huerta's U.S. representative. However, Huerta's internment at Fort Bliss, Texas, and his death shortly thereafter ended Baca's hopes.

At the end of World War I Elfego Baca was elected sheriff of Socorro County and held that position intermittently during the 1920s. In the 1920s Baca was sufficiently well known statewide that he was occasionally mentioned as a possible candidate for the governorship of New Mexico. His vote-getting potential came to the attention of the leading New Mexican liberal politico, Bronson Cutting,* and a political alliance was made between the two. During the Cutting era of New Mexican politics Baca published a Spanish-language weekly in his support and also did some political detective work for him. After Cutting's death in 1935 Baca continued his career as detective and lawyer.

FURTHER READING: Kyle S. Crichton, *Law and Order Limited: The Life of Elfego Baca*, Santa Fe, New Mexico: New Mexican Publishing Co., 1928; William A. Keleher, *Memoirs: 1892-1969; A New Mexico Item*, Santa Fe, New Mexico: Rydal Press, 1969.

BACA-BARRAGÁN, POLLY (1941-), politician. Born in a small town near Greeley, Colorado, Polly Baca-Barragán graduated in political science from Colorado State University and then worked as editor on two union publications. Between 1967 and 1972 she was active in a number of political groups and several federal agencies. In 1974 she was elected to the Colorado House of Representatives and four years later was successful in her race for the state senate, becoming the first Chicana to be elected to that office. Polly Baca-Barragán has been the recipient of numerous honors and awards; she remains active in many political and Mexican American organizations, especially those related to housing.

BÁEZ, JOAN (1941-), folksinger and antiwar activist well known for her commitment to nonviolence and her opposition to United States involvement in the Vietnam War.

Joan Báez is one of three daughters of Dr. Albert V. Báez, Mexican-born U.S. physicist and Professor Joan Báez, a dramatics teacher. While growing up, Joan excelled in music, learning to play the guitar and singing in the Palo Alto (California) High School choir. When her father received a joint appointment to the Massachusetts Institute of Technology and Harvard, and the family moved to Boston, Joan's interest in folk music was aroused by visits to Boston expresso shops where amateur folk musicians entertained. Because of the social content of many folk songs and her own experiences in racial prejudice, she quickly developed a social awareness and soon began her own career as a folksinger.

Her simple style and pure soprano voice brought her a nationwide following within a few years. In the late 1960s and early 1970s she was a frequent participant in antiwar rallies and demonstrations for equal rights for blacks and farm workers. Her interest in world peace led to her founding the Institute for the Study of Nonviolence and to her participation in the work of Amnesty International. In 1979 her "Open Letter to the Socialist Republic of Vietnam," published in five U.S. newspapers, denounced the victors in the Vietnam War for their violation of human rights in treatment of political prisoners.

BAKKE CASE (1978), concerned with the issue of special treatment in institutions of higher education for minority students, and particularly important to Mexican Americans, because, unlike blacks, they lack their own colleges.

Alan Bakke, an Anglo applicant for admission to the Medical School of the University of California at Davis and rejected in 1973 and 1974, filed suit against the university, claiming reverse discrimination. His suit argued that he was denied admission although his grades were higher than those of some minority applicants for whom sixteen of the one hundred annual medical school admissions places were reserved.

The California state courts and the United States Supreme Court (June 1978) upheld Bakke's suit. The California courts ruled that the use of race as a factor in admission decisions of a public institution was unconstitutional, but the Supreme Court held that, while a specific quota was discriminatory and therefore generally illegal, race and ethnic background were valid considerations in school admission policies. Bakke entered medical school at Davis.

Because of its implications for the education of Mexican Americans, the Bakke case aroused considerable interest in Mexican American communities, and many prominent Chicano leaders criticized the decisions of the courts, which they saw as weakening Anglo resolve to make up for past discrimination.

BANDITRY, lawlessness characterizing a large part of the Southwest from before the United States-Mexican War to about 1920. This lawlessness varied considerably in nature, ranging all the way from simple robbery to social banditry and political fund-raising. In California, stemming in large measure from the gold rush and frontier conditions, banditry was important from 1849 to the 1880s; in Texas, New Mexico, and Arizona it arose from conditions along the western frontier and the border with Mexico and peaked in this area between the 1860s and the end of World War I. Banditry resulted from a variety of causes, but when it involved Mexican Americans, banditry was often a reaction to Anglo racism and economic and cultural dominance. Numerically a majority of bandits in the Southwest was probably Anglo since that area became the last refuge for rascals from all over the United States, especially as the frontier moved rapidly westward after the Civil War.

In California Anglo racist excesses in the gold fields and the taking of Californios'* lands often led to reprisals and acts of personal revenge. This upsurge of "banditry," as it was called, brought on an equally extralegal reaction; vigilante committees, often merely lynch mobs, meted out their own justice to those they considered guilty—whippings, shootings, hangings. Skin color was often important evidence of guilt. These aggressions and indignities greatly embittered Mexicans and Californios, and in retaliation they sometimes resorted to personal interpretations of justice. Anglo highwaymen expanded the banditry scene, and the 1850s saw numerous small-time banditti operating, mostly in the gold fields. After some slackening toward the end of the decade there was a resurgence in the 1860s—mostly cattle and horse stealing by outlaw gangs in the Coast Range and Central Valley. Many gang members were displaced Mexicans who decided to live off the new society and claimed nationalism as their motivation, thereby combining outlawry and patriotism.

In California the two most widely known Mexican bandits were the at least partially legendary Joaquín Murieta* and the very real Tiburcio Vásquez,* last of the great California robber-bandits. There were in addition many others—Juan Soto, Bartolo Sepúlveda, Narciso Bojorques, Jesús Tejada, Salomón Pico, and Juan Flores, who declared he was starting a revolt against the hated gringo.* With the capture of Tiburcio Vásquez and his band and the execution of Vásquez in 1875, California banditry tapered off considerably.

In Texas the leading figures among those commonly designated as Mexican bandits by Anglos were Juan Nepomuceno (Cheno) Cortina* (1860s and 1870s) and Catarino Garza* (1890s), both of whom were probably more revolutionaries than bandits. Much of so-called banditry in Texas was the result of border disputes or of racial antagonisms and retaliatory attacks. A great deal of banditry in Texas arose from the fact that the state formed a one-thousand-mile border with Mexico in a frontier area that was generally geographically and climatically more hospitable to gangs than the one-thousand miles of desert from El Paso west to the Pacific Ocean.

Until 1890 the United States-Mexican border was a wide-open, lawless frontier; robbers, cattle thieves, smugglers, and a variety of desperados infested the lower Rio Grande, and bandits and Indians inhabited the rugged border area west of Laredo. In the early 1880s Mexico and the United States reached an agreement whereby forces of either country might cross into the territory of the other while in hot pursuit of bandits. By the end of the decade these forces had virtually wiped out hidden outlaw sanctuaries, especially in Rio Grande "islands" created by channel changes and claimed by both countries. In the early 1890s there were occasional outbursts of trouble that the Mexican government blamed on American-domiciled bandits who crossed into Mexico, while the United States imputed them to Mexico-resident bandits who crossed over into Texas.

New Mexico had little of the kind of outlawry and banditry that plagued California and Texas. Possibly the speed with which the Anglos dominated California and Texas helped bring on there a banditry that was at least partly socially inspired. In New Mexico most of the desperadoes appear to have been Anglos, and the lawless element was mostly cattle thieves. In the post-Civil War era New Mexico had its share of uprooted rowdies and villains who found it difficult to settle down, and occurrences like the Elizabethtown gold strike in 1869 brought in some Anglo toughs. Toward the end of the following decade the Lincoln County War* kept local scoundrels "employed" and also brought in gunmen, but not bandits. The White Caps* of the 1890s were in part a response to recent Anglo intrusion and change, and their activities might be considered a form of organized social marauding. But there was little social banditry by individuals such as exemplified by Tiburcio Vásquez or Cheno Cortina.

On July 12, 1862, a *Daily Alta California* correspondent reported about Arizona that "This territory has been the refuge and paradise of rascals of every type, who have made it unsafe for them to dwell elsewhere. Escaped convicts from California and desperadoes from Texas and New Mexico comprise the majority of its population, who scruple not at the commission of the most hideous crimes and excesses of iniquity. Dreading each other, for they are ranged in cliques, they make common cause against the native inhabitant, whom they murder without ceremony." This description forms a good contrast to the common nineteenth-century stereotype of the Mexican bandit in the Southwest. More accurately perhaps, there was a circular pattern of violence, counterviolence, suspicion, and retribution between Anglo and Mexican which time after time forced innocent Mexicans to flee across the border into Sonora to save themselves and their families.

The end of the Civil War turned loose in the Southwest a widely assorted lot of delinquents, rascals, ruffians, scoundrels, hoodlums, felons, exconvicts, cutthroats, outlaws, and gunmen who preyed on all, Anglo and Mexican alike, but more on the latter because they were more defenseless. By the end of the century the decline in frontier isolation had mostly eliminated this lawless group.

FURTHER READING: Joseph H. Jackson, *Bad Company*, New York: Harcourt Brace and Company, 1939; Pedro Castillo and Alberto Camarillo, *Furia y Muerte: Los Bandidos Chicanos*, Los Angeles: University of California, 1973; Stanley Crocchiola, *Desperadoes of New Mexico*, Denver: World Press, 1953; Carlos Cortés, "El bandolerismo social chicano," in David Maciel and Patricia Bueno, *Aztlan: historia del pueblo chicano (1848-1910)*, Mexico City: SepSetentas, 1975, 111-122.

BAÑUELOS, RAMONA ACOSTA (1925-), Treasurer of the United States. Born on March 20, 1925 in Miami, Arizona, she "repatriated" to northern Mexico with her parents during the Great Depression.* Returning to the United States in 1944, she settled in Los Angeles and five years later began a small tortilla factory. Successful in this enterprise, she later expanded into the banking business, and in 1969 was selected Outstanding Businesswoman of the Year in Los Angeles.

With her inauguration on December 17, 1971, as Treasurer of the United States, she became the first Mexican American and sixth woman to hold this post.

BARELA, CASIMIRO (1847-1920), senator and businessman. Born in Embudo, New Mexico, Casimiro Barela came to the attention of his pastor (later archbishop) Jean B. Salpointe who attended to his education hoping he would enter the priesthood. At Casimiro's suggestion in 1867 his family moved to southern Colorado, to the town today named after him. Two years later he entered public life by being elected Justice of the Peace and continued to be elected to various offices in the territorial government, including the Colorado House of Representatives. In 1875 he played an important role as a delegate to the constitutional convention. He secured provisions in the Colorado constitution for publication of all laws in Spanish for twenty-five years as well as protection of the civil rights of the Spanish-speaking.

Casimiro Barela was elected to the first state senate and was repeatedly reelected thereafter. A strong Democratic leader in southern Colorado, he was twice elected president of the senate by his fellow legislators. He was also elected and appointed to various national, state, and local offices of importance and was even appointed Mexican consul at Denver. In recognition of his long record of public service and of his political integrity he was known as "El Padre del Senado del Estado de Colorado" and "El Senador Perpetuo." His lengthy and successful political career made him an object of great pride and a role model for Colorado Mexican Americans.

FURTHER READING: José Fernández, *Cuarenta años de legislador: biografía del Senador Casimiro Barela*, reprint, New York: Arno Press, 1976.

BARELA, PATROCINIO (1900?-1964), artist and santero. Barela was born in Bisbee, Arizona, and lost his mother while he was still a small child. Barela spent his early years in a succession of farms and camps where his itinerant laborer father was employed. When his father settled near Taos, New Mexico, and remarried, Patrocinio was able to attend school, where he was encouraged by the teacher to draw, carve, and mold clay figures. At age eleven he ran away from home because he did not get along with his stepmother and as a result was boarded for a while with a black family in Denver, Colorado, by the juvenile authorities. Here he learned English and Anglo culture.

As soon as he was old enough, Patrocinio became an itinerant laborer, traveling around the West for years and earning a bare living. In 1930 he returned to New Mexico and settled in Cañón, the little village near Taos in which he had attended school. He soon married a woman with three children and to support his new family did odd jobs. One of these jobs was repairing an old wooden statue of a santo* (saint) and in the process he found he had a great interest in and talent for woodcarving. Almost compulsively he carved santos, although there was little market for his wares and he was artistically misunderstood.

When the New Deal came to New Mexico in the 1930s Barela was one of many Nuevo Mexicanos who found employment in the federal program. Here his carving skills were brought to the attention of the federal art project director, who transferred Barela to the project in Taos. In the FAP Barela evolved his style and expanded his subject matter to include *bultos*, figures expressing the universal themes of birth, suffering, and death. He also carved doors and massive Spanish colonial-style furniture. His work gradually achieved recognition, and in 1939 a collection of his carvings was exhibited at the New York World Fair.

In 1943 the federal art project was terminated and Barela set up a workshop near his house, where he continued to carve bultos when he was not working as a field hand to support his family. During the post-World War

II period he usually acted as his own salesman, in emergencies sometimes selling his work for almost nothing. In late October 1964, Barela died as the result of a fire that broke out in his workshop.

Patrocinio Barela was a self-taught carver of bultos whose work has been characterized by art critics as combining the external naturalism of a primitive style with a sophisticated internalized expression of his inner self.

BARRIO, literally district; in the United States it is used to refer to the quarter of town inhabited by Mexican Americans or other Hispanic Americans. Barrio has the double meaning of ghetto or slum and also of neighborhood or community.

Barrios have had varied origins. The downtown, central city barrio had its origins in the many cities of the Southwest established by Mexicans and Spaniards. These cities were organized around a plaza area, which served a variety of functions. The advent of railroads and the establishment of new settlements by Anglos caused many of these plazas to be bypassed when transportation terminals and commercial centers developed some distance away. As new urban growth gravitated around these terminals, the plaza area remained as a backwater. These plazas came to constitute the focus of many contemporary downtown barrios, for example, that in Albuquerque, New Mexico.

Additional central barrios resulted from former agricultural labor communities being enveloped by rapid urbanization. The shift of agricultural land to urban use meant that Mexican Americans were also absorbed, as happened with the Mayfair area of San José, California.

Former labor camps were yet another source of today's barrios, for often a small population remained after the purpose for which the labor camp had been established was achieved. An example is the Sawtelle area in West Los Angeles.

The barrio can be characterized as a place of widespread poverty; a high incidence of disease, illness, poor dental hygiene, and alcoholism; low-cost substandard homes; economic exploitation; political powerlessness; limited city services; isolation from and neglect by city or county authorities; and a lack of hope and aspirations.

BARRIO, RAYMOND (1921-), novelist, teacher. Born in New Jersey, Barrio has lived most of his life in California. He studied at City College of New York, the University of Southern California, and Yale and has both a B.A. in Humanities and a Bachelor of Fine Arts. Specializing in etching, he has taught art at Ventura College, the University of California at Santa Barbara, and West Valley College.

Barrio has published numerous articles and books and is especially known as the author of *The Plum Plum Pickers*, considered to be one of the leading novels of the contemporary Chicano literary renaissance. In *The Plum Plum Pickers* Barrio presents a fictitious portrayal of Mexican American migrant experiences that elaborates in a historical way the group's struggle for a better way of life. He is also author of *Mexico's Art and Chicano Artists.*

FURTHER READING: Raymond Barrio, *The Plum Plum Pickers*, New York: Harper & Row, 1971; and *Mexico's Art and Chicano Artists*, California: Ventura Press, 1975.

BEAR FLAG REVOLT, (June and July, 1846) an uprising of short duration which preceded the Mexican War.* In early 1846 the California political situation was in a state of great flux. There were rumors of an American takeover of California and of Mexican preventive action. These led to heightened tensions between Mexicans and Anglos; many Anglos believed they would soon be attacked by Mexicans.

In March 1846 an expedition led by John Charles Frémont, his third, was ordered out of California by Mexican military commandant José Castro; however, Frémont lingered in the Sacramento Valley area where his presence acted to provoke resistance to Mexican authority. Many settlers began to talk belligerently of hostilities with the Mexican government.

On June 10 a party of Anglo settlers and trappers seized a herd of 150 horses being driven south for Castro's militia. Emboldened by this action, on Sunday morning, June 14, a party of over thirty armed Americans led by William B. Ide and Ezekiel Merritt rode into Sonoma and took pro-American General Mariano Vallejo* as a "prisoner of war." He was subsequently sent "under arrest" to Sutter's Fort where he was kept prisoner in a cell for two months by Frémont. At Sonoma, Ide and the other Americans declared their independence and raised the homemade flag of their new republic—a white cloth with the name of their republic, a star, and a grizzly bear from which the revolt took its name.

Subsequently Castro sent about fifty men from the south San Francisco bay area to Sonoma, and on June 24 there was a brief skirmish south of Sonoma that became known as the Battle of Olompali. Frémont now assumed command of the Bear Flaggers and merged them with his men. Declaring California under martial law, he marched south and on July 1 took over the ruined San Francisco presidio. Meanwhile the United States had declared war on Mexico, and a week later Commodore John D. Sloat captured Monterey without bloodshed, officially raising the American flag. By July 11 the American flag had replaced the Bear flag at Sutter's Fort. Thus the Bear Flag republic lasted less than a month, but it left among many Californios a heritage of bitter feelings toward Anglos and the American government.

FURTHER READING: Allan Nevins, *Fremont, the West's Greatest Adventurer*, 2 vols., New York: Harpers, 1928; Cardinal Goodwin, *John Charles Frémont, an Explanation of His Career*, Stanford, Calif.: Stanford University Press, 1930.

BEAUBIEN, CARLOS (1800-1864), a merchant, landowner. Born in Canada, Beaubien moved to St. Louis where he became employed in the fur trade at a young age. In 1823 with a fellow fur trapper and trader he went to New Mexico, recently opened by the Santa Fe trade.* He developed a lucrative business in Taos, married a Nuevo Mexicana, and became a Mexican citizen. At the beginning of the 1840s in partnership with Guadalupe Miranda he received a maximum-sized land grant later known as the Maxwell Grant.*

When the United States took over New Mexico he became a strong supporter of the new government and was named judge by Colonel Stephen Kearny.* He presided at the trial of those Nuevo Mexicanos arrested in the Taos Rebellion.* Despite his death sentence for the leaders (some of whom had slain his son), until his death he remained a figure of great popularity and influence even among Nuevo Mexicanos.

BENAVIDES, SANTOS (1827- ?), soldier, merchant. Born to a prominent Laredo Tejano family, Santos Benavides's mercantile position and education brought him to the mayoralty of that city in 1857. When the United States Civil War broke out a few years later, he joined the Confederate forces which dominated Texas. During the war years Benavides was prominent in recruiting Chicanos for the South and in protecting the important cotton trade with Mexico, which supplied the Confederacy with badly needed war supplies. By the end of the war he had been promoted to brigadier general. In the post-Civil War era Benavides returned to active political life, serving many years in various leadership positions in the Laredo area and in the legislature. He also was a founder and president of the Alianza Hispano-Americana,* established to promote acculturation while protecting Mexican American civil rights and cultural identity.

BENT, CHARLES (1799-1847), trader, landowner, and politician. Born in Virginia, Charles Bent joined the Missouri Fur Company as a young man and spent seven years in the western fur trade before turning to the Santa Fe trade in 1829. In the next year he organized Bent, St. Vrain, and Company with posts at Santa Fe and Taos, and a few years later he built Bent's Fort on the Arkansas River for trade with the plains Indians. In 1837 his company built Fort St. Vrain on the South Platte River.

During the 1830s Bent's interest in New Mexico sharpened, and he moved to Taos where he soon married María Ignacia Jaramillo. He also became associated with the governor, Manuel Armijo,* who awarded large land grants to Bent, Ceran St. Vrain, and others.

When the United States-Mexican War developed, Bent favored the American takeover and was named first U.S. governor of New Mexico by Stephen Kearny.* His expanding interest in acquiring land seems to have been a factor in his murder during the Taos revolt* of January 1847.

BERREYESA FAMILY, an early Californio* family left landless and penniless as a result of the American takeover of California in 1848. The Berreyesas, besides holding title to the New Almaden mercury mine, owned over five thousand acres of land, today northeast San Jose and Milpitas, California. Harassed by vigilantes and plagued by Anglo squatters and lawsuits, the Berreyesas not only lost all their lands, in addition, during the 1850s eight members of the family were murdered, lynched, or otherwise met untimely ends at the hands of Yankees, some of whom were claimants to their lands. Other members of the family were to flee to southern California and Mexico for their safety.

BICULTURALISM, the combination of two cultures, or the internalization of two totally different sets of norms of behavior and value systems. These distinct norms presumably allow individuals to organize their real and phenomenal world with its beliefs and value systems in order to make life more predictable and rewarding. The combination or coexistence of two distinct cultures in a single person, region, or society in relatively equal proportions has perhaps existed only in limited cases. A truly bicultural person has to be able to switch codes of behavior and values as he or she switches linguistic codes. However, the internalization of some values and norms (in some domains) of two cultures makes a person bicultural, just as a person with proficiency in some facets of language (phonetics, syntax, semantics) is considered bilingual.

After 1848 a partial or modified biculturalism did develop in the Southwest as some Anglo Americans immersed themselves in Mexican culture and Mexican Americans like Miguel Otero, Sr.* and Solomon Luna* became as much at home in Anglo society as in their own. Moving equally well within the two cultures, they expressed themselves in modes of behavior and life-styles that were unique to each of the two cultures. This living together of two cultures continued to some degree down to the turn of the century. By 1900, however, observers saw the overpowering influence of Anglo domination ending this half century of biculturalism and felt that behavioral patterns that characterized a Mexican way of life were fast disappearing.

These changes arose from the fact that in real life a given sociolinguistic and cultural environment is tapped by individuals for specific purposes with great ingenuity and functional economy. If a person needs only one language for a given purpose, he or she does not use two. But if a person in a social group needs two languages for specifically diverse purposes, those languages remain strong to the extent that such functions as language performs are needed.

In the case of cultural pluralism, when the sociocultural environment requires interaction among diverse groups because there is a particular value to their interaction, single individuals will develop the capacity to interact effectively in two or more cultural settings in specific social contexts. Thus a person can be not only bicultural, but multicultural. Many Mexican and Anglo Americans dealing with diverse groups are able to acquire bicultural or multicultural attributes and harmonize them into a single system of behavior by keeping behavioral domains separate and by internalizing the functional relevancy of the cultural code that corresponds to each domain (for example, business, religious, and family life).

It appears very likely that in the near future many more Chicanos will not only regain, retain, and increase their dual language skills, but will also regain, retain, and increase their bicultural capacity as well. This development will undoubtedly accelerate as Spanish-speaking countries such as Mexico gain greater economic standing and industrial significance. The need for and the status attached to interaction with members from those cultural groups will be drastically increased in a modern world whose problems of industry, energy, defense, and basic resources are becoming increasingly international. As a result biculturalism appears to be destined to expand.

See also HISPANO SUBCULTURE and BORDER CULTURE.

FURTHER READING: Ward H. Goodenough, *Culture, Language and Society*, Reading, Mass.: Addison-Wesley Publishing Company, 1971; Henry T. Trueba, "Implications of Culture for Bilingual Education," in *Bilingual Multicultural Education and the Professional: From Theory to Practice*, H. T. Trueba and Carol Barnett-Mizrahi, eds., Rowley, Mass.: Newbury House, 1979. *H.T.T.*

BILINGUAL EDUCATION, sometimes seen as an extension of the political civil rights movement of the 1960s and 1970s intended to increase educational opportunities for language minority groups in the United States. Some authors view bilingual education as a highly controversial, but also unsuccessful experimental instructional technique. Others see it as a major conceptual breakthrough in a new philosophy of education fitting more realistically the demands of modern pluralistic societies.

Instruction in languages other than English has been known in this country since the eighteenth century and the more recent use of German, French, Spanish, Chinese, Polish, Japanese and a number of North American Indian languages is well documented. In the Southwest instruction in

Spanish was not unusual in the second half of the nineteenth century. However, the first programs with recognized national impact were established in Dade County, Florida, in 1963, and in Webb County, Texas, in 1964. In subsequent years many programs were started in Texas, California, New Mexico, Arizona, and other states with large ethnolinguistic populations.

Bilingual education, looked at from an international and enrichment perspective, is not merely a new curriculum—not a remedy to cure the presumed deficits of culturally different and educationally disadvantaged children. Bilingual education is indeed a pedagogical option that involves use of the students' mother tongue along with the school language, which is the language of mainstream society. Bilingual instruction, as the main component of bilingual education, is congruent with the democratic principles of respect for other languages and cultures as well as with the psychological requirements for learning, in so far as any person can learn most effectively in the language he or she knows best.

Bilingual education, in its broadest sense of a democratic philosophy of education for pluralistic societies, is given different attributes by opposing constituencies. Minority groups see in it a unique opportunity for each group to obtain educational equity and ultimately recognition, status, and the good life that presumably comes with education. Some educators and government officials see bilingual education as a mechanism to speed up the delayed assimilation of certain ethnic groups into mainstream society so that culturally and linguistically different students may participate fully in social, economic, and educational resources. In other words, these latter interpretations of bilingual education see assimilation as the immediate result and the sine qua non for future social, economic, and educational equity.

Because the body of knowledge about utilization of two languages within a classroom setting is fairly limited, local education agencies implemented their bilingual programs by superimposing techniques, materials, and curricula designed for monolingual English classrooms. Among the problems that resulted from this superimposition are confusion and lack of continuity. Objectives for the curricular content areas are vague, if defined at all; language proficiency of teachers often is questionable. In fact, non-English proficient children may be sometimes better off in English-only classrooms, even if they do not understand the language, because of better-trained teachers, well-defined goals, and better curricular materials. Bilingual children in bilingual classrooms for the most part are still achieving below the academic norm.

The boundaries of bilingual education and its relationships with other fields have not yet been well-defined. In general, however, linguistics has had great impact on the conceptualization of bilingual education. The literature of the mid-1950s, with work by Robert Lado, W. E. Lambert,

Einar Haugen, and many others, focused on critical methodological and conceptual issues, on the nature of research in bilingualism, its implication for school, and its relationships to historical aspects of language use. Valuable contributions were to come a decade or two later with the works of Joshua A. Fishman, Wallace E. Lambert and G. R. Tucker, Uriel Weinreich, W. Labov, Dell Hymes, and others who had begun looking at the social context of language learning, use, and contact in a dynamic diachronic fashion. The historical research on language policy in this country by Heinz Kloss and A. H. Leibowitz, has been enlightening and instrumental in redirecting linguistic research in bilingual education.

Efforts to establish bilingual education programs have reflected the weak empirical basis for the typologies developed by Bernard Spolsky, Rolf Kjolseth, Fishman and Lovas, William Mackey, Christina Paulston, G. F. Drake, José González, Henry Trueba, and others. Because past social science research efforts have neglected the social context in the learning activities of ethnolinguistic-minority children, there is no clear understanding of their social behavior. It is simply inconceivable to assess the potential achievement of children in a bilingual program without being familiar with what the children bring with them to school: their family life, cultural and physical survival skills, roles and obligations, world view, sources of self-esteem, and health and general welfare, to mention just a few.

Bilingual education is not a panacea, nor can it be expected to work miracles that will cure social evils resulting from societal inequities, economic exploitation, disease, and racism. We cannot measure academic progress of children in bilingual programs by instruments which primarily evaluate the degree of acculturation to the Anglo-American cultural milieu.

Many studies of bilingual education give evidence of a clear bias against ethnolinguistic minority students themselves. When a study seeks to explain behavior already labeled as failure, it is biased; when the cause of such failure is attributed to an inherent trait, quality, or condition of the child—whether cultural, linguistic or genetic—then the victim is being blamed for his or her own suffering.

In its variety, research to date has performed several important functions; it has revealed important lacunae in existing knowledge about and relevant to bilingual education; it has revealed significant biases that have warped research and thwarted educational effort; and it has begun to suggest avenues for fruitful research.

FURTHER READING: T. Andersson and M. Boyer, *Bilingual Schooling in the United States*, 2 vols., Washington, D.C.: Government Printing Office, 1970; Joshua A. Fishman, *Language and Nationalism: Two Integrative Essays*, Rowley, Mass.: Newbury House, 1972; Joshua A. Fishman, *Language Loyalty in the U.S.*, New York: Humanities Press, 1966; Heinz Kloss, *The American Bilingual Tradition*, Rowley, Mass.: Newbury House, 1977; Rolf Kjolseth, "Bilingual Education

Programs in the United States: For Assimilation or Pluralism?'' in B. Spolsky, ed., *The Language Education of Minority Children*, Rowley, Mass.: Newbury House, 1972; Wallace Lambert and R. Tucker, *Bilingual Education of Children. The St. Lambert Experiment*, Rowley, Mass.: Newbury House, 1972; Henry T. Trueba and Carol Barnett-Mizrahi, eds., ''Bilingual Education: Models, Types and Designs,'' *Bilingual Multicultural Education and the Classroom Teacher: From Theory to Practice*, Rowley, Mass.: Newbury House, 1978; Uriel Weinreich, *Languages in Contact*, The Hague: Mouton, 1966.

H.T.T.

BILINGUAL LEGISLATION, mandated by law in the context and as a consequence of the Civil Rights movement of the 1950s and 1960s. Historically the children of many immigrants encountered difficulties in American schools because of language problems; however, this inequality of opportunity was somewhat tempered by the existence of private, often church-related, schools in which instruction was given in a foreign language. The racial separation that developed from the *Plessy* v. *Ferguson* case, the ''separate but equal'' position, was consistently applied to all educational settings until challenged in the famous *Brown* v. *Board of Education of Topeka* lawsuit. The Supreme Court decision in this case (1954) laid the foundations for many court decisions dealing with equal educational opportunity issues and the promulgation of Civil Rights legislation in the late fifties and early sixties.

However, bilingual instruction did exist before this time, either privately or governmentally supported. German, French, Spanish, Polish, Chinese, and Japanese were used for instruction in the United States for a long time before federal monies were allocated for that purpose. The organized and systematic teaching of English and other languages with federal dollars is traced back to 1963 in Dade County, Florida, and 1964, in the San Antonio School District in Texas.

A bilingual education bill was introduced in the U.S. House of Representatives by James Scheuer of New York in May 1967 and later modified and presented as an amendment to the Elementary and Secondary Education Act, Title VII, and passed on January 2, 1968. The bill was again amended and presented on October 9, 1973 by Senators Cranston, Kennedy, and Montoya. Finally, with additional minor amendments it was again presented by Kennedy and Cranston in 1978 and approved for an additional period of five years. The essence of the Bilingual Education Act has not changed since its original approval. It mandates that children from diverse language backgrounds be instructed in two languages and that teachers be trained, materials be developed, and research be done to help these children move as rapidly as possible from bilingual education to regular all-English-language instruction classrooms.

Meanwhile, in February of 1974, the Supreme Court upheld the right of non-English-speaking students to educational programs that meet their needs, thus creating a presumption in favor of bilingual education. The Lau* decision in 1974 has legitimized and given impetus to a new interpretation of equal educational opportunity, an opportunity that takes into consideration the linguistic differences of students, when compared with the educational opportunities open to all English-speaking students. The most recent version of the Bilingual Education Act, Title VII, states in section 702:

> . . . the Congress declares it to be the policy of the U.S., in order to establish equal educational opportunity for all children, (A) to encourage the establishment and operation, where appropriate, of educational programs using bilingual educational practices, techniques, and methods, and (B) to provide financial assistance to local educational agencies, and to State educational agencies for certain purposes, in order to enable such local educational agencies to develop and carry out such programs in elementary and secondary schools, including activities at the preschool level, which are designed to meet the educational needs of such children; and to demonstrate effective ways of providing, for children of limited English proficiency, instruction designed to enable them, while using their native language, to achieve competence in the English language.

This mandate was implemented by Congress which authorized and appropriated federal dollars in the last ten years as follows:

U.S. CONGRESS APPROPRIATIONS FOR TITLE VII, OBE, USOE
1969-1978

Year	*Amount of Appropriation (In Millions)*
1969	7.5
1970	21.2
1971	25.0
1972	35.0
1973	45.0
1974	58.3
1975	85.0
1976	99.9
1977	115.0
1978	135.0

In the last ten years Congress has appropriated over $626 million for bilingual education.

FURTHER READING: Henry T. Trueba, "Bilingual-Bicultural Education: An Overview," in L. J. Rubin, ed., *Handbook on Curriculum*, Boston: Allyn and Bacon, 1977; Henry T. Trueba, "Research, Journalism or Politics," in H. T. Trueba and Carol Barnett-Mizrahi, eds., *Bilingual Multicultural Education and the Professional: From Theory to Practice*, Rowley, Mass.: Newbury House, 1979.

H.T.T.

BIRTHRATE, among the Mexican American population of the United States, has been growing more rapidly than that of any other ethnic group. In the period 1950 to 1960 the annual rate of increase was 4.1 percent as compared to 3.1 percent for Anglo Americans. A household survey done in Los Angeles and San Antonio for *The Mexican American People* indicated that a majority of Chicano respondents agreed with the statement that "the most important thing" that a married woman could do was to have children.

FURTHER READING: Leo Grebler, Joan W. Moore, and Ralph C. Guzmán, *The Mexican American People*, New York: The Free Press, 1970, p. 361.

BISBEE "DEPORTATIONS," from Bisbee, Arizona. Two months after the United States entry into World War I in 1917, copper miners in southeastern Arizona walked out on strike. Vigilante action led to the rounding up of more than a thousand strikers, mostly Mexican, and their being shipped out of Arizona by rail. These deported men had to find their way back to Arizona on their own. Although court charges were brought against the vigilantes because of this inhumane treatment, no court action resulted.

BISHOPS COMMITTEE FOR THE SPANISH SPEAKING. *See* SECRETARIAT FOR THE SPANISH SPEAKING.

BISHOPS COMMITTEE ON FARM LABOR, an ad hoc committee formed in February 1970 during the grape strike at Delano to mediate between growers and striking workers. *See* GRAPE STRIKE, DELANO.

BLACK BERETS, a somewhat nationalistic paramilitary youth group that emerged in the Chicano student movement during 1969 and was involved in high school demonstrations and walkouts. Although never achieving the success of the very similar Brown Berets,* the organization developed both in California and New Mexico. Based in part, at least, on ideas from the Black Panthers, the Berets, like the Panthers, were the "shock troops" for the movement, but they also were involved in various community service projects. Because of an alienated, radical, anticapitalist stance, the Black Berets never attracted a large following in the Mexican American community, even though most of their projects were highly laudable.

BLISS BILL (1931), a proposal in the California legislature which would have given school districts the power to establish separate schools "for Indian children, whether born within the United States or not, and for children of Chinese, Japanese or Mongolian parentage." The bill was viewed by many Mexican Americans as anti-Mexican in light of the contemporary repatriation movement. The bill passed the assembly but was killed in the Senate Committee on Education.

BLOODY CHRISTMAS CASE (1951), involving police detainment and beating of Chicano youths. On Christmas Eve 1951 seven young Chicanos were arrested after an altercation with police and taken to the Lincoln Heights police station in Los Angeles, where they were charged with battery and interfering with the officers. Early in 1952 a Los Angeles grand jury indicted eight policemen for brutally beating the seven during a Christmas Eve drinking party at the station. As a result of subsequent trials some of the officers were convicted and given prison sentences. All were reprimanded and disciplined by the police department.

BOGARDUS, EMORY S. (1882-1973), sociologist, and seminal scholar in Mexican American studies. Born in northeastern Illinois, Bogardus graduated from Northwestern University in 1908 and received his doctorate in sociology at the University of Chicago three years later. Subsequently he was the recipient of four honorary degrees. Professor Bogardus began his teaching career in 1911 at the University of Southern California, where he founded the department of sociology and the school of social work and ended it there thirty-five years later by becoming dean of the Graduate School. In addition to his teaching, he found time to research and write twenty-four books (including revised editions) and hundreds of articles. He was the founder, and for forty-five years editor, of the *Journal of Sociology and Social Research*.

While many of Bogardus's books concerned general sociological topics, his particular areas of interest were race relations, social (ethnic) distance, leadership, and immigration. During the 1920s he was director of the Pacific Coast Race Relations Survey and was intimately involved in the development of the All Nations Foundation in Los Angeles, of which he was a board member for many years. His studies in the Los Angeles area on race relations and juvenile delinquency considerably influenced attitudes and reactions to these issues there.

Among his better known works are: *Development of Social Thought*, 4th ed., New York: Longman, 1960; *Immigration and Race Attitudes*, Englewood, N.J.: Ozer, 1971, reprint of 1928 publication; and *The Mexican in the United States*, New York: Arno Press, 1970, reprint of 1934 edition.

BONANZA, usually a lucky strike in mining or prospecting, and in a broader sense any stroke of good fortune. The basic meaning of the Spanish word is success, prosperity, fair weather.

BORDER CONFLICT, in the period from the end of the United States-Mexican War (1846-1848) until the beginning of this century prevalent along the twelve-thousand mile border between the United States and Mexico. Among the principal factors in this unrest were: a long and in many areas not clearly marked border, Anglo-American filibustering, widespread rustling and smuggling, long-standing animosity between Anglo Americans and Mexicans, the fact that the area on both sides of the border was a wild, untamed frontier, and the inability of the two countries until the last decades of the nineteenth century to impose a rule of law in the area. Among the notable high points in this conflict were the Carbajal incidents* (1851), Raousset de Boulbon's filibusters* (1852 and 1854), the Ainza-Crabb filibuster* in Sonora (1857), the Cart War* (1857), Juan Cortina's* raids (1859-1860), and the Salt War* (1877).

Part of the border difficulties in the 1850s was the incursion into Mexico of Texas slave owners for the purpose of recovering runaway slaves who often found sympathetic acceptance in Mexico. These raids sometimes included looting Mexican villages and robbing individuals. Another repeated cause of conflict was the extensive filibustering of the 1850s, especially the efforts to create a República de la Sierra Madre on Mexico's northern frontier. Intrusions into Mexico by United States Army units and Texas Rangers formed a further irritant to border relations. Sometimes border troubles in the third quarter of the nineteenth century became excuses for demanding extension of United States territorial control to large parts of northern Mexico, and this further exacerbated relations.

The advent of the strong Porfirio Díaz administration in Mexico in the 1870s and the winding down of Indian fighting in the United States brought a degree of peace to the border. However, some banditry continued as the border area became the last refuge of unsavory American badmen who organized bands of border raiders. By the 1890s opposition to the Porfirian dictatorship led to the organization of anti-Díaz bands which always fled back to the safety of the United States when pursuit got too hot. Because these groups usually enjoyed wide Mexican American sympathy United States troops had difficulty in dealing with the problem. The outbreak of the 1910 Revolution led to heightened border tension, the highlight of which was Francisco Villa's* raid on Columbus, New Mexico, in 1916 and the almost year-long invasion of Mexico by American troops under General John J. Pershing seeking Villa. In the twentieth century the chief causes of border conflict have been division of border river waters, narcotics smuggling, and rapidly rising undocumented immigration* into the United States.

FURTHER READING: Clarence C. Clendenen, *Blood on the Border*, New York: Macmillan Co., 1969; also *The United States and Pancho Villa*, Ithaca, N.Y.: Cornell University, 1961; Walter P. Webb, *The Texas Rangers*, Austin: University of Texas Press, 1965; Robert D. Gregg, *The Influence of Border Troubles on Relationships Between the United States and Mexico, 1876-1910*, Baltimore: John Hopkins Press, 1937.

BORDER CULTURE, technically, existing along the border that is a boundary line between the Republic of Mexico and the United States. The border is also used as a synonym for the borderlands, a larger area encompassing all border states of the U.S. and Mexico. The binational border is a two-thousand-mile line extending from the Pacific Coast to the Gulf of Mexico; the western half being a semiarid desert and the eastern portion a river valley (Rio Grande). Throughout this sparsely populated borderland area are somewhat isolated cities and an occasional fertile valley dedicated to agriculture. Its people live on the lowest family incomes in any region of the United States and have little political power within their states or in the federal government to change this condition.

Some ten-to twelve-thousand years ago southern Arizona was a rain-soaked swampland with lush vegetation supporting giant mammoth, short-horned bison, dire wolf, horses, and camels which were pursued by Clovis hunter bands. By 5000 B.C. these animals were near extinction and the human nomadic bands had followed the herds northward or to the Great Plains. At the beginning of the Christian era, small agricultural communities, ancestors of Pueblo culture, were found in various stages of development. Some five hundred years later Athapaskan-speaking peoples (Navaho/Apache) began to arrive in the borderlands preying on the more stabilized agricultural societies.

Between 1000 and 1300 A.D. a completely preplanned urban community was built in northern New Mexico—Pueblo Bonito. Casas Grandes, in Chihuahua, was a dominant trade center with influence throughout the entire Borderland. In the Central Valley of Mexico, the capital city of the Aztec Empire, Tenochtitlán, was liberating itself from being a tribute-paying city, while in the mound culture city of Cahokia (St. Louis, Missouri) a population of 30,000 had reached its zenith.

When the Spaniards arrived in North and South America indigeneous cultures and land rights were systematically ignored. The Spaniards were extremely successful in establishing themselves in the Central Valley of Mexico, which had been part of earlier Olmec, Zapotec, and Toltec empires followed by a short Aztec rule. The Spaniards sought land on which established people were available to carry out their needs. The indigenous cultural legacy of the Maya, Olmec, Zapotec, and Toltec empires converged, but historical accounts mistakenly focused on the mythical Aztec cosmology as if these were real historical events. The full-blooded Indian groups were soon decimated through war, maltreatment, starvation, and disease, and increasing numbers of mestizos* took their place. Mining policies superseded all others as Spain financially supported its European bid for power from New World resources.

Land claims were symbolically maintained by scattered missions and military presidios, while larger claims northward to Oregon, then to the northern border of Arizona-New Mexico, became less secure. The Spaniards' efforts to establish the feudal system among sedentary cultures of the Central Valley were relatively successful, but they were unable to duplicate this among the nomadic hunting and gathering societies of the borderlands, and their control of this vast area waned. Throughout North and South America, New-World elites took the reins of power from Old-World elites in independence movements. After only a dozen years of Mexican rule, wealthy Spanish families and prominent Anglos combined to reject the faraway centralist leaders of Mexico City as Texas and California territories followed in the independence trend. Subsequent western European immigration into Texas shifted this alliance to one of Anglo dominance, the "redneck" philosophy, which persists in institutionalized form to the present. In New Mexico the traditional Spanish elite maintained their dominant position against immigrant Mexican peasants but were politically and economically infiltrated by Anglo entrepreneurs. The Californios,* transferring the mission lands to secular authority, in turn fell victim to the economic and legal procedures of the ever-expanding Anglo society.

Unlike the Spanish exploitation of the New World by selective migration of temporary administrators, those who arrived on the eastern shores of the United States were mostly the rejected and landless poverty classes of western Europe, permanently here seeking a piece of land without any people on it. Based upon a Biblical interpretation that mankind was to "subdue" the land, farmers claimed "unused" lands periodically occupied by hunting and gathering Indian clans. As compared to the thirty million inhabitants of Mexico's Central Valley, an estimated one million indigenous people occupied the area now designated as the United States. Fragmented into 600 societies speaking 125 different languages and dialects, they were fair game for land-hungry immigrant groups. To save them from physical extinction, they were collected onto government-controlled lands (reservations) without regard for tribal, language, and cultural differences with the result that most of their traditional culture was lost, except for that of the more stable sedentary groups of the Southwest.

Immigration exclusion laws were first passed by the United States in the 1880s to curtail the flow of illegal Chinese aliens crossing from Mexico to the United States. No constant immigration policy has been maintained toward Mexicans. The waves of Mexican families fleeing from the Mexican

Revolution* of 1910 came temporarily, but many stayed and their descendants comprise the majority of all Mexican Americans in the U.S. today. As the need for field laborers increased, Mexicans were invited to come in. Throughout the Great Depression,* when any jobs were scarce, they were cast out to fight starvation and deprivation or to return to Mexico. Some were forceably deported from California to avoid paying them welfare to which they were otherwise entitled under universal coverage at that time. Immigration and emigration ebbed and flowed in cycles, depending upon the strength of the U.S. economy, without much regard for immigration statutes.

Prior to World War II, Mexico had begun to mechanize its agriculture and to break up some of the giant land holdings of traditional families. Endentured servitude was supplanted by large-scale migration from rural to urban centers, principally to the federal capital and cities on the northern border. From 1940 to 1960 the per decade growth rate of Mexican cities on the Texas border was 150 percent, while that of Tijuana was 255 percent. Traditional border life became more and more the concern of Mexican and American federal agencies and regulations. The task of coordinating traditional border functions necessitated local circumvention of awkward national procedures and substituting for these local informal agreements because border jurisdictions are symbiotically dependent upon one another —economically, socially, traditionally, and through kinship linkages. In fact, Mexican American borderlands residents are often caught between loyalty to Mexican values and kinfolk and the acceptance of these same people as competitors for their jobs. In a similar dilemma, some governmental agencies try to make the border an insurmountable barrier to protect the territorial integrity of the nation, while others are working just as feverishly to create a permeable membrane between the nations through which people, goods, and services might flow freely. Border peoples are caught within this mosaic of contradictory policy and procedures.

Of all borderlands peoples, Native Americans have the highest level of poverty. Two families in five earn less than the poverty minimum, and the largest border minority, Mexican Americans, have one family in five living in poverty, as compared to only one in eleven within the larger society. Educational attainment, as well as social and economic immobility also reflect this trend. Clearly, the borderlands are not yet capable of offering minorities economic parity or part of the American Dream. Federal mandates to correct this situation, though well-intentioned, are often counterproductive when developed in other areas and applied to the unique conditions of a border society.

Inasmuch as most borderlands scholarship has been conducted by individual researchers or small coordinated groups, many of the best materials dealing with the borderlands have been scattered unpublished professional papers, research reports, fugitive materials, and archival collections awaiting a research historian. At the present time, perhaps the best general reference to borderlands materials and literature is *The Borderlands Sourcebook*, a collection of more than fifty bibliographical essays on various salient border topics.

FURTHER READING: Edward H. Spicer, *Cycles of Conquest: The Impact of Spain, Mexico and the United States on the Indians of the Southwest, 1533-1960*, Tucson: University of Arizona Press, 1962; Ellwyn R. Stoddard, ed., "The Status of U.S. Mexico Borderlands Studies: A Symposium," *Social Science Journal*, 12 & 13 (October 1975/January 1976): 1-112; Ellwyn R. Stoddard, Richard L. Nostrand, and Jonathan P. West, eds., *The Borderlands Sourcebook*, Norman: University of Oklahoma Press [1981]; Oscar Martínez, *Border Boom Town*, El Paso: University of Texas, 1978; Raul A. Fernández, *The United States-Mexican Border: A Politico-Economic Profile*, Notre Dame, Ind.: University of Notre Dame Press, 1977.

E.R.S

BORDER INDUSTRIALIZATION PROGRAM (BIP), a program begun by the Mexican government after World War II to relieve the unemployment problem in northern Mexico by creating industrial jobs along the border. Through the Border Industrialization Program, of which maquiladoras* came to form the most important element, Mexico hoped to raise the standard of living in its northern states. Although it was not designed to attract runaway plants seeking cheap labor, it has had that effect to some degree. In addition to providing industrial jobs for local workers, the program tended to attract labor from all over Mexico. The influx of these workers rapidly expanded the population of Mexico's border towns, placing tremendous pressure on housing and social services. Many of the people thus attracted to the border region crossed over into the United States where most became competitors with Mexican Americans for low-paying jobs and added to the social and economic problems of the Southwest.

FURTHER READING: Donald W. Baerresen, *The Border Industrialization Program of Mexico*, Lexington, Mass.: D. C. Heath and Co., 1971.

BORDER PATROL, a United States federal agency created in 1924 to supervise and control the flow of migration, especially of Mexicans, into the United States. Since its inception, the agency has been criticized by Mexican American organizations for undue harassment and violation of civil rights in its treatment of Mexican Americans.

BORDER TOWNS, first established in the mid-seventeenth century. Spaniards made initial contact with indigenous peoples of the United States—Mexico border region in the early sixteenth century, but it was not until the mid-seventeenth century that New Spain pioneers succeeded in founding the first permanent settlement along the present border. After several northward expeditions through the central corridor leading to Santa Fe, New Mexico, missionaries established the mission of Nuestra Señora de Guadalupe at the Pass of the North on the south bank of the Rio Grande in 1659. Two decades later the Franciscans founded nearby Ysleta, Senecú, and Socorro when New Mexican settlers fled southward during the Pueblo revolt of 1680. These communities flourished with a strong agricultural economy, and by the mid-eighteenth century about four thousand people lived in the area. One hundred years later Anglo Americans took possession of the territory, and the people at the Pass wound up in two nations: El Paso (which started as a rancho* in 1827), Ysleta, Socorro, and San Elizario became part of the United States by virtue of their location on the north bank of the Rio Grande, and El Paso del Norte, or Ciudad Juárez (renamed after Mexican president Benito Juárez in 1888), remained in Mexico due to its location on the opposite shore.

Successful European colonization of the lower Rio Grande Valley occurred in the mid-eighteenth century when the government at Mexico City induced migrants to move northward with the promise of generous land grants, tax privileges, and travel assistance. Camargo and Reynosa, founded in 1749, became the first permanent colonies in the new province of Nuevo Santander, soon followed by Revilla, 1750; Mier, 1752; Dolores, 1755; and Laredo, 1755. By 1800 Nuevo Santander contained fifteen thousand relatively self-sufficient people supported by agriculture and stock-raising activities. Following Mexican independence from Spain in 1821, the lower Rio Grande Valley became part of the province of Tamaulipas. After Texas declared itself an independent republic in 1836, the area between the Rio Grande and the Nueces River emerged as disputed territory between the rebel Texans and Mexico. Eventually a skirmish which broke out between U.S. and Mexican troops across the Rio Grande from Matamoros erupted into the War of 1846-1848. This outbreak occurred a year after the annexation of Texas by the United States.

European expansion into the far western borderland region began early, but permanent occupation came late. Spanish sailors explored Baja California in the first half of the sixteenth century, founding a colony at La Paz in 1535. The mission at San Diego, California, however, was not established until 1769. The beginnings of Tijuana date to the early nineteenth century, when a rancho was established in the area. By 1840 six ranches constituted the Tijuana pueblo. In the Sonora-Arizona frontier, Father Eusebio Francisco Kino* founded countless missions in the late seventeenth and early eighteenth centuries, but the dry and barren nature of the terrain prevented the development of large settlements.

Following the ratification of the Treaty of Guadalupe Hidalgo* in 1848, new towns emerged on both sides of the boundary. Texas communities like Brownsville, Rio Grande City, Roma, Edinburgh, and El Paso* (known as Franklin in the early 1850s) evolved from old Spanish or Mexican ranchos or former U.S. military forts established during the War of 1846-1848. On the south bank of the Rio Grande, Mexican refugees from the United States founded such towns as Nuevo Laredo and Guadalupe (near Paso del Norte). West of the Pass of the North, the border region remained sparsely populated throughout the nineteenth century.

As Anglo Americans moved into the border area in greater numbers, ranching and commercial activities accelerated, leading to sharp economic competition between U.S. and Mexican towns. Along the Texas frontier the American communities threatened to absorb the older settlements across the boundary, prompting state governments in Tamaulipas and Chihuahua to institute the border *Zona Libre*, or Free Zone, in the 1850s. With free-trade privileges the Mexican frontier communities withstood the American commercial challenge. Boom conditions ensued in Matamoros and nearby Mexican towns in the 1860s during the Civil War in the United States when American southerners exported their cotton and received arms and supplies via the Free Zone. By 1885 Mexico's federal government extended the Zona Libre across the entire frontier, allowing border residents to cope with added American competition brought on by the arrival of railroads into the region. Yet political pressure from the United States and opposition on the part of merchants and industrialists in Mexico's interior led to the abolition of the Free Zone in 1905. Thereafter the Mexican border communities found it exceedingly difficult to compete with their counterpart cities across the political line for the area's trade.

As frontier conditions waned along the border in the late nineteenth and early twentieth centuries, the U.S. border region experienced considerable economic growth. In the Texas lower Rio Grande Valley, Europeans and American southerners arrived to conduct mercantile operations and to settle on inexpensive land. Growers introduced new crops such as sugar cane, tobacco, and citrus. After 1903 towns mushroomed between Corpus Christi and Brownsville and westward upriver in the wake of extensive railroad expansion. Soon land-development companies transformed the region into an agricultural oasis prompting an increase in farming activity with the aid of cheap Mexican labor. Winter truck crops, cotton, and citrus became the mainstay of the area's economy after World War I. On the Mexican side isolation from the interior and disruption resulting from the Revolution of 1910* kept development at a minimum. During the 1920s, however, border tourism increased with the onset of Prohibition in the United States.

At El Paso-Juárez the turn of the century brought a profound transformation. Because of El Paso's location as a strategic crossroads for north-south and east-west patterns of traffic, within a few years after the arrival of the railroads this city evolved into an important transportation center. By 1900 El Paso had become a leading supply, processing, smelting, and refining site for the rich mining districts in the surrounding territory. Commerce, industry, and agriculture also prospered from the infusion of new capital and the growing trade with Mexico. By 1930 El Paso's population had increased to over one-hundred thousand, and the city had achieved a prominent position among urban centers in the U.S. Southwest. During the 1900-1930 period neighboring Juárez lost considerable ground to El Paso due to the former's lack of integration with the Mexican interior, abolition of the Free Zone, absence of natural resources, decline in agriculture (stemming from recurring shortages of water), and instability resulting from the Mexican Revolution. As in other Mexican border towns, the Prohibition era brought temporary prosperity to Juárez.

The border towns west of El Paso-Juárez remained small and isolated until the World War II period. However, the western region did not escape involvement in the internal strife of Mexico between 1910 and 1920, nor was its economy unaffected by Prohibition. In the 1920s Tijuana achieved fame as a favorite resort for Southern Californians and other American tourists. Yet by 1930 this town had a permanent population of only eight thousand, being surpassed in size by Nogales, Sonora and Mexicali, Baja California. On the U.S. side Nogales, Arizona and Calexico, California remained even smaller than Tijuana. In San Diego an 1870 gold strike in the mountains to the northeast, the arrival of the railroads, and several land booms caused the population to swell to forty thousand by the 1880s, but a fall in real estate enterprises triggered a drop to eighteen thousand by 1900. San Diego recovered quickly, however, and by 1930 this city had grown to one hundred and forty-eight thousand residents.

The Great Depression* brought serious stagnation to the border economies. Conditions were especially grave on the Mexican side as tourism declined drastically. The end of Prohibition in the United States in 1933 and subsequent moral reform by the Mexican government sealed the fate of bars, gambling casinos, and related industries for the remainder of the 1930s. When Tijuana's economy tumbled after Prohibition's end, Mexico City reestablished the Zona Libre in Tijuana and Ensenada, and eventually this institution was extended to the entire Baja California peninsula and to a portion of Sonora. North of the boundary the Depression triggered a massive southward migration into Mexico of destitute people who were pressured out of the United States to alleviate unemployment and welfare problems.

World War II supplied the stimulus to lift the border region out of the Depression. Mexico's frontier cities benefited greatly from the impetus which this global conflict provided for the Mexican economy and from the stress placed by the Mexican federal government on development in the nation's northern states after 1940. Attracted by the peso devaluations of 1948 and 1954, increasing numbers of American shoppers purchased greater amounts of Mexican goods, thus fostering local commerce and industry. Most important of all, the Mexican side received an extraordinary economic boost from tourist-related activities as a result of visits by American servicemen stationed in the U.S. borderlands and from the U.S. vehicular traffic bound for Mexico's interior. Lured by this prosperity, as well as by the possibility of emigrating to the United States as legal residents, contracted braceros,* and undocumented workers, migrants from Mexico's interior, began congregating at the border in unprecedented numbers in the 1940s and 1950s. With Mexico's initiation of border development programs such as the Programa Nacional Fronterizo (PRONAF) and the Border Industrialization Program (BIP)* after 1960, migration northward accelerated, leading to a population explosion on the frontier. While Mexico's population grew by 87 percent from 1950 to 1970, that of the border municipalities increased by 168 percent. By 1950 about 800,000 Mexicans lived on Mexico's frontier, and by 1970 that figure had soared to 2.3 million, resulting in a border annual growth rate of 5 percent during the 1960s, compared to the national rate of 3.2 percent.

On the U.S. side, the population of the border counties increased from 1.5 million in 1950 to 2.6 million by 1970. This growth resulted from immigration from the Mexican side as well as Anglo migration from other parts of the United States. Economic activities north of the boundary which served as strong stimulants for growth in the last few decades include increased governmental expenditures in military installations and boundary-related regulatory agencies, expanded trans-border wholesale and retail trade, increased agricultural production, the spread of textile manufacturing, the establishment of twin plants to support industrial operations south of the border, and proliferation of tourist-related enterprises. Modernization and urbanization have spread to such an extent in the twentieth century that the area has assumed a prominent place in the national pictures of both Mexico and the United States.

FURTHER READING: Seymour U. Connor, *Texas: A History*, New York: Thomas Y. Crowell Co., 1971; Paul F. Horgan, *Great River: The Rio Grande in North American History*, two volumes, New York: Holt, Rinehart and Winston, 1954; Oscar J. Martínez, *Border Boom Town*, El Paso: University of Texas, 1978; Oscar J. Martínez, "Chicanos and the Border Cities: An Interpretive Essay," *Pacific Historical Review*, 46 (1977), 85-106.

O.J.M.

BOX BILL (1926), introduced in the House of Representatives in 1926 by John C. Box, a strongly restrictionist Democratic congressman from Texas and member of the House Immigration Committee, to amend the 1924

Immigration Act. The Box Bill arose out of mounting concern over unexpectedly high levels of Mexican immigration in 1923 and 1924. It would have included Western Hemisphere countries in the 1924 quota system and would have limited Mexico to about two thousand emigrants per year.

The House Immigration and Naturalization Committee held hearings on the proposal at which representatives of growers, railroads, cattlemen, and others testified that such a quota would drive them to near bankruptcy. The hearing clearly showed that southwestern employers favored unlimited migration from Mexico because it provided them with cheap, unaggressive, exploitable labor. State Department representatives also spoke out against the bill as being inimical to the fledgling Good Neighbor Policy that Washington had just initiated. Only labor-union spokesmen favored passage of the bill, which failed to pass into law.

BOX, JOHN. *See* BOX BILL.

BOYCOTT, GRAPE, During the Delano grape strike* the United Farm Workers (UFW)* initiated a boycott against all table grapes when it was discovered that Giumarra Vineyards* was using other growers' labels on its grapes as a way of avoiding the impact of the UFW strike against Giumarra. The boycott spread in mid-1968 to the entire United States and became a national issue in the fall presidential elections as well as in local elections in California. By late fall the embargo had extended outside the United States. In the following May it centered on Safeway grocery stores in one hundred cities across the nation. The boycott is usually heavily credited for the success of the Delano strike. An attempt to use the boycott against nonunion lettuce in the Salinas* lettuce strike of 1970 proved much less successful.

BRACERO, Spanish for day-laborer, from brazo (arm). The term bracero usually refers to temporary Mexican agricultural and railway workers brought to the United States beginning during World War II (1939-1945) under government-to-government agreements. These arrangements, which lasted in various forms from 1942 to 1964, are referred to collectively as the bracero program* and were implemented by Public Law 45,* 78,* and others.

The term is also used in a wider sense to refer to Mexican workers legally brought into the United States, and in its widest sense it refers to any unskilled Mexican workers in the U.S.

BRACERO PROGRAM, a program for bringing Mexican workers into the United States. In July 1942, not long after the bombing of Pearl Harbor and the entry of the United States into World War II, the presidential administrations of Franklin D. Roosevelt and Manuel Avila Camacho entered into a bilateral agreement (designated formally as the Mexican Farm Labor Supply Program and informally as the Bracero Program) permitting the entry of Mexican farm workers into the United States to work in the agricultural fields of the Southwest. The wartime draft in the United States and the lure of better-paying jobs in war-related industries quickly depleted the rural work force north of the Rio Grande. The Bracero Program was thus seen as an important Mexican contribution to the Allied war effort, and Mexican migrants soon assumed a major role in the planting and harvesting of southwestern crops.

When the war ended the Bracero Program continued, and Mexican laborers ventured north from the border region to begin harvesting crops in the states of Minnesota, Michigan, Wisconsin, and Indiana. The number of postwar migrants increased markedly rather than declined, and the issue of Mexican workers became a focal point of national debate in both the United States and Mexico. The complex arguments posited did not result in clearly defined United States and Mexican positions. To the contrary, the bracero issue polarized special interest groups in both countries.

Influential spokesmen in both countries urged its continuation. United States growers argued that braceros would put in an honest day's work for an honest wage while United States citizens preferred welfare checks to work in the fields. Some Mexican Americans, appreciating the exigencies of recent arrival from Mexico, argued that the Bracero Program helped to keep the ports of entry open. Even officials of the United States Immigration and Naturalization Service argued that abrogating the program would increase the flow of undocumented workers, a phenomenon which had begun to manifest itself graphically in the 1950s. Other interest groups in Mexico supported continuing the program as well, but for other reasons. Mexican economists quickly calculated that the dollars the braceros remitted to family and creditors in Mexico constituted a new, important source of national wealth, not far behind tourism and cotton sales, the two leading sources of the nation's foreign exchange earnings. National planners in Mexico City also found benefits in the program, as each bracero who entered the United States, relieved, albeit slightly, the tensions of unemployment and underemployment in rural Mexico. Finally, the braceros themselves found that the economic opportunity that awaited them more than compensated for the psychological wounds of dislocation, the disintegration of family ties, and in many cases, the trauma of expatriation.

Countervailing arguments were voiced as well. Labor economists and union leaders in the United States held that the ready supply of bracero labor depressed the wages of rural workers in the United States. Farm workers, including many Mexican Americans, expressed similar resentment when braceros threatened or seemed to threaten their livelihood, and some immigration officials began to suggest that the Bracero Program should be ended, as it encouraged illegal Mexican immigration to the United States. In Mexico, too, opposition to the continuation of the program grew in the 1950s. Mexican growers, experiencing temporary labor shortages at the crucial harvest season, urged Mexico City to reconsider its support. Social activists reported that in many cases working conditions were intolerable, that discrimination against the braceros was rampant, and that in spite of the program's guarantees, the braceros' most basic human rights were violated with impunity. These charges were supported by Mexico's most powerful labor union, the Confederación de Trabajadores de México, and by opposition political parties. In spite of these undeniable hardships, the program continued to be attractive to Mexico's rural work force; but ultimately the Mexican government, realizing that it reflected poorly on its ability to provide reasonable employment opportunities for its own population, withdrew its enthusiastic support.

The proponents of the Bracero Program prevailed for twenty years. The program was extended in 1947 and again in 1951. But by the time of John F. Kennedy's New Frontier and Lyndon B. Johnson's Great Society a consensus had been reached that it had outlived its usefulness. It was unilaterally terminated by the United States in December 1964. During the twenty-two years of its existence, more than 4.8 million Mexican workers had come to the United States.

Periodically since 1964 attempts have been made to revive the Bracero Program or to create something similar. The Mexican government has suggested repeatedly that a new program, with special safeguards, might prove to be a partial solution to the undocumented worker issue. United States congressmen, representing a constituency of southwestern agricultural interests, have introduced bills in the House of Representatives aimed at restoring the program. As of 1981, however, chances for passage of such legislation appeared slim. The focus of debate for the 1980s will be undocumented Mexican workers rather than braceros.

FURTHER READING: Richard B. Craig, *The Bracero Program: Interest Groups and Foreign Policy*, Austin: University of Texas, 1971; Robert C. McElroy and Earle E. Gavett, *Termination of the Bracero Program*, Washington, D.C.: Department of Agriculture, 1965; Wayne D. Rasmussen, *A History of the Farm Labor Supply Program, 1943-47*, Washington, D.C.: Department of Agriculture Monograph No. 13, 1951; Ernesto Galarza, *Merchants of Labor: The Mexican Bracero Story*, Chicago: Rand McNally, 1966; Juan Rámon García, *Operation Wetback: The Mass Deportation of Mexican Undocumented Workers in 1954*, Westport, Conn.: Greenwood Press, 1980.

M.C.M.

BRAVO, FRANCISCO (1910-), physician, philanthropist, and civic leader. Francisco Bravo was born in Santa Paula, California, of parents who had left Mexico to find a better way of life. In elementary and high school he was a good student, but he budgeted his time carefully because he had to help at home and also worked at odd jobs around town. During the summers he followed the crops with his parents. After completing high school Francisco entered the University of Southern California to study pharmacy. His college years were filled with study and work to support himself, while each summer he followed the migrant circuit.

Finally, with his degree in hand, Bravo got a position as a pharmacist. While he worked in a drugstore he continued his education in sociology, earning a master's degree. Then the young pharmacist-sociologist decided to study medicine. After six years at Stanford University he received his M.D., and then he did four years of post-graduate work in surgery.

Having completed his residency, Dr. Bravo returned to Los Angeles and set up a private practice. He also opened a free medical clinic for Mexican Americans. His work was interrupted by World War II, when Dr. Bravo joined the U.S. Medical Corps, serving for over three years in the South Pacific. At the war's end he returned to his civilian practice and his clinic. At this time he became active in clinics for braceros.* He also set up scholarships for students of Mexican descent, enabling them to study pharmacy, medicine, nursing, dentistry, and teaching.

Believing strongly in participation in community affairs, Dr. Bravo has taken an active role in politics and in 1967 was appointed by the mayor of Los Angeles to serve on the committee to revise the city charter. He has also served on numerous local, regional, and national commissions and boards.

BROWN BERETS, one of the few Chicano* organizations advocating physical measures to defend rights of the Chicano community. The Brown Berets was founded in Los Angeles late in 1967 by David Sánchez, Carlos Montez, and Ralph Ramírez, all former members of Young Citizens for Community Action. The organization's initial goal was to ease the strained relationship between the community and the police, but the Brown Berets soon evolved from a community-service organization to a quasi alert patrol. Mostly young people, often high school dropouts rather than educated or middle-class Chicanos, were attracted to its ranks. Members sported brown berets, army fatigues, and boots to symbolize militancy and to accentuate the organization's role as a forceful element in the Chicano search for liberation. Organized throughout the Southwest, the Brown Berets was especially active in California and in Texas.

Seeking to unite the community and to insure that Chicanos were treated justly, the Brown Berets was committed by its laws to keep informed of political and social issues affecting Chicanos; members usually were present at meetings and other events of concern to the community. By exposing insensitivity and corruption among public officials and basic undemocratic attitudes toward Mexicans, the Brown Berets aroused fear among Anglo Americans that a Chicano group would counter oppression with violence. Panicked police officials reacted with widespread and forceful attempts to destroy the Brown Berets and to invalidate the membership in the eyes of both the Anglo and Chicano communities.

The Brown Berets received wide public attention in 1968. Rallying to high school blowouts, demonstrations, and protests during the week of March 5, 1968, they sought to awaken the Mexican American community to the poor quality of education its children were receiving and generally to focus attention on problems facing Chicanos in the Southwest. Instead, they were accused by police and others of inciting students to riot, of using narcotics, and of being communists. Charges of conspiracy to instigate a riot were filed against members. The Brown Beret conspiracy trial that ensued demonstrated that the group had become representative of brown power.

The Brown Berets operated the East Los Angeles Free Clinic with financial aid from the Ford Foundation. On October 6, 1971 La Caravana de la Reconquista, created by the Brown Berets to disseminate their ideology, began its first tour; deployed from Palm Springs, California, it encountered mainly negative reactions.

In August 1972 twenty-six members of the Brown Berets invaded and occupied Santa Catalina Island off the California coast. According to spokesman David Sánchez, the purpose of the invasion was to protest the illegal American occupation of land rightfully belonging to Mexicans. Sánchez seemed to base his accusations on the claims of both Mexicans and Chicanos that Mexico never ceded the Channel Islands to the United States at the end of the Mexican War. The Treaty of Guadalupe Hidalgo* made no specific mention of them when describing the Mexican territory to be annexed by the United States. The Brown Berets renamed the island "Aztlán Libre" and stayed twenty-four hours until, surrounded by sheriff's deputies, they were forced to return to the mainland.

The Brown Berets' inability to define clearly their role in society resulted in their failure to develop specific plans to achieve their demands, and their tendency to react to crisis rather than to remain in control of a situation caused the group to become a disorganizing influence in the Chicano movement. Late in 1972 founder David Sánchez announced the disbanding of the organization.

At its peak the Brown Berets had an estimated five thousand members in some ninety chapters. However, scarcity of funds, a lack of political sophistication, and a stance far to the left of most Mexican Americans prevented the organization from playing a more central role of leadership in the barrio.* Despite these basic weaknesses, the Brown Berets was viewed by many Mexican Americans as symbolic of their protests.

C

CABALLEROS DE LABOR, an organization modeled on the Noble Order of the Knights of Labor, a nationwide union founded in Philadelphia in 1869. When the Knights began to attract a large membership throughout the United States in the early 1880s it became the pattern for the Caballeros de Labor in the Southwest.

Under the leadership of Juan José Herrera, a district organizer for the Knights of Labor, about twenty assemblies of the Caballeros de Labor were established in San Miguel County, New Mexico, but they were never given charters by the national organization. Because land ownership was far more important at the time to Mexican Americans in the Southwest than the eight-hour work day goal of the Knights, these organizations devoted their attention mainly to resisting Anglo land-grabbing. Many of the members as well as leaders were also involved in the White Caps,* and much of their activity lay in the political arena—with only moderate success.

CABEZA DE VACA, ÁLVAR NÚÑEZ (1490?-1557?), explorer, conquistador, and government official. Cabeza de Vaca is the best-known and most important survivor of the ill-fated 1528 Pánfilo Narváez expedition to Florida. The expedition was wrecked off the Texas coast, and Cabeza de Vaca and some companions wandered for eight years across the Southwest of the present-day United States. After a four-year sojourn among the Indians of eastern Texas, he and three companions began a journey that early in 1536 brought them to Culiacán, then the northernmost Spanish outpost on the west coast of Mexico. The search for the legendary seven cities of Cíbola,* especially by the Coronado* and De Soto expeditions, was the direct outcome of Cabeza de Vaca's explorations. From this search the Spaniards obtained a much clearer idea of the geography and native populations of the Southwest.

In 1542 Cabeza de Vaca was appointed governor of Asunción (Paraguay), but he was unsuccessful in that office and returned to Spain where he died. In one of the vagaries of history he is generally known by his mother's family name, Cabeza de Vaca, rather than his father's, Núñez.

CABEZA DE VACA, EZEQUIEL (1864-1917), teacher, editor, and governor. Born near Las Vegas, New Mexico, Ezequiel Cabeza de Vaca attended local schools and completed his college education at the Jesuit St. Regis College in Denver. After first teaching in rural New Mexican one-room schools for several years, he accepted a position as a railway postal clerk. In 1890 he went to work on *La Voz del Pueblo*, the leading New Mexican Spanish-language newspaper controlled by Félix Martínez,* a prominent local businessman and politician. In the following year he became associate editor. When the populist party, Partido del Pueblo Unido,* was founded, Cabeza de Vaca and Martínez were among the principal organizers, and its success carried Martínez to political preferment, but not Cabeza de Vaca. However, the latter accompanied Martínez as his assistant when he was named secretary of the federal district court.

In 1900 Cabeza de Vaca became quarter-owner of *La Voz del Pueblo* when Martínez moved to El Paso, Texas, and his eminence as editor gained him a powerful position in New Mexican politics. By 1910 he had become chairman of the county Democratic party, in which role he opposed the 1910 New Mexican constitution as not sufficiently protective of Nuevo Mexicano* rights. When the first New Mexican state elections were held in 1911 Cabeza de Vaca was elected lieutenant governor on the Democratic ticket. After serving an uneventful term as lieutenant governor, in 1916 he was nominated by the Democratic party for the governorship, despite his increasing ill health, and he was elected. Less than two months after assuming office, he died. Although he had little opportunity as governor to implement his ideas, Ezequiel Cabeza de Vaca had shown that he would have been a strong advocate of full civil and educational rights for all citizens.

CABEZA DE VACA, FERNANDO E. (1937-), La Raza* leader. In 1974, upon appointment by President Gerald Ford as his special assistant, Fernando Cabeza de Vaca became, at age 37, the youngest and highest-ranking Mexican American federal executive. His background included experience as regional director in the Department of Health, Education, and Welfare; special assistant to the Chairman of the U.S. Civil Service Commission; and commissioner of the New Mexico Department of Motor Vehicles.

CABINET COMMITTEE ON OPPORTUNITIES FOR SPANISH SPEAKING PEOPLE, a high-level federal committee, successor to the Inter-Agency Committee on Mexican Americans created by President Lyndon Johnson in 1967. The Cabinet Committee on Opportunities for Spanish Speaking People was founded in 1969 for a five-year period to assure that Spanish-speaking people were acquainted with federal programs aimed at their needs and to develop new programs necessary for their economic advancement. It had a broader mandate than the Inter-Agency Committee, but had diminished support from the new president, Richard M. Nixon. Headed by Henry Ramírez for most of its five-year life, the committee was often widely criticized by the Spanish-speaking. At the time of its demise in December 1974 the National Council of La Raza* characterized the agency as having had few substantive accomplishments; nevertheless, some groups, including the G.I. Forum,* had urged its continuance.

CABORA, LA NIÑA DE. *See* URREA, TERESA.

CACIQUE, a political boss, from the Caribbean term for chief, imported into Mexico in the sixteenth century. It is used among Mexican Americans to apply to a wide variety of officials, usually those exercising power arbitrarily.

CAHUENGA TREATY (1847), an agreement signed by John Charles Frémont and a group of rebel Californios* in 1847. During the U.S. occupation of California in 1846 in the course of the Mexican War,* southern Californios rebelled against the unnecessarily harsh and oppressive control of tactless Lieutenant Archibald Gillespie. Led by Captain José María Flores, Andrés Pico, and others, the Californios gained control of Los Angeles late in September 1846, and despite internal dissension, a shortage of powder, and loss of hope for a Mexican victory over the United States, they held the city until January 10, 1847. Flores then fled to Sonora, Mexico, and Andrés Pico surrendered the rebellious forces to John Charles Frémont. In the conciliatory capitulation or Treaty of Cahuenga signed by Frémont and Pico, the Californios agreed to lay down their arms and keep the peace. Frémont in turn gave full pardon to all the rebels, promising them equality with the victors and guaranteeing their persons and property.

CALIFORNIA, first visited by Spanish-speaking persons during the sixteenth and seventeenth centuries. These Spanish seamen explored the coast, but actual colonization of Alta California, as it came to be known, did not commence until 1769 when Junípero Serra* founded the first mission at San Diego. For over fifty years the foundation and economic mainstay of California was a chain of twenty-one Franciscan missions that stretched up the coast from San Diego to San Francisco Bay. Despite efforts to promote civilian settlement, especially through the founding of pueblos at San Jose and Los Angeles, Spain had difficulty attracting lay colonizers to California.

When Mexico won its independence from Spain in 1821, California became part of the new Mexican Republic. Although often isolated from independent Mexico because of unsettled political conditions in the capital, California felt the impact of its reforms. Mission secularization, a basic tenet of the revolution, was begun in 1834 during the governorship of José Figueroa. The redistribution of developed mission properties and other lands to civilian settlers aimed at building up the underpopulated and underdeveloped province. Although emancipated mission Indians profited little from secularization, the distribution of vast tracts of land to inhabitants of the pueblos and presidios created a new ruling elite in California. After mission secularization rancheros dominated California politically and economically. Allied with them was a group of newly arrived

Anglo American merchants who settled in Mexican California and married into the new landed Californio* upper class. At the top of California's stratified society stood the ranchero-merchant elite and its large patriarchal families. These included northerners like Mariano Vallejo,* José Castro, and Juan Alvarado and southern Californians such as Juan Bandini, Pío Pico, José Carrillo, and José de la Guerra. In the middle of the California social scale was a small middle class of artisans and shopkeepers living in the pueblos, and at the bottom was a large lower class of Indian peon workers. The bulk of Mexican California's non-Indian population was a combination of Spanish, Indian, and mestizo elements.

Livestock-raising was essential to survival in California. It was also California's main industry. From the 1820s on hides and tallow were exported through foreign maritime merchants. As a consequence, California's inhabitants became increasingly dependent upon traders from abroad, especially Yankee merchants from the United States, for manufactured goods.

Mexico's tenuous hold on its remote northern province ended in 1848 when California was annexed to the United States following the U.S.-Mexican War. The Americanization of California brought racial and labor conflict in its wake. It also heralded a loss of political and economic power by the Californios. In spite of the Treaty of Guadalupe Hidalgo* that guaranteed them rights of citizenship and title to their property, many of the ranchero elite were separated from their lands in the turmoil that prevailed after the American conquest and the discovery of gold. Californios, Mexicans, and Latin Americans frequently were driven out of the gold-mining region by their Anglo competitors. Some were victims of violent racial persecution. In northern California, where the influx of miners and squatters was greatest, the decline of the Californios was rapid. In southern California they retained power longer, but the passing of a pastoral economy and the dawning of a new economic order during the 1860s and 1870s gradually reduced the Californios there, too, to a small minoirty with little economic or political influence. By the end of the 1880s, Spanish-Mexican culture in the south had nearly disappeared.

Some native Californios were assimilated into the majority society. A few, like Juan Flores,* Tiburcio Vásquez,* and the legendary Joaquín Murieta,* turned to banditry. Most Californios found themselves isolated and living apart in Spanish-speaking ghettos.

By the late nineteenth century, California's Mexican American population was also increasingly concentrated at the bottom of the state's racially stratified labor force. This phenomenon became more apparent after 1900 with the arrival of large numbers of Mexican immigrants into the state. Although the migration of Mexican nationals into California had been underway since the gold rush, unrest in Mexico and the mushroom growth of California's economy at the turn of the century created a pull-push environment that prompted a massive exodus northward. The Mexican Revolution of 1910 led some middle-class persons and workers to immigrate, and during the 1920s hundreds of thousands of unskilled and semiskilled laborers left Mexico to join the seasonal migratory labor force that harvested the crops of California's booming agricultural industry. By 1930 California's Mexican population, including citizens and noncitizens, had climbed to over three hundred and sixty thousand.

The Great Depression brought a sudden, if only temporary, halt to the influx. In hopes of relieving domestic unemployment, the United States government not only barred further immigration during the 1930s, it also supervised a massive program of deportations and repatriation of Mexican laborers back to Mexico. In 1931 alone, over fifty thousand persons were shipped at government expense from the city of Los Angeles back across the border.

With the outbreak of World War II, however, California's industries once again drew upon Mexico's large labor reserve. To replace the ranks of farm workers who had gone into military service and into wartime industries, Mexican nationals were again urged to migrate northward. In 1942 Mexico and the United States inaugurated the bracero program* whereby hundreds of thousands of Mexican workers were brought across the border on temporary labor contracts. Although begun as a wartime expedient, the bracero program was allowed to continue until 1964. Its termination did not, however, spell the end of Mexican migration as is shown by the fact that thousands of undocumented workers continued to pour illegally across the border, seeking employment in California and the Southwest.

California's Mexican American population grew dramatically during the war years as a result of immigration both from Mexico and from the American Southwest. It was a highly urbanized population, the majority of which lived in southern California. By 1945 Los Angeles housed a Mexican population second in size only to that of Mexico City itself. The 1940s also witnessed increased racial tension between Latinos and the dominant society. Anti-Mexican prejudice, illustrated by the "Sleepy Lagoon"* murder trial in 1942, and violence in the form of antipachuco* or "zoot-suit"* riots the following year, erupted in the barrios of Los Angeles.

In the mid-1960s Mexican Americans became an awakened minority. Under the banner of La Raza,* Chicanos participated in the drive of minority groups throughout the nation for their rights. In 1962 Los Angeles councilman Edward R. Roybal* was elected to Congress. Politically active and aggressive groups like the Mexican American Political Association

(MAPA),* the Brown Berets,* and the Movimento Estudiantil Chicano de Aztlán (MECHA)* protested the subservient status of Mexican Americans in employment, education, welfare, and government. Cesár Chávez,* Dolores Huerta,* and others led the movement for farm-labor unionization that resulted in the formation of the National Farm Workers Association.* During the 1970s the campaign for social justice and for full participation in pluralistic American society continued on many fronts. Many colleges and universities developed ethnic studies programs with courses in Chicano history, politics, sociology, and literature. Growing numbers also gave California's Chicano population increased political influence. In 1980 President Carter appointed Julian Nava* U.S. ambassador to Mexico, the first Mexican American to be named to such an important diplomatic post. By the end of the decade, Mexican Americans, the second largest ethnic minority in the United States, numbered over 3.5 million in California.

FURTHER READING: Albert Camarillo, *Chicanos in a Changing Society: From Mexican Pueblos to American Barrios in Santa Barbara and Southern California, 1848-1930*, Cambridge, Mass.: Harvard University Press, 1979; John W. Caughey, *California: A Remarkable State's Life History*, Englewood Cliffs, N.J.: Prentice-Hall, 1970; Matt S. Meier and Feliciano Rivera, *The Chicanos: A History of Mexican Americans*, New York: Hill & Wang, 1972; Leonard Pitt, *Decline of the Californios: A Social History of the Spanish-Speaking Californians, 1846-1890*, Berkeley: University of California Press, 1970; Edward Staniford, *The Pattern of California History*, San Francisco: Canfield Press, 1975. *G.M.*

CALIFORNIA AGRICULTURAL LABOR RELATIONS ACT (1975), called for by Governor Brown at his inauguration in 1975. California Governor Jerry Brown asked for farm labor legislation fair both to labor and growers and called the legislature into special session to write such a law. The result was the passage in May 1975 of the Agricultural Labor Relations Act by a vote of sixty-four to ten in the State Assembly. It gave California agricultural workers essentially the same benefits that the National Labor Relations Act (1935) guaranteed all industrial workers, and the law particularly provided for secret elections to let workers decide which union, if any, they wanted to represent them. Despite the unhappiness of both labor and growers with aspects of the act, it has been successful in reducing strife in California fields.

CALIFORNIA ANTI-VAGRANCY ACT (1855), a law passed in 1855 by the California State Legislature, decidedly anti-Californio,* aimed at restricting the freedom of Americans of Mexican descent. Because Section Two of the Anti-Vagrancy Act specified that persons, "commonly known as Greasers," especially should be watched in the application of this law, it was sometimes referred to as the Greaser Law. Even though the legislature removed the objectionable reference to Greasers in 1856 by an amendment to the act, the law so read and was applied for a full year.

CALIFORNIA MISSIONS. *See* MISSIONS.

CALIFORNIA RURAL LEGAL ASSISTANCE (CRLA), established in 1966, a nonprofit California corporation funded by the Office of Economic Opportunity to provide free legal services. With emphasis on cases that would benefit large numbers of people, it vigorously pushed for the legal rights of its poverty-level clients, many of whom were Mexican Americans. In its first year it handled nearly one thousand cases. As a result of its active role CRLA aroused active opposition from Governor Ronald Reagan and state conservatives. Because of its excellent record the CRLA was successful from 1968 to 1971 in fighting off vicious annual attempts to terminate its funding. During the 1970s, with the election of Jerry Brown as governor, life in the CRLA became less hectic. At the beginning of the eighties it employed 160 people in 12 offices located throughout the rural areas of California and handled over thirteen thousand cases annually. It also has a task force studying legal needs in education, housing, agricultural work, and other employment areas. From its San Francisco headquarters the CRLA publishes a bimonthly *Noticiero*.

CALIFORNIANOS, LOS, a statewide society founded in 1969 and made up of descendants of early Spanish-Mexican settlers in California. The purpose of the group is to preserve the history of early California, to conduct research, and to interpret the Spanish period in California for present-day Californians.

CALIFORNIO, also Californiano. A Californian of Mexican descent. Usually the term refers to Mexicans who were living in California when the United States seized the area in 1846 and to their descendants. The term is sometimes used in a more restricted sense to apply to the upper class of eight hundred or so California Mexican landowners of the 1840s and members of their families. In this latter sense it was used in Mexican California as the equivalent of gente de razón.*

CALÓ, a dialect used by the lower class in slums and barrios* of Spanish-speaking countries. In the United States, Caló is the Spanish idiom spoken in Mexican American communities, especially by the youths. Commonly referred to as slang, Caló is very ingenious linguistically, being a mixture of archaic Spanish, neologisms, anglicisms, and even some Nahuatl.*

CAMA. *See* COMMITTEE FOR THE ADVANCEMENT OF MEXICAN AMERICANS.

CAMPA, ARTHUR LEÓN (1905-1978), folklorist, professor. Born in Guaymas, Mexico, of American missionary parents, Arthur Campa grew up on a ranch near El Paso and continued his education at the University of New Mexico. Upon graduation he taught one year at Albuquerque High School and then went on for his M.A. in 1932 at the University of New Mexico. For the next decade he taught at the University and worked on his doctorate which he received at Columbia University in 1940. Six years later he moved to the University of Denver, where he taught and was chairman of the Department of Modern Languages and Literature until his retirement in 1972.

During World War II Professor Campa served in Italy and North Africa as a Combat Intelligence Officer and subsequently served in various capacities for the Department of State. As the result of State Department sponsorship as a lecturer in Spain, he was named a corresponding member of the Real Academia Hispano-Americana at Cádiz.

Among his better-known publications are *A Bibliography of Spanish Folk-lore in New Mexico,* Albuquerque: University of New Mexico, 1930; *Spanish Religious Folktheatre in the Southwest,* Albuquerque: University of New Mexico, 1934; *Treasure of the Sangre de Cristos,* Norman: University of Oklahoma Press, 1962; and *Hispanic Culture in the Southwest,* Norman: University of Oklahoma Press, 1979.

CAMPESINO, literally countryman or countrywoman. Person who tills the land. Today it is most commonly used in the United States for farm worker. Suffering a virtual feudal existence, and oppressed and exploited in Mexico, campesinos came to the United States in significant numbers after the Mexican Revolution of 1910. They were similarly exploited in the United States, until César Chávez* and his nonviolent labor organization made significant efforts to ameliorate their plight beginning in the 1960s.

CANALES, ANTONIO (1800?-1852), soldier, politician. Canales was born in Monterrey, Mexico, and studied for a law career. Like most northern Mexican leaders, he opposed Antonio López de Santa Anna's* assumption of centralist powers in the mid-1830s. As commander of the armed forces in Tamaulipas, he was prepared to join with the Texans in their revolt against Santa Anna until their intent to establish complete independence became evident. Later he supported the creation in northeastern Mexico of a Republic of the Rio Grande* which would have included the area between the Nueces River and the Rio Grande. After a second attempt to establish the republic in 1840 failed, he abandoned his allies to make his peace with Mexican centralism. Rewarded with a commission as a general in the Mexican army, he fought against his former friends and during the United States-Mexican War led guerrilla forces against General Zachary Taylor's* army. After the war he became governor of Tamaulipas, a position he still held when he died.

CANALES, JOSÉ, a member of the Texas Legislature from Brownsville, Texas, who filed formal charges against the Texas Rangers* on January 31, 1918, over the mistreatment of Mexican Americans. This action contributed to the rangers being reduced greatly in size—to only five companies.

CANNERY AND AGRICULTURAL WORKERS INDUSTRIAL UNION (CAWIU), an important radical union of the early 1930s, affiliated with the communist Trade Union Unity League (TUUL).* Formally created in mid-1931, it grew out of the earlier Agricultural Workers Industrial League, a TUUL affiliate. It dominated the strike scene in California agriculture from late 1932 to early 1934. In 1933 the CAWIU led three-fourths of the 31 agricultural strikes in California involving some 38,400 workers—two-thirds of all agricultural strikers in the United States that year. By the middle of 1934 wages of agricultural workers in California had improved substantially as the result of grower enlightened self-interest, and the appeal of the CAWIU correspondingly declined. In mid-1934 it was involved in the famous San Francisco General Strike, and its Sacramento offices were raided and many of its leaders arrested under California's criminal syndicalism laws. After June 1934 the CAWIU quickly dwindled away, and in the following year its parent organization, the TUUL, was formally ended.

During its short existence the CAWIU led dozens of agricultural strikes involving thousands of workers, a majority of them Mexican Americans. As a result, some improvement in wages and working conditions was achieved, and many Mexican Americans learned organizing skills and techniques which made Mexican unions the most effective California agricultural unions in the second half of the thirties.

FURTHER READING: Stuart Jamieson, *Labor Unionism in American Agriculture*, Washington, D.C.: U.S. Government Printing Office, 1945; reprint, New York: Arno Press, 1976.

CARBAJAL DISTURBANCES. *See* JOSÉ MARÍA JESÚS CARBAJAL.

CARBAJAL, JOSÉ MARÍA JESÚS (also CARVAJAL) (?-1874), born in San Antonio, Texas. As a young man Carbajal worked and studied in Kentucky and Virginia and returned to Texas as surveyor for empresario* Martín de León. He became active in government, acted as secretary to the

San Antonio municipal council, and early in 1835 was elected to the state legislature. During the Texas revolt against Mexico he aided the rebels and was captured, imprisoned, and escaped. After Texas independence, he continued to fight for an independent republic along the Rio Grande—against Mexico in 1839, and against the United States in 1846. After leading some American filibusters* and merchants in border clashes (sometimes called the Carbajal disturbances) in the early fifties, he settled in Tamaulipas where he fought against the French and became governor in 1865. Later he moved across the border to Hidalgo County, Texas, and in 1872 recrossed the Rio Grande to Tamaulipas where he died two years later. His life illustrates the confusion and anarchy along the Texas border, especially during the period between the United States-Mexican War* in the mid-1840s and the calming of the area by the late seventies.

CARD CHECK, a check-off to discover which workers in an organization are union members in order to determine if the union has majority support.

CARNAL. *See* CARNALISMO.

CARNALISMO, ethnic kinship based on a collective consciousness created by a common experience. An important philosophical and moral ideology that became formulated with the advent of the Chicano movement* in the late 1960s and early 1970s. The term, not common in formal Spanish usage, today remains part of the Pachuco* argot, and signifies a spiritual, unifying force shared by Chicanos who have come to know themselves and their culture.

CARR, VICKI (Florencia Bicenta de Casillas Martínez Cardona) (1940-), popular singer. Born in El Paso, Texas, and raised in southern California, Vicki Carr grew up singing. In high school she was active in all musical programs and sang with local bands on weekends. Her rise to musical fame was steady, and by the early 1960s she had become one of the top female vocalists in the United States. For her contributions to the Chicano community she has received numerous honors including the award of a doctorate in Law from the University of San Diego and in 1970, the Los Angeles *Times* Woman of the Year award.

CARRILLO, LEO (1881-1961), stage and screen actor. Born in Los Angeles to a prominent Californio family, Carrillo first became a cartoonist and in 1913 entered vaudeville from which he quickly graduated to Broadway. He played a variety of romantic stage roles during the 1920s and moved naturally into films at the end of the decade. In Hollywood he played both romantic leads and (especially later) an exuberant, talkative, sidekick to the hero. He played in more than fifty films between 1930 and 1950 and is probably best remembered for the role he played many times as the witty, fractured-English-speaking partner of the Cisco Kid.

Carillo in many ways personified the romantic idea of a southwestern Spanish-Mexican way of life often referred to as the "fantasy heritage." He was a frequently seen figure in California fiestas, rodeos, and parades, smiling and waving from his ornately caparisoned mount. He was also genuinely interested in California's past, read much of its early history, and transmitted a good deal of the Californio oral tradition that he had heard from his elders. With a great sense of pride in his ethnic background, he authored an autobiographical work, *The California I Love*.

FURTHER READING: Leo Carrillo, *The California I Love*, Englewood Cliffs, N.J.: Prentice-Hall, Inc., 1961.

CARSON, CHRISTOPHER (KIT) (1809-1868), mountain man, scout, military commander, and rancher. Carson was born in Kentucky and grew up on the Missouri frontier. While still a teenager he joined an expedition to Santa Fe and Taos, New Mexico. For a decade Carson explored the Southwest with some outstanding mountain men in search of beaver. In 1842 he met John C. Frémont* and became a guide for his three expeditions in the far west, thereby becoming involved in the Bear Flag Revolt.*

Carson married Josefa Jaramillo of Taos, and after the Mexican War became a rancher in the area. In 1853 he took a large flock of sheep to southern California where he sold them at a great profit as a result of the demand created by the gold rush.

Carson was an active figure in the Anglo American community of New Mexico and also exercised considerable influence among pro-Anglo Nuevo Mexicanos. In the quarrel between Bishop Jean Lamy* and Father Antonio José Martínez* he strongly supported Lamy. During the Civil War* he served as commander of the New Mexican volunteers and was breveted brigadier general for his action at Valverde, the first important Civil War battle in New Mexico which occurred in February 1862. After the war Carson moved from Taos to southern Colorado, where he died in May of 1868, just a month after his wife Josefa.

FURTHER READING: Christopher Carson, *Kit Carson's Own Story as Dictated to Colonel and Mrs. D. C. Peters About 1856-57*, Santa Fe: Museum of New Mexico, 1926.

CART WAR (1857), a Mexican border incident which attained international importance in 1857. Mexican teamsters controlled the lucrative trade between the Texas coast and San Antonio from colonial times. In an 1857 attempt to take over this profitable business Anglo businessmen, unable to compete economically, focused their anger and bitterness on Mexican teamsters along the route between San Antonio and Indianola, Texas. As a result the Mexicans were the victims of violent assaults of such proportions that finally the Mexican Minister to the United States protested in October 1857. As a result a company of Texas Rangers was dispatched to the area by the legislature, and by December 1857 the Cart War ended.

CARTA EDITORIAL, a Los Angeles-based newsletter founded in the mid-1960s. Published by a Chicana, Francisca Flores, it commented on the many problems plaguing Mexican Americans in the Los Angeles community. In 1970 it merged with *Regeneración.**

CASA. *See* CENTRAL DE ACCÍON SOCIAL AUTÓNOMA.

CASTAÑEDA, CARLOS EDUARDO (1896-1958), historian, educator. Castañeda was born in Ciudad Camargo, Chihuahua, Mexico. In 1906 his family moved to Brownsville Texas, where he began his American education. Although his parents died while he was in the eighth grade, he managed to graduate in 1916 from the Brownsville High School. He was the class valedictorian and only Mexican American.

Hard work and excellent grades earned him an academic scholarship and in 1917 he entered the University of Texas. Early the next year he enlisted in the U.S. Army and served as a machine-gun instructor for the duration of World War I. After the war he returned to the University, only to drop out after a few months for lack of funds. Spending a year working with an oil company, he returned to his studies in 1920, and in 1921 earned his bachelor of arts degree and membership in Phi Beta Kappa. After two years of graduate work, he received his M.A. in 1923 and was appointed associate professor at William and Mary College in Virginia.

In 1927 Castañeda returned to the University of Texas as a librarian, and while working in the Biblioteca Nacional in Mexico, he discovered Fray Juan Morfi's "lost" *History of Texas*. A critical English translation of this work became his doctoral dissertation, which he completed in 1932, when he received his Ph.D. in history. Dr. Castañeda's editing of Morfi's history brought him considerable fame and led directly to what was to become his magnum opus. In 1933 he was commissioned by the Knights of Columbus to write a history of the Catholic church in Texas for the Texas centennial. This became his monumental *Our Catholic Heritage in Texas*. It was a six-volume work completed in Austin between 1936 and 1950. The title is somewhat misleading, since it is a complete history of Texas from 1519 to 1836 and the history of the Church only since 1836. While he worked on this long narrative history, Dr. Castañeda continued to teach at the University of Texas. In 1939 he finally became a member of the History Department and seven years later he was promoted to full professor. For the 1939-1940 term he was elected president of the American Catholic Historical Association, and he was appointed to editorships on the *Hispanic American Historical Review*, *The Americas*, and *The Handbook of Latin American Studies*.

Throughout his life he wrote articles and books on Mexican history and culture and on the Southwest. Few American historians have received more honors than Dr. Castañeda. A life devoted to historical scholarship produced twelve outstanding books and over eighty-five articles. He died on April 4, 1958.

FURTHER READING: Félix D. Álmaraz, Jr., "The Making of a Boltonian: Carlos E. Castañeda of Texas—the Early Years," *Red River Valley Historical Review*, 1 (Winter 1974): 329-50.

CASTILLO, LEONEL J. (1939-), first Mexican American to be appointed commissioner of the U.S. Immigration and Naturalization Service. Born in Victoria, Texas, on June 9, 1939, he received his B.A. from St. Mary's University in Texas in 1961 and a M.S.W. (Masters in Social Work) degree from the University of Pittsburgh in 1967. Prior to his appointment in 1977, as head of the Immigration Service, he served as city controller for Houston, Texas, and treasurer of the Texas Democratic party. In the 1960s he served as Peace Corps supervisor in the Philippines and worked as director in various community projects.

CASTRO, RAÚL (1916-), lawyer, politician, and diplomat. Born to indigent parents in the copper-mining city of Cananea, Sonora, Mexico, Raúl Castro became the first Mexican American to be elected governor of the state of Arizona.

Castro's early years were spent in Pertleville, Arizona, and after his father died in 1929 he worked as migrant worker, boxer, schoolteacher, miner, and ranchhand to finance his education.

After graduating from Arizona State College at Flagstaff in 1939, he worked for the State Department in Washington, D.C. He returned to Arizona in 1946 and taught Spanish at the University of Arizona while studying for a law degree. Completing his law degree, he practiced law in Tucson for five years, and at the same time entered politics. After serving in various elected positions including county attorney and county judge, he was appointed United States ambassador to El Salvador in 1964, and in 1968, became ambassador to Bolivia.

In 1969 Castro responded to requests from friends and community leaders and returned to Arizona to run for governor. After losing his bid for governor in 1970, he returned to practicing law in Tucson and prepared for the 1974 election. Successful this time, on November 5, 1977, he became the fourteenth governor of the State of Arizona. Offered the ambassadorship to Argentina in 1977, he accepted and resigned as governor.

CASTRO, SAL, teacher. Castro emerged in March 1968 as the symbolic leader of the Chicano students' walkout and their demands for better education, more Chicano teachers and administrators, bilingual education, and the removal of racist teachers and administrators. This Los Angeles student walkout, which served as a catalyst for similar demonstrations throughout the United States, caused Castro to be removed from his teaching position for over five years. His reassignment as a classroom teacher in 1973 was a victory for the Raza* movement.

CATHER, WILLA (1873-1947), writer. Although born in Virginia, Willa Cather grew up in the high plains of Nebraska, an area with which she later became almost completely identified. After graduating from college she became an editor for *McClure's* Magazine, but quit in 1912 to take a trip to the Southwest. This visit aroused her interest in the area, and the Southwest became the locale for her writing. In the following years she published a number of novels and short stories based on western themes.

Perhaps her best-known work is *Death Comes for the Archbishop* (1927), based on the conflict between the first Anglo archbishop in New Mexico and his Mexican American clergy and their followers. It is a highly favorable, fictionalized life of Archbishop Jean Baptiste Lamy* of Santa Fe, detailing his difficulties in reorganizing the Catholic church among Nuevo Mexicanos and especially his quarrel with Father Antonio José Martínez.* It was one of the earliest novels to deal with a Mexican American topic.

CATHOLIC BISHOPS COMMITTEE ON FARM LABOR. *See* BISHOPS COMMITTEE ON FARM LABOR

CATÓLICOS POR LA RAZA (CPLR), a militant group founded in Los Angeles in 1969. On Christmas Eve, 1969, members of Católicos Por La Raza, demanding that the church become more involved in Mexican American economic and social problems, picketed St. Basil's cathedral in Los Angeles and attempted to enter the church. They were expelled by ushers armed with clubs, and some were arrested for disturbing the peace and assaulting police. Most Mexican Americans disapproved of this violent confrontation.

CATRON, THOMAS B. (1840-1921), New Mexican landowner and political leader in the last third of the nineteenth century. Catron was born in Missouri, spent his youth there, and was a graduate of the state university.

After serving on the side of he Confederacy during the Civil War, he moved to Santa Fe, New Mexico where he was admitted to the bar in 1867. In addition to his law practice, he was active in railroading, banking, mining, and land speculation. In 1894 he owned an estimated two million acres and had some interest in an additional four million acres. Most of his land was acquired from Spanish and Mexican land grantees as fees for his services in defense of their claims.

After his 1872 appointment as a United States attorney he also became one of the leading political figures in New Mexico. Through the Santa Fe Ring,* a shifting alliance of powerful Anglos and wealthy Nuevo Mexicanos, and by his dominance of the territorial Republican machinery, Catron exercised tremendous economic and political power. He served in the constitutional convention of 1910, and when New Mexico achieved statehood in 1912, he was elected one of the two first U.S. senators from the new state. His political hold was finally broken by Bronson Cutting.*

FURTHER READING: Howard Lamar, *The Far Southwest, 1846-1912*, New York: W. W. Norton and Co., 1966.

CATTLE INDUSTRY. *See* LIVESTOCK INDUSTRY

CAUSA, LA, the cause. A term sometimes used interchangeably with el movimiento, the movement, to designate the general objectives of many Mexican Americans to achieve greater parity with Anglos in civil rights, economic conditions, and social acceptance. La Causa also represents the objective of Mexican Americans to retain their distinctive cultural heritage.

CAWIU. *See* CANNERY AND AGRICULTURAL WORKERS INDUSTRIAL UNION.

CENSUS, DATA, on Mexican Americans, of only limited value for comparison because of the varying bases used for enumerating persons of Mexican descent. Until 1930 the census counted only those born in Mexico or who had at least one Mexican parent. In the 1930 census, in an effort to ascertain more precisely the Mexican American population, census takers listed as Mexican all persons of Mexican origin who were not definitely white, Negro, Indian, or Oriental. Because this count still excluded many persons of Mexican descent, particularly in New Mexico, the Census Bureau in 1940 identified Mexican Americans as those who spoke Spanish in early childhood. This still proved to be inadequate since it excluded a sizeable population of Mexican origin that spoke only English from childhood.

In 1950 and 1960 the Bureau of the Census changed its counting system again, now using Spanish surnames as the determinants for identifying Mexican Americans in the five Southwestern states. This base, like the earlier ones, was not completely satisfactory since it excluded all females of Mexican origin who had married Anglos and their children as well. It also lumped together Puerto Ricans, Cubans, and other Latin Americans, as well as Spaniards, with Mexican-origin Americans. Braceros* who were in the United States when the enumeration took place were also included in the count.

The 1970 census continued the practice of Spanish-surname identification, and in a special sample, persons of Spanish cultural origins were identified no matter how far removed generationally from their country of origin. As a result of the 1970 census, the bureau was able to publish more social and economic statistical information on the Mexican-descent population than in any previous census. However, many Mexican Americans still contended that the 1970 count understated their numbers by as much as 10 percent.

In the 1980 census there is a category called Español-Hispano which includes a breakdown into Mexican American, Chicano, Mexican, Cuban, Puerto Rican, and other Spanish-Hispanics. Every household will be asked a question on Spanish-culture origin or descent. This may finally give a more precise count of Americans of Mexican descent. In 1960 there were perhaps 4 million Mexican-descent Americans according to the census; in 1970 that figure rose to over 6 million; the 1980 census may show that there are as many as 11 million.

CENSUS 1970, including the following statistics: 9.6 million Spanish-speaking persons, plus half a million non-Spanish-speaking persons with Spanish surnames. (This total of 10.1 million persons is generally accepted as an undercount, the only question being the degree of undercount). Of this group about 5.3 million were of Mexican origin, 1.5 million of Puerto Rican origin, .63 million of Cuban origin, and 1.8 million of other origins. Of the 5.3 million of Mexican origin, 2.3 million were immigrants or first generation. The overwhelming bulk of Mexican-origin Americans lived in the five southwestern states, but sizeable numbers were located in the Chicago area, northern Ohio and Indiana, and southern Michigan. Over 80 percent lived in metropolitan areas, but many of these were migrant farmworkers with an urban base.

The median age was eighteen years and 28 percent were children under ten. The median years of school completed (in the five southwestern states) ranged from 7.2 years in Texas to 10.6 years in California, and the number of high school graduates entering college ranged from less than 1 in 6 in Texas to 1 in 3 in New Mexico. The unemployment rate for Mexican Americans was 6.9 percent compared to 4.1 percent for Anglo Americans; while for Mexican American women it was the highest for any group—8.5 percent. In the area of annual family income, Mexican Americans averaged $7,486 compared to $10,285 for all families, and in the five southwestern states the average for individual Mexican Americans was $5,963 compared to $7,875 for Anglo Americans.

See Appendix table: Hispanic American Population, by Various Identifiers: April, 1970 and map: Distribution of Spanish-speaking Americans, 1970.

CENSUS 1980, viewed by Hispanics with considerable concern, especially two issues that relate to Mexican Americans: a concern that all Spanish culture-descent persons be identified and counted, and the question whether undocumented aliens should be counted. The counting of illegal aliens was favored by city and state agencies which depend in part on revenue-sharing for funds and was opposed by some state political leaders who saw the counting of aliens as possibly leading to reapportionment and thereby to dilution of representation. This latter view was strongly supported by an organization known as the Federation for American Immigration Reform.* A suit filed to impede the counting of undocumented* aliens was rejected by a federal panel of judges at the end of February 1980, and on March 17 the Supreme Court effectively ended the controversy by refusing to issue an injunction against the enumeration of illegal aliens.

Estimates of the size of the Spanish-descent population varied considerably. The estimated total number ranged from a high of twenty million to a low of twelve million, with the Census Bureau opting for a middle-range figure of fourteen to fifteen million. Preliminary 1980 census reports indicate over fourteen and a half million persons who classified themselves as of Spanish origin. Of this total approximately nine million are Mexican Americans. However, there are almost certainly undocumented Spanish origin persons who were not included in the count.

Finally, many organizations, spearheaded by the Mexican American Legal Defense and Education Fund,* have participated in efforts to publicize the census and its potential benefits for Hispanics. In view of the widespread conviction that the 1970 census undercounted minorities by over five million, the Census Bureau and these organizations made great efforts to overcome Hispanic fears of the census taker and to insure a more accurate count. The 1980 census asked *all* Americans if they are of Spanish descent.

CENTRAL DE ACCIÓN SOCIAL AUTÓNOMA (CASA), a left-wing organization of Mexican workers in Los Angeles. The organization is concerned with radical labor causes and has especially involved itself with the problems of undocumented workers.

CENTRO CAMPESINO CULTURAL, INC., (CULTURAL FARMWORKERS' CENTER), largely the creation of Luis Valdez, originating in the Delano grape strike* in the late 1960s. Intensely committed to the development and improvement of Mexican American cultural heritage through the theatrical arts, it produces plays, films, and music; conducts theater workshops, and is best known for the Teatro Campesino.*

CENTRO DE SERVICIOS PARA MEXICANOS, INC. (CENTER FOR SERVICES FOR MEXICANS), a social service agency established and financed by the Catholic archdiocese of Kansas to provide help to immigrants and Spanish-speaking citizens in becoming self-sufficient. The Centro provides a wide variety of social services and acts as intermediary with various state, federal, and private bureaucracies. It has a registered lobbyist in the Kansas legislature.

CHACÓN, FELIPE M. (1873-?), publisher and writer. Born in Santa Fe, New Mexico, he was the son of an important early northern Nuevo Mexicano newspaper publisher, Urbano Chacón. Although he was orphaned at age thirteen, Felipe had the advantage of a good education at Santa Fe, first in the public schools and then in the Colegio de San Miguel. As an adult he was engaged in various business enterprises and, like his father, edited a number of local Spanish-language newspapers from about 1911 onward. He also wrote poetry and essays of high literary quality in both Spanish and English. In 1924, while publishing and editing *La Bandera Americana* in Albuquerque, he wrote and published an excellent example of his literary skills titled *Obras de Felipe Maximiliano Chacón, El Cantor Nuevomexicano: Poesía y Prosa*.

CHARGIN, GERALD S., Judge of the County of Santa Clara, California, Juvenile Court. Chargin became well known to the Mexican American community after a vicious racial outburst during a trial over which he was presiding on September 2, 1969. Chargin proclaimed:

> Mexican people, after thirteen years of age, think it is perfectly all right to go out and act like an animal. We ought to send you out of the country—send you back to Mexico. You belong in prison for the rest of your life for doing things of this kind. You ought to commit suicide. That's what I think of people of this kind. You are lower than animals and haven't the right to live in organized society—just miserable, lousy, rotten people.
>
> Maybe Hitler was right. The animals in our society probably ought to be destroyed because they have no right to live among human beings.[1]

Although an effort was made to remove him from office, Chargin continued to serve as a member of the judicial system, administering justice, until his retirement from the bench several years later.

[1]Rodolfo Acuña, *Occupied America, The Chicano's Struggle Toward Liberation*, San Francisco: Canfield Press, 1972, pp. 270-71.

CHAVES, JOSÉ FRANCISCO (1833-1904), politician and soldier. Born near Albuquerque, as a teenager Chaves was sent to school at St. Louis, Missouri, by his father so he would be able to cope with the Anglo Americans who were pushing inexorably westward in response to "manifest destiny." During the United States invasion of New Mexico in 1846 he served under General Stephen W. Kearny* as interpreter and after the American takeover fought in various Indian campaigns and in the Civil War.*

After the Civil War Chaves was elected to the New Mexico territorial legislature and reelected for thirty years until his death in 1904. During this time he was elected president of the legislature eight times. He was also elected to serve three terms as New Mexican delegate to the U.S. Congress. In 1904 he was murdered by an unknown assailant.

CHAVES, MANUEL ANTONIO (1818-1889), trader, rancher, scout, and Indian fighter. Chaves was born during the revolution for Mexican independence at Atrisco, near Albuquerque, New Mexico. Although he was a nephew of Governor Manuel Armijo,* he was forced to flee to Saint Louis, Missouri, at the end of the thirties because the governor had made threats against his life. In 1841 he returned to Santa Fe, married, and settled down to trading and ranching.

When the United States-Mexican War* broke out he became involved early in the plotting of the first Taos Rebellion;* as a result he was arrested, charged with treason but acquitted in January 1847 and released. When the Taos revolt broke out a week later he was one of the Nuevo Mexicanos who helped suppress it. After the war Chaves returned to trading with Chihuahua merchants and to stock raising.

In the early fifties Manuel Chaves participated in a number of expeditions against hostile Indians, and by 1857 he was appointed chief of scouts in the Gila expedition against the southern Apaches. In 1861 he was given command of Fort Fauntleroy in northwestern New Mexico. Meanwhile the Civil War* had broken out, and a strong Texas Confederate force was pushing up the Rio Grande toward Albuquerque and Santa Fe, which the Confederates took despite valiant New Mexican resistance. In a most brilliant action against the Confederate invaders Chaves, as chief scout, led a Colorado volunteer force under Major John Chivington through Glorieta Pass southeast of Santa Fe to flank the Confederate army and capture its supply train. This action forced the Confederates to withdraw southward along the Rio Grande and marked the beginning of the end for Confederate military efforts in the west.

At the end of the Civil War Chaves returned home to rebuild his cattle herds which had been depleted by Indian raids during the war. In the decade following the war his stock-raising activities became profitable, as the Indian tribes were pacified.

In 1876 Chaves moved his family to a new frontier in southwestern New Mexico where a half-brother had settled earlier. Here in his sixties he again built up an extensive ranch despite considerable pain from old wounds that had never completely healed. Till his death in 1889, El Leoncito, the Little Lion, as he was known, remained a company commander in the territorial militia.

FURTHER READING: Marc Simmons, *The Little Lion of the Southwest*, Chicago: The Swallow Press, Inc., 1973.

CHÁVEZ, FRAY ANGÉLICO, (1910-), author, poet, historian, clergyman (Franciscan). Born at Wagon Mound, New Mexico, in east central Mora County and christened Manuel, Chávez was educated in Mora public schools staffed by the Sisters of Loretto. He then attended the Franciscan order's preparatory seminary in Cincinnati, Ohio, and in 1933 graduated from Duns Scottus College in Detroit. Four years later he was ordained as a Franciscan priest with the name Angélico. He then began a career devoted to Indians and Nuevo Mexicanos in his native state. After serving as a missionary in Rio Grande Indian pueblos for six years, he entered the United States Army in 1943, serving as a chaplain in the South Pacific until the end of the war. In 1946 Fray Angélico returned to his busy missionary life among the Rio Grande Pueblo Indians of New Mexico and to his writing. In 1959 Angélico Chávez was named pastor of the church at Cerrillos near Santa Fe. In the early seventies he separated from the Franciscan order and in the mid-seventies was appointed archivist of the archdiocese of Santa Fe by Archbishop Robert F. Sánchez.*

Fray Angélico Chávez has written numerous articles and poems, and is the author of over a dozen books. The best known of his published works are *Origins of New Mexico Families in the Spanish Colonial Period*, Santa Fe: Historical Society of New Mexico, 1954; *Our Lady of the Conquest*, Santa Fe: Historical Society of New Mexico, 1948; *When the Santos Talked*, Santa Fe: William Gannon, 1977 reprint of 1957 edition; *Coronado's Friars: The Franciscans in the Coronado Expedition*, Washington, D.C.: Academy of American Franciscan History, 1968; and *My Penitente Land*, Albuquerque: University of New Mexico Press, 1974.

CHÁVEZ, CÉSAR (1927-), organizer and labor leader. Born near Yuma, Arizona, César Chávez came from the typical milieu of a migrant farmworker family in southwestern United States during the 1930s. Growing up in farm labor camps, he attended nearly thirty schools and eventually reached the seventh grade. He served two years in the navy at the end of World War II and after being mustered out returned to the migrant life briefly but settled down in San Jose, California, after marrying Helen Fabela of Delano in 1948.

In San Jose, Chávez became acquainted with Fred Ross* who was organizing Community Service Organizations (CSO).* Ross quickly became convinced of Chávez's leadership potential and persuaded him to become a CSO organizer. In his new activities Chávez not only organized CSO chapters and voter-registration drives but also filled in some of the holes in his education by reading. By 1958 he had been named general director of the CSO in California and Arizona, and soon he began to advocate a program for organizing agricultural workers. When his proposal to develop a farmworkers' union was rejected at a 1962 meeting of the CSO, Chávez resigned from the directorship.

At age thirty-five Chávez moved his family to Delano* and in California's great Central Valley began to develop his concept of a farm labor organization with the help of Fred Ross, Dolores Huerta,* and others. The National Farm Workers Association (today the United Farm Workers,* AFL-CIO) evolved slowly as the result of long hours spent in contacting workers and persuading them that they could improve their conditions by joining the union.

In September 1965 Chávez's fledging union had about seventeen hundred members and an invitation from Larry Itliong* of the heavily Filipino Agricultural Workers Organizing Committee (AFL-CIO) to join his organization in a strike of the Delano grape fields. Chávez took the NFWA into the strike, which he was to dominate.

Chávez viewed the strike as part of a broad movement for social justice and human dignity, as indicated by the Spanish term used—La Causa. He based his leadership of La Causa on two principles: nonviolence and widespread appeal for outside support. His twenty-five-day march from Delano to Sacramento early in 1967 served to dramatize the strike and give it front-page publicity. In the continuing struggle with Di Giorgio Fruit Corporation* and Giumarra Vineyards,* Chávez's tactics included a long fast of rededication to nonviolence and the decision to initiate a general table-grape boycott. After five years of struggle Chávez was successful in obtaining contracts with twenty-six Delano grape growers in July 1970. He then turned his attention to the plight of workers in the Salinas lettuce fields.

In the lettuce strike and the boycott which was part of it César Chávez continued to demonstrate his leadership qualities. Ten years later Chávez's struggle for recognition of the NFWA as agent for the lettuce workers continues. Meanwhile, the Chávez union has lost some of its grape farm labor contracts.

More than any other person César Chávez was responsible for the 1975 California Agricultural Labor Relations Act* which provides secret ballot union elections for farm workers.

Despite this legislation, the fight for farm workers' rights goes on, and Chávez remains in the forefront. Because of his unrelenting efforts, a revolution has come to the "factories in the fields," and it is clear that as a result of his leadership most California farm workers of the future will be union members. César Chávez continues to challenge agriculture's insistence on its right to an unlimited supply of cheap labor. To his opponents he apears to be a stubborn, relentless, labor organizer; his supporters see him as a dedicated, ascetic, twentieth-century saint.

FURTHER READING: Peter Matthiessen, *Sal Si Puedes. César Chávez and the New American Revolution*, New York: Random House, 1969; Jean M. Pitrone, *Chávez: Man of the Migrants*, New York: Pyramid Communications, Inc., 1972; Lynn Faivre, *Chávez: One New Answer*, New York: Praeger, 1970; Jacques E. Levy, *César Chávez: Autobiography of La Causa*, New York: W. W. Norton and Co., 1975; Florence White, *César Chávez: Man of Courage*, New York: Dell Publishing Co., 1975; Ronald Taylor, *Chávez and the Farmworker*, Boston: Beacon Press, 1975.

CHÁVEZ, DENNIS (1888-1962), senator and humanitarian. Baptized Dionisio, Dennis Chávez came from a large, poor, New Mexican family—a factor which put him in the labor market at age thirteen. An interest in history and biography after he left school at the end of the eighth grade led him to politics even before he reached voting age. Chávez supported a successful Democratic senatorial candidate, who brought him to Washington, D.C., where he completed a Bachelor of Laws degree at Georgetown University in 1920. At the same time he clerked in the Senate.

Chávez then returned to practice law in Albuquerque and to pursue actively a career in state politics. He was easily elected to the state legislature and in 1930 successfully campaigned for a seat in the U.S. House of Representatives. After one reelection he set his sights in 1934 on the United States Senate seat held by Bronson Cutting.* Narrowly defeated, Chávez challenged the senator's reelection and carried his challenge all the way to the U.S. Senate. While his petition was still pending in that body, Cutting was killed in an airplane crash and Chávez was appointed interim senator until the next election in 1936. In that election he was overwhelmingly elected to finish out the four years of Cutting's term.

As senator, Dennis Chávez was a staunch New Dealer, supporting all of Franklin D. Roosevelt's legislative programs. Only in one area was his support of F.D.R. less than enthusiastic; on the eve of World War II he initially opposed the administration's Lend-Lease bill to help the Allies and favored a strict neutrality policy. During the war some of his votes in the Senate were controversial among his constituents, often because of his support of liberal social legislation, including an equal rights amendment which he cosponsored.

In the postwar years the loyalty of his Nuevo Mexicano supporters enabled him to win election term after term. During these years his greatest contribution to his constituency and to the country was his strong leadership in creating a permanent Fair Employment Practices Commission. Despite setbacks, he continued to fight for greater economic and social equality for all, opposing exemption of farm labor from provisions of the National Labor Relations Act and working quietly to help the cause of the American Indian.

Dennis Chávez was one of New Mexico's most important political leaders in the twentieth century, fighting for human equality and a better quality of life.

CHICAGO, an important midwestern lodestone for Mexicans and Mexican Americans. The early years of the twentieth century saw the beginning of a movement of Mexicans and Mexican Americans out of the Southwest into the industrial centers of the Midwest. Soon after World War I* broke out in Europe in 1914 the first Mexicans arrived in Chicago, most of them railroad workers. Beginning in 1917 the railroads set up a number of camps for this labor force. Six of these camps were within the city limits. Gradually some of these railroad workers left for other jobs, especially in the steel mills and meat-packing plants, and separate Mexican neighborhoods developed around these three industries. The big steel strike of 1919 brought in more Mexican workers as strikebreakers, and by the following year Chicago had a Mexican/Mexican American population of approximately four thousand. During the 1920s additional thousands of workers came to Chicago out of the labor reservoirs* of the Southwest and spread out into restaurant, hotel, and other service positions. By 1930 there were nearly twenty thousand Mexicans and Mexican Americans living in Chicago.

Most of these immigrants were young, unskilled, single men; about half were from Mexico and half were Mexican American. In 1924 the first Mexican church, Our Lady of Guadalupe, was established in south Chicago among the steel workers by a Jesuit priest, William T. Kane; and at about the same time various social clubs and mutualist societies were organized. By 1928 there were 1,660 Mexican children enrolled in Chicago's elementary schools. The Great Depression* and repatriation of the thirties caused a decline in single Mexican workers, and thereby increased the percentage of families in the Mexican American population of the city. By 1940 Chicago counted about sixteen thousand persons of Mexican descent, most of whom seemed on their way to assimilation.

World War II,* with its labor needs, brought a renewed and much greater influx of workers from Mexico and the Southwest. Despite the adverse effects of the 1954 drive against illegal aliens in "Operation Wetback,"* the number of Mexican-origin Chicagoans continued to rise rapidly, especially in the 1960s. By 1970 there were nearly one hundred and ten thousand Mexican Americans in Chicago. Meanwhile there has also been a rapid growth of other Spanish-speakers, principally Puerto Ricans and Cubans, who swelled the total Hispanic population to a quarter million in 1970. By 1978 Chicago had an estimated Hispanic population of between four hundred thousand and eight hundred thousand, not including illegal aliens. Despite this impressive number, between 15 and 25 percent of the total population, the Spanish-speaking did not have a single Hispanic alderman. Chicago's Mexican Americans have not seen themselves as a single entity whose political organization might give them power in city government.

FURTHER READING: Anita Jones, *Conditions Surrounding Mexicans in Chicago*, San Francisco: R & E Research Associates, 1971; *Chicago's Spanish-Speaking Population: Selected Statistics*, Chicago: Department of Development and Planning, 1973.

CHICANA FORUM, functioning primarily through advisory committees in El Paso, Los Angeles, and Albuquerque. The Forum endeavors to increase female Mexican American participation in the economy and to act as a center for information on government contracts. It was organized in 1976 and is funded by federal grants.

CHICANA SERVICE ACTION CENTER, INC. (CSAC), a southern California agency which provides employment training for low income, educationally disadvantaged Mexican American women through its offices in the greater Los Angeles area. Its goal is to raise them above the poverty level by developing and upgrading their vocational skills.

CHICANISMO, a concept based on self-awareness, compadrazgo,* and carnalismo,* and enriched by unique qualities of Chicano and Mexican heritage. Ideologically identified with La Causa,* Chicanismo became the primary driving force of the Chicano movement* as articulated by its leadership.

CHICANO, controversial term made popular by activists in the 1960s referring to Mexican Americans and especially to those who demonstrate a militant pride in their ethnicity. The term apparently derives from the word Mexicano, by elision to Xicano (with the X pronounced in the Nahuatl as S/SH), and then to the current spelling, Chicano. In the late-nineteenth century it was a pejorative term used by upper-class Mexicans to refer to the lower class. The term was adopted with pride by young Mexican Americans during the 1960s.

In its broadest sense Chicano means simply Mexican American and has been widely used in this meaning by the news media because of its shortness and simplicity as compared to terms like Spanish-speaking, Spanish-surnamed, or Mexican American. In its narrowest meaning it signifies a proud, militant ethnicity with connotations of self-determination, rejecting accommodation and assimilation, and favoring confrontation strategies.

A recent (1978) limited study of rural south Texas youths indicated that the most favored self-referent term was Mexican American (50 percent); Chicano was both the second most favored (25 percent) and the most disliked (43 percent). Some Mexican Americans reject the term because of its former pejorative and/or its current militant connotation. It is probably most popular in California.

CHICANO ASSOCIATED STUDENTS ORGANIZATION (CASO), an activist student group founded at New Mexico Highlands University in Las Vegas during the late 1960s. Originally called Spanish American Students Organization, in 1969 it was successful in its demands for educational changes, especially development of multicultural programs, including a Chicano studies program and the hiring of more Mexican American professors. Its crowning success was the hiring of an Hispano descent university president, Dr. John Aragón.

CHICANO LIBERATION FRONT, a radical organization active in the Los Angeles area at the beginning of the 1970s.

CHICANO MOVEMENT. *See* MOVIMIENTO.

CHICANO POLICE OFFICERS ASSOCIATION (CPOA), an organization in the Albuquerque, New Mexico, police department formed in 1973 in order to protect the civil rights of Mexican American officers in hiring and promotion policies. By filing suits alleging discrimination, the CPOA secured a review of recruiting, hiring, and promotion procedures.

CHICANO PRESS ASSOCIATION, an informal organization of Chicano community newspapers with headquarters in Los Angeles. Members of the association, representing about fifty Chicano publishers, cooperate to exchange and disseminate information, stories, photographs, and graphics of interest to Mexican Americans. The association also is dedicated to the support of the Chicano struggle against discrimination and for cultural self-determination.

CHICANO SOCIAL STUDIES ASSOCIATION, an organization founded during 1973 in New Mexico to fill the need for social intercourse among

Mexican Americans in the various professions. It enables Chicano social scientists to meet to pool information, and exchange views and makes possible continuing interchange of professional information of interest to members of the association.

CHICANO TRAINING CENTER, a social service organization organized in Houston, Texas, during 1971. It provides specialized training programs for mental health and social service personnel in order to improve the quality of these services. It also provides bicultural social services through a clínica de consulta familiar, which serves also as a training center.

CHICANOS UNIDOS PARA JUSTICIA (CUPJ), an activist student group in the Las Vegas, New Mexico, school protest of 1973 and the Montezuma (N.M.) 1974 demonstration. Chicanos United for Justice helped establish an alternative school in Montezuma. Its militant demonstrations frightened and alienated many moderate Hispanos.

CHICANO WELFARE RIGHTS ORGANIZATION (CWRO), a pressure group of people on welfare which lobbies at the state level for the interests of welfare participants. Founded in November 1973 at Las Vegas, New Mexico, the CWRO later became a chapter of the National Welfare Rights Organization. It provides its members and all people on welfare with support in their dealings with the welfare bureaucracy.

CHICANO YOUTH ASSOCIATION (CYA), a high-school student group in New Mexico which organized walkouts at the beginning of the seventies in Albuquerque and Roswell schools in protest against the lack of courses relating to Mexican American culture and against prejudiced faculty and administrators. The students were successful in obtaining curriculum and policy changes.

CHILEANS, during the gold rush period numbering about five thousand in California. Because of their general mining experience Chileans were often among the more successful miners. This success and their language and culture caused them to be discriminated against along with Mexicans, with whom they were sometimes confused under the general denigrative term "greasers."

CHOLO (CHOLA), during the Spanish and Mexican periods in the Southwest a mestizo* or an acculturated Indian, commonly having a lower-class or inferior connotation. In modern times it has been used to refer to a member of a pachuco* gang.

CHURCH, THE, especially in its Roman Catholic form, always of symbolic importance in the consciousness of Mexican Americans. For some it has played a positive and for others a negative role. For this reason the relationship between the church and Mexican Americans is a problematic one. Probably the best approach is to view the Mexican American as an ethnic minority within a large American religious institution. Here the Chicano can be seen as a nonparticipant in the official structures of the church and as an object of missionary care. Of fifty-nine thousand American priests today, less than two hundred are Chicanos. Another 385 Hispanic priests have been brought into the United States from Spain or countries other than Mexico. The situation with regard to Hispanic religious sisters and brothers is quite the same.

It was during the late 1960s that Chicanos began to overtly resist their position in the church. From one end of the Southwest to the other, protests and confrontations took place. In San Jose, California, the Chicano Priests' Organization, which had been formed in May of 1969 to provide ministerial and political support to the Chicano movement, picketed the dedication of the multimillion dollar St. Mary's Cathedral in San Francisco. Many considered this church an extravagant expense in a time of great social need. Near San Diego Católicos por la Raza* occupied church-owned Camp Oliver on November 29, 1969, and demanded a better distribution of church resources for the poor. In Los Angeles on December 24 of that year another group by the same name demonstrated in front of the new St. Basil's Cathedral. In Las Vegas, New Mexico, Chicanos occupied the vacant Montezuma Seminary on August 26, 1973. In Arizona during most of 1975 a protracted dispute occurred between the Bishop of Phoenix and a coalition of Indians and Chicanos.

Protests also occurred within the national church structure. Early in 1970 Chicano priests formed PADRES, an acronym for Padres Asociados para Derechos Educativos y Sociales,* as a vehicle for communication with the bishops. Hispanic nuns formed Las Hermanas* on April 3, 1971.

The response from the official church was to make concessions that included diocesan offices for the Spanish-speaking and service centers in the barrio.* Two national gatherings, called Encuentros de Pastoral, took place; one in 1972 and another in 1977. With the exception of Mariano Garriga,* appointed Bishop of Corpus Christi diocese in 1936, no Chicano was elevated to the office until Patricio Flores was consecrated on May 5, 1970. By the middle of 1979 eight others had been appointed, four of whom were of Mexican origin (Gilbert Chávez of San Diego, Robert Sánchez of Santa Fe, Raymund Peña of San Antonio, and Manuel Moreno of Los Angeles). Only three of the Hispanic bishops, however, were heads of dioceses.

The evolution of this problem can best be understood through historical and sociological analysis. When the United States finished taking over the entire Southwest in 1848 it had also assumed the resident Mexican population. The Mexican church was in a weakened condition as a result of the aftermath of Mexico's revolt from Spain and because an indigenous clergy had never been fully developed. Thus there were few local priests in the newly acquired Southwest. The first bishop for California was not appointed until 1840, and he died in 1846, just before the arrival of the Americans. A very capable Mexican Franciscan priest, José María González Rubio, governed ecclesiastical matters, but it was clear that the next bishop would be American. The first invitation went to Fr. Charles Montgomery of Kentucky, but he declined; then the American provincial of the Dominicans, Joseph S. Alemany, was selected. Alemany was born in Spain but had become an American citizen. His knowledge of Spanish was of great help, but the sheer numbers of the new Euro-American population made him direct his main efforts to that group.

Within a decade of the American takeover, Mexicans had become marginal to both the church and general society. American clergy soon supplanted Mexican priests. The latter are pictured by contemporary American sources as being of low character, but recent research has begun to indicate that much of the conflict between the American and Mexican clergy was of a cultural and political nature. The dispute between Bishop Thaddeus Amat of Los Angeles and the Mexican Franciscans of Santa Barbara in the 1860s seems to have been of this type.

In northern New Mexico the future archbishop of Santa Fe, Jean Baptiste Lamy, arrived in 1851 and the first order of business was to upbraid the native clergy for their lack of morals, laziness, and general disobedience. Eventually four of the native priests were excommunicated. Little credit has been given to these priests for their efforts to preserve the culture and political integrity of their people. Among these, Father José Manuel Gallegos* had been elected to the Forty-second Congress of the United States and Fr. Antonio José Martínez* had been an outstanding student of canon law, a community leader, and an instructor for native vocations in his own seminary.

A similar situation occurred in Texas, although there were fewer native priests there, and the Mexican population was scattered in ranchos and villages. Research is now beginning on the efforts of the Mexican people to preserve their faith through religious services conducted by laymen and through their religious shrines at home. Once again, American churchmen of the time have described the Mexican priests in negative terms. The new American vice-prefect, John Odin, deposed the only two Mexican priests in Texas in 1840 for their "neglect of priestly duties" and their "immoral life." Little credit is given these men, Refugio de la Garza and José Antonio Valdez, for their advocacy of the rights of their people. De la Garza had been a delegate to the state legislature and another priest, Antonio Díaz, was killed in a battle between Texan and Mexican forces.

The attitudes of the large number of Mexicans who entered the U.S. in the early 1900s ranged from bitterly anticlerical to intensely Catholic. The American church, however, was culturally unprepared to deal with this new large group. Here and there, signs appeared in back of Catholic churches saying "Last three rows for Mexicans."

Conditions changed somewhat between 1940 and 1960. The Bishops' Committee for the Spanish-Speaking* was formed in 1945; but its low budget and the lack of cooperation from many pastors indicated that is success was limited. Towards the end of this period, a group of Anglo diocesan priests in northern California, calling themselves the "Spanish Mission Band," did pioneer work among the Mexican people. Other individual priests, both Anglo and Chicano, also began working more closely with the Mexican American community. By and large, however, the Church has remained a paternalistic institution. Only Vatican II saved it from being completely unprepared for the changes required by the new consciousness of the 1960s and 1970s.

FURTHER READING: Antonio R. Soto, *The Chicano and the Church in Northern California, 1848-1978*, Ph.D. dissertation, Berkeley: University of California, 1978; Michael Neri, *Hispanic Catholicism in Transitional California . . .*, Ph.D. dissertation, Berkeley: University of California, 1974; Juan Hurtado, *An Attitudinal Study of the Social Distance between the Mexican American and the Church*, Ph.D. dissertation, San Diego: United States International University, 1976; José R. Juárez, "La Iglesia Católica y el Chicano en Sud Texas, 1836-1911," *Aztlán* 4 (Fall 1973): 217-56; *La Raza and the Church in the 70's*, Milwaukee: n.p., 1971; César E. Chávez, "The Mexican American and the Church," *El Grito* 4 (Summer, 1968): 9-12.

A.R.S.

CÍBOLA, the location of seven cities founded, according to an old Spanish tale, by seven bishops and their flocks fleeing from the Moorish conquest of the Iberian peninsula. Originally located in the fabled islands of Antillia, the location shifted over the centuries, and Cíbola acquired the repute of being the site of a rich civilization. In 1536 Álvar Núñez Cabeza de Vaca* told of hearing from the Indians about populous cities to the north. These were identified as the Seven Cities of Cíbola and immediately became one of the attractions drawing Spanish explorers like Francisco Coronado* to explore the Southwest. The towns alluded to by the Indians are usually identified as a group of Zuñi pueblos in western New Mexico and eastern Arizona.

FURTHER READING: Stephen Clissold, *Seven Cities of Cíbola,* New York: C. N. Potter, 1962.

CIBOLEROS, buffalo hunters of the late eighteenth and early nineteenth centuries who made short trips from northern Nuevo México into the southern Great Plains where they obtained hides, dried meat, and tallow. They carried on small trade with the plains Indians and with the Anglo Americans after the latter penetrated the high plains area. *See also* COMANCHEROS.

CINCO, LOS, also referred to as Cinco Candidatos, a group of five working-class Mexican Americans who won election to the city council of Crystal City,* Texas, in 1963 thereby ending the long domination of city government by Anglos.

See also CRYSTAL CITY.

CINCO CANDIDATOS. *See* CINCO, LOS.

CINCO DE MAYO, the Fifth of May. This holiday commemorates the defeat of the invading French army at the city of Puebla, Puebla in 1862 by Mexican forces under Texas-born General Ignacio Zaragoza* and is the second most important civic holiday in Mexico. The day has been celebrated by Mexican Americans since the latter part of the nineteenth century.

CISNEROS, JOSÉ (1910-), artist. Born in Durango, Mexico, and driven northward by the 1910 revolution, José Cisneros moved to El Paso when in his mid-twenties. By this time he was a self-taught artist of some ability and was able to get some of his drawings accepted for publication. From the 1940s onward he made drawings for books, greeting cards, and other printed materials. His drawings, which use the borderlands as their theme, have been displayed in many museums in the Southwest.

CITIZENSHIP. *See* NATURALIZATION.

CIVIC UNITY COUNCIL, a Los Angeles civic organization arising out of the Sleepy Lagoon* affair and the Zoot-suit riots.* The Council was created in 1944, as the result of liberal demands, for the purpose of providing cross-sectional input at city hall. It soon became dominated by conservative interests and was ended in 1948.

CIVIC UNITY LEAGUES. *See* UNITY LEAGUES.

CIVIL RIGHTS. Mexican Americans share with other minorities the twin and related problems of poverty and discrimination. The fact that some do not understand English well creates special problems and can cause minor incidents to escalate into serious situations.

Mexican Americans have considerable potential political power but have only recently begun to organize to put it to use. Mexican American organizations have been weak in financing and in other resources necessary to pursue political activities. Although more than 85 percent of the Mexican American population is native born, their political participation, except in special instances, has been low. In some instances a variety of techniques, ranging from intimidation to restrictive or confusing legislation, has been used to keep Mexican Americans from voting. (Only in 1966 was the Texas poll tax declared unconstitutional.) While there have been voter-registration drives by Mexican American organizations like the Community Service Organization,* Mexican American Political Association* and Bishops Committee for the Spanish Speaking* (especially since World War II), until 1960 neither Democrats nor Republicans concerned themselves with the Mexican American vote. Gerrymandering* has also been used effectively to reduce Chicano voting power when Mexican Americans have overcome the problems of registration and getting out the vote.

Following the Civil Rights Act of 1964 there occurred a considerable push toward improving Mexican Americans' civil rights, and they have recently had considerable success in local elections, such as in Crystal City,* Texas. However, in 1979 there were only five Mexican Americans in the United States Congress; and California, with 29 percent of the U.S. Hispanic population, had none in statewide elective offices. Grossly underrepresented ethnically in both state and national political jobs, they have had greater success in obtaining appointive positions at these levels since the mid-1960s.

In the courts serious and widespread underrepresentation on juries and exclusion from jury duty have also been common complaints among Mexican Americans. Preemptory challenges are used frequently to eliminate Mexican Americans from jury service. All southern states except New Mexico have a requirement that jurors be able to speak and understand English. Underrepresentation of Mexican Americans on juries has resulted in their distrust of the impartiality of verdicts as well as in a general alienation from the Anglo American legal system, which many view as a device to create and perpetuate injustice. Often Mexican Americans have not had access to their judicial rights. Many cannot afford to hire lawyers; and court-appointed counsel, required in felony cases, is sometimes inexperienced or unconcerned. Also there is evidence that Mexican Americans are more likely to be burdened with excessive bail and receive more severe sentences than Anglos for the same offenses.

In many situations police actions are discriminatory and often paternalistic. There are complaints against excessive patrolling in barrios,* dragnet arrest techniques, use of excessive force, selective application of the law, indiscriminate body searches, especially of youths, and use of condescending language and attitudes toward all age levels. The net result is that many Mexican Americans feel harassed. Sometimes the police have greatly exceeded their authority by interfering with Mexican Americans' right to assemble, protest, and organize. There have been instances of police use of *agents provocateurs* and of police retaliation against complaints about excesses of law enforcement officers.

In May 1968 the Ford Foundation, recognizing the problems of Mexican American civil rights, established the Mexican American Legal Defense and Education Fund* to inform Mexican Americans of their legal rights and to prepare civil rights cases for court. In the 1970s there have been some improvements, but as a group Mexican Americans have faced great difficulty in their efforts to move into the political and economic mainstream of America. They are still heavily concentrated in the lowest paying jobs, partly because of low levels of skills and education and partly because of discrimination both in jobs and in unions. They suffer from widespread underemployment, and their unemployment rate is nearly twice that of Anglo Americans. Since World War II Mexican Americans have made gains in certain employment areas; in others (for example, electronics, aircraft, and communications) they are considerably underrepresented. In the area of federal, state, and local government employment Chicanos make only a slightly better showing than they did at the end of the war. In addition to discrimination in employment, there continues to be widespread discrimination in promotion. Federal agencies have sometimes been less than energetic in applying laws that require equality of opportunity for all Americans.

There is widespread housing segregation, which varies in degree and intensity from area to area. Generally speaking, segregation decreases as one goes westward, that is, there is more in Texas and least, perhaps, in California. There is comparatively less segregation for Chicanos than for blacks, party because of color and, partly, because barrios* have historically developed, not in the central city, but on the edges of towns. However, until rather recently such practices as segregated seating in theaters and churches, exclusion from restaurants, swimming pools, and toilet facilities, and even segregation in cemeteries, were not unusual.

As a group Chicanos have had difficulties in the past in obtaining good educations. Until World War II few finished the eighth grade and fewer were encouraged to go on to high schools, even when their families could afford to do without their labor. Along with blacks, Chicanos have been highly segregated in the public schools. After World War II lawsuits like the Méndez* case in California and the Delgado* case in Texas brought about some improvement in Chicano conditions, but their educational needs have been largely ignored, and Chicanos continue to have two serious complaints: Mexican American pupils are severely isolated by school district and within school districts and Mexican Americans are considerably underrepresented on school staffs and boards of education.

FURTHER READING: Helen Rowan, *The Mexican American*, a Paper Prepared for the U.S. Commission on Civil Rights, Washington, D.C.: The Commision, 1968; U.S. Commission on Civil Rights, *Mexican Americans and the Administration of Justice in the Southwest*, Washington, D.C.: Government Printing Office, 1970.

CIVIL RIGHTS ACTS. The 1957 Civil Rights Act, the first since the Civil War, was passed as the result of President Dwight Eisenhower's recommendations in his 1956 and 1957 State of the Union messages. Emphasizing the absence of voting rights among blacks, it created the Civil Rights Commission to investigate and report on abridgment of citizens' voting rights because of race, creed, color, or national origins and to assess federal legislation and policy in this area. It also prohibited voting interference and established simplified procedures for requesting federal protection. One effect of the law was to create a new civil rights division in the Justice Department.

The 1960 act, also the result of President Eisenhower's recommendations, stressed voting rights and strengthened the Civil Rights Commission. The use of force or threats of violence to obstruct court orders was made a federal offense, and the courts were given power to appoint federal referees to protect voting rights.

The comprehensive Civil Rights Act of 1964, the result of President John F. Kennedy's proposals but passed after his assassination, went far beyond voting rights. It created the Equal Employment Opportunity Commission (EEOC) to prevent job discrimination and prohibited discrimination in employment because of sex as well as race. It also forbade discriminatory practices in hotels, restaurants, and other places of public accommodation; in the implementing of election legislation; and in activities involving expenditure of federal funds by state and local governments. This last clause led to school desegregation on a broad scale.

The 1968 Civil Rights Act further extended the protection of the federal government to minority groups by prohibiting discrimination in housing. It also concerned itself with some aspects of civil riots by making various acts in promoting riots federal offenses, and it extended the usual protection of citizen rights to Indians on trial in tribal courts.

CIVIL WAR (1861-1865), the culmination of a conflict between the North and South, fought on the high seas, the Mississippi River, in the Seaboard states, the Midwest, and the Far West. Although there was little significant military activity in the Far West during the Civil War, inevitably the struggle did have an impact on Mexican Americans. The majority of Mexican Americans was barely aware of the North-South quarrel and did not understand it; as a result most were unionist, although indifferently so.

However, a small but important minority of Mexican American landowners, primarily in New Mexico, identified slavery with their own use of peonage and felt empathy for the Southern view and way of life. New Mexican Democratic leader Miguel Antonio Otero, Sr.,* who was married to a Southern Anglo and had been proslavery before the war, was ready to ignore both the North and the South and suggested forming a Pacific states confederacy. In late 1861 Southern sympathizers in the Mesilla Valley of Arizona planned to create a separate Confederate territory out of the southern half of New Mexico and Arizona. Some Unionist Nuevo Mexicanos were influenced by their fear and dislike of Texans, who had joined the Confederacy.

Most Nuevo Mexicanos remained loyal to the Union, and many served in the five infantry and one cavalry militia units that were formed. When a Confederate force invaded New Mexico late in 1861, it was repulsed with the help of Colorado volunteers in the battle of Glorieta Pass* southeast of Santa Fe the following March. As a result the Confederate army was forced to withdraw, being harassed by hostile Nuevo Mexicanos as it retreated southward along the Rio Grande to Texas.

In Texas there were savage Confederate attacks on Mexican and Mexican Americans in the triangle formed by the Rio Grande and the Nueces rivers. Many fled across the Rio Grande to safety in Mexico. On the other hand, some Tejanos were drafted into the Confederate army, while others became "Yankees" because Anglo Texans were Confederates. Some Tejanos took advantage of war conditions to "liberate" Confederate cotton, cattle, and horses.

Because of its geographical location, California's direct involvement in Civil War fighting was minimal. Californios too were divided by the war, but the overwhelming majority remained loyal to the North. Some California Mexican Americans served in the Union forces; especially notable was the battalion of 450 Californio cavalry, led by Captain Salvador Vallejo, which patrolled the Mexican border and held the Apaches in check during the war.

FURTHER READING: Stanley F. L. Crocchiola, *The Civil War in New Mexico*, Denver: The World Press, Inc., 1960.

CLAMOR PÚBLICO, EL, the first Los Angeles Spanish-language newspaper, edited and published weekly from 1855 to 1859 by Francisco P. Ramírez. Decrying the widespread discrimination against Mexicans and Californios,* it gave voice to complaints of mistreatment of Latins in southern California by the dominating Anglo minority. In its columns Ramírez described the expulsion of Mexicans and Californios from the mines, their difficulties in the courts, the lynchings, and unequal treatment before the law. He also urged them to work towards political participation, education, and acculturation.

CLIFTON-MORENCI STRIKE OF 1903, one of the earliest copper-mine strikes in the Southwest. A strike by Mexican and Mexican American miners that occurred in the first two weeks of June 1903 but failed in part because Anglo workers abstained from striking, and because a disastrous flash flood swept through Clifton on June 9. *See also* LABOR ORGANIZATION.

COCONUT, a pejorative term for a Mexican American who abandons his Mexican roots and assimilates or tries to assimilate into the majority society. The image is that of a person who is brown on the outside but white on the inside.

CODE-SWITCHING, also code-alternation or code-mixing; a sociolinguistic term used to describe the alternation or intermixing of two languages by bilingual speakers. Occurring with individuals fluent in two languages, code-switching is a natural and legitimate form of communication explained within a social psychological framework.

This linguistic phenomenon expresses itself in a variety of forms and, depending on the linguistic ingenuity of the speaker, can be simple or complex. The speaker interchangeably uses clauses, phrases, words, or whole sentences from both languages without losing continuity of thought and understanding. In this way code-switchers develop their own language or a third language.

Many Mexican American bilinguals frequently use code-switching to communicate. They effectively intermix English and Spanish without phonological interference in a natural conversation, among family and friends capable of the same phenomenon. Bilinguals who switch code are individuals who have acquired Spanish and English in a bilingual environment usually within the family. No linguistic evidence exists to indicate that mixing two linguistic systems affects the speaker's ability to function independently in Spanish or English.

Casual observers of code-switching comment that intermixing of two languages is random and caused by the inability of bilinguals to speak either language fluently and correctly. These perceptions indicate a limited knowledge of this highly complex phenomenon. Code-switching is not a random process but is complex and governed by rules. Unfortunately, negative views by critics of code-switching have caused widespread feelings of linguistic inferiority among bilingual Mexican Americans.

FURTHER READING: Jan-Petter Blom and John J. Gumperz, "Social Meaning in Linguistic Structures," in John J. Gumperz and Dell Hymes, eds., *Directions in Sociolinguistics*, New York: Holt, Rinehart and Winston, 1972; John J. Gumperz and Eduardo Hernández-Chávez, "Bilingualism, Bidialectalism, and Classroom Interaction," in Courtney Cazden, Vera John, and Dell Hymes, eds., *Functions of Language in the Classroom*, New York: Teachers College Press, 1972; Donald M. Lance, "Spanish-English Code Switching," in E. Hernández-Chávez, A Cohen, and A. Beltramo, eds., *El Lenguaje De Los Chicanos*, Virginia: Center for Applied Linguistics, 1975. *G.M.B.*

COFRADÍA, a religious society organized to carry out the required devotions to honor a particular saint. The members of the cofradía arrange the celebration of the saint's day with a special mass, procession, or other devotion. Members of a cofradía feel a special relation to each other deriving from their membership.

COLEGIO CÉSAR CHÁVEZ, a Chicano institution of higher education directed by Salvador Ramírez. The school was formerly Mt. Angel College and is located in the Oregon town of that name. A private, four-year institution, it grants both associate of arts and bachelor of arts degrees. It has less than one hundred students.

COLFAX COUNTY WAR, an armed conflict during the 1870s between factions struggling for control of the Maxwell land grant.* Basically the "war" (largely made up of ambushes) pitted settlers, small ranchers, and their supporters against members of the Santa Fe Ring* with its political and financial backers. As vaqueros* and small landowners many Mexican Americans became caught up in the hostilities.

COLONIA, literally colony, settlement, plantation, or colonized country. It is a small settlement or area of a muncipality inhabited by a particular ethnic or immigrant group. The term is also used to refer to a particular ethnic or national group within a greater population. Within the Mexican American experience, colonia preceded barrio.* Today a barrio is a Mexican American district, whereas the colonia historically had been inhabited by recent Mexican arrivals.

COLORADO INTER-AMERICAN FIELD SERVICE COMMISSION, an organization established in the fall of 1948 in the state of Colorado. Charged with developing a more positive attitude towards Spanish-speaking people and with stimulating grass-roots democracy in Spanish-speaking communities, the commission quickly disbanded after failing to achieve positive results.

COMADRE, the title by which a godmother and mother of her godchild address each other. *See* COMPADRAZGO.

COMANCHERO, a Mexican or Anglo trader who dealt with the southern plains Indians, especially the Comanches. The trade, much of which was illegal, consisted in exchanging cheap whiskey, guns, and trade goods for stolen horses and cattle. It began in the late 1700s and lasted to the mid-1800s, when the buffalo herds were wiped out and Indians were put on reservations. Many of the comancheros were lawless men who had fled from more organized and stable society and who became horse and cattle thieves when the trade ended. As a result the term comanchero was one of disrepute by the end of the century.

COMISIÓN FEMENIL MEXICANA NACIONAL, INC., formed in 1970, concerned with advancing the Chicana* image and calling attention to issues affecting the Mexican American family. With headquarters located in Los Angeles, the organization is largely limited to California, but has chapters in several southwestern states. To help Chicanas prepare for and seek leadership roles, it provides leadership information and training. Self-financed, it publishes a bimonthly newsletter and operates two bilingual child-development centers.

COMISIÓN HONORÍFICA MEXICANA, an organization established in the Southwest by Mexican consuls to assist Mexican nationals until help could be obtained from the nearest consulate. Founded in Texas in about 1920 and in the following year in southern California by local consuls because of problems created by the post-World War I economic downturn, commissions were made up of Mexican citizens of some standing in Mexican American communities. In the 1920s and 1930s these organizations provided leadership oriented toward preserving loyalty to Mexico. They became an important part of Mexican American society and in post-World War II have placed a heavy emphasis on education as an important avenue to economic and social upward mobility for Mexican Americans.

COMMISSION ON CHICANO RIGHTS, a Mexican American organization based in San Diego County whose principal objective is the defense of the civil rights of undocumented aliens.

COMITÉ MEXICANO CONTRA EL RACISMO (CMCR), the Mexican Committee Against Racism. Formed in August 1944, it is an example of the effect of World War II on Mexican American attitudes. It published a journal called *Fraternidad*.

COMMITTEE FOR THE ADVANCEMENT OF MEXICAN-AMERICANS (CAMA), the name of one of the early California Chicano student organizations organized in the late 1960s that became part of the Movimiento Estudiantil Chicano de Aztlán (MECHA)* in 1969.

COMMUNISM. Although there was considerable effort on the part of the American Communist party to win support in Mexican American communities, especially in the late 1920s and in the 1930s, the ideas of communism never had any wide attraction for Mexican Americans. The major effort of the communists was in the field of labor through the Trade Union Unity League* and the Cannery and Agricultural Workers Industrial Union,* both of which were affiliated with the Communist party.

COMMUNITIES ORGANIZED FOR PUBLIC SERVICE (COPS), an organization founded in San Antonio, Texas, in 1974 largely through the efforts of Ernesto Cortés, Jr., and several young Catholic priests to improve living conditions among the city's Mexican Americans. Quite similar to the Community Service Organization,* COPS shows the influence of the community organizing ideas of Saul Alinsky* and his Industrial Areas Foundation. COPS' strength is based on local Catholic church support, the support of civil service employees, especially at Kelly Air Force Base, and the organization's ability to harness the political power of San Antonio's large Chicano community. COPS does not officially endorse political candidates but does support its friends in city and county government.

COMMUNITY SERVICE ORGANIZATION (CSO), a nonpolitical, nonpartisan organization concerned with community relations and improvement in the general welfare. Heavily based on the community organizing ideas of Saul Alinsky* and his Industrial Areas Foundation and initiated in California under the leadership of a West Coast disciple in nonviolent confrontation tactics, Fred Ross,* the CSO goals are to make community members aware of their civic and social rights and responsibilities, to use the power of the ballot to promote social action programs, and to improve relations among all ethnic, national, and religious groups in the community.

The CSO is a broad-based organization having no language or citizenship requirements. As indicated by the absence of the word Mexican in its name, the CSO has a broad general goal of assimilation and integration into

American society and culture. Membership ranges from the young to the elderly, from recent immigrants to descendants of sixteeth-century Nuevo Mexicanos, from college professors to illiterate migrants.

Partly an offshoot of local Unity Leagues,* the CSO was first organized in the late 1940s, largely under the leadership of Fred Ross, to assist Edward Roybal* in his 1947 candidacy for a seat on the Los Angeles city council. With his election in 1949, the CSO turned to problems of the Mexican American community and was successful in pursuing civil rights violations as well as in conducting various citizenship, English language, and get-out-the-vote programs. From Los Angeles it soon spread to San Jose and other California urban centers, as well as to metropolitan areas outside the state. In the 1960s when financial and personnel support from the Industrial Areas Foundation was withdrawn, the CSO suffered a considerable setback. This decline was aggravated by increased competition from other organizations for Mexican American loyalties and by the more activist and radical mood of the late sixties, which found the CSO too moderate. When Mexican American community attitudes moderated in the 1970s, the CSO regained both some of its community support and some of its earlier membership. Strongest in California and Arizona, the organization at the end of the seventies had about thirty chapters in the two states.

COMMUTER, a person who lives in Mexico and crosses the border regularly (daily, weekly, or periodically) to work in the United States. Commuters may be American citizens, greencarders,* whitecarders,* or simply undocumented* entrants. The precise number of commuters is unknown since there is no reliable data on them; but it certainly exceeds one-hundred thousand. The overwhelming majority live in Mexican border cities like Juárez and Tijuana and work in American cities just across the frontier. Commuters find employment largely in agriculture or in sales and service industries, and about 25 percent are in heavy industry and construction. Commuter labor tends to displace American labor along the border, and especially Mexican American labor. This has had a depressing effect on border-region wages and working conditions. Commuters have also been used as strikebreakers in U.S. border towns.

The commuter system has come under increasing denunciation from organized labor and welfare groups, but there is considerable dispute about the overall impact of commuters on American society and the economy. In November 1974 in the case of *Saxbe* v. *Bustos*, the United States Supreme Court, by a five to four vote, upheld the Immigration and Naturalization Service practice of admitting commuters. Despite efforts by the Mexican government to reduce the problem (through a border development program and establishment of in-bond factories—maquiladoras*), the number of commuters has steadily increased since the end of the bracero program in 1964. Today the majority of commuters are greencarders.

FURTHER READING: Lamar B. Jones, "Alien Commuters in United States Labor Markets," *International Migration Review* 4, no. 3 (Summer 1970): 65-86; United States Commission on Civil Rights Staff Report, "The Commuter on the United States-Mexican Border," *Hearings* in San Antonio, Texas, December 9-14, 1968, Washington, D.C.: Government Printing Office, 1968, pp. 983-1006.

COMPADRAZGO, coparenthood, a religious-ritual-kinship system in which there is established a three-way relationship between godparents, godchild, and the godchild's parents. Among Mexican Americans godparents are used on three important religious occasions: baptism, confirmation, and marriage. While the religious bond established between godparents (padrinos) and godchild (ahijado) is basic, there is also a social relationship, often more important, between the godparents and the parents of their godchild, who refer to each other as compadre or comadre. The system is known by this relationship.

The compadrazgo system serves to reaffirm old ties of friendship and to create new ones. There is evidence that the urbanization of the Mexican Amerian has led to a decline of the role of compadrazgo in the culture. Although still used and viable, its part in kinship and community interrelations now is minor. The common casual use of the word compadre to mean buddy is some indication of its reduced importance.

COMPADRE, cofather, the title by which a godfather and father of his godchild address each other. *See* COMPADRAZGO.

COMPROMISE OF 1850, a description given to a series of laws concerning the western half of the United States passed by the U.S. Congress to postpone the divisive effects of the slavery issue. After the U.S.-Mexican War* the former Mexican areas of California and New Mexico drew up state constitutions and applied for statehood. Their admission to the Union as states was complicated by the rising national importance of the slavery issue and the likelihood that California would become a free state and New Mexico a slave state. Further muddling the issue was the claim of Texas to all of New Mexico east of the Rio Grande and the reluctance of the Union to grant statehood to an area where the population was overwhelmingly Mexican as in New Mexico.

Ultimately, by a series of congressional acts in 1850, California was admitted as a state; New Mexico, including the land east of the Rio Grande, was admitted as a territory; and Texas was awarded $10 million to satisfy its claims to eastern New Mexico. Nuevo Mexicanos, of course, were disappointed in the results of the compromise, as many had expected early statehood, given the area's large population.

CON SAFOS, an expression of Pachuco origin meaning "the same to you" or "forbidden to touch." In Chicano graffiti, when a threatening slogan is written, writing "con safos" or "C. S." next to the slogan reverses the threat or insult. However, if a poem, mural, or other art form is signed "con safos," it signifies a warning that the creation merits respect and is not to be defaced. *Con Safos** is also the name of a Chicano periodical that supports the liberation of La Raza.*

***CON SAFOS*,** an important literary magazine with strong political and ethnic emphasis begun in June 1968. *Con Safos* did not cover regular news stories, but published poetry, short stories, and political and historical essays which reflected life in the barrio. With a strong intellectual approach and feeling, *Con Safos* was, during its short life, a major outlet for creative Chicano literature. It ceased publication in 1971.

CONFEDERACIÓN DE UNIONES DE CAMPESINOS Y OBREROS MEXICANOS. *See* CONFEDERATION OF UNIONS OF MEXICAN FARM LABORERS AND WORKERS.

CONFEDERACIÓN DE UNIONES OBRERAS MEXICANAS. *See* CONFEDERATION OF UNIONS OF MEXICAN WORKERS.

CONFEDERATION OF UNIONS OF MEXICAN FARM LABORERS AND WORKERS (Confederación de Uniones de Campesinos y Obreros Mexicanos, CUCOM), growing out of the El Monte Berry strike* which began in May 1933 in Los Angeles County. Early in June leaders of the Mexican Farm Labor Union, an affiliate of the Confederation of Mexican Workers Unions (CUOM),* officially called a strike, demanding a 25-cent-per-hour minimum wage. A struggle developed between the Mexican American and outside leadership as the strike spread in Los Angeles County and beyond into Orange County. With the enlargement of the strike the Mexican Farm Labor Union grew rapidly, and some leaders trained in the CUOM formed the nucleus of a new worker organization, the CUCOM.

Early in July the El Monte strike ended with a small wage increase and recognition of the CUCOM, which then became a permanent organization. By the year's end it was the largest and most active California agricultural union, with over five thousand members in about fifty locals. In 1935 the CUCOM led one-third of the eighteen strikes in California agriculture, most in southern California, and also was able to achieve some gains without striking. Early in the following year the CUCOM furnished leadership for the organization of the Federation of Agricultural Workers Unions of America. In 1936 and 1937 the CUCOM took part in various conferences to establish a statewide federation of agricultural workers, but this move was not successful. In July 1937 most Mexican unions, including the CUCOM, sent delegates to the first national convention of agricultural unions in Denver, and many joined the CIO's United Cannery, Agricultural, Packing and Allied Workers of America (UCAPAWA).* By the late 1930s a combination of aggressive grower opposition, use of state criminal syndicalism legislation, jurisdictional disputes between the AFL and the CIO, and a surplus of workers led to a decline in union activities and union strength in California agriculture.

FURTHER READING: Stuart Jamieson, *Labor Unionism in American Agriculture*, Washington, D.C.: U.S. Government Printing Office, 1945; reprint, New York: Arno Press, 1976.

CONFEDERATION OF UNIONS OF MEXICAN WORKERS (Confederación de Uniones Obreras Mexicanas, CUOM), one of the first Mexican American labor organizations, founded in the 1920s in the Los Angeles area largely because of the potential threat from continuing heavy Mexican bracero immigration. It developed out of a meeting in 1927 of the Los Angeles Federation of Mexican Societies which resolved to encourage the organizing of workers of Mexican origin into unions. As a result the following year a number of unions were created, as well as a confederation of these unions modeled on the Regional Confederation of Mexican Workers (Confederación Regional Obrera Mexicana, CROM) in Mexico. In its tactics the CUOM wavered between revolutionary exhortation and peaceful reform via businessmen of enlightened self-interest. At its peak in 1928 the CUOM represented about three thousand workers in twenty-two local unions, but it rapidly declined and disappeared in the 1929 crash and subsequent depression. The CUOM was important for its consitution which clearly articulated the objectives of La Raza* workers and for the experience it gave leaders who later founded the important Confederation of Unions of Mexican Farm Laborers and workers* (Confederación de Uniones de Campesinos y Obreros Mexicanos, CUCOM). *See also* AGRICULTURAL LABOR AND LABOR ORGANIZATIONS.

CONGRESO DE PUEBLOS DE HABLA ESPAÑOLA, a congress of Spanish-speaking people, it was one of the early national Chicano civil rights organizations. The congress was founded in 1938 by Bert Corona,* Luisa Moreno,* and others and soon attracted a membership of several thousand students, union members, teachers, and politicians. Its first meeting, held in 1938 in Los Angeles, was well attended despite the fact that the congress was labeled subversive by local officials. Because of the activist position held by the congress, its members were often subjected to FBI investigation and this, plus the advent of World War II, caused its decline by the mid-forties.

CONGRESS OF MEXICAN AMERICAN UNITY (CMAU), an umbrella organization formed in 1968 to represent approximately three hundred southern California Chicano organizations. It took part in the September 16, 1970, march in Los Angeles. The CMAU later declined in influence, but it did continue to serve as a conduit for community concerns until its demise largely as a result of reaction to the frequently dogmatic inflexibility of its young leadership.

CONGRESSIONAL HISPANIC CAUCUS, a group made up of the handful of Hispanics in Washington plus about 150 honorary Anglo congressional members. Formed in mid-1977, the Caucus's aim is to highlight the achievements of Spanish-speaking people in the United States by calling attention to accomplishments of Hispanics in various fields and by informing the nation about issues of special interest to them. The Caucus concerns itself with the executive and judicial branches of the federal government as well as legislative action. It is privately funded and publishes *Avance*, a monthly newsletter.

CONTRACT LABOR. *See* AGRICULTURAL LABOR.

CONTRATISTA. *See* LABOR CONTRACTOR.

CONQUISTADOR, sixteenty-century Spanish conqueror of the New World, typified in Mexico by Hernán Cortés.*

CORONA, BERT (1918-), union organizer and political activist. A long-time leader in the Chicano community and labor movement, Corona was born on May 29, 1918 in El Paso, Texas, attended El Paso city schools, the University of Southern California, and the University of California at Los Angeles, where he majored in commercial law.

A pioneer in the areas of social reform and greater educational opportunites for Chicanos, Corona contributed to the development of the following organizations: the Mexican American Youth Conference, the Community Service Organization* and the Mexican American Political Association (MAPA).*

Between 1936 and 1942 he particpated in numerous union activities in the southwest. As a member of the Congress of Industrial Organizations, he contributed to organizing cannery and warehouse workers and gained invaluable experience.

Together with Edward Quevedo he called a meeting in Fresno in 1959 to discuss the possible avenues available for furthering Mexican American political interests. The general feeling of those attending was that Mexican Americans were taken for granted, and as a result, a separate political vehicle, the Mexican American Political Association, was founded.

Bert Corona's extensive experience and record attest to his leadership qualities. Besides the organizations already mentioned, he has organized Hermandad General de Trabajadores, Mexican American workers in the Los Angeles area; and the National Congress of Spanish-speaking People, the first national organization created to protect the civic, political, and civil rights of the Mexican population in the Southwest. Furthermore, he has served in varied and numerous positions of authority and leadership. For example, in MAPA alone, Corona has held the offices of California state secretary, vice president, and president. In 1966 he represented MAPA at Albuquerque, New Mexico, in support of Tijerina* and the Alianza Federal de Pueblos Libres's participation in the Tierra Amarilla courthouse raid. Until March 1978 Corona also served as president of the Association of California School Administrators.

FURTHER READING: Bert Corona, *Bert Corona Speaks*, New York: Pathfinder Press, 1972.

CORONA, JUAN, labor contractor (contratista). Corona was arrested in late May 1971 and charged with having killed twenty-five migrant farm workers whose bodies were found buried in peach orchards near Yuba City, California. Corona was found guilty of first-degree murder on twenty-five counts January 18, 1973, and sentenced to twenty-five consecutive life terms. During the trial charges of racial prejudice were made by individuals and some Mexican American groups, and national attention was focused on difficulties Mexican Americans often face in the courts in obtaining equal treatment before the law.

On May 8, 1978, a court of appeal overturned Corona's convictions and ordered a new trial, largely on the basis that he was inadequately represented in court and that some evidence was erroneously suppressed.

CORONADO, FRANCISCO VÁSQUEZ DE (1510-1554), explorer and governor. As a result of Álvar Núñez Cabeza de Vaca's report on the Southwest and of Spanish interest in an "otro México" (another wealthy Indian civilization), Coronado, the youthful governor of Nueva Galicia in northwestern Mexico, was sent northward on an exploratory expedition in the spring of 1540. Coronado's two-year exploration of the Southwest indicated to the Spaniards that there were no otro México, but it also gave them a fairly clear idea of the physical and human geography of the area from the eastern boundary of California to western Kansas.

CORONEL, ANTONIO (1817-1894), educator, civic leader, and politician. Born in Mexico City, Coronel moved to Los Angeles, Alta California, when he was seventeen as a member of the Padrés and Hijar colony. Here Coronel began an early career of service to society. Under the Mexican government he served as schoolteacher, territorial deputy, street commissioner, and member of an electoral commission and of the Los Angeles irrigation board. After the United States-Mexican War (1846-1848)* he became an equally active American citizen and continued to serve on the Los Angeles city council and the irrigation board.

At the beginning of the gold rush, Coronel was one of the few fortunate ones who made a modest fortune in the mines in 1848. Encountering a rising tide of anti-Mexicanism in the gold fields, in 1849 he returned to Los Angeles where he resumed his teaching and soon was elected again to the city council. He was also appointed superintendent of schools. In the 1850s and early 1860s he served in many positions in the city and county government including that of mayor, from which office he led a movement that initiated a public school system. During the post-Civil War period he attained local status as a Mexican American elder statesman and was elected state treasurer in 1867 on the Democratic ticket. He held this position until the mid-seventies when he was elected to the state senate, where he acted as a principal Californio spokesman.

During the 1870s and 1880s Antonio Coronel continued his activities in civic affairs and in state politics. At the same time he made important contributions to Mexican American historiography by preparing a lengthy memoir of his life and of California history from 1830. He also provided Helen Hunt Jackson with background information for her famous novel, *Ramona*.* In 1890 in one of his last public appearances he was a guest of the Native Sons of the Golden West* at an Admissions Days celebration.

On April 17, 1894, Coronel's long and distinguished public service career came to an end. He had been an outstanding civic leader in both the Mexican and American periods, and in the latter had served as a focus of political power among southern Californios. Unlike many fellow Californios, he adapted well to the Anglo environment and remained financially solvent, having considerable income from his real estate, grape-growing, and money-lending activities.

CORPORACIÓN ORGANIZADA PARA ACCIÓN SERVIDORA (COPAS), a Santa Fe, New Mexico, barrio organization. Formed in the mid-1970s, COPAS administered a number of federally funded Model Cities social service programs. Today its board of directors coordinates and directs the overall program, but each director is responsible for a specific program. Despite efforts of Santa Fe Model Cities officials to secure control of COPAS finances, it has been able to secure private funding to continue operations. COPAS is an example of a successful effort by a Chicano group to deal with community problems.

CORPORATION IN ACTION FOR MINORITY BUSINESS AND INDUSTRIAL OPPORTUNITY (CAMBIO), a minority business organization established in New Mexico in 1970 to help small businessmen participate more effectively in the free enterprise system by supplying technical and managerial know-how, as well as help in obtaining business capital. Beginning with twenty members, CAMBIO (the acronym means change) quickly grew to more than fifteen hundred and has an ultimate goal of ten thousand members. Most of its members are Nuevo Mexicanos, many of whom CAMBIO has helped with advice and business skills.

CORRIDO, folk ballad, a form of literature put to music which reflects and captures folk peoples' reactions to human actions, events, and dominant personalities. The corrido tells a story simply and swiftly without much embellishment.

As a significant historical document, the corrido can be a rich source for interpretive study of Mexican and Mexican American history. Archetypically the Mexican corrido can be traced to the period of Mexican independence in the early 1800s.

Today corridos are written and enjoyed by folk-oriented Mexicans and Chicanos. Their popularity as a medium of expression continues to grow in Mexican American communities with the most popular being those of the Mexican Revolution of 1910.

CORTÉS, HERNÁN (1485?-1547), explorer, conqueror. Cortés was born in Medellín, Extremadura, in southwestern Spain of a relatively poor hidalgo family. After two-years study at the University of Salamanca, he sailed for Hispaniola in 1504 and from there went to Cuba seven years later. In 1518 Cortés was selected by Governor Diego Velásquez of Cuba to head an expedition to follow up the earlier slave-hunting trips of Hernández de Córdoba and Juan de Grijalva. With about seven hundred men in ten ships Cortés crossed over to Yucatan and sailed along the Tabasco coast where he was given, among other slaves, a girl named Malinche,* who became his mistress and mother of the mestizo Martín Cortés.

By November 1519 Cortés had entered Tenochtitlán (today, Mexico City), capital of the Aztec federation, where he was welcomed by Moctezuma II,* head of state; however, he soon was forced to leave for the coast to deal with Pánfilo de Narváez, sent by Velásquez to supersede him. Returning to the Aztec capital, Cortés found the Aztecs hostile as the result of a bloody Spanish attack on a religious festival. Virtual prisoners, the Spaniards were soon without food and water, and Cortés's effort to calm the Indians by having Moctezuma appeal to them led only to the latter's death from stoning by his own people. With the Aztecs now in full revolt and the Spanish position desperate, Cortés decided to sneak out of Tenochtitlán by night. In June 1520 Cortés and the Spaniards left the city, this time in wild disarray and with heavy losses in both men and material as the Aztecs discovered their flight and attacked on what became known as La Noche Triste (the sad night). Retreating to the territory of his Indian allies, the Tlaxcalans, Cortés began six months of preparation for the second battle of Tenochtitlán. In December he initiated the first stages of his plan by moving to the edge of the large lake that surrounded the Aztec capital and there assembling thirteen brigantines previously constructed in the land of the Tlaxcalans. After subduing the numerous towns on the lake shore, at the end of April 1821 Cortés began his attack on the city itself. By August, after a long battle of reconquest in which most of Tenochtitlán was razed, the Spaniards were masters of the city and Cortés began the rebuilding process.

Cortés and his captains quickly extended their conquest in all directions from Tenochtitlán-Mexico, now the capital of New Spain. One of these men, Cristóbal de Olid, reverted to Velásquez, and from 1524 to 1526 Cortés made a remarkable but disastrous expedition to Honduras to force his submission. Two years later he returned to Spain to defend his rule at the royal court and returned in 1530 laden with honors and lands but not confirmed as governor and prohibited from making Mexico City his headquarters. For the next decade Cortés was involved in various exploratory activities, especially in the Gulf of California. In 1539 he returned to Spain where he remained until his death.

FURTHER READING: Hernando Cortés, *Five Letters, 1519-1526*, New York: W. W. Norton and Co., 1962; Francisco López de Gómara, *Cortés: The Life of the Conqueror by his Secretary*, Berkeley: University of California Press, 1964; Salvador Madariaga, *Hernán Cortés, Conqueror of Mexico*, Chicago: Henry Regnery Co., 1955.

CORTEZ, GREGORIO (1875-1916), border folk-hero who came to symbolize the conflict between Mexican Americans and Anglos in Texas. In

1901 Cortez killed the sheriff of Karnes County, Texas, when the sheriff attempted to arrest him and his brother for horse stealing. Forced to flee, Cortez was pursued by a large posse which he managed to elude or fight off for over a week while trying to reach the Mexican border. He was finally captured and brought to trial.

His exploit was seen by most Mexican Americans as an understandable reaction to the double standard of justice for Anglos and Mexicans; many Mexican Americans supported and helped finance his four-year court battle for justice. Eventually he was acquitted of the charge of killing the sheriff but was convicted for the death of a member of the posse. Pardoned in 1913, he died a few years later. For his resistance to Anglo racism he became enshrined as a folk hero in the ballad, "Corrido de Gregorio Cortez."

FURTHER READING: Américo Paredes, *With his Pistol in his Hand: A Border Ballad and its Hero*, Austin: University of Texas, 1958; Pedro Castillo and Alberto Camarillo, *Furia y Muerte: Los Bandidos Chicanos*, Los Angeles: University of California, 1973.

CORTINA, JUAN NEPOMUCENO (1824-1892), rancher, bandit-revolutionary, Mexican governor. A controversial figure, Cortina has been seen by some as simply a border bandit and cattle thief; others have viewed him as a social revolutionary fighting against Anglo repression. Born at Camargo on the south side of the Rio Grande, Cortina came from an upper-class land-owning Mexican family with traditions of power and responsibility. As a young man he fought in the Mexican War* against the United States invasion forces and later developed a ranch on family land near Brownsville, Texas. In this heavily Mexican area he soon became aware of the inferior economic and social position that Mexican Americans were being forced into after the Treaty of Guadalupe Hidalgo.*

In July 1859, while on the road, Cortina encountered a former family employee being mistreated by a Texas marshall. When the marshall refused to stop abusing the Mexican, "Cheno" Cortina fired a shot which wounded him and then released the exemployee. This exploit immediately made him a hero to the poor Mexicans and Mexican Americans of the area. He soon crossed into Mexico to escape almost certain imprisonment and likely death.

Cortina's actions stirred up the Mexican border population, and as a result he soon found himself with a sizeable force of eager volunteers. In September he recrossed the border at Matamoros with some Mexican followers, rode into Brownsville, and took over the city, raising the flag of Mexico. He then issued a "declaration of grievances" that stressed Anglo mistreatment of Mexicans and Mexican Americans. Throughout his ensuing fight with the local militia, Texas Rangers, and United States Army forces under Robert E. Lee, Cortina emphasized his commitment to social justice for Mexicans and continued resistance to oppression and the failure of the law to protect them. By mid-1860 Cortina was forced again to flee across the Rio Grande into Mexico. His well-intentioned effort to better conditions for La Raza* turned out to be counterproductive when it was twisted by some Anglo Texans into a Mexican attempt to reconquer Texas.

In Mexico Cortina developed into an important figure in the northeastern state of Tamaulipas and became an officer in the Liberal army fighting against French intervention. During this time he briefly became acting governor of Tamaulipas and was promoted by President Benito Juárez to the rank of general. His anti-Confederate position during the American Civil War led to an effort by Union factions to obtain a pardon for him after 1865. That effort failed.

In the mid-1870s he was evidently sufficiently out of favor with the Mexican federal authorities to be arrested for cattle rustling and jailed without trial in Mexico City. As a result of his support of General Porfirio Díaz in 1876, he was able to return to the border area, only to be rearrested and returned to Mexico City where he lived out his life under local arrest. In 1890 he was allowed to return briefly to the northern border area to visit relatives and friends.

Neither a rogue nor a saint, Cortina seems to have been a product of his time and place. He is an example of the border folk-hero who was seen by many as defending the rights and interests of poor and powerless Mexican Americans.

FURTHER READING: *Juan N. Cortina: Two Interpretations*, New York: Arno Press, 1974.

COS, MARTÍN PERFECTO DE, (1800-1854), soldier. Cos was the brother-in-law of Antonio López de Santa Anna,* who, as president of Mexico, sent him to Texas in the fall of 1835 to bring the Texans under Santa Anna's centralist government in Mexico City. Forced to surrender by the Texans at San Antonio, Cos was released on his promise not to fight further against them. In the following spring Cos returned with Santa Anna, fought at the siege of the Alamo, and was taken prisoner at the battle of San Jacinto. He later fought in the United States-Mexican War.*

COTTON STRIKE, SAN JOAQUIN, in many ways a prototype of the grape strike* at Delano over thirty years later. The San Joaquin cotton strike broke out in October 1933. It was the largest and best organized of a long series of labor disputes during the early thirties led by the radical Cannery and Agricultural Workers Industrial Union (CAWIU).* In the face of high unemployment and extreme job competition, in September growers agreed upon a picking rate of 60 cents per hundred pounds, up 20 cents from a year earlier, but at least 40 cents under the rate of the late twenties. As a result, on October 4 cotton pickers at Corcoran walked out of the fields, and the strike quickly spread throughout Tulare, Kern, and King counties until between twelve thousand and eighteen thousand pickers were demanding a one dollar rate. Evicted from growers' camps, the pickers set up a strike city on a rented forty-acre farm on the outskirts of Corcoran.

In addition to evicting cotton pickers, growers responded to the strike by mass meetings, protective associations, armed intimidation, and more violent methods. On October 12 the killing of two strikers and wounding of others at Pixley, when the union hall was riddled by rifle fire, aroused intense feelings against the growers. This violence and blanket condemnation of the strike as led by "reds" and "outside agitators" served only to unify the striking pickers. The strikers, about three-fourths Mexican and Mexican American, faced the Herculean task of picketing several thousand ranches in an area of over one hundred miles, in addition to dealing with constant vigilante encounters. At first the growers flatly refused mediation, and when their early tactics failed, they brought in Mexican consul Enrique Bravo to try to persuade the pickers to return to work. The tense situation caused California governor James Rolf to mobilize the National Guard and to create a fact-finding board made up of Archbishop Edward J. Hannah, President Tully Knowles of the University of the Pacific, and Dr. Ira B. Cross of the University of California. The board recommended a compromise settlement of 75 cents per hundred pounds and condemned grower violation of strikers' civil rights. Both sides accepted the compromise with some reluctance and by the end of October most pickers had returned to work. In the aftermath of the struggle some union activists found themselves blacklisted and some growers, vociferous in their opposition earlier, now found it difficult to hire pickers.

FURTHER READING: Stuart Jamieson, *Labor Unionism in American Agriculture*, reprint, New York: Arno Press, 1976.

COUNCIL OF MEXICAN AMERICAN AFFAIRS (CMAA), organized in Los Angeles in 1954 as a council of all Mexican American organizations in the city. Its goals were the development of Mexican American leadership and the coordination of efforts among its member organizations for the advancement of Los Angeles-area Chicanos. Although at one point the CMAA claimed forty-four member organizations, it soon became evident that the concept of a high-level professional umbrella organization was too grandiose and that internal dissension was rife. The Council did organize some conferences on youth and drug problems, job training and opportunities, education, and delinquency. Its education committee, which sought improved opportunities for Chicano students and professors, was also temporarily successful.

COUNCIL ON SPANISH-AMERICAN WORK (COSAW), an agency of the National Council of Churches, founded in 1912 for cooperative missionary work among Spanish-speaking persons, especially Mexicans who immigrated to the United States. During the 1960s its ecumenical viewpoint led to recommendations that member churches broaden their social Christianity role in the Southwest and deepen their acculturative functions. Its activities have had limited results.

COURT OF PRIVATE LAND CLAIMS, (1891-1904), established in March 1891 by the United States Congress because confirmation of Mexican and Spanish land grants was proceeding too slowly and was too much subject to political pressures. The Court consisted of five judges whose decisions could be appealed only to the United States Supreme Court; it had jurisdiction over claims in New Mexico, Arizona, and Colorado. (California had a separate board of land commissioners between 1851 and 1856.) During its existence the Court reviewed about three hundred claims covering some thirty-five million acres. The court found some forgery supporting fraudulent claims, and many cases of illegal enlargement of boundaries. The extensive loss of legal documentation and records made it difficult to prove titles in court, though many claims undoubtedly were valid. The court confirmed only about one-third of the claims for a total of a little more than two-million acres. Of course, some five-million acres of private and pueblo grant land in the area had been confirmed earlier.

FURTHER READING: Richard W. Bradfute, *The Court of Private Land Claims. The Adjudication of Spanish and Mexican Land Titles, 1891-1904*, Albuquerque: University of New Mexico Press, 1975.

COYOTE, from the Nahuatl *coyotl*. In colonial Mexico, a coyote was the product of a mixed marriage. Today it is a locution used when referring to a professional smuggler who smuggles Mexicans into the United States. It is sometimes used synonymously with contratista and enganchista.

CREPÚSCULO DE LA LIBERTAD, the first newspaper printed in New Mexico. It was published by Antonio Barreiro for about one month in the summer of 1834 at Santa Fe, with Jesús Baca as the printer. Later the press was bought by Father Antonio José Martínez* and moved to his parish in Taos where he used it to print school manuals and pamphlets.

CRIOLLO, a colonial Spanish-American term designating a person born in the New World; technically, a person of pure Spanish ancestry. The term is used more broadly today to describe a person who is nationalistic or an aspect that is typical of a country.

LA CRÓNICA, a Spanish-language weekly published in Los Angeles. Begun in 1872, it had a life span of two decades.

CRUSADE FOR JUSTICE, one of the most successful civil rights organizations, founded in Denver, Colorado, in 1966 by Rodolfo "Corky" Gonzales. Gonzales established the Crusade because he saw the need for an organization completely independent of all economic and political ties and independent of government agencies.

The Crusade originally conducted its affairs from an old red-brick building at 1265 Cherokee Street. Since it was basically a civil rights organization, its early demands were similar to those of other related organizations. These demands included better housing, more educational opportunities for Spanish-speaking people, and jobs. The organization printed and published its own newspaper, *El Gallo: La Voz de la Justicia*, through which it reported the activities of the Crusade and other related events throughout the Southwest.

In 1968 the group bought a structure which had formerly been the Calvary Baptist church and school. This building, located at 1567 Downing Street, was renamed El Centro de la Cruzada Para La Justicia (The Center for the Crusade for Justice). Purchased through loan pledges of Crusade members, the structure accommodated Crusade administration offices; a five-hundred-seat auditorium used for theatre skits, plays, film previews, and lectures; and a three-thousand square-foot ballroom. The facility also contained a dining room and kitchen; a Mexican gift shop; an art exhibition and working area; a gymnasium, nursery, library, and classrooms. Through this center the Crusade provided the Mexican American community with social services, cultural programs, and leadership education classes.

In the late sixties Crusade members led protest marches and attempted to end discrimination against Chicanos in the Denver public schools. At the height of the student walkouts and demonstrations, Crusade members attended a Denver school board meeting in November 1968 to present a list of demands to the board of education. One of the most violent student demonstrations occurred at West Side High School on March 20, 1969. Crusade for Justice leader Gonzales led the protest and demanded the hiring of Chicano teachers and administrators in the Denver school system. The walkout, originally called to demand the firing of an Anglo teacher for making racist remarks in the classroom, lasted three days. In that short period of time street riots broke out, and a fierce battle with police officials occurred. Armed with riot equipment, the police attacked demonstrators and jailed twenty-five people, including ten juveniles and Gonzales.

To Chicano youths in Denver and to those active in the Chicano movement throughout the Southwest, the Crusade for Justice had become the most visible symbol of protest and defiance. The Crusade for Justice appealed especially to Chicano youths. It was a nationalistic organization and not given to mere rhetoric and slogans. In an effort to create unity among Chicano youths, the Crusade sponsored and hosted the first national Chicano Youth Liberation Conference in Denver on March 27 through 31, 1969. The event was held at El Centro de la Cruzada. Panel discussions, workshops, lectures, and seminars focused on two main areas: social revolution and cultural identity. The conference proceedings addressed the question: Where do the barrio youth, the student, the rural Chicano, and the campesino fit into the Chicano movement? Topics discussed in the area of social revolution included organizational techniques, Chicano politics and philosophies, methods of self-defense against the police, and the organizing of protests and demonstrations. In the cultural identity sessions, workshops centered around topics such as Chicano art and literature, newspapers, and music. The general theme of the liberation conference was one of ethnic nationalism and ethnic pride. Crusade members conducted the general sessions and provided the youths with opportunities to express their views on self-determination. Total attendance at the conference was estimated at fifteen hundred youths, representing groups such as UMAS (United Mexican American Students),* MAYA (Mexican American Youth Adelante),* the Brown Berets,* and the Young Lords Association.

The conference produced a document which will continue to serve as a plan or ideology to unite other Mexican Americans and Hispanics at various conferences in years to come. This document is *El Plan Espiritual de Aztlán*.* It presented a clear demonstration of the growing concept of ethnic nationalism and a self-determination among Chicanos in the entire Southwest. It also stressed the need for Chicanos to control their own communities, schools, and political structures. A commitment to the concepts of the Plan de Aztlán and to the Chicano movement implied a commitment to educational, political, social, economic, and cultural independence.

The Crusade for Justice played a major role in the history of ethnic relations in Colorado and in the Southwest. The organization became the major vehicle through which the Chicano movement articulated the demands and the objectives of its aggressive leaders and members. Thus, the organization became a tool for an ethnic movement whose objectives included the creation of Chicano identity and cultural pride. During the second half of the 1970s the Crusade for Justice played a much less active role on the national political scene. Even within Colorado its activities were low-key.

FURTHER READING: Ann Novotny, "People and Events from Mexican and Mexican-American History," in Rodolfo Gonzales' *I Am Joaquín*, New York: Bantam Books, Inc., 1972; "Chicano on the Move. Crusade Buys New Center," *El Gallo: La Voz De La Justicia* [Denver Colorado], 1, no. 12 (September 1968): 4-5;

Rubén Salazar, "Chicanos Hold 5-State Event in Colorado," *Los Angeles Times*, March 30, 1969; Christine Marín, *A Spokesman of the Mexican American Movement: Rodolfo "Corky" Gonzales and the Fight for Chicano Liberation, 1966-1972*, San Francisco: R & E Research Associates, 1977. *C.N.M.*

CRYSTAL CITY (Cristal), a special place in the history of Chicano politics because of two political revolts by the Chicano people against the dominant Anglo minority of this community. Located in the heart of the Winter Garden area of southern Texas, the town contains slightly less than 10,000 people and is over 85 percent Chicano.

The first revolt occurred in 1963, when a slate of five (Los Cinco*) working-class Mexican Americans ousted the Anglos from city government by winning city council election, making Crystal City the first community in North America where such an event had occurred. Organized and mobilized by the Teamsters Union* at the local Del Monte cannery and by the Political Association of Spanish-speaking Organizations (PASO),* the new Mexican American city government quickly ran into severe difficulties because of Anglo intimidation and the inexperience of Los Cinco. Juan Cornejo, the mayor, eventually lost his job with the Teamsters Union, and bitter factionalism hid the fact that the new government had made considerable progress in ending discrimination against the Spanish-speaking majority in city jobs and through city improvements. After two years of rule the Mexican Americans were defeated by a mixed Anglo-Mexican American slate backed by the original Anglo rulers. This coalition ran the community for four years, but in 1969 a second revolt led to more permanent changes in the town.

Beginning as a protest against discrimination in the schools, a strike ended with the Chicano students winning broad changes. Simultaneously a Chicano political party, La Raza Unida,* was organized by José Angel Gutiérrez (himself a native of Crystal City), and a number of other young educated Chicanos. This organization recaptured the city government from the Anglos and gained control of the schools as well, with Gutiérrez becoming head of the school board. Thus Crystal City also became the first community in the United States to have a Chicano third party controlling the local government.

In the decade since La Raza Unida gained power, many changes occurred, and nearly all elective and appointive offices were won by the party, including such crucial ones as county sheriff, city attorney, city manager, and school superintendent. As many Anglos have left the community, Chicano activists from across the region were willing to come to the community to teach, gain political and administrative experience, and continue mobilizing the local Chicano population. With the help of federal funds, many new programs in education (bilingual and bicultural), housing, and city government were inaugurated. But the city remains heavily dependent on federal aid and has had great difficulties creating enough local jobs to stem the continuing migration of Chicanos from Crystal City to larger cities where better employment opportunities exist. As county judge, Gutiérrez and La Raza Unida also gained control of the government of Zavala County, but after several years of rule, the Raza Unida leadership became badly factionalized over both issues and personalities. By 1981 the party was in serious decline, having lost most of its power, and in February Gutiérrez resigned his position as county judge. Crystal City was thus a laboratory for Chicano government. While considerable improvement for the Chicano people occurred in the decade of Raza Unida rule, the town remained poor. A visit to socialist Cuba by many of the party's leaders emphasized their commitment to basic changes in the economic structure of the community and the nation, but because of limitations on the autonomy of local governments and a lack of many resources, more fundamental economic changes (such as developing cooperatives and restructuring the tax system) were very difficult to carry out.

Crystal City was in the vanguard of the Chicano movement, and the lack of many comparable successes elsewhere in the Southwest emphasize the unique and fragile factors that seem to account for this town's successes. These include (1) the large number of migrant workers (at one time more than half the Chicano population), who, when mobilized, became more radical than most other Mexican Americans, (2) the absence of a conservative, upper-class "Spanish" leadership in the town, (3) a generally intransigent Anglo community which allowed little opportunity for moderation, (4) a heavy Chicano voting majority in the town, and (5) very adroit, talented Chicano political leadership.

FURTHER READING: Lyle Brown and Thomas Charlton, Interviews with José Angel Gutiérrez, Baylor University Oral History Project, Waco, Texas: University Archives; John S. Shockley, *Chicano Revolt in a Texas Town*, Notre Dame, Ind.: University of Notre Dame Press, 1974; José Angel Gutiérrez, *Toward a Theory of Community Organization in a Mexican American Community in South Texas*, Ph.D. diss., Austin: University of Texas, 1976; Douglas Foley et al., *From Peones to Politicos: Ethnic Relations in a South Texas Town, 1900-1977*, Monograph No. 3, Center for Mexican American Studies, Austin: University of Texas, 1977. *J.S.S.*

CSO. *See* COMMUNITY SERVICE ORGANIZATION.

CUAUHTÉMOC (1502-1525), last ruler of the Aztec state. The sources conflict as to the details of Cuauhtémoc's life. He was born in either Tenochtitlán or Tlatelolco (both now part of Mexico City) between 1496 and 1502. His father and mother were most likely Ahuizotl, the eighth Aztec emperor, and Tiyacapatzin, a Tlatelolcan princess. He was, therefore, a cousin of Moctezuma II, who ruled the Aztecs when Hernán Cortés entered Mexico in 1519.

Despite his young age, in 1521 his noble lineage and his role as military governor for the Aztecs in Tlatelolco enabled him to succeed Cuitláhuac, who had reigned after Moctezuma II was killed in 1520. Cuauhtémoc then led the defense of Tenochtitlán and Tlatelolco. His capture in 1521 brought the military conquest of the Aztecs to a conclusion. He was subsequently tortured by the Spanish in an attempt to make him confess the location of Aztec treasures. His stoic resistance is regarded as a model of fortitude in the face of adversity.

After the conquest Cuauhtémoc acted as an intermediary between the Aztecs and the Spaniards. He also appears to have collaborated with the Spanish by providing troops for the defeat of the natives of Pánuco and the Maya regions. In 1525, while accompanying the Spaniards to Honduras, he was accused of conspiring against Cortés, who then summarily executed him. Reports of the exact location and circumstances of his death vary.

The enigmas surrounding his life and death, coupled with his legendary stance against the Spaniards, have made him the most important hero in the folklore and nationalist histories of Mexico. Among Mexican Americans, who celebrate his name, Cuauhtémoc represents a symbol of defense by natives against the oppression of foreigners.

FURTHER READING: Josefina Muriel, "Divergencias en la biografia de Cuauhtémoc," *Estudios de Historia Novohispana* I (1966): 53-119. *J.J.K.A.*

CUCOM. *See* CONFEDERATION OF UNIONS OF MEXICAN FARM LABORERS AND WORKERS.

CUENTISTA. *See* CUENTO.

CUENTO, a story, folk legend or fairy tale. The cuento is an important part of the Mexican and Mexican American oral tradition of education and entertainment. In Mexican American communities, "tell me a story" is heard much more than "read me a story." Cuentos often illustrate religious beliefs and standards of social conduct. A cuentista (storyteller) is often an individual honored for sagacious advice and folk wisdom who illustrates his point with stories.

CULTURE OF POVERTY. *See* POVERTY, CULTURE OF AND OFFICE OF ECONOMIC OPPORTUNITY.

CUOM. *See* CONFEDERATION OF UNIONS OF MEXICAN WORKERS.

CURANDERISMO, folk curing; healing of physical, psychological, and psychiatric illnesses by curanderos, folk doctors who use herbs, massages, diet regulation, and religious rituals in administering to their clientele.

Aztecs believed that angry dieties used disease, hunger, and other misfortunes to punish violations of moral codes and neglect of religious duties. Spanish priests brought the Roman Catholic religion, Spanish herbs, and Hippocratic medicine to Mexico, all of which influenced Aztec medical methods. European beliefs in natural and preternatural causes of illness were combined with Indian practices leading to a combination of cures used by curanderos.

Curanderos advise patients and do not order them to submit to treatment. They administer personalized, friendly treatment, which touches all aspects of the patient's life. In curanderismo the patient is usually considered a passive, innocent victim of malevolent environmental forces. Emotional disorders are viewed similarly to the psychosomatic illnesses of Western medicine.

Today, although folk healing is still a reality in Mexican American communities, methods have been modified and folk theories underlying their use often have been forgotten.

FURTHER READING: Ari Kiev, *Curanderismo*, New York: The Free Press, 1968.

CURSILLO MOVEMENT, a Spanish religious movement brought to the United States in the late 1950s. Members meet periodically for three days in a religious retreat atmosphere with an emphasis on self-reform and individual responsibility for others. While not designed as a social-action agent, the Cursillo movement does motivate its members toward community involvement. The Cursillo movement has had some impact in the colonias* of the Southwest and has made male Mexican American participation in church activities more acceptable in a culture which emphasizes individualism and machismo.* Approximately one-half of Cursillo members have Spanish surnames; among them is César Chávez.*

CUTTING, BRONSON M. (1888-1935), senator and journalist. Born in New York, educated at Groton and Harvard, Cutting was forced to leave Harvard because he had turberculosis. For his health he went to California and then to New Mexico, where he quickly learned Spanish and took an interest in local economic, social, and political problems. With the purchase of the *Santa Fe New Mexican* in 1912 (which also published a Spanish-language weekly, *El Nuevo Mexicano*), he soon made himself the champion and spokesman of Nuevo Mexicanos,* a role he filled the rest of his life.

Having organized the New Mexico Progressive Republican League in 1911, in the next year Cutting left the Republicans for the new Progressive party in which he took an active role. After service in World War I he resumed his journalistic activities in Santa Fe as well as his political career in the Republican Party, despite some old-line opposition. His large following of Hispanic-American voters gave him power in the party, and in 1927 Republican governor Richard Dillon appointed him to fill a United States Senate vacancy. He was then twice elected to that body in which he vigorously spoke out for honest, liberal government with concern for the "little man." In May 1935 he was killed in an airplane crash while on his way from Santa Fe to Washington. A man widely interested in history, archeology, music, and literature, Cutting was a great admirer of the Hispanic culture of the Southwest and interested in its preservation.

D

DE LA GARZA, ELIGIO, "KIKA" (1927-), politician. Born in the extreme south of Texas at Mercedes, Kika de la Garza was educated at nearby Edinburg Junior College and St. Mary's University, San Antonio, where he received his Bachelor in Laws degree in 1952. After serving in the navy at the end of World War II and spending two years in the army in the Korean conflict, de la Garza began practicing law and a career in Democratic politics. With a political power base in Hidalgo County, he was elected to the state House of Representatives in 1952 and was reelected regularly until 1964 when he successfully won a seat in the United States House of Representatives. He was reelected to each succeeding congress through 1980. Representative De la Garza has been active in veterans' and businessmen's organizations. He is chairman of the United States-Mexico Inter-Parliamentary Group, vice chairman of the House Committee on Agriculture, and a member of various other House committees. In 1978 President José López Portillo awarded De la Garza Mexico's highest award to a foreigner—the Order of the Aztec Eagle.

DEGANAWIDAH-QUETZALCOATL UNIVERSITY (DQU), a Native American and Chicano university located seven miles west of Davis, California, on 650 acres, a former U.S. Army communications center. Organized during the 1960s, DQU became a reality after the organizers agreed that Native Americans and Chicanos shared many common characteristics and were not interested in assimilating into the Anglo culture. After incorporation on July 13, 1970, a long legal battle to acquire the former communications center ensued. Proponents of DQU developed a highly effective strategy of court action with support from political lobbyists. Native Americans and Chicanos occupied the intended site for the university in early 1971, and finally the deed was transferred to DQU on April 2, 1971. DQU has about two hundred students and provides outreach courses through five centers in California.

DELANO, a town in the southern San Joaquin Valley, the focal point of César Chávez's* organizing of agricultural labor and of the subsequent grape strike in 1965 through 1970. A fruit and grain center about 30 miles north of Bakersfield, Delano was founded in 1873 when the Southern Pacific Railroad reached that point.

In 1970 it had a population of 14,559, many of whom opposed the grape strike and the National Farm Workers'* union. Some even appeared on television to condemn the strike, and a group called Citizens for Facts from Delano was organized.

DELGADO, ABELARDO BARRIENTOS (1931-), poet, community organizer, usually known simply by the single name, Abelardo. Abelardo Delgado is unquestionably the most widely known Chicano poet. Born in the state of Chihuahua, he came to El Paso, Texas, when he was twelve and began his formal education there. After marriage, college, and ten years' work in an El Paso youth center, Delgado continued working at various jobs with juvenile delinquents and migrants while he began to write poetry. He remains very much concerned with improving the conditions of the least favored members of La Raza* and much of his poetry expresses this concern. Delgado is the author of more than one thousand poems, many of which have been published in various anthologies. His best-known work is probably *Chicano: 25 Pieces of a Chicano Mind*, La Causa Publications, 1971.

DELGADO CASE, a Texas lawsuit concerning school segregation. After World War II the League of United Latin American Citizens (LULAC)* chose as one of its goals the elimination of the segregation of Mexican American children in Texas schools. In *Delgado* v. *The Bastrop Independent School District*, filed by LULAC, the federal court at Austin in June 1948 handed down its decision that school segregation of Chicanos was contrary to the Fourteenth Amendment and therefore unconstitutional. The court did allow segregation in the first grade, only because of language difficulties.

This court decis was followed by a conciliatory policy statement from the Texas State Board of Education and by instructions to local school districts to eliminate Chicano segregation. One result of these events was a considerable increase in the number of children of undocumented Mexicans attending school. *See also, DOE* v. *PLYER*.

DENVER, COLORADO, first populated in 1859 when thousands of fifty-niners descended on the area in hopes of striking it rich in the gold fields. Denver was incorporated in 1861 and boosted by land speculators and town promoters. Denver's favorable location and the achievement of territorial status by Colorado in that same year brought more people to the area. With the passage of the Homestead Act and the promotion of Colorado as farming country, Denver became a natural warehousing and distribution center. Although subsequently bypassed by the Union Pacific Railroad, Denver's civic leaders made up that loss by building three railroads out of Denver. The silver boom of the 1870s and 1880s brought new investments, businesses, and citizens to Denver. When the city became the state capital in 1881 it attracted more people. By 1890 Denver had more than one hundred thousand inhabitants, and by 1920 there was a quarter of a million.

Silver mining and later coal mining in southern Colorado brought Mexican miners into the area toward the end of the nineteenth century and during the first two decades of the 1900s. Development of the sugar beet industry in these same decades at first brought north Mexican Americans from southern Colorado and by 1916 was beginning to attract Nuevo Mexicanos and Mexican nationals. Soon the sugar beet companies were encouraging their workers to "winter over" rather than return to border areas, and as a result Denver became an important labor reservoir of Mexican Americans. From 1930 to 1970 Denver's population nearly doubled to 514,678, of whom 16.8 percent, or approximately 86,000, were of Mexican heritage. A center of federal government agencies for the Rocky Mountain region, Denver also has many defense-related industries and is a busy skiing, hunting, fishing, and camping center. All of this growth has brought with it problems: congestion, dirty air, and social dislocation. Many Denver Mexican Americans, along with blacks, still live in squalid barrio* conditions and suffer from lack of equal opportunity.

DI GIORGIO CORPORATION, a conglomerate with early interests in fruit auctions, fruit and grape growing, and wine-making. The Di Giorgio Corporation was established by Joseph Di Giorgio, who came to the United States from his native Sicily in 1888. Having had some experience with citrus on his father's farm, he soon became a fruit jobber and in 1904 founded the Baltimore Fruit Exchange. After a long and unsuccessful struggle with United Fruit Co., in 1910 he bought the Earl Fruit Co. of California and came west. By the end of the decade he had bought Florida citrus acreage and also about six thousand acres near Delano, California. In 1946 Di Giorgio was one of the largest fruit growers in the United States, especially important in grapes, plums, and pears. He employed about eight hundred people on an annual basis and sixteen hundred more for harvest operations. Di Giorgio also was a large stockholder in a number of fruit exchanges, owned an Oregon lumber and box company, and had a one-third interest in Italian Swiss Colony winery.

In 1962 Robert Di Giorgio became president of the family-dominated corporation and led the company into further diversification. By the early 1970s Di Giorgio represented produce and grocery distribution, specialty food products, canned and frozen foods, ethical and proprietary drugs, recreational vehicles, plastic cutlery, aluminum doors, windows, and screens, and lumber and wood products. Agriculture and other land use accounted for about 1 percent of total sales.

Di Giorgio was involved in two important strikes involving large numbers of Mexican Americans. In 1947 the National Farm Labor Union* struck Di Giorgio's Arvin, California, farms in a struggle that finally collapsed in 1950, and fifteen years later César Chávez's* National Farm Workers Association* renewed the fight and finally signed a contract with Di Giorgio in 1967. In the course of the NFWA strike, because of intensive competition from the Teamsters Union,* Chávez felt constrained to join with the Agricultural Workers Organizing Committee of the AFL-CIO, forming the United Farm Workers Organizing Committee in order to obtain that body's financial support. Subsequently, because of a previous agreement with the Secretary of Interior related to the 160-acre limitation law, Di Giorgio sold most of its Delano and Arvin properties.

DIEZ Y SEIS DE SETIEMBRE, September 16 (1810), the date of the Grito de Dolores,* which initiated the Mexican independence movement. It is the most important Mexican holiday, and is observed only second to the Cinco de Mayo* by Mexican Americans.

DIMAS INCIDENT, occurring during a 1966-1967 strike in the lower Rio Grande valley. On June 1, 1967, Ranger Captain Alfred Y. Allee and other rangers arrested a United Farm Workers* Organizing Committee member named Magdaleno Dimas after breaking into a Rio Grande City house where Dimas was hiding. Allee admitted hitting Dimas over the head with his shotgun. Medical examination indicated that Dimas had suffered a severe blow to the lower back and multiple bruises and lacerations as well as a brain concussion. The Rangers denied allegations of brutality; but state senator Joseph J. Bernal, who investigated the affair, asked Governor John Connally to remove the rangers from the valley, citing Dimas's arrest and other ranger violations of civil rights. However, Connally took no action.

FURTHER READING: Julian Samora, Joe Bernal, and Albert Peña, *Gunpowder Justice: A Reassessment of the Texas Rangers*, Notre Dame: University of Notre Dame Press, 1979.

DISCRIMINATION, the act or policy of prejudicial treatment against a person or group; usually based on racial, religious, or cultural differences.

Throughout their history from 1848 many Mexican Americans have suffered repeatedly from economic, political, educational, and social discrimination as indicated in numerous histories, newspaper and periodical articles, and local, state, and federal government reports.

FURTHER READING: Arturo S. Almanza, *Mexican-Americans and Civil*

Rights, Los Angeles: County Commission on Human Relations, 1964; Mario Barrera, *Race and Class in the Southwest: A Theory of Racial Inequality*, Notre Dame, Ind.: University of Notre Dame Press, 1979; California. Governor, *Citizens Committee Report on the Zoot Suit Riots*, Sacramento, Calif.: State Printing Office, 1943; Thomas P. Carter, *Mexican Americans in School: A History of Educational Neglect*, New York: College Entrance Examination Board, 1970; Everett Ross Clinchy, *Equality of Opportunity: Latin Americans in Texas,* Ann Arbor, Mich.: University of Michigan Press, 1954, reprinted, New York: Arno Press, 1974; Nancy L. Geilhufe, *Ethnic Relation in San Jose: A Study of Police-Chicano Interaction*, Stanford, Calif.: Stanford University Press, 1972; Margaret M. Mangold, ed., *La Causa Chicana: The Movement Towards Justice*, New York: Family Service Association of America, 1972; Joan W. Moore and Frank Mittelbach, *Residential Segregation in the Urban Southwest*, Los Angeles: University of California, 1966; United States Commission on Civil Rights, *Mexican Americans and the Administration of Justice in the Southwest*, Washington, D.C.: U.S. Government Printing Office, 1970; United States Commission on Civil Rights, *The Mexican American*, Washington, D.C.: U.S. Government Printing Office, 1968.

DIVERSITY, the condition of being different or having differences. Despite a basic cultural unity, the historical experience of Mexican Americans has created three distinct subcultures: those of the Californio,* the Nuevo Mexicano,* and the Tejano.* Some would add a fourth, the subculture of those who came to the United States since World War II. These groups have been affected differentially by their economic and social backgrounds in Mexico, by the dates of their coming to the United States, and by their interaction with people and geography since their arrival. Within each of these groups further subgroups can also be distinguished. For example in Texas there are descendants of early Tejano families, descendants of Mexican Revolution emigrés, and braceros,* who came during World War II.

Many Mexican Americans in Texas think of themselves as Latin Americans, while those in New Mexico and southern Colorado call themselves Hispanos, and most in California prefer the term Mexican American. Many of the young refer to themselves as Chicano. In addition to these different ways of looking at themselves, Mexican Americans vary tremendously in economic and social class, all the way from doctors and scientists to unskilled urban workers and migrant agricultural harvesters. This differentiation in social, economic, and cultural status appears to be growing.

Although a broad consensus about social and economic goals exists among Mexican Americans, there are widely diverging views about the means to attain full enjoyment of civil and political rights, with the young favoring more direct action than their elders. Mexican American leaders have articulated the common aspirations of La Raza* from time to time, but they have been unable to unite all their followers in the pursuit of these goals. Diversity continues to plague the movement.

FURTHER READING: Leo Grebler et al., *The Mexican-American People*, New York: The Free Press, 1970.

***DOE* v. *PLYER*,** a case filed against the Tyler, Texas, school district in 1977 by the Mexican American Legal Defense and Education Fund* to prohibit the district from charging tuition for undocumented children. The district court declared that the action was an irrational way of saving money and was unconstitutional. The state of Texas appealed this verdict, and in October 1980 a federal appeals court decision upheld the lower court's ruling, holding that treating undocumented children differently was a violation of the equal protection clause of the Fourteenth Amendment.

DOMINGO, PLÁCIDO (1941-), operatic singer. Although born in Madrid, Spain, Plácido Domingo's formative years were spent in Mexico, where his parents settled when he was eight. At twenty he made his operatic debut as a tenor in *La Traviata* at Monterrey, Nuevo León, in northeastern Mexico. In the succeeding years he sang operatic roles in Dallas, Fort Worth, and Tel Aviv. Returning to the United States in 1965, Plácido joined the New York City Opera where he soon won critical acclaim. In 1968 Domingo made his official debut at the Metropolitan Opera House. Since then he has sung in opera houses throughout the United States and Europe. He is considered by many to be the leading lyric-dramatic tenor in the world today.

DQU. *See* DEGANAWIDAH-QUETZALCOATL UNIVERSITY.

DRYING OUT, used to describe the process whereby illegal (undocumented) Mexican aliens in the United States were given legal status. Because of the rapidly rising volume of illegal immigrants by 1947 and the concern of both the U.S. and Mexican government over mistreatment of these aliens, officials reached an understanding by which undocumented Mexicans in the United States might be returned across the border into Mexico where they would be given contracts enabling them to reenter the United States legally. This March 10, 1947, agreement was followed by a similar August 1949 agreement. By the end of 1950 more than two hundred thousand illegal aliens had been legitimatized under these two agreements.

Supporters of drying out emphasized that it served to protect the rights of undocumented workers, while its opponents pointed out that it merely compounded the problem by encouraging illegal entrance by holding out the hope for legalization of their status.

DURST RANCH. *See* WHEATLAND RIOT.

E

ECONOMIC OPPORTUNITY ACT (1964), federal legislation in President Lyndon B. Johnson's "War on Poverty." It authorized creation of a Job Corps, created a community-action program, and organized a Peace Corps-like agency called Volunteers in Service to America (VISTA). All three of these programs were of special interest to Mexican Americans in their efforts to improve their economic and social position.

EDUCATION, among the Mexican American population. Estimates of the total number of Hispanics in the United States range from ten to sixteen million; over fifty percent of adults have not completed four years of high school. Interpretations of socioeconomic data on Mexican-descent people indicate that they (1) achieve poorly in school, (2) drop out earlier, (3) speak Spanish, (4) complete fewer years of schooling, and (5) earn less income. The theory of cultural deprivation has been used most frequently to explain these problems. The home and neighborhood are interpreted as chief causes of limited educational and social achievement.

Today's Mexican Americans are characterized by: (1) their diversity within the group (2) their differences in English and Spanish language abilities (3) their differences in individual identity with ethnic culture, and (4) their differences in psychocultural orientation.

Recent national legislation has provided a base for court rulings on issues of equality of opportunities and access to education. The 1964 Civil Rights Act* is basic to understanding the progress minorities have made recently. The *Lau* v. *Nichol** decision in San Francisco is an example of a case which has affected bilingual education* programs throughout the country. The school district was directed to provide bilingual-bilcultural instruction to Chinese-speaking students. This is necessary, the Court ruled, if equality of educational opportunities are to be provided for all children. In *Lujan* v. *Colorado State Board of Education* the court ruled that disparities in financial resources between rich and poor school districts denied children in the poor districts equal protection under the law. Court cases on school finances have also been tried successfully in California, Connecticut, New Jersey, and West Virginia.

Today bilingual education is the focus in developing instructional programs for Hispanics. Debate continues on the merits of using World Spanish or one of the various forms of Spanish known as barrio, Spanglish, pochismos, pachuquismos, or caló. Much controlled research needs to be designed and carried out on these issues.

Fundamental concepts for bilingual education are that: (1) basic concepts of learning are initiated in the child's home language, (2) language development is in the child's dominant language, (3) language instruction is provided in the second language, (4) learning content and concepts are taught in the child's dominant language, (5) subject matter and concepts are also taught in the second language, and (6) the child's positive identity with his cultural heritage is promoted.

Limited enrollment in national higher education is also a subject of attention. Some progress in the number and percentage of total Hispanics in undergraduate education can be noted in the following statistics: 1970: 100,000 (2.1 percent), 1974: 158,000 (2.8 percent), 1976: 264,000 (4.4 percent). While gains in enrollment over the 1970-1976 year span are evident, gains for Hispanics have not been dramatic.

Reacting to limited higher education opportunities, Chicano college and university students have demonstrated for educational as well as community issues. Students have developed campus organizations such as UMAS (United Mexican American Students),* MASC (Mexican American Student Confederation),* MAYO (Mexican American Youth Organization),* MECHA (Movimiento Estudiantil Chicano de Aztlán).* These and other student organizations are to be found throughout the United States and concern themselves with cultural identity and educational issues.

Civic-oriented organizations such as LULAC (League of United Latin American Citizens),* American G.I. Forum,* and AMAE (Association of Mexican American Educators)* are also active. At the political action level are PASSO (Political Association of Spanish-Speaking Organizations),* MAPA (Mexican American Political Association),* and others. With the exception of the G.I. Forum, perhaps, which is a veteran-based organization, no one group operates effectively on a national scale.

Federal and philanthropic fundings have encouraged educational programs. National Association for Bilingual Education (NABE) is active on a national scale today and a host of state-level affiliates are also appearing. Professional interests of these organizations center on second language and cultural awareness in education.

Demonstrative activities of Chicanos and other Hispanics have raised levels of institutional awareness. Part of this awareness is exemplified by the question which many Hispanics are asking: "What do I call myself (you)?" Preliminary reports indicate that Bureau of the Census surveys, in preparation for the 1980 National Census, find no ethnic consensus on label usage. These surveys indicate that Mexicano or Mexican seems to be most frequently preferred. Other labels, such as Mexican American, Spanish-American, Hispano, Latino, and Chicano, of Hispanics are preferred labels among smaller percentages of Hispanics. For the moment, the label Chicano appears to be an elitist, political, or student preference.

Critics of educational traditions urge reform. José A. Cardenas formulated his Theory of Incompatibilities in which the educational failure of Mexican

Americans is attributed to the lack of compatability between the culture and language characteristics of these children and the traditional American school culture and curriculum.

Chicano professionals are also beginning to fight issues through court action. Dr. José A. Perea, removed as Administrative Vice President of a community college campus, filed a discrimination suit. The court ruled that invidious discrimination had occurred and that Perea was expected to perform in a way not required of other campus vice presidents. To help both students and professionals the Hispanic Higher Education Coalition, with a broad membership, has organized to influence national politics and legislation.

The 1980s begin with an expectant view that educational programs at all levels will improve for Mexican Americans. Serious critics concede the need for a clear, sound, and consistent theory of education to be formulated and tested. According to Zappert and Cruz, few of the reports today on bilingual programs satisfy criteria of good research design. They conclude that "the research demonstrates that bilingual education improves, or does not impede oral language development, cognitive functioning, and self image."

FURTHER READING: Y. Arturo Cabrera, *Emerging Faces: The Mexican-Americans*, Dubuque: Wm. C. Brown Co., 1971, reprint 1978; *Minorities in Higher Education: Chicanos and Others*, Niwot, Colo.: Sierra Publications, 1978; *Strategies for Education of Chicanos*, Niwot, Colo.: Sierra Publications, 1978; Y. Arturo Cabrera and José A. Perea, *Community College Conflict: Chicano Under Fire*, Niwot, Colo.: Sierra Publications, 1979; Thomas P. Carter, *Mexican Americans in School*, New York: College Entrance Examination Board, 1970; Leo Grebler, Joan W. Moore, and Ralph C. Guzmán, *The Mexican-American People*, New York: The Free Press, 1970; Laraine Testa Zappert and B. Roberto Cruz, *Bilingual Education: An Appraisal of Empirical Research*, Berkeley Unified School District, California, 1977.

Y.A.C.

See also Appendix: EDUCATION: YEARS OF SCHOOL COMPLETED.

EDUCATIONAL OPPORTUNITY PROGRAM, initially established in 1964 by the regents of the University of California and the state college system. The purpose of the program was defined as follows: to provide access and academic support services for students with demonstrated potential, who, for socioeconomic reasons, might not otherwise have pursued higher education; to increase the number of students from ethnic and economic groups underrepresented in the university; and to increase the cultural diversity of the university's enrollment.

EL MEXICANO PREPARADO, LISTO, EDUCADO Y ORGANIZADO (EMPLEO), translated as The Prepared, Ready, Educated and Organized Mexican. This organization, whose acronym spells "employment," was begun by Chicano convicts in San Quentin prison in 1966. As the name indicates, its aim is to prepare prisoners for successful employment after their release from jail. It also hopes to improve treatment of Spanish-surnamed convicts as well as to foster goals of cultural awareness, education, self-development, discipline, and self-esteem—all based on ethnic identity and a sense of obligation to La Raza.* After several unsuccessful efforts at acceptance, the concept of a bilingually based education program for Chicano inmates succeeded in obtaining prison administration approval for this first Chicano self-help cultural group.

EL MONTE BERRY STRIKE, organized in 1933 in the El Monte area northeast of Los Angeles. In May about seven thousand berry pickers and onion and celery workers, many of who were earning less than ten cents per hour, voted to go on strike. There were grower's accusations of communist leadership among the strikers and some struggle between local Mexican American leaders and outsiders for control of the strike. Leaders with experience gained in the Confederation of Unions of Mexican Workers* began forming the nucleus of a new Chicano organization. Early in July the strike was settled with a new wage agreement of $1.50 for a nine-hour day and a twenty-cents hourly rate for shorter periods. Out of this strike experience the important Confederation of Unions of Mexican Farm Laborers and Workers* (CUCOM) was established on July 15.

EL PASO INCIDENT (1948), a border violation by local U.S. immigration officials. As the cotton harvest of 1948 approached, Texas growers offered a pay scale of from $2.00 to $2.50 per 100 pounds to Mexican nationals. The Mexican government responded that the going rate was $3.00 and adamantly insisted on that pay rate if the Texas growers wanted Mexican workers. An impasse ensued. Early in October the local immigration authorities were told that unless Mexican nationals could be hired, the cotton would soon rot in the fields. On October 13 American immigration authorities unilaterally opened the border at El Paso, and in the following five days between six and seven thousand undocumented cotton pickers crossed into the United States, despite Mexican government efforts to stop them. On the American side they were placed under technical arrest and turned over to the United States Employment Service which loaded them into trucks of the growers' agents. On October 18 the Immigration Service again closed the border.

The Mexican government protested this violation of a February 1948 U.S.-Mexican agreement on workers, as did the AFL, the CIO, LULAC, and other Mexican American organizations. Mexico abrogated the February pact, and later the United States government expressed its regrets at the El Paso incident to the Mexican government. But the cotton had been picked at the growers' rates, and the illegals returned to Mexico.

EL PASO, TEXAS, among the major cities of the Southwestern United States, unique because of its border location and the makeup of its population. Chicanos have constituted the majority in this city throughout the twentieth century, currently comprising approximately 62 percent of the four hundred thousand residents. On the other side of the Rio Grande is Ciudad Juárez, Chihuahua, with an estimated population of eight hundred thousand.

El Paso-Juárez began as the mission of Nuestra Señora de Guadalupe in 1659. Missionaries established the settlement on the south bank of the river after the area had assumed importance as a desert oasis inhabited by friendly Indians on the northward trail from New Spain. Juan de Oñate, the Spanish colonizer of New Mexico, appropriately called the site the "Pass of the North." In the early 1680s other colonies bearing New Mexico names (Ysleta, Senecú, Socorro) were established a few miles downriver as refugees fled the Pueblo Indian revolt to the north. By the mid-eighteenth century four thousand people lived in the area, supported by a strong agricultural economy in a fertile valley.

Following the U.S.-Mexico War of 1846-1848, El Paso, which started as a rancho* in 1827, became part of the United States along with Ysleta, Socorro, and San Elizario by virtue of its location on the north bank of the Rio Grande. Paso del Norte, or Ciudad Juárez (renamed after Benito Juárez in 1888), remained in Mexico due to its location on the opposite shore. Between 1850 and 1880 El Paso's population, made up mostly of Mexican Americans, grew from about 300 to 736 persons.

The smallness and isolation that characterized this locality was altered when the railroads arrived in the early 1880s. Because of its location as a strategic crossroads for north-south and east-west patterns of traffic, within a few years El Paso evolved into an important transportation center. The economy of El Paso received strong stimulus as the demand for raw materials increased in the eastern United States. By 1900 El Paso had become a leading supply, processing, smelting, and refining site for the rich mining districts in the surrounding territory. Commerce, industry, and agriculture also prospered from the infusion of new capital and the growing trade with Mexico. By 1910, El Paso's population had increased to almost forty thousand persons, and the city had achieved a prominent position among urban centers situated in the U.S.-Mexico borderlands.

These developments brought some important changes to the lives of Chicanos native to the El Paso area. These people had involuntarily become subjects of a new country, and soon the Anglo minority which moved in relegated them to a position of relative powerlessness. Uneasy relations resulted from this state of affairs. Shortly after 1848 land-hungry individuals from the east aggressively acquired property in the area, often disregarding local rules and traditions. Frequently lawless elements (*See* Banditry) raised havoc in the Mexican American settlements with little interference from established Anglo authority. The foremost example of ethnic tensions and conflict during the period is the Salt War* of 1877-1878, when native residents from San Elizario violently resisted the takeover by Anglo entrepreneurs of nearby salt beds, which had been public property since Spanish days. As larger numbers of the dominant society moved into the area after 1880, the subordination of the Chicanos became more accentuated. The decline of their political influence in El Paso County is exemplified by the highly questionable but successful election campaign of 1883 that shifted the county seat from Ysleta, then the area's largest town with a preponderant Mexican American population, to El Paso, where Anglos had become solidly entrenched.

In the twentieth century El Paso has grown at an impressive rate, and Mexican Americans have played a decisive role in that process. By 1900 persons of Mexican descent regained the majority status they had temporarily lost during the late nineteenth century when Anglos arrived in large numbers. Immigrants from Mexico and their descendants have constituted the predominant element in El Paso's Mexican American population since 1900. One period when this ethnic group experienced particularly rapid growth was the era of the Mexican Revolution between 1910 and 1920. During this time the influx of middle- and upper-class refugees from Mexico altered the character of the Chicano community, although many of the wealthy newcomers returned to Mexico when the political climate stabilized. An incident that reveals attitudes toward Mexican immigrants then current occurred in 1916. Following the Villista massacre of fifteen American engineers at Santa Ysabel, Chihuahua, on January 13, a mob of one thousand revenge-seeking Anglos marched on the Chicano community in El Paso, vowing to drive out its residents. Street fighting broke out, resulting in injuries to twenty-five Mexicans and an undetermined number of Anglos. Military authorities averted a major riot by establishing a dividing line between the two groups and ordering a curfew.

As in other areas throughout the Southwest, historically El Paso has welcomed Mexican migrants into the city in time of economic progress but has repelled them during hard times. Due to this pattern, El Paso's Mexican American population decreased significantly during the Great Depression of the 1930s, when thousands were pressured into returning to Mexico. After 1940 the local Mexican American population entered a period of steady growth.

Since 1900 Mexicans from south of the border as well as Anglos from all over the United States have been attracted to El Paso by the economic development which the area has experienced. The locally often-cited four Cs—cattle, copper, cotton, and climate (as a health attraction)—provided an early and continuing impetus for growth. Seldom mentioned (in public) is a fifth C—Chicanos, whose low paid labor has been a strong factor in luring employers to the region. Major local industries which have evolved over the decades include ore smelting, oil refining, and cement and textile manufacturing. Production of natural gas, leather goods, and lumber have also been important. Wholesale and retail trade have flourished due to the city's large hinterland, which extends far into Mexico. Large financial institutions have developed to meet local as well as regional needs. El Paso continues to be a major railway and trucking terminal, and related secondary industries have evolved due to this factor. Heavy federal investments in the form of military installations and border-related agencies (e.g., Customs, Immigration Service) have likewise spurred local growth. Finally, the "Old West" frontier heritage and the presence of Ciudad Juárez across the Rio Grande have made El Paso a major regional tourist attraction for Americans as well as for Mexicans.

Prior to the World War II period, with few exceptions, Chicanos in El Paso were relegated to the lowest rung on the socioeconomic ladder and had little political representation. In the last few decades, however, conditions have changed somewhat, and today there is a growing middle class that has managed a greater presence in El Paso's major institutions. Since 1957 two of El Paso's mayors have been of Mexican ancestry, and numerous Chicanos have served in elective and appointed positions at various levels of government. In spite of such advances, however, a 1978 survey revealed that of the top thirty "influentials" in the city, not a single one was of Mexican extraction. Thus, while El Paso is well known in the Southwest as a city where Mexican Americans are very visible, much remains to be done before they achieve participation and representation proportionate to their numbers. The preliminary 1980 census figures show a Spanish origin population of 265,819, which forms 62.5 percent of the total population.

FURTHER READING: Seymour U. Connor, *Texas: A History*, New York: Thomas Y. Crowell Co., 1971; Oscar J. Martinez, *Border Boom Town*, El Paso: University of Texas, 1978; also "Chicanos and the Border Cities," *Pacific Historical Review* 46 (February 1977): 85-106. *O.J.M.*

EMIGRANT AGENCY LAW (1929), the second of two Texas laws attempting to make it difficult for out-of-state recruiters to obtain Texas farm laborers. By the early 1920s sugar-beet companies were recruiting Mexican and Mexican American workers in Texas. Irritated by this practice, Texas farm interests were able to get the state legislature in May 1929 to pass a law requiring out-of-state recruiters to pay a large occupational tax. Since sugar interests got a federal injunction against implementing this legislation, the second session of the legislature passed the Emigrant Agency Law. It established a ten-dollar license fee and a thousand-dollar occupational tax, plus a five-thousand-dollar bond and employment license required by an employment agency law. Finally, the law provided for a tax to be paid to the county in which the agent recruited. The Emigrant Agency Law did little to reduce the outflow of Mexican-origin labor in Texas.

EMPLOYMENT, an area in which, in comparison to Anglo Americans, Mexican Americans are grossly overrepresented in unskilled and low-skill jobs and heavily underrepresented in white-collar and skilled occupations. In the Southwest the proportion of Chicanos in low-skill manual occupations is approximately twice that of Anglo workers. The reasons for this difference lie in education levels, recency of immigration, and discrimination. The earlier rural, agricultural orientation of Mexican Americans was once another factor for Mexican Americans being in low-skill occupations, and, even though they have become highly urbanized since the 1930s, a relatively large percentage has continued to work in occupations in and related to agriculture. Of all groups in American society, Mexican Americans have the highest percentage employed as farm workers—about 8 percent of males and 3 percent of females.

In industrial employment Chicanos have been strongly affected by the presence or absence of union organizations. Generally speaking, they have been able to obtain employment more widely in nonunionized industries and in industries organized in industrial rather than craft unions. It is in the area of industrial employment that Mexican Americans have made the greatest strides in recent decades; however, they have made fewer gains in those industries dominated by craft unionism, for example, the construction industry. Obviously this assessment excludes the category of common labor. Large numbers of Chicanos work as truck drivers, delivery men, laundry workers, and service employees.

In professional and technical areas the unfavorable position of Mexican Americans is even more notable, and the bulk of those who do work in professional and technical occupations have the lower-prestige and lower-paying jobs. There are more social workers than physicians, more draftsmen than architects, more technicians than engineers. Comparatively few Mexican Americans work in petroleum, aircraft, and chemical industries. Despite nondiscrimination policies and some efforts to recruit minorities, Mexican Americans have not fared too well in city, state, and federal government employment. They are generally heavily underrepresented in California but better represented in Texas; in both areas they have better representation in federal positions than in state and local government, and are in lower-category jobs rather than in higher ones.

In all occupational areas there has been some progress in recent years. Discrimination has lessened somewhat, and the improving educational status of Chicanos has enabled them to qualify for more prestigious employment. More of them are becoming lawyers, university professors, high-level government employees, scientists, and joining other professions.

See also Appendix: EMPLOYMENT STATUS AND DISTRIBUTION OF WORKERS BY TYPE OF WORK, 1976.

EMPRESARIO, in the Mexican period (1821-1846) of southwestern history, a land grantee who agreed to settle a minimum of one hundred families on a grant within a six-year period. The empresario was to receive a large land grant for himself for the successful completion of this undertaking. This system was used by the Mexican government in the 1820s to encourage settlement on the Indian-plagued northern frontier, especially in Texas.

The majority of empresarios there were Anglo Americans and the most successful and best known was Stephen F. Austin.* Empresarios often functioned as intermediary agents between their colonists and Mexican governmental red tape. The system was very successful in bringing settlers into Texas—so successful that the Mexican government became alarmed at the large number of American colonists who settled there during the 1820s and took measures in 1830 to restrict further immigration from the United States.

ENGANCHADO. *See* LABOR CONTRACTOR.

ENGANCHADOR. *See* LABOR CONTRACTOR.

ENGANCHISTA. *See* LABOR CONTRACTOR.

ENGLISH AS A SECOND LANGUAGE, (ESL), programs teaching English to nonnative speaking people. These programs used to be referred to as English for the foreign-born or English for foreign students. During the second half of the 1960s the title English as a second language was widely used because of the perceived negative implication of the term foreign. Today, some ESL programs are being retitled English language acquisition because ESL is seen as implying inferiority or a lack of education.

EOP. *See* EDUCATIONAL OPPORTUNITY PROGRAM.

EQUAL EMPLOYMENT OPPORTUNITY COMMISSION (EEOC), established by the Civil Rights Act of 1964 to prevent discrimination in employment. As an independent agency in the executive branch, it has been of considerable help to Mexican Americans and other minorities in reducing, if not completely eliminating, discrimination in employment by race or sex.

E.S.L. *See* ENGLISH AS A SECOND LANGUAGE.

ESPARZA, CARLOS (1828-1885), literateur and leader. Born in Matamoros, Mexico, Esparza spent his entire life on the troubled Rio Grande border. He was an important local literary figure and poet as well as a successful rancher and businessman. A long-time financial supporter of the border leader, Juan N. Cortina,* and a part of his information system, he nevertheless found the struggle disturbing to his world of literature and poetry.

ESPARZA, FRANCISCA (1883-1962), descendant of an old Tejano family. In the 1940s and early 1950s Francisca Esparza waged a long and unsuccessful struggle in Texas to regain lost Spanish and Mexican grant lands for herself and other descendants of grantee families.

FURTHER READING: Carlos Larralde, *Mexican American Movements and Leaders*, Los Alamitos, California: Hwong Publishing Co., 1976.

ESPINOSA, FELIPE (?-1863), leader of a bandit gang that terrorized much of south-central Colorado in the early 1860s. He was killed by U.S. troops in 1863. The name is also spelled Espinoza.

ESQUIROL, a colloquial Mexican term meaning a strikebreaker or scab.

F

FAIR EMPLOYMENT PRACTICES COMMITTEE, (FEPC) established in 1941 in the Office of Production Management by executive order. Since over a third of all complaints in the Southwest involved Mexican Americans, President Franklin D. Roosevelt appointed the Texas historian, Dr. Carlos Castañeda,* to the FEPC as special assistant for their concerns. The committee had the authority to investigate charges of discrimination in employment by private companies with government contracts and to take measures to eliminate these discriminatory employment practices. At the end of World War II the U.S. Senate terminated the agency, rejecting President Harry S. Truman's proposal that it be made permanent. The FEPC had succeeded in improving treatment of Mexican Americans in industry, especially in terms of job opportunities and promotions.

With the demise of the FEPC various states created similar commissions; in 1949 New Mexico passed a fair employment practices act due largely to LULAC's* fight against discrimination in that state. A decade and a half later the U.S. Congress established the Equal Employment Opportunity Commission,* which was essentially a re-creation of the FEPC.

FANTASY HERITAGE, the extravagant literary image of the Spanish-Mexican way of life in the Southwest developed at the end of the nineteenth century. Given birth by the publication in 1884 of Helen Hunt Jackson's *Ramona** and nurtured by Charles F. Lummis with his *Land of Poco Tiempo* (1893) and *The Spanish Pioneers* (1893), it presented a heavily romantic, sentimentalized version of the Spanish and Mexican periods of Southwest history which heavily stressed Spanish heritage and largely ignored Mexican and mestizo contributions. This literary movement led to the formation of associations to preserve Spanish place names and to organize fiesta days and fiesta parades in Santa Barbara and on Olvera Street in Los Angeles, California, Santa Fe, New Mexico, and elsewhere.

It angers many Mexican Americans that this mythic carefree Spanish world of gallant dons and flashing-eyed senoritas was and is glorified, while the mundane world of real live Mexican Americans with its many problems in contemporary Anglo society was and still is largely pushed to one side, if not entirely ignored.

FARAH STRIKE (1972-1974), a strike and nationwide boycott initiated on May 3, 1972, by about one-third of the ten thousand employees of Farah Manufacturing Company, a clothing manufacturer in the Mexican border region of Texas. The basic cause of the strike was the insistence of owner William Farah on his unrestricted right to hire and fire employees, an overwhelming majority of whom were Chicanas, and on Farah's antiunionism. The strikers were represented by the Amalgamated Clothing Workers of America (ACWA) and were supported by various churches and other groups. The strike was characterized by a series of unfair labor practices suits by the union and antiboycott suits by Farah, in which most of the court decisions favored the workers. Early in 1974 discussions were quietly begun between Farah and the ACWA. The strike came to an end in late February when a vote indicated that two-thirds of the workers clearly wanted the ACWA to represent them. The boycott and all litigation then were called off.

FEDERAL MIGRANT HEALTH ACT, legislation passed in 1962 providing some health services for migrant workers.

FEDERATION FOR AMERICAN IMMIGRATION REFORM (FAIR), an organization formed to support changes in the U.S. immigration policy. Early in 1980 the organization filed suit in the Washington, D.C., district court to compel the Census Bureau to conduct a separate tally of undocumented aliens, arguing that unfair congressional reapportionment might otherwise result. In February, the suit (*FAIR* v. *Klutznick*) was dismissed by the court and FAIR then asked the U.S. Supreme Court to enjoin the census-taking until an appeal could be filed and heard. On May 17, 1980, the Supreme Court denied the request. *See also* CENSUS.

FILIBUSTERS, semimilitary or military adventurers who invaded Mexican territory in the aftermath of the United States-Mexican War.* Among the more important filibusters were Joseph Morehead, who invaded Sonora and Baja California in mid-1851, Raousset de Boulbon who led 250 men in a landing at Guaymas, Sonora, in 1852 and made a second invasion in 1854; William Walker, who invaded both Baja California and Sonora in 1853; and Henry A. Crabb, who led a colonizing-filibustering intrusion into Sonora in 1857. All of these invasions of northern Mexico ended in failure, but they served to keep the border region in turmoil and to create friction between Anglo and Mexican Americans.

FURTHER READING: J. Fred Rippy, "Anglo-American Filibusters and the Gadsden Treaty," *Hispanic American Historical Review* 5 (May 1922): 155-80.

FILIPINOS, large numbers of whom came to California beginning in the 1920s, attracted by jobs in agriculture where they competed with Mexican workers. Many returned to the Philippines in the depression era of the 1930s but some remained, largely in migratory agricultural labor. They played a catalytic role in the 1965 Delano Grape strike,* which they initiated under the leadership of Larry Itliong* of the AFL-CIO Agricultural Workers Organizing Committee.

FLORES, JUAN (?-1857), bandit. In the mid-1850s Juan Flores organized an outlaw band of young toughs in the Los Angeles area where he began holding up stores. The gang's ambush and killing of Sheriff James Barton led to organization of an Anglo-Californio posse of about one hundred which captured Flores and most of his gang. Eventually Flores and eleven of his gang were executed without benefit of trial. Several dozen other Mexicans who were rounded up by the posse and jailed were subsequently released.

FLORES, PATRICK (1929-), Archbishop of San Antonio, Texas. Born to a farm-worker family on July 20, 1929, in Ganado, Texas, he became a pioneer Mexican American church leader. He was ordained Bishop of El Paso on May 24, 1979, and appointed Archbishop of San Antonio, Texas, on October 13, 1979. Archbishop Flores has been noted for his support of the Chicano struggle for social justice, and especially of César Chávez* and the farmworkers.

FLORES MAGÓN BROTHERS. *See* FLORES MAGÓN, RICARDO.

FLORES, MAGÓN, RICARDO (1873-1922), journalist and political leader. Ricardo and his brothers Enrique and Jesús were leaders in the early movement against President Porfirio Díaz of Mexico that led to the 1910 Mexican Revolution. Of humble parentage, Ricardo studied law but became a journalist in the 1890s and in 1901 organized the Liberal Reformist Association. Exiled from Mexico three years later, Ricardo began publishing *Regeneración* in San Antonio, Texas, with his brother Enrique. Persecuted by Díaz agents, the brothers moved to St. Louis, Missouri, where they organized El Partido Liberal and published its anti-Díaz program. By 1906-1907 Ricardo had become an anarchist, and his extreme viewpoints made it increasingly difficult for him to attract Mexican American and Mexican refugee support. In 1907 he moved to Los Angeles where he published a paper called *Revolución*.

After the Francisco Madero revolution began in 1910, Ricardo launched a campaign into Baja California, but it failed. Increasingly isolating himself by his radicalism, Ricardo was arrested in 1918 by American authorities and sentenced to twenty years in federal prison for violation of United States neutrality laws. He died in prison four years later. His impact on Chicano and Mexican workers in the Southwest and their unionization was considerable.

FURTHER READING: James D. Cockcroft, *Intellectual Precursors of the Mexican Revolution, 1900-1913*, Austin: University of Texas, 1968.

FOLKLORE, the unofficial or informal heritage of a people and including oral traditions such as folk narratives, proverbs and riddles, traditional arts such as music, dance, and folk medicine, and other elements such as magic, superstitions, and social customs.

The study of Mexican American folklore properly begins with Aurelio Espinosa whose first publication, a version of the New Mexico folk drama "Los Comanches," appeared in 1907. Before Espinosa various writers on the Mexican Southwest, including John Bourke and Charles Lummis, had described certain oral traditions and customs but generally lacked the expertise and intense interest to explore Mexican American folklore rigorously. Espinosa exhibited both these qualities in a career that spanned nearly half a century and was devoted largely to establishing the peninsular origins of New Mexico Spanish and folklore.

A scholar committed to scrupulous techniques of collection, classification, and analysis, Espinosa traced the beginnings of hundreds of folktales, songs, proverbs, and even particular Spanish words and phrases from New Mexico. He concluded not only that New Mexico folk culture was rooted in the oral traditions of sixteenth- and seventeenth-century Spain, but that it had survived into the twentieth century practically untouched by Indian and other "foreign influences." Borrowing from the Spanish scholar Ramón Menéndez Pidal, Espinosa developed a theory of Spanish cultural dominance that became a cornerstone of the notion of New Mexico's special Hispanicism.

Not the least of Espinosa's achievements was the stimulations of folklore scholarship not only in New Mexico but throughout the Southwest. Juan Rael, a student of Espinosa's, collected folktales from New Mexico and

Colorado and generally reaffirmed his master's theories of southwestern Hispanicism. But other younger scholars emerged to challenge Espinosa, notably Arthur Campa, who in the 1930s turned his attention to New Mexican folk songs and concluded that many had made their way north from the Mexican interior. In investigations of other types of New Mexico folklore, he again discovered overwhelming evidence of Mexican origins and influences. Campa's most succinct rejection of Espinosa's Hispanicism came in this statement: "I believe it is stretching the imagination too far to try to make Spain out of a country that was called *Nuevo México*."

In Texas, interest in Mexican American folklore soon approximated that in New Mexico. John Lomax, for example, published several versions of border corridos (ballads) as early as 1915. The following year, the Texas Folklore Society began its publication series and since then has issued a steady stream of Mexican American folk materials. In presenting this lore, the Texas folklorists—many of whom have been amateurs of varying talent—have aimed to demonstrate the richness and diversity of Texas culture but too frequently have regarded Mexican American traditions as curiosities of a primitive people. Furthermore, their fieldwork and analysis can be rather casual, certainly not up to the scientific standards of Espinosa. Still, the Mexican American folk materials published by the Texas Folklore Society are invaluable. The collection of corridos by Paul Taylor are a striking example. Other notable contributors to the publication series include J. Frank Dobie, Mody Boatright, and Jovita González.

The study of Mexican American folklore advanced greatly in the late 1950s with the first publications of Américo Paredes, whose contributions have enriched several areas. He has demonstrated how folklore, particularly legends and songs, can be of great use to the cultural historian. He has also shown how ethnographers frequently misrepresent Mexican American culture because they are unaware of the performance element of Mexican American behavior. But Paredes' greatest achievement has been to delineate the distinctiveness of Mexican American culture. His two great predecessors in the field of Mexican American folklore, Espinosa and Campa, both saw their subject as essentially derivative, either from Spanish or Mexican traditions. Paredes, however, has determined that much of Mexican American lore evolved from special cultural conditions of the Southwest and, instead of deriving from Mexican traditions, in fact helped to shape them. As a result of Paredes' work, the conventional argument that Mexican American culture is essentially a diluted hodgepodge of that found in Mexico is no longer tenable. Many classic Mexican corridos originated in Texas and points farther north; so did certain words and phrases and many Mexican perceptions of Anglo character. Paredes has focused specifically on the southward movement of selected folkloric phenomena but his work suggests a much broader range of cultural exchange.

Presently folklore scholarship remains vigorous along several fronts. The traditional task of gathering and annotating such materials as folk narratives continues, as exemplified by the collections of Elaine Miller and Stanley Robe, from Los Angeles and New Mexico respectively. Anthropological approaches to folklore illumine such issues as levels of ethnic identity and intercultural conflict. Literary scholars are studying the ways in which creative writers transform folklore into fiction and historians appropriate folk materials to reconstruct the past from the ground up. Scholars have come to understand that much of Mexican American culture has been preserved primarily in oral tradition, and so for them folklore has become an indispensable tool.

FURTHER READING: Espinosa's bibliography runs to over 175 items but a good beginning point is his "Romancero Nuevo-mexicano," *Revue Hispanique* 33, no. 84 (April 1915): 446-560. Campa's work is also voluminous but particularly important is his *Spanish Folk Poetry in New Mexico* 1946; Paredes' major books are the classic study of a Texas corrido, *With His Pistol in His Hand*, 1958; and *A Texas-Mexican Cancionero*, 1976. A notable publication of the Texas Folklore Society is J. Frank Dobie, ed. *Puro Mexicano*, 1935. The best bibliography of Mexican American folklore is Michael Heisley, *An Annotated Bibliography of Chicano Folklore from the Southwestern United States*, 1977. *R.A.P.*

FOREIGN MINERS' LICENSE TAX (1850-1851), a tax instituted during the California gold rush to restrict the mining area to white Americans. In the spring and early summer of 1849 there occurred large-scale expulsion of Mexicans and other foreigners from the northern mines by vigilante groups, and the first California Assembly (1849-1850) asked the United States Congress to bar from the mines all foreigners, including naturalized citizens (Californios).

As a result of this anti-Mexican feeling, the California legislature early in the spring of 1850 passed the Foreign Miners' Tax Law. This legislation, which went into effect on May twentieth, imposed a twenty-dollar-per-month license on all foreign miners and was expected to bring in about $2.5 million per year. The tax collectors had great difficulty in collecting the monthly fee and also in protecting the mining rights of those who had paid. As a result of these problems and the punitively high tax rate, there soon developed wide-scale avoidance and defiance of the tax—which in turn quickly led to vigilante action on the part of Anglo miners. Scores of Mexicans and Mexican Americans were murdered or lynched. There was, of course, retaliation. The bulk of Spanish-speaking miners fled the mines, and as they fled many were further harassed and molested. A few Anglos, revolted by this persecution, spoke out against it.

Early in 1851 the tax was repealed, but it had already had its effect. Spanish-speaking people were eliminated from the mines, and immigration was greatly reduced. The license had failed completely to protect foreigners and brought in only twenty-six thousand dollars in revenue over a six month period. It convinced many Mexican Americans that Anglo guarantees of their rights as citizens were only empty promises.

FURTHER READING: Leonard M. Pitt, *Decline of the Californios*, Berkeley: University of California, 1966.

FORUM OF NATIONAL HISPANIC ORGANIZATIONS, a nonpolitical umbrella organization of nationwide groups with Spanish-speaking constituencies formed in 1974. The first formal meeting of the Forum was held in Kansas City, in 1975, and has been followed by annual assemblies. At recent Forum conventions a principal topic of discussion has been the creation of a more defined structure in order to better carry out objectives. The group's goals are: to promote justice and eliminate discrimination, to provide a forum for discussion and formulation of Hispanic views, to develop a unified voice for Hispanic communities, to influence national policy, and to promote awareness of the history, culture, and contribution of Hispanic communities.

At present the Forum is made up of two representatives from each of sixty-two national organizations. In a current restructuring plan there is a proposal to broaden its base by extending membership to regional and local Hispanic organizations and to establish permanent headquarters in Washington, D.C. The Forum hopes to speak for the estimated fourteen to twenty million Hispanics in the United States.

FREDONIA REVOLT (1826). On December 16, 1826, Benjamin Edwards, accompanied by a handful of men, rode into Nacogdoches, Texas, and as a revolutionary act against Mexico, proclaimed the empresario* grant of his brother Haden to be the Republic of Fredonia. He took this initiative because he felt that the Mexican government was treating Haden unfairly in the latter's disputes with earlier settlers in the grant area.

The only hope of success for the revolt lay in support from the United States or from Stephen Austin's* large group of colonists. No support materialized from either. In fact, Austin urged his colonists to stand by the Mexican government and raised a militia of several hundred who joined with Mexican forces in a march on Nacogdoches. The willingness of the Edwards brothers to develop an alliance with the Cherokees further alienated Anglo colonists. The revolt collapsed with a single minor skirmish, but the Edwards brothers continued the hopeless struggle until the end of the year. In January 1827 the remnants of the rebels fled across the border into Louisiana.

Despite some playing up of the Anglo versus Mexican aspect of the revolt both in Mexico City and in the United States, it was a minor, abortive affair and showed that a majority of Mexico's Anglo Texans were reasonably loyal to their adopted government at that time.

FRÉMONT, JOHN CHARLES (1813-1890), politician, soldier, and western path-marker. Born in Savannah, Georgia, and educated in the South, Frémont joined the U.S. Topographical Corps and in 1838 was commissioned a second lieutenant. As a result of his marriage to the daughter of an influential senator, Thomas Hart Benton, he was appointed to head three expeditions to the far West and his reports and maps from these trips soon made his name virtually a household word.

The third expedition, in 1845, led him into California where he not only defied the Mexican government by refusing to leave but also assumed an important and controversial role in the Bear Flag revolt.* In the ensuing war with Mexico his disagreement with General Stephen Kearny* led to his recall, court-martial, and eventually a presidential pardon. Resigning from the army, he returned to California where he had purchased from Juan B. Alvarado his forty-four-thousand-acre ranch. Frémont was later elected one of the state's first two senators. In 1856 Frémont became the first presidential candidate of the newly formed Republican party, but lost to James Buchanan.

With the outbreak of the Civil War, Frémont was appointed head of the Department of the West where his radical antislavery policies soon led to his removal by President Lincoln. After the war Frémont's activities in railroad promotion ended in financial failure. However, he was appointed territorial governor of New Mexico from 1878 to 1883. Shortly before his death in New York City in 1890 he was restored to his former military rank of major general and received a pension.

FURTHER READING: John C. Frémont, *Memoirs of my Life*, Chicago and New York: Belford, Clarke and Co., 1887.

G

GABACHO (GAVACHO), a pejorative term for an Anglo American. The word originally designated a Frenchman from the slopes of the Pyrenees and was then extended to all Frenchmen. Today it is used by Chicanos as a more pejorative term than gringo to refer to an Anglo American.

GABALDÓN, GUY (1927-), World War II hero. Born in Los Angeles, at the age of eleven Gabaldón was adopted by a Japanese family after his mother died. At seventeen he enlisted in the Marines and became a hero during the battle for Saipan Island in the South Pacific in 1944. Using the

Japanese he had learned as a youth, Gabaldón captured more than one thousand enemy soldiers during a period of eight months. At the end of the fifties Hollywood made his story into the film *Hell to Eternity*.

In 1970 Gabaldón returned his Navy Cross and Purple Heart medals as a protest against discrimination against minorities in the United States. After living in Baja California for a number of years after the war, in the early 1970s Gabaldón moved to Albuquerque, New Mexico, where he operates a motel.

GADSDEN TREATY (1853), the agreement between the United States and Mexico by which in 1854 the United States acquired a twenty-nine-million-acre triangle of territory in southern Arizona and New Mexico known to the Mexicans as the Mesilla Valley. The Gadsden Treaty is sometimes referred to in Mexican history as the Treaty of La Mesilla.

The United States Minister to Mexico, James Gadsden, was instructed by Secretary of State William Marcy to buy as much of northern Mexico as he could for two purposes: a transcontinental railroad route across the south, and U.S. expansion. When Gadsden urged cession of five Mexico border states and Baja California on President Antonio López de Santa Anna and the latter demurred, two thousand American troops were sent to the New Mexican border "to preserve order." Politically weakened by lack of government funds and fearful of a possible U.S. filibuster* attack, Santa Anna agreed to the treaty of purchase and it was signed on December 30, 1853. The treaty was ratified by the United States Senate on June 29, 1854, with a purchase price of $10 million.

By the treaty hundreds of Mexicans who had crossed the old border in 1848 rather than remain in the United States were now living in the United States again. While the treaty recognized land claims protected under the Treaty of Guadalupe Hidalgo,* it also expressly stated that only titles recorded in Mexican archives were to be held valid.

FURTHER READING: Odie B. Faulk, *Too Far North, Too Far South: The Controversial Boundary Survey and the Epic Story of the Gadsden Purchase*, Los Angeles: Westernlore Press, 1967; Paul N. Garber, *The Gadsden Treaty*, Philadelphia: University of Pennsylvania Press, 1923; J. Fred Rippey, "The Boundary of New Mexico and the Gadsden Treaty," *Hispanic American Historical Review* 4 (November 1921): 715-42.

GALARZA, ERNESTO (1905-), labor expert, author, sociologist, and educator. Galarza was born near Tepic, capital of Nayarit, in the Sierra de Nayarit. Because of the Mexican Revolution his family moved frequently settling for a time in Tepic, Mazatlán, Nogales, Tucson, and finally in Sacramento, California, where he began school. When he was suddenly left without an immediate family Galarza, still in high school, supported himself with odd jobs.

Upon completion of high school Galarza entered Occidental College in Los Angeles and from there went on to graduate work in history at Stanford University, receiving his M.A. in 1929. He later received his Ph.D. from Columbia University with honors. He then worked in a number of jobs in the fields of education, labor, and Latin America. From 1936 to 1940 Galarza was a research assistant in education for the Pan American Union. During that time he became an American citizen.

Galarza was promoted to Chief of the Division of Labor and Social Information, of the Pan American Union in 1940. This brought him to the area that was to be his main interest for the rest of his life—labor. Seven years later Galarza left the PAU to become research director with the newly organized National Farm Labor Union,* AFL, and moved to San Jose, California. In his twelve years with the NFLU he was intimately involved with all the problems of agricultural workers and became union secretary-treasurer and vice president.

In the 1960s Dr. Galarza was occupied as a consultant, as editor of *Inter-American Reports*, and as university professor and visiting lecturer. He was also busy writing several books on agricultural labor—the products of his experience in the field. Among his works in this genre the best known are *Strangers in our Fields,* (Washington, D.C.: Joint United States-Mexican Trade Union Committee, 1956; *Merchants of Labor: The Mexican Bracero Story*, Santa Barbara, Calif.: McNally and Loftin, 1964; *Spiders in the House and Workers in the Field*, Notre Dame: University of Notre Dame Press, 1970; and *Farm Workers and Agri-Business in California, 1947-1960,* Notre Dame: University of Notre Dame Press, 1977.

In the 1970s Dr. Galarza became active in the development of Spanish-language teaching materials and bilingual education programs. In this new field he wrote among other books *Zoo Risa*, *La Mula No Nació Arisca*, and *Rimas Tontas*.

GALLEGOS, JOSÉ MANUEL (1815-1875), priest and politician. Born in northwestern New Mexico, Gallegos' career closely paralleled that of his colleague, Antonio José Martínez.* Gallegos studied for the priesthood in Durango where he was ordained. He then returned to work among the people of New Mexico. He was elected to the New Mexican provincial legislature and served from 1843 to 1846. After New Mexico became a part of the United States he was elected to the 1850 constitutional convention and the 1851 Territorial Council.

When Jean Baptiste Lamy* was appointed to head the Catholic Church in the Southwest, Gallegos, then pastor at Albuquerque, was excommunicated by him for concubinage. As a prominent opponent of Lamy he was supported by most Mexican clerics and their flocks. Separated from the church, Gallegos married and devoted himself to a political career. With the support of the Penitentes* he was elected territorial delegate to the U.S. Congress in

1853. However, in the following election Gallegos lost to Miguel Otero, Sr.,* who had Archbishop Lamy's support. At the beginning of the 1860s he was elected to the territorial legislature and Speaker of the House. After an interlude as a Confederate prisoner of war, he became territorial treasurer in 1865 and three years later Superintendent of Indian Affairs. In 1870 he was again elected delegate to the United States Congress, but was defeated two years later.

EL GALLO: LA VOZ DE JUSTICIA, a monthly news journal published in Denver by the Crusade for Justice.* Its primary purpose was to publicize organization activities and to keep Crusade members informed about Chicano efforts in the struggle for social justice throughout the Southwest.

GALLUP INCIDENT (1935), a riot by miners in Gallup, New Mexico, early in 1935 which resulted from attempts to evict striking Mexican and Mexican American miners from housing on former property of the Gallup American Coal Company. Three deaths occurred during the riot. Attempts were made to coerce the miners by cutting off relief payments, and excitement ran high for several weeks as outside support for the miners poured into Gallup. Among the miners' supporters was Jesús Pallares who had earlier founded La Liga Obrera de Habla Española* (The Spanish-Speaking Workers' League). More than one hundred miners were arrested, mostly under New Mexican criminal syndicalism legislation. Eventually the criminal syndicalism charges against the strikers were dropped, and they won rights to relief.

GAMIO, MANUEL (1883-1960), outstanding Mexican anthropologist. The founder of modern indigenist studies in the Western Hemisphere, Dr. Gamio was also one of the first persons to study Mexican immigration to the United States. With a grant from the Social Science Research Council in 1926-1927, Gamio made an in-depth study of the Mexican in the United States at the time of his peak movement northward in the mid-1920s. This study resulted in two outstanding works, still very useful today: *The Mexican Immigrant: His Life Story,* Chicago: University of Chicago Press, 1931; reprint, Arno Press, 1969; and *Mexican Immigration to the United States,* Chicago: University of Chicago Press, 1930; reprint, Dover Publications, Inc., 1971.

GARCÍA, HÉCTOR PÉREZ (1914-), doctor, Texas politico. Born in Mexico and educated in the United States, Dr. García served in the Medical Corps during World War II, earning the Bronze Star with six Battle Stars. At the end of the war he entered private practice at Corpus Christi and early in 1948, partly as a result of the Longoria* incident, he organized the American G.I. Forum,* whose aim was to defend the civil rights of Mexican

Americans, especially veterans. He was elected first national chairman of the Forum. García was active in other Mexican American civil rights organizations and politics as well. He became a member of the Texas State Democratic Committee and in 1954 was appointed to the Advisory Council of the Democratic National Committee. In 1955 he was given the outstanding Democracy Forward award by the Texas Conference of Negro Organizations. He was also active in LULAC* and in 1960 was a founder and first national president of PASO.

During the 1960 election Dr. García was a leader in the J. F. Kennedy campaign in Texas and became the National Coordinator of the Viva Kennedy clubs.* He was appointed to various national positions by both President Kennedy and his successor, Lyndon Johnson. President Johnson appointed Dr. García presidential representative and special ambassador to the inauguration of President Raul Leoni of Venezuela in 1964 and three years later made him alternate delegate to the United Nations with rank of ambassador. He also appointed him as the first Mexican American member of the United States Commission on Civil Rights. As a result of his long involvement in the civil and human rights movement he has also been the recipient of many other honors from regional and national organizations. In 1965 Panamanian President Marco Robles awarded García the Order of Vasco Núñez de Balboa in recognition of his services to humanity.

GARCÍA DIEGO Y MORENO, FRANCISCO (1785-1846), first bishop of the Californias. Born in the Mexican town of Lagos (later Lagos de Moreno), he came from a distinguished family, and at the age of ten entered the minor seminary in Guadalajara. In 1801 he went to the Franciscan College at Zacatecas and was ordained a priest eight years later.

In 1832 the Mexican government ordered native-born Mexican clergy of the Zacatecas College to take over the California missions from Spanish-born friars. Thus began García Diego's thirteen years of service in California. Arriving in 1833 as Father President, he quickly arranged for the transfer of control of eight northern California missions to the Zacatecan friars. At the petition of the Zacatecan missionaries and the Mexican government, the Holy See created a new diocese of Both Californias (Ambas Californias) a few years later.

In 1840 San Diego became the seat of the first bishopric in what is now the western United States, and García Diego became its first bishop. He ordained the first priests in California in June 1842 at Mission Santa Barbara and two years later established the first seminary in California near Mission Santa Inés.

FURTHER READING: Francis J. Weber, *Francisco García Diego, California's Transition Bishop*, Los Angeles: Dawson's Book Shop, 1972.

GARRIGA, MARIANO S. (1886-1965), bishop. Born in Port Isabel, Texas, he grew up there and in Brownsville and was ordained a Catholic priest in 1911. After missionary work in west Texas and service as a chaplain in World War I, Garriga became pastor of Saint Cecilia Church in San Antonio. In 1936 he was appointed coadjutor bishop of the Corpus Christi diocese and thirteen years later succeeded to the episcopal see, becoming the first Mexican American bishop. In 1959, in recognition of his role as a historian and bishop, he was named "Mr. South Texas."

GARZA, CATARINO (1859-1902?), journalist and revolutionary. Born on the Texas border a decade after the United States-Mexican War, Catarino Garza was educated both in Mexico and the United States. Early in his career Garza worked on or published a number of papers in border-area towns including Laredo, Eagle Pass, Corpus Christi, and San Antonio. In the late 1880s he published an anti-Diaz newspaper in Nueces County called *El Libre Pensador* and quickly became a leader of Mexican revolutionary elements along the border.

In September 1891, with a half-revolutionary, half-bandit force he had assembled, he invaded Mexico, but his band was easily dispersed by Mexican troops. When he recrossed to the northern side of the Rio Grande he was pursued by United States troops, but was able to elude them because of widespread support from Texas Mexican Americans. Eventually Garza was forced to flee to Cuba and from there went to the isthmus of Panama, where he was killed fighting for that area's independence from Colombia.

See also BORDER CONFLICT.

GARZA, ELIGIO (KIKA). *See* DE LA GARZA, ELIGIO (KIKA).

GENTE, LA, a Santa Fe, New Mexico, Chicano group, organizationally based somewhat on the Black Panthers' ministry system. Developed in late 1970, La Gente (The People) was made up mostly of young people concerned with social and economic problems in the barrio. In addition to attempting to influence local federally funded programs, the group organized barrio schools, a free clinic, and street fiestas. Its "Ministry of Justice" was especially concerned with police-community relations and overall the organization stressed its service role to the barrio.

GENTE DE RAZÓN, literally, people of reason or rational people. The term originally applied to Europeans (especially Spaniards) and to anyone (mestizo or Indian) who adopted Spanish language and culture. On the northern frontier of colonial New Spain (Mexico) the term referred to any settlers of European culture, whatever their racial background. In a more restricted sense it is sometimes used to refer to the upper classes of this frontier region.

GERRYMANDERING, the dividing of a voting area in such a way as to create political advantage. Many Mexican American leaders assert that solidly Chicano areas, as in East Los Angeles, for example, are politically divided so as to reduce the predominance of Chicano political power. To illustrate the seriousness of the problem, at the beginning of the 1980s more than one hundred lawsuits over gerrymandering in Texas are in the planning stage.

G.I. FORUM. *See* AMERICAN G.I. FORUM.

GIUMARRA VINEYARDS, INC., one of the largest table-grape growers in the United States in the late 1960s, producing about two and one-half million lugs of grapes a year on five thousand acres near Bakersfield, California, and employing about three thousand workers during the peak harvest season.

After the United Farm Workers* Organizing Committee had won the right to represent field workers at Di Giorgio's* farms, it set its sights on organizing Giumarra's workers in August of 1967. Giumarra's response was that its workers were perfectly happy and did not want a union. Early the following spring the UFWOC charged that 75 percent of Giumarra's workers were greencarders,* and in May César Chávez said that greencarder and commuter strikebreakers were the largest obstacle to farm unionization in California. Giumarra admitted to using greencarders (but claimed they were not strikebreakers) and to using other growers' labels for his grapes. This grower's tactic led to the famous grape boycott.* The strike and boycott dragged on until mid-1970 when Giumarra and 25 other table-grape growers signed three-year contracts with UFWOC.

See also GRAPE STRIKE.

GLORIETA PASS, BATTLE OF (1862), a critical Civil War* battle in New Mexico. After Confederate forces from Texas under General Henry Sibley's command had captured Santa Fe, early in 1862, they headed eastward to take Fort Union. At Glorieta Pass in the Sangre de Cristo mountains, about twelve miles southeast of Santa Fe, they encountered Union forces and a group of Colorado volunteers. A running battle from March 26 to 28 resulted in the discovery and destruction of all seventy-three wagons of the Confederate supply train through the excellent scouting of Manuel Cháves.* The Texans eventually were forced to withdraw from New Mexico to Texas virtually ending Civil War fighting in the territory.

GOLIAD, TEXAS, county seat of Goliad County in south central Texas. In 1721-1722 a presidio was established at the mouth of the San Antonio River near the mission of Espiritu Santo de la Bahía and was referred to as

La Bahía. Later the presidio was moved upstream, and by 1800 it had become a town of about nine hundred inhabitants, second in size in Texas to San Antonio. After the 1810 Mexican revolution for independence the name was changed from Bahía to Goliad, allegedly an anagram of (H)idalgo, clerical leader and hero of the revolution.

During the Texas Revolt* against Mexico (1835-1836), two weeks after the fall of the Alamo, Goliad was the scene of a second Texas defeat (March 1836) and the execution of over three hundred Texans at General Santa Anna's* orders. The result was that Goliad and the Alamo became rallying points in the war.

GONZALES, RAYMOND J. (1938-), educator, legislator. Born in Bakersfield, California, he received his early college education there and graduated from San Francisco State College, continuing his graduate studies at the University of the Americas in Mexico. Between 1965 and 1972 Gonzales taught at several California colleges and also did some radio and magazine news reporting. In 1971 he was awarded a Ph.D. in Latin American Studies at the University of Southern California. After his election in the following year to the California Assembly, he was appointed to the Education Committee of the Assembly, becoming the first freshman assemblyman ever to be named chairman of that committee. After several appointments to various state and federal educational agencies, in 1976 he was assigned by Governor Brown to the Public Employment Relations Board, and two years later President Carter named him to the National Advisory Commission to the United Nations Education, Science, and Cultural Organization (UNESCO).

GONZALES, RICHARD ALONZO (PANCHO) (1928-), tennis champion. Gonzales was born in Los Angeles into a family of seven children and grew up in southern California. He was active in sports during his high school days. In 1945, after leaving school, he joined the United States Navy and upon his discharge two years later began playing tennis more seriously—especially after his marriage in the following year.

In 1948 and 1949 he won the U.S. men's singles championships and in 1949, England's men's doubles championship. He turned professional in 1949 and was a top-ranking professional tennis player from 1954 to 1961. He is noted for his personal approach to tennis, for which he has never taken a lesson, and his aversion to systematic training. In recent years he has done tennis exhibition work.

GONZALES, RODOLFO (1929-), political activist. In the mid-1960s, an urban civil rights and cultural movement called the Crusade for Justice* was formed in Denver, Colorado. Its founder and principal spokesman, Rodolfo Gonzales, a former boxer, businessman, and official of the Democratic party, soon became one of the central leaders in the Chicano movement and a strong proponent of Chicano nationalism.

Rodolfo ("Corky") Gonzales was born in a barrio* of Denver. Since his parents were seasonal farm workers, at an early age he joined them in the sugar-beet fields. His education was a mixture of formal and barrio experiences that later affected the direction of his personal and professional life. He became a fighter, as many other poor men have done to escape poverty. Rated as the third-ranking contender for the World Featherweight title, he nevertheless quit the ring, becoming a successful businessman, Democratic leader, and director of poverty programs. Frustrated by traditional politics, he soon abandoned these roles and terminated his affiliation with the Democratic party. Soon thereafter, in 1965-1966, he established the Crusade for Justice, through which objectives and priorities of the Chicano movement were articulated and carried out.

In the late sixties and early seventies "Corky" Gonzales organized and supported high school walkouts, demonstrations against police brutality, and legal cases on behalf of arrested Chicanos. He also organized mass demonstrations against the Vietnam War.

With Reies Tijerina,* in 1968 Gonzales led a Chicano contingent in the Poor People's March* on Washington. While there, he issued his "Plan of the Barrio" which called for better housing, education, barrio-owned businesses, and restitution of pueblo lands; he also proposed forming a Congress of Aztlán to achieve these goals. One of the most important roles played by Gonzales was as organizer of the annual Chicano Youth Liberation conferences,* an ambitious effort to create greater unity among Chicano youths. These conferences brought together large numbers of Chicano youths from throughout the country and provided them with opportunities to express their views on self-determination. The first conference in March 1969 produced a document, *El Plan Espiritual de Aztlán** (*The Spiritual Plan of Aztlán*) which develops the concept of ethnic nationalism and self-determination in the struggle for Chicano liberation. The second Chicano youth conference in 1970 represented a further refinement in Corky Gonzales's theories on Chicano self-determination. Following the 1970 conference, Gonzales launched the Colorado Raza Unida party.*

On August 29, 1970, while participating in a mass demonstration against the Vietnam War in Los Angeles, Gonzales and twenty-eight members of the Crusade were arrested. After posting $1,250 bail he was released and returned to Denver. Later he was exonerated of all charges.

Gonzales is well known as the author of the epic poem *Yo Soy Joaquín,* which created a considerable impact on the Chicano community and especially on Chicano youths. When the poem is recited, few Chicanos are left unstirred, because Gonzales has skillfully woven myth, memory, and desire into a master poem.

In many ways "Corky" Gonzales has greatly influenced the Chicano movement. His key to "liberation" for the Chicano community is to develop a strong power base, and he has placed heavy reliance on nationalism among Chicanos. His contributions as a community organizer, youth leader, political activist, and civil rights advocate have helped to create a new spirit of Chicano unity and the concept of self-determination for all Chicanos.

GONZÁLEZ, HENRY B. (1916-), lawyer and congressman. Born in 1916 in San Antonio, Henry González attended San Antonio public schools and later enrolled at Saint Mary's University, from which he received a law degree. After graduation he occupied various positions, including that of chief probation officer for Bexar County.

Elected to the San Antonio city council in 1953, he introduced an ordinance that removed all laws permitting segregation in San Antonio. In 1956 he became the first Mexican American to be elected to the Texas state senate in 110 years. While a senator, González was an outspoken champion of equal rights for minorities in Texas.

In November 1961 González won election to the United States House of Representatives, where he became the first Texan of Mexican American background to be elected to the Congress. Many of his Spanish-speaking constituents regarded him as their leading spokesman in defense of their rights as American citizens. In Congress he sponsored bills supporting adult basic education, Puerto Rican rights, a youth conservation corps, benefits for farm workers, adequate housing, manpower training and development, and a minimum wage. In 1964 he contributed to the defeat of the long-term bracero bill providing government protection and subsidies for temporary workers from Mexico.

Although Henry González received a great deal of liberal support when he first sought election to the Congress, today he is regarded as conservative by many Mexican Americans. He, on the other hand, criticizes these groups as being reverse racist organizations and self-aggrandizing.

FURTHER READING: Eugene Rodríguez, *Henry B. González: A Political Profile*, New York: Arno Press, 1976.

GONZÁLEZ PARSONS, LUCÍA (c. 1852-1942), feminist, labor leader. Lucía González was born and grew up in north central Texas in a small community just south of Fort Worth. When she was about nineteen she married Albert Parsons, and in the early 1870s they moved to Chicago where Parsons, a journalist, soon became an important figure in the local labor movement. Lucía and her husband both came to be ardent socialists and prominent figures in the Workingmen's party and then in the socialist party. During the first half of the 1880s Lucía, or Lucy as she was commonly known, joined the Chicago Working Women's Union and led women's marches to demonstrate for the eight-hour workday and for women's rights.

When the famous Haymarket riot occurred in Chicago early in May 1886 Parsons was one of eight leaders indicted, and one of the seven given the death sentence. After his conviction Lucy led a year-and-a-half futile fight to reverse the jury's verdict. Although she worked to support her children, she found time to make speaking tours to raise popular support for the convicted men. She was unsuccessful in reversing the verdicts.

After her husband's execution she continued her activities in support of radical labor leaders and was one of the founders of International Labor Defense, which later fought for the labor activists Tom Mooney, Warren Billings, and the McNamara brothers. She was also one of the founders of the Industrial Workers of the World* at the beginning of this century and traveled widely in the western United States recruiting members. She continued throughout her life to be active in the ongoing struggle for women's rights and justice for the worker; even in her eighties she remained a vital figure in the International Labor Defense. She died at ninety, as the result of a fire that razed her home. Lucía González Parsons is an important early radical Chicana reformer whose life spanned nearly a century from the American takeover of the Mexican Southwest to World War II.

FURTHER READING: Carolyn Ashbaugh, *Lucy Parsons*, Chicago: Kerr, 1976.

GOOD NEIGHBOR COMMISSION, a result of Mexican refusal to allow braceros* to be sent to Texas during World War II because of extreme racial discrimination. Governor Coke Stevenson authorized the organization of the Texas Good Neighbor Commission in September 1943. The commission had some success during the war years in bringing about better Anglo understanding of Mexicans and Mexican American culture and in reducing discrimination, but not enough to induce the Mexican government to reverse its position against braceros for Texas. In January 1945 a program was inaugurated by the commission to make farm labor more attractive to domestic workers by improving working conditions, housing, and overall treatment.

In 1947 the Texas Good Neighbor Commission was made a permanent state agency, but Governor Stevenson's successor had different interests, and by 1950 the Good Neighbor Commission was primarily active at the visiting dignitary level. It had become a state diplomatic agency rather than one with a concern for problems of Mexican and Mexican American workers.

GORRAS BLANCAS. *See* WHITE CAPS.

GOVERNMENT, UNITED STATES. The historical relationship of Mexican Americans to their government has been strained, with many, perhaps a majority, having varying degrees of suspicion and fear of governmental agencies, even those created to serve them or to right racial and economic inequalities of the past. Governmental bodies like the Immigration and Naturalization Service,* the Border Patrol,* and the Texas Rangers* have created particularly negative images in the minds of most Mexican Americans. However, even agencies like the Census Bureau* and the Federal Bureau of Investigation are viewed with great suspicion and some fear.

At lower levels relations between law enforcement agencies and Mexican American communities have ranged from mediocre to poor, with frequent and intense friction. All too often narrowly stereotypical perceptions of Mexican Americans and racists assumptions have embittered these relations. Governmental acknowledgment of basic civil rights and recent expanded concern for political and social rights of Chicanos have often been nullified or lessened by the day-to-day attitudes and actions of its agents. Mexican American experience with government has caused many to feel ambivalent about the political process as a way to social and economic improvement. Their problems have been further exacerbated at times by a language barrier. Lacking until recently the kind of organizational development to deal with government agencies, most Mexican Americans developed a pattern of coping with such agencies by withdrawal, accompanied by feelings of fear and suspicion. The mixture of police and welfare roles in some government agencies as in the Immigration and Naturalization Service continues to affect Mexican Americans and helps to account for a lower than average level of naturalization* and a continuing alienation from American society.

GRAPE STRIKE, DELANO. Early in September 1965 Filipino grape pickers of the Agricultural Workers Organizing Committee, AFL-CIO, led by Larry Itliong,* decided to strike Delano, California, grape growers for union recognition and higher wages. Because growers then began to use Mexican American strikebreakers, Itliong went to César Chávez,* head of the fledgling National Farm Workers Association (today the United Farm Workers*), and asked for his support. Despite Chávez's apprehension about his small and weak union, on September 16 the NFWA voted unanimously to join the strike. The Delano strike was to alter permanently Chicano consciousness.

César Chávez and the NFWA molded the Delano strike, making it not only a strike but also a movement for social justice via nonviolence. Recognizing that the American liberal conscience had been aroused by the Civil Rights movement, Chávez made the strike a moral issue and sought the support of a full range of civil rights and religious groups. His most important appeal was to college and university students. A steady stream of students, ministers, nuns, priests, and civil rights workers poured into Delano, helping the strikers to resist local pressures and giving the strike national publicity. Chávez also involved political leaders such as Robert Kennedy and Governor Edmund G. Brown, at times somewhat against their wills. His encouragement of Catholic heirarchy support and the adoption of the figure of the Virgin of Guadalupe as the patron of the strike made the charges of communist involvement seem a bit silly. Chávez's eventual success can be attributed to the boycott, which brought national pressure on Delano grape growers. Schenley Industries and Di Giorgio Corporation,* both major Delano grape* growers, received only a small part of their total corporate income from farming operations and therefore saw the adverse publicity of the boycott as highly damaging nationally.

NFWA demands centered on three issues: recognition of the union as bargaining agent, an increase in wage rates from $1.20 an hour plus 10 cents per 25 to 30 pound lug of grapes to $1.40 an hour plus 25 cents per lug, and enforcement of standard field working conditions as prescribed by state law. In the first weeks of the strike some growers raised the wage rate to $1.40 per hour but most reacted with a strongly emotional rejection of union goals and with the cry of communism. Many Delano townspeople, including Mexican Americans, were strongly opposed to Chávez and the NFWA and organized a publicity agency called Citizens for Facts from Delano.

Early in the strike the NFWA claimed that as many as five thousand workers had walked off the job, while growers asserted that only a few hundred had left the fields. However, within a week strikebreakers began to come in from Fresno, Bakersfield, and the Los Angeles area. Later they were brought in from as far away as New Mexico, Texas, and northern Mexico. Chávez tried to impress upon the strikers the importance of his policy of nonviolence; nevertheless because of provocation there was some intimidation and beating up of strikebreakers, and piles of grape boxes did catch fire. General labor support, and especially financial help from Walter Reuther's United Automobile Workers, make it possible for the NFWA to survive the long strike.

By December 1965 César Chávez had decided on a nationwide boycott of Schenley products, and workers were sent to large cities to set up boycott centers. Early in 1966 he also planned a three hundred-mile march from Delano to Sacramento to dramatize the strike to a national audience and thereby to help the Schenley boycott. Shortly before the marchers reached the state capital, Schenley corporation agreed to recognize the NFWA and to discuss its demands. This first success brought Christian Brothers Winery to the bargaining table, and the Di Giorgio Corporation became the next target. Here an announcement by the International Brotherhood of Teamsters* that it was organizing field workers considerably changed the strike picture. Favored by Di Giorgio and other growers, the teamsters began a high-powered campaign to win the field workers, and thus forced Chávez to take the NFWA into the AFL-CIO by merging it with the AWOC* to form the United Farm Workers Organizing Committee (UFWOC). Charging bad faith Chávez boycotted the first vote on representation held on June 24 at Di Giorgio's, and in the second vote on August 30 the UFWOC won the field workers by a vote of 530 to 331, initiating seven months of contract negotiation. A January 1967 UFWOC-Teamster no-raiding agreement caused other California wine-grape growers to agree to elections.

With most wine-grape growers signed up, the UFWOC turned to the table-grape growers, and especially the largest grower, Giumarra Vineyards* near Bakersfield. Giumarra rejected a Department of Labor request to meet and discuss the strike, asserting that its workers did not want union representation.

Later it admitted to using large numbers of greencarders,* but denied that they were strikebreakers. It also admitted illegal use of other growers' labels to ship its grapes. This admission led to a complete grape boycott by the UFWOC, and early in 1968 growers responded by organizing the California Table Grape Commission to promote sales. By late 1968 the boycott had spread even abroad, with California grapes being embargoed by a number of European and Latin American countries. In May of the following year the boycott was extended to Safeway grocery stores all across the United States.

The first sign of a break in the strike came in mid-1969 when Coachella grape growers began negotiations with the UFWOC. As early as 1966 the U.S. Catholic bishops had been interested in the farm workers' struggle, and in February 1970 the National Conference of Catholic Bishops created an ad hoc Delano committee. This Bishops' Committee on Farm Labor was instrumental in April 1970 in bringing about three contracts with Coachella growers and two months later played an important role in a contract with Roberts Farms, employer of five thousand California workers. Finally the Bishops' Committee brought twenty-six Delano growers and the UFWOC to the bargaining table. On July 29 John Giumarra, Sr., signed a three-year contract as representative of the table-grape growers thus ending the long Delano grape strike. In 1973 many Delano growers refused to renew their UFW* contracts and signed up with the Teamsters union.

FURTHER READING: John Gregory Dunne, *Delano*, New York: Ferrar Straus

& Giroux, 1971, revised; Mark Day, *Forty Acres: César Chávez and the Farm Workers*, New York: Praeger Publishers, 1971; Dick Meister and Anne Loftis, *A Long Time Coming: The Struggle to Unionize America's Farm Workers*, New York: Macmillan Co., 1977; Paul Fusco and George D. Horowitz, *La Causa, The California Grape Strike*, New York: Macmillan Co., 1970; Jacques E. Levy, *César Chávez: Autobiography of La Causa*, New York, W. W. Norton & Co., 1975; Sam Kushner, *The Long Road to Delano*, New York: International Publishers, 1975.

GREASER, pejorative Anglo American term for Mexican American, and especially during the 1800s an epithet used to label all Latin Americans in California. Greaser is an abusive term that can be attributed to various origins. In early American history a greaser, usually a Mexican and later a Mexican American, ran besides carts and wagons with a bucket of tallow greasing the hubs of dry, creaking wheels. United States army troops, when referring to Mexicans, continued the abusive phrase during the Mexican War. Also the word assumes a connection between the hair and skin of Mexicans and grease. Mexican food, too, is thought to be greasy by many Anglo Americans.

More recently greaser has been used disparagingly to refer to Chicanos' hairstyles and mode of dress.

GREASER LAW. *See* CALIFORNIA ANTI-VAGRANCY ACT.

GREAT DEPRESSION, the period of economic decline in the United States usually bounded by 1929 and World War II, although some economic indicators had begun to show downtrends as early as 1927. The stock market crash of October and November 1929 is often cited as the beginning of the depression. The economy continued to slow down until 1933 and then began a slow recovery interrupted by a short but sharp recession in the second half of 1937.

As a result of the Great Depression many Mexican Americans lost their jobs or found themselves competing with Anglo workers for the fewer, low-paying jobs available. The depression also uprooted many Mexican Americans and drove them into the migrant agricultural circuits of Texas and California. Many unemployed urban Mexican Americans tried to return to their rural roots but found that difficult or impossible. Some rural Mexican Americans lost their farms because of their inability to pay taxes, and overall the depression encouraged the already ongoing movement of Chicanos to an urban environment.

As a result of the depression as many as four hundred thousand Mexican nationals (and their American children) returned to Mexico—voluntarily, semi-voluntarily, or repatriated. Initiated by concern over the high level of unemployment, congressional legislation to limit Mexican entrance into the

United States was debated during the mid-thirties but was defeated, largely by southwestern agricultural interests. The experience of Chicanos and Mexican nationals during the Great Depression served to confirm their mistrust of Anglo society and to alienate them even further.

FURTHER READING: Abraham Hoffman, *Unwanted Mexican Americans in the Great Depression*, Tucson: University of Arizona Press, 1974.

GREBLER, LEO (1900-), economist, Emeritus Professor of Land Economics, at the University of California at Los Angeles. He received his Ph.D. in Economics from the University of Giessen, Germany, in 1926. Before his 1957 appointment at UCLA he taught at Columbia University.

In early 1964 the University of California at Los Angeles embarked on a comprehensive study of the socioeconomic situation of Mexican Americans in the Southwest. Supported by a generous grant from the Ford Foundation, this research effort, directed by Leo Grebler, became known as the Mexican American Study Project. Preceded by eleven published book-length advance reports on various topics, the final publication of this study, *The Mexican American People* (New York: The Free Press, 1970) became an outstanding interdisciplinary resource on Mexican Americans.

GREENCARDER, a person possessing an alien registration card (green until 1965, now blue) as proof of immigrant status in the United States. This card, Form I-151, is a permanent document which allows the owner to live and work anywhere in the United States. Many greencarders live in the border area of Mexico and commute on a regular basis to jobs in the United States. In 1971 there were more than nine hundred thousand greencarders in California over half of whom were Mexicans. The term greencarder is also used loosely to refer to United States citizens of Mexican descent who work north of the border but live in Mexico.

GRINGO, a mildly pejorative Mexican term for an Anglo American. The origin of the term appears to be the Spanish word *griego*, meaning "Greek" and therefore foreign. It is noteworthy that in Argentina gringo refers to Italians, the predominant foreigners in that country. Gringo is often used to describe a cultural attitude rather than a racial type. In this sense it refers particularly to a paternalistic, ethnocentric Anglo.

GRITO, EL, the shout. El grito refers to the cry of Father Miguel Hidalgo, when he called upon his parishoners to rise up in revolt against the mother country, Spain, on September 16, 1810. It is usually given as: Long live Our Lady of Guadalupe! Long live Mexico! And his flock allegedly responded: Death to the Gachupines (Spaniards)!

GRITO, EL: A JOURNAL OF CONTEMPORARY MEXICAN AMERICAN THOUGHT, one of the earliest and most serious Chicano journals, founded in 1967 and edited until its demise in 1974 by Octavio Romano-V.* and Nick Vaca in Berkeley, California. Begun as an independent forum through which Chicanos could articulate their sense of self-identity, it provided an outlet for young writers and poets and published writings of such outstanding novelists as Tomás Rivera,* Rudolfo Anaya,* and Rolando Hinojosa.* Some issues were devoted to specific themes. It was published by Quinto Sol Publications, which went out of business in 1974. *El Grito del Sol*, begun in 1976 and edited by Octavio Romano-V., was in many ways its successor.

GRITO EL, DEL NORTE, a Chicano newspaper established in Española, New Mexico, by militants who came there to join Reies López Tijerina* in the 1960s. At first it was edited by feminist Chicanas Enriqueta Vásquez and Betita Martínez. It has served to help unite the rural Hispano poor of northwestern New Mexico and given them an instrument for airing their grievances.

GRITO DEL SOL, EL. See *GRITO, EL: A JOURNAL OF CONTEMPORARY MEXICAN THOUGHT.*

GUADALUPE, VIRGIN OF, the Virgin Mary as a mestiza (a person of mixed European and Indian blood; *see* MESTIZAJE) venerated in the shrine of the same name on the outskirts of Mexico City. According to the sixteenth-century oral tradition, the Virgin appeared on the hill of Tepeyac to an Indian named Juan Diego in December 1531. To prove that she was truly the Virgin Mary, she caused her image to appear miraculously on his cloak—the image of a dark-skinned Virgin.

A special devotion to Guadalupe quickly developed. She was particularly attractive to the recently converted Indians both because of her skin coloring and because Tepeyac had been sacred to the Aztec goddess Tonantzin (Our Mother). However, the cult of Our Lady of Guadalupe transcended racial and cultural bounds; she was venerated widely by criollos, mestizos, and Indians and gradually became a symbol of Mexican nationalism. By mid-1600 there is physical evidence of this symbolism in associations of Guadalupe with the nopal cactus and the Mexican eagle in various art forms.

By the 1810 Revolution for Independence the Virgin had become, along with the last Aztec emperor Cuauhtémoc and the Mexican eagle, a rallying point for anti-Spanish sentiment. It was therefore natural that the army of revolutionary leader Father Miguel Hidalgo should make her image its standard; later Father José María Morelos who succeeded Hidalgo declared that anyone who would not pay homage to Guadalupe was a traitor to the Mexican insurgent cause. Over the years the cult of the Virgin of Gaudalupe became the strongest cement for Mexican nationalism. In 1737 Our Lady of Guadalupe was declared "Patroness of the Mexican nation," and in 1895 she was crowned "Queen of Mexico." Even during the most difficult years of church-state conflict in the 1920s no government ever dared to interfere with her veneration.

This special devotion to Guadalupe has been carried into the Southwest by the settlers who came there from northern and central Mexico and from the late sixteenth century on down to the present. When the Southwest became a part of the United States in 1848 by the Treaty of Guadalupe Hidalgo,* the Virgin continued to serve as a unifying symbol. The Mexican cultural content of the devotion to Guadalupe helps to maintain a distinctive Mexican American culture in an overwhelming Anglo environment. As pressures on Mexican Americans to Americanize have increased in this century, many have seen the Virgin as assuming an increasingly important role in helping Mexican Americans retain their ethnic identity. An excellent example of the unifying role of the Virgin of Gaudalupe among Chicanos can be seen in the Delano grape strike of 1965-1970.

FURTHER READING: Matt S. Meier, "María Insurgente," *Historia Mexicana*, 23:3 (January-March 1974), 466-82.

GUADALUPE HIDALGO, a town on the outskirts of Mexico City where the treaty of the same name was written. *See* GUADALUPE HIDALGO, TREATY OF.

GUADALUPE HIDALGO, TREATY OF (1848), negotiated by President Polk's emissary Nicholas Trist and signed in the small town of the same name outside of Mexico City. The treaty brought the Mexican-U.S. War to an end in February 1848. By its terms the United States acquired an area of about one million square miles including the present states of California, Nevada, Arizona, New Mexico, Utah, Texas, and half of Colorado. The new boundary between the U.S. and Mexico was the Rio Grande to the southern boundary of New Mexico, then westward to the Gila River, down the Gila to its juncture with the Colorado River, and thence west to the Pacific Ocean, one league south of San Diego.

Mexico received $15 million in partial compensation for the loss of about half of her national territory (plus $3 million in claims); she lost less than 1 percent of her citizens in the transfer. By the terms of the treaty the approximately eighty thousand Mexicans living in the ceded area were to have the choice of remaining Mexican citizens (by declaring their intent within one year) or of becoming citizens of the United States at a time deemed proper by the U.S. Congress. Both groups were to enjoy protection of their liberty and property and the "free exercise of their religion without restriction." By the second protocol to the treaty legal titles to land grants and other property were those recognized as legitimate under Spanish and Mexican law.

All except some two thousand Mexicans became U.S. citizens. While the treaty gave all some legal protection, it provided no protection for their culture and language.

FURTHER READING: George P. Hammond, ed., *The Treaty of Guadalupe Hidalgo, 1848*, Berkeley, Calif.: Friends of the Bancroft Library, 1949; Julius Klein, *The Making of the Treaty of Guadalupe Hidalgo, February 2, 1848*, Berkeley, Calif.: University of California, 1905; Geoffrey P. Mawn, "A Land Grant Guarantee: The Treaty of Guadalupe Hidalgo or the Protocol of Querétaro?," *Journal of the West* 14, no. 4 (October 1975): 49-63; Antonio Peña y Reyes, ed. *Algunos documentos sobre el Tratado de Guadalupe y la situación de México durante la invasión americana*, México, 1930.

See Appendix H, MAPS: TEXAS CLAIMS AND MEXICAN WAR RESULTS; Appendix B: TREATY OF GUADALUPE HIDALGO.

GUTIÉRREZ, JOSÉ ANGEL (1944-), activist, political leader, and judge. Son of a doctor who had fought in the 1910 Mexican Revolution, Gutiérrez was born in Crystal City, Texas, to an upper-class Mexican immigrant family. His father died when he was twelve years old, forcing his mother into farmwork in and around Crystal City. Gutiérrez received his early education in Crystal City, where he became an outstanding debater, and went on to complete his undergraduate college education at Texas Arts and Industries University at Kingsville. After briefly studying law at the University of Houston, he completed his master's degree in Political Science at St. Mary's University in San Antonio in 1968, writing his M.A. thesis on "La Raza and Revolution: Emperical Conditions of Revolution in Four South Texas Counties." In 1976 he finished his doctorate in Political Science at the University of Texas at Austin. His dissertation "Toward a Theory of Community Organization in a Mexican American Community in South Texas" indicated the evolution of his political ideas.

In 1967 Gutiérrez, Mario Compeán, and others organized the Mexican American Youth Organization (MAYO)* and Gutiérrez became its first president. Returning two years later to Crystal City, he began implementing some of his ideas about organizing Chicanos to achieve economic and political power. Following a boycott of city schools, Gutiérrez organized Mexican Americans into La Raza Unida party* during the 1970 Crystal City elections. As a result, he and two other Chicano candidates were elected to the city council. With Gutiérrez as president, the new school board immediately began a series of innovative bicultural and bilingual programs. La Raza Unida's success at Crystal City inspired further efforts in the southwest to win local political control in areas of Chicano majorities.

In 1972, despite Gutiérrez's reluctance to take La Raza Unida to the rest of the Country, a national convention was held at El Paso, Texas. A struggle for control of the party between Gutiérrez and "Corky" Gonzales resulted in the latter's defeat when José Angel was elected national president of La Raza Unida party. In 1974 Gutiérrez was elected judge of Zavala County, Texas, a position he resigned in 1981.

GUTIÉRREZ-MAGEE EXPEDITION (1812-1813), an effort on the part of José Bernardo Gutiérrez de Lara,* Augustus Magee (a former United States military officer), and about three hundred others from the Texas-Louisiana border to free Texas from Spanish control. After initial success in the fighting, Magee's death and dissension between Anglo and Mexican members of the expedition led to its defeat and dissolution.

GUTIÉRREZ DE LARA, JOSÉ BERNARDO (1774-1841), early leader in the Mexican 1810 revolutionary movement on the Texas-Tamaulipas frontier. In 1812-1813 the Gutiérrez-(Augustus) Magee expedition* briefly freed Texas from Spanish control. For the next decade he carried on anti-Spanish revolutionary activities from his Louisiana exile. After Mexican independence in 1821 he returned to the northeastern Mexican state of Tamaulipas where he was appointed governor and commandant general. By the end of 1825 he had resigned from both positions and retired from public life.

H

HACIENDA. *See* RANCHO.

HARRIS BILL, introduced in Congress early in 1930 by U.S. Senator William J. Harris of Georgia to place all Western Hemisphere countries except Canada under quotas such as were applied to the rest of the world by the 1924 Immigration Act. The bill was debated hotly by those who feared the racial debasement of America as a result of Mexican immigration and emphasized the United States' right to do whatever it thought best for itself despite the feelings of other hemisphere countries and the demands of Pan-American diplomacy. Agricultural and other southwestern interests lobbied against this legislation to exclude Mexican workers. Numerous amendments were added to the bill in attempts to defeat it; Senator Harris himself finally introduced an amendment to apply the quota only to Mexico. This amendment was passed by a vote of 56 to 11 and the Harris Bill was then passed without further discussion by the Senate. However, the bill failed to pass in the House of Representatives where state department representatives testified against the singling out of Mexico for quotas and argued that administrative restriction was a sufficient device to reduce Mexican immigration. The congressional session ended without action on the Harris Bill in the House. During the 1930s opposition to Mexican immigration continued, but the problems of the depression years and the repatriation of thousands of Mexicans made it much less virulent.

FURTHER READING: Robert A. Divine, *American Immigration Policy, 1924-1952*. New Haven: Yale University Press, 1957.

HERITAGE, SPANISH. Modern Mexico, and therefore the Mexican American, have been legatees of the complex Iberian culture. Mexican culture was and is primarily Spanish-European with some important contributions from Indian and to a lesser extent black societies. From Spain Mexican Americans in the Southwest inherited their language, religion, and most of their laws, architecture, education, political attitudes, personalism, mysticism, sense of human dignity, and an almost anarchic individualism. The cattle and sheep industries of the Southwest were completely Iberian in origin, and mining was largely so. So was the cultivation of fruits and the vine. In foodstuffs and agriculture (and perhaps in psychosomatic medicine) the Indian contribution looms large.

Some Chicano* activists have tended to denigrate this Spanish inheritance in favor of their Indian cultural background. Taking the 1857 and 1910 revolutions in Mexico as high points in Mexican history, Chicano and other historians have explained the Mexican past as pointing toward those two events. In this view of history those Mexicans who admired the Hispanic past and its heritage were seen as villains and enemies of the Mexican people. As a result many Mexican Americans have muted their Spanish heritage while emphasizing the very real glories of Indian America.

HERMANAS, LAS, an organization of Hispanic-American nuns loosely paralleling PADRES* in its goals. The group is concerned about developing Christian humanism and about the Catholic Church's sometimes obtuseness in understanding Hispanic needs. It hopes to further social change and religious intensity for Spanish-speaking people and publishes a professional newsletter titled *Las Hermanas*.

HERMANDAD, also known as cofradía, a brotherhood which performs a religious function, often organizing feast days of the Church, but which also may have fraternal or mutualist aspects as well, particularly through an insurance program. The best known of these hermandades is the group called Los Hermanos Penitentes or simply Penitentes.*

HERNÁNDEZ, BENIGNO CÁRDENAS (1862-1954), politician, businessman. Born and educated in Taos, New Mexico, Benigno Hernández moved west to the Rio Arriba area while still a teenager and was employed there in sheep-raising and merchandising. Between 1882 and 1912 he became active in the mercantile business in various towns of north central New Mexico.

In Rio Arriba County Hernández served as probate clerk, sheriff, and county treasurer during the period from 1900 to 1912, and in the latter year and again in 1916, he was a delegate to the Republican National Convention. In 1914 he was also elected to the United States House of Representatives and was reelected in 1918 after a two-year absence. At the end of his second term the new Republican administration appointed him Collector of Internal Revenue for New Mexico, a position he held until Democrat Franklin D. Roosevelt took office in 1933. After his resignation Hernández, in his early seventies, retired from active politics. Shortly after moving from New Mexico to Los Angeles, California, in the early fifties, he died there.

HERNÁNDEZ, BENIGNO CARLOS (1917-), ambassador, judge. Born in Santa Fe, New Mexico, son of Benigno Cárdenas Hernández, he grew up in a family active both in politics and the Presbyterian church. He was educated at the University of New Mexico and De Paul University, where he received a Doctor of Jurisprudence in 1948 after a hiatus of four years' service in World War II. Admitted to the New Mexico bar in the following year, he set up law practice in Albuquerque and in 1962 became a partner in the law firm of Hernández, Atkinson and Kelsey. Five years later he was appointed Ambassador to Paraguay by President Lyndon B. Johnson—a position he held for two years. Upon his return to New Mexico he was elected judge of the New Mexico Court of Appeals. In 1972 he was appointed a member of the New Mexico Judicial Standards Committee and has been extremely active as a member of numerous judicial and educational boards. In 1975 Judge Hernández was recipient of the Distinguished Alumni Award from De Paul University.

HERNÁNDEZ, MARÍA L., Chicana community leader. Born in Mexico at the beginning of the twentieth century, she moved to Texas where she became an outstanding civic, political, and social leader. She has long written about and spoken out for educational opportunities and civil rights for Mexican Americans. More recently she strongly supported José Angel Gutiérrez's* Raza Unida party* in Texas.

HERNÁNDEZ* v. *TEXAS (1953), a crucial case in the post-World War II struggle for Chicano civil rights in which the U.S. Supreme Court held that Pete Hernández, convicted of murder, had been denied equal protection under the law because the jury that convicted him did not include Mexican

Americans. The court found that out of six thousand jurors selected in the past twenty-five years no persons of Mexican descent had served on juries in Jackson County, Texas, where Hernández was convicted, despite the fact that the county was 14 percent Chicano. *Hernández* v. *Texas* was the first Mexican American discrimination case to reach the U.S. Supreme Court as well as the first to be argued by Chicano attorneys.

HERRERA, EFRÉN, football player. Herrera was born in Mexico and came to the United States as a teenager, where he quickly became a sought-after football player. After a successful college athletic career at the University of California at Los Angeles, he turned professional in 1974 and played for the Dallas Cowboys where he won spots on the All-Rookie team and later the All-Pro team. In 1977, as a result of his request, he was traded to the Seattle Seahawks.

HIDALGO, a nobleman, a member of the oligarchy and by extension a person who has the bearing, concepts, and attitudes of that class.

Also, Father Miguel Hidalgo y Costilla, the initiator of the 1810 Mexican revolution for independence from Spain. By giving the Grito de Dolores* and championing the Mexican cause, he became a leading Mexican and Mexican American culture hero.

HIDALGO (KUNHARDT), EDWARD (1912-), Secretary of the Navy, lawyer, public official. Born in Mexico City, Edward Hidalgo came to the United States while a small child. He received a Doctor of Jurisprudence from Columbia Law School and also a degree in civil law from the Universidad Nacional Autónoma de México. Hidalgo became an American citizen in 1936 and began to practice law; he continued in this profession until the Second World War. During World War II he served in the United States navy and was awarded the Bronze Star. In 1946 he resumed law practice. His career has included both government service (serving as special assistant to two secretaries of the Navy) and his private law practice. Hidalgo received the Knighthood of the Royal Order of the Vasa from the government of Sweden for his legal services. After serving as Assistant Secretary of the Navy for Manpower, Reserve Affairs and Logistics for two years, Edward Hidalgo was appointed by President Carter as Secretary of the Navy in 1979.

HINOJOSA-SMITH, ROLANDO (1929-), educator, novelist, born in Mercedes, Texas, in 1929. Hinojosa earned his B.S. from the University of Texas in 1953, his M.A. from New Mexico Highlands University in 1963, and his Ph.D. in Spanish from the University of Illinois in 1969.

Following a family tradition, Hinojosa has devoted much of his time to education. He has taught at the University of Illinois, Trinity University, and Texas Arts and Industries University where he was chairman of the Department of Modern Languages. After serving as Dean of the College of Arts and Sciences and later as Vice President for Academic Affairs of Texas A&I University at Kingsville, Hinojosa accepted the chairmanship of the Department of Chicano Studies at the University of Minnesota at Minneapolis.

Hinojosa is one of the most prolific and well-known Chicano writers. He is recognized internationally for his ability to write dialogue that captures the flavor of the popular idiom as well as for the rich imagery of his descriptive prose. In his novels, poetry, and short stories Hinojosa seeks to preserve and transmit the diverse personalities and experiences of the south Texas Chicano. His novels, *Estampas del valle y otras obras* (which received the Third Annual Premio Quinto Sol National Literary Award in 1972) and *Klail City y sus alrededores* (which was awarded the Premio Casa de las Américas in 1976), provide the reader with a mosaic of convergent stories involving the collective experiences of those who populate a fictitious Belken County in the Valley of the Rio Grande. *F.J.*

HISPANO, also HISPANO AMERICAN AND HISPANIC AMERICAN, term used by most Mexican Americans in New Mexico when referring to themselves. The term implies an attitude of superiority. Many New Mexican Hispanos consider themselves pure Spaniards in comparison to Indians or mestizos who have recently immigrated from Mexico. The term is of twentieth-century origin and is explained sociopsychologically rather than culturally.

HISPANO SUBCULTURE. The Hispanos* of New Mexico are culturally distinctive among members of the larger Spanish-speaking minority for two reasons. First, their ancestors came earlier and more directly to the borderlands than did those of Tejanos or Californios, and they brought certain archaic Iberian forms that have remained peculiar to them. Second, after initial colonization, the Hispanos remained isolated. This factor fostered certain indigenous attributes. Because Anglo and Mexican intruders were far fewer in the Hispano area than where Tejanos and Californios resided, their culture has remained relatively undiluted and intact.

Both reasons explain the distinctiveness of the Hispano's Spanish language. Juan de Oñate* and his colonists took a largely Castilian dialect of Spanish with them to New Mexico in 1598. As the several Spanish dialects evolved in Spain and her empire, many now-archaic forms were preserved in isolated New Mexico. "I believe there is no modern Spanish dialect, either in Spain or America," wrote famed Stanford University linguist, Aurelio Espinosa, "that can surpass the New Mexican in archaic words and expressions, constructions and sounds." In his glossary of New Mexican Spanish, F. M. Kercheville noted under archaic words *truje* (rather than *traje*) for "I bought," and *facer* (rather than *hacer*) for "to do" or "to make." After colonization certain colloquialisms also came to characterize New Mexican Spanish; Kercheville gave *cajete* (as opposed to *baño*) for "tub," and *puela* (as opposed to *sartén*) for "frying pan."

The Hispano's Spanish surnames are also distinctive, but for reasons that are much less clear. Hispanos have surnames like Garcia, Gonzales(z), Lopez, Martinez, and Sanchez (accents are usually dropped in the United States) that are among the most common in the Spanish-speaking world, yet they also have surnames such as Abeyta, Archuleta, Barela, Maestas, and Tafoya that differentiate them from the larger southwestern minority, Puerto Ricans, Cubans, and others. The onomatologist Robert W. Buechley has identified thirty-nine such distinctively New Mexican names. Yet it seems unlikely that these peculiar Hispano surnames are found only in the New Mexico section of the borderlands because a given Spanish source area was unique to Hispanos. Thirty-five of Buechley's thirty-nine names apparently either originated in or are most frequently found in some ten diverse parts of Spain. Rather it is likely that families with these names converged in Mexico whence some members joined the New Mexico colonization enterprise but not the subsequent borderlands expeditions. More easily explained are the Hispano's distinctive given names. Some, such as Esquipula, Secundino, Onofre, and Belarmino, are archaisms, whereas others; for example, Miterio, Ologia, and Abrelio, derive from phonetic changes in New Mexico.

Most of the Hispano's folklore—for example, his tales, ballads, riddles, proverbs, nursery rhymes, myths, and superstitions—diffused from Iberia to New Mexico where it has been preserved in an oral tradition. Comparative studies apparently have not been made that reveal whether archaic or unique examples of this peninsular folklore persist only among Hispanos. But there is evidence that, after colonization, indigenous folk materials developed. For example, at least two folk plays are New Mexican; *Los Comanches* and *Los Tejanos* celebrate Spanish victories over the dreaded Comanches in about 1777 and the hated Texans in 1841. During the nineteenth century the décima, so named for its four ten-verse stanzas that follow a four-verse introduction, was at its height in popularity, and many were composed for all occasions and then sung in monotonous tunes by the ubiquitous village troubadours. After the arrival of Anglos some troubadours turned to writing bitter yet good-natured protest folk poetry, some of it in the form of the décima.

The most celebrated of Hispano folk arts, the carved and painted religious images known collectively as santos, is neither some archaic craft that was preserved in New Mexico nor an indigenous creation. It stems instead from an attempt by local santeros (those who produce santos) to satisfy a need for such icons by imitating seventeenth-century-style santo prototypes fashioned in Spain and Mexico. However, because this art form flourished in New Mexico during the century prior to the American takeover, and because a growing literature on the topic associates Hispanos with the craft, santos may be regarded as another culturally distinctive Hispano attribute. In New Mexico santos were made as flat or modeled panels often used as altar pieces *(retablos)* and as free-standing statues *(bultos)*; both were carved from pine or cottonwood, were coated with a white gesso made from native gypsum, and were painted in tempera colors. Most santos are now in private hands or in museums, but they were once venerated in homes and churches and were carried in religious processions including those of the Penitentes.*

The Penitente Brotherhood, a lay Hispano society organized for penance and mutual aid, seems not to have been some archaic institution that was preserved in the upper Rio Grande basin, but whether it evolved in New Mexico about 1800 or diffused to New Mexico about that time is in dispute. Following Bishop Jean Baptiste Lamy's* arrival in 1851, the prevailing thought among Catholic clergymen and others was that the brotherhood derived from the Third Order of St. Francis founded in 1221. Diarist Gaspar Pérez de Villagrá's report that Juan de Oñate had scourged himself (a Third Order practice) en route to New Mexico in 1598 seemed to confirm the Third Order's long-standing existence in New Mexico; and after its introduction Third Order practices were thought to have degenerated into the "bloody flagellations and similar tortures" witnessed by Anglos.

Marta Weigle, the most recent scholar to review the existing evidence, cautiously reaffirms that Penitentes likely evolved from lay interpretations of Franciscanism, particulary the Third Order, in the late eighteenth century. However, this Franciscan theory of origin is rejected by Fray Angélico Chávez, who documented: 1) that the brotherhood did not exist anywhere in New Mexico in 1776, yet did exist, at least in the Santa Cruz area, in 1833; 2) that, after it came into existence, Penitente rites in New Mexico were strikingly similar to those practiced, even to this day, in Seville; and from this he inferred 3) that, in about 1800, the Seville-type institution was transplanted to New Mexico, probably via Mexico where Penitente activities were undergoing a resurgence. If, on the one hand, Weigle and her like-minded "Third Order" predecessors are correct, then the brotherhood is a relatively recent, and to some degree indigenous, development, and is therefore a culturally distinctive Hispano attribute. If, on the other hand, Chávez' "late transplant" theory is correct, the brotherhood, like santos, may still be considered as a culturally distinctive Hispano phenomenon, for in all the borderlands New Mexico alone was the "hotbed of penitenteism," as Bourke expressed it in 1896. Indeed, Lamy, as bishop and then archbishop, was unsuccessful in his attempts to suppress the brotherhood. His successor, Archbishop Jean Baptiste Salpointe,* finally ordered the society to disband in 1889, yet the brotherhood flourished well into the twentieth century before membership finally declined, extremist rites were abandoned (or practiced covertly), and the brotherhood was reinstated by the Catholic Church. Priests today willingly accept invitations to celebrate Mass in Penitente moradas (lodges) which are located on the outskirts of many villages.

Several additional attributes differentiate Hispanos culturally. For example, the Patron Saint of Hispanos, as of all persons of Spanish-Indian or Mexican descent, is the Virgin of Guadalupe, but for Hispanos, La Conquistadora, under whose watcheye New Mexico was conquered and reconquered, has equal importance. Another example is the heavily seasoned ground dried chili pepper content of many Hispano dishes. The Harvard anthropologist Evon Z. Vogt, who was raised in Ramah, New Mexico, once observed that he had sampled enough food in Mexico and in the borderlands to know that Mexican food becomes more picante the closer one gets to the northern boundary, and that it has its greatest chili content in New Mexico. This chili consumption, as Edmonson pointed out, typifies Hispano cuisine. Finally, Hispanos, unlike the larger minority of Spanish-speaking southwesterners, reject that which is Mexican. This can be seen in that they do not observe Mexican Independence Day and Mexico's Cinco de Mayo holiday, and by the fact that they take umbrage at being called Mexican Americans. Instead, they self-consciously assert their Spanishness.

FURTHER READING: Robert W. Buechley, "Characteristic Name Sets of Spanish Populations," *Names* 15 (1967): 53-69; Fray Angélico Chávez, "The Penitentes of New Mexico," *New Mexico Historical Review* 29 (1954): 97-123; Munro S. Edmonson, *Los Manitos: A Study of Institutional Values*, New Orleans: Middle American Research Institute, Tulane University, 1957; Aurelio M. Espinosa, *The Spanish Language in New Mexico and Southern Colorado*, Santa Fe: New Mexican Printing Company, 1911; José E. Espinosa, *Saints in the Valleys: Christian Sacred Images in the History, Life and Folk Art of Spanish New Mexico*, Albuquerque: University of New Mexico Press, 1960; F. M. Kercheville and George E. McSpadden, *A Preliminary Glossary of New Mexican Spanish, Together with Some Semantic and Philological Facts of the Spanish Spoken in Chilili, New Mexico*, Albuquerque: University of New Mexico Bulletin, Language Series, Vol. 5, No. 3, Whole No. 247, 1934; and Marta Weigle, *Brothers of Lights, Brothers of Blood: The Penitentes of the Southwest*, Albuquerque: University of New Mexico Press, 1976.

R.L.N.

HOUSTON, SAMUEL (1793-1863), politician and solider. Born in Virginia, at age fourteen Houston moved to Tennessee where he grew up to become a lawyer and leading political figure. In 1827 he was elected governor of that state, but resigned two years later and fled to the Cherokee country of the Southwest because of a disastrous and unhappy marriage.

After several trips into Texas he settled at Nacogdoches and joined other settlers in late 1835 in their revolt for federalism against the Mexican central government. Elected commander of the Texas army, Houston was responsible for General Santa Anna's* defeat at the Battle of San Jacinto* in April 1836, thereby assuring Texas independence.

Twice elected president of the Texas Republic, he also became one of her first two senators when Texas was admitted to the Union in 1846. Houston ran for governor in 1859 and was elected. As a strong unionist Houston found himself at odds with a majority of his fellow-Texans as the Civil War approached and stepped down when the Texas convention voted to secede in February 1861. He died two years later in retirement on a farm near Huntsville, Texas.

HUELGA, literally strike. It usually refers to the Great Strike organized on September 16, 1965, in Delano, California. César Chávez* with eleven hundred members of the National Farm Workers Association voted to join the strike begun by Larry Itliong* and the AWOC* against the Di Giorgio* Fruit Corporation.

HUELGA EAGLE, the black eagle taken by César Chávez* and his union in the late 1960s as a symbol of their struggle for social justice. Derived from the Mexican eagle, it was, and is, widely used on banners carried by striking members of the United Farm Workers.*

HUERTA, DOLORES FERNÁNDEZ (1930-), vice president, lobbyist, organizer, and chief negotiator for the United Farm Workers.* Born in Dawson, a mining town in northeastern New Mexico, she spent most of her early life in Stockton, California. During the early 1950s Huerta met Fred Ross* who was helping Mexican Americans develop chapters of Community Service Organizations,* CSO. In 1955 she met César Chávez, and since then she has dedicated her time to serving farm workers.

Dolores spent most of the early 1960s organizing migrant workers around Stockton and Modesto, California. She then went to work in Delano within the central headquarters staff of UFWOC.* Gaining experience in all aspects of organizing, she worked in such varied jobs as picket captain and contract negotiator and quickly became César Chávez's most trusted and able associate.

An effective speaker and politician, she has gained an international reputation and today serves the UFW* as lobbyist in Sacramento, California.

I

ILLEGAL ALIEN. *See* UNDOCUMENTED.

IMAGE, acronym for Involvement of Mexican Americans in Gainful Employment, a San Antonio-based national organization. Through local chapters IMAGE works to improve the educational, social, and economic position of Chicanos. Chapters operate a variety of youth-oriented programs and centers.

"I AM JOAQUÍN" (Yo soy Joaquín), a Chicano epic poem by Rodolfo "Corky" Gonzales* first published in 1967. The Chicano hero of the poem in his painful outburst indicates the author's acceptance of his plural roots by self-identification with both Malinche* and Cuauhtémoc* and with Hernán Cortés* and the Mexican Emperor Maximilian of Hapsburg. In the poem Gonzales draws upon ancestral Indian myths to express symbolically his journey in search of self-understanding. "I am Joaquín" is the best-known piece of Chicano literature, an historical search and an affirmation of Chicano mestizaje.*

IMMIGRATION. Migration from central Mexico into the American Southwest has an old and regular pattern that makes it one of the great population movements in world history. Over the decades this migration has been of the greatest variety: legal and illegal; temporary and permanent; consisting of braceros* on contract and on their own initiative; involving daily, regular, and seasonal commuters; men and women; old and young; refugees, tourists, businessmen, and students. For the most part it has not been a move from one culture to another, but a move within the same culture on both sides of the border.

From the late 1500s onward settlers moved from central and northern Mexico across the Rio Grande into New Mexico and later into Texas and California. During the nineteenth century the unregulated and unimpeded flow of migrants across the border in both directions was of little interest to either the United States or Mexico. Yet sheepherders, cowboys, miners, farmhands, and political refugees took economic and political advantage of the border. Until 1900 permanent legal immigration was relatively light, as it was easy to move back and forth across the border informally. The United States began keeping records of border immigration only in 1907, just when the first big wave of immigration was beginning. How many migrated northward between 1848 (the date of the Treaty of Guadalupe Hidalgo) and 1900 is an unanswered question. But perhaps of greater importance is the fact that this regular flow had established the pattern of emigration for the twentieth century.

For historical convenience this great and continuous migration may be viewed as taking place in three distinct waves. Several factors precipitated the first and smallest of these waves, which began at around the turn of the century. These were deteriorating economic conditions in central Mexico, economic development in the United States, particularly in the Southwest, the reduced availability in the U.S. of cheap Oriental labor in the wake of the Chinese exclusion laws of 1882, 1892, and 1902, and the Gentlemen's Agreements of 1900 and 1907 with Japan. At this time the immigrants came largely from central and eastern border areas of Mexico and went mostly to Texas. Among those who migrated at this time were political leaders like the Flores Magón* brothers and Francisco I. Madero. The census of 1910 showed that since 1900 the number of Mexican-born persons in the United States had more than doubled to a total of approximately a quarter of a million.

The outbreak of the Mexican Revolution* in 1910 and of World War I four years later initiated the second wave. The Mexican Revolution inaugurated a decade of indescribable violence and confusion during which about one and a half million Mexicans lost their lives. In these chaotic years there was a large-scale exodus from rural to urban Mexico, and to the United States as an even safer alternative. Pulled first by the needs of World War I and in the 1920s by an American demand for cheap agricultural and industrial labor, the two decades of this second wave left at least another quarter million Mexicans in the U.S., most in the Southwest. A majority of these immigrants were simply uprooted, displaced persons, but early among them were supporters of Mexican President Porfirio Díaz and later members of various revolutionary factions. About half of this group came from the same region as the first wave, and the other half from the area of west-central Mexico. Large numbers, probably a majority, came in as contract workers to supply the labor demands of Southwest agriculture, mining, and the burgeoning defense industry. Before the turn of the century Mexican nationals had been recruited by Texas cotton growers, and by the time of American entrance into World War I in 1917 Arizona cotton farmers, Colorado sugar beet growers, and railroad companies were avidly following this example. While the primary attraction for this second wave was employment in agriculture, there was an increasing pull from industry as new job opportunities presented themselves.

The post-World War I period first saw a temporary decline in immigration and then, after 1923, a continued high level of immigration from Mexico. During the 1920s, when the immigration quota system was established, there was an unsuccessful effort to include Mexico in quota legislation (see Box Bill). During the 1920s an average of about fifty thousand Mexicans came in legally each year, and probably an equal number entered illegally. As a result, this second wave spread over the United States from California, Oregon, and Washington in the west to the great Mississippi Valley, with a part of this group reaching industrial centers such as Chicago, Detroit, and Pittsburgh. Proportionately many more immigrants of this group came to California than had members of the first wave, and its large volume helped to create labor reservoirs* in cities like El Paso, San Antonio, Denver, and Los Angeles. The Great Depression of the thirties resulted in a sharp decline in legal immigration and in considerable repatriation of undocumented Mexicans, but the number of nationals entering the United States illegally remained high.

This second wave reinforced and renewed the existing Mexican American culture, and because of its volume and the historical matrix in which it took place, it gave that culture much of its present-day shape and content. The attitudes and culture of small farmers, tradesmen, and artisans were dominant, although a tiny minority might have been classified as capitalist. This latter group led to the beginnings of a small upper-middle class all along the border, but they did not become a dominant element in the Mexican American community.

The third wave was set into motion by World War II and was composed of immigrants, braceros, and undocumented* workers who came during and after that worldwide cataclysm. This last and heaviest wave came from no particular geographic area in Mexico, but did come primarily from a distinct socioeconomic group, the upwardly mobile element in the lower class and lower-middle class. During the two decades between 1931 and 1950 only eighty-three thousand Mexicans entered the United States as permanent residents, while in the 1950s and 1960s three quarters of a million came in, settling chiefly in urban areas of California and Texas. As a result of tremendous demands for labor, the United States and Mexico inaugurated a government-to-government Bracero Program* to employ temporary contract workers in agriculture and on the railroads. Between 1942 and 1964 approximately 4,750,000 braceros were brought into the United States and at least that many undocumented workers entered. How many of these remained in the country is impossible to say.

In the postwar years, undocumented Mexicans were not merely replacing those Mexican Americans who managed to move out of field labor, they were also driving them out because of their willingness to work for low wages and under poor conditions. Increasingly, illegals moved into service industries and border sweatshop factories. To try to reduce their numbers the Mexican and United States governments agreed in 1949 upon a program of legalizing undocumented Mexicans. This program was continued, with some interruptions, until renewal of the government-to-government Bracero Program in 1951 with the passage of Public Law 78.* Despite this new agreement, or perhaps because of its advertising, the number of undocumented, as well as braceros, increased greatly in the 1950s. As a result the attorney general in 1954 ordered what became known as "Operation Wetback"* during which more than one million undocumented Mexicans were rounded up and deported and perhaps an equal number left on their own. During the period between 1950 and 1955 about 3.7 million illegals were sent back to Mexico; during the same period some 1.4 million braceros were admitted. Termination of the Bracero Program at the end of 1964 as the result of public pressure in the United States led to a dramatic increase in the number of undocumented workers. By the end of the 1970s estimate of the number of undocumented in the United States ran from three to twelve million, of whom probably 90 percent were Mexican.

In 1965 the U.S. Congress passed a new immigration act replacing the national origins quota system of the 1920s. Under this new legislation, which went into effect in 1968, Western Hemisphere countries are allowed a total of 120,000 permanent immigrants, and in 1976 an amendment to the 1965 law assigned Western Hemisphere countries an individual maximum of 20,000 per year, the same as Old World countries. However, because the law exempts certain classes of immigrants from that limit, annual immigration from Mexico during the 1970s was actually about fifty thousand per year. Nevertheless, a Mexican immigrant who wants to bring his wife and children into the United States legally can expect a wait of seven or eight years.

The aspect of Mexican immigration to the United States that is both least documented and most discussed is the entrance of undocumented, or illegal aliens. The end of the Bracero Program and the passage of the 1965 immigration act in the same decade undoubtedly put heavy pressures on clandestine immigration, pushed at the same time by high levels of unemployment and underemployment in Mexico. A just solution to this very serious problem remains a matter of highest priority between Mexico and the United States.

FURTHER READING: Leo Grebler, *Mexican Immigration to the United States: The Record and Its Implication*, Los Angeles: University of California, 1966; George C. Kiser, *The Bracero Program: A Case Study of Its Development, Termination and Political Aftermath*, Boston: University of Massachusetts, 1974; Lawrence A. Cardoso, *Mexican Emigration to the United States, 1897-1931: Socio-Economic Patterns*, Tucson: University of Arizona Press, 1980; Paul R. Ehrlich, Loy Bilderback and Anne H. Ehrlich, *The Golden Door: International Migration, Mexico, and the United States*, New York: Ballantine Books, Inc., 1979; Manuel Gamio, *The Mexican Immigrant: His Life Story*, Chicago: University of Chicago Press, 1931.

See also Appendix C.

IMMIGRATION ACTS. *See* IMMIGRATION LEGISLATION.

IMMIGRATION AND NATURALIZATION SERVICE, created by the U.S. Congress in 1891. The INS was given the responsibility of administering legislation concerning admission, exclusion, naturalization, and deportation of aliens. It provides information to aliens seeking to become citizens, inspects and examines them for entrance, guards the border against illegal entrance, works to stem drug smuggling, and apprehends and repatriates aliens illegally in the United States. The Border Patrol* is an enforcement agency of the INS and at the end of the 1970s had about twenty-one hundred agents to patrol the two-thousand-mile border with Mexico.

IMMIGRATION LEGISLATION. Immigration to the United States was unregulated until the latter 1800s when concern began to develop about the large volume of cheap labor immigration from southern and eastern Europe and from Asia. In 1882 Congress passed a Chinese Exclusion Act prohibiting the immigration of Chinese laborers for a ten-year period. This law was renewed until 1904 when it was reenacted without a termination date. In 1882 Congress also passed a general immigration act, set up a federal immigration service, imposed a fifty-cent head tax on each waterborne immigrant, and specifically excluded idiots, lunatics, convicts, and persons likely to become public charges. Three years later Congress forbade the importation of contract labor. In 1891 a congressional act created an office of superintendent of immigration and led to the establishing of the Bureau of Immigration in 1906. To the list of ineligibles Congress also added polygamists, prostitutes, and people with certain diseases. All of this legislation affected only those who came to the United States by boat; there was no control or regulation of immigration across the southern or northern land boundaries.

Because of continuing high levels of immigration from southern and eastern Europe, some nativists attempted to pass further restrictive legislation in the 1890s and the first two decades of the twentieth century. Passed by Congress, these bills were vetoed by presidents Cleveland, Taft, and Wilson; however, in 1917 Congress repassed, over Woodrow Wilson's second veto, a law establishing a literacy requirement.

As a result of need for workers in southwestern agriculture, in May 1917 the United States Department of Labor suspended the head tax, literacy requirement, and contract labor prohibition and explicitly authorized the importation of Mexican workers to engage exclusively in agricultural labor. A year later this waiver was extended to workers for railroads, mining, and government construction. Over fifty thousand Mexican workers were admitted under these exemptions before the waiver was finally terminated in June 1920, by which time a postwar recession had set in.

During and at the end of World War I there was considerable apprehension that the United States would be inundated by refugees from war-devastated Europe. Spearheaded by demands from organized labor, restrictionists were able to pass the Emergency Immigration Act of 1921. This legislation established a yearly quota of 10 percent of each nationality as counted in the 1910 census and set a total maximum of 357,000. Western Hemisphere immigration was exempted from this quota system. In 1924 Congress passed a new quota law which favored immigrants from northern and western Europe. It set the annual quota at 2 percent of each nationality in the United States at the census of 1890, with the total maximum 150,000. The act of 1924 excluded completely those aliens ineligible for citizenship—mainly Japanese—and exempted the nations of the Americas as before.

The 1924 immigration act remained in effect until 1952 when Congress, in the midst of Senator Joseph McCarthy's anti-communist crusade, passed the McCarran-Walter Immigration and Nationality Act.* This legislation, which continued the quota system and removed the ban on Asiatics, stressed screening devices to keep out subversives and other radicals and gave the government the right to deport politically dangerous aliens and naturalized citizens.

In 1965 Congress passed new immigration legislation to go into effect in June 1968. This law for the first time established a quota system for the Western Hemisphere. The Americas were given an upper limit of 120,000 (with 170,000 for the rest of the world); there were no individual country quotas, but the maximum from any single Western Hemisphere country was set at 20,000 in 1976. The act separates immigrants into two groups: those subject to the 20,000 limit and those not subject to it; about 40 percent enter under the second category. For example, in 1977, 44,079 permanent resident aliens were admitted from Mexico. Obviously more than half belonged to the second category. In the first category preference is given to close relatives of U.S. residents, to professionals, scientists, people with special skills, and refugees.

IMPERIAL VALLEY, a fertile agricultural region bordered by Arizona, California, and Mexico. It was an important area of activity in the early unionization of Mexican farm workers.

Prior to World War I agribusiness recruited workers from Baja California and Sonora, Mexico, to cultivate cotton in the Imperial Valley. The postwar depression in the early 1920s caused a shift to lettuce and citrus crop production. This important shift necessitated a great increase in labor and large fees were paid to contratistas* and enganchistas* for the recruitment of farm workers. Commuter workers, easily imported from across the Mexican border, began to be used, depressing the wages of local workers. By 1928 over 90 percent of workers in the Imperial Valley were Mexicans.

Labor disputes and union activity began in 1928 with cantaloupe pickers who established el Únion de Trabajadores del Valle Imperial, which later became the Mexican Mutual Aid Society (MMAS)* of Imperial Valley. The union demanded elimination of contratistas, a minimum wage of seventy-five cents an hour, improved housing and sanitary conditions. When their demands were turned down they refused to work and many were jailed. After many violent encounters with agribusiness, MMAS finally achieved a contract.

Later the Imperial Valley area once again became the focus of union activity when, in 1959, the AFL-CIO established the Agricultural Workers Organizing Committee, AWOC,* to organize lettuce workers in the valley. This successful drive toward unionization of farm workers, which began in the Imperial Valley, would later culminate with César Chávez's* efforts in Delano,* California.

INDEPENDENT FARM WORKERS UNION (IFWU), a company union organized after the Delano grape strike began in September 1965. Two of the five directors of the union were labor contractors for grape growers. Despite grower preference for the IFWU over the NFWA,* it shortly collapsed.

INDEPENDENT WORKERS ASSOCIATION (IWA), a union organized by Eugene Nelson in the Rio Grande Valley in 1966 and affiliated with César Chávez's National Farm Workers Association.* Originally working with Chávez in the Delano grape strike,* Nelson went to Texas to help farm workers who were among the lowest paid in the nation. The IWA sparkplugged a 1966 march to Austin, the state capital, from Rio Grande City, following the example of a similar march to Sacramento in the California grape strike.*

INDIAN, the name applied by the early Spanish explorers to the first inhabitants of the Americas. They came in waves from Asia across a land bridge at the Bering Strait beginning possibly as early as 50,000 B.C., but the majority probably came between 25,000 and 8,000 B.C. By the time Columbus and early Spanish explorers arrived at the end of the 1400s, they had long since spread all the way to the tip of South America. While the physical type remained remarkably uniform (because of minimal admixture with other populations), they developed over one thousand separate languages and many dialects and varied tremendously in culture from the highly civilized Maya of southern Mexico and Guatemala to the more primitive tribes of Baja California and other desert areas.

About 10,000 B.C. the first Indians began to settle in what is today the southwestern United States, and in the third millennium B.C. the inhabitants of this area began to cultivate corn, and later squash and beans, through agricultural techniques acquired from the highly developed civilizations of central Mexico. From this same central Mexican culture they also adopted pottery, basketry, weaving, metallurgy, platform temples, ball courts, and religious practices. The Pueblo Indians of New Mexico and Arizona, who had four different language groups and additional dialects, were the most highly civilized of these people, living in villages of apartment-like structures that housed as many as several thousand dwellers. Apache groups moved into this southwestern area only shortly before the Spaniards arrived, and most remained at least seminomadic warriors who raided Pueblo villages and later Spanish towns. The Indians of California never developed agriculture and as a result showed little of the cultural growth made by Indians in the rest of the Southwest. Because of these cultural differences the Spaniards intermixed less with the California Indians and more with those of New Mexico.

Mexico was the site of two of the largest and more highly developed Indian civilizations—the Maya* and Nahua.* Since the Mexican population is about 90 percent Indian most Mexican Americans are of part Indian ancestry.

INDIANISM, an intellectual and political movement that views the Indian and his past as providing the roots of Mexican nationalism and culture. While Indianism is a broad movement in a number of Latin American countries, the Mexican revolution of 1910 established it as a central cultural theme in that country. Indianism seeks to improve the material life of Indians and to incorporate them into national life without destroying their culture. Indianism is often expressed by praising the Indian contributions to Mexican culture while minimizing European aspects.

INDUSTRIAL WORKERS OF THE WORLD (IWW), a militant, radical labor organization founded in Chicago in 1905. It had direct links with the Western Federation of Miners and wanted one big union to carry on the class struggle against capitalism.

The IWW was most successful in the West where it appealed to unorganized, unskilled, and migratory workers in agriculture and lumbering, many of whom were Mexican and Mexican Americans. One of the important western strikes the IWW was involved in was the Wheatland Riot* of August 1913; it was also active in the Southwest among copper mine workers. The IWW at one time claimed ten thousand to twelve thousand workers, principally in California agriculture, and introduced many Mexican and Mexican American workers to organizing skills and to the potential benefits of unionization.

FURTHER READING: Stuart Jamieson, *Labor Unionism in American Agri-*

culture, Washington, D.C.: U.S. Department of Labor, 1945; reprint, New York: Arno Press, 1976.

INSIDE EASTSIDE, a Los Angeles newspaper in the late 1960s aimed at Chicano high school students with the goal of developing ethnic solidarity.

INTER-AGENCY COMMITTEE ON MEXICAN AMERICAN AFFAIRS, established in June 1967 by presidential memorandum to assure that federal programs were reaching Mexican Americans and providing them with necessary services. In December 1969 it was expanded to the Cabinet Committee on Opportunities for Spanish-Speaking People* headed by Henry A. Quevedo.

INTERNAL COLONIALISM, a term used to describe the relationship of Chicanos to the dominant society. It argues that American political and economic structures hold Chicanos, as they do Third World peoples, in permanent subservient positions from which they cannot escape. They are a colonized people, permanent second-class citizens. It also says that conflict between Chicanos, blacks, and other minority groups are more the result of competition for scarce resources than reflective of cultural differences. Anglo leadership, it adds, whether Republican or Democrat, liberal or conservative, uses a divide and rule technique by keeping Chicanos isolated from other minorities. It follows then that the Chicano's course of action must be a continuous struggle for liberation. Probably the best-known exponent of the internal colonial model is Dr. Rodolfo Acuña,* author of *Occupied America: The Chicano's Struggle Toward Liberation* (San Francisco: Canfield Press, 1972).

INTERNATIONAL BROTHERHOOD OF TEAMSTERS, CHAUFFEURS, WAREHOUSEMEN, AND HELPERS OF AMERICA (IBT), labor union closely involved in the rise of Mexican American union development in the 1960s and 1970s. Begun in 1899, the Teamsters union has always been internally divided on the issue of local control of its member unions. In the 1970s the Teamsters' conflict with the United Farm Workers* in the grape strike* and the lettuce strike* in Salinas arose in part out of this high degree of local union control in the Teamsters and an aggressive and expansive jurisdictional policy. On several occasions when agreement had been reached by the United Farm Workers* with national Teamster leadership, locals refused to abide by the national decision.

On the other hand, in 1963 at Crystal City* local Teamsters supported the political efforts of Los Cinco.*

FURTHER READING: Steven Brill, *Teamsters*, New York: Simon and Schuster, Inc., 1978.

ITLIONG, LARRY, head of the Agricultural Workers Organizing Committee that initiated the grape strike* at Delano in 1965. From the time that César Chávez and his Mexican American organization joined the strike, Itliong and his Filipinos were pushed into a minority-within-a-minority role. While Itliong expressed great admiration for Chávez and his goals, he preferred the more orthodox labor unionism of the AFL-CIO to the social movement ideas of Chávez and his brain trust. Filipino resentment came to a head in 1971, and Itliong resigned from active leadership but made no effort to persuade other Filipino workers to leave the union. Itliong then joined Agbayani Village, the United Farm Workers* low-cost housing project for Filipino retirees.

J

JARAMILLO, MARI-LUCI (1928-), diplomat, professor. Born in Las Vegas, New Mexico, Jaramillo grew up there and completed her A.B. (magna cum laude, 1955), M.A. (with honors, 1959), and Ph.D. (1970) at New Mexico Highlands University. From 1972 to 1977 she was Professor of Education, and for part of that time she was chairman of the Department of Elementary Education at the University of New Mexico. During this time she was active as a consultant and a conference keynote speaker in the field of education and also authored various articles. In 1977 she was appointed United States ambassador to Honduras by President Carter.

JARAMILLO, PEDRO (c.1850-1907), curandero.* "Don Pedrito" Jaramillo is perhaps the best-known Mexican American folk healer, or curandero. Born near Guadalajara in Mexico, he came to Texas in the early 1880s and continued to practice folk medicine there as he had done in Mexico. In an area where there were few doctors, his fame quickly spread, and people came from far for his treatment and remedies. After half a century of service he died and was buried in a small cemetery near Falfurrias in southern Texas. His grave became a shrine visited by the many people he had helped.

FURTHER READING: Ruth Dodson, *Don Pedrito Jaramillo: Curandero*, San Antonio, Texas: Casa Editorial Lozano, 1934.

JOVA, JOSEPH C. (1916-), ambassador, foundation executive. Joseph Jova was born in Newburgh, New York. After graduation from Dartmouth College in 1938 he worked for four years for the United Fruit Company in Guatemala and then served in the navy during World War II. In 1947 he joined the United States Department of State and filled a succession of posts as vice-consul in Basra, Iraq; Tangier, Spanish Morocco; and Oporto, Portugal. After four years of service as first secretary in the United States embassy at Lisbon and four more years as deputy chief of mission in Santiago, Chile, from 1961 to 1965, he was appointed ambassador to Honduras. After five years at that post, he became ambassador to the Organization of American States and then served as ambassador to Mexico from 1974 to 1977. Jova is a member of the Mexican Academy of History, the Mexican Academy of International Law, and the Mexican Institute of History and General Studies. Among his many honors are the Order of the Aztec Eagle from the Mexican government and the Order of Morazán from the Honduran government. He is also a Knight of Malta.

JUÁREZ-LINCOLN UNIVERSITY, a school founded in Austin, Texas, to provide an academic program designed for Chicanos. Headed by Dr. Leonard Mestas, it operates a program for migrants and for the National Farmworker Information Clearinghouse in Austin. Through the Mexican American Cultural Center of San Antonio and Antioch College, it also makes available a master's degree in education.

JUSTICE. *See* CIVIL RIGHTS.

K

KEARNY, STEPHEN W. (1794-1848), U.S. army officer who, as commander of the Army of the West, with its three hundred regulars and twenty-four hundred recruits, invaded New Mexico in 1846 when the United States declared war on Mexico. Eventually he entered Santa Fe unopposed and announced the U.S. intention of annexing New Mexico. After organizing a civil government and appointing Charles Bent* as acting governor, in late September Colonel Kearny left for California with three hundred dragoons. On the way he met Kit Carson,* who informed him that California had already been taken by U.S. forces. Kearny pressed on with only one hundred men, who, upon arrival in southern California, helped put down the southern Californio uprising against Lt. Archibald Gillespie's oppressive rule.

After serving as governor of California for three months Kearny returned to Washington, D.C. He was assigned to Veracruz, Mexico, as civil governor and there contracted yellow fever, of which he died in October 1848 shortly after his reassignment to the United States.

FURTHER READING: William H. Emory, *Notes of a Military Reconnaisance from Fort Leavenworth in Missouri to San Diego in California*, Washington, D.C.: Wendell and Van Benthuysen, 1848; Dwight L. Clarke, *Stephen Watts Kearny: Soldier of the West*, Norman, Okla.: University of Oklahoma Press, 1961.

KINO, EUSEBIO FRANCISCO (1644-1711), missionary and explorer. Born in Italy but educated and trained as a Jesuit in Germany, Father Kino arrived in Mexico as a missionary in 1681. His missionary field was the area of northern Sonora and southern Arizona into which he introduced European agriculture and ranching. Over a period of a quarter century he also explored and mapped a large part of Sonora, Arizona, and northern Baja California, and proved conclusively that Baja California was a peninsula and not an island as had been commonly believed.

By the time of his death in 1711 he had established twenty-four missions, the most notable of which is San Javier del Bac, south of Tucson. More than any other person, Father Kino was responsible for the Spanish-Mexican settlement of the area of northern Sonora and southern Arizona (Pimería Baja and Pimería Alta) and for the beginnings of many present-day cities in that region.

FURTHER READING: Herbert E. Bolton: *The Padre on Horseback*, Chicago: Loyola University Press, 1963 (reprint); Herbert E. Bolton, *Rim of Christendom: A Biography of Eusebio Francisco Kino*, New York: Macmillan Co., 1936; Ernest Burrus, *Kino Reports to Headquarters*, Rome, Italy, 1954.

KNIGHTS OF AMERICA, a Mexican American organization in San Antonio, Texas that broke away from the Order of Sons of America* in the mid-1920s. In 1929 it recombined with the Sons of America and the newer League of Latin American Citizens* to form the enduring League of United Latin American Citizens (LULAC).*

KNIGHTS OF LABOR. *See* CABALLEROS DE LABOR.

KNOW-NOTHING PARTY, an anti-Catholic and antiimmigrant nativist movement of the 1840s in the United States that was revived in the following decade as an important political force officially called the American party. At its peak in the mid-1850s, it was blamed by some of the Texas press during the Cart War* for attempts to deny Mexicans their rights and for outrages against them, especially in Goliad and Karnes counties.

L

LABOR. *See* AGRICULTURAL LABOR, SOUTHWESTERN and LABOR ORGANIZATION.

LABOR CONTRACTOR, known to most Mexican Americans and Mexicans as a contratista, enganchador, or enganchista. Labor contractors, who were usually Mexicans or Mexican Americans, operated on both sides of the border arranging to provide workers for growers, railroads, and other industries. Usually they were free-lance agents, but some worked for railroads, cotton growers associations, sugar beet processors, and other employers of large numbers of unskilled workers. Many United States border towns had one or more contract labor offices.

The labor contractor often provided workers to the grower for a flat fee of between fifty cents and one dollar each, or he acted as supervisor in the harvest. In this latter case he and the grower agreed upon a task rate or a wage rate that the enganchados (contracted workers) were to be paid, and the contractor then received a percentage of the total wages or he simply paid his workers a lower rate than the one agreed upon. The contractor on a large job also could make a considerable profit by supplying meals to the workers. Among workers the labor contractor often had a reputation for sharp deals and cheating as is indicated by corridos* sung by migrants. Today the activities of labor contractors are more closely regulated by law and licensing.

FURTHER READING: Arthur F. Corwin (ed.) *Immigrants—and Immigrants*, Westport, Conn.: Greenwood Press, 1978.

LABOR ORGANIZATION. Although labor-union development among Mexican American workers dates as far back as the immediate post-Civil War era, it was not until the 1920s that organizing really began on a more systematic basis. In the period of World War II and especially in the post-war period a considerable expansion of Mexican American unions took place. Throughout nearly this entire period and especially from World War I until after World War II the development of unions by Spanish-speaking persons was impeded by two important factors: Mexicans and Mexican Americans were concentrated in a nonindustrial area in which American unionism had little interest and activity, and when it did, Spanish-speaking people were either ignored or excluded. Because of early mechanization and industrialization in California and Texas, the states of greatest Mexican American concentration, these two areas have seen the most activity in union formation.

In the immediate post-Civil War years, the Mexican American stevedores of the port of Galveston were among the first to try to unionize. During the early 1880s there was also some temporary organizing among the employees of large (some foreign-owned) cattle companies in central Texas, and at the end of the eighties some organizing was attempted among Mexican railroad workers. However, the Caballeros de Labor,* which was founded in the early 1880s, had become largely political and economic in orientation by the 1890s and had little impact on Mexican workers. During this same decade Chicanos became an important labor element in Texas cotton and Louisiana sugarcane fields, and after the turn of the century importation of Mexican strikebreakers into Texas gives evidence of some organizing. The anti-Mexican bias of the Texas State Labor Federation encouraged the formation of Spanish-speaking unions, mostly socialist oriented, as did the encouragement, example, and leadership of exiles like the Flores Magón* brothers, Praxedis Guerrero, and other Mexican radicals.

The expansion of mining in southeastern Arizona, southwestern New Mexico, and southern Colorado during the late 1880s led in 1896 to the formation of the radical Western Federation of Miners* and, since so many of the miners were Spanish-speaking, to the formation of Mexican unions. Here also the influence of the Flores Magón brothers and their associates was very important. As a result of this unionization, there was a series of labor difficulties in these mining areas from the Clifton-Morenci (Arizona) strike* of 1903 to the copper-mine strikes during World War I. In the early decades of the 1900s southwestern labor organizations generally remained weak, with the exception of the railroad unions. Those unions that did manage to survive usually excluded Mexicans and Mexican Americans or relegated them to common labor and other physically strenuous, low-paying jobs.

The Mexican Protective Association,* founded in 1911 in Texas, was one of the earliest agricultural unions and was something more than a union as its name indicates. However, by the outbreak of World War I it was in decline because of its ineffectiveness. A decade and a half later, in 1930, the Catholic Workers Union of Crystal City was founded by the local priest, but was also only temporarily successful. It was followed three years later by the Asociación de Jornaleros, which included industrial workers as well as farm laborers. In 1936 this organization was given new life by reorganizing it as a chartered AFL local, the Agricultural Workers Labor Union. Despite depression difficulties, in 1937 an Agricultural Workers Organizing Committee was established in Corpus Christi and developed some locals that soon joined the CIO's United Cannery Agricultural, Packing and Allied Workers of America,* which was recruiting in Texas. The AFL continued its organizational efforts with no great success. Throughout this period attempts at collective action were local, sporadic, and uniformly unsuccessful.

In California the first evanescent Mexican unions seem to have been formed only at the beginning of the 1920s. As more Mexican workers came into the state during World War I, an increasing interest in unionization developed, and in 1927 the Confederación de Uniones Obreras Mexicanas* (COUM) was founded in Los Angeles. Although it lasted only a few years, CUOM was an important expression of Chicano determination to unionize. The formation during the 1928 Imperial Valley* melon strike of the Mexican Mutual Aid Society* (MMAS) was also important—as one of the earliest agricultural unions in California. At the same time, in Colorado the Industrial Workers of the World* (IWW) was helping to organize Mexican American coal miners, and Clemente Idar, an AFL organizer, was working with Spanish-speaking beet workers. Both the early California and Colorado agricultural workers' organizations floundered in the 1929 stock market crash and following depression.

The depression era of the 1930s was a time of great worker unrest; in California alone there were over one hundred and fifty agricultural strikes between 1930 and 1938. It was also a time of radical union leadership, with the communist Trade Union Unity League* (TUUL) and Cannery and Agricultural Workers Industrial Union* (CAWIU) taking active roles. The numerous agricultural strikes of the 1930s involved large numbers of Mexican Americans both as leaders and as followers, but most of the unions they developed were short-lived. The notable exception was the Confederación de Uniones de Campesinos y Obreros Mexicanos* (CUCOM) which developed out of the 1933 El Monte Berry Strike* and which, under the presidency of Guillermo Velarde, remained important until the outbreak of World War II both in supplying leadership and in spearheading strikes.

The year 1933 was a busy one. Out of sixty-one agricultural strikes in the United States involving 56,816 workers, California accounted for thirty-one involving 48,005 workers. Growers responded by forming the Associated Farmers* to combat the swelling move toward unionism, using all the means at their command from legislation to vigilantism. The second half of the thirties was marked by less labor conflict in the fields, due in part to activities of the Associated Farmers.

The oubreak of World War II brought a greatly expanded demand for America's agricultural products at a time when labor was being drawn off the farms and into the factories. This led to an arrangement between the United States and Mexico for workers under the Bracero program.* The access of growers to unlimited numbers of workers from Mexico made labor union organizing virtually impossible. However, in 1947 organizers from the Southern Tenant Farmers Union came west to California under a new name, the National Farm Labor Union,* an AFL affiliate. Led by Hank Hasiwar and Ernesto Galarza,* and made confident by post-World War II interest in unionizing and by local labor council support, they tackled Di Giorgio farms, the largest grower in California and perhaps the strongest foe of unionization. They had no great difficulty in signing up a majority of Di Giorgio's workers and forming a local (218), but the strike that then ensued at Di Giorgio's Arvin ranch proved to be long and unsuccessful. In 1950 it was ended. Subsequently the NFLU organized three locals in the Imperial Valley and in 1952 also led a partially successful strike (using the boycott) against Schenley and less productive activities in the Salinas lettuce fields.

In 1952 the National Farm Labor Union was reorganized as the National Agricultural Workers Union (NAWU), but during the rest of the decade it gradually declined as it struggled against the United Packinghouse Workers of America, use of braceros, and the Teamsters* drive to organize field workers. In 1959 the AFL-CIO used its resources and power to create the Agricultural Workers Organizing Committee to replace the NAWU. A year later the NAWU was merged with the Amalgamated Meat Cutters and Butcher Workmen of America, leaving California's fields to AWOC. Two years and half a million dollars after its founding, the AWOC was virtually gone, its staff having been disbanded by AFL-CIO president George Meany.

By 1962 César Chávez's* disagreement with the Community Service Organization* over the issue of organizing farm workers had caused him to quit the CSO and to begin organizing the National Farm Workers Association in the great Central Valley of California. The Delano grape strike* of 1965 began with the NFWA supporting an AWOC action and before its end found the NFWA merging with the AWOC to form the United Farm Workers Organizing Committee which in 1972 became the United Farm Workers,* AFL-CIO. Passage of the California Agricultural Labor Relations Act* in 1975 muted somewhat the bitter rivalry between the United Farm Workers and the Teamsters* union, and two years later a successful no-raiding pact was agreed upon by the two groups.

Elsewhere in the Southwest, local Chicano labor organizing has been less successful. However, in Texas, impelled by UFW organizational success, Eugene Nelson began the Independent Workers Association in 1966, and ten years later the Texas Farm Workers Union had about three thousand members but no contracts. No other southwestern state has followed California's lead in adopting comprehensive farm labor legislation. In fact, the signing of a farm labor law by the governor of Arizona in 1972 led to a demand for his recall, and in 1978 a move to establish farm workers' rights to bargain collectively was defeated in the Texas legislature.

Outside of agriculture and mining, Mexican Americans have played an important role in labor organizing in the border garment industry. The International Ladies Garment Workers Union began organizing in Texas in the late 1930s but has had at best limited success. In 1974 the Amalgamated Clothing Workers of America had somewhat greater success in the 1972-1974 Farah strike.*

FURTHER READING: Stuart Jamieson, *Labor Unionism in American Agriculture*, Washington, D.C.: U.S. Government Printing Office 1945; reprint 1976; Dick Meister and Anne Loftis, *A Long Time Coming: The Struggle to Unionize America's Farm Workers*, New York: Macmillan Co., 1977; George Greene, "ILGWU in Texas, 1930-1970," *Journal of Mexican American History*, 1:2 (Spring 1971); Juan Gómez Quiñones, "The First Steps: Chicano Labor Conflict and Organizing, 1900-1920," *Aztlán* 3 (Spring 1972); Mario Trinidad García, *Obreros: The Mexican Workers of El Paso, 1900-1920*, San Diego: University of California, 1975.

LABOR RESERVOIR, an area with a large population of unskilled and semi-skilled Mexican Americans and Mexican nationals; these areas became, therefore, centers for recruiting workers for other areas—which in turn attracted more laborers. The Southwest generally, and Texas especially, had become such a reservoir by 1920 with El Paso and San Antonio as the earliest centers for recruiting. By the end of the 1920s Los Angeles had developed into a West Coast reservoir, supplying migrant workers not only for California but also for Oregon, Washington, and even Alaskan fish canneries. In Colorado, Denver held a similar position for the Northwest beet-growing area, and Kansas City, Missouri, had become an important labor source for the railroads, particularly the Santa Fe Railroad. In these labor reservoirs workers were recruited also for Midwest stockyards, meat-packing plants, and steel mills, as well as for temporary agricultural work.

LAFOLLETTE COMMITTEE (1936-1940), also known as the LaFollette Civil Liberties Committee. This was a U.S. Senate subcommittee to investigate practical hindrances to the right of labor to organize by the denial of civil liberties on which that right depended. Headed by Senator Robert LaFollette, Jr., the subcommittee began its task by studying the issue in the steel, auto, and mining industries. In 1939, partly prodded by publication of John Steinbeck's *Grapes of Wrath* (1939) and Carey McWilliams's *Factories in the Fields* (1939), the committee turned its attention to the same issue in California agriculture. During December 1939 and January 1940 the committee's staff of thirty-five held twenty-eight days of public hearings in San Francisco and Los Angeles.

The LaFollette Committee's report came out in October 1942, but as a result of the onset of World War II it had litle impact at that time. It found considerable use of violence on the part of growers and shocking misery among workers. It charged the Associated Farmers* with violent and flagrant infringement of the civil liberties of agricultural workers by use of espionage, blacklisting, and vigilantism. The committee's recommendations included passage of an agricultural employment stabilization law, an agricultural labor recruitment act, an agricultural labor relations act, and an agricultural labor standards act and also the creation of an agricultural wage board to determine a fair wage for farm workers. None of these recommendations was implemented; the wartime concern was for greater agricultural production, not workers' rights.

LAMY, JEAN BAPTISTE (1814-1888), bishop and archbishop. Born in France where he entered the priesthood, Lamy came to the Ohio frontier as a missionary in 1839 and in July 1850 was appointed vicar apostolic to establish his headquarters in Santa Fe and to reorganize the Catholic church in the Southwest. Three years later, as bishop of the newly created vast diocese of Santa Fe which extended over New Mexico, Arizona, and part of

Colorado, he began laboring to reform the Hispanic-Mexican church of the area. His insistence on tithing, his strict, even Jansenist, views, and his lack of appreciation for Mexican culture quickly broght him into conflict with many of the small number of Mexican clergy in his diocese. Most notable were his difficulties with a number of New Mexican padres, especially José M. Gallegos* and Antonio José Martínez,* both of whom he eventually declared excommunicated. He also attempted to reduce and suppress the Penitente brotherhoods* which until that time had escaped Church discipline. Finding only nine priests in New Mexico when he arrived at Santa Fe, Bishop Lamy brought in a large number of missionary priests from France and several other European countries, built schools for Anglos and Nuevo Mexicanos,* and pushed an ambitious building program including construction of a stone cathedral.

In 1885 Lamy resigned from the archbishopric after thirty-five years of episcopal endeavor, during which time he had, with some success, moved toward a blending of the three southwestern cultures: Anglo, Mexican, and Indian. The life of Bishop Lamy has been presented in American literature in a very sympathetic fashion by the Western novelist Willa Cather* in *Death Comes to the Archbishop* (1927).

FURTHER READING: Paul Horgan, *Lamy of Santa Fe*, New York: Farrar, Straus & Giroux, 1975.

LAND ACT (1851), a law passed by the United States Congress establishing a three-man commission known as the Board of Land Commissioners, which sat in San Francisco from January 1852 to March 1856. The act required California grant holders to appear within this period to prove their titles. Both rejected and unclaimed land would revert to the public domain and would be opened to settlers. The board's function was to weed out invalid titles as determined by Spanish and Mexican law, provisions of the 1848 Treaty of Guadalupe Hidalgo,* principles of equity, and precedents of the United States Supreme Court.

Prior to 1851 most good land in California was held by Californios* but pressure from increasing numbers of immigrants motivated political leaders to seek a solution to the problem of extensive squatting on the part of the immigrants by questioning the validity of land titles. Seeking a legal means to vacate as many of them as possible, California congressmen persuaded the United States Congress to pass the Land Act. As a result of the biases of the board, unscrupulous lawyers, the Californios' confusion, and debts incurred trying to defend their titles, an estimated two-fifths of the rancheros' lands were lost. To Californios, these land transfers meant an end to much of their economic power and position in California.

FURTHER READING: Leonard Pitt, *The Decline of the Californios*, Berkeley: University of California Press, 1966.

LAND GRANTS. During the seventeenth and eighteenth centuries, Spain occupied what is now the American Southwest to protect the northern boundaries of New Spain, now Mexico, from possible foreign intrusion. The legal procedures developed by the Spanish government to grant land in her American colonies, including the Southwest, developed out of practices devised by the Christian monarchs of Spain to populate lands conquered from Spanish Moslems during hundreds of years of warfare. The fundamental principle of this evolving body of land law was that all conquered and explored lands belonged to the Spanish Crown to be disposed of as the monarchs directed. In order to attract colonists, settle towns and villages, develop natural resources, and populate colonies, the Spanish kings extended to their viceroys and governors (including those of California, New Mexico, and Texas) the right to grant or to sell land within their jurisdiction. When Mexico became independent in 1821 public lands belonged to the Mexican nation to be granted or sold by the government, and Mexican governors of states and territories were granted the right to sell or to dispose of land according to national law.

The basic function of Spanish and Mexican land law, like that of American homestead legislation, was to populate the country and develop flourishing farms, ranches, plantations, towns, and villages. Although both Spanish and Mexican governments hoped to support their treasuries through sale of public lands, this goal was subordinate to populating vacant lands. They therefore granted lands to prospective settlers under relatively generous terms. According to Spanish and Mexican law, three basic types of land grants were made: private, communal, and empresario.*

Communal land grants were given to encourage formation of towns and villages in conquered or newly explored territory. Relatively large grants of land were made to ten or more family heads. Private land grants were made for the purpose of developing farms, ranches, plantations, or for other private purposes. Empresario grants were large extensions of land granted conditionally to persons of wealth or high social position who promised to attract settlers and found towns and villages. Communal land grants were most common in mountainous northern New Mexico and southern Colorado where many farm villages inhabited by numerous small farmers came into existence. Private land grants were dominant in eastern and southern New Mexico, and in Arizona, California, and Texas. On these private land grants substantial ranching population developed. Empresario grants were limited for the most part to Texas, although smaller colonial grants awarded for the same purpose were not unknown in southern New Mexico.

The Spanish government developed a set of uniform procedures to be followed by persons requesting land. These procedures with few changes were adopted by the Mexican government. Applicants for land grants submitted a written petition to the territorial governor. The petitions signed by applicants and their witnesses listed the names and residences of the petitioners, their reasons for wanting the land, a description of the land desired, and a statement that the land was not occupied nor needed by any Indian tribe or other third party. The Spanish or Mexican governor, upon receipt of the petition, required the nearest local official to investigate the statements of the petition and advise other inhabitants of the region that a land grant had been requested in their area. Upon receipt of the report of the local official and if no protests had been made, the Spanish governor alone and the Mexican governor with the advice of the local territorial council granted the land through a formal statement signed by the governor and his witnesses in the Spanish period and by the governor, the president of the territorial council, and their witnesses during the Mexican period. If protests were made, a hearing was held.

In the case of a communal land grant, the local official conducted the petitioners to the site of the grant, read to them the governor's order granting the land, selected the site of settlement, located the public square, distributed house sites, and then measured a portion of the arable lands for each family. The portion received by each family depended upon its size and social position. Watering places, grazing lands, forests, rivers, mountains, and streams were defined as communal lands belonging to the community as a whole. Every resident of the community had the right to use these lands, and they could not be separated from the community for any reason. The grantees were usually required to build their homes around the public square, to construct irrigation systems and a church, and if there was any danger from attack, to build a wall around the settlement. The house sites and farmlands could be sold after five years residence. If the settlement was abandoned, title to the grant reverted to the government. Settlers could be forced to reoccupy the grant or the land could be regranted to other groups. A copy of the order making the grant was given to community leaders and another copy was filed in territorial archives.

The act of possession for private land grants was similar although simpler. The petitioner for a private land grant received a copy of the order granting the land and another copy was filed in the territorial archives. He was expected to establish residence upon his grant. If he did not do so or if he abandoned his grant, it could be, and often was, regranted to another party. Empresario grants also reverted if empresarios did not fulfill the terms of their grants. Since the function of land grants was to settle territory, those given lands in the Southwest who did not settle upon them usually lost them if the lands remained unoccupied for several years.

At the close of the war with Mexico, the United States promised through Article 8 of the Treaty of Guadalupe Hidalgo* to protect the property rights of the population of the Southwest. Unfortunately, the United States never fully implemented the provisions of the treaty. Caught in a strange and alien Anglo American political, economic, legal, and social system, Mexican Americans were not able to defend their land grants and lost them to Anglo Americans, often through legal manipulations, force, and fraud.

Congress could have authenticated titles to land grants in the Southwest that were occupied at the time of the American occupation. Or it could have required the government to bear costs of litigation essential to settling land grant titles. Instead it forced claimants to Spanish and Mexican land grants to appear before courts and commissions staffed by Anglo American judges and commissioners unfamiliar with the Spanish language and with Spanish and Mexican land law. Mexican American landholders were forced to hire expensive Anglo American lawyers, and carry on complicated and prolonged litigation, often lasting for twenty years or more, before a final legal decision was secured. They also had to prove that they had followed all the minutia of Spanish and Mexican law. The judges and commissioners somehow overlooked the Spanish law that permitted grant owners with title defects to remedy the defects by paying a fee to the government. The burden of proving that their land grant titles were legal was simply beyond the power of most Mexican American landowners. At the mercy of a complex, expensive legal system and of greedy, often corrupt, Anglo American lawyers, politicians, government officials, surveyors, and judges, they lost most of their land grants.

From California to Texas many Mexican Americans faced with land loss, discrimination, and downward social mobility turned to social banditry that still finds an echo in Mexican American folklore. In spite of their protests, Mexican American landowners in California and Texas were overwhelmed by waves of Anglo American and Mexican migration. But in northern New Mexico and in southern Colorado, lack of mineral discoveries and Indian resistance delayed the entrance of large numbers of Anglo Americans until the coming of the railroads in the 1870s. By the 1920s most of the range lands of the land grants had been lost to Anglo Americans. Land loss, resultant impoverishment of the Spanish-speaking people, and the depression of the 1930s helped to create a major depressed region in New Mexico and southern Colorado.

From the 1880s to the present, many movements protesting the loss of land grants have occurred in this area, the latest being the Alianza Federal de Mercedes* in the 1960s. As resentment over the loss of the grants is deeply embedded in the local Spanish-speaking population, more protest movements can be expected. The land grant problem could be resolved by the government buying up the community land grants and restoring them to the village populations to whom they once belonged. The problem of the land grants in this part of the Southwest is a social issue that refuses to vanish.

FURTHER READING: *Spanish and Mexican Land Grants* (An original anthology), New York: Arno Press, 1974; Paul W. Gates, "Adjudication of Spanish-Mexican Land Claims in California," *Huntington Library Quarterly* 21, no. 3 (May 1958): 213-36; William C. Jones, *Land Titles in California. Report on the Subject*, Washington, D.C.: Gideon & Co., 1850; William A. Keleher, "Law of the New Mexico Land Grant," *New Mexico Historical Review* 4 (October 1929): 350-71; Clark S. Knowlton, "Causes of Land Losses Among the Spanish Americans in Northern New Mexico," *Rocky Mountain Social Science Journal* 1 (5 April 1963): 201-11; Clark S. Knowlton, "Land Grant Problems Among the State's Spanish-Americans," *New Mexico Business* 20 (June 1967): 1-13; Olen E. Leonard, *The Role of the Land Grant in the Social Organization and Social Processes of a Spanish American Village in New Mexico*, Ann Arbor: University of Michigan, 1943; Matthew G. Reynolds, *Spanish and Mexican Land Laws, New Spain and Mexico*. St. Louis: Buxton & Skinner Stationery Co., 1895; William W. Robinson, *Land in California*, Berkeley: University of California, 1948, reprint ed., 1979; Ivy Belle Ross, *The Confirmation of Spanish and Mexican Land Grants in California*, San Francisco: R and E Research Associates, 1974. *C.S.K.*

LAREDO, TEXAS. Founded in 1755 by Tomás Sánchez, and named Villa de San Agustín de Laredo seven years later when a mission was established close by. The existence of a ford across the Rio Grande at the location led to Laredo's becoming the hub of a number of roads both from Texas and the south and to a steady increase in population from about one thousand in 1800 to seventeen hundred by 1835. Laredo's citizens had little contact with Anglo American settlers in Texas and remained a de facto part of Mexico after the Texas revolt* of the 1830s. During the United States-Mexican War, Texas government was extended to the area and in 1848 it became the seat of Webb County. However, Laredo remained heavily Mexican in culture and feeling because of its role as the main port of entry from Mexico. The beginnings of market agriculture in the lower Rio Grande Valley, the completion of the Mexican National Railway to Laredo in 1882, and the construction of an international bridge in 1889 all helped to retain the Mexican cultural flavor of the town. At the end of the nineteenth century all public signs were in Spanish and most residents spoke that language.

In 1910 the Mexican Revolution* saw an augmented flow of refugees northward through Laredo and the settlement of some in the town and its surrounding area. Discovery of oil and gas in Webb County, plus some industrial development brought Laredo's population to 22,000 by the end of World War I; by 1950 Laredo had 51,694 inhabitants, over 70 percent of whom were of Mexican descent. According to the 1970 census, the total population reached 69,024, of which 86.4 percent was of Mexican origin, making it culturally the most Mexican city of large size in the United States.

LARRAZOLO, OCTAVIANO A. (1859-1930), Nuevo Mexicano* politician, lawyer, and educator. Born in Chihuahua, Mexico, Larrazolo, who expected to become a priest, came to Tucson, Arizona with Bishop Jean B. Salpointe* in 1870 and accompanied him to Santa Fe fifteen years later. Larrazolo studied law and also worked as a teacher and high school administrator while still in his early twenties. Admitted to the bar in El Paso County, Texas, he later served as district attorney of the county.

In 1895 Larrazolo returned to central New Mexico where he set up a law practice. In the first decade of the 1900s he ran three times for territorial delegate to Congress but lost narrowly each time. When the New Mexico State Constiution* was being developed he spoke out for safeguarding the rights of Hispanic Americans and helped get the protection of Article VII, Section 3, and Article XII, Sections, 8, 9, and 10 written into the document.

In 1911 Larrazolo switched his allegiance from the Democratic party to the Republican party and began emphasizing Mexican culture in his political appeal, supporting Hispanic American candidates for office. After helping elect Ezequiel Cabeza de Vaca* governor two years previously, he was himself elected governor of New Mexico in 1918. He proved an able executive, strongly supporting measures to help La Raza, especially bilingual education, but was not renominated by the Republicans for another term. He continued to be active in state politics and in 1928 was elected to the United States Senate where he served until his death.

FURTHER READING: Paul A. Walter, "Octaviano Ambrosio Larrazolo," *New Mexico Historical Review* (April 1932): 97-104. For the State Constitution *see* NEW MEXICO.

LATIN AMERICAN, a person from Latin America. Largely a term of convenience rather than one of accuracy. Latin America as a geographical entity includes all of the continent of South America, Central America, and Mexico, as well as Cuba, Haiti, Puerto Rico, and other islands of the Caribbean.

Latin American is used in Texas mostly by Anglo Texans and middle-class Mexican Americans when referring to Mexicans and Mexican Americans. In existence since the late 1920s, but not widely used until the early 1940s, the term often denotes a condescending attitude toward Mexican Americans. By avoiding the word Mexican Texas usage implies a resistance to recognizing and acknowledging the Mexican heritage of Texas and the descendants of this heritage. It is also used simply to avoid the term Mexican, which many racist Texans use as an epithet.

LATIN AMERICAN RESEARCH AND SERVICE AGENCY (LARASA), a consciousness-raising and ethnic-organizing association founded early in the 1960s at Denver, Colorado, by Lino López* and other Mexican American leaders.

LATIN AMERICAN STUDENT ORGANIZATION, established in Chicago at the end of the 1960s by Mexican American students together with other Latino students, especially Puerto Ricans.

LATINO, a broad term which became increasingly popular in the late 1970s as an alternative to the terms Spanish-speaking or Spanish surname in referring to Mexican Americans. However, it is a blanket term that includes all persons of Spanish American origin and descent. This latter use is especially common in the East and Midwest.

LATINO POLITICAL TASK FORCE, a California Chicano federation representing a number of organizations including La Confederación de La Raza* and the Mexican American Political Association.* The basic objective of the group is to present a united effort in political education, voter registration, election campaigns, and other activities aiming at organizing Spanish-speaking persons for political participation and success. The task force was formally organized in October 1979.

***LAU* v. *NICHOLS*,** a United States Supreme Court decision handed down in January 1974. The Court held that the San Francisco (California) Unified School District discriminated against a non-English speaking student, Kinney Lau, by failing to provide a program to deal with his language problem and thereby denying him meaningful participation in the educational program. This decision has helped Mexican Americans secure more bilingual programs in primary schools. *See also*, BILINGUAL EDUCATION, BILINGUAL LEGISLATION.

LEAGUE OF LATIN AMERICAN CITIZENS, a Texas Mexican American political organization that developed out of the Order of Sons of America.* In August 1927 a group of Mexican American leaders met in Harlingen in an effort to create a more widely based organization than the Sons of America. Their efforts to unite with the Sons of America were rejected, so the group then created the League of Latin American Citizens which, in 1929, combined with the Sons of America and the Knights of America* to form the League of United Latin American Citizens.*

LEAGUE OF UNITED CITIZENS TO HELP ADDICTS (LUCHA), a self-help barrio* organization founded in Los Angeles in the late 1960s by exconvicts to assist exconvicts with drug problems by use of workshops, clinics, psycho-drama, counseling, and jobs. Militant, but ideologically moderate, it did not support more radical barrio elements in the La Raza movement, and enjoyed wide community support. It operated with rather precarious funding into the early seventies. The acronym means struggle or fight.

LEAGUE OF UNITED LATIN AMERICAN CITIZENS (LULAC). The League or LULAC, as it is more commonly known, is one of the largest Mexican American organizations. It was established in 1929 as the result of a meeting at Corpus Christi of representatives of three earlier established organizations: Order of Sons of America,* Knights of America,* and League of Latin American Citizens.* Its original objectives emphasized the social, political, and economic rights and duties of Mexican Americans; it was not primarily interested in direct political action. LULAC projected a fairly conservative image with its membership largely middle- and upper-class Mexican Americans. During the post-World War II period, however, LULAC became more activist oriented and especially pursued the goals of getting Mexican Americans on juries and ending school segregation. LULAC was important in the success of the Méndez case* in southern California (1946) and of the Delgado case* in Texas (1948); it was also influential in the passage of a New Mexico state fair employment practice law (1949).

By the early 1970s LULAC had grown to about 240 active councils, mostly but not solely in the Southwest. At its 1973 national convention in Albuquerque about 5,000 out of its more than 100,000 members were in attendance. LULAC continues to be one of the more influential of the Mexican American organizations in the pursuit of its goals of equality in government, law, education, business, and opportunity. It sponsors thirteen LULAC National Education Service Centers in ten states serving about 5,000 college and university students with counseling, assistance, and advocacy. It also publishes the monthly *LULAC News* and holds an annual convention. In 1980 its membership was estimated to be in excess of 200,000.

LETTUCE BOYCOTT. *See* LETTUCE STRIKE, SALINAS.

LETTUCE STRIKE, SALINAS. As soon as the United Farm Workers Organizing Committee (UFWOC) under César Chávez* had signed contracts with a majority of California's Central Valley table-grape growers on July 29, 1970, UFWOC turned to the Salinas lettuce fields south of San Jose to organize the workers because of lettuce workers' requests. When Chávez announced this move, some seventy Salinas lettuce growers signed five-year contracts with the International Brotherhood of Teamsters* without elections or card checks.* The UFWOC denounced these as "sweetheart contracts"* and went to court charging the Teamsters with denying workers the right to choose their own union. Some seven thousand workers went on strike early in August despite the Teamster contracts, and a few corporations signed with UFWOC.

On August 12 the UFWOC and the national Teamsters reached an agreement on spheres of union activity—field workers would belong to UFWOC and packing shed workers to the Teamsters. This agreement was never accepted by Teamster locals. As a result, late in September Chávez launched a national boycott on nonunion (UFWOC) lettuce, which was followed by a court injunction against UFWOC's secondary boycott* of one of the largest lettuce firms, Bud Antle. On December 4 Chávez was jailed on contempt charges for refusing to call off the boycott of Antle lettuce, and remained in prison until December 23.

In early March 1971 UFWOC-Teamster discussions began to settle what seemed to many to be essentially a jurisdictional dispute, that is, one between the two unions; and in two weeks a new agreement, very similar to the August 12 pact, was worked out with the Teamsters' Western Conference Headquarters. On March 28 the California Court of Appeals held that the UFWOC strike was jurisdictional and therefore illegal. UFWOC appealed this decision to the state Supreme Court. Meanwhile, Teamster locals did not accept the new pact, and while the boycott was suspended, UFWOC negotiations with growers lasted all summer long, only to break down in November.

The strike and lettuce boycott continued into 1972, an election year in which California voters had a chance to express their views via Proposition 22, which outlawed secondary boycotts and harvest strikes but provided for secret ballot agricultural worker elections. In November Proposition 22 went down in defeat by a 58 to 42 percent vote. The Bishops Committee on Farm Labor,* which had been very effective in the Delano grape strike,* tried to mediate between the Teamster and the United Farm Workers (formerly UFWOC), but then the Teamsters announced an all-out effort to organize agricultural workers. The UFW responded by declaring a step-up in the lettuce boycott. On December 29 the California Supreme Court in a six to one decision reversed the lower court, holding that the strike was not jurisdictional and that the UFW might legally picket growers with Teamster contracts.

When the UFW's grape contract renewals came up in 1973 there was a deemphasis on the Salinas strike, while the Teamsters continued their campaign to organize California agricultural workers. In April the Teamsters signed up thirty major Southern California Coachella Valley grape growers as their UFW contracts expired. On August 10 César Chávez angrily walked out of UFW-Teamsters discussions when he learned that on the day before the Teamsters had signed up thirty Delano growers whose UFW contracts were now expiring.

By November the Teamsters appeared to have completely reneged on their earlier accord with the UFW, and the lettuce (and grape) boycott went on through 1974. The boycott was clearly less successful than the earlier grape boycott, and César Chávez toured the country urging support for the boycott, followed by a Teamster "truth squad." The election of Jerry Brown as governor of California in November seemed to hold some promise for the UFW, and after his inauguration he did call a special session to write a state farm labor law. The result was passage of California's Agricultural Labor Relations Act* under which union elections would be scheduled. Through these elections the UFW regained some of its lost contracts, winning 65 percent of the elections held.

During 1977 a major agreement between the Teamsters and the UFW was worked out with the promise of an end to Teamster raiding of the UFW, and in February of the following year César Chávez ended the lettuce boycott, declaring it had served its purpose. However, in February 1979 some 3,000 UFW members struck eight Salinas lettuce companies with wages as their main issue. Late in July Chávez led a 150-mile march from San Francisco to Salinas to publicize the UFW boycott against Sun Harvest's parent company, United Brands, Inc. By September the UFW had been successful in signing contracts with West Coast Farms, Sun Harvest, and six other Salinas growers for a basic wage of $5.00 per hour, plus benefits, and the boycott was ended.

FURTHER READING: Dick Meister and Anne Loftis, *A Long Time Coming: The Struggle to Unionize America's Farm Workers*, New York: Macmillan Co., 1977.

LIGA OBRERA DE HABLA ESPAÑOLA, a coal miners union composed of Mexicans and Mexican Americans. This Spanish-speaking workers league was organized in late 1934 and early 1935 by Jesús Pallares and others interested in establishing a miners union in central New Mexico. Pallares was a coal miner who had come from Mexico during World War I, encouraged by the war-time labor shortage. His league, which served the miners' needs in the deepening economic slowdown of the depression, soon had a membership of about eight thousand but was unable to obtain recognition as bargaining agent for the miners. When a criminal syndicalism bill was introduced into the state legislature to hinder unionizing efforts, the league was able to mount a convincing march to the capital in opposition, and the bill was defeated. However, the unionization movement eventually failed, and because of his leadership in it Pallares was deported to Mexico as an undesirable alien in June 1935.

LIGA PROTECTIVA MEXICANA, a Mexican American organization formed in Kansas City, Missouri, in the post-World War I recession of 1921 because of rumors of general deportation of all Mexicans. The protective association lasted until 1923, by which time the threat had passed.

LIGA PROTECTORA LATINA, a fraternal and mutual aid society formed in Arizona in 1915 and incorporated in that state in August of the following year. Providing burial funds for its deceased, financial support to unemployed and sick members, and social and educational aid to their families, the organization grew rapidly, and by the time of its January 1917 convention it had some thirty lodges.

During the Arizona copper mine strikes of 1917 the league played an important role in uniting Mexican and Mexican American miners. Expressing its support for the United States war effort during World War I, by implication it condemned the militant and disruptive tactics of the Industrial Workers of the World in the copper mines. As the war came to an end in 1918 the league held its third convention in Tucson and reported lodges in Texas and New Mexico as well as in Arizona; by 1920 it could report members in California and a lodge even in Philadelphia. But the league had reached its zenith and quickly began to decline in membership because of internal dissension and increases in fees and dues. The lodges continued downhill steadily during the 1920s and disappeared in the depression years of the 1930s.

LIMÓN, JOSÉ ARCADIO (1908-1972), dancer. José Limón was from the generation of Mexican Americans who came to the United States when their families were driven out of Mexico by the Mexican Revolution* of 1910. His father, a musician and orchestra director, brought the family from Culiacán, Sinaloa, first to Arizona and finally settled in Los Angeles. José grew up wanting to become a painter but found quickly that his taste, which ran to an intense, mystical style, was out of phase with an artistic world that followed French modernism. He gave up painting as a result and, finally, persuaded by friends that dancing could be dignified and masculine, he took to modern dance with a dedication that soon brought him moderate success. In the late 1930s he developed a number of dances based on Mexican and Spanish themes. During 1940 to 1942 he toured the West Coast in a concert program that included some of his own choreography, and by 1943 he was being labeled as one of the outstanding contemporary dancers.

Out of the United States army after two years of service, in 1945 he reorganized his dance company and within a short time was at his peak. Between 1947 and 1949 he went from artistic success to artistic success, but the financial rewards were so small that he taught at numerous institutions to support himself and his wife. In 1950 he turned down the Mexican government's invitation of a permanent post, but did some important choreographic work there for several years. Limón's reputation resulted in engagements in France, South America, Central America, the Near East, and Far East. Much of this work was under U.S. State Department auspices. He was also the recipient of numerous honors and awards.

Rejecting the dance as an exhibition of technical prowess, José Limón viewed it as the highest expression of man's humanity. Among his best-known dance works are *Lament for Ignacio Sánchez Mejías*, *La Malinche*, *The Moor's Pavane*, and *Danza de la Muerte*.

LINCOLN COUNTY WAR (1878), a bloody cattlemen's range war illustrative of the instability and lawlessness of the southwestern frontier that often resulted in violence in which Mexican and Mexican American vaqueros* were caught in the middle. In this case it was a struggle between rival cattlemen Lawrence Murphy of the Santa Fe Ring* and the famous New Mexican "Cow King" John Chisum. Conflict between supporters and opponents of the Santa Fe Ring* soon escalated to ambushes and killings by both sides and to the bringing into play of political power, including that of the territorial governor. Meanwhile toughs and gunmen poured into Lincoln County to rob, steal, and kill in the name of one side or the other. Among them was the notorious Billy the Kid who fought on the Chisum side. The climax came in the battle of Lincoln from July 16 to 19, 1878, during which the anti-Murphy supporters were virtually wiped out when the house they were fighting was set on fire. Billy the Kid escaped.

As large numbers of settlers fled the Lincoln County violence, a special investigator named Frank Angell was sent to look into the fighting, and finally in early October President Rutherford B. Hayes declared a state of emergency and sent Lew Wallace as the new territorial governor. By awarding amnesty to all who would cease fighting and testify to the events of the "war" Governor Wallace was able to bring it to an end.

FURTHER READING: William A. Keheler, *Violence in Lincoln County, 1869-1881*, Albuquerque: University of New Mexico, 1957; Maurice G. Fulton, *History of the Lincoln County War*, Tucson: University of Arizona, 1968.

LITERATURE, CHICANO. A literature written by Mexicans and their descendants living or having lived in what is now the United States. This literature, written in Spanish, English, or a combination of both languages, had its origins when the Southwest was settled by the inhabitants of Mexico during colonial times and has continued uninterrupted to the present.

Chicano literature can be broadly divided into three general literary periods: (1) that of the Spanish colonial and Mexican national periods, ending in 1848; (2) that of the period beginning in 1848 and ending in the late 1950s; and (3) that period which Philip Ortego has called the "Chicano literary renaissance" which begins in the 1960s and extends to the present.

The early Spanish colonial period is characterized, for the most part, by historical writings, mostly in the form of letters, diaries, and memoirs, which describe Spanish explorations of the region now known as the Southwest. One of the most significant works of this epoch is Gaspar Pérez de Villagrá's *Historia de la Nueva México* (1610), a rhymed history of thirty-four cantos describing the founding of New Mexico by Juan de Oñate.*

During the seventeenth, eighteenth, and nineteenth centuries a folk literature developed and flourished; and as early settlers from Mexico moved to the Southwest, they brought with them such popular forms as the pastorela (shepherd's play), the corrido (ballad) and the cuento (folktale). These were widely cultivated in Arizona, California, southern Colorado, New Mexico, and Texas. Several pastorelas were staged at missions, among them a *Pastorela en dos actos* which dated from 1828. The corrido is a popular poetic form, the Mexican equivalent of the Spanish *romance*. It became widely used among Mexican Americans living in the Southwest where its form was naturally suited for transmitting oral tradition and experiences. Equally important was the cuento, a legend encapsulated in brief story, often dealing with mysterious characters and miraculous events. These folktales were and continue to be cultivated extensively in rural Spanish-speaking communities of the American Southwest.

By 1848, the beginning of the second period (considered by some to be the beginning of the development of Chicano literature), Mexican Americans of the Southwest possessed a rich literary tradition deeply rooted in popular Spanish forms. The people continued to produce pastorelas, corridos and cuentos using the basic forms that had been passed on orally from generation to generation. Yet, in many cases, they modified folktales and ballads and created new ones.

Much of the literature written by Mexican Americans between 1848 and 1950 was published in local and regional newspapers. Research undertaken by Lupe Castillo and Herminio Ríos has revealed that 380 Chicano newspapers were in existence in the United States between 1848 and 1958. A wealth of Chicano literature is buried in these materials. The most significant publication during this period, perhaps, is the novel *Pocho* (Doubleday, 1959) by José Antonio Villarreal.* This autobiographical work, set in Santa Clara, California, was the first Chicano novel published by a major American publishing company and was the forerunner of the Chicano literary renaissance.

The Chicano literary renaissance emerged from the Chicano movement of the 1960s. The proliferation of Chicano literature was made possible and encouraged by the establishment of hundreds of Chicano literary outlets, from mimeographed magazines to such sophisticated publications as *El Grito: A Journal of Contemporary Mexican American Thought.** This journal published 135 Chicano authors between 1967 and 1972.

Initially, Chicanos regarded literature as a means by which to articulate their own sense of identity by exploring their roots in history and culture. This emphasis on self-definition came as a result of a strong disillusionment with the writings that stereotyped Chicanos. This quest for identity is best illustrated by Rodolfo "Corky" Gonzales's* *Yo soy Joaquín* (1967).

In many works written in the late 1960s, Chicanos identify themselves almost exclusively with their Indian past. Thus Chicano writers appropriated Aztec and Mayan figures for their literary symbols, including the Aztec calendar stone. Names of newspapers and journals such as *Aztlán* (Los Angeles), *Bronce* (Oakland), *El Azteca* (Kingsville, Texas), attest to their close adherence to pre-Columbian culture.

Just as Chicano writers view their Indian past with pride, they express the reality of the present—their life in the United States—with a critical perspective. In works like *The Plum Plum Pickers* (Ventura Press, 1965) by Raymond Barrio, Chicanos point out and criticize socioeconomic injustices in American society.

National interest in Chicano literature quickly developed in the late 1960s and early 1970s. Several anthologies were published, three by major publishing houses. The publication of Tomás Rivera's* award winning novel *. . . y no se lo tragó la tierra* (Quinto Sol, 1971), initiated the current generation of Chicano novels. Several of these, including Rolando Hinojosa-Smith's* *Klail City y sus alrededores* (La Habana: Casa de las Américas, 1976), have earned an international reputation, and are being translated into French, Italian and German. The Chicano short story as well as the Chicano theatre have also gained wide recognition.

As Chicano writers explore new themes and literary techniques, Chicano literature becomes increasingly more heterogeneous and thus more representative of the diversity of Chicano culture. However, within this diversity, certain common concerns are evident: (1) the search for identity, (2) the resistance to assimilation into Anglo American culture, (3) the encouragement of self-assertion and self-determination, (4) the preservation of oral tradition, and (5) the recording of Chicano history and culture.

Even though contemporary Chicano literature expresses common concerns, there is no literary manifesto in existence today that unifies this body of literature. Some writers continue to restrict themselves to social realism while others are more concerned with creating a work of art. In either case, Chicano literature continues to be an important part of America's literary heritage.

FURTHER READING: Francisco Jiménez, ed., *The Identification and Analysis of Chicano Literature*, New York: The Bilingual Press, 1979; Francisco A. Lomelí and Donaldo W. Urioste, *Chicano Perspectives in Literature*, Albuquerque, N.M.: Pajarito Publications, 1976; Joseph Sommers and Tomás Ybarra-Frausto, eds., *Modern Chicano Writers*, Englewood Cliffs, N.J.: Prentice-Hall, Inc., 1979.

F.J.

LIVESTOCK INDUSTRY. The introduction of major pastoral industries into the Southwest brought to the area a legacy directly derived from Spain.

Cattle and sheep constituted the major elements of these industries, while horses comprised the basic ancillary support necessary for continuation of a pastoral tradition. As legatees of this great tradition, American cattlemen who later trailed immense herds from Texas to Kansas often failed to recognize the roots of their enterprises. In part this came from a widespread feeling of anti-Mexicanism and from a sense of cultural superiority.

As early as the twelfth century, the livestock industry in Spain had become institutionalized. Transfer of traditions and institutions to Mexico after 1522, especially the Mesta, and availability of large landed estates in the north allowed continuation of transhumance of livestock. Institutional guarantees existed to prevent the ravaging of Indian lands by roaming cattle, and disputes that arose were adjudicated by the stock-raiser's association, the Mesta. In the sixteenth, seventeenth, and eighteenth centuries, the livestock industry of New Spain left an indelible imprint on the cultural traditions of those areas in which it was most prevalent in the southwest.

Introduction of domesticated animals to New Spain in the sixteenth century provide clear evidence that Spain's principal intent in the region was one of permanent colonialization. Hernán Cortés,* for example, almost immediately after the fall of Tenochtitlán, arranged for the importation of horses, cattle, and Merino sheep. In 1522 Gregorio Villalobos brought cattle from the island of Española and helped establish the cattle industry in Mexico. Clearly the intent of Cortés and subsequent colonizers was to become self-sufficient through the production of meat, hides, and wool. Horses provided transportation, as did the jacks and jennets used for the hybridized cross that produced mules.

In large measure the pastoral economy of northern Mexico and the Southwest was limited by the number of acres required for year-round pasturage. In a time when supplemental feeding was unknown, it required an average of seventy-five acres per cow-calf unit. For sheep, the figure was considerably less. By the end of the eighteenth century, permanent expansion into Texas, New Mexico, and California had transferred traditions of large landholdings and a pastoral economy to those areas. Thus, by 1800 major livestock industries existed on both sides of the Río Bravo del Norte.

Haciendas,* while major producers of sheep, cattle, and horses, were not the only enterprises devoted to pastoral industries. Small ranchos* (not to be confused with the large ranchos in California) also contributed to the development and expansion of the livestock industry.

Mexican independence in 1822 did not alter patterns of development in the livestock industry in what had formerly been Spanish domain. Livestock producers continued to graze their herds of cattle, horses, and sheep on open range, requiring huge tracts of lands for the extensive and profitable production of livestock. Between 1822 and 1848 continued and increasing contact with Anglo Americans occurred in Mexican territory, and with the ultimate separation of the Southwest from Mexico in 1848 and its annexation to the United States, formerly Mexican stockmen transmitted a livestock culture and its traditions to incoming Anglo cattle raisers.

Between 1848 and 1900 Anglo interest in the livestock-growing regions of the West grew. With only a few exceptions in northern New Mexico and parts of southern Colorado, former large Spanish land grants eventually were transferred to Yankee ownership. Stock husbandry methods, however, did not change.

Anglo ranchers utilized the expertise of Mexican vaqueros* (cowboys) and caporales (foremen) in the handling of their large herds. Roundups, branding, ear notching, and other related management practices continued in the latter part of the nineteenth century. The King Ranch in the Lower Rio Grande Valley, for example, was formed from the original Santa Gertrudis grant and continued to employ almost exclusively Mexican and Mexican American ranch hands. When control of the ranch transferred from Captain Richard King to the Kleberg side of the King family, the Klebergs too continued to use the expertise of the kineños (Mexican American vaqueros on the ranch).

Mexican and Mexican American vaqueros provided the prototypes for a myriad of objects related to the livestock industry. Rawhide ropes, reins, chaps, hats, saddles, and bridles all had their origins in the Mexican tradition.

Methods of handling cattle involved extensive use of horses. In order to train a responsive cow horse, Spanish and Mexican horse trainers employed techniques that have been perpetuated in California and Texas schools of hackamore training. The ultimate product was a horse that was light and responsive to cues and one that worked cattle with undiminished energy. Rawhide hackamores and horsehair reins constitute a part of this tradition.

A salient feature of the livestock industry with its Mexican American vaqueros was the cultural reenforcement that came from Mexico. The employment needs of livestock owners in the Southwest created opportunities for Mexicans to immigrate there, and thus created a constantly renewed labor and cultural pool that continued to give a distinctive character to livestock raising in the Southwest. Additionally, the importation of feeder cattle from Mexico continued to rise throughout the nineteenth century and into the twentieth century as the United States demand for more and better beef increased.

Major expansion in sheep-herding in New Mexico and Texas in the late nineteenth century provided additional opportunities for Mexican American sheepherders who competed with imported Basque herders for jobs handling the large flocks. In eastern Montana, for example, sheep and cattle ran simultaneously, and vaqueros from Texas helped provide some of the managerial skills in the handling of these animals.

United States annexation of Texas, New Mexico, and California led to increased institutionalization of the livestock industry. Creation of the U.S. Forest Service in 1891 and subsequent federal regulation of range lands within the public domain had a direct impact on Mexican American sheep and cattle raisers in northern New Mexico. Accustomed to free range and unregulated use of that range, livestock producers in the area often found themselves in direct conflict with federal authorities. In the twentieth century increasing federal takeover of public lands and their subsequent regulation through either the Forest Service or the Bureau of Land Management precipitated heightened conflict. In part, the grievances in northern New Mexico expressed by Reies López Tijerina* grow from the disruption imposed on New Mexico livestock raisers through federal regulation of the public domain.

The influence of Mexico and of Mexican Americans on the livestock traditions of the West remains strong even today. Modes of dress, methods of handling cattle (within the technological constraints of modern animal husbandry), and the essentially individualistic attitudes of the original cattlemen of the area—Spaniards and Mexicans—continue to mold the culture of a region centered in, but extending beyond the original cessions of 1848.

FURTHER READING: Robert C. Cleland, *The Cattle on a Thousand Hills*, San Marino, California: Huntington Library, 1941; Edward E. Dale, *The Range Cattle Industry*, Norman: University of Oklahoma, 1960; Tom Lea, *The King Ranch*, Boston: Little, Brown & Co., 1957; Arnold Rojas, *California Vaquero*, Fresno, California: Academy Library Guild, 1953; Charles A. Siringo: *Riata and Spurs: The Story of a Lifetime Spent in the Saddle as Cowboy and Ranger*, Boston: Houghton Mifflin Co., 1927; J. J. Wagoner, *The History of the Cattle Industry in Southern Arizona, 1540-1940*, Tucson: University of Arizona, 1952.

M.A.M., Jr.

LONGORIA, FELIX, a Mexican American soldier killed on Luzon in the Pacific during World War II. In 1948 his body was returned to his widow in Three Rivers, Texas, for reburial, and a bitter squabble over his burial ensued. In the confusion the only mortician in Three Rivers apparently did not want to hold services in his chapel for Longoria because he was a Mexican American, and the story made newspaper headlines all over the country. Texas sentiment was widely and overwhelmingly against the alleged position of the funeral director, and the Texas Good Neighbor Commission* declared his attitude was discriminatory. Intervening in the situation, young Lyndon B. Johnson, who had just been elected to the U.S. Senate, was able to secure Longoria's burial in Arlington National Cemetery.

LÓPEZ, FRANCISCO, a Mexican herdsman who discovered gold on March 19, 1842, in Feliciano Canyon near Los Angeles. Mexican Californians worked various diggings along the coast range from Los Angeles to

Santa Cruz for years prior to James Marshall's bonanza at Sutters Mill on January 24, 1848, which led to the California gold rush.

LÓPEZ, LINO (1910-1978), civic leader, lecturer, educator, and social worker. Born in Mexico to poor farm-worker parents who moved to the United States, Lino worked as a youth in migrant agriculture to help the family and to finance his early education. Later the family moved to Chicago where he worked his way through Loyola University, earning his A.B. in the social sciences. He also did some postgraduate work at the University of Tennessee in Nashville in the mid-fifties.

After graduation and a brief stint in the grocery business Lino, seeing the need for social change in the Mexican American community, went to work for the Illinois Welfare Department. During the mid-1940s he became deeply involved with the important Bishops Committee for the Spanish-speaking* in Chicago. Then a heavy Chicano youth delinquency rate in San Antonio took him to that Texas city where he worked as a juvenile officer for the Bexar County court until 1948 when he moved to Pueblo, Colorado, to take a more positive role as director of a Catholic Youth Center.

In 1953 López moved to Denver where he served La Raza* for a decade both as a member of the mayor's Commission on Human Relations and as a consultant with the public schools. In this new role he continued to open doors for Mexican Americans and to urge them to join civic and ethnic organizations. While there he helped organize the Latin American Research and Service Agency (LARASA),* established a dozen chapters of the American G.I. Forum,* and played an important role in other Mexican American organizations.

In 1963 Lino López moved to San Jose, except for Los Angeles, the California city with the largest Chicano population, to establish the Mexican American Community Services Project (later Agency). During his years in San Jose he also worked extensively with students, helping them organize Mexican American Youth Organization* (MAYO) clubs in twenty-five Santa Clara Valley high schools.

Five years later Lino moved to Redlands University in southern California as an instructor, and continued his work with young people. After a car accident there in which he was seriously injured, he suffered a stroke and left California in 1974 to return to Denver and semiretirement. He lived there until his death.

Lino López was a man of vision, dedicated to raising La Raza* pride and to persuading Mexican Americans to organize in order to improve their economic and social conditions. During his life he developed projects in California, Colorado, Illinois, Indiana, and Texas and promoted organizational work in other midwestern and southwestern states. A gentle but firm man, he seldom raised his voice but was uncompromising in fighting bigotry and discrimination. He held influential positions in numerous Chicano organizations and was recipient of many honors including a posthumous service award from the Latin American Educational Foundation.

LÓPEZ, NANCY (1957-), golfer. Born in Roswell, New Mexico, Nancy López won her first golf tournament before she was out of primary school, and by the time she graduated from high school she had won the New Mexico amateur championship four times. Her golfing skills won her a scholarship to the University of Tulsa and later a four-year $10,000 Colgate Golf Scholarship. At the end of her sophomore year Nancy dropped out of the university to become a professional golfer. In July 1977 she joined the Ladies Professional Golf Association and in the following year she was the top LPGA prize money winner, breaking the previous LPGA record by earning $189,813. During 1979 she played in twenty-two tournaments, placed within the top ten in eighteen, won eight, and earned $215,987, breaking the LPGA record she had set the year before. On the golf course she is usually followed by a large group of vociferous and admiring young supporters who are known as "Nancy's Navy."

LÓPEZ, TRINI(DAD) (1937-), singer Trinidad López was born in Dallas of parents who had crossed the Rio Grande ten years earlier without documentation in search of a better life. Trini acquired his interest in playing the guitar and singing from his father and was encouraged by him to develop his musical skills. While still in high school Trini organized a small combo that played hotels, nightclubs, and country clubs in Texas. In 1960 he moved to southern California where, after some initial difficulties he became successful. In 1963 his first recording, "If I Had a Hammer," was an instant hit, and its sales soon passed the four million mark. It was followed by other successful recordings and led to several foreign tours in the mid and late sixties. At the same time he made concert and television appearances all over the United States.

Trini López's style is described as a pleasant Latin folk rock, and his repertoire contains an upbeat blend of blues, ballads, Latin folk, and sophisticated rock.

LOS ANGELES, CALIFORNIA. The area that is now Los Angeles was first sighted by Europeans in 1540 when Juan Rodríguez Cabrillo explored the California coast; however, settlement was not begun until 1769 when an expedition was undertaken by Father Junípero Serra* and Gaspar de Portolá. Twelve years later Governor Felipe de Neve established El Pueblo de Nuestra Señora de los Angeles de Porciúncula with forty-four mestizos and castas (mixed bloods) and two Spaniards from the lower classes of Sinaloa on Mexico's west coast. By 1800 the town had grown to slightly more than three hundred inhabitants living in some thirty adobe homes—the largest settlement in Alta California, but barely able to supply its own basic needs.

The 1810 revolution for independence in Mexico brought little change to this frontier town, which remained isolated on the northern fringe of the new republic which was created in 1824. During the Mexican period (1821-1848) the first handful of Anglo American merchants and adventurers began to arrive. Men like Abel Stearns, William Wolfskill, and Joseph Chapman became naturalized Mexican citizens, acquired land grants from the government, and many married into well-to-do landed Mexican families. The secularization of the missions in the midthirties added to the economic opportunities of this upper-class combination of Mexican landowners and Anglo entrepreneurs. When the United States-Mexican War* broke out in 1846, Los Angeles was taken over by invading American naval forces without great difficulties. However, the harsh and arbitrary acts of the Anglo military government quickly led to an Angeleno* revolt which was ended by the Cahuenga Treaty* of January 13, 1847.

In the aftermath of the Treaty of Guadalupe Hidalgo* Los Angeles became the county seat, but the discovery of gold to the north, and the subsequent rush to the mines left the town a small frontier community heavily Mexican in culture. While the north quickly became Anglo-dominated, Angelenos retained some control over their destinies despite Anglo inroads on their economic and then political power. Until the 1860s the mining region's demand for cattle brought some prosperity to the city, but it dwindled and finally collapsed in the prolonged drought of the sixties. The arrival of the Southern Pacific Railroad in 1876 and the Santa Fe Railroad in 1885 marked the beginning of the end of Angeleno control as thousands of midwestern Anglo settlers poured in. By the time the southern real estate boom collapsed at the end of the eighties, Los Angeles's population had ballooned to fifty thousand, and its Californio* population had been reduced from a majority to a small minority. By the end of the century Los Angeles had a total population of more than one hundred thousand, of whom about sixteen thousand were of Mexican descent. Of these just about half were Sonoran immigrants and half were Californios, and the majority of immigrants lived in the central area often called Sonora-town. Most worked as unskilled laborers, farmers, butchers, barbers, and seamstresses; upper-class Californios tended to merge into the dominant Anglo culture.

As Anglos moved into Los Angeles some Spanish-speaking people began moving eastward out of Sonoratown, especially the recent arrivals from Mexico who in increasing numbers "wintered over" in the Los Angeles area after the harvest migration ended. The Mexican Revolution* of 1910 and the economic spur that resulted from World War I brought large numbers of Mexicans to Los Angeles both for the expanding industrial work there and for its position as a labor reservoir. By 1920 there were nearly thirty thousand, over 40 percent of whom lived in the central area; and, as the ingress continued during the boom years of the twenties, the 1930 census showed their numbers had more than tripled during the decade as they got jobs in iron and steel foundries, meat-packing, cement, and tile factories. A majority now lived in the inexpensive Boyle Heights, Belvedere, and Hollenbeck areas, which came to be known as East Los Angeles. Within this barrio* there developed a culture and way of life that had little to do with the affairs of the Anglo-dominated larger community.

In the 1930s the alienation of the Los Angeles Chicano population reached new heights with the repatriation,* often under coercion, of thousands of Mexican workers and their families, many of whom were American citizens by birth. A decade later, during World War II, a new climax of bitterness and antagonism resulted from the Sleepy Lagoon* murder trial in 1942 and the Zoot Suit riots* of July 1943. At the same time the war years swept many young Angelenos more into the mainstream of American life. Expanded wartime industries in Los Angeles opened their doors a bit wider to Mexican Americans, and the armed services often recognized their talents that had been ignored in civilian life.

After the war, returning veterans showed Los Angeles a new facet of her Chicano citizens. Self-confident and ambitious, they entered college, bought homes, entered the professions, and started their own businesses. Interested in community affairs and especially in the education of their children, they began to voice concern about educational problems in barrio schools during the 1950s. In 1949 they helped elect Edward Roybal* to the city council and later sent him to Congress as their representative. In the midsixties Los Angeles Chicano students, resentful of continuing discrimination and low-quality education, initiated a series of school "blowouts" in the area high schools. At colleges and universities in greater Los Angeles their older brothers and sisters successfully pushed administrators to hire more Chicano professors; to establish classes in Chicano history, literature, and culture; and even to create new departments of Chicano studies. At both levels they organized into groups with acronyms like MASA* and UMAS* and supported each other's demands. Their enthusiasm also spilled over into anti-Vietnam War demonstrations like the one at Laguna Park in March 1970 at which Rubén Salazar* was killed.

As the eighties, the "decade of the Hispano," approached, some improvements in the Los Angeles Chicano community were evident. Spanish surnames increasingly appeared in the professions; there was some movement from the barrio; but a majority of the three-quarter million of Mexican-descent population (1970) still lived in East Los Angeles, one of the country's extreme poverty areas.

FURTHER READING: John W. Caughey, *California: A Remarkable State's Life History*, Englewood Cliffs, N.J.: Prentice Hall, Inc., 1970; Carey McWilliams, *Southern California: An Island on the Land*, Santa Barbara, Calif.: Peregrine Smith, Inc., 1973; Leonard Pitt, *The Decline of the Californios*, Berkeley: University of California, 1966; Eshref Shevky and Marilyn Williams, *The Social Areas of Los Angeles, Analysis and Typology*, Berkeley: University of California Press, 1949; Richard Griswold del Castillo, *The Los Angeles Barrio, 1850-1890; a Social History*, Berkeley: University of California Press, 1979; Ricardo Romo, *Mexican Workers in the City: Los Angeles, 1915-1930*, Los Angeles, University of California, 1975.

LUCEY, ROBERT E. (1891-1977), bishop. Born in Los Angeles, Robert Lucey was educated for the priesthood in California and at the North American College in Rome, Italy. Ordained in 1916, he served as pastor in a number of California parishes. In 1934 he was appointed Bishop of Amarillo, Texas, and seven years later was raised to Archbishop of San Antonio. Active in promoting the interests of agricultural workers, he was appointed in 1950 to the President's Commission on Migratory Labor* and was prominent in the founding and directing of the Bishop's Committee for the Spanish Speaking.* He served as executive chairman of the latter from its founding in 1945 until his retirement.

Archbishop Lucey had a national reputation as a champion of social justice and civil rights and was especially concerned with the plight of poverty-stricken Mexican Americans in southwest Texas. He fought for child-labor legislation and for inclusion of migrant agricultural workers in the protection of federal labor laws. In his own diocese he insisted on employing only union labor and supported farm worker strikes for union recognition and better wages. During the 1966 march of the Rio Grande City melon strikers to Austin, he urged them to stand up and defend themselves against discrimination and oppression.

Although a liberal in socioeconomic matters, Archbishop Lucey was quite conservative in the ecclesiastical sphere, and his attitudes toward changes in the church led to conflict with many of the clergy, especially the younger ones. Some of them virtually revolted against his leadership and petitioned his removal. In 1969 he asked to be relieved because of his age, and was retired, being named to a titular see in June of that year. He died in retirement eight years later.

LULAC. *See* LEAGUE OF UNITED LATIN AMERICAN CITIZENS.

LUNA, SOLOMON (1858-1912), politician, rancher, and businessman. Member of a wealthy and prominent family, Luna was born in Los Lunas, New Mexico. After graduating from St. Louis University, he entered local politics as a Republican and held a variety of offices in Valencia County, whose political life he came to dominate. He played a prominent role in Republican politics in the territory and nationally, and was a regular member of the Republican National Committee from New Mexico.

Actively interested in New Mexican statehood,* Luna helped organize wide support for that movement and was elected to the 1910 constitutional convention. As a representative of Hispano Americans in that body, he endeavored to get included in New Mexico's constitution guarantees for the Spanish language and Nuevo Mexicano culture. His efforts, combined with those of others like Octaviano Larrazolo,* resulted in inclusion of the safeguard clauses of Article VII, Section 3 and Article XII, Sections 8, 9, and 10. These clauses included the provision that those clauses, which dealt with rights of Mexican Americans, could be amended only by a vote of three-fourths of voters in the entire state and two-thirds of the voters in each county. He lived to see New Mexico enter the Union as the 47th state in 1912.

M

MCCARRAN-WALTER IMMIGRATION AND NATIONALITY ACT (1952), passed by the United States Congress to continue the quota system set up by the immigration acts of 1921 and 1924. The new law liberalized the earlier acts by providing small quotas for immigrants from Asia and the Pacific islands and by making it possible for them to become naturalized citizens; it also gave special status to immigrants of certain skills and education. However, its provisions for exclusion and deportation of politically undesirable aliens and naturalized citizens was viewed by President Harry Truman as a potential threat to civil rights by overzealous interpretation, so he vetoed it. Congress repassed the bill over his veto. The McCarran-Walter legislation has sometimes been used to deport Mexican immigrants active in labor organizing.

The law also provided that any person in continuous U.S. residence since June 1924 could become a legal immigrant without leaving the United States. In 1957 the base year for this privilege was changed to 1940. Many Mexican residents took advantage of this relaxation of the law to legalize their status.

MCGOVERN BILL, HR 11211 (1960), a bill introduced by Representative George McGovern (Democrat, South Dakota) in mid-1960. It proposed reducing the number of Mexican braceros* allowed entrance into the United States by 20 percent yearly until 1965 when the program would have been terminated completely. Despite McGovern's argument that the widespread use of bracero labor caused a decline in both wages and working conditions, and despite support at hearings from representatives of the AFL-CIO and the National Council of Churches, the bill failed of passage.

MCWILLIAMS, CAREY (1905-1980), lawyer, author, and editor. Born in northern Colorado McWilliams grew up on the family cattle ranch. McWilliams's family moved to Los Angeles a few years after World War I. Because of his interest in journalism, he took a job with the Los Angeles *Times* while he went to law school at the University of Southern California. After receiving his law degree in 1927 McWilliams entered law practice and later developed a special interest in labor law as the result of President Franklin D. Roosevelt's New Deal. At the same time the young lawyer was writing his first books. His biography of the important California writer, Ambrose Bierce, appeared in 1929; and *Factories in the Fields*, the result of his developing interest in farm labor, was published in 1939, gaining him national attention.

The expertise he developed in researching *Factories in the Fields* helped get McWilliams appointed by Governor Cuthbert Olson as chief of the Division of Immigration and Housing for California in 1939. In the following year he became president of the Committee for the Protection of the Foreign Born. Following a period of government service that included a stint in the Office of Inter-American Affairs where he devised a program to improve Anglo-Mexican American relations, he settled down to writing, which resulted in *California Country* (1946), *California, The Great Exception* (1949), and *North from Mexico* (1949).

During this time McWilliams had become deeply interested in the problem of racism, which he explored in depth as it affected Mexican Americans, in his book, *North from Mexico*. His vigorous and outspoken involvement with their civil rights led him in 1943 to a leadership role in the Sleepy Lagoon* Defense Committee, which financed the appeal that brought about in the following year a reversal of the lower court's conviction of seventeen of the Mexican American defendants.

In 1951 McWilliams went to New York to help with a special issue of *The Nation* on civil liberties and remained as a staff member. In 1955 he was made editor of *The Nation*, a post he filled until his retirement at the end of 1975. Throughout his long career he was constantly active in defense of minorities and of the rights of the foreign born.

FURTHER READING: Carey McWilliams, *North from Mexico*, Philadelphia: J. B. Lippincott Co., 1949; reprinted edition, Greenwood Press, 1968.

MACHISMO, literally maleness, from the Spanish macho. Machismo is the term for the cult of masculinity in Latin America, especially Mexico, identified with a masculine aggressiveness, self-confidence, and courageousness.

A cultural misunderstanding exists with the popular usage of the term in the United States by both Anglo Americans and Mexican Americans. Machismo is misinterpreted as being associated only with arrogance, selfish sexual satisfaction, extramarital sexuality, and as an overcompensation for personal insecurity. It is true that some men exhibit and use machismo for these purposes, which have much in common with lower-class attitudes toward masculinity. On the other hand, in the Latin American social and cultural ambience machismo also expresses honor, responsibility, dependability, dedication, and generosity.

MADSEN, WILLIAM (1920-), anthropologist, professor, author. Born at Shanghai, China, and first educated in Manila, Madsen later received his B.A. from Stanford University. After graduate work at the Escuela Nacional de Antropología in Mexico City he was awarded his Ph.D. by the University of California at Berkeley. Madsen served in World War II and taught at the University of Texas and the University of California at Berkeley, before becoming a professor of Anthropology at the University of California at Santa Barbara in 1966. He is a member of the Sociedad Mexicana de Antropología.

Madsen's publications include *Christo-Paganism: A Study of Mexican Religious Syncretism* (1957), *The Virgin's Children: Life in an Aztec Village Today* (1960), *Society and Health in the Lower Rio Grande Valley* (1961), and *The Mexican Americans of South Texas* (1964). These last two publications have come under increasing criticism for stereotyping Mexican Americans as existing in a culture of poverty.

MAGOFFIN, JAMES W. (1799-1868), frontier merchant, pioneer, and United States representative. Magoffin was born on the Kentucky frontier. When he was in his mid-twenties he developed a successful trading business in northeastern Mexico and in 1825 was named American consul at Saltillo. Early in the following decade he moved to Chihuahua, the southern end of the Santa Fe trail, where he soon became a leading figure because of his convivial personality, command of Spanish, and his Mexican wife, María Valdez. Just before the Mexican War* he moved again, this time to the other end of the Santa Fe Trail at Independence, Missouri.

When the Mexican War began he was selected by President James Polk to facilitate the American takeover of New Mexico. In this capacity he conferred with his wife's cousin, Governor Manuel Armijo*, before American forces arrived at Santa Fe. Since his negotiations were secret it is not possible to say how much the peaceful initial occupation of New Mexico was his doing. Generally historians have felt his influence was not that great, and the story that he bribed Armijo not to resist the U.S. forces is unsubstantiated.

After the Mexican War he moved to El Paso where his business experience and connections again made him a successful merchant. When the Civil War reached the Southwest he enthusiastically supported the Confederate cause and with its defeat retired to San Antonio.

MAGÓN, RICARDO FLORES. *See* FLORES MAGÓN, RICARDO

MALCRIADO, EL, a newspaper founded in December 1964 by César Chávez* at Delano, California. *El Malcriado* was published semimonthly by the National Farm Workers Association with the principal objective of publicizing the farm workers' struggle for a better way of life. It still carries news of el movimiento.*

MALDEF. *See* MEXICAN AMERICAN LEGAL DEFENSE AND EDUCATION FUND

MALINCHE, LA (1502?-1527?), interpreter and adviser to Hernán Cortés* during the conquest of Mexico. La Malinche was most likely born to a Nahua family who ruled the town of Painalla in the province of Coatzacoalcos. While she was still a child her father died, and her mother remarried. Her parents, wishing to deprive her of her lawful inheritance in favor of a newborn son, gave her to some traders from Xicalanco. They in turn passed her on to some natives from Tabasco.

In 1519, after the Spaniards defeated the Indians in Tabasco, they were given twenty Indian women to assist them. One of these, La Malinche, was then given by Cortés to a fellow conqueror. She was baptized, and her name was changed from Malinalli(?) to Marina. When it became known she could speak both Maya and Nahuatli, Cortés took her for himself as both interpreter and mistress. With the aid of a Spaniard who could speak Maya, Cortés was then able to communicate with the Aztecs.

Malintzin, Malinche, or Doña Marina (variant forms of her name), as she came to be called, served Cortés as an interpreter of native customs, beliefs, and political alignments. This position allowed her to exercise a great influence over Cortés and the course of the conquest. In 1522 she bore Cortés a son, and in 1524 she married a high government official. They settled in Mexico City where she died sometime near 1527.

Long a synonym in Mexico for betrayal and seduction by things foreign and still so viewed, La Malinche has become among Mexican Americans, particularly among Chicanas, a symbolic mother of the new mestizo race and an outstanding historical figure.

FURTHER READING: Bernal Díaz del Castillo, *The Conquest of New Spain*,

Baltimore: Penguin Books, Inc., 1963; Adelaida R. del Castillo, "Malintzin Tenépal: A Preliminary Look into a New Perspective," in *Essays on La Mujer*, Rosaura Sánchez and Rosa Martínez Cruz, eds., Los Angeles: University of California, 1977.

J.J.K.A.

MANIFEST DESTINY, an expression of American nationalism used to justify, rationalize, and explain United States expansionist efforts during the nineteenth century.

In essence Manifest Destiny suggested that the American people were destined and had the God-given right to extend their way of life throughout the North American continent. Nineteenth-century politicians and writers, conscious that the United States had embarked upon an extensive course of expansion, transformed the idea of Manifest Destiny into a significant expression of American nationalism and purpose.

More than just an expression of aggressive expansion, Manifest Destiny proclaimed a national mission to the oppressed, justifying and rationalizing in terms of a higher good the nation's alleged right and duty to dispossess neighboring countries of their territory.

The annexation of Texas and the subsequent war with Mexico provided the necessary events that brought all the elements of Manifest Destiny together. The subsequent acquisition of one-half of Mexico's territory, after the Mexican War, became the most notorious historical expression of Manifest Destiny.

FURTHER READING: Frederick Merk, *Manifest Destiny and Mission in American History*, New York: Alfred A. Knopf, Inc., 1966. Albert Weinberg, *Manifest Destiny*, Chicago: Quadrangle Books, 1967.

MANO NEGRA, a secret organization that developed in New Mexico in the early 1900s. Its members, who were mostly Nuevo Mexicano* small landowners, used terroristic tactics to frighten Anglo homesteaders who were moving into the Rio Arriba area of northwestern New Mexico and were fencing in the land.

MANUEL, HERSCHEL T. (1887-   ), educator, psychologist. Manuel was born and grew up in the Midwest. A graduate of DePauw University, he completed an M.A. at the University of Chicago and his Ph.D. at the University of Illinois in 1917. After teaching and directing research in educational testing and measurement at several universities, he joined the University of Texas at Austin. There he served first as a professor and later as director of testing and guidance. A course he taught on individual differences and exceptional children led to an interest in the educational problems of Spanish-speaking children, and in 1930 he published *The Education of Mexican and Spanish-Speaking Children in Texas* at the University of Texas Press.

Manuel became especially noted for his areas of special interest and competence: bilingual testing and the education of Spanish-speaking children. Nearly thirty years later, with a Hogg Foundation grant, he culminated his research, and in 1965 his broader study, *Spanish-Speaking Children of the Southwest*, was published by the University of Texas Press at Austin. Manuel was one of the pioneers, along with George I. Sánchez* and Lloyd Tireman,* in studying the problems of Spanish-speaking children in an English-speaking educational environment.

MAPA. *See* MEXICAN AMERICAN POLITICAL ASSOCIATION.

MAQUILADORAS, factories, mostly in Mexican border towns, to which materials are brought under bond for completion or assembly by Mexican workers and are then returned to the United States. This program of in-bond factories, as they are sometimes called, was designed by the Mexican government in 1965 and 1966 as a substitute for the Bracero Program* which ended the year before. Through it, goods, about two-thirds of them electric and electronic materials, rather than Mexican workers, move across the border. In many instances there are dual factories, one on each side of the border, with the U.S. side specializing in capital-intensive operations and the Mexican factory doing the labor-intensive work. As a result of this arrangement, the program is sometimes referred to as the twin plant concept.

United States labor unions have been highly critical of maquiladoras because they undermine the gains of American workers by providing industry with cheap labor. American corporations have argued that the program competes, not with U.S. labor, but with Hong Kong, Taiwan, and other inexpensive labor markets and has enabled them to remain competitive. The Mexican government has appreciated the creation of badly needed jobs—about one hundred three thousand jobs in four hundred plants by 1979—but has been concerned with the increasing Americanization of her border area. Unquestionably the program has taken many jobs from Mexican Americans, as American industry has taken advantage of the nearby availability of cheap labor.

MARCH TO AUSTIN (1966), a march of farm workers in July and August 1966 from Rio Grande City to the capitol building in Austin. Led by Eugene Nelson, a follower of César Chávez,* Father Anthony González of the Oblates of Mary Immaculate, and a Baptist minister, Reverend James Novarro, the event was primarily to petition that Governor John Connally support farm worker demands to be included in the Texas $1.25 per hour minimum wage by calling a special session of the legislature. The march began on July 4, and the marchers reached the capital on Labor Day. On the way there were addressed at various times by Archbishop Robert E.

Lucey* and Texas Senator Ralph Yarborough, both of whom spoke strongly in favor of a minimum wage for farm workers, and by Governor Connally, who told them he would not meet them in Austin and would not call the legislature into special session. Although the 1967 legislature rejected farm worker inclusion in the minimum wage law, the march did serve to call attention to the Texas workers' plight and there was some improvement in farm wages.

MARCH TO SACRAMENTO (1966), a march designed to serve various objectives, but especially to publicize the National Farm Workers Association* boycott against Schenley Industries.* Beginning on March 17, 1966, about sixty marchers began the three-hundred-mile, twenty-five-day trek from Delano, California, to the state capital carrying the banner of the Virgin of Guadalupe.* Along the way they were joined by local supporters who marched with them for a while and who helped arrange for their sleeping quarters each night. In each town rallies were held, efforts were made to set up local strike committees, and in the evenings the Teatro Campesino* put on satirical skits. On the day before Easter, when they were due to arrive in Sacramento, the marchers learned that Schenley had agreed to recognize the NFWA as sole bargaining agent for its field workers and would discuss contract terms. With this happy news the marchers entered the capital the following day as eight thousand spectators and supporters watched. The governor, Edmund G. (Pat) Brown refused to meet them and was out of town. Chávez* announced that Schenley had settled and that the next target would be the Di Giorgio Corporation,* at the time one of California's largest grape and fruit growers.

MARTÍNEZ, ANTONIO JOSÉ (1793-1867), New Mexican priest, politician, civic leader, landowner, and rebel. Born in Abiquiu on the upper Rio Grande, the eldest son of an economically and politically powerful family, Martínez was ordained a priest in 1822 and four years later was sent to the Taos parish where he was to spend the rest of his life. In 1833 he established a school in which he trained students, many of whom became future civil and religious leaders of New Mexico. For this school he acquired the first printing press west of the Mississippi River. During the Mexican period he served as territorial deputy during several years and was a candidate for national deputy.

In the years immediately preceding the Mexican War,* Father Martínez was the principal leader of the anti-American faction in New Mexico, warning both civil and religious superiors that an American takeover was imminent. He also was opposed to large land grants being made to members of the local "American party" and their northern friends; however, by the early 1840s this group largely dominated the Taos region. At the American invasion, Martínez initially favored a policy of resistance, but later accepted the fait accompli of American control and sought to exploit those aspects of the new system that he saw as beneficial to his people. He therefore took an active role in the American territorial legislature and in the 1848 statehood convention of which he was elected president. In subsequent years he was repeatedly elected to the territorial legislature and in that body he appears to have fought ably for the good of Nuevo Mexicanos.*

In the affair of the 1846 insurrection plot and the murder of Governor Charles Bent* and others, Father Martínez's role and position are not clear. He was unquestionably sympathetic to the rebel cause and must have been aware an insurrection was brewing, but there is no evidence to connect him with it.

A further aspect of his cultural leadership role was his quarrel with his new bishop, Jean Baptiste Lamy,* over the latter's reintroduction of tithing and his reliance on Americanos (as the Nuevo Mexicanos* called the French priests Lamy brought in). Martínez believed Lamy was prejudiced against the Nuevo Mexicano clergy. Lamy's appointment of an anti-Mexican Spanish priest to replace Martínez, rather than the Nuevo Mexicano suggested by him, led to the final break between the strong-willed priest and his equally unyielding bishop. In mid-1857, after a period of suspension for continuing to exercise his priestly functions despite Lamy's express prohibition, Father Martínez was formally excommunicated by the bishop; but, supported by many Nuevo Mexicanos, he continued to head his own schismatic church until his death. Father Martínez died 28 July 1867 at Taos and was buried from his private chapel by his friend, Father Mariano de Jesús Lucero, His schism died with him. The actions of Martínez in the 1840s and 1850s are an excellent example of Nuevo Mexicano leadership promoting local ethnic interests against a rising tide of Anglo ascendancy.

FURTHER READING: E. K. Francis, "Padre Martínez: A New Mexican Myth," *New Mexico Historical Review* 31 (October 1956); Pedro Sánchez, *Memorias sobre la vida del presbítero Don Antonio José Martínez*, Santa Fe: Compañia Impresora del Nuevo México, 1903; Pedro Sánchez, *Memories of Antonio José Martínez*, Santa Fe: Rydal Press, 1978.

MARTÍNEZ, FÉLIX, JR. (1857-1916), political leader, businessman, publisher. Born in the small town of Penasco, near Taos, Martínez grew up in northern New Mexico and southern Colorado. After seven years' experience as a clerk in the mercantile business, in 1878 he began his own store in a partnership that became quite successful. During the following years his mercantile activities expanded considerably until 1886 when he sold his interest, investing in real estate.

Meanwhile he had also become interested in politics, and after being defeated in 1884, ran in the following election to win the job of county assessor. Martínez's purchase in 1890 of a controlling interest in *La Voz del Pueblo*, a leading Spanish-language weekly, was part of his political activity. After moving the paper from Santa Fe to Las Vegas he quickly made it the voice of the Democratic party in New Mexico. In the elections of 1890 and 1892 he was active in the populist third party movement known as El Partido del Pueblo Unido* and was elected to the territorial council in the second election. He then served as court clerk of the Fourth Judicial District between 1893 and 1897.

Two years later he moved to El Paso, Texas, but retained his controlling interest in *La Voz del Pueblo*. In El Paso he bought and published the *El Paso Daily News* and was active in numerous business ventures. As a strong advocate of the very important Elephant Butte Dam and Irrigation Project on the lower Rio Grande, he played an important role in securing the Mexican government's approval of the project. Partly because of this success he was appointed United States Commissioner General to South America and was sent on a number of goodwill missions by President William Howard Taft. At his death he was widely recognized as a pioneering entrepreneur, an important Texas businessman, and international figure.

MARTÍNEZ, JAVIER (1869-1943), painter. Born in Guadalajara, Javier Martínez became an immigrant to the United States when his foster father was appointed Mexican consul general at San Francisco in 1892. Having shown early aptitude in art, he was soon enrolled in the Mark Hopkins Institute of Art from which he was graduated with honors in 1897. After further art training in Paris and elsewhere in Europe, Martínez returned to San Francisco at the beginning of the century and set up a studio which quickly became the center for lively discussions by a group of artists, literary figures, and political mavericks including Jack London. Out of this group evolved the California Society of Artists.

Martínez was on his way to national artistic success when his studio and most of his paintings were destroyed by the 1906 San Francisco earthquake and fire. He moved across the bay to Oakland and established a new studio in Piedmont, soon accepting a job that was to lead to a lifetime teaching career at the California College of Arts and Crafts. During the World War I years and in the 1920s Martínez exhibited extensively in California and New York galleries. His work in this period served to gain even wider recognition of his talent, especially in the area of dramatic landscapes based on California, Southwestern, and Mexican vistas. In addition he published some poetry and articles on philosophy and pre-Columbian culture in *Hispano América*, a San Francisco Spanish-language newspaper and often emphasized his Indian blood, calling himself "the Aztec."

MARTÍNEZ, VILMA (1944-), president and general counsel of the

Mexican American Legal Defense and Education Fund* (MALDEF), the major civil rights organization for Chicanos. Miss Martínez, the daughter of a carpenter, was born in San Antonio, Texas; after high school she worked her way through the University of Texas and Columbia Law School.

A former staff attorney for the NAACP Legal Defense Fund and the New York State Division of Human Rights, she has been associated with MALDEF since its beginnings in 1968. In 1973 Miss Martínez went to San Francisco to head the organization. In her presidency she has worked to broaden MALDEF's funding base and to emphasize its activities in the areas of education, employment, and political access. As general counsel for MALDEF she has argued skillfully for Chicano rights and in 1974 won a case guaranteeing the right to bilingual education for non-English-speaking children in the public schools. In 1976 Governor Brown appointed Miss Martínez a member of the University of California Board of Regents. Her term expires in 1990.

MASA. *See* MEXICAN AMERICAN STUDENT ASSOCIATION.

MASC. *See* MEXICAN AMERICAN STUDENT CONFEDERATION.

MAXWELL LAND GRANT, originally made in 1841 to Carlos Beaubien and Guadalupe Miranda, two prominent Nuevo Mexicanos,* by the then governor of New Mexico, Manuel Armijo.* When Beaubien died in 1864, his son-in-law, Lucien B. Maxwell, bought out all other claimants including Miranda, and five years later sold the grant of ninety-seven thousand acres in Colfax County in northeastern New Mexico to a joint New Mexican-Coloradan group for $1.35 million. These speculators, who obviously expected to expand their claim, formed the Maxwell Land Grant and Railroad Company and moved to make a profit on their investment. On the basis of a new survey, the company sought confirmation of its grant and now claimed 2 million acres; but, previous to confirmation, sold the grant to a group of English speculators in April of 1870.

In the following year the Secretary of the Interior ruled that the grant was limited to ninety-seven thousand acres. The company clearly needed political power to gain its economic ends; thus the Santa Fe Ring,* composed of influential Anglos and Nuevo Mexicanos, was formed. Despite their political efforts and influence the Maxwell Company had considerable difficulty, including conflict among the various stockholder groups and with settlers, ranchers, and miners, of which the Colfax County War* (1875) was a part. In 1879 the company was granted patents to 1,714,765 acres and finally during the decade of the 1890s this award was upheld by the U.S. Supreme Court.

FURTHER READING: Jim B. Pearson, *The Maxwell Land Grant*, Norman:

University of Oklahoma Press, 1961; Howard Lamar, *The Far Southwest 1846-1912*, New Haven, Conn.: Yale University Press, 1966.

MAYA, term used to identify a number of Central American Indian groups by language. Most Mayan Indians live in the peninsula of Yucatan, the southeastern Mexican states of Chiapas and Tabasco, and neighboring Guatemala. Because the ancestors of most Mexican Americans came from central and northern Mexico, relatively few are of Mayan descent.

MAYO. *See* MEXICAN AMERICAN YOUTH ORGANIZATION.

MECHA. *See* MOVIMIENTO ESTUDIANTIL CHICANO DE AZTLÁN.

MECHANIZATION, FARM, the substitution of machinery for human muscle. The mechanization of agriculture began in the second half of the nineteenth century with the application of technology to the harvesting of wheat in the high plains area of the Midwest. But mechanization of the crops that the Southwest specialized in did not really get underway until the middle of the present century. It began with cotton. In the late twenties experiments were undertaken to develop a mechanical picker and a decade later success was achieved. In 1950 the latest improved version of the mechanical picker could pick a field at a rate of 2.5 miles per hour with 90 percent efficiency, and six years later 90 percent of all cotton in California was machine picked. A similar experience occurred in Arizona and Texas cotton fields. Since one machine could do the work of twenty-five men, the labor force dropped by 60 percent in the decade of the fifties, and the cotton-picking season was cut by eight weeks.

Similar developments took place in most other crops. By the early 1950s sugar beets were being sown, weeded, thinned, and harvested by machine; potatoes were similary being dug, sorted, and packed; and an experimental tomato-picker was being tried out. At the beginning of the 1960s the tomato-picking machine was a success, and wine grapes were being harvested, untouched by human hands. By the midsixties, in addition to these most important cash crops, machines were harvesting or partially harvesting asparagus, onions, celery, lettuce, pears, peaches, plums, and walnuts. Some fruit trees were being pruned with a maneuverable bank of circular saws, and a pneumatic pruner enabled one man to trim nearly one hundred acres of grapes per day.

The results of this application of machines to agriculture were far-reaching. Many packing operations could be moved from the sheds to mobile rigs in the fields and packers might be reclassified as field workers at a lower pay scale. In addition to reducing unit costs per acre in production, harvesting, and packing, mechanization also led to hiring of workers with experience operating machinery, and as higher skills and fewer workers came to be required, a kind of ethnic bias became apparent, discriminating against Mexicans, blacks, and other minorities. At the same time women were substituted for men in some shed jobs. Finally, the decline in the demand for hand labor brought about the beginning of the end of family work units. Mechanization generally tended to creat full-time, year-around jobs—but for many fewer workers. Mechanization also eliminated many family farms, which were no longer able to compete because they could not afford or take advantage of expensive machinery. This trend accelerated the concentration of farm production into fewer and fewer hands.

In December 1979 Robert Bergland, Secretary of Agriculture, announced that his department would stop "the use of federal money to finance labor-saving research." Some people in agriculture see this as a beginning of a trend to slow down, if not reverse, the mechanization of farming.

FURTHER READING: "Machines Take Over Braceros' Jobs," *Business Week*, January 8, 1966, pp. 108-10.

MEDIERO, a sharecropper. In New Mexico, especially during the Spanish and Mexican eras, a poor Nuevo Mexicano* who worked a farm on shares for its owner.

MEDINA, HAROLD R. (1888-), jurist and author. Of Yucatecan and Dutch ancestry, Harold Medina was born in Brooklyn, New York, and attended PS44 and a prep school. At Princeton University he was both an outstanding scholar and athlete, graduating with high honors in French. He went on to study law at Columbia University, from which he was graduated in 1912 with the Ordronneaux Prize for highest standing in the law school. From 1915 to 1947 he taught law at Columbia and at the same time practiced law, winning a number of famous cases. The best known of these was the Cramer treason case during World War II, in which Anthony Cramer, a Brooklyn stoker, was accused of befriending two Nazi spies. Medina first lost the case in the lower courts and then won on appeal to the United States Supreme Court.

After the war Medina was appointed federal district court judge. He sat on the emotion-laden conspiracy trial of eleven members of the National Committee of the Communist party. At the end of the 1950s Judge Medina retired to devote himself to the defense of the First Amendment to the U.S. Constitution. He is the author of numerous books on the American juridical system published between 1922 and 1959. His latest book is a personal description of his judicial experiences titled *The Anatomy of Freedom*, 1959. Holder of honorary degrees from twenty-five colleges and universities, Judge Medina has also been the recipient of numerous prestigious awards.

***MEDRANO* v. *ALLEE*,** a class action suit brought against the Texas Rangers and Captain A. Y. Allee following the 1966-1967 farm-workers strike in the lower Rio Grande Valley. The suit charged that the Rangers had interfered in a variety of ways with the workers' right to organize and strike, depriving them of constitutional rights guaranteed by the First and Fourteenth amendments. In 1972 a federal district court ruled in favor of the farm workers as represented by Francisco Medrano and enjoined the Rangers from interfering with peaceful organizing and from arresting people without probable cause. On appeal, the United States Supreme Court two years later upheld the lower court's findings that the Rangers both had used Texas statutes that violated constitutional guarantees and had unconstitutionally used valid laws in their efforts to intimidate strikers.

MENCHACA, JOSÉ ANTONIO (1800-1879), born in San Antonio, where he grew up to become a prominent townsman. Menchada fought on the Texas side in the Texas revolution* against Mexico and remained in the Texas army after independence. He served on the San Antonio city council for several terms and was briefly mayor pro-tem in 1838. He was elected sergeant at arms of the Texas lower house in the early 1860s and at the time of his death was public weigher in San Antonio.

MÉNDEZ ET AL.* v. *WESTMINSTER SCHOOL DISTRICT ET AL. In 1945 a group of Mexican American parents in the Westminster and Modeno school districts in California filed suit against four Orange County elementary school districts. Led by Gonzalo Méndez, the parents charged that school officials in these districts were continuing to practice segregation against approximately five thousand children by regulation and custom solely because these children were of Mexican descent. They also argued that this segregation violated constitutional guarantees of due process and equal protection of the law under the Fifth and Fourteenth amendments of the U.S. Constitution.

On March 21, 1945, federal judge Paul McCormick ruled that the segregation was illegal both under California statute and under the equal protection clause of the Fourteenth Amendment and also cited social benefits of desegregation. The school districts appealed this decision to the higher courts, and in 1947 the Ninth Circuit Court in San Francisco upheld the lower court's decision. It also instructed the Los Angeles federal grand jury to review the situation for possible indictment of the school board. The school districts finally complied with the court's ruling.

FURTHER READING: Charles Wollenberg, "Méndez vs. Westminster: Race, Nationality and Segregation in California Schools," *California Historical Quarterly* 53, no. 4 (Winter 1974): 317-32.

MÉNDEZ, RAFAEL (1906-), musician. Born in Mexico into a musical family and growing up playing the trumpet, Rafael left for the United States in the mid-1920s, just in time to be caught in the hard times of the Great Depression.* Fortunately he was hired by the band leader Russ Morgan in whose company he perfected his musical skills. In 1964 he became the first trumpet player to play a solo performance at Carnegie Hall.

MESTER, JORGE (1935-), musical conductor. Born of musically inclined Hungarian immigrant parents in Mexico City, Jorge Mester grew up in both a Mexican and American culture as a result of higher education in southern California. At twenty-two he became the youngest teacher/conductor at the Juilliard School of Music and was for six years conductor at the Juilliard Opera Theatre. Appointed conductor of the Louisville Orchestra in 1967, he made it one of the top city orchestras in the country. In the following year Mester became a United States citizen and won the annual Naumberg Award to record a major American composer in an important composition. In 1970, as a result of his impressive conducting credits, he was named director of the annual Aspen Festival. Equally at home with traditional and avant-garde music, he has conducted premiere recordings of more than fifty twentieth-century works.

MESTIZAJE, the blending and overlapping of races, cultures, and life-styles which occurred when Spain encountered and conquered the indigenous peoples of the Western Hemisphere. The Mexican American, a product of three hundred years of racial, cultural, and linguistic mingling, is a prime example of mestizaje. Mexican Americans are a mixture of indigenous and Spanish; but the racial aspect is not predominant, although it is complicated when one considers the number of Indian nations with whom the Spaniards intermixed. More important are the cultural and linguistic factors which have created La Raza's* life-style, a collage of indigenous and Spanish traditions permeated by the language of the latter.

MESTIZO, a person of mixed Indian and European ancestry; also a person who may be racially Indian but has adopted aspects of European culture. Sometimes the phrase "culturally mestizo" is used. *See* MESTIZAJE.

METZGER, SIDNEY M. (1902-), educator, clergyman, bishop. Born in Fredricksburg, Texas, Metzger received his education and clerical training in Texas and in Rome where he was ordained a priest in 1926. Returning to Texas, Metzger became a professor at St. John's Seminary in San Antonio and later was appointed rector. In 1940 he was made auxiliary bishop of Santa Fe and in the following year was transferred to El Paso as coadjutor bishop. In 1942 he became bishop of El Paso. Very much interested in the working man, he actively supported Mexican American efforts to improve their standard of living by forming unions, especially in agriculture. He has been the recipient of numerous awards, including Grand Cross of King Alfonso X, St. Joseph the Worker award (Texas AFL-CIO), and John Casey Labor Man of the Year award.

FURTHER READING: Emilia F. Carrillo, *Bishop Has Kept His Word*, New York: Carlton Press, 1966.

MEXICAN, a person who is a citizen of the United Mexican States. In contemporary literature of the nineteenth and early twentieth centuries the term is often used to refer to Mexican Americans as well. Prior to Mexican independence in 1821 the term was used to refer to a person who spoke the Mexica language.

MEXICAN AMERICAN, a citizen of the United States of America either by birth or naturalization who is of Mexican descent, usually of mixed European (largely Spanish) and Indian origins. There are approximately nine million Mexican Americans, most of whom live in the Southwest—Texas, New Mexico, Arizona, California, and Colorado. There are also large communities of Mexican Americans in Chicago, Detroit, Gary, Omaha, Des Moines, and Kansas City. More than three-fourths of Mexican Americans are native-born and about 80 percent are urban dwellers. Some members of the group prefer to be called Spanish Americans,* Chicanos,* Latinos,* Latin Americans* (especially in Texas), and Hispanos* or Hispanics (especially in New Mexico).

Occasionally one still finds the term Mexican* used to describe members of the group, a practice which was common up to World War II.

MEXICAN AMERICAN AFFAIRS UNIT, an agency of the United States Office of Education headed by Armando M. Rodríguez. Founded in 1969, it became the Office for Spanish Speaking American Affairs in January 1970 when it was placed in the Office of Special Concerns of the Commissioner of Education. It was responsible for administering educational programs like Project Head Start, Upward Bound, and Follow Through.

MEXICAN AMERICAN ANTI-DEFAMATION LEAGUE, an organization concerned especially with the cultural and civil rights of Chicanos. Recently the name was changed to Institute for the Study of Hispanic American Life and History. It sponsors seminars and works through the media to expose and eliminate stereotyping and publishes a monthly newsletter on its activities.

MEXICAN AMERICAN CULTURAL CENTER, founded in San Antonio as the result of the Texas Catholic Conference there in 1971. A center for research, education, and leadership development, it conducts workshops in community organization and development at the center and provides a Master of Education degree through Juárez-Lincoln University.*

MEXICAN AMERICAN JOINT COUNCIL, a politically minded group founded in 1967 by Tejanos* from various Texas Mexican American organizations. An organization of politically oriented activists, it was initially headed by Professor George I. Sánchez.* Among the resolutions passed at the first meeting of the Council at Austin in January 1967 was one calling for the dissolving of the Texas Rangers.* Its overall goal was to achieve for Mexican Americans more social and economic benefits accruing from political power by involving them more extensively and intensively in local, state, and national politics.

MEXICAN AMERICAN LEGAL DEFENSE AND EDUCATION FUND (MALDEF), an organization dedicated to the protection of legal rights of Chicanos and to assisting (with an educational grants program) in the education of Chicano lawyers to carry on this work. Founded in 1968 and supported in its first years under Pete Tijerina's* leadership by a $2.2 million Ford Foundation grant, MALDEF has since played an important role in civil rights cases affecting Mexican Americans. In the early 1970s, under Mario Obledo,* it concerned itself mostly with cases of school segregation, job discrimination, jury exclusion, rights under welfare and Social Security legislation, and with various consumer issues.

In 1973 Vilma Martínez* took over the financially ailing MALDEF and soon pumped new fiscal blood into its veins. Under her vigorous leadership MALDEF has stressed cases dealing with bilingual educaton, voter disenfranchisement, and the 1970 undercount of Chicanos, as well as continuing its earlier objectives. MALDEF also does research and analysis of public policy, counsels groups concerning their legal rights, and encourages Chicanos to enter the legal profession. MALDEF's headquarters are in San Francisco, and it maintains offices in Los Angeles, San Antonio, Albuquerque, Denver, and Washington, D.C. Financed by government grants and private donations, it publishes a quarterly newsletter called *MALDEF*.

MEXICAN AMERICAN LIBERATION ART FRONT (MALAF), a Chicano artist group founded in San Francisco, to help aspiring Chicano artists and to encourage painting that represents the Chicano movement.

MEXICAN AMERICAN POLITICAL ASSOCIATION (MAPA). As a result of feeling left out of the two-party structure in the United States, a group of politically active Chicanos met at Fresno, California, in 1959 to discuss what they might do to advance La Raza* interests. Led by Eduardo Quevedo and Bert Corona,* they formed the Mexican American Political Association, a nonpartisan pressure organization, which has consistently leaned toward the Democratic party. MAPA's goals were almost exclusively political and ethnic: to take stands on issues; to lobby for Mexican American interests; to seek out, endorse, and help finance Chicano candidates; to get out La Raza votes; and to help Mexican Americans in their dealings with state and federal bureaucracy.

First headed by Eduardo Quevedo, MAPA became an important force in California politics, pointing out to Mexican American voters that they did not have their fair share of elected and appointed officials. Partly as a result of MAPA support, Edward Roybal* was elected to the United States Congress in 1962, and other Mexican Americans were elected to the California legislature. Several Mexican American judges were also appointed to municipal and state courts in the 1960s.

In 1966 when Quevedo stepped down, Bert Corona was elected to replace him as chairman, as MAPA continued its political, education, and supportive role. MAPA's early success in electing officials and in influencing both the Republican and Democratic parties aroused wide interest in the Southwest and led to the founding in Texas of Mexican Americans for Political Action* (Texas MAPA). However, changing attitudes of the seventies and internal factionalism led to a considerable decline in MAPA's membership and influence.

In the late 1970s there was a revival under the presidency of Edward Sandoval and at the end of the decade MAPA claimed five thousand members in sixty chapters—a bit short of its goal of at least one chapter in each of California's eighty assembly districts. Despite a 1979 effort to spread MAPA nationally (to Chicago and Kansas City as well as the Southwest), it has remained essentially a California organization. Organizations like MAPA are especially important in rural areas because they lend external support to local Chicanos attempting to assert their civil and social rights.

MEXICAN AMERICAN STUDENT ASSOCIATION (MASA), a Chicano student organization which was founded at East Los Angeles College in 1967 and spread to other Los Angeles institutions. Its goal was almost exclusively Chicano progress through higher education, and its major activity was fund-raising for tutoring and scholarships. It later became a part of United Mexican American Students* (UMAS) established by students at the University of California at Los Angeles.

MEXICAN AMERICAN STUDENT CONFEDERATION (MASC), one of the numerous Chicano student groups that developed in the late 1960s. MASC was organized by students in the San Francisco Bay area.

MEXICAN AMERICAN UNITY COUNCIL (MAUC), a Texas organization founded by young Chicanos of the Mexican American Youth Organization* (MAYO) in San Antonio at St. Mary's University in 1967. While its principal goals were community development and self-help economic improvement for Tejanos,* it also inevitably became involved in the politics of the Chicano community. After funding by the Ford Foundation in 1968, it developed community programs in low-cost housing, health care, and new career development despite early opposition from Texas* leading Mexican American politician, conservative Senator Henry B. González.* Among its most successful undertakings is its business development effort, especially a McDonald's franchise in San Antonio. Working with MAYO,* La Raza Unida party,* Communities Organized for Public Service,* and other organizations, it has achieved real, if modest, improvements in the lives of San Antonio's Mexican American population and shows the extreme importance of cooperative efforts by Chicano organizations.

MEXICAN AMERICAN WAR. *See* MEXICAN WAR.

MEXICAN AMERICAN WOMEN'S NATIONAL ASSOCIATION (MANA), an organization founded in 1976 to promote the status of women of Mexican descent. Its immediate goals are to expand Chicana leadership and to develop equality with men. MANA holds an annual convention to discuss issues affecting Mexican American women, and at its Washington, D.C., headquarters it publishes a monthly newsletter devoted to the same issues.

MEXICAN AMERICAN YOUTH ADELANTE (MAYA), a federation of south El Paso Chicano gangs organized in the second half of the 1960s to attack the problem of juvenile delinquency. By channeling the energies of members toward goals of Chicano cultural nationalism, education, employment, better housing, and equality of opportunity, its members hope to escape the trap of poverty and discrimination. Although MAYA includes a radical, confrontation-conscious element, it has been led by a board of directors that is aware that more can be achieved by accommodation and cooperation, while still maintaining cultural goals.

MEXICAN AMERICAN YOUTH ORGANIZATION (MAYO), founded in 1967 in San Antonio, Texas, by José Angel Gutiérrez,* Mario Compeán, and other young Chicanos with Gutiérrez as its first president. A strongly activist organization, it especially attracted college- and high school-aged Chicanos and by 1974 numbered one thousand members. Its objectives were to make Tejanos* aware of their civil rights and to encourage political activity. MAYO especially concerned itself with Texas educational policies and political practices as they affected Chicanos. In the period 1967-1969 it played a leading role in various school "walkouts" and in 1970 was an important element in Chicano success in the Crystal City* school board elections. MAYO took the initiative in the formation of La Raza Unida party* in Texas in the early 1970s.

MEXICAN AMERICANS FOR POLITICAL ACTION (MAPA, Texas). *See* POLITICAL ASSOCIATION OF SPANISH-SPEAKING ORGANIZATIONS.

MEXICAN ASSOCIATION, a somewhat shadowy, possibly revolutionary organization flourishing in New Orleans circa 1805-1810. It appeared to have had connections with General James Wilkinson, Aaron Burr, and the latter's conspiracy and may have had some impact on the subsequent Mexican revolution* for independence in the Texas area.

MEXICAN CIVIC COMMITTEE, a Chicago community-based organization founded in the 1940s by Frank M. Paz. The committee is concerned with the status of Mexican Americans in the Chicago area.

MEXICAN MUTUAL AID SOCIETY, an organization developed during the 1928 Imperial Valley melon pickers' strike. With the help of the Mexican consul at Calexico the melon pickers, mostly Mexican nationals, developed in advance of the strike an organization first known variously as the Unión de Trabajadores del Valle Imperial and Unión de Obreros Unidos del Valle Imperial. Organized through the Benito Juárez Mutual Aid Society of El Centro, by April 1928 the group was incorporated as the Mexican Mutual Aid Society. The MMAS dominated the melon strike and, although unsuccessful in its major objectives, continued to be a cohesive force for Mexicans in the Imperial Valley in opposition to the Trade Union Unity League* (TUUL) and its organizing efforts.

MEXICAN PERIOD IN THE SOUTHWEST (1821-1848). A variety of factors and events in the Mexican period paved the way for the later American takeover of the Mexican northern frontier region. First and foremost, the internal political dissension in central Mexico and sometimes petty political squabbling made it virtually impossible for the new, independent government to assume any real control of the distant frontier regions. In addition, the Mexican congress's unwillingness to establish a sound system of taxation weakened the central government. In a few words, the frontier regions were forced to rely largely on themselves for governance, defense, and taxation. The resulting heady localism (patria chica feeling) made the federal system of the United States government very appealing, and to this was added a variety of economic inducements.

In California mission secularization by the new Mexican government quickly led to development of large private ranchos raising cattle whose tallow and hides found a market in the United States. In New Mexico, Mexican approval of the Santa Fe trade* not only resulted in business ties with the developing American Midwest but also made the territory completely independent of Mexico City, both economically and from a tax standpoint. In Texas, Mexican encouragement of (American) empresarios* quickly led to a heavy influx of American settlers and cotton growers and thereby also to close economic ties with a rapidly expanding United States. It can be seen that both political developments in central Mexico and economic growth in the northern borderlands during the Mexican period made American takeover more palatable to local leadership.

MEXICAN REVOLUTION. The first of the twentieth-century nationalist social revolutions, the Mexican Revolution erupted in November 1910 as a political movement to overthrow the thirty-four year dictatorship of Porfirio Díaz. It evolved into a full-fledged social upheaval characterized by agrarian reform, anticlericalism, nationalism, and a strong xenophobia. It was a historic culmination of the Mexican search for identity and of the struggle to create a modern nation.

Inevitably the conflict affected the United States and particularly the border region. American lives and property were endangered not only in Mexico but also along the border as fighting for key frontier towns occurred and as the unsettled conditions and absence of effective political control facilitated raiding and banditry. The border region was the staging area for many of the military movements during the revolution and the source of arms and supplies. It also was an asylum for political exiles and for those seeking to escape the destruction and violence of civil war.

It was the Mexicans and Mexican Americans in the border area who were most affected by what was happening in Mexico. It affected friends and family, it aroused sentiments of ethnic solidarity and stimulated feelings of reform and of revenge. The growing Mexican population in the area increased the demand for news of what was happening in Mexico, and those anxious to disseminate ideas created a communications network of Spanish-language newspapers.

The Flores Magón brothers,* who had moved during the initial decade of the century from liberalism to anarcho-syndicalism and had three times attacked the Díaz regime, sought sanctuary in the border region and used it for launching their rebellions. The Magonistas endeavored to organize Mexican and Mexican American workers on both sides of the border and to enlist them in their movement against the dictatorship. Their 1910 effort coincided with the liberal democratic movement headed by Francisco I. Madero, which received a sympathetic and supportive response from the population of Mexican origin in the border area. Madero's Plan of San Luis Potosí to overthrow Díaz was drafted in San Antonio and from there he launched an armed movement that by May of 1911 had captured Ciudad Juárez and toppled the Díaz regime.

With the election of Madero, the revolution assumed power. However, Mexico was not ready for democracy, but very much in need of reform. The old regime fought back in the legislature, the press, and on the battlefield. And impatient agrarian revolutionaries rebelled, including Emiliano Zapata* in the south. However, most of the armed movements came from the north and involved conservative elements. During the civil war of the decena trágica in February 1913, Madero was undermined by the American Ambassador Henry Lane Wilson's interference and betrayed by General Victoriano Huerta. Madero and his vice president were deposed and then killed.

Huerta's counterrevolutionary regime was opposed by Venustiano Carranza and Francisco Villa* in the north and by Zapata in the south and by President Woodrow Wilson in Washington. Madero, in his martydom, unified the revolutionaries. Huerta was forced out, bringing a more conservative exile element to the border region, but not before American troops occupied Veracruz in what has been called an "affair of honor" and an effort to prevent arms from reaching Huerta. Revolutionary unity disappeared along with the common foe, and the Convention forces of Villa and Zapata opposed the Constitutionalists of Carranza. Both sides promised reforms in an effort to attract peasants and workers to their camp. In the end, Carranza triumphed militarily and was recognized by the United States. Villa, on the other hand, raided Columbus, New Mexico, and provoked the Punitive Expedition led by General Pershing* which succeeded in dispersing, but not capturing and destroying the Villistas. It was Carranza who accepted the reformist Constitution of 1917, which provided a legal framework for the revolution and chartered its course in the succeeding decades.

President Woodrow Wilson, in his effort to get additional information about the Mexican situation and to influence the course of events, sent a number of personal envoys to Mexico. His second fact-finding emissary was Reginald(o) Del Valle, a Los Angeles native, who was a political ally of Secretary of State William Jennings Bryan. Despite his heritage and knowledge of Spanish, Del Valle had a disdain for the Mexican masses, little faith in the workability of democracy in Mexico, and was unsympathetic to the revolutionary leaders. Worse still, he was indiscreet and his mission became a fiasco necessitating his recall.

The Mexican Revolution brought turbulent conditions to the border region, in part attributable to the absence of effective control in the region and in part due to an irredentist movement under the Plan of San Diego.* That movement, which produced over two dozen raids into the south Texas border area in the summer and fall of 1915, may well have started as part of a Huertista effort to return to power. It is probable that Germany—later to offer Mexico an alliance and the return of her lost provinces in the 1917 Zimmerman note*—sought to encourage and built on it; and the movement could not have continued as long as it did without encouragement by Carranza who used it as leverage to obtain recognition from the United States. However, the movement would never have occurred but for the racial bitterness and resentment of discrimination along the border and the historical antagonism against the United States, both of which were stimulated by the Mexican Revolution with its goal of equality for Mexicans and its anti-United States orientation. The plan called for an independent republic to be set up in the former Mexican territories which, when appropriate, would be annexed to Mexico.

The Plan of San Diego was bizarre and quixotic. However, it did generate rumors, fear, and hysteria. Ironically, it accentuated the existing prejudice and discrimination and provoked retaliation against Mexican Americans, which cost more lives than did the raids. In the end the movement came to nothing which is not surprising since its goal was an impossibility.

Perhaps the most important effect of the Mexican Revolution was that it resulted in the first large-scale Mexican migration to the United States—a movement that has continued with only minor interruptions ever since. Many fled the chaos and destruction of their native land. Others sought political asylum from their foes. The revolution accelerated the process begun by the railroads of freeing the rural workers from the land. Some joined revolutionary bands; others went northward. And many chose to remain, sharing both their historic movement and their revolutionary heroes with the Mexican Americans and other Mexican residents in the border region.

FURTHER READING: Rodolfo Acuña, *Occupied America: The Chicano's Struggle Toward Liberation*, San Francisco: Canfield Press, 1972; Charles Cumberland, "Border Raids in the Lower Rio Grande Valley—1915," *Southwestern Historical Quarterly* 57 (January 1954): 285-311; Charles H. Harris, III and Louis R. Sadler, "The Plan of San Diego and the Mexican-United States War Crisis of 1916: A Reexamination," *Hispanic American Historical Review* 58, no. 3 (August 1978): 381-408; Manuel A. Machado, Jr., *Listen Chicano! An Informal History of the*

Mexican American, Chicago: Nelson Hall, 1978; Matt S. Meier and Feliciano Rivera, *The Chicanos: A History of Mexican Americans*, New York: Hill and Wang, 1972.
S.R.R.

MEXICAN PROTECTIVE ASSOCIATION, an early Mexican American labor organization, founded in south Texas in 1911. Essentially mutualist* in character, it was composed of small farmers, tenant farmers, and day laborers. It had minimal impact on the Mexican American labor movement in Texas, which tended to follow more radical leadership.

MEXICAN WAR (1846-1848). Following a growing sense of "manifest destiny" throughout the country and an increasing interest in Mexico's northern provinces of Texas, Nuevo México, and California, the United States declared war on Mexico on May 13, 1846, citing boundary disputes, Mexico's failure to pay U.S. claims, and clashes between Mexican and U.S. forces in the Nueces triangle in southeastern Texas as her reasons. General Zachary Taylor* moved southwestward from the lower Rio Grande, capturing Matamoros, Monterrey, and Saltillo, while Colonel Stephen Kearny* with his Missouri volunteers invaded New Mexico and took Santa Fe without a fight. In California Commodores John Sloat and Robert Stockton, with help from John Charles Frémont,* the Bear Flaggers,* and eventually Kearny, defeated the pro-Mexican forces. In both California and New Mexico American takeover was facilitated by a decade of disaffection with the ineffectual centralist government in Mexico City as well as by a vanguard of American traders and settlers.

In March 1847 American forces landed at Veracruz and advanced on the Mexican capital, which was captured in September after the Battle of Chapultepec with Los Niños Héröes.* On February 2, 1848, the Treaty of Guadalupe Hidalgo* was finally concluded; its ratification by Mexico late in May concluded the hostilities. The results of the war were far-reaching. It gave the United States the Southwest and eighty thousand Mexican Americans. See maps in Appendix H.

FURTHER READING: K. Jack Bauer, *The Mexican War, 1846-1848*, New York: Macmillan Co., 1974; John E. Weems, *To Conquer a Peace: The War Between the U.S. and Mexico*, Garden City, N.Y.: Doubleday & Company, 1974.

MEXICO, MEXICAN AMERICAN ATTITUDES TOWARD. Mexican American views of Mexico are, perhaps inevitably, ambivalent. Obviously most Mexican Americans or their ancestors, whether economic or political refugees, left Mexico because in one way or another life in the United States was more attractive. Evidence suggests that most Mexican Americans tend to regard Mexico in a stereotypical or romantic fashion. This explains why so many young Chicanos who went to Mexico in the late 1960s and early 1970s to discover their "roots" met with disappointment in that quest and were surprised at their Mexican reception and at their own Americanism.

In any event, Mexico and Mexican culture have exerted and continue to exert a strong influence on Mexican Americans. The Spanish language and Mexican literature are unquestionably important ingredients in this attraction, as is devotion to the Virgin of Guadalupe,* Mexico's patron saint and a powerful symbol of Mexican nationalism. In addition, religion, customs, and manners in Mexico are seen by many Mexican Americans as preferable to corresponding attitudes in the United States. On the negative side, views of Mexican economic and political conditions appear to be much more realistic and hold no attraction for Mexican Americans. There are, of course, differences of views within the ethnic community based on age and distance, both physical and temporal, from Mexico, as well as other factors. *See also* NATIONALISM.

MIDWEST COUNCIL OF LA RAZA, a Mexican American organization serving a broad area of the Midwest and concerned with a wide variety of problems that Mexican Americans encounter. Founded at Notre Dame University in the early 1970s, the council is governed by an elected board of directors from the ten midwestern states in which it has members. Despite a problem of limited funds it continues to work effectively for its membership. It also works closely with the Centro de Estudios Chicanos E Investigaciones Sociales, a social action organization, and publishes *Los Desarraigados (The Uprooted)*.

MIDWEST MEXICAN AMERICANS, a twentieth-century phenomenon that began in the early 1900s with the northward migration of seasonal agricultural workers, mostly from Texas. For decades Mexican Americans traveled northward from their permanent homes in the Southwest to harvest crops in the Midwest. Only within the past four decades have large numbers of these persons remained as permanent residents after the end of the harvest season. Affected by the process of urbanization, some remained in agricultural-related work in small rural towns, but most settled in communities with industrial employment opportunities. Midwest areas with a large concentration of Mexican Americans are the Chicago, Illinois-Gary, Indiana area; Milwaukee, Wisconsin; St. Paul, Minnesota; Detroit, Michigan; Toledo, Ohio; and many others.

MIGRA. *See* IMMIGRATION AND NATURALIZATION SERVICE.

MIGRANT HEALTH ACT OF 1962, federal legislation authorizing the appropriation of funds to be used for grants to both public and private agencies for health services to domestic migratory farm workers. Because migratory workers may travel interstate, their health problems pose a potential threat to the national health. Congress felt that this fact justified federal action, which resulted in the law that President John F. Kennedy signed in September. The legislation has helped improve the quality of life for Mexican American migrant workers.

MIGRANT MINISTRY, an interdenominational Protestant ministerial group financially supported principally by the National Council of Churches. The Migrant Ministry was established in 1920 to deal more adequately with the social problems of poor housing, inadequate sanitation, low literacy levels, and moral laxity among migrant farm workers. Despite considerable hostility from local churchmen, in the early 1960s the ministry turned more of its attention to union organizing and in the second half of the decade was very important in the Delano grape strike* and unionizing efforts in Texas. The Migrant Ministry strongly identified with César Chávez* and his largely Mexican American migrant farm-worker followers in the Central Valley of California, even though most of them are Catholic.

MIGRATION, INTERNAL. The decline in tenant farms in the Southwest at the end of the nineteenth century, the expansion of a market economy of seasonal crops, and the movement to large-scale agribusiness inevitably led to a need for large numbers of workers for harvest periods. This demand caused the development of a pattern of internal migration and a heavy influx of Mexican seasonal workers. From 1900 to 1930 a reasonable estimate of Mexican immigration to the United States, legal and undocumented, is one million.

The large number of laborers willing to work for low wages reduced local employment available to Mexican Americans in the Southwest and almost inevitably impelled them to join the migrant circuit, since they spoke English and had familiarity with the area. As market agriculture became increasingly a large-scale operation accompanied by a considerable amount of mecahnization* in some phases and requiring large numbers of workers for short time periods, even heavier pressures were put on Chicanos to follow the harvests.

Three migrant patterns or streams involving Mexican Americans developed in the United States from the 1880s to the present time. The Eastern Stream is a mixed group, partly Mexican Americans with increasing numbers of Puerto Rican and black workers. Their southern home bases are mainly Florida and Puerto Rico; their northern home bases are New Jersey and New York. They migrate to the Central Atlantic states, and often also work from July to October in the Northeast. The Midcontinent Stream is made up almost exclusively of Mexican Americans who winter in Texas and then migrate to work in four areas: Arkansas, Indiana, Illinois, Ohio, and Michigan; Wisonsin and Minnesota; Colorado, Idaho, and Montana; and

Washington and Oregon. The Western Stream has a majority of Mexican Americans with some Filipinos, blacks, and poor whites. This group has been greatly reduced in recent years by farm mechanization and less than 25 percent of this group is migrant now. Most of those who are migrate from the Imperial Valley of southern California to agricultural centers in Arizona, to the Salinas Valley, to the San Joaquin Valley, and then return home. Conditions are better for migrants in this stream than in the other two, principally because of the efforts of the United Farm Workers* in California since the 1960s.

Over the years many southwestern Mexican Americans developed regular patterns of harvest work, going from one farm to the next as past experience dictated. This annual migratory trek of many Mexican Americans in family groups made it additionally difficult for them to obtain adequate education for their children or to escape the poverty cycle. *See also* MIGRATORY LABOR and AGRICULTURAL LABOR.

FURTHER READING: Carey McWilliams, *Migrants and Migratory Labor in the United States*, Boston: Little, Brown & Co., 1942.

MIGRATORY LABOR, agricultural workers—singles, families, or crews—who move from place to place following the harvests. Migratory workers might start in March in the Imperial Valley of California on the Mexican border and as the summer proceeds move northward, and then into Oregon and Washington as fall advances. Or they might begin in the lower Rio Grande Valley of Texas in early spring, move up into Arkansas and end the picking season in Wisconsin or Michigan, returning to Texas in October.

Migratory labor patterns began to develop at the beginning of the twentieth century as a result of wider availability of automobiles and trucks, decline of family farming, decline of tenancy and share-cropping, development of large-scale "factories in the fields," and the increasing importance of green vegetable and fresh fruit crops. As new areas of agricultural employment opened up, the highly seasonal nature of their harvests and partial mechanization created the need for a large, mobile work force for a relatively short period of time.

By the early 1880s Mexican nationals were crossing the border to work in Texas cotton harvests where they began to replace black Americans. By World War I Texas crews of Mexican Americans were moving from harvest to harvest within the state and by the early 1920s were beginning to discover better-paying jobs outside of Texas especially in the sugar beet industry. In California a variant pattern developed in the post-World War I era as Mexican workers moved more slowly northward harvesting various fruit and vegetable crops as they matured. During the depression years of the 1930s more families went on the migrant circuit as more people acquired automobiles. At this time the labor force was also expanded when Anglo workers, especially from Arkansas and Oklahoma, who lost their farms to dust storms or to the tractors of large-scale agriculture, joined the migrant circuit. The 1930s were especially hard years for migrant Mexican Americans.

The advent of World War II and concomitant manpower needs failed to help these Mexican Americans economically as much as might be expected because in 1942 the United States and Mexico concluded an agreement by which Mexican workers, called braceros,* were brought in. Although the Bracero Program was initiated as a wartime emergency arrangement, it was not terminated officially until 1964.

Texas alone had about 100,000 migrant agricultural workers in the mid-1960s, about two-thirds of whom left the state for better wages and treatment elsewhere. Their places in Texas were increasingly taken by undocumented* workers and commuters.* Since 1965 the unionization movement among farm workers in Texas and California has led to increased wages and therefore to more mechanization* and decline in the numbers of migrant agricultural workers hired.

Although statistics on migrants are not highly reliable, there are about one million migrants and their dependents in the United States, and the largest single group is Mexican American and Mexican. Their annual family incomes range from less than $2,000 to about $4,000 per year, and their way of life, economically and socially, is highly unsatisfactory. Migrants have always suffered from a number of problems: extremely low wages, poor working conditions, poor health conditions and treatment, substandard housing, exploitation both by crew leaders and employers, lack of economic and political power, lack of community, minimal social and educational opportunity for themselves and their children, to cite the most important. The federal Migrant Health Act of 1962* provides limited health services to migrants, and the 1964 Economic Opportunity Act includes some benefits. Federal minimum wage legislation applies to some agricultural workers, and over half the states have passed laws to meet some of the pressing needs of migrant workers. Conditions are probably best in California and poorest in Texas.

FURTHER READING: Harry Schwartz, *Seasonal Farm Labor in the United States*, New York: Columbia University Press, 1945; Vernon M. Briggs, Jr., *Chicanos and Rural Poverty*, Baltimore: John Hopkins University Press, 1973; George O. Coalson, *The Development of the Migratory Farm Labor System in Texas: 1900-1954*, San Francisco: R & E Research Associates, 1977; Carey McWilliams, *Migrants and Migratory Labor in the United States*, Boston: Little, Brown & Co., 1942.

MIGRATORY LABOR AGREEMENT OF 1951. *See* PUBLIC LAW 78.

MINING INDUSTRY. The mining industry in the Southwest today is based on a combination of techniques used in Spain and in Mexico. Metallurgy and mining, two of Spain's economic mainstays, were highly developed on the Iberian peninsula before the conquest of America. Mines in Galicia and Asturias in Spain had been worked for centuries before the discovery of America. Spain had improved on Egyptian methods of grinding, smelting, and extracting ores and by the Middle Ages had developed mining codes and laws. Mining codes, originated for the mines in Castile in 1584, were later carried to the New World, and they remained the fundamental law until the Mining Ordinances of 1783, which were part of the general eighteenth-century Spanish reforms.

After the conquest, Spaniards prospected over most of Central and South America, Mexico, and what is today the southwestern United States. These centuries of mining yielded a considerable body of knowledge concerning mining techniques, which was later brought to Arizona, New Mexico, and California by Mexicans.

It was the discovery of the New Almadén* mines in the early 1800s, near San Jose, California, that unlocked the gold and silver resources of California and the West. Since mercury was essential to the reduction of gold and silver ores, subsequent discoveries of gold and silver would have meant little had it not been for the important discovery of the New Almadén mercury deposits. Until 1887 more than half of the world's mercury came from the New Almadén mines.

In 1736 the discovery of Arizonac, a silver mine just below the present international boundary, attracted hundreds of miners and prospectors. Within five years, however, this silver rush came to an end when ores were exhausted. Nevertheless, this mining rush gave Arizona its name and brought hundreds of prospectors northward from the interior of Mexico.

In the Southwest copper mining became important after Juan Carrasco discovered the Santa Rita copper deposit in southern New Mexico. By 1804 more than six hundred Mexican miners were working this tremendous copper deposit. Later, whenever larger mines were discovered in Arizona, mining companies hired Mexican miners and adopted many of the techniques first devised at Santa Rita.

In California after the Mexican War,* when James Marshall struck gold at Sutter's Mill, thousands of Americans poured into northern California to work the diggings. Most of these adventurers knew nothing about mining but quickly learned techniques from Mexican Sonorans,* who established the town of that name and brought Spanish mining techniques to California. Many laws adopted during these early days to settle disputes and problems resembled the Spanish mining laws of Mexico.

Early mining methods and techniques learned from the Mexicans served prospectors in Nevada, Colorado, New Mexico, Arizona, and California. The legal mining code evolved in California in the late 1840s spread across the West and beyond to Alaska and even to Australia. In 1866 the U.S.

government imposed laws on mining in the public domain, and it adopted into federal statute the miner's code almost verbatim.

Today many of the technical terms in America's mining law and vocabulary are of Spanish and Mexican origin. Furthermore, Mexican Americans represent over 65 percent of all mine labor in the Southwest and western part of the United States.

FURTHER READING: Rodman W. Paul, *California Gold*, Cambridge, Mass.: Harvard University Press, 1947; *The Mining Frontiers of the Far West 1848-1880*, New York: Holt, Rinehart and Winston, 1963.

MISSION. The basic justification for the Spanish conquest of the New World was Christianization of its Indian population, and the principal means of undertaking this on the frontier was through the mission. A mission was essentially a pueblo* created by friars, having a church, infirmary, library, living quarters for the missionaries, dwellings for the Indian neophytes who were to be brought together, storehouses, and workrooms, and surrounded by fields and corrals. Artisans brought from central Mexico taught the Indians skills like masonry, carpentry, smithing, weaving, and leatherwork. Among the largely seminomadic Indians of Mexico's northern frontier the mission was a particularly important institution and controlled large areas of good agricultural land in the name of its neophytes. In theory each mission was to complete its work of converting the nearby Indians to Christianity and making them culturally into Europeans (gente de razón*) in a ten-year period and then to release them from missionary control. This time limit was almost never met.

The first missions on the north Mexican frontier were established in New Mexico beginning with the Oñate* expedition of 1598. These New Mexico missions differed somewhat from the description above in that the Spaniards found the Pueblo Indians sedentary and already congregated in villages. The New Mexico mission church and friars' quarters were usually built on the edge of the pueblo and often were physically separated from it by a wall. Thus here the mission establishment really was more like a normal village church than the mission on the rest of the frontier. The Franciscan missionaries in New Mexico never exercised the control over the Pueblo Indians that they did over the Chumash, Costanoan, Miwok, and other coastal Indians in the California missions. With the Hopis, Navajos, Zuris, and Apaches they had even less success.

In the late 1600s Jesuit Father Eusebio Kino* began his missionary activity among the Upper Pima Indians and by 1700 had founded missions Tumacácori and San Javier del Bac in southern Arizona. Partly because of Apache raiding and low population density, missionary work in Arizona went slowly, and by 1767, when the Jesuit missionaries were expelled from all Spanish possessions, the area had only eight missions, all in Sonora. The subsequent attempt of Franciscan friars to establish two missions among the Yuma Indians on the route to Alta California quickly ended in failure with the Yuma Revolt of 1781. Soon after Mexican independence mission secularization began. In 1828 most of the remaining missionaries were ordered out of the country by the Mexican government because they were Spaniards and refused to take the oath of allegiance to Mexico. The missions declined further and were gradually abandoned.

The first Texas mission, San Francisco de los Tejas, was established south of Nacogdoches in 1690 by Spanish friars, and during the following century they founded some twenty-seven missions in that vast area. One of the more successful Texas missions was San Antonio de Valero, founded in 1718 and better known today as the Alamo.* However, generally the Indian neophytes of the Texas region were too nomadic to adapt well to mission life, and Comanche and Apache raiding made missionary endeavors additionally difficult. After the mid-1750s the northeast expansion from central Mexico had ended, and Spanish Texas was on the defensive; by the end of the century there were only six functioning missions with nine missionaries. Among the missions that had closed down was San Antonio de Valero; in 1793 it was secularized and the mission lands were distributed.

The California missions date from 1769 when Father Junípero Serra* established Mission San Diego de Alcalá. Before his death in 1784 Fr. Serra had founded nine missions, and his successors built twelve more—the last one, San Francisco Solano, was built in 1823 during the Mexican Period in the Southwest.* The Alta California missions were different from those in New Mexico and Texas in that, in addition to the normal financial support from the Spanish Crown, they had income from the Pious Fund created earlier by the Jesuits for the Baja California missions. These California missions were materially the most successful of the north Mexican frontier, with outstanding agricultural development and stock raising. By the mid-1830s, when secularization finally ended the mission system, there were sixty friars, mostly Spaniards, and over thirty thousand Indians in twenty-one missions, which still supplied much of the food for all Alta California.

A simplistic, black and white evaluation of the mission system is not possible. In a spirit of not always benevolent paternalism, the Indians were overseen and cared for by the friars, who saw them as permanently retarded children. Some of the friars were stern disciplinarians in an era when punishments were often inhumane, and as a result the Indians often suffered for "wrongdoing" of which they were unaware. Certainly the missions failed to make any large number of them into gente de razón. On the other hand, the missions provided a degree of security that was attractive to tribes harassed by more warlike brethren, such as the Apache and Comanche. Also it often protected them from the exploitive rapacity of Spanish-Mexican settlers, most of whom saw Indians only as a potential labor force. Economically, culturally, and religiously many a mission was a tiny island cut off from contact with the outside world.

FURTHER READING: John Francis Bannon, *The Spanish Borderlands Frontier, 1513-1821*, New York: Holt, Rinehart and Winston, 1970; Edward H. Spicer, *Cycles of Conquest*, Tucson: University of Arizona, 1962; Zephyrin Engelhardt, *The Missions and Missionaries of California*, 4 vols., San Francisco: The James H. Barry Co., 1908-1915.

MITCHELL, HARRY L. (1906-), agricultural labor leader. Growing up in Tennessee, Mississippi, Alabama, and Arkansas, Mitchell at an early age became acquainted with the problems of the small farmer, especially the tenant farmer. In 1934 he became one of the founders of the Southern Tenant Farmers Union (STFU), which worked for the betterment of conditions among agricultural workers. In 1947 Mitchell developed the National Farm Labor Union,* an AFL affiliate, out of the STFU and became its president. Mitchell's new union was especially active among the agricultural workers of California during the 1950s. Mitchell served on several governmental committees in the 1930s and has published articles in the *New Republic* and *The Nation*.

MOCTEZUMA II (?-1520), also spelled Motecuhzoma and Montezuma. Moctezuma Xocoyotzin was the leader who governed the Aztec confederation from 1502 until 1520. Trained for the priesthood but elected ruler, he expanded Aztec influence and control to its widest limits. His efforts to reduce the power of the warrior clans resulted in the increasing authoritarianism and despotism of his rule. Generally he seems to have been a good leader, but his religious concerns caused him to deal equivocally with the Spaniards. As a result, after welcoming Hernán Cortés* and his men to Tenochtitlán he soon became their hostage and finally was killed, apparently stoned by his own people, while pleading the Spanish cause.

Because he has generally been interpreted by Mexican historians as weak and vacillating in dealing with the Europeans, Moctezuma has not achieved the cultural hero role among Mexican Americans reserved for Cuahtémoc,* Emiliano Zapata,* and Francisco Villa.*

MOJADO ("Wetback"). *See* UNDOCUMENTED.

MONDRAGÓN, ROBERTO (1940-), politician. Mongragón was born at La Loma in New Mexico of a poor family and received his early education in a traditional one-room school. In high school he was elected sophomore class president in one school and senior class president in another. After high school graduation in 1958 and two years of electronic training he became a laboratory technician. In 1966 Mondragón was elected to the state house of representatives and four years later he was chosen lieutenant governor of New Mexico. Quite active in the Democratic party at the national as well as state level, in 1972 he was named vice-chairman of the Democratic National Committee.

MONTALBÁN, RICARDO (1920-), actor. Ricardo Montalbán was born in Mexico City, but his family shortly moved to Torreón, Coahuila, where he received his early education. He then joined an older brother in Los Angeles where he attended Fairfax High School and began to take part in school plays.

Deciding to make acting his life's work, he moved to New York where he got his first break in the New York play, *Her Cardboard Lover* (1940). Montalbán's career progressed slowly in motion pictures and on the stage, his roles limited by his Latin appearance and accent. Often he was cast as the hero's buddy, but seldom as the hero unless the role called for a foreigner.

Partially as a result of this personal experience, in 1969 Montalbán founded a small organization called *Nosotros** (we) whose main goals were equal opportunity in motion picture and television employment for Mexican Americans and improvement of the La Raza* image in both media. Over the past thirty years Montalbán has achieved a high level of long-term success in an area where employment is notably erratic. In addition to his career in films, he has acted in such stage plays as *Don Juan in Hell* and *The King and I*. In the summer of 1976 he received excellent reviews for his role in a touring company of *Accent on Youth*. In recent years he also broke new ground by becoming the first La Raza actor to star in a television commercial.

MONTOYA, JOSÉ (1932-), artist. Born in rural New Mexico and greatly influenced in his painting by his childhood experiences there, José Montoya had the typical fragmented early education of migratory farm workers' children. After service in the U.S. Navy during the Korean War, he began his formal art education at San Diego City College in the late fifties and went from there to the California College of Arts and Crafts in Oakland for a B.F.A. and Sacramento State University for an M.F.A. He first taught fine arts at the Wheatland (California) High School and since 1971 has taught at Sacramento State University. He also has been largely responsible for a program of barrio* art in Sacramento, in which the Mexican American experience is related to universal human experience through the arts and crafts.

MONTOYA, JOSEPH M. (1915-1978), United States Senator from New Mexico, born in Peña Blanca, New Mexico, on September 24, 1915. After four years in high school in Bernalillo, New Mexico, Joseph Montoya attended Regis College in Denver, where he graduated with a Bachelor of Arts degree in 1934. In 1938 he received his law degree from Georgetown

University. At age twenty-one and while he was still a university student, Montoya was elected to the New Mexico House of Representatives, the youngest representative in New Mexico's history. Two years later he scored another first when he was reelected and named Democratic floor leader. From the house of representatives Montoya moved into the state senate, serving a total of twelve years in both houses.

From 1947 to 1957 he served as lieutenant governor for New Mexico, and at forty-two years of age he was elected to the first of four terms in the United States House of Representatives. During his fourth consecutive term as congressman, Montoya was appointed to the United States Senate to fill the term of Dennis Chávez* who had died. In 1965 he won his own seat in the Senate.

Senator Montoya's voting record in the Senate earned him high ratings from farm and labor organizations; he was also an early opponent of American involvement in Vietnam. Particularly interested in consumer protection legislation, he advocated measures to aid the poor, Indians, and the elderly.

MOORE, JOAN W. (1929-), sociologist, author, professor. Born in New York City, Joan Moore received her Ph.D. from the University of Chicago in 1959. Later Professor Moore taught at the University of Chicago, University of California, Riverside, University of Southern California, and in the latter 1960s served as associate director of the Ford Foundation's Mexican American Study Project at the University of California, Los Angeles.

Joan Moore continues to have an interest in Mexican Americans. Her publications on Mexican Americans include, as coauthor with Leo Grebler and Ralph Guzman, *The Mexican American People*, New York: Free Press, 1970; *Mexican Americans*, Englewood Cliffs: Prentice Hall, 1970; revised second edition, 1976; and *Homeboys*, Philadelphia: Temple University Press, 1978.

MORENO, LUISA, union organizer. Born in Mexico or Central America, Luisa Moreno worked in the early 1930s in New York. Later in the 1930s she worked as a labor union organizer and editor for the United Cannery, Agricultural, and Packing Workers of America* and was also active in El Congreso de Pueblos de Habla Española.* During the early 1940s she was involved in the Sleepy Lagoon* Defense Committee and in efforts to organize Chicano workers in agriculture and related industries. Her activist and radical stance made her a natural target for McCarthyism in the early 1950s and she was deported under the terms of the McCarran-Walter Immigration Act.*

MORÍN, RAUL R. (1913-1967), author, civic leader. Born in Lockhart, Texas, and growing up there and in nearby San Antonio, Morín early showed artistic skills that led him to a commercial art education. After service in the Civilian Conservation Corps in Arizona during the 1930s he settled in California, eventually opening a sign shop in Los Angeles. World War II led to his being drafted, and he served as an infantryman in the seventy-ninth Division of the Seventh Army until a battle wound in the Battle of the Bulge put him into the hospital for nearly two years.

After his discharge Morín returned to his sign painting business, but with a much greater awareness of the discrimination Mexican Americans still suffered in the Los Angeles area. Asking himself what he might do to make all Americans more aware of Mexican American contributions to our society, he decided to write of Chicano service and valor in World War II. After long and arduous research and writing, his book was finally completed but he found publishers singularly uninterested in it. Nearly ten years later, in 1963, through the efforts of the American G.I. Forum,* his *Among the Valiant* was finally published.

During the 1950s and 1960s Morín was also very active in Mexican American organizations, in Democratic politics, and in veteran organizations. As a result of his constant struggle for the social welfare of La Raza* he was singled out for a number of board and commission appointments—most importantly to the Los Angeles Mayor's Advisory Committee. By the time of his death in 1967 he had become widely recognized as one of the pioneers in working for greater dignity and equality for Mexican Americans, and in the following year a veterans' memorial at Brooklyn and Lorena streets in East Los Angeles was officially dedicated as the Raul R. Morín Memorial Square.

MOVIMIENTO, EL, literally the movement, a vaguely defined, amorphous concept to cover all the activities of Chicanos in their efforts to achieve ethnic consciousness and separate identity. It is especially used in references to such activities since World War II and embraces a wide variety of political, social, and economic ideologies—from the extreme left to the right. It includes such disparate elements as the student demonstrations of the 1960s, the Chicano literary and artistic explosion, and the United Farm Workers' grape and lettuce strikes.

The Chicano movement exemplifies the potential force existing within the Mexican American community to improve itself and its position in American society. More than an economic and political rights campaign, the Chicano movement is also an assertion by Chicanos that they are an important entity in the United States and that their culture and heritage have contributed significantly to American life and culture.

Actively working for greater recognition of Mexican American culture, language, and traditions, the movement plays an important role in three major areas: educating people on their political and economic status; educating them on their history and heritage; and promoting educational programs in the barrios.*

MOVIMIENTO ESTUDIANTIL CHICANO DE AZTLÁN (MECHA), the Chicano Student Movement of Aztlán. *Mecha* means "wick" in Spanish and "match" in Caló.* The organization is a potential spark to ignite Chicano educational, economic, and political change.

In 1969 many existing but separate activist student organizations, including UMAS,* MASA,* MASC,* and MAYO,* reorganized as MECHA. The reorganization took place at the University of California's state-wide convention of the Chicano Coordinating Council on Higher Education, held at Santa Barbara, where the Plan de Santa Bárbara* was formulated and first articulated.

MECHA describes its function as further socialization and politicization for liberation on all campuses. Members of MECHA are encouraged to work both on and off campus to achieve educational, cultural, and socioeconomic liberation for the community.

FURTHER READING: *El Plan de Santa Bárbara*, Santa Barbara: La Causa Publications, 1969.

MOVIMIENTO FAMILIAR CRISTIANO, a husband and wife organization affiliated with the Christian Family movement, with the goal of improving the quality of family life in U.S. Spanish-speaking communities. Founded in 1969, it operates a three-year program of study and dialogue and publishes a monthly bulletin as well as leadership materials at its Houston, Texas, headquarters.

MUJERES, an organization of Chicano exnuns related to PADRES* and LAS HERMANAS,* and having goals of services to the community.

MURIETA, JOAQUÍN (also Murrieta), California folk hero and bandit. In 1848 gold was discovered in California and quickly attracted thousands of prospectors from all over the world. As the result of this heavy influx, prospecting became much more chancy, and in 1850 the California legislature passed the Foreign Miners Tax law.* This legislation and the vigilantism which accompanied it had the effect of virtually eliminating the Spanish-speaking population from the California mines within a year. Some of these displaced miners joined with ruffians attracted by gold to form bandit gangs that soon infested the California hills. Many Californios* and

Sonorans* who were forced out of the mines understandably saw these bandits as Robin Hoods or social revolutionaries who were merely retaliating for the abuses they were suffering at the hands of Anglos. The California legislature took a different view and in the spring of 1853 created a temporary state ranger group with orders to capture bandits known as the five Joaquíns, who were identified by the legislature as Joaquín Valenzuela, Joaquín Ocomorenia, Joaquín Carillo, Joaquín Botellier or Botilleras, and Joaquín Muriati or Murieta.

Under the leadership of a transplanted Texan named Harry Love this ranger force was to rid California of the Joaquíns within three months and thereby collect a one thousand dollar reward. Since there was little by which to identify the five Joaquíns, Californios bitterly protested that this was a license to hunt Mexicans. Nevertheless, the ranger force was organized. Late in July Love's rangers, with only days left to their mandate, encountered a small group of Mexicans.

When the shooting ended the rangers had two corpses later identified as those of Joaquín and a wanted criminal known as three-fingered Jack García. The hand of García and head of Joaquín were removed and placed in jars of alcohol. From the beginning there was some doubt about these facile identifications and especially the later tacking of the name Murieta onto the jar containing the head of Joaquín, but the head and hand became an instant success as touring curiosities, and Governor John Bigler paid Love and his rangers the promised reward as well as their three-months' wages. The head was finally destroyed in the San Francisco earthquake and fire of 1906.

In 1854 John Rollin Ridge, a writer, published *The Life and Adventures of Joaquín Murieta, the Celebrated California Bandit* in San Francisco, and the legend of Murieta was on its way. At least 90 percent fiction, this slim paperback used a Robin Hood motif and became such an instant success that it was pirated both in the United States and abroad, dramatized, made into an epic poem and a biography, rewritten and embroidered on, and was much later Hollywood's basis for the Cisco Kid and Zorro. Toward the end of the nineteenth century the Murieta legend received historical sanction by being included in the works of Hubert Howe Bancroft and Theodore Hittell.

Since then the Joaquín Murieta story has been kept alive by numerous reprintings and rewrites. Among the many questions about Murieta is that of his origins. Various authors have described him as a Californio, a Sonoran, and a Chilean. The most recent work is a play titled *Fulgor y Muerte de Joaquín Murieta* by the noted Chilean poet Pablo Neruda. In his introduction to the play Neruda writes "Pero Joaquín Murieta fue chileno, Yo conozco las pruebas." ("But Joaquín Murieta was a Chilean, I have the proof.") Nevertheless, the discussion goes on.

FURTHER READING: Joseph Henry Jackson, *Bad Company,* New York: Harcourt, Brace and Co., 1939; Remi Nadeau, *The Real Joaquín Murieta,* Corona del Mar, Calif.: Trans-Anglo Books, 1974.

MUSIC, CHICANO, the result of a blend of various elements from pre-Columbian Mexico as well as from later developments in Mexican music history, including European, black, and folk admixtures. Indian and Spanish musical influences evolved in the Mexican colonial period and later national era. During the nineteenth and twentieth centuries additional western and third-world musical elements blended in to create results which can be seen in today's Chicano music. The threads of Chicano music, then, must be traced with the autochthonous, folk, and European admixtures in mind.

With the arrival of the Spaniards, Mexico began to develop a mestizo style, evidenced in both its dances and folk songs. Subtle blends of Indian/black, Indian/European, or Indian/black/European elements are evident. Most of the popular folk song language was handed down by oral tradition, so the written sources for this music are scarce. The dance also formed an important musical element in colonial Mexico. While European-influenced dances such as the pavane existed in early Mexico, Indian and black dances developed and survived side-by-side with them; the tocotín and portorrico de los negros are examples of each. There were other dances and songs as well—cumbees with black elements and examples of various European models. In the nineteenth century both Mexican independence and development of the romantic movement led to an interest in and a revival of Aztec musical forms.

Popular themes and national tunes such as Las Mañanitas and La Paloma made their way into Mexican concert music in the nineteenth century. The most popular Mexican vocal form to emerge, however, was the corrido. This oral newspaper, usually sung, but sometimes recited, had a stylized form including a salutation and a farewell; but most important were the contents, which told with considerable historical accuracy, exact times, dates, and places of the heroic deeds of generals, revolutionaries, and those who fought for independence. Examples such as the famous corrido of Gregorio Cortez* were printed as broadsides in Mexico City with variants passed along by oral tradition to the northern border areas. Nationalism had considerable effect on Mexican music during the 1910 revolutionary period. Corridos continued to be popular, but indianism* became one of the most important elements in Mexican art and music and persisted well into the 1940s. Also, in the 1920s Mexico took part in a worldwide avant-garde musical experimentation.

Although Mexicans had been consciously expressing their roots in music for decades, it was not until after 1945 that Mexican Americans and Mexicans in the United States began in a systematic way to express their origins musically. While individuals have been writing, singing, recording, and collecting Chicano music since before 1945 in the United States, little study of early regional Chicano musical expression has been done.

Southwestern culture contains numerous examples of Chicano music. In New Mexico cylinder recordings go back as far as 1890. Discographies from this area can be found, as well as anthologies of folk music. Recently Albuquerque was described in *Newsweek* magazine as the Nashville of Spanish-American music, but the whole state is in fact a lively center for the recording industry. The Cantemos and Taos labels have produced many albums of folk songs for both adults and children. In Albuquerque itself, the Hurricane label of Sra. Bennie Sánchez and her sons, Al, Morrie, and Gaby has been very successful. Important artists are Al Hurricane, Tiny Morrie, Baby Gaby, Gloria Pohl, Miguel Archibeque, Debbie "La Chicanita" Martínez, Lorenzo Martínez, Bonnie Martínez, Nick and Jane, Los Chavos, the Purple Haze and Robert Griego, Clem García, Baltazar López, Luisa Mendoza, Eulogio Montoya, Los Populares del Norte, Charlie Sauceda, Edelmiro Zúñiga, Los Álvaros, and Rudy García.

In Texas the trend is more toward corridos and especially music of border conflict. The most prolific composer of corridos is José Morante whose subjects include Russian satellites, the Austin police and the Vietnam War. The border music of Lydia Mendoza began around 1928; her recent recordings are of love, courtship, and marriage. In the norteño area of Texas the twelve string rhythm guitar is typical of the German-Bohemian-Mexican admixtures of the conjuntos polkeros. The polka, and to some extent the waltz, schottish, and mazurka are typical of this region. In the 1930s pioneers in Tex-Mex music were Narciso Martínez, Santiago Jiménez, Bruno Villarreal, Jesús Casiano, José Rodríguez, and Lolo Cavazos.

A contemporary perspective with jazz rhythms, improvisation, and virtuosity has been offered by Flaco Jiménez and Ry Cooder on *Chicken Skin Music*, as well as by Tony de la Rosa, Steve Jordan, Wally Gonzales, and the Conjunto Cuatro Espadas de Mingo Saldívar.

The best known Texan of Hispanic origin in the world of song is, of course, Freddy Fender (born Baldemar Huerta in San Benito, Texas, in 1936). His bilingual "Before the Next Teardrop Falls" in country-western style caused him to soar to national prominence. Fender has retained his identity by singing in both English and Spanish.

Arizona and Colorado are also regional centers for Chicano music, but even more has happened in California. From the 1930s to the 1950s Edward "Lalo" Guerrero recorded the Chicano classics "Pancho Claus," "Tacos for Two," "Mario from the Barrio," and "Elvis Pérez." One recording that has had more impact that any other was *Viva la causa!—Songs and Sounds from the Delano Strike* (referring to the 1965 strike of César Chávez's* United Farm Workers).* Two effective Chicano songs are "El Louie," in Spanish, English, and Caló* and "The Ballad of Richard Campos."

Los Angeles is a center for Chicano culture and music. Many mariachi groups have based themselves there—for example, Los Camperos de Nati Cano. Manuel S. Acuña has also influenced Chicano music with his compositions. East Los Angeles Chicano rock groups of the 1960s influenced those of the 1970s: for example, Tierra, Tango, Yaqui, Macondo, Sapo, Azteca, and El Chicano. Redbone is another famous group, whereas in San Francisco the Santana brothers Carlos and Jorge have achieved international recognition.

Lastly, five well-known popular singers of Mexican extraction have reached national prominence: Andy Russell, Vikki Carr,* Joan Báez,* Linda Ronstadt* and Trini López.* These artists all have included Spanish-language songs in their recordings.

FURTHER READING: Gerard Behague, *Music in Latin America: An Introduction*, Englewood Cliffs, N.J.: Prentice Hall, 1979; Guy Bensusan, "Some Current Directions in Mexican American Religious Music," *Latin American Research Review* 10/11 (Summer 1975): 186-90; Dan Dickey, *The Kennedy Corridos: A Study of the Ballads of a Mexican American Hero*, Austin: University of Texas, 1978; Américo Paredes, *A Texas-Mexican Cancionero, Folksongs of the Lower Border*, Champaign-Urbana: University of Illinois Press, 1976; John Storm Roberts, *The Latin Tinge, The Impact of Latin American Music on the United States*, New York: Oxford University Press, 1979; Phil Sonnichsen, "Chicano Music," *The Folk Music Sourcebook*, New York: Broadcast Music, Inc., 1976, 44-59; David K. Stigberg, "Jarocho, Tropical and 'Pop': Aspects of Musical Life in Veracruz, 1971-72," in *Eight Urban Musical Cultures*, ed. Bruno Nettl, Champaign-Urbana: University of Illinois Press, 1978, pp. 260-65.

MUTUALISM, the theory of mutual benefit and protective associations formed by the Mexican Americans. By pooling their meager resources, Mexican immigrants to the United States learned they could provide each other with low-cost funeral and insurance benefits, low-interest loans, and other forms of economic assistance. Dating back to the Spanish and Mexican eras, mutual-aid societies, called mutualistas, also provided a forum for discussion and a means of organizing the social life of the community. Mutualistas often provided the foundations for labor and civil rights organizations which followed in later years. *See also* ORGANIZATIONS.

N

NAHUA(TL), term used to identify various Mexican Indian groups by language. Most prominent among the Nahua peoples were the Toltecs and Aztecs. The spelling Nahuatl is used usually when referring to the language and Nahua when referring to the culture. However, there is no absolute rule for this.

NATIONAL AGRICULTURAL WORKERS UNION. *See* NATIONAL FARM LABOR UNION.

NATIONAL ASSOCIATION FOR BILINGUAL EDUCATION, an organization founded in 1975 and headquartered in Dallas, Texas. Made up of educators, community people, and students, it promotes and publicizes bilingual education, compiles statistics, and operates a placement service. It also publishes a quarterly journal and holds annual meetings to promote public awareness of outstanding bilingual programs.

NATIONAL ASSOCIATION FOR CHICANO STUDIES (NACS), formed in 1972, an organization made up mostly of people in education who are interested in working to promote cultural, educational, and political awareness among Mexican Americans. The group advocates study programs which emphasize Hispanic history, achievement, and contributions. In addition, NACS is concerned with involving Chicanos as a group in the governmental processses.

Financed from dues and fees, NACS has chapters in the Midwest and Southwest. Its headquarters are in Pueblo, Colorado, but its largest membership is in California.

NATIONAL ASSOCIATION OF LATINO ELECTED OFFICIALS (NALEO), an organization founded in 1975 by Spanish-surnamed politicians to encourage Hispanic participation in the voting process and to develop a national lobby for legislation to benefit Spanish-speaking Americans. Still essentially in its organizing and developing stage, NALEO is politically nonpartisan and welcomes as members all who support its goals. It is financed by dues and donations and publishes a newsletter, *NALEO Washington Report*, at its Washington headquarters.

NATIONAL CHICANO COUNCIL ON HIGHER EDUCATION (NCC HE), founded in 1975 in Los Angeles as a result of a meeting of representatives of the Chicano academic community and funded by a Ford Foundation grant. Recognizing the need for an organization to come to grips with the problems of Chicanos in higher education, NCCHE has two main goals: to discuss and develop positions on educational issues affecting Chicanos, and to develop and sponsor research and other academic activities among Chicanos. To attain these goals NCCHE has commissioned a study entitled "Chicanos in Higher Education: Status and Issues," and sponsors a postdoctoral fellowship program through a Ford Foundation grant for the express purpose of increasing the number of Chicanos obtaining tenured positions in higher education.

NATIONAL CHICANO HEALTH ORGANIZATION, formed in 1972 by Chicano medical students, with regional offices in Los Angeles, Oakland, Denver, Albuquerque, San Antonio, and Chicago. Its program begins at the high school level, where it counsels and recruits Mexican American students for careers in public health and medicine. It also operates at the university level, organizing chapters which serve to recruit and find financial support for Chicano students in health care professions. It publishes a quarterly newsletter, *Salud y Revolución Social*, for its six thousand members.

NATIONAL CHICANO MORATORIUM. On August 29, 1970, more than twenty thousand Chicanos and their friends assembled in Belvedere Park in East Los Angeles and marched to Laguna Park to protest the high percentage of Mexican American casualties in the Vietnam War. Organized by Rosalio Muñoz, former student body president of the University of California at Los Angeles, the march was supported by an overwhelming majority of Chicano organizations. The Moratorium committee provided monitors to maintain order and avoid possible confrontation at the march and rally. However, some rock and bottle throwing and the looting of two stores along the line of march, according to the police, caused them to declare the situation critical at 3:10 in the afternoon and to begin to disperse the crowd. At Laguna Park, where the earlier marchers had found places on the lawn to listen to music and speakers, sheriffs moved in with tear gas to disperse the crowd of men, women, and children and created panic and hostility by what many considered unwarranted harassment.

In two hours the melee was over. At the peak of the violence over five hundred police and sheriffs were involved, of whom forty were injured by flying debris thrown by the angry crowd. Twenty-five police cars were damaged, mostly broken windshields or windows. There were three fatalities, the most controversial being that of Rubén Salazar* who was killed in a bar by a tear gas cannister; and hundreds of Moratorium participants were injured, many from panic created by the police sweep of the park. About a dozen stores on Whittier Boulevard were burned by Chicanos. After the event there was a long-lingering feeling of hostility toward law and the government, especially when an investigation into the death of Rubén Salazar proved unproductive. Chicanos were left with a feeling of anger and powerlessness.

FURTHER READING: Rodolfo Acuña, *Occupied America: The Chicano's Struggle Toward Liberation*, San Francisco, Calif.: Canfield Press, 1972.

NATIONAL COUNCIL OF LA RAZA, a private, nonprofit service corporation whose goal is the social and economic betterment of Hispanic-descent

Americans. Begun with private funding in 1968 as the Southwest Council of La Raza,* the organization was first devoted to organizing and strengthening community-based groups in the southwestern states. One of the organization's areas of emphasis was advice, support, and seed-funding for local groups in their efforts to obtain financing for housing and economic development. The Council also has undertaken studies of Chicano voting patterns and of Los Angeles social services, in addition to a number of bilingual-bicultural education projects. During 1978 and 1979 it conducted a special study for the Department of Labor to pinpoint the employment problems and other needs of Hispanic youths.

In 1970, after the Ford Foundation withdrew its financing because of strictures in the Tax Reform Act of 1969, the Southwest Council moved to Washington, D.C., and three years later became the National Council of La Raza in keeping with its more national focus. It has offices also in Texas, New Mexico, Arizona, and Illinois. As the principal national Hispanic organization headquartered in Washington, the National Council has developed affiliate relationships with over one hundred community organizations and in the past decade has become increasingly important as a voice for Mexican Americans, and other Hispanics as well. Today its principal activities can be subsumed under three headings: advocacy of Chicano goals at the national level, research and analysis, and technical assistance to local organizations in program development, funding, and operation. The National Council publishes a bimonthly magazine titled *Agenda* as well as some pamphlet materials and books.

NATIONAL ECONOMIC DEVELOPMENT ASSOCIATION (NEDA), a national organization for Mexican American businessmen, formed in 1970. NEDA is a private nonprofit corporation whose principal goal is the development of Chicano-owned businesses. Operating with a $5 million annual budget, NEDA has its national headquarters in Los Angeles and has grown from nine to twenty-five offices in California, New Mexico, and twelve other states. From these centers it provides information on business opportunities, proposal writing, securing finances and credit, and management know-how to minority businessmen and potential businessmen. NEDA, which is funded through contracts with state and federal agencies such as the Office of Minority Business Enterprise, has been particularly successful in generating new Chicano businesses and in securing financial assistance for them. It publishes a bimonthly newsletter titled *Impact*.

NATIONAL EDUCATION TASK FORCE OF LA RAZA, organized in 1970 by a group of Mexican American academicians to provide increased educational opportunities for Chicanos. The task force conducts training institutes, primarily in the Southwest. Functioning through a number of regional offices, it is also involved in developing more effective community relations.

NATIONAL FARM LABOR UNION (NFLU), an AFL-affiliated agricultural union formed in 1947 out of the earlier Southern Tenant Farmers Union founded in 1934 by Harry L. Mitchell.* Under the leadership of organizers Hank Hasiwar and Ernesto Galarza* in California, the NFLU tried to unionize the fields of the San Joaquin Valley. In the year 1947 its Local 218 initiated a strike against the Di Giorgio Corporation,* which eventually failed and was called off by Mitchell in May 1950. By that time the NFLU was busy organizing workers far to the south in the Imperial Valley and in the next year initiated a strike against Valley melon growers which lasted into 1952 without achieving NFLU recognition. A 1952 strike against Schenley Corporation's grape growing operation in the San Joaquin Valley was equally unsuccessful despite use of the passive boycott technique.

At an NFLU convention that same year the organization was renamed the National Agricultural Workers Union (NAWU). At its peak the union had perhaps four thousand members in twenty California locals, but by the mid-1960s it had dwindled to a membership of about two hundred in six locals. Having struggled unsuccessfully against bracero use, the International Brotherhood of Teamsters competition, and the newly created AFL-CIO Agricultural Workers Organizing Committee as well as agribusiness, the organization was terminated in 1964 by merger with the Amalgamated Meat Cutters and Butcher Workmen of America, which took over its charter.

FURTHER READING: Ernesto Galarza, *Farm Workers and Agri-business in California, 1947-1960*, Notre Dame, Ind.: University of Notre Dame Press, 1977.

NATIONAL FARM WORKERS ASSOCIATION. *See* UNITED FARM WORKERS.

NATIONAL IMAGE, INC. Begun in 1972 National IMAGE (an acronym for Incorporated Mexican American Government Employees) was organized to counter discrimination against the Spanish-speaking persons, especially in government hiring. Its goal is population percentage parity in the public sector, and its program includes the recruiting of Hispanics and the evaluation and establishing of educational qualifications for jobs. Formed mostly by federal employees, National IMAGE's principal approach is to seek support of influential congressmen, to disseminate information about job vacancies, and to encourage Mexican Americans to apply for jobs.

By contract with the Department of Labor, in 1978 it began an outreach program to attract qualified candidates for openings in that agency. Although strongest in the Southwest, National IMAGE has over one hundred chapters in thirty-four states and a membership of about five thousand. The Washington, D.C., office operates a Hispanic talent bank to facilitate placing Hispanics in available government positions and also publishes a quarterly newsletter. *See also* IMAGE.

NATIONALISM, CHICANO. Chicano nationalism has a broad spectrum of interpretation. Some Chicano militants like Reies López Tijerina* envisioned a new national state in the Southwest, Aztlán, the legendary homeland of the Aztecs, or the Republic of San Joaquín del Río Chama.* Tijerina even attempted to internationalize his movement by appealing to the United Nations for recognition of Indo-Hispanos' (Tijerina's term) right to establish an independent republic in the Southwest based on Spanish and Mexican land grant claims.

On the other hand, one of the leading Chicano nationalists, Rodolfo "Corky" Gonzales,* defines Chicano nationalism as an internal symbolic feeling, a commitment to a degree of economic, social, and cultural separation from the majority society, and a dedication to the La Raza* concept of Aztlán. This view includes political and economic control of Mexican American communities by Mexican Americans and is firmly based on Gonzales' theory of a common history, culture, language, and oral tradition. His ideas are lyrically expressed in his famous poem "I am Joaquín."*

Some militants questioned the worth of working within the Anglo system and opted for independent action, but José Angel Gutiérrez* took a somewhat different position. While recognizing the problems involved, he chose to use the system, at the same time taking a strongly anti-Anglo rhetorical stance. Real independence he saw as impossible, but cultural nationalism was a useful base for organizing Mexican Americans to take their rightful places in political and economic spheres. The Raza Unida party* was based on this ethnic nationalism.

Many staunchly Catholic Mexican Americans, lay or clerical, support cultural nationalism because they see it as a force working against the disintegrative affects of the American milieu. The retention of cultural values and attitudes, which are seen as superior to Anglo equivalents, and of the Spanish language, which envelopes the culture, are viewed as supporting the retention of the Catholic religion. This perception is not without validity since conversion to Protestantism has often been associated with complete assimilation.

In summation there appears to be a widespread desire among Mexican Americans to preserve many aspects of their cultural identity. By and large the Mexican American community has supported milder aspects of Chicano nationalism—retention of language, customs, and culture—but has consistently failed to subscribe to the views of more radical nationalists. It has generally supported policies of working through normal channels rather than policies of confrontation.

NATIVE SONS OF THE GOLDEN WEST, a California society organized in 1875 by General Albert M. Winn to perpetuate memories of the days of 1849. Originally membership was restricted to white males born in California after the U.S. takeover. In the early 1900s the organization was asked to develop a list of men who had grown up with Los Angeles; the resultant list included no Californios.* The society still is considered by many to reflect a racist Americanism, although less forthrightly than at an earlier time.

NATIVISM, a policy of favoring native-born citizens; in U.S. history a policy of favoring persons of Anglo-Saxon origin over those of other backgrounds. American deprecation of things foreign and of foreigners who maintained large parts of their culture gave many Americans a sense of superiority over immigrants.

Since the mid-nineteenth century nativism has contributed to violence against foreigners in the United States and in the 1880s was an important factor in the development of restrictive immigration legislation.* Throughout the nineteenth and twentieth centuries, this xenophobic attitude has been particularly violent and oppressive against Mexican Americans as culturally, racially, and religiously different. Ethnocentrism, a major element in nativism, supported a belief in the cultural inferiority of Mexican Americans and provided justification for their shameful treatment. Nativistic sentiment against Mexican Americans culminated in and supported the massive repatriation* of Mexicans and Mexican Americans during the 1930s, and the Zoot Suit Riots* of the 1940s. *See also* DISCRIMINATION.

FURTHER READING: John Higham, *Strangers in the Land*, New York: Atheneum, 1971.

NATURALIZATION. One of the important characteristics of Mexican immigration to the United States has been the low levels of Mexican naturalization compared to that of European immigrant groups. According to the 1910 Census only 11,000 of the 102,000 foreign-born Mexican males in the United States had become citizens, or about 10.7 percent as compared to 45.6 percent for all foreign born males. In 1930, of 320,000 Mexican-born males and females over twenty-one counted by the census-takers, only 18,000, or 5.5 percent were naturalized as compared to 49.7 percent of all foreign born.

Up to World War II the low level of interest in naturalization by Mexican immigrants was often fostered by consuls who acted as their spokesmen from time to time and organized them into the Comisión Honorífica Mexicana,* which fostered a continuing loyalty to Mexico. The Second World War marked a beginning of change in attitude toward naturalization. From 1952 onward, provisions of the new Immigration and Naturalization Act of that year enabled those over fifty and those whose legality of entrance was doubtful to qualify more easily for citizenship. Many Mexican immigrants took advantage of this liberalizing of the law, and naturalization rates for the 1950s rose as a result. However, by the sixties the rate of naturalization had again subsided, to about 2.5 percent.

A number of factors help to account for the relatively low level of naturalization among Mexican immigrants. Perhaps the most important single factor is the recency of heavy Mexican immigration compared to other (European) immigration. A second factor of importance has been the closeness of the mother country and a long history of seasonal border crossing for the purpose of working in the United States. As a result of the proximity of the border and ease of returning, as well as historical tradition, many immigrants intended to return to Mexico even after decades of living in the United States. Another factor in the low naturalization rate has undoubtedly been the high number of undocumented* among Mexican immigrants. Obviously the undocumented, being unable to establish legal entrance to the United States, could not seek naturalization.

Additionally, the Southwest, where Mexican immigrants settled overwhelmingly, had historically received little of the earlier heavy European immigrant influx and as a result was lacking in institutions for naturalization. At the same time the concentration of their settlement in the heavily Mexican Southwest tended to make naturalization seem less important. Naturalization was also made more difficult for many Mexicans by mutually reinforcing economic and social patterns: low levels of income, instability, mobility, and seasonality of jobs, low levels of education, isolation from the dominant society, and lack of facility with the English language. Lastly, Anglo attitudes toward Mexican immigrants, their virtual exclusion from the political processes, the custom of considering them as Mexicans no matter how many years—or for that matter how many generations—they had been in the United States, discouraged many from becoming naturalized citizens. In fact, naturalization promised few, if any, benefits. Generally, naturalization rates seem to be related to occupation, levels of schooling, and length of residence in the United States. On all these counts, a lower level of naturalization among Mexican immigrants is understandable. Clearly the potential political power of Mexican Americans has been reduced by the low naturalization rate of Mexican immigrants. *See* IMMIGRATION LEGISLATION.

FURTHER READING: Patrick McNamara, *Mexican Americans in Los Angeles County: A Study in Acculturation*, San Francisco: R & E Research Associates,

1975; Leo Grebler, "The Naturalization of Mexican Immigrants in the U.S.," *International Migration Review* 1 (Fall 1966): 17-32.

NAVA, JULIAN (1927-), diplomat, historian, author, and educator. Julian Nava was the second son in a family of eight children whose parents fled Mexico during the Mexican Revolution* of 1910. After a fairly typical childhood in East Los Angeles he volunteered for naval service in World War II and after the war decided to use the G.I. Bill for a college education. An outstanding student and student body president at East Los Angeles Junior College, he went on to Pomona College for his A.B. and then to Harvard where he received his doctorate in history in 1955. After a two-year teaching stint at the University of Puerto Rico Nava accepted a position at California State University at Northridge where he has taught ever since except for a year in Spain on a Fullbright scholarship and another in Bogotá, Colombia, as organizer of a college consortium program.

At Northridge Professor Nava has been involved in the rising interest in Chicano problems, especially in education, and in 1967 he ran for the Los Angeles school board. He won an impressive victory and later was elected president of the board. At the end of his first four-year term he was re-elected to the board of education—a feat he repeated in 1975. He also was a member of the board of the Plaza de la Raza and the Hispanic Urban Center and on the advisory committee of the Mexican American Legal Defense and Education Fund (MALDEF).* In addition, he has served on various educational committees. Nava has written a public school textbook: *Mexican Americans: Past, Present, and Future* (1969), and edited two books of readings: *The Mexican American in American History* (1973), and *Viva La Raza! Readings on Mexican Americans* (1973). His most recent research and writing have stressed bilingualism.*

In January 1980 Julian Nava was nominated by President Jimmy Carter as the new ambassador to Mexico—the first Mexican American to be selected for that important post. He was confirmed in that post by the United States Senate on March 4.

NAVARRO, JOSÉ ANTONIO (1795-1871), political leader, merchant. Born in San Antonio, Texas, Navarro was the son of an immigrant army officer turned merchant on the Texas frontier. While growing up in the confused days of the Mexican revolution for independence, he managed to get a rudimentary education and also worked in the family business. By 1828 he was sufficiently well known as a businessman to be elected to the Coahuila-Texas state legislature where he worked to ease the rising tensions between Anglos and Mexicans in Texas.

As a strong federalist Navarro was one of three Mexican Texans who signed the Texan declaration of conditional independence from General

Santa Anna's* centralist government in Mexico City in November 1835. He also helped to write a constitution for the new country. After the war Navarro returned to rebuild his mercantile business and his ranches.

When Texas president Mirabeau B. Lamar planned the ill-fated Texas-Santa Fe Expedition* of 1841, Navarro agreed to be one of four commissioners who accompanied the three hundred men and twenty-one wagons. When the expedition ended in a fiasco Navarro, as a former Mexican and now prisoner, was singled out for special treatment. Originally condemned to death as a traitor, he was instead given a sentence of life imprisonment. When all the other Texas prisoners were released, he was sent to San Juan de Ulúa, the worst prison in Mexico. Only after Santa Anna's overthrow did he manage to escape and return to Texas.

Upon his return he barely had time to recoup his health when he was elected to the convention to write a state constitution, and following Texas annexaton to the United States he was elected to the state senate. Increasingly disturbed by the racial and ethnic intolerance of many Anglos, Navarro decided not to run for reelection when his senate term ended in 1849 and instead retired to private life. Not even the devisive events leading up to the Civil War drew him from his family and business interests. During this time he wrote a number of short articles on early Texas history, although increasingly plagued by poor health. When he died in 1871 he was relatively well off with twenty thousand acres of ranch land, some town property, and two houses in San Antonio. In 1960 the governor of Texas declared the birthday of this "co-creator of Texas" to be an officially noted day.

FURTHER READING: Joseph M. Dawson, *José Antonio Navarro: Co-creator of Texas*, Waco: Baylor University Press, 1969.

NEVADA ASSOCIATION OF LATIN AMERICANS, INC., an organization founded at Las Vegas in 1969 to provide a variety of social services including citizenship education, consumer protection, legal services, counseling, and job placement. It also provides child-care services for working parents, a senior citizens meal program, and a scholarship fund for students. A nonprofit corporation, it is funded by governmental and private grants.

NEW ALMADÉN, mine and mining town a few miles south of San Jose, California. In the latter half of the nineteenth century New Almadén became the world's second largest producer of quicksilver.

In 1845 Andrés Castillero, a Mexican army captain with mining expertise, recognized mercury in the red cinnabar rocks. He immediately formed a partnership to develop the mines and began to dig a few tunnels with the help of local Indian and Mexican workers, but the lack of capital and the eruption of war between Mexico and the United States put an end to his venture. By 1850 the British firm of Barron and Forbes had bought the mine and they, in turn, were taken over by the newly formed New York Quicksilver Mining Corporation by the end of the decade.

John Russell Bartlett, a surveyor for the international boundary between the United States and Mexico who visited New Almadén, wrote just before 1850 that he found the laborers, who made forty to fifty trips a day, emerging every minute from the mine, bent under the weight of their loads. He added that all the work was performed by about two hundred Mexicans and Californios,* employed by contractors and overseers who were their countrymen. By 1864 nearly two thousand persons were living and working at the mines, five-eighths of whom were Mexicans or Californios. Some insight into the nature of this population can be gained from the fact that so many had originated in the state of Sonora, Mexico.

People had started to move north from Sonora into California long before 1846, but the discovery of gold suddenly brought greater numbers. Records show that in 1849 alone, four thousand Sonorans* left their homeland. Although the nativism* associated with the gold rush forced many of these people to return to Mexico, others moved into urban areas or into places such as New Almadén. Here they lived in Mexican Town and soon became indispensable for the operation of the mines.

The Sonoran people were essentially conservative and traditional in politics and religion, but there is a record of strikes led by Mexican workers in New Almadén during 1865, 1866, and 1868. They were joined in these labor stoppages by their coworkers who had been brought in from Cornwall, England, and who lived close by in English Town. Other forms of resistance took place with regard to education and politics. This is indicated by the comment by a mine official that a new school was established after Mexicans strongly protested that they were not receiving fair treatment at the English school.

Political organizations were also formed, although these were concerned more with issues current in Mexico than in the United States. Self-help organizations appeared such as the Sociedad Filantrópica y de Ahorros de Nuevo Almadén (1879), and the society Nuestra Señora de Guadalupe (1873).

By the 1880s substitutes had been found for quicksilver and the mines went into decline. By the early 1900s most of the Mexican population had dispersed to other areas. Some headed for work in other mines in California or out of state, while others formed colonias* on the outskirts of urban areas such as San Jose. A number intermarried into the Anglo population or otherwise became acculturated into it. All of these groups together became the resident Mexican American population that awaited the coming of a yet greater migration from Mexico after 1910.

FURTHER READING: John R. Bartlett, *Personal Narrative of Explorations and Incidents in Texas, New Mexico, and California*, four volumes, New York: Appleton Company, 1854; "Down in the Cinnabar Mines," *Harpers New Monthly Magazine* 31 (October 1865): 549, 552; Colette Standart, O.P., "The Sonora Migration to California, 1848-1856: A Study in Prejudice," *The Southern California Quarterly* 58 (Fall 1976).
A.R.S.

NEW MEXICO, a part of the United States by terms of the Treaty of Guadalupe Hidalgo,* and an act of Congress on September 9, 1850. Five years after the American occupation, a territorial government was established that included New Mexico and parts of Arizona, Utah, and Nevada. The act of Congress which set up the territorial government was known as the organic act and served in place of a state constitution until 1912 when New Mexico became a state.

In contrast, Congress admitted California as a free state without its ever having gone through the territorial stage; but it denied a similar process for New Mexico because most of the numerous residents in 1850 were as yet unamericanized. Instead, Congress created a territorial government for New Mexico, which included Arizona.

Throughout the long territorial period until 1912, the people of New Mexico worked for statehood. Attempts in 1850, 1867, and during the 1870s failed completely. A constitution was drawn up in 1889 by a Republican dominated convention but was decisively defeated by the voters because of cultural, religious, and political provisions of the document. Joint statehood for Arizona and New Mexico was attempted in 1906 but was rejected in Arizona. However, an enabling act passed by Congress in 1910 resulted in the calling of a constitutional convention which drafted the constitution ratified by the voters in January 1911.

At the same time that New Mexico achieved statehood, the Mexican American community began to see an erosion of its political influence and economic status, and faced threats to its civil rights and culture. Yet in New Mexico Mexican Americans remained the numerically dominant group until the 1930s.

In the 1880s Anglo-American scholars, writers, and artists discovered New Mexico and began referring to the area as Spanish, largely ignoring the considerable Mexican heritage of the region. The development of this Anglo American appreciation for the Southwest's "Spanish" heritage helped lead to a New Mexican tendency to distinguish between things Spanish and things Mexican and to Hispanicize their heritage. After 1910, if not before, Spanish-speaking New Mexicans began referring to themselves as Spanish American or Hispano* in order to disassociate themselves from the term *Mexican*, which by that time was being used with pejorative connotation in American society.

Although Mexican Americans have suffered under Anglo American political and economic dominance, they still have managed to preserve a stronger economic and political position in New Mexico than have Mexican Americans in Arizona, California, Colorado, or Texas. The success of Nuevo Mexicanos in maintaining political power is illustrated by the large numbers of Spanish American judges, county commissioners, mayors, powerful members in the state legislature, heads of local, federal, and state public agencies, senators, and congressmen. For many years, Spanish Americans from New Mexico were the only Spanish-speaking representatives in the United States Congress.

However, with the end of World War II large numbers of Anglo Americans of mostly Texas, Oklahoma, and Kansas origins migrated to the state and today dominate the state politically and economically. In spite of this, New Mexico is the only area within the United States where a Spanish cultural tradition has continued unbroken since colonial times. As a result, feelings of inferiority and loss of cultural identity are far less severe here than among Mexican Americans elsewhere in the United States.

FURTHER READING: Warren A. Beck, *New Mexico: A History of Four Centuries*, Norman: University of Oklahoma Press, 1962; Francisco Domínguez, *The Missions of New Mexico, 1776*, Albuquerque: University of New Mexico Press, 1956; Richard N. Ellis, ed., *New Mexico Historic Documents*, Albuquerque: University of New Mexico Press, 1975.

NEW MEXICO STATEHOOD. *See* STATEHOOD, NEW MEXICO.

NEWSPAPERS. *See* PRESS.

NFLU. *See* NATIONAL FARM LABOR UNION.

NFWA. *See* UNITED FARM WORKERS; *also* GRAPE STRIKE, DELANO

NIÑA DE CABORA, LA. *See* URREA, TERESA.

LOS NIÑOS HÉRÖES (the heroic children), teen-age students of the Mexican military school on Chapultepec hill outside Mexico City who fought in the last battle of the United States-Mexican War.* According to popular history, some of the survivors of the battle, on facing defeat by the Americans, jumped from the heights to their deaths rather than surrender. Because of this defiant stand against the United States forces, Los Niños Héröes have become cultural heroes to some Chicanos, especially the more militant.

NORTHERN FRONTIER, the region of northern Mexico and the southwestern United States, sometimes known in Spanish colonial times as the frontera septentrional or in the late-eighteenth century as the Provincias Internas del Norte. Herbert Eugene Bolton used the term Spanish Borderlands in 1921, but meant only the northern Mexican states or the four states of what today constitutes the southwestern United States. Occasionally the northern frontier includes the Pacific Northwest, the Southeast, and the Mississippi Valley. It was this northernmost frontier of earlier Hispanic culture that the United States encountered in its westward movement.

Spanish expansion northward began in the decade following the conquest of Mexico by Hernán Cortés* in 1521. It continued over the next three centuries, reaching its apogee in 1790 with the establishment of the military post at Santa Cruz de Nutka (Nootka Sound) on Vancouver Island, and declining but not ending before Mexican independence in 1821. The term northern frontier of New Spain (colonial Mexico) may be applied to different regions at different times. By 1530 it was in the modern Mexican states of Sinaloa, Guanajuato, Zacatecas, Hidalgo, San Luis Potosí, and the Pánuco region of Veracruz. A half century later Nueva Vizcaya (primarily Durango), Nuevo León, and Coahuila were settled. By 1700 the frontier reached Sonora, Baja California, and even New Mexico with the founding of San Juan de los Caballeros on the upper Rio Grande. In the eighteenth century Spain reached its northernmost limits with the occupation by settlers of Tamaulipas (then known as Nuevo Santander), Chihuahua (part of Nueva Vizcaya), Alta California,* Pimería Alta (southern Arizona below the Gila River), Texas, Louisiana, and the Mississippi River Valley. With the abandonment of Nootka Sound in 1795, Spanish expansion declined, but the frontier experience continued until 1821. By then the earlier frontiers were integral parts of the Kingdom of New Spain.

Spain's frontier experience may be divided into two eras: exploration and settlement. The earlier age was usually of short duration and heroic figures: Cortés, Nuño de Guzmán, Francisco de Ibarra, Álvar Núñez Cabeza de Vaca,* Fray Marcos de Niza, Francisco Vásquez de Coronado,* Hernando de Soto, Sebastián Vizcaíno, and Juan Rodríguez Cabrillo. Motivated by searches for mythical kingdoms (Gran Quivira, El Dorado), advanced Amerind civilizations, and the rumored Strait of Anián connecting Atlantic and Pacific oceans, these expeditions were transitory ventures. While they familiarized Spain with the land and people of North America, with the exception of Ibarra in Durango and Guzmán at Culiacán they usually failed to plant permanent settlements on the northern frontier.

Actual colonization occurred after the age of exploration, sometimes immediately but often much later (half a century later in New Mexico, nearly two centuries later in Alta California). Diversified motives promoted this permanent occupation. Silver mining in Nueva Vizcaya (Durango and Chihuahua), Sonora, and San Luis Potosí led to the establishment of mining districts and agricultural and stock-raising enterprises to support them. Religion was also a factor. The proselytizing mission of Catholicism among the Amerinds was partially responsible for the occupation of Baja California, Sinaloa, Sonora, New Mexico, Alta California, Pimería Alta, Texas, and Coahuila. Economic advancement and improved social status constituted the principal motives for the majority of those who came to the frontier to stay—farmers, stock-raisers, landowners, artisans, day laborers, merchants, and shopkeepers. Large private land holdings (haciendas) were established in Coahuila and Nuevo León, but small individual plots prevailed in New Mexico, Texas, Tamaulipas, and Sonora. Since Spanish occupation threatened the Amerind population already present and came into conflict with foreigners, defense was important on the frontier. For half a century Spain struggled with the Chichimecas of Zacatecas, using peaceful persuasion and war to pacify the Gran Chichimeca country. Spain established military garrisons on farflung frontiers, many of which became centers of Spanish civilization to counter the resistance of tribal groups known collectively as indios bárbaros. Fear of the English promoted the settlement of San Agustín, Florida; defense against French efforts partly contributed to the establishment of Texas; and fear of Russian and English activity on the Pacific Coast brought the settlement of California at San Diego (1769) and Monterey (1770) and the exploration of the Northwest Coast as far as modern British Columbia and Alaska.

The Spanish frontier experience contributed greatly to the overall development of Spain's kingdoms in America and the formation of an Hispanic heritage in North America. Spain succeeded in adapting and planting permanent societal, cultural, economic, and political institutions in a huge geographical area from Cape Horn to California, Texas, New Mexico, and Florida. By the end of the colonial period some 473,000 Spanish-speaking people lived in the ten-state region of what then comprised the northern frontier. About 10 percent of them lived in what today is the southwestern United States. New Mexico alone had 36,579 people by 1817. Permanent settlements were founded at Durango, Chihuahua, Hermosillo, Monterrey, Saltillo, San Antonio, San Agustín, Pensacola, Santa Fe, Albuquerque, Tucson, San Francisco, San Diego, San Jose, Los Angeles, Monterey, and El Paso del Norte (modern Ciudad Juárez). Settlers introduced crops and farmed; raised cattle, sheep, mules, horses, goats, and swine; practiced Catholicism, established cofradías (lay brotherhoods), and developed special religious ceremonies, penitente rites for example; and intermarried with the pacified Amerinds; and preserved customs, food, dress, architecture, folk art, legends, superstitions, and music. Through presidios,* Francisan and Jesuit missions, civil communities, and rural landholding institutions, Spain established the nucleus of the Hispanic settlement tradition on the northern frontier and even a degree of administrative unity with the Comandancia General de las Provincias Internas del Norte in 1776. These contributions were passed on to the Mexican nation in 1821.

With little opposition all of the northern frontier provinces joined independent Mexico. For the next quarter of a century (1821-1846) they experienced settlement dispersal, religious neglect, internal dissension, irregular trade, inadequate military protection, intensified warfare with hostile tribes, personal scrambles for power (Manuel Armijo* in New Mexico, Pío Pico* and José Castro in California), and increasing penetration by foreigners (empresarios* and American settlers in Texas, the Santa Fe trade, and merchants in California). Instability and conflict prevailed, reflecting conditions throughout the new republic. Anglo Americans in Texas outnumbered Mexicans by three to one and differences of attitudes developed toward religion, Negro slavery, land ownership, trade, customs, and administration. This hostility resulted in the Texan Revolt* of 1835, the Lone Star Republic, and annexation to the United States a decade later. In California Commodore Thomas ap. Catesby Jones erroneously seized Monterey (1842) and four years later norteamericanos were prominent in the Bear Flag Revolt* against Mexico. Manifest Destiny* in the United States reached a climax in the war with Mexico (1846-1848), during which General Stephen Watts Kearny* occupied New Mexico and assisted naval forces in the conquest of California, while General Zachary Taylor* invaded Nuevo León and Coahuila. By the Treaty of Guadalupe Hidalgo* (1848), Mexico recognized the Rio Grande as her northern boundary and ceded New Mexico and California to the United States. Thus ended over three centuries of Spanish and Mexican experience on the northern frontier.

FURTHER READING: Herbert E. Bolton, *The Spanish Borderlands*, New Haven, Conn., 1921; Hubert H. Bancroft, *The Works of Hubert Howe Bancroft*, San Francisco: H. H. Bancroft Co., 1883-1890; especially vols. 15-16 on *The North Mexican States*, vol. 17 on *Arizona and New Mexico*, and vols. 18-24, *California*; John F. Bannon, *The Spanish Borderlands Frontier, 1513-1821*, New York: Holt, Rinehart and Winston 1970; Charles E. Chapman, *The Founding of Spanish California: The Northwestward Expansion of New Spain, 1687-1783*, New York: Macmillan Co., 1916; Philip W. Powell, *Soldiers, Indians, and Silver: The Northward Advance of New Spain, 1550-1600*, Berkeley: University of California Press, 1952; Oakah L. Jones, ed., *The Spanish Borderlands—a First Reader*, Los Angeles: L. L. Morrison, 1974; Oakah L. Jones, *Los Paisanos: Spanish Settlers on the Northern Frontier of New Spain*, Norman: University of Oklahoma Press, 1979. *O.L.J.*

NOSOTROS, a community self-help organization, founded in 1971 by barrio* people of Las Vegas, New Mexico. Based on the idea that the poor best know their own needs and can establish and operate programs to fulfill them effectively, Nosotros, with funds from various social service agencies, initiated an extensive program that included family counseling, various services for teens and the aged, criminal rehabilitation, and day care centers. The organization was terminated in 1974 when its funds were reduced, but some of the valuable programs initiated by Nosotros were continued.

Nosotros is also the name of a Hollywood organization of Mexican American actors founded in 1969 by Ricardo Montalban.* Although small in membership (two hundred), Nosotros makes its views on the hiring of Hispanic actors and on the portrayal of Chicanos on television and in films known widely through branch offices in Dallas, Chicago, and Miami.

NOVARRO, RAMÓN (1899-1968), actor. The son of a dentist, Ramón Novarro was born in the Mexican mining and transportation center of Durango, and was baptized Ramón Gil Samaniega (family name). Like many other Mexican families, his parents fled to the United States in 1913 to escape the perils of the Mexican Revolution* and settled in Los Angeles. Because the family was desperately poor and his father was ill, Ramón began working at an early age. Among his many jobs were small acting and dancing parts in films and plays. His work as a dancer came to the attention of Hollywood director Rex Ingraham, who hired him to play a leading part in the *Prisoner of Zenda* in 1923. Novarro was an instant success and was quickly starred in several successful films.

Novarro's career developed at a very inopportune time for him in that he came along just when Rudolph Valentino and John Gilbert had between themselves established a virtual monopoly as Latin male sex symbols. Nevertheless, Novarro continued to be a reasonably successful box office draw in films like *Ben Hur* (1926) and *The Student Prince* (1927). Valentino died suddenly and soon afterwards the lushly romantic films of the mid-twenties also died as depression seized the land. On top of these changes came the talkies. Novarro, who had a good singing voice, survived the change better than many other movie stars, and in 1932 he costarred in *Mata Hari* with Greta Garbo. He followed that with *The Son-Daughter* (1933) opposite Helen Hayes, and *The Cat and Fiddle* (1934), probably his best film.

After the mid-1930s Novarro made no more important films, but did some theater and concert work and occasionally did character roles in films and on television. He also spent a good deal of his time traveling, administering real estate investments in Mexico and the Los Angeles area, and painting and writing. In October 1968 Novarro was murdered in his Hollywood Hills home.

NUEVO MEXICANO, a New Mexican of Mexican-Spanish descent. The term often is used to refer to the inhabitants of the Spanish and later Mexican province of Nuevo México and is also used to apply to their descendants. In a broad sense it may also be used to refer to any New Mexicans of Spanish or Mexican descent even though they are not descended from ancestors living there before the American takeover in 1848.

O

OBLEDO, MARIO G. (1932-), politician. Born in San Antonio, Texas, into a family of twelve children, Obledo lost his father at age five. With his brothers and sisters he did odd jobs as a youth to help support the family. During the Korean War he served as a radarman in the U.S. Navy. In 1957 he completed a B.S. in Pharmacology at the University of Texas and then earned a Bachelor of Law degree and a Doctor of Law degree at St. Mary's University in San Antonio, working as a pharmacist while he studied law. Upon completing his legal studies, Obledo became Texas Assistant Attorney General in 1965 and later a law professor at Harvard University. In 1975 he was appointed head of California's Department of Health and Welfare.

OCHOA, ESTEBAN (1831-1888), merchant and civic leader. Ochoa was born in Chihuahua, Mexico, raised on the Nuevo México frontier, and educated and trained for business in Missouri. After the Treaty of Guadalupe Hidalgo* young Ochoa became a partner in a successful trading business. Just before the Civil War the partnership was dissolved and he moved to Tucson, making it the hub of his extensive freighting business.

During the Civil War Ochoa abandoned Tucson and his property rather than take an oath of allegiance to the Confederacy, but he was fortunate in recovering most of his goods when the Confederate forces withdrew. To take advantage of expanding Arizona mining activities, Ochoa organized Tully, Ochoa, and Company which, in the post-Civil War period, became the leading freight company in the Southwest. Ochoa's position made him a natural spokesman for the Raza* population of southern Arizona and he acted as an intermediary between it and Anglo society. In addition, he was elected to the territorial legislature and also mayor of Tucson. More than any other person, except possibly the governor, he was responsible for the establishment of a public school system in the Arizona Territory. In the 1880s his fortunes declined considerably as the railroads took over much of his earlier business. He died a relatively poor, but highly respected, man.

OEO. *See* OFFICE OF ECONOMIC OPPORTUNITY.

OFFICE OF ECONOMIC OPPORTUNITY (OEO), an agency created to direct programs established under the Economic Opportunity Act of 1964, a part of the war on poverty during the administration of President Lyndon B. Johnson. OEO is headed by a director who is appointed by the president with the advice and consent of the Senate. Programs administered by OEO include Job Corps, VISTA, and CAP. Job Corps essentially is a job-training program to help disadvantaged youths find employment. VISTA, Volunteers in Service to America, works with migrant laborers, on Indian reservations, in urban and rural community action programs, slum areas, hospitals, and schools. CAP, Community Action Programs, is the primary program of OEO. With federal funds, local groups (Community Action Agencies) combining the efforts of local government, business, labor, civic, and religious organizations, and of the poor themselves mobilize local resources to alleviate poverty.

OFFICE OF INTER-AMERICAN AFFAIRS, established July 30, 1941, as the Office of the Coordinator of Inter-American Affairs and later shortened by dropping "of Coordinator" from the name, it was headed during World War II by Nelson Rockefeller. In April 1942 a Spanish-Speaking Peoples Division was organized with Carey McWilliams* as operational officer. To reduce discrimination against Mexican Americans McWilliams set up conferences, workshops, and fellowships to help Mexican Americans participate more fully in the American way of life; however, his program was never fully implemented. In April 1946 the Office of Inter-American Affairs was terminated by President Harry Truman. Some functions were closed down and others, having to do with international relations, were transferred to the State Department.

OLD SPANISH TRAIL, a route linking New Mexico to California. To avoid the Grand Canyon the Old Spanish Trail ran northwest from Santa Fe, up the valley of the Chama River, across the southwest corner of Colorado and southeastern Utah, southward along the Colorado River, entering California at present-day Needles, and went on to Los Angeles via Cajon Pass. Pioneering of this trail began on the eve of Mexican independence. The first expedition to reach Los Angeles via this route was led by Antonio Armijo, a trader from Santa Fe, and arrived in 1830. In the 1830s and 1840s the Old Spanish Trail was an important southern pack train route into California but it came too late to link the two Spanish-speaking areas firmly and was little used after the Mexican War, except as a route for driving sheep and other stock.

OLIVÁREZ, GRACIELA (1928-), born near Phoenix, Arizona, and educated there, she got her first job in the radio industry. During the civil rights movement of the 1960s she met Father Theodore Hesburgh, president of the University of Notre Dame, who invited her to come to Notre Dame law school. Despite the gaps in her educational background, she entered law school and graduated in 1970.

Returning to the Southwest, Olivárez taught law, was active in the civil rights movement, and worked for local and state government agencies. In 1975 she was appointed Director of Planning for New Mexico. Two years later President Jimmy Carter named her director of the Community Services Administration in Washington, a position she held for three years. In 1978 she received a Juris Doctor degree from Notre Dame University Law School and in 1980 left the Community Services Administration to become senior consultant with the United Way of America, a national service organization.

OÑATE, JUAN DE (1549?-1624), founder of New Mexico.* From a wealthy and influential Spanish family long involved in the conquest and settlement of Zacatecas on the north Mexican frontier, Oñate was awarded a contract to lead a colonizing expedition into New Mexico in 1595. The assumption was that Oñate, whose family had made its fortune from mining, would exploit the silver mines reported by Antonio de Espejo in 1583, and in the process, Christianize the native population. Extensive privileges and exemptions were granted to colonists who were willing to settle in the area. After months of frustration Oñate finally set out in February 1598 with approximately four hundred soldiers and colonists, ten Franciscans, a number of slaves, over eighty wagons, and seven thousand head of stock.

The expedition marched through Chihuahua and crossed the Rio Grande at El Paso early in May. Near Mesilla Oñate selected sixty of his best men and pressed forward in advance of the main body of colonists, subduing various Indian pueblos and taking formal possession of the land as he went. On July 11 he came to a beautiful valley at the junction of the Chama and the Rio Grande rivers. Here Oñate decided to establish his headquarters, which he called San Juan de los Caballeros. Later, as a result of Indian hostilities, this capital was moved to San Gabriel and then to Santa Fe in 1609.

Almost from the beginning the colony was plagued by dissension due to scarcity of provisions and the bleak prospects for amelioration of conditions. In spite of rebellion among the Acoma Indians and protest from his own colonists, Oñate nevertheless laid the foundations for the colonization of New Mexico. When he resigned as governor in 1607, his colony was in shambles and might have been abandoned had not the Crown decided to maintain the area as a missionary province. Oñate's greatest achievement in these early years was the conversion of thousands of Pueblo Indians with the aid of the Franciscans. His greatest disappointment was his failure, shared with his predecessors and successors, to find great wealth for the Crown.

FURTHER READING: George P. Hammond, *Don Juan de Oñate, Colonizer of New Mexico, 1555-1628*, Albuquerque: University of New Mexico Press, 1953;

George P. Hammond and Agapito Rey, *The Rediscovery of New Mexico 1580-1584*, Albuquerque: University of New Mexico Press, 1966.

OPEN BORDER, immigration policy by which there is little or no restriction on Mexican workers who wish to cross the border to work in the United States, or on labor agents who wish to bring them in. The open border policy characterized the United States-Mexican border especially until the establishment of the Border Patrol* in 1924. Since then the term has also been used to describe the border policy views of southwestern agricultural labor employers and others who favored a maximum access to Mexican immigrant labor despite federal legislation to control border crossing.

"OPERATION WETBACK." In the years following World War II the flow of undocumented* Mexican workers northward into the United States became a torrent as the demands of southwestern agribusiness and of border factories for cheap labor increased rapidly. This burgeoning use of illegals rather than Mexican contract labor was sharply reversed in June 1954 by strict enforcement of immigration legislation and by a massive roundup and deportation of undocumented aliens. Attorney General Herbert Brownell, Jr., gave as his reason for this action the possible illegal entrance of subversives. Highly publicized in advance, "Operation Wetback," as it was called, was meant as much to encourage undocumented aliens to leave voluntarily as to deport them. In the year 1954 over one million illegal aliens were collected in a gigantic dragnet by the attorney general's special mobile force and returned to Mexico.

While Operation Wetback probably served to improve the economic lot of Mexican Americans, it also had dubious and negative social results. In the process some civil liberties and basic human rights of the undocumented and their families were ignored, and their physical treatment all too frequently was marked by rudeness and intimidation. Husbands and wives were separated, and children saw their fathers taken from them. The roundup did not stop the flood of undocumented Mexicans into the Southwest; after the end of the Bracero Program* in 1964 illegal entrances again began to rise.

ORD, ANGUSTIAS DE LA GUERRA (1815-1880), historian. Born into a Californio* presidial family, Angustias de la Guerra received a meager frontier education in Santa Barbara. At age fifteen she married Manuel Jimeno Casarín, who held various important government offices in the twilight of the Mexican period. As a result of her marriage, she lived for twenty-five years in Monterey at the center of Californio politics. Although her family opposed the American takeover in 1846, after her husband's death she married Dr. James L. Ord, a physician in United States Army. Two years before her death she dictated to Mr. Thomas Savage (for historian Hubert H. Bancroft) her recollections of events in California from her early childhood until the United States takeover. In addition to their use for Bancroft's histories, these have been published as *Occurrences in Hispanic California,* Washington, D.C.: Academy of American Franciscan History, 1956.

ORDEN DE HIJOS DE AMÉRICA. *See* ORDER OF SONS OF AMERICA.

ORDER OF SONS OF AMERICA, a middle-classs Mexican American organization founded in San Antonio, Texas in 1921. It marked the transition from earlier, mutualista-type societies to the politically oriented Chicano organizations that came after it. In 1929 it was incorporated into the League of United Latin American Citizens,* which its leaders helped found.

ORGANIZATIONS. There has been a wide variety of Mexican American organizations with an equally wide divergence of goals, which range all the way from economic to political and from retention of a Mexican way of life to complete assimilation into American society. While their goals were generally a synthesis of Mexican and Anglo American cultural traits rather than either extreme, they have appealed to La Raza* heavily in terms of ethnic symbolism (e.g. use of the Virgin of Guadalupe*). These groups generally have been characterized by leadership* that is limited and not infrequently personalist in nature (e.g. Reies López Tijerina*), and that for the most part represented the Mexican American middle class. Few efforts were made to recruit mass membership. Development of Mexican American organizations may be schematically described under four overlapping goal and chronology subdivisions: mutualist (1848-1920), assimilationist-citizenship (1920-1945), political pressure (1945-1970), and political party (1970-) organizations.

In the group of mutualist organizations were a large number of small, local groups like the Alianza Hispano-Americana founded at Tucson, Arizona, in the 1890s. In addition there were many others such as the Sociedad Española de Beneficencia Mutua, Sociedad Ignacio Zaragoza, Sociedad Benito Juárez, and the Fraternal Aid Union.

After serving in World War I many returning Mexican American veterans decided to organize civic clubs to teach other Mexican Americans about their political rights. In many cases these efforts were frustrated by the local Mexican American leader who often used his political power for his own personal benefit rather than to help La Raza. One result of such attitudes was some retardation of Mexican American political consciousness;

however, in some areas, especially in New Mexico, membership in veterans' organizations like the American Legion led to a degree of political strength. The most enduring of these equality-seeking, self-improvement, assimilationist groups developed in Texas. The Order of Sons of America* (1921), Knights of America, and League of Latin American Citizens eventually coalesced in 1929 into the League of United Latin American Citizens.* But there were other civic-oriented groups like the Good Citizens League of Houston (1945).

World War II was a powerful influence in awakening Chicanos to their rightful place in American politics and society. Educative wartime service plus the development of a new generation of urbanized and assimilated Mexican Americans made available a leadership with heightened skills and knowledge. Self-reliant and little disposed to accept continued discrimination, this leadership strongly emphasized active participation in politics, and therefore changed the goals of Mexican-American organizations. Beginning with the Community Service Organization* (1947) in California and the American G.I. Forum* (1947) in Texas, these groups became more strictly political pressure organizations with the establishment of the Mexican American Political Association* (1959) in California, the Political Association of Spanish-Speaking Organizations* (1960) in Texas, and the American Coordinating Council of Political Education* (1960s) in Arizona. Paralleling pressure groups was the development after the mid-sixties of a wide variety of student organizations which had both educational and political goals and which used pressure and confrontation as tactics in achieving objectives.

In 1970 a Chicano third party, La Raza Unida,* was formed in south central Texas, initiating the fourth stage of direct political participation. Foreshadowed by the short-lived Partido del Pueblo Unido* (1890) and the equally ephemeral People's Constitutionalist party* (1968), both in New Mexico, La Raza Unida aimed at winning local elections in areas of Mexican American majorities and influencing the final outcome of elections in area where Chicanos could provide a balance-of-power vote. This most recent development in Mexican American organizations has brought into clearer focus the relationship of the ethnic minority to the majority society and the manner in which that relationship can be molded and changed.

ORTIZ, RAMÓN (1813-1896), diplomat, priest. Born in Santa Fe, New Mexico, and trained in the Durango seminary, Ortiz was ordained in 1833 and sent to El Paso del Norte (Juárez). During the 1840s he worked for better United States-Mexican relations and helped the survivors of the Texan Santa Fe expedition* of 1842 as well as many American traders and officials. A member of the Mexican Chamber of Deputies, he was also appointed to superintend the removal of those Nuevo Mexicanos who wished to live in Mexico after the Treaty of Guadalupe Hidalgo.*

OTERO, MIGUEL A., SR. (1829-1882), outstanding Nuevo Mexicano* political and business figure. Born near Albuquerque and educated in New Mexico* and Missouri, Otero graduated from Pingree's College in New York and studied law in New York City and in Missouri where he was admitted to the bar. In 1852 he returned to New Mexico, opened up a law office, and was elected to the territorial legislature. Three years later he defeated José M. Gallegos* for the position of New Mexico territorial delegate to Congress, an office to which he was reelected in the following two elections.

Meanwhile Otero, a Democrat, married Mary Blackwood of South Carolina, who reinforced his rico* views of peonage and slavery. In 1859, as a result of his leadership, New Mexico legislated a slave code, and in the following year he supported Senator John H. Crittenden's compromise to avoid the Civil War by extending slavery in territories south of 36°30′, which embraced New Mexico. Otero also favored the idea of a separate confederation of western states but did not support the southern Confederacy. At this time Otero declined his nomination as Minister to Spain by President Lincoln in favor of appointment as Secretary of the Territory of New Mexico, which the Senate then failed to confirm.

During the Civil War* Otero devoted himself to merchandising and freighting, forming Otero, Sellar & Co. Later he was a pioneer in extending railroads to the territory, especially the New Mexico and Southern Pacific Railroad of which he was a founder. He also founded and was first president of the San Miguel National Bank and a director of the Maxwell Landgrant and Railroad Company and of the Atchison, Topeka, and Santa Fe Railroad. Two years before his death he ran for territorial delegate to the U.S. Congress but was defeated, and in 1881, due to poor health and a long quarrel with John Sellar, he liquidated Otero, Sellar & Co.

OTERO, MIGUEL A., JR. (1859-1944), governor, banker, businessman. The second son of Miguel A. Otero, Sr.,* young Otero was educated in St. Louis, at Annapolis, and at Notre Dame University. However, poor health and no great enthusiasm for formal education caused Miguel to obtain most of his education in the streets of frontier towns like Leavenworth, Kansas, and in the offices of Otero, Sellar & Co. His business experience as cashier and bookkeeper stood him in good stead when his father died and he took a leading role in the family business interests. In addition to being active in ranching, real estate, and mining, he naturally turned to politics, but as a Republican rather than a Democrat like his father.

From his late twenties onward Miguel was politically involved and held a series of appointive and elective positions in New Mexico until 1912. In 1894 he was named as a candidate for the Republican vice presidential nomination, but lost. Three years later, at age thirty-seven, he was appointed the youngest governor of the New Mexico Territory by President William McKinley. He was a vigorous leader and developed strong Nuevo Mexicano* support and an efficient political organization. During the Spanish-American War Otero raised four cavalry companies for the Rough Riders and was himself made an honorary member of that group after the war.

In his second term the statehood issue arose, and he strongly supported separate statehood for New Mexico and Arizona, calling a statehood convention in 1901. His opposition to President Theodore Roosevelt's National Forest policy caused much Republican resentment as his second term drew to an end, and Roosevelt decided not to reappoint him. Otero switched his allegiance to the Democratic party and stepped down from the governorship in January 1907.

After a European trip Otero returned to New Mexican political life, being appointed territorial treasurer in 1909. Republican defeat in the 1912 presidential election brought Woodrow Wilson to the White House and political preferment to Otero, who was appointed United States Marshal of the Panama Canal Zone in 1917. After a brief flirtation with the Progressive party he continued active in Democratic politics in the 1920s, leading Canal Zone delegations to the national convention in 1920 and 1924. During World War II he died at the age of eighty-four. He was the author of the autobiographical *My Life on the Frontier, 1864-1882,* New York: Press of the Pioneers, 1935, *My Life on the Frontier, 1882-1897,* Albuquerque: University of New Mexico Press, 1939, and *My Nine Years as Governor of the Territory of New Mexico, 1897-1906,* Albuquerque: University of New Mexico Press, 1940.

P

PACHECO, GOVERNOR ROMUALDO (1831-1899), twelfth and only Californio* governor of American California. Son of an aide to Mexican Governor Manuel Victoria (1830-1831), he was born at Santa Barbara and partially educated in Honolulu. As a young man he worked as a sailor in the California-Hawaii trade and then held various local and state offices in the 1850s. During the post-Civil War period he was active in Republican politics, becoming state treasurer from 1863 to 1867. In 1871 he was elected lieutenant governor. When Governor Newton Booth persuaded the California legislature to elect him to the United States Senate in 1875, Pacheco filled out the remaining nine months of Booth's governorship, thereby becoming the only Californio governor of the American period.

Pacheco failed to secure the Republican nomination to the governorship in the next election, but was elected to the U.S. House of Representatives (1876-1883). In December 1890 he was appointed envoy extraordinary to Central America, his last important office.

PACHUCO, a term of unclear origins applied in the 1940s and 1950s to Mexican American youths in the urban Southwest, especially in the Los Angeles area, who adopted a certain life-style that included zoot suits* as a kind of uniform, tatooing on the hand, membership in a palomillo (gang), and the self-referent "pachuco." Often these youth groups formed groups known as "pachuco gangs." George I. Sánchez,* the outstanding Nuevo Mexicano* sociologist, saw pachuquismo arising out of the economic exploitation of, and blatant racial and ethnic discrimination against, Mexican Americans. Pachucos saw themselves as defenders of their barrios,* their women, and their culture.

The term *pachuco* is also used to refer to a Spanish dialect originating in the El Paso area in the early twentieth century and consisting of a mixture of archaic Spanish, neologisms, and Anglicisms.

FURTHER READING: George I. Sánchez, "Pachucos in the Making," *Common Ground* 4, no. 1 (Autumn 1943): 13-20.

PACHUCO RIOTS. *See* ZOOT-SUIT RIOTS.

PADRES. *See* PADRES ASOCIADOS PARA DERECHOS RELIGIOSOS, EDUCATIVOS, Y SOCIALES.

PADRES ASOCIADOS PARA DERECHOS RELIGIOSOS, EDUCATIVOS, Y SOCIALES (PADRES), originally a local association of Chicano Catholic priests, founded in San Antonio, Texas, in 1968. During the following year PADRES was expanded nationally and in 1970 held its first national convention at Tucson, Arizona. PADRES argued for the need for Spanish-speaking leadership in the church as well as in government and business.

Now an association of about three hundred Spanish American Catholic priests, PADRES goals are the political, educational, and social development of Spanish-speaking people and especially the arousing of poor Mexican Americans to an awareness of their power to bring about social and economic change and to control their own futures. It concerns itself with the problems of farm workers, migrants, and the Mexican-United States border and with legislation to protect and aid farm workers and illegals. It publishes a newsletter and occasional socioeconomic documents developed by its members.

PADRINO, a godparent, chosen by the parents of a baby, to act in place of the parents if something should happen to them. The padrino also serves to help and advise the godchild. *See* COMPADRAZGO.

PALLARES, JESÚS. *See* LIGA OBRERA DE HABLA ESPAÑOLA.

PALOMILLA, derived from *paloma* (dove, pigeon), literally meaning a "flock of doves." In Mexican American communities the term *palomilla* is used to refer to an association of boys, a gang, or peer group.

PALOMINO, CARLOS (1950?-), boxing champion. Born in Sonora, Mexico, Palomino immigrated to Long Beach, California, with his family after a two-year wait in Tijuana. In school he excelled in mathematics and baseball and on weekends played semiprofessional baseball with a Mexican team. After high school he was drafted into the army where his boxing career began. By the time he left the army he had won the World Military Champion title, winning thirty-one of his thirty-four fights. Back in southern California, Palomino decided to turn professional in 1972 and after a string of thirty victories to a single loss, in June 1974 he won the World Welterweight championship. During this time he also completed a college degree in recreational education. Palomino has made numerous appearances at high schools and civic groups to encourage students to complete their education.

PARLIER, CALIFORNIA, a small town in central California where in 1972 for the first time in California history, Mexican American voters replaced an all-Anglo American city council with all-Mexican American members. According to the 1970 census, Parlier's population was 1,993: its Mexican barrio,* West Parlier, had a population of 1,954, 98 percent Mexican American. All available land was owned by non-Mexican Americans, and discrimination against Chicanos was strong and overt. As a result the Chicano population was restless long before the events of 1972.

Precipitating the Chicano political revolt in Parlier was the death of the police chief who had been in office for over twenty years. Next in line for the vacant position was a Chicano. Instead of naming this man to the office, the city council appointed an Anglo American from outside the community. Chicanos protested without results.

A program of politicization and mobilization was organized; boycotting intensified and petitions were initiated for recall elections, and voter registration and education drives began. By June 1972 all city council members had been replaced with Mexican Americans.

PARTIDO DEL PUEBLO UNIDO, EL. (United People's party), a group organized in 1890 by Mexican Americans in San Miguel County, New Mexico, as a result of their unhappiness with the two major political parties. Although the party, allied locally with the Caballeros de Labor* and with the Populist party at the national level, was successful in county offices in 1890 and again in 1892, it declined afterwards and was disbanded by the next election.

PARTIDO SYSTEM, a "sharecropping" system in New Mexico in which a landowner supplied a tenant with a breeding flock of sheep. The tenant agreed to return one lamb for each five ewes at the end of the year, to rent breeding rams from the owner, to sell his lambs and wool through the owner, and to return on demand a flock equivalent to the one supplied. By the partido system some tenants were able to acquire large flocks of their own, as Manuel Armijo* did. The partido system reached its peak at the end of the 1800s and dwindled away with reduced access to open range lands.

PASO. (PASSO) *See* POLITICAL ASSOCIATION OF SPANISH-SPEAKING ORGANIZATIONS.

PATERO, literally a person who cares for ducks. It is used to describe a boatman who ferries undocumented Mexicans across the Rio Grande. *See also* POLLERO.

PATRÓN, JUAN B. (1855-1884), political leader. Patrón was born in Lincoln, New Mexico, and educated in Santa Fe and at Notre Dame University in Indiana. In 1873 he took over his father's general store when the latter was killed at a dance by anti-Mexican Texas ruffians. Patrón also became the Lincoln schoolmaster. After time as a probate court clerk, in 1876 Patrón was elected to the territorial legislature and soon became a leader of local Nuevo Mexicanos.*

Both Patrón's official position and his community role brought him into conflict with the dominant Anglos. In the mid-seventies he was shot in the back while arresting Anglos involved in the killing of two Mexicans, and in 1878 he was an important figure in the (John S.) Chisum faction during the Lincoln County War.* Increasingly concerned for the safety of his family and himself, Patrón left Lincoln during the fall of 1878 and later went into business in Puerto de Luna, N.M., with his wife's uncle. Late one evening after work he was murdered by a stranger at the local saloon. His assailant was tried, but the jury could not reach a verdict and it was unclear whether his murder was a result of the feuding connected with the Lincoln County War or not.

PATRÓN-PEÓN SYSTEM, a relationship that was a very important part of the economic and social structure in the New Mexico-Colorado area from the latter days of Spanish-Mexican settlement until the end of the American Civil War.* The patrón was commonly either a powerful, large landowner or an important village leader; the peón was a worker who usually owed his patrón debts he was unable to pay. By law a debtor was obliged to work out his debt if he could not pay it. The rate of pay set by the patrón was usually quite low. Frequently the result was life-time servitude by the peón.

The patrón-peón system provided minimal economic security at the expense of economic and social freedom. In addition to economic advantages accruing to the patrón, there were benefits for the peón since the patrón was expected to protect, look after, and provide for the peón and his family. Some poor Nuevo Mexicanos* deliberately became peones in order to obtain this protection and help. The patrón-peón relationship was based on attitudes and values of Hispanic society and included unwritten understandings and agreements as to the reciprocal obligations of each person. The system's effects were softened somewhat by the fact that often the patrón and peón were related by blood and/or compadrazgo.*

Early in the American period the system gave the patrón a considerable amount of political power since he was able to direct the vote of his peones. The ability of Nuevo Mexicano leaders to retain political power far into the American period rested, in part, on the patrón's control of the peón vote. For example, during the entire territorial period the Territorial Council's makeup ranged from 25 to nearly 100 percent Nuevo Mexicano. On the economic side, since a majority of the leading Anglo politicians in New Mexico were southerners, they had little difficulty accepting the concept of peonage. After the Civil War, however, in March 1867, the United States Congress passed legislation ending all forms of servitude, and a month later Territorial governor Robert B. Mitchell issued a proclamation freeing all peones in New Mexican territory. That this act did not immediately end the system is indicated by the fact that in the next year General William Tecumseh Sherman ordered an army investigation of the lingering practice. Eventually the army enforced the statute.

FURTHER READING: Alvin R. Sunseri, *Seeds of Discord: New Mexico in the aftermath of the American Conquest, 1846-1861*, Chicago: Nelson Hall, 1979; Clark Knowlton, "Patrón-Peón Pattern Among the Spanish Americans of New Mexico," in Renato Rosaldo, et al., eds. *Chicano: The Evolution of a People*, Minneapolis: Winston Press, 1973, pp. 232-37.

PAZ, OCTAVIO (1914-) Mexican poet and essayist, born in Mexico City. Today Paz is considered one of Mexico's most prominent literary figures. In 1943 Paz studied Spanish-American poetry in the United States under the auspices of a Guggenheim Fellowship. He was awarded the International Grand Prize in poetry in 1963, and held the Charles Eliot Norton Chair of Poetry at Harvard from 1971 through 1972. The period of his greatest literary activity coincided with the assumption of several high government posts, including one as Mexico's representative to UNESCO and another as ambassador to India.

Besides being recognized as a leading poet, Paz has distinguished himself as an essayist. In 1950 he published *El laberinto de la soledad* in which he provides a complex analysis of the Mexican character. Taking as his point of departure the *pachuco*, he then goes back historically to trace the historical and psychological roots of the Mexican from the time of the conquest to the present. Paz's analysis reveals a Mexico in quest of a national identity. This sociological, poetic essay, widely read in the United States, became popular among Chicanos in the 1960s as they sought to articulate their own sense of identity by exploring their roots in history and culture. *El laberinto de la soledad* has been brought up to date with the publication of *Posdata* in 1970.

FURTHER READING: Octavio Paz, *El laberinto de la soledad,* México: Fondo de Cultura Económica, 1959. *F.J.*

PECAN SHELLERS' STRIKE (1938), a response to low wages in the pecan-processing industry. The Texas pecan industry, with its center in San Antonio, dated back to the late 1800s, when the gathering, cracking, and shelling of the nuts was first organized. The work was farmed out to contractors who employed many Mexican American families to crack and shell the pecans in their homes. Others assembled the workers in poorly lit and poorly ventilated factories to process the nuts. In the mid-1930s San Antonio pecan shellers were paid as little as two and three cents per pound for pecan shelling—plus all they cared to eat. The average sheller earned about two dollars a week. Even the wage provisions of the New Deal's National Recovery Administration of 1933 failed to help pecan workers, since the industry rejected an NRA code.

By 1937 these conditions had led to the organization of several unions representing perhaps ten to twelve thousand workers; among these the largest was the Texas Pecan Shelling Workers Union which became an affiliate of the CIO's radical United Cannery, Agricultural, Packing and Allied Workers of America.* The announcement of a 15 percent wage cut in January 1938 led to a spontaneous strike movement which left-wing organizers rapidly extended and dominated. Emma Tenayuca,* who became a Communist because she felt only the Communist party was doing anything to help Mexican Americans, was the firebrand of the women strikers. As the strike went on week after week, the struggle became extremely bitter, with the authorities treating it as a riot and a Communist revolutionary movement. Over one thousand of the six thousand strikers were arrested, and tear gas, raids, and vigilantism were widely used. Conservative groups like the League of United Latin American Citizens,* the local Mexican Chamber of Commerce, and both Catholic and Protestant clergy failed to support the radically led strike.

In March the strike was settled by arbitration which gave the strikers union recognition with only a 7.5 percent *decrease* in wages. This agreement was rendered obsolete in October by the Fair Labor Standards Act, which set a 25 cents per hour minimum wage. Under this new condition the plants mechanized as quickly as possible, and only about two thousand workers retained jobs in the pecan-shelling industry. The union declined and by the post-World War II period had collapsed.

FURTHER READING: Stuart Jamieson, *Labor Unionism in American Agriculture*, Washington, D.C.: U.S. Department of Labor, 1945, reprint, New York: Arno Press, 1976; Carlos Larralde, *Mexican American Movements and Leaders*, Los Alamitos, California: Hwong Publishing Co., 1976; Selden C. Menefee and Orin C. Cassmore, *The Pecan Shellers of San Antonio*, republished in *Mexican Labor in the United States*, New York: Arno Press, 1974.

PENITENTES, a common and sometimes pejorative name for the Brothers of Our Father Jesus Nazarite. The Penitentes are largely men of Hispanic descent who belong to this loosely organized lay religious society of the Roman Catholic church. Although much diminished today, the brotherhood, known in Spanish as La Fraternidad Piadosa de Nuestro Padre Jesús Nazareno (also La Hermandad or La Cofradía), claims a few thousand members, located mostly in northern New Mexico and southern Colorado.

Members and their auxiliaries participate in devotions, primarily rosary, way of the cross, and Tenebrae services, during Lent and Holy Week, provide mutual aid throughout the year, and act as a community worship resource and welfare agency (though much less so today)—organizing wakes and funerals and performing numerous charitable acts for needy neighbors. These social and ritual services substantially benefited isolated communities but were usually overlooked by outsiders who sensationally reported only the earlier public penitential processions of the group which involved self-flagellation, cross-bearing, and other types of self-mortification. Nevertheless, the Brothers' dual commitment to the passion of Jesus and to Christian charity played a crucial role in maintaining Hispanic villages and traditions both before and after Anglo American occupation in 1846.

Because of scant documentation, no single theory of the Brotherhood's origin in the late 1700s or early 1800s can be established. The first unequivocal reference to the organization is in a special condemnatory decree by Bishop Antonio Zubiria of Durango, Mexico, on July 21, 1833. Before and after his visitation, New Mexican settlers suffered from a chronic lack of clerical services—both from the Franciscans who were the first missionaries and from the secular priests who partially took over in the late eighteenth century. Consequently, colonists increasingly came to rely on such rituals as they could provide for themselves. Most of these forms are basically Franciscan, probably derived from the lay Third Order of St. Francis which had early been organized in the province. However, a case can also be made for the later influence of a Mexican penitential confraternity, likely one related to the Cofradía de Nuestro Padre Jesús Nazareno de Sevilla y Santa Cruz en

Jerusalém. Certain evidence further suggests that the controversial Taos priest, Antonio José Martínez* strongly influenced the early course of the brotherhood.

After 1850 New Mexico was placed under American Catholic jurisdiction, and the French priest Jean Baptiste Lamy* was sent to implement the changeover. During his administration and that of four subsequent French archbishops of Santa Fe, most notably his successor, Archbishop Jean Baptiste Salpointe,* brotherhood strength and secrecy increased significantly. Local chapters, called moradas, incorporated under territorial laws. Some organized as councils of moradas, and most acquired both legal and political expertise. Brotherhood independence and circumspection led to strained relations with the church, which culminated in several official denunciations during the 1890s. Protestant denominations, especially Presbyterians, also pressured the brothers, who, like all native Hispanos, suffered the encroachment of Anglo immigrants following completion of the railroads in the 1880s.

The effects of World War I, several droughts, and the 1930s Depression radically altered Hispanic village life. Fewer men became brothers, and moradas could not significantly ameliorate deteriorating social conditions. Outsiders more frequently disrupted Holy Week observances, and previously public rites had to be conducted covertly.

Local priests' attitudes toward parishioner brothers varied considerably throughout the territorial period and after statehood. It was not until January 1947 that a systematic organization of councils and chapters was officially reinstated by Archbishop Edwin V. Byrne. His proclamation marked the culmination of two decades' work by Don Miguel Archibeque, who became the first Hermano Supremo Arzobispal, and several others. Nor all moradas joined the archbishop's Supreme Council. Because of its overall adaptability and the individual variability and independence of local chapters, the Penitente movement has managed to survive. In turn, the Brothers have helped preserve the Spanish language and many Hispanic traditions in New Mexico and southern Colorado.

FURTHER READING: Marta Weigle, *Brothers of Light, Brothers of Blood: The Penitentes of the Southwest*, Albuquerque: University of New Mexico Press, 1976; Alexander M. Darley, *The Passionists of the Southwest: Or the Holy Brotherhood*, Glorieta, New Mexico: Rio Grande Press, 1968; Marta Weigle, *A Penitente Bibliography*, Albuquerque: University of New Mexico Press, 1976.

M.W.

PEÓN. *See* PATRÓN-PEÓN SYSTEM.

PEOPLE'S CONSTITUTIONAL PARTY (Partido Constitucional del Pueblo), a third-party Hispano American political organization formed during mid-1968 by leaders of the Alianza Federal de Pueblos Libres.* It selected Reies López Tijerina* as its candidate for the governorship of New Mexico at a founding convention in August at Albuquerque; however, in early October the New Mexico Secretary of State declared that eight of its candidates, including Tijerina, were disqualified. After a New Mexico Civil Liberties Union suit against the disqualifications, the state supreme court ordered that the names of all but Tijerina be replaced on the ballot. In the ensuing election PCP candidates received less than three thousand votes; but in several contests their vote was larger than the difference in votes between the Democratic and Republican candidates.

Quiescent between elections, in 1970 the PCP again developed a party platform stressing cultural self-determination and pledging support of goals for the poor and politically impotent. Although the party again ran a full slate of state officers, it failed to improve materially on its showing two years previously. In July 1971 the Partido Constitucional del Pueblo announced its end.

PEREGRINACIÓN A SACRAMENTO. *See* MARCH TO SACRAMENTO.

PERSHING EXPEDITION, an American military expedition into Mexico between March 1916 and February 1917, led by General John J. Pershing. As the result of border raiding and especially the March 9, 1916, attack by supporters of Francisco Villa* on Columbus, New Mexico, President Woodrow Wilson ordered American forces to pursue the attackers, presumably headed by Villa. Pershing led about six thousand troops on a difficult chase across the barren and dry mountainous region of northern Mexico despite the objections of the Mexican government under Venustiano Carranza. Although feelings were enflamed by clashes between Pershing's forces and Mexican federal troops as well as Villistas, war between the United States and Mexico was avoided, and talks between the two nations were initiated in September. After over four months of discussion, the Pershing expedition was finally withdrawn on February 5, 1917.

PICO, PÍO DE JESÚS (1801-1894), politician, and both fifth and last Mexican governor of California. Born at Mission San Gabriel into a typical Californio* family, Pico became an influential businessman in Los Angeles while still in his early twenties. In 1828 he was elected to the territorial legislature, thereby initiating a controversial career as a southern Californio political leader. He was governor briefly for the first time during January and February 1832, and he subsequently became a civilian administrator of Mission San Luis Rey. In March 1845, following the ouster of Mexican governor Manuel Micheltorena, he again assumed the governorship with headquarters in Los Angeles, but compromised with northern leaders by appointing José Castro as military commander with headquarters at Monterey.

During this period he made many controversial grants and sold mission lands, even after the U.S. invasion.

As governor when the Americans invaded California, Pico organized resistance, but as the situation became hopeless, he announced that fact and fled south into Baja California and then Sonora. After the Treaty of Guadalupe Hidalgo,* Pico returned to California and settled down to the routine of a southern ranchero. In order to defend his land titles in court, he mortgaged his property, but eventually lost all his landholdings.

Under the new American government Pío Pico continued to be active politically in the Los Angeles area, being elected city councilman and county tax assessor. During the Civil War* he was staunchly Unionist and in the postwar period built and operated a large hotel, Pico House. He died penniless at age 93, having lost his last piece of land a few years before.

PICO, SOLOMÓN, California bandit who was active in the Santa Barbara region from the late 1840s to the middle of the following decade. Allegedly turning to a life of crime because he had been cheated out of his land, he specialized in assaulting Anglo gold miners and cattlemen. Because of support from local Californios,* he was seldom apprehended. By the mid-fifties his bandit activities ceased, and his subsequent history is not known.

PIKE, ZEBULON M. (1779-1813), American explorer and army officer. Pike was an able and courageous leader with considerable ambition to achieve fame. In 1805 he was sent by his superior, General James Wilkinson to explore the upper Mississippi River, seeking its headwaters and surveying its mineral, animal, and human resources. In mid-1806, shortly after his return from the foregoing survey, Pike was again sent by Wilkinson on an exploratory expedition—this time west rather than north. Traveling through Missouri, Nebraska, and western Kansas he crossed over into Spanish territory (Colorado) in the late fall. Early the following year, after crossing the Sangre de Cristo Mountains, he reached the upper Rio Grande where his force was taken prisoner by Spanish soldiers and brought to Santa Fe for interrogation. The men were then taken to the regional capital, Chihuahua, for more questioning and finally returned to American soil at Natchitoches, Louisiana, in July 1807. During the War of 1812 Pike, now promoted to a general, was killed by a powder magazine explosion. There has been some suspicion that Pike's activities in the 1806-1807 expedition might have some connection with the intrigues of Aaron Burr or General Wilkinson to form an independent state in the Southwest, but there is no proof of this.

FURTHER READING: W. Eugene Hollon, *The Lost Pathfinder*, Norman: University of Oklahoma Press, 1949.

PLACER, Spanish for sand bank. This was the most common form of gold mining in the mid-nineteenth century. The gold was free, mixed with sand and gravel in a river bed (or former river bed), and was separated from the sand and gravel by washing the mixture in a shallow pan (a batea in Spanish) so that the heavier gold remained behind. This technique of panning gold was introduced into the California gold fields by Sonora miners.

PLAN DE SAN DIEGO (1915), a program for an uprising by Mexican Americans along the Mexican border and the creation of a republic, with possible eventual union with Mexico. The Plan was found in the possession of a person of Mexican descent arrested in January 1915, at the height of the Mexican Revolution* and border unrest and raidings. It called for a general uprising on February 20, 1915, under the leadership of a Supreme Revolutionary Congress of San Diego, Texas, and mandated the killing of all Anglos over sixteen, except the elderly. The Plan caused considerable alarm among Anglos along the Texas border, and in the ensuing months of 1915 a number of raids and some rioting were allegedly connected with it, but the evidence is inconclusive. It led to some Anglo vigilante action against Mexicans and increased military and border patrols. By autumn the scare had passed.

FURTHER READING: Juan Gómez-Q(uiñones) "Plan de San Diego Reviewed," in *Chicano: The Evolution of a People*, Rosaldo Renato, et al. eds., Minneapolis: Winston Press, 1973, pp. 123-27; Charles H. Harris, "The Plan of San Diego and the Mexican-United States War Crisis of 1916: A Reexamination," *Hispanic American Historical Review* 58 (August, 1978).

EL PLAN DE SANTA BÁRBARA (1969), a plan that describes the philosophy, organization, and function of the Movimiento Estudiantil Chicano de Aztlán.* Since the initiation of this plan, moderate success has been attained for Chicanos* at a number of institutions of higher learning.

According to the plan's philosophy, the university is important to the Chicano movement because it generates and distributes knowledge, which is power. Thus, institutions of higher learning should contribute to the liberation of the Chicano community by producing knowledge applicable to the Chicano movement. Under this plan, Chicanos were charged with developing strategies and tactics for the purpose of realigning the Chicano community's structural relationship to Anglo American society.

FURTHER READING: *El Plan de Santa Bárbara,* Santa Bárbara: La Causa Publications, 1969.

PLAN DEL BARRIO (1968), a program issued by Rodolfo "Corky" Gonzales* in Washington, D.C. during the 1968 Poor People's March. It called for greater cultural nationalism, for better education, and especially for education in the Spanish language, for better housing to fill Mexican American needs, for land reforms, particularly return of pueblo lands wrongfully taken from Mexican Americans, and for the development of more Chicano-owned businesses in the barrio.*

PLAN ESPIRITUAL DE AZTLÁN (1969), announced by Rodolfo "Corky" Gonzales* at the first annual Youth Liberation Conference* held in Denver, Colorado, on March 31, 1969. Gonzales called for Chicanos to work together and organize a new political party based on Chicano nationalism.

PLUNKETT, JIM (1947-), football player. Plunkett was born and raised in San Jose, California, of German-Irish and Mexican ancestry. In high school he was an above average student and an outstanding all-around athlcte. He received a football scholarship from Stanford University when he graduated in 1966. For three years he played on the Stanford team, studied political science, and spent his spare time giving career and life counseling to Chicano youths, both in groups and individually.

In 1970 Jim Plunkett won the Heisman trophy, awarded to the best college football player in the United States. After completing his college studies he began playing professional football, being drafted by the Boston (now New England) Patriots. In 1976 he was traded to the San Francisco 49ers and thus returned to California.

PLURALISM, a theory which states that political, social, and cultural systems may be composed of a number of autonomous, possibly opposing, and independent units. Each of these systems is held to be equally valid and may constitute a significant part of the social order.

Chicanos have criticized the inadequacy of the pluralistic model especially in the political and social realms in the United States. Generally Chicanos have argued that for them real pluralism does not exist in American society. For example, in the political area they have held that politicians are not concerned with the Chicano community because they do not perceive Chicanos as a legitimate political force.

POCHO, literally short, small; pejorative term used especially by Mexicans for Chicanos and also to describe their nonstandard language. It is pejoratively applied to Mexican Americans who do not speak Spanish, or if they do, mix it with English and who have adopted Anglo American customs and dress. Originally, when Mexico lost one-half of her territory to the United States in 1848, the inhabitants and progeny were "cut short" of being all-Mexican. Subsequently, these people were referred to as pochos or pochitos.

Linguistic variations of Pocho are multiple and complex, both philologically and syntactically. Characterized by code switching* Spanish and

English, and also by Hispanicizing English words or Anglicizing Spanish words, Pocho serves to identify Chicanos from Anglo Americans, and especially other Spanish-speaking groups.

POLITICAL ASSOCIATION OF SPANISH-SPEAKING ORGANIZATIONS (PASO/PASSO). The success of the Viva Kennedy clubs* in the 1960 election led Texas Mexican Americans, especially Dr. Hector P. García,* to transform these ad hoc organizations into permanent ones initially called Mexican Americans for Political Action (Texas MAPA), but quickly changed to Political Association of Spanish-speaking Organizations in order to appeal to a broader spectrum of American groups. The purpose of the organization was to act as an umbrella for all Texas groups of Spanish-American cultural orientation. In its constitution PASO called on all persons to unite in seeking political means for solving economic and social problems of Spanish-speaking persons. The leaders of PASO, most with experience in The League of United Latin American Citizens* and American G.I. Forum,* moved to become a decisive force in Texas politics. However, the 1962 Texas primary elections showed that PASO had little effect on the balloting, and in the general elections many PASO leaders squabbled among themselves.

After the elections PASO moved to reunite and regroup its membership, seeking an occasion to demonstrate its political power. This occasion came in Crystal City,* Texas, early in the following year. Here, with help from the local Teamsters union, PASO was successful in electing Chicanos to all five city council positions. However, the chaotic rule of Los Cinco,* lacking political know-how and harassed by Anglo economic pressures, served further to discredit PASO. In the middle and late 1960s PASO worked with black organizations in San Antonio and Houston to elect minority candidates, but its importance as a Chicano organization declined. At the same time, efforts to expand PASO membership to other parts of the Southwest, especially Arizona, met with little success, and it failed to become the umbrella organization envisioned by its founders. Reduced largely to Texas membership, PASO eventually lost many of its members to the rising tide of La Raza Unida,* which proved to be a far more attractive organization to Chicanos.

FURTHER READING: Robert Cuellar, *A Social and Political History of the Mexican American Population of Texas, 1929-1963*, San Francisco: R & E Research Associates, 1974.

POLITICAL PARTIES. In the United States political history clearly shows that, with limited exceptions, traditional political parties have systematically ignored Mexican Americans or excluded them from roles of any importance in party hierarchy, initially perhaps partly because of Chicano* rural dispersal.

Not only have Chicanos lacked a share in the direction of party apparatus and in the development of party platforms, but their political clout has often been softened by gerrymandering* of political districts. Historically the result of this has been to reduce Chicano interest in the political process (since they saw little chance of influencing it) and also to bring about a very low level of participation in electoral contests.

After World War II and the development of a new generation of Chicano leaders, there was an outburst of politically oriented organizational development. Earlier Mexican Americans had limited themselves to developing self-help and assimilationist groups; but now political pressure groups like the G.I. Forum,* Community Service Organization,* Mexican American Political Association,* Political Association of Spanish-Speaking Organizations,* and the Alianza Federal de Pueblos Libres* emerged. These organizations, while generally separating themselves from existing political parties, used their political power to influence the outcome of the electoral process.

Mexican American political organizing was relatively limited until the founding of La Raza Unida* party. In 1890 Nuevo Mexicanos organized El Partido del Pueblo Unido* in conjunction with the national third party Populist movement. It endured for only two elections. Much more recently the Alianza Federal de Pueblos Libres* formed the People's Constitutional Party* during 1968 and ran candidates in New Mexico in that year and in 1970. In the following year it was disbanded. Begun originally as a Texas political party in early 1970, La Raza Unida, after local successes in Crystal City, Cotulla, and Carrizo Springs, quickly spread to Colorado and California. In the presidential election year of 1972 it held its first national convention at El Paso and ran a slate of candidates. Since that first bloom of enthusiasm, La Raza Unida has taken a somewhat more limited view of its possibilities, seeing itself as able to win elections only in local areas where Chicanos are in a majority, but also as able to provide a swing vote between the two major parties in many electoral contests. *See also* POLITICS.

POLITICS, MEXICAN AMERICAN, all the activities by Americans of Mexican ancestry which are attempts to influence public authorities and public policies and/or redistribute political power in America. Chicanos* are a relatively disadvantaged and powerless group in the United States and therefore have had a difficult time in securing the socioeconomic and political perquisites which are available in the American system to many other groups.

Yet, from the time that the United States took over the northernmost part of Mexico and the Treaty of Guadalupe Hidalgo* was signed in 1848,

Chicanos have been engaged in political struggles to protect, secure, and advance their interests. Some Chicanos continued to struggle against the American forces even after that military conquest of the mid-nineteenth century. In many cases, Chicano rights protected in the Treaty of Guadalupe Hidalgo were not honored by American governors. In some areas such as Texas, Chicanos were brutally suppressed at times. Because political officials would not enforce the laws designed to protect Chicanos, several organizations arose to protest this treatment. Protest organizations such as Las Gorras Blancas* of the 1890s and protest leaders such as Tiburcio Vásquez* and Juan Cortina* continued to challenge physically the political domination of the Anglo conquerors. This period of adjustment between the United States and Mexican American communities was marked by suspicion, hostility, and physical violence on both sides. Therefore the dominant motif of Chicano politics was one of alienation and withdrawal. This style was not one of choice; it was simply a reflection of the Chicanos' relatively powerless position.

By World War I many Mexican Americans had accepted their status as disadvantaged United States citizens. A small minority had begun to improve their economic and social position and also to adapt themselves to the political style of the nation. However, their attempts at accommodation usually did not meet with acceptance from the American power structure. During this era several organizations were formed which engaged in political activities even though they usually did not consider themselves explicitly political. The first of these organizations was the Orden Hijos de América* (The Order of Sons of America). This group was founded in San Antonio, Texas, in 1921 primarily by middle-class Mexican Americans. In 1929 several Chicano groups, including the OSA, met in Corpus Christi, Texas, and formed a new organization, the League of United Latin American Citizens* (LULAC). LULAC was formed to present a united front to the Anglo-American community. The group emphasized its members' adaptation to the American system and engaged in political activities within a pragmatic accommodationist context. The first quarter of the century also saw a great many struggles by Chicano-based mine, railroad, and agricultural workers' unions.

The post-World War II period marked an important watershed in the history of Chicano politics. Chicanos had participated in the war effort and moved into urban areas of the country. These experiences, plus continued discriminatory treatment by the core culture, spurred the Mexican American community to new political organizations and new strategies. For example, in California the Community Service Organization* (CSO) mobilized the community around issues such as health, housing, employment, and police-community relations. For these purposes it mounted intense voter registration and political education projects. In Texas the American G.I. Forum* was organized, which, as well as serving the community or providing the necessities of life and legal assistance, also engaged in openly political activities such as protesting injustices perpetrated against Chicanos and organizing and carrying out voter registration drives and get-out-the-vote campaigns. In 1958 Mexican Americans in Texas formed the Political Association of Spanish-Speaking Organizations* (PASO). In California, the Mexican American Political Association* (MAPA) was born. Both of these organizations were formed to function as nonpartisan pressure groups to articulate Mexican American demands to the political parties and to help Mexican Americans attain elective and appointive offices. Both groups enjoyed considerable success during the 1950s and 1960s in helping elect Mexican Americans to office and in influencing the internal affairs of both major parties. By the 1960s many Chicanos were no longer willing to accept the system on its own terms. Attempts at engaging in accommodation politics had advanced the cause of the Chicano people disproportionately little compared to the effort that had been expended. Chicanos were still grossly underrepresented among political decision-makers, and public policies enacted in behalf of the Chicano people were few and far between.

Dissatisfaction with the slow pace of progress, and awareness of the political successes of other ethnic groups such as the Afro-American, turned the thrust of Chicano political activities towards a new direction. The Chicano Movement* was the result. Several events in the mid-1960s marked the initiation of the movement. The efforts and organization by César Chávez* and the farm workers and the resultant strike of 1965 were factors leading to an expanded political consciousness by Chicanos. On campuses across the Southwest Chicano students became increasingly politically aware, formed organizations, and engaged in various kinds of political activities. Activists organizations such as the United Mexican American Students* (UMAS), the Movimiento Estudiantil de Chicanos de Aztlán* (MECHA), and the Mexican American Youth Organization* (MAYO) brought pressures to bear on decision makers both on and off campus. In New Mexico, the Alianza Federal de Pueblos Libres* led by Reies López Tijerina* increased its demands for a return of Mexican and Spanish land grants to the people of the area. The 1966 raid on the courthouse in Tierra Amarilla* nationally publicized the needs and demands of the Chicanos in this area. In south Texas José Angel Gutiérrez,* MAYO, and the Raza Unida party* became very active in the politics of several towns. In 1967 these efforts were rewarded by Chicanos being elected to the school board and the city council of Crystal City, Texas. In the Colorado area the Denver-based Crusade for Justice* led by Corky Gonzales* aroused the spirit of Chicano nationalism by calling for an independent Chicano nation of

Aztlán. In the barrios* of California Chicano students and others engaged in school walkouts and protests. Similar blowouts also occurred in other parts of the Southwest, demonstrating to educational authorities the dissatisfaction of Chicanos with the inferior education available to them.

The Chicano Movement* of the late 1960s and early 1970s was best known for its dramatic and radical political tactics. These activities provided a relatively powerless group with political resources that it otherwise lacked. The movement had some favorable effects, as several programs were initiated which benefited Chicanos. Various relief and welfare programs for barrio and rural Chicanos were enacted; and some educational reforms, including increased bilingual-bicultural education,* also were initiated. Various job-training programs and educational scholarships were instituted. An increasing number of Chicanos were appointed to positions of authority or hired by major institutions. In California legislation was passed which gave farm workers the same rights as other laborers. While these dramatic political activities did advance the cause of the Chicano people, they also raised the political consciousness of Mexican Americans throughout the country and enhanced the effectiveness of more conventional political efforts by Chicanos.

In the late 1960s and early 1970s Chicanos advanced economically, educationally, and politically. An increasing number of Chicanos were elected to public office. Chicano representation in state legislatures and city councils of the Southwest had been almost nonexistent before the 1960s. Chicanos also were found increasingly in administrative positions, on school boards, and in other governmental agencies. Two Mexican American governors were elected in 1974 as Jerry Apodaca* became governor of New Mexico and Raul Castro* became governor of the state of Arizona. In some of the smaller towns in Texas and California, Chicanos became a majority on city councils and school boards. By 1979 the major metropolis of San Antonio had a proportionate number of Mexican Americans on the city council and El Paso had a Chicano mayor. In April 1981 Henry Cisneros was elected mayor of San Antonio.

These results were at least partially the effect of increased participation in systemic politics. Several voter registration and education projects, the passage of the Voting Rights Act of 1965, plus the heightened political consciousness of the Chicano movement resulted in significant increases in Chicano voter registration in the 1960s and 1970s. Many other institutional barriers to voting such as the literacy test, residency requirements, and poll taxes were abolished. Consequently in the late 1970s Chicano voter registration rates approximated those of non-Chicanos. However, voter turnout rates among Chicanos continued to lag substantially (15 to 10 percent less) behind those of non-Chicanos. When Chicanos have turned out, they have continued to support the Democratic party. Over the years, for example, support for Democratic congressional candidates has remained fairly constant at about an 80 percent rate. Chicanos have complained that the Democratic party takes their vote for granted and has not rewarded Chicano people commensurate to their party support. The Republican party has flirted with Chicano voters, hoping to build its status from a minor party by recruiting dissatisfied Chicano Democratic supporters. However, the GOP has not been able to make significant inroads into Chicano support primarily because it has not offered the kinds of meaningful policy alternatives that are needed to attract Chicano voters.

One significant institutional product of the Chicano movement was the establishment of the various La Raza Unida* parties. Their greatest electoral successes have been in small towns with majority Chicano populations such as Crystal City,* Texas and Parlier,* California. However, they have also played a significant role in pressuring the two major parties to make concessions to Chicanos. In addition, state La Raza Unida parties have served an important political educative function as they have continually publicized the needs and wants of the Chicano people and have called attention to the lack of responsiveness by major political organizations in the United States.

In the late 1970s Chicano politics began to take new forms. Pressure organizations such as LULAC, G.I. Forum,* and student groups continued to attempt to exert influence on major policy-making institutions. The various Raza Unida parties in the Southwest continued to serve as coalition organizations which could present a united front for Chicano political demands. Efforts at national Chicano organization also continued as attempts were made to form national political coalitions either within the Democratic party or outside its ranks. The most radical and dramatic manifestation of Chicano politics had subsided by the late 1970s. However, the newly aroused political consciousness of the Chicano people guaranteed that Chicanos would continue their efforts to secure a fair share of collective power and influence.

FURTHER READING: Rodolfo Acuña, *Occupied America: the Chicano's Struggle Toward Liberation*, San Francisco: Canfield Press, 1972; F. Chris García and Rudolph O. de la Garza, *The Chicano Political Experience*, North Scituate, Mass.: Duxbury Press, 1977; F. Chris García, ed., *La Causa Política: A Chicano Politics Reader*, Notre Dame, Indiana: University of Notre Dame Press, 1974; Ralph C. Guzmán, *The Political Socialization of the Mexican American People*, New York: Arno Press, 1976; Richard Santillán, *La Raza Unida*, Los Angeles: Tlaquilo Publications, 1973; John Staples Shockley, *Chicano Revolt in a Texas Town*, Notre Dame, Indiana: University of Notre Dame Press, 1974; Maurilio Vigil, *Chicano Politics*, Washington, D.C.: University Press of America, 1977. *F.C.G.*

POLLERO, literally a chicken-tender. The term is used to describe a person who guides undocumented Mexicans across the border. *See also* PATERO.

POLLOS, literally chickens. This term is used along the United States-Mexican border to describe Mexicans without documents who hope to cross into the United States. They are taken care of, or "hooked" by polleros* on the Mexican side, entrepreneurs who specialize in guiding the uninitiated across the border through a maze of paths and thickets.

POOR PEOPLE'S CAMPAIGN (1968), a march on Washington, D.C., during May and June 1968, organized by Ralph Abernathy and Martin Luther King. Before his death King had named Reies López Tijerina* to head a delegation from the Southwest. Possibly because of King's death and Abernathy's less commanding personality, Tijerina, as the head of a Chicano* contingent, proved to be an independent and aggressive leader in the campaign. He fostered meetings to reduce ethnic friction between blacks, Chicanos, and Indians, but also accused the black leadership of neglecting Mexican American participants and threatened to withdraw unless amends were made. Tijerina took advantage of the opportunity to stage a confrontation with the State Department over the Treaty of Guadalupe Hidalgo* and attempted to involve the Mexican embassy in his land claims under that treaty. Rodolfo "Corky" Gonzales* also took part in the Poor People's march and used the occasion to issue his Plan del Barrio* from Washington, D.C.

POPÉ REVOLT, (1680), a serious uprising of New Mexican Pueblo Indians under the leadership of one of their medicine men, Popé, against the Spanish-Mexican settlers and missionaries. As a result of a unified, sustained campaign by the Indians, all settlers and missionaries were forced to retreat southward along the Rio Grande to El Paso (today Ciudad Juárez, Mexico). Not until the mid-1690s were the Spanish able to reconquer and resettle New Mexico.

POPULATION. During the Spanish and Mexican eras the Mexican population of what is today the Southwest grew slowly. The first settlements took place in New Mexico beginning at the end of the 1500s, but the settlers were completely expelled in 1680 by the Pueblo Indians. After the reconquest of New Mexico in the early 1690s, Spanish control was painstakingly reestablished. Continued incursions by nomadic Navajos, Apaches, and Comanches during the rest of the colonial period delayed population growth. By the end of the colonial era, at the beginning of the nineteenth century, there were perhaps ten thousand Europeanized people in what is today New Mexico, Arizona, and southern Colorado.

Spanish-Mexican settlement in Texas began almost exactly a century after it did in New Mexico with the establishment of two missions on the Neches River. Here too population growth was slow because of hostile Indian tribes, including the Comanches, and at the end of Spanish control there were approximately thirty-five hundred Tejanos* in the vast area. The first Mexican settlers did not arrive in Alta California until 1769, nearly a century after Texas, and population growth was only slightly more rapid. By the time Mexico threw off Spanish control, there were no more than twelve hundred gente de razón* in California.

During the brief Mexican period (1821-1848) a relatively more rapid population growth took place in the Southwest. When the United States took over the former Mexican territory, there were between seventy-five and eighty thousand Spanish-speaking inhabitants: some sixty thousand in New Mexico, eight thousand in California, five thousand in Texas, and two thousand in Arizona and Colorado. During the next half century immigration from Mexico, while relatively small, was actually fairly heavy in relation to the sparse population in the Southwest border area. The census of 1900 showed about 103,000 persons of Mexican birth in the United States, about 95 percent of whom were in the Southwest: Arizona, 14,171, California, 8,086; Colorado, 274; New Mexico, 6,649; and Texas, 71,062. In addition, 3,168 lived outside the Southwest. Adding estimates for American-born of Mexican descent gives the following totals: Arizona, 29,000; California, 33,000; Colorado, 15,000; New Mexico, 122,000; and Texas, 131,000.

The 1910 Revolution in Mexico* was the most important factor in the heavy emigration northward during the first three decades of the twentieth century. From 1900 to 1930 probably well over a million Mexicans came to the United States, and the 1930 census, taken on the basis of Mexican origin, showed these Mexican American totals: Arizona, 114,173; California, 368,013; Colorado, 57,676; New Mexico, 59,340; Texas, 683,681; other, 226,612, with a grand total of 1,509,495. Most authorities would add to this another one-half million because of undercount. The decade of the 1930s saw little immigration, but during World War II and after it picked up with results indicated in the 1970 census. Based on Spanish as the home language, it showed: Arizona, 333,349; California, 3,101,589; Colorado, 286,467; New Mexico, 407,268; Texas, 2,059,671, giving a total of 6,188,344 for the Southwest. Possibly as many as a million of these are of other-than-Mexican origin; however, it is necessary to add about six hundred thousand for persons of Mexican descent living outside the Southwest, giving a rough grand total of five million eight hundred thousand. Most authorities would add another two to three million for undercount, undocumented, and perennial transborder migrants. Statistics on the Mexican American population are not precise; authorities disagree widely on some numbers. *See also* Appendix tables: TOTAL U.S. AND SPANISH ORIGIN POPULATION BY AGE BRACKETS: MARCH 1976 and TOTAL AND SPANISH ORIGIN POPULATION FOR THE FIVE SOUTHWESTERN STATES BY AGE BRACKETS: 1976.

FURTHER READING: Arthur Corwin, "¿Quién Sabe? Mexican Migration Statistics," in Arthur Corwin, ed. *Immigrants—and Immigrants: Perspectives on*

Mexican Labor Migration to the United States, Westport, Conn.: Greenwood Press, 1978.

POVERTY, CULTURE OF, a life-style attributed to those living in poverty. It is often used to describe both Mexican and Chicano* cultures. People living within a culture of poverty adopt one or more of the following characteristics: the extended family affects their entire lives and interactions; they are nonjoiners in voluntary associations; they are tied to tradition and observe traditional male and female roles; they express little interest in activities considered cultural; they do not support schools or school activities; they are present oriented, and extremely fatalistic in their view of the world.

POVERTY PROGRAMS. *See* OFFICE OF ECONOMIC OPPORTUNITY.

PRESIDENT'S COMMISSION ON MIGRATORY LABOR, a presidential commission, first created in June 1950 by Harry S. Truman. The commission held twelve regional public hearings and filed a report in 1951 recommending, among other things, that legislation be passed to make employment of undocumented workers unlawful, contracting of braceros* more orderly, and efforts to use the domestic labor force more effective. Bishop Robert Lucey* of San Antonio was a commission member.

PROTOCOL OF QUERÉTARO. *See* QUERÉTARO, PROTOCOL OF.

PUBLIC LAW 45 (1943), congressional legislation of April 29, 1943, which financed and regulated the World War II Bracero Program,* the international agreement reached in July of the previous year by the United States and Mexican governments. To some extent P.L. 45 was designed to bypass wage and working condition agreements of the 1942 United States-Mexican accord. As the bill was discussed in Congress, its provisions were shaped to express the views of large-scale agricultural interests in the West, especially in regard to their desire for an open border* policy. Under provisions of P. L. 45, the Commissioner of Immigration was authorized to issue one-year permit cards to Mexican workers, a violation, in spirit at least, of the July, 1942 international agreement. Early in May 1943 he used this power. The Mexican government protested the violation of the 1942 agreement, and the issuing of cards were discontinued after some two thousand braceros had crossed into the United States.

PUBLIC LAW 78 (1951), congressional legislation introduced by Senator Allen Ellender of Louisiana and Representative William R. Poage of Texas and passed July 12, 1951, to implement the importation of bracero* laborers from Mexico. Sometimes it is referred to as the Migratory Labor Agreement of 1951. It was based on the alleged need for manpower during the Korean War as well as the persistent demands of southwestern agriculture and had strong support in Congress from employer organizations. P.L. 78 authorized the Secretary of Labor to certify a need for workers, to recruit farm labor in Mexico, to arrange transportation and processing, to help negotiate contracts with employers, and to guarantee employer compliance with contracts. It also provided for the contracting of undocumented workers with five years or more United States residence. Employers were to reimburse the government for transportation and had to agree to minimum conditions of work, pay, and housing.

Despite continuing criticism from labor organizations, social workers, church groups, and Mexican American organizations, P. L. 78 was regularly renewed, with minor modifications, until 1964 when it was finally allowed to lapse by Congress because of mounting pressures. Although progrower in orientation, P.L. 78 was criticized by employers who complained of red tape, excessive safeguards, and contracts that were overly favorable to the Mexican braceros. Clearly they would have preferred an open border.*

PUEBLO, a Spanish word meaning village or town. It was used to designate an agricultural center on Mexico's northern frontier. Eventually settlements around many presidios, missions,* and mining centers became pueblos.

The term was also applied by the Spaniards to the settlements of sedentary Indians of New Mexico and Arizona who lived in terraced, apartment-like structures. These agricultural, basket and pottery-making Indians also became known as Pueblo Indians or Pueblos.

Q

QUERÉTARO, PROTOCOL OF (May 26, 1848), an explanatory note to the Treaty of Guadalupe Hidalgo* written in the Mexican town of Querétaro, capital of the State of Querétaro, where the Mexican government was located during the United States occupation of Mexico City. Nathan Clifford and Ambrose H. Sevier, the two American commissioners entrusted with the task of obtaining Mexican ratification of the Guadalupe Hidalgo Treaty as amended by the Senate of the United States, were instructed to explain to Mexican officials why the Senate had made the changes in the treaty. After the Mexican Chamber of Deputies and Senate had approved the treaty (with the amendments) on May 19 and 25, Clifford was presented to the president of Mexico and subsequently discussed the amendments with the minister of foreign affairs and other officials. At the suggestion of the minister, Luis de la Rosa, the substance of their exposition was put into the form of a protocol. The exchange of treaty ratifications then took place on May 30. Neither the United States nor the Mexican government ever ratified the protocol, and it therefore imposed no obligation on either government. Within a year the question arose whether the protocol modified the treaty. The United States position was that it was merely explanatory and did not modify or change any provision of the treaty. *See* Appendix C, TREATY OF GUADALUPE HIDALGO and the PROTOCOL OF QUERÉTARO.

QUINN, ANTHONY (1916-), actor, writer, painter. Born in the middle of the Mexican Revolution of a Mexican mother and an Irish-Mexican father, Anthony Quinn joined the revolution-inspired exodus to the United States at a young age. The Quinn family stopped temporarily at El Paso, but in 1920 moved on to Los Angeles where his father, Francisco, worked in a movie studio. When his father was killed in an accident five years later, Anthony began working at odd jobs to help support the family.

His mother's remarriage when he was fourteen relieved Quinn of further family responsibility just as the Great Depression hit. During those difficult years he worked at a wide variety of jobs including boxer, custodian, electrician's helper, ditch digger, and migrant farm laborer. Acting had always interested Quinn, and for a while he worked in the Federal Theater Project. After an operation on his tongue to correct a speech defect, he also acted in local theater groups and was picked to play the lead in a Los Angeles production of *Clean Beds*.

In 1936 Quinn heard Cecil B. DeMille was looking for actors to play some important Indian roles in his new film, *The Plainsman*. He convinced DeMille he was a Cheyenne Indian and got the part, which rocketed him to stardom. For the next ten years he was in constant demand; most of the parts casting him as an Indian, a swarthy villain, or a Valentino-type. During this time Quinn continued to improve his acting by working with local theater groups and in summer stock. His initial Broadway debut was a disaster, but he later starred as Stanley Kowalski in *A Streetcar Named Desire* for two years.

In the 1950s Quinn divided his time between Hollywood and Italy, making *Viva Zapata!*, *The River's Edge*, *La Strada*, and *Attila the Hun*. Following these films he did his best work in *Lawrence of Arabia*, *Shoes of the Fisherman*, *Requiem for a Heavyweight*, *Lust for Life*, and *Zorba the Greek*. Twice Quinn has won an Oscar for his work, first for *Viva Zapata!* in 1952, and again in 1956 for *Lust for Life*.

Anthony Quinn has always been proud of his Mexican cultural heritage. In the 1940s he raised funds for the Sleepy Lagoon* Defense Committee and in recent years has strongly supported the United Farm Workers.* In addition to his success on the American stage and in films, Quinn has found time to paint, write, sculpt, and produce films. He has a personal library of over five thousand volumes and owns a valuable collection of modern paintings.

FURTHER READING: Anthony Quinn, *The Original Sin: A Self-Portrait*, Boston: Little, Brown, 1972.

QUINTO SOL PUBLICATIONS, an organization founded by a group of Mexican American writers (Octavio Ramano-V* and Herminio Ríos) at Berkeley, California, in the fall of 1967. Quinto Sol provided a forum for self-definition and expression on issues of relevance to Mexican Americans. Its most important contribution to the Chicano* movement was perhaps its publication of *El Grito,** the outstanding Chicano literary and cultural journal. In 1974 Quinto Sol went out of business. The name originates in Aztec mythology, referring to people of the Fifth Sun, destined to perish as a result of a major world disaster.

QUIVIRA, also **GRAN QUIVIRA,** a legendary, wealthy Indian settlement sought by Francisco Coronado* during his 1540-1542 exploration of the Southwest. Led by an Indian informant, Coronado looked for it in the Kansas-Nebraska area, only to be disappointed when he found a simple Indian village. Myths such as that of Quivira encouraged widespread exploration of the Southwest in the sixteenth century.

R

RACISM, attitudes and actions that adversely discriminate against those deemed racially alien in a given society. A racist society allows social policies, procedures, decisions, habits, and acts to subordinate one race or group of people, and permits another race or group to maintain control over them. Racism may be expressed by individual acts or by institutional practice.

Racism has caused Mexican Americans historically to be denied positions of control and leadership in schools, businesses, unions, and other associations. More important, it has excluded them from legal and political institutions in American society.

RAILROAD INDUSTRY. Circa 1900 United States railway companies began recruiting Mexican workers at El Paso, Texas, and sending them northward on six month contracts. The Southern Pacific Railroad and the Atchison, Topeka, and Santa Fe were particularly active along the border and by 1906 these companies were bringing two to three carloads of Mexican track workers into California weekly. By the end of 1908 about sixteen thousand Mexican railway workers were employed in California, New Mexico, Texas, Arizona, Colorado, Wyoming, Montana, Oregon, and Washington. Railroad recruitment of Mexican workers reached its peak between 1910 and 1912, and in the latter year a Department of Labor investigator reported that most Mexicans and Mexican Americans he encountered had worked for the railroads at one time or another.

In the early summer of 1917, shortly after the United States entered World War I, railroad as well as agricultural employers began pressuring the government to permit recruitment of Mexican nationals, warning that troop and supply movements might otherwise be endangered by lack of track maintenance. As a result a series of waivers was made that allowed the railroads to bring in Mexican workers. Some of these railroad workers went as far north and east as Chicago and Pittsburgh. The waivers allowing railroads to bring in Mexicans ended in December 1918.

Late in 1941, even before Pearl Harbor, the Southern Pacific Railroad had requested permission from the Immigration and Nationalization Service to again bring in Mexican workers. Because of considerable union opposition, the application was temporarily withdrawn but then reactivated the following May with the assertion that nearly one thousand workers were needed. No action was taken on the request, and retired railroad workers were recruited to fill the jobs. However, a year later recruitment of railway workers began in Mexico as a part of the Bracero Program.* During the World War II years a total of 80,273 Mexican nationals were employed on 32 American railroads; more than half worked for the Southern Pacific and the Santa Fe. In August 1945 recruitment ended despite railroad requests for renewals and extensions. The railroads then delayed repatriation of the workers for months. Finally, after complaints from the Mexican Secretary of Labor and the American Federation of Labor, the railroad braceros were repatriated—the last by April 1946.

RAMÍREZ, FRANCISCO. *See CLAMOR PÚBLICO, EL.*

RAMÍREZ, HENRY M. (1929-), educator, politician. Henry M. Ramírez was appointed in 1971 to be chairman of President Nixon's Cabinet Committee on Opportunities for Spanish-Speaking People.* Born in Walnut Creek, California, to migratory farm worker parents, Ramírez graduated from St. John's High School, and later received his B.A. degree from St. John's College in 1952, and his Ph.D. from Loyola University.

Dr. Ramírez was summoned to Washington, D.C. in 1968 to become director of the Mexican American Studies Division for the U.S. Commission on Civil Rights. Then, as Nixon began to be concerned about securing more Mexican American votes in the 1972 elections, Ramírez was chosen to fill the vacant position of chairman of the Cabinet Committee on Opportunities for Spanish-Speaking People. His appointment was followed by the appointment of several other Mexican Americans to high-level positions.

The Cabinet Committee on Opportunities for Spanish-Speaking People has been disbanded, and Dr. Ramírez is no longer a member of the president's staff.

RAMONA (1884). Helen Hunt Jackson's highly romantic novel emphasizing Anglo land grabbing and mistreatment of Indians and Mexican Americans. The success of *Ramona* at a time when Anglo Americans were ignoring the condition of contemporary Indians and Mexican Americans led to the creation of a romantic Southwest inhabited by "beautiful people" who were all noble, handsome, and Spanish and ate Spanish rather than Mexican or Indian foods. In contrast it placed Mexicans and Mexican Americans in an inferior position. *See also* FANTASY HERITAGE.

RANCHO, stock-farm, small farm, ranch; the basic landed property of the north Mexican frontier, officially limited to a legal maximum (often exceeded) of eleven leagues square (48,400 acres). The rancho, used primarily for raising cattle in California and sheep in New Mexico, tended to be larger in California than in New Mexico. In both areas larger rancho grants were given out during the Mexican era (1821-1846) than earlier in the Spanish colonial period.

Associated with rancho is the term ranchería, which refers to an area usually located on the perimeters of a hacienda. Ranchería refers to the common dwelling area for peasants, Indians, or peones.

RANGERS, special state police forces in many western states often created for a specific task and for a limited time period. Two outstanding examples of such ranger forces are the band authorized by the California state legislature and recruited in 1853 by Captain Harry Love for the pursuit of the five Joaquins and the permanently organized Texas Rangers.*

RAZA, LA, literally the race; however, the term is used in a cultural, rather than a biological sense and has the meaning of folk or brotherhood. La Raza in its widest use includes all peoples of the Americas with some Spanish cultural roots, as in Día de la Raza (Columbus Day). In the Southwest it oftentimes has a more limited meaning, applying to all people of Mexican descent. Its widespread and sometimes strident use there by militants since the late 1960s as a term of racial superiority inevitably has carried some political connotations. Today it is widely used in a spirit of cultural pride.

RAZA, LA, a Los Angeles news magazine begun in 1970 which focuses its attention on problems of the East Los Angeles barrio.* Political in orientation, it carries information on various Chicano* organizations, especially the Brown Berets.* Although it emphasizes local concerns, it has covered a wide variety of national and international news topics, not all directly related to the Chicano. *La Raza* also publishes an occasional piece of creative literature.

RAZA NATIONAL BAR ASSOCIATION, LA, founded in 1972, an association whose membership is composed of judges, lawyers, and law students who have two principal goals: to advance Mexican American civil rights and to promote legal careers among Chicanos.* The organization also is concerned with raising the levels of competence among Spanish-speaking attorneys. Privately funded, it publishes a quarterly newsletter, *La Raza News*, at its Torrence, California, headquarters.

RAZA UNIDA CONFERENCE (1966), a counterconference organized by Chicano* activists in El Paso to protest the Johnson administration's refusal to acknowledge Mexican American demands for a greater voice in government programs affecting them. *See also* ALBUQUERQUE WALKOUT.

RAZA UNIDA PARTY, LA. At various times Hispanics in the United States have formed their own political parties. The Partido Liberal Mexicano of Ricardo Flores Magón* operated in the Southwest and was headquartered for a time in St. Louis, Missouri, during the Mexican Revolution* of 1910. Puerto Ricans have their Socialist party today. Some three hundred Chicanos met in Crystal City, Texas, on January 17, 1970, at Campestre Hall and formed the Raza Unida Party. By 1972 the RUP had organizing activities, active chapters, and registered state affiliates in seventeen states and the District of Columbia. At its first national convention in El Paso, Texas, held during the 1972 Labor Day weekend, delegates elected José Angel Gutiérrez* first national president of RUP and established a national executive committee, El Congreso de Aztlán, comprised of three delegates from each state.

The RUP has filed candidates for election in numerous states since 1970. The Texas RUP, however, remains the most successful at getting its candidates elected to office. In 1970, although the party was denied access by the state courts to the ballot, it elected its first officeholder, County Commissioner Roel Rodríguez in La Salle County in November by an organized write-in campaign. Previously, in April 1970, in three municipal and school district at-large and nonpartisan elections which were held in Crystal City, Carrizo Springs, and Cotulla, Texas, sixteen RUP candidates won in fifteen contests. Minority representation was obtained in two cities, and majority control was gained of both the school board and city council in Crystal City. On April 3, 1971, the RUP candidates won control of the city council in San Juan, located deep in southern Texas. A month later Colorado formed a RUP and filed statewide candidates. Boosted by these initial successes, candidates filed in 1972 under the RUP banner in Los Angeles, Tucson, New Mexico, Colorado, Chicago, and Texas.

The Texas RUP gubernatorial candidate, Ramsey Muñiz, polled nearly 250,000 votes for 6 percent of the total vote in 1972. His vote total caused the first election of a governor by less than a majority vote. Again in 1978 the RUP gubernatorial candidate, Mario Compeán, polled just under 2 percent of the total vote and caused the election of the first Republican governor in Texas in over 104 years. In a 1972 congressional race in Chicago the RUP candidate, Angel Moreno, lost to the Democratic nominee but out-polled the Republican challenger. Statewide races by RUP candidates in Colorado and New Mexico have not met with significant success, but various candidates to local office have succeeded. For example, Sal Carpio, a delegate to the El Paso RUP convention, is now a city councilman in Denver; Alfredo Gutiérrez, a partisan in the early 1970s, ran as a Democrat and presently is a state senator in Arizona and is also the senate majority leader. Similarily, Irma Mireles of Texas won election to a six-year term on the San Antonio River Authority in 1976; Ciro Rodríguez was elected to the Harlandale Independent School District in San Antonio, Texas, as was Pablo Escamilla elected to the Edgewood Independent School District (ISD) in the same city in 1975. Frank Shaffer-Corona, the representative of the Raza Unida Party in the District of Columbia, was elected to the board of education of the District in 1977. In the November 7, 1978, elections in Zavala County, Texas, the RUP slate of twelve candidates won all twelve races.

The name, La Raza Unida, means "the United People" and had been used previously by Juan Nepomuceno Cortina* in 1848. La Raza Unida was also used by the Mexican American Youth Organization* of Texas in the late 1960s and was the name used for the rump conference held in El Paso as a protest to the White House Conference on Spanish-Speaking Affairs of 1966.

La Raza Unida Party of 1970 was formed to organize the masses of unregistered Mexicano voters into an independent political bloc that could elect candidates to office in areas where Chicanos could be a voting majority. Chicanos could also act as the balance of power between candidates of the major parties in areas where they were less than the majority, and could raise issues of concern for the Hispanic community across the country.

The record of the Raza Unida over the last ten years is mixed. In areas of Mexicano voting majorities, the party has enjoyed success. In nonmajority areas the party candidates have lost but have forced the Democratic party to file Mexican American candidates who have been successful. La Raza Unida has been instrumental in focusing the attention of the American public on critical issues of our time. For example, the party accepted an invitation to tour Cuba in 1975. Upon its return the nineteen-person delegation urged the cessation of the blockade against Cuba, the normalization of relations with the island, and reunification of Cuban families. Excellent relations have been developed with the government of Mexico since 1972.

In October 1977 in San Antonio, Texas, the Raza Unida Party, together with other political organizations and groups, held a conference in opposition to President Carter's immigration plan. The Carter plan was prevented from becoming law. More recently, in March 1979, Raza Unida Party delegates were among those invited to celebrate the fiftieth anniversary of Mexico's Partido Revolucionario Institucional (PRI).

La Raza Unida continues to be a force influencing the politics of Chicanos and the United States.

FURTHER READING: José Angel Gutiérrez, *El politico: The Mexican-American Elected Official*, El Paso, Texas: Mictla Publications, Inc., 1972; José Angel Gutiérrez, *La Raza and Revolution*, San Francisco: R & E Research Associates, 1972; Miguel Pendas and Harry Ring, *Toward Chicano Power: Building La Raza Unida Party*, New York: Pathfinder Press, 1974; Raza Unida Party, *Raza Unida Party Rules*, [n.p., 197-?]; Richard Santillán, *Chicano Politics: La Raza Unida*, Los Angeles: Tlaquilo Pubs., 1973; John S. Shockley, *Chicano Revolt in a Texas Town*, Notre Dame: University of Notre Dame Press, 1974; Irma I. Ulloa, *Awakening of a Sleeping Giant: La Raza Unida Party in Perspective*, Thesis, Tempe: Arizona State University, 1974.

J.A.G.

RECLAMATION ACT OF 1902, also called the Newlands Act after Senator Francis Newlands, a Nevada conservationist and politician who sponsored it. It was a landmark law in western agricultural development, which, for the first time, placed the federal government in the business of building dams and accessory irrigation construction. It led to a rapid expansion of agriculture in the semiarid lands of the Southwest. *See also* AGRICULTURE, SOUTHWESTERN.

RECONQUISTA, NEW MEXICO (1681-1696). Having been driven completely out of the province of New Mexico in 1680 by the successful Popé revolt* of the Pueblo Indians, the Spanish-Mexican settlers began the attempt at reconquest late in the following year under the leadership of Governor Antonio de Otermín. This first effort was soon abandoned when the Indians refused to submit peacefully, and the force returned to its base at El Paso del Norte.

The second attempt at a reconquest was not undertaken until 1688, and like its predecessor it proved to lack the manpower needed to subdue the Indians. However, in that same year Diego de Vargas was appointed as the new governor and captain general with the specific goal of recovering New Mexico. Not until 1692 was he able to assemble a force large enough for the task at hand, and for the following four years the struggle of reconquest went on. Finally at the end of 1696 Vargas was able to write to the viceroy in Mexico City that the repossession of New Mexico had been virtually completed.

REGENERACIÓN, a Chicano* magazine founded in 1970 in Los Angeles, originally emphasizing issues and events affecting La Raza.* In the following year *Regeneración* modified its objectives to emphasize recurring basic political themes the editors felt earmarked the Chicano movement, and in 1972 it expanded its format to include articles of a more literary nature. The name of the magazine was taken from the journal of the same name published by Ricardo Flores Magón* at the beginning of the twentieth century.

REGIONAL ORIGINS OF MEXICAN IMMIGRATION. In 1980 there were approximately eight to ten million persons of Mexican descent or of Mexican birth residing in the United States. Of these perhaps one and one-half million can trace their ancestry to the one hundred thousand or so Hispanic peoples who were living in Mexico's northernmost regions prior to the acquisition of this area by the United States after the Mexican War of 1846* and the Gadsden Purchase* of 1853. The remainder are descendents of Mexican immigrants or immigrants themselves.

Most of the Mexicans who have immigrated, crossed into the United States after 1910 from regions north of Mexico City in the Central Plateau and northeastern and northwestern Mexico. The reasons for massive emigration from Mexico during this century are varied, but an instrumental cause was the building of a railroad network in the United States Southwest and into central Mexico. Railroads made possible a radical transformation of an economy on both sides of the border heretofore based largely on pastoral pursuits, artisanry, and local trade. As the new economy, characterized by large-scale exportation of mining and agricultural products by railroad, expanded, larger labor forces were required and the logical source was Mexico. Mexican workers were induced to move northward by the very forces of change wrought by the railroads. As finished goods from centralized manufacturing centers in both Mexico and the United States penetrated the countryside, much of the traditional rural economy based on limited money exchange was destroyed, and workers became more and more dependent on wages for survival. In order to obtain currency, former peasants, artisans, and hacienda peons* migrated to the Mexico City area, Veracruz, to the north, and increasingly into the United States to work in textile mills, railroads, commercial agriculture, mines, and foundries.

This very process of economic change also determined a discernable regional origin-destination pattern for Mexican immigrants. One reason for this is that immigration increased steadily as railroad building penetrated deeper and deeper into Mexico. Between 1880 and 1900 railroad lines connected El Paso and Laredo to Mexico City, and Nogales to Jalisco. The first immigrants, owing to railroad penetration, came from the Mexican north and settled in the U.S. border regions of California, Arizona, New Mexico, and Texas. As railroad tracks were laid farther and farther south, immigrants from Durango, San Luis Potosí, Zacatecas, and Sinaloa came to the United States, sometimes leap-frogging the border communities where earlier immigrants had saturated labor markets and established cultural hegemony in the barrios,* and settling in Dallas, Houston, Kansas City, or Los Angeles, where by the turn of the century the need for Mexican labor was becoming more apparent.

The Revolution of 1910 created even more causes for emigration; and, as a result of deteriorating economic conditions and violence, between 1910 and 1930 hundreds of thousands of Mexicans abandoned west central Mexico at a time when traditional sources of labor for industrial America were drying up in Europe. Consequently these workers, unlike earlier Mexican immigrants,* went to midwestern industrial centers. Ironically, the farther from the border that immigrants originated in Mexico, the farther north in the United States their destinations became. Thus Chicago and Detroit's Mexican colonias* were inhabited primarily by natives of Jalisco, Guanajuato, and Michoacán, while Mexican immigrants in Tucson were in the vast majority from Sonora and in Corpus Christi Mexicans from Tamaulipas and Nuevo León dominated the barrios.

This pattern has changed somewhat in recent years as advanced transportation technology has made it possible for immigrants from all of Mexico to come to the United States and also because now, 1981, most of Mexico's workers are wage dependent at a time when the U.S. economy cannot keep pace with a growing population. Still, recent studies by Gilberto Cárdenas, Wayne Cornelius, and others indicate that the regional origin-destination pattern established in earlier decades remains basically the same, primarily because of the informal network of information established by earlier arrivals.

FURTHER READING: Wayne A. Cornelius, "Mexican Migration to the United States: The View from Rural Sending Communities," *Migration and Development Study Group*, Cambridge, Mass.: Center for International Studies, Massachusetts Institute of Technology, 1977; Arthur F. Corwin, ed., *Immigrants—and Immigrants: Perspectives on Mexican Labor Migration to the United States*, Westport, Conn.: Greenwood Press, 1978.
F.A.R.

RELIGION. Most Mexican Americans consider themselves Catholics.

Mexican American perception of the church* and their role in it has been conditioned by the fact that many immigrants from Mexico were largely untutored in the Catholic faith and practiced a folk religion and had only limited loyalties to the institutional church. Many did not follow usually accepted church practices and made no effort to seek out the church upon settling in the Southwest. The Catholic church (and Protestant religious groups too) perceived Mexican immigrants as uninstructed in religion and therefore appropriate candidates for missionary activity. In this missionizing work the church in the Southwest was severely hindered by frontier conditions and lack of funds and missionaries.

As a result of historical background, large numbers of Mexican Americans today who call themselves Catholic conform minimally to the accepted norms of the church. As a group their Sunday mass attendance is appreciably lower than the national average for Catholics, and there is a particularly low level of attendance by males. Mexican Americans show a lower level of church marriages and of acceptance of Catholic teaching on birth control, and are less likely than most Catholics to send their children to parochial schools. For many, being Catholic is largely cultural rather than religious. One result is that relatively few Mexican Americans have converted to Protestantism; the majority of those who have, have seen membership in a Protestant church as one means of becoming accepted by the majority society and as a way to upward social mobility.

REPATRIATION, 1800s. When the United States took over the region acquired from Mexico by the Treaty of Guadalupe Hidalgo* and the Gadsden Purchase,* the Mexican government made an effort to help its citizens living in this area to move southward into Mexican territory. In 1848 a decree was issued sending Mexican commissioners to California, New Mexico, and Texas; however, one went only to New Mexico. Father Ramón Ortiz,* who arrived in April 1849, traveled around New Mexico offering land in Mexico and equipment for agriculture to those who would repatriate. He was accused by the territorial governor of inciting unrest and was required to return to Santa Fe to carry out his mission from there. The Mexican government protested this action as an effort to discourage repatriation.

Again in 1855 Mexico offered land in Sonora to Mexicans in California who were willing to return, and in the late 1870s there was still some encouragement of repatriation. In all, somewhere between one and two thousand (out of a total of about seventy-five thousand Mexicans are estimated to have repatriated, and even some of them later returned to the American Southwest.

REPATRIATION, 1930s. With the onset of the Great Depression, there began a large-scale return to Mexico of Mexicans in the United States. Of an estimated three million Mexicans in the United States in 1930, almost a half million left the country in the decade between 1929 and 1939. They left under a variety of circumstances. The chief cause for the decision to return to Mexico was the loss of jobs and the difficulties of obtaining new employment in a period of prolonged economic depression. Coupled with the lack of employment was the reluctance of local welfare agencies to provide assistance over a lengthy period of time. Many of the Mexicans who became involved in repatriation had lived in the United States for a number of years, and families included children who were American-born citizens. Nevertheless, Mexicans and Mexican Americans alike were pressured to repatriate themselves to Mexico.

Repatriation occurred in several phases. In the first year of the Depression, from late 1929 to the end of 1930, Mexicans largely repatriated themselves. They gathered up their possessions, including items acquired in the United States such as radios and furniture, loaded everything into trucks or automobiles, and left for Mexico. They departed mainly from the Southwestern states, especially California* and Texas,* but also from such areas as the Great Lakes region and scattered enclaves in the East. The pathways of migration led to such key border crossings as El Paso/Ciudad Juárez and Nogales, Arizona/Sonora. In the fifteen months following the collapse of the stock market and increasing unemployment, as many as eighty-five thousand Mexicans left the United States for various points in Mexico, usually the town or village of origin.

In about 1931 a climate extremely hostile toward Mexicans and other nationals began to develop in the United States. A key motivation for this attitude on the federal level was the belief, stated by the secretary of labor, that removal of illegal aliens from the United States would help end the Depression by freeing jobs for American citizens. The federal government supported this belief by carrying out antialien drives across the country. The effort was particularly felt in southern California, where the Spanish-speaking population was subjected to harassment and detention by federal and local authorities. Relatively few illegal aliens were actually apprehended in the deportation drive, but the climate of fear it created helped drive thousands of Mexicans from the region. As many as seventy-five thousand Mexicans may have left southern California by 1932 because of the deportation drive.

While the Department of Labor's immigration agents cooperated with sheriffs and police agencies in driving Mexicans from the Los Angeles area, Los Angeles County welfare authorities adopted a policy of offering free train rides to Mexico for families willing to undergo repatriation. With the assistance of the Mexican consulate, a series of train trips was organized from March 1931 to April 1934. The Los Angeles Bureau of County Welfare sent over thirteen thousand Mexicans to Mexico, ignoring the fact that many of them, particularly children, were Mexican Americans. The county claimed to have saved over two million dollars through this program, but estimates as to the actual savings in welfare costs are contradictory. Similar smaller programs were initiated in other parts of the country. Welfare departments in such cities as Detroit, Gary, and East Chicago practiced some degree of coercion in urging families on relief to accept repatriation.

Although many local welfare agencies and federal officials pressured Mexicans to leave the United States one way or another, such efforts did not occur unilaterally. The Mexican government had long endorsed a policy of repatriation for its citizens living in other countries, and especially those in the United States. Certain irrigation and agricultural projects in Mexico offered employment to repatriated Mexicans. The magnitude of the 1930s repatriation, however, surpassed Mexico's ability to absorb the numbers moving south of the border. For example, over one hundred, thirty-eight thousand repatriates returned to Mexico in 1931, with over twenty thousand returning in the month of November alone, many under conditions of hardship. Government attempts to deal with the repatriates proved ineffectual; most of them simply returned to the place they had left years before.

As the Depression years wore on, the number of repatriates declined. It became increasingly difficult for welfare agencies to locate families willing to accept repatriation. New Deal employment programs helped many Mexicans decide to remain in the United States despite the hardships. Others experienced family pressures as teenaged children viewed Mexico as the foreign country and the United States as the homeland. The numbers continued to dwindle as each month passed, and by 1938 the movement had lost most of its drive. The Mexican government sponsored a campaign in early 1939 to attract Mexicans living in the United States, but it met with few takers. With the entry of the United States into World War II, U.S. attitudes toward Mexican workers changed, and many Mexicans who had left the United States in the depths of the Depression found it once again relatively easy to cross the border northward. The effect of the repatriation experience upon the integration of Mexican immigrants into American society, however, was disruptive and traumatic.

FURTHER READING: Neil Betten and Raymond A. Mohl, "From Discrimination to Repatriation: Mexican Life in Gary, Indiana, During the Great Depression," *Pacific Historical Review* 42 (August 1973): 370-88; Mercedes Carreras de Velasco, *Los mexicanos que devolvió la crisis, 1929-1932*, México, D.F.: Secretaría de Relaciones Exteriores, 1974; Abraham Hoffman, "Mexican Repatriation During the Great Depression: A Reappraisal," in *Immigrants—and Immigrants: Perspectives on Mexican Labor Migration to the United States*, ed. Arthur F. Corwin, Westport, Conn.: Greenwood Press, 1978; Abraham Hoffman, "Mexican Repatriation Statistics: Some Suggested Alternatives to Carey McWilliams," *Western Historical Quarterly* 3 (October 1972): 391-404; Abraham Hoffman, *Unwanted Mexican Americans in the Great Depression: Repatriation Pressures, 1929-1939*, Tucson: University of Arizona Press, 1974; George C. Kiser and David Silverman, "Mexican Repatriation During the Great Depression," *Journal of Mexican American History* 3 (1973): 139-64; Mark Reisler, *By the Sweat of Their Brow: Mexican Immigrant Labor in the United States, 1900-1940*, Westport, Conn.: Greenwood Press, 1976.

A.H.

REPUBLIC OF SAN JOAQUÍN DEL RIO CHAMA, a "republic" set up by Reies López Tijerina* late in 1966 after he and a group of followers tried to take over part of Carson National Forest in north-central New Mexico. Tijerina and his aliancistas* based their claims to the area on the fact that Carson National Forest had been formed, in part, out of ancient Spanish community land grants.

REPUBLIC OF THE RIO GRANDE (1840). After Texas independence from Mexico in 1836, Mexican federalists in the northeast continued their struggle against Mexican centralism. In 1839 General Juan Pablo Anaya, an important federalist leader in Mexico, visited Texas with some expectations of obtaining Texas support, and shortly thereafter General Antonio Canales,* who had raised the banner of federalism in the border state of Tamaulipas, established his headquarters on the Nueces River. After raising a mixed Texas-Mexican force, Canales recrossed the border at the end of September. Although his forces had some success in northern Mexico, Canales finally had to retreat across the Rio Grande into Texas early in January 1840. On January 18 Canales proclaimed the organization of a federalist Republic of the Rio Grande with Jesús Cárdenas as president and himself as commander in chief; then he proceeded to reinvade Mexico, only to be forced once again a month later to cross over into Texas to avoid a severe defeat.

At his headquarters in San Patricio on the Nueces River he recruited about seven hundred Mexicans and Texans—including Juan N. Seguín*—under the flag of the Republic of the Rio Grande, and in June again invaded Tamaulipas. Capturing Laredo and a number of other Rio Grande towns, Canales's army on August 17 captured Ciudad Victoria, the capital of Tamaulipas, and organized a new state government. An effort to capture the important mining and agricultural center of Saltillo in adjacent Nuevo León ended in failure when most of Canales's Mexican troops marched over to the centralist side. The remaining soldiers, largely Texans, were forced to withdraw to Texas. In November, after two months of inactivity, General Canales capitulated to the centralist government with the stipulation that his men were to be given life and liberty.

Thus ended the effort of north Mexican federalists to create a Republic of the Rio Grande. Canales was able to enlist about two hundred mettlesome Texans in his army of liberation, but the anticipated Texas government support never materialized. *See also* TEXAS REVOLT.

RICOS, literally the rich ones. Landowner and merchant class in New Mexico, who, with Anglo Americans, controlled the New Mexico area economically and politically during the nineteenth and early twentieth century.

RINCHES. *See* TEXAS RANGERS.

RIO ARRIBA, a term dating back to the colonial period to designate that part of the Rio Grande* in New Mexico* north of Albuquerque. The area south of that down to El Paso became known as Rio Abajo.

RIO BRAVO DEL NORTE. *See* RIO GRANDE.

RIO GRANDE. Beginning in southern Colorado and flowing southward through the center of New Mexico, the Rio Grande then turns in a more easterly direction, becoming the boundary between the United States and Mexico from El Paso to the Gulf of Mexico. From the very beginning of Spanish-Mexican settlement in New Mexico and Texas, it has played an important role in the history of the Southwest and of the people who have lived there. To the Nuevo Mexicano* settlers it provided water to irrigate their crops. From time to time a provincial boundary for Spain and Mexico, the Rio Grande's political role became important with Texas independence and the United States-Mexican War. To slaves in the expanding cotton fields of Texas it meant safety in flight, and marauding Indian bands used it in a similar fashion. At the end of the nineteenth century the Rio Grande became the goal of political dissidents in Porfirian Mexico and continued in that role during the long years of the Mexican Revolution* begun in 1910. In addition to Mexican patriots, bandits from both the United States and Mexico for many years found it a welcome sight as they fled their pursuers. In this century it became the goal of hundreds of thousands of Mexican emigrants, legal and undocumented, and in the second half of the 1900s the quality and use of its waters became a matter of increasing importance and mutual concern to both the United States and Mexico.

FURTHER READING: Paul Horgan, *Great River: the Rio Grande in North American History*, New York: Holt, Rinehart & Winston, 1954. Two volumes.

RIO GRANDE VALLEY. The valley of the Rio Grande extends from southern Colorado (about 37° north) almost due south through the center of the state of New Mexico. At New Mexico's southern border it turns in a southeasterly direction toward the Gulf of Mexico. The term Rio Grande Valley is used most frequently to refer to the last 150 miles of the river valley as it approaches the coast. This section has become a rich agricultural region sometimes referred to as the winter garden area. The term is also used to refer to the area along the river in central and southern New Mexico. In New Mexico the part north of Albuquerque is often referred to as the Rio Arriba* region, while that south of the capital is called Rio Abajo.

RIVERA, RAFAEL (1811-?), pioneer scout, discoverer of Las Vegas Valley, Nevada. Scouting for Antonio Armijo's* trading party from Albuquerque, New Mexico, in January of 1830, Rivera ascended Vegas wash and blazed a route to the Mojave River in California by way of the Amargosa River.

Rivera's pioneering route became the vital link in the Old Spanish Trail* with Las Vegas Springs, an essential stop on this popular way to southern California. Three years later, following an extension of the path to Salt Lake Valley, the route became known as the Mormon Trail, Today, highway Interstate 15 closely parallels the Old Spanish Trail.

RIVERA, TOMÁS (1935-), educator and novelist. Rivera was born in Crystal City, Texas. He grew up as part of the migrant labor stream that went from Texas to various parts of the Midwest. His earliest education was acquired in Spanish-instruction barrio* schools, and he was graduated in 1954 from Crystal City High School.

An English major in college, he earned an A.A. from Southwest Texas Junior College and by 1964, a bachelor's and master's degree in Educational Administration at Southwest Texas State University, and then a Ph.D. in Romance Languages and Literature at the University of Oklahoma in 1969.

Rivera has held various teaching and administrative positions. He taught English and Spanish in Texas secondary schools and served as chairman and instructor in the Department of Foreign Languages at Southwest Texas Junior College. At Sam Houston State University he was an associate professor of Spanish, Director of the Division of Foreign Languages, Literature, and Linguistics, Associate Dean of the College of Multidisciplinary Studies, and Vice President for Administration. In 1978 he became Executive Vice President of the University of Texas at El Paso. Rivera was appointed Chancellor of the University of California at Riverside in 1979, the first minority chancellor in University of California history.

Concurrent with Rivera's career in education has been a successful writing career. Poet, novelist, and literary critic, he has had numerous works published in journals and anthologies. His novel, *Y no se lo tragó la* *tierra/And the Earth Did Not Part*, (Quinto Sol, 1971), won the Quinto Sol National Chicano Literary Award for 1969-1970. This work initiated the current "generation" of Chicano* novels. The novel reflects Rivera's own experiences as a farm worker growing up on the migrant circuit. *F.J.*

RODEO, a periodic roundup of range cattle or horses to determine ownership of calves and colts, to brand them, to cut out those to be slaughtered or taken to market, and to care for the injured or diseased. In addition to being a basic part of ranch management, rodeos became important occasions for social intercourse in a society of scattered dwellings in the Southwest.

RODINO BILL (1973), legislation introduced in the House of Representatives by Peter Rodino of New Jersey early in 1973 to make it unlawful for an employer knowingly to hire illegal aliens. The bill set a fine of $500 for each undocumented worker employed and $1000 and/or up to one year in prison for a second conviction. Although Mexican American leaders, such as César Chávez,* had called for such legislation earlier, most opposed the Rodino bill arguing that it would discriminate against Mexican and Mexican American workers by singling them out and requiring only them to prove that they were legal residents. The bill was not passed.

RODRÍGUEZ, ARMANDO M. (1921-), educator, college president. From the state of Durango, Mexico, Armando Rodríguez's family came to the United States at the beginning of the Great Depression in the 1930s, and he grew up in San Diego, California. After serving in World War II, Rodríguez used the G.I. Bill to obtain a college education and entered the teaching profession. In the 1950s and 1960s he moved from teacher to principal to consultant in the Sacramento, California city school system and on to the United States Office of Education in Washington. In 1971 he resigned as assistant commissioner to become president of East Los Angeles College.

President Rodríguez has been active in numerous educational organizations and other boards and commissions related to La Raza.* An early supporter of bilingual* and bicultural* education, he has made major speeches and written important articles advocating his ideas. The best known of these is perhaps "Speak Up, Chicano" in the May 1968 issue of *American Education*.

RODRÍGUEZ, CHIPITA (?-1863). Arrested in 1863 for the murder near Goliad, Texas of an Anglo horse trader named John Savage, Rodríguez was indicted by the grand jury. She was found guilty of first-degree murder and, despite a mercy recommendation by the jury because of her age and the weakness of evidence against her, was hanged, becoming the only woman legally hanged in Texas.

ROLAND, GILBERT (1905-), actor. Born in Chihuahua, Mexico, and christened by his family Luis Antonio (his family name was Alonso), Roland spent his first years in that city and Ciudad Juárez on the border. In 1911 when Pancho Villa* attacked Juárez, the Alonsos crossed the Rio Grande* into El Paso. Here Luis went to school, learned English, and saw his first motion picture. At thirteen he hopped a freight train to Los Angeles and was soon working as a movie extra. After years of bit parts he won a leading role in *Plastic Age* (1925) with Clara Bow. Two years later Norma Talmadge picked him to star opposite her in *Camille*. Working for United Artists, he became a Hollywood fixture along with Douglas Fairbanks, Gloria Swanson, John Barrymore, and others. Because of his accent the advent of talking pictures set back his career; however, by 1933 he was again back in lead roles in *We Were Strangers* and *The Bullfighter and the Lady*. The years since then have given him one of the longest careers in show business with some sixty films and even more television performances in shows like *Bonanza*, *Gunsmoke*, and *Playhouse 90*. In addition Roland is a short story writer of some note.

Although not an activist, Gilbert Roland spoke out against discrimination and stereotyping of Mexicans long before the 1960s. On occasion he has threatened to walk off a film set rather than portray an unrealistic or stereotypical Mexican character. He was awarded commendations by both the California legislature and the City of Los Angeles for his faithful portrayals and his promotion of better U.S.-Mexican relations. In his work he consistently tries to present the feeling of dignity that is so much a part of Mexican culture.

ROMANO-V., OCTAVIO (1932-), anthropologist, professor, and editor of Quinto Sol Publications* in Berkeley, California. Dr. Romano-V. received a B.A. and M.A. from the University of New Mexico and a Ph.D. in Anthropology from the University of California at Berkeley in 1964. He was one of the first proponents and supporters of Chicano* literature at a time when literary experts seriously questioned its existence.

Quinto Sol's first publication, a quarterly called *El Grito*,* came out in the fall of 1967 and was a great success. By publishing materials concerning La Raza,* Quinto Sol has introduced Chicano writers and Chicano perspectives to the literary world.

In 1969 Romano-V. published *El Espejo-The Mirror*, illustrating Chicano diversity and complexity and providing a literary view of the thoughts and feelings of different Chicanos. It quickly went through five printings.

At present Romano-V. is professor of Behavioral Science in the School of Public Health at the University of California at Berkeley.

ROMERO, EUGENIO (1837-1920), freighter, businessman, politician. Romero, whose long life spanned both the Mexican and American eras, was a member of an important Las Vegas freighting family. After an early private education in Santa Fe, as a teenager he began working on the family freight run between New Mexico and Missouri. With the coming of the railroad to New Mexico at the end of the 1870s, Romero concentrated on the family trading business and developed extensive cattle and sheep holdings. During the following decade he expanded into the lumber and contracting businesses.

One of the founders of the Republican party in New Mexico, Romero was a dominant political leader in San Miguel County and a member of the Republican Executive Committee. He held numerous political posts in city, county, and state government during the last quarter of the nineteenth century and played an active role in the 1910 constitutional convention where he led the successful fight for guarantees for Nuevo Mexicanos.* He was prominent in opposing the belligerent confrontation tactics of the White Caps,* and they reciprocated by cutting his fences and burning some of his property.

RONSTADT, LINDA (1946-), singer, born in Tucson, Arizona, of Mexican and German ancestry. In 1964 she dropped out of the University of Arizona and went to Los Angeles to seek a career in music. After several years of singing in a group called the Stone Poneys, she began making record albums as a soloist (with various backup musicians) and during the late 1960s and early 1970s toured the United States, opening concerts for big name singing groups. She had her first platinum record (sale of a million copies) in 1974. Since then she has attained status as a female rock music superstar. In January 1977 she was invited to sing at President Jimmy Carter's inaugural concert and in the following month was awarded her second Grammy Award. Linda Ronstadt is credited with creating a genuinely contemporary (1970s) pop style—a mix of rock, folk, and country-western music—which gives her a broad appeal to many social sectors.

ROSS, FRED W. (1910-). Born in San Francisco, Ross moved to Los Angeles as a boy when his father became automotive editor of the *Herald Express* there. After high school he worked his way through the University of Southern California, graduating in 1936 in the middle of the Great Depression. Unable to secure a teaching job as he had hoped, Ross went to work for the California relief administration and in the late 1930s managed a Farm Securities Administration migrant camp at Arvin, California. When the United States entered World War II, he worked in an Idaho relocation camp for Japanese Americans.

After the war Ross returned to Southern California where he took a job with the American Council on Race Relations developing Unity Leagues* in the Los Angeles area. He also became acquainted with Saul Alinsky* and worked in development of Community Service Organizations.* While working for the CSO he met César Chávez* in San Jose and in 1954 persuaded Alinsky to hire him as a CSO organizer. When Chávez left the CSO and became involved in the Delano Grape Strike* he lured Ross from semi-retirement. Ross headed the United Farm Workers* Organizing Committee in the Di Giorgio* election and was a major force in the victory there in 1966.

Throughout the following decade Fred Ross had the responsibility of training organizers for the Farm Workers, as well as the management of campaigns against California Proposition 22 in 1972 (outlawing secondary boycotts) and for Proposition 14 in 1976 (modifying California's Agricultural Labor Relations Board). In addition to these activist roles, Ross also has been working on a manuscript titled *The Education of an Organizer*, a personal account of his experiences.

ROYBAL, EDWARD R. (1916-   ), one of Los Angeles's most consistently reelected members of the United States Congress, from California's 25th District. Roybal was born in Albuquerque, New Mexico, into a typical lower-middle-class Mexican American family. His family moved from New Mexico to Los Angeles where he attended public schools and graduated from Roosevelt High School in 1934. Soon after, he continued his education in Business Administration at the University of California and in the late 1930s obtained a position as a public health educator with the California Tuberculosis Association.

During 1944 and 1945 he served in the armed forces and after the war accepted the position of Director for Health Education in the Los Angeles County Tuberculosis and Health Association.

In post-World War II Los Angeles, despite the Sleepy Lagoon* case and zoot suit riots,* discrimination against Mexican Americans continued. However, returning veterans refused to accept second-class citizen status and, among other accomplishments, formed an organization to elect a Mexican American to the Los Angeles City Council. Roybal was their candidate in 1947, but he failed in his bid for the vacant city council seat.

The group intensified its efforts in the next election, and with the help of Fred Ross* the members created the Community Service Organization (CSO), a grass-roots community political movement. In 1949 CSO registration and get-out-the-vote drives in East Los Angeles were successful, and Edward

Roybal, elected to the city council, became the first Mexican American to serve on that board since 1881.

Roybal was repeatedly reelected to the city council, twice without opposition, serving a total of over thirteen years, until 1962 when he was elected to the United States House of Representatives. Since then he has been reelected in every election. In the House of Representatives he continued his work for economic and social reforms, speaking out for tax reform, expanded federal efforts to reduce unemployment, improved pension benefits, and programs to establish a national health insurance system. He has also proposed a law to bring oil and natural gas resources under public regulation and introduced a bill to protect the privacy of individuals in the area of credit reports.

In almost twenty years in Congress, Roybal has served on a number of important committees. Initially he was assigned to the Interior and Insular Affairs Committee and the Post Office and Civil Service Committee. After his reelection in 1964 he was appointed to the Committee on Foreign Affairs where he specialized in inter-American affairs and Middle East policy. Five years later he was made a member of the Committee on Veterans' Affairs, serving on the subcommittees on education and training, and housing and hospitals. In 1971 he became a member of the House Appropriations Committee, and at present he sits on three subcommittees of this key committee, the most important being the Subcommittee on Labor, Health, Education and Welfare.

In his congressional work Edward Roybal has been especially concerned about the problems of Mexican Americans. In 1967 he introduced and won approval for the first federal Bilingual Education* Act. The following year he proposed a cabinet-level committee on Opportunities for Spanish-Speaking People which was established in 1969. Since then he has introduced legislation to create a federal bilingual court system, to require the accumulation of current social and economic data on Spanish-speaking Americans, and to protect their voting rights.

The many groups in which Roybal has been active include: Community Service Organization, American Legion, Boy Scouts, United States-Mexico Health Association, County Committee on Human Relations, Metropolitan Recreation and Youth Services Council, and the Welfare Planning Council of Metropolitan Los Angeles. He is also a vice chairman of the Democratic National Committee and a member of the Democratic Advisory Council of Elected Officials.

Among Edward Roybal's achievements are honorary Doctor of Law degrees from Pacific States University and Claremont Graduate School and a Visiting Club Fellowship from Yale University.

Throughout six terms of congressional service in the House and twenty-five years of public life, Roybal has consistently advocated stronger citizen participation in party politics and in federal and local government. Currently he continues to work toward the development of community based organizations to encourage citizen involvement in governmental decision-making.

RUMFORD ACT (1963), a California open housing law, prohibiting discrimination in the sale of real estate. Introduced into the California Assembly by Byron Rumford, it was enacted into law in 1963, but revoked in the following year by an amendment to the California state constitution (Proposition 14). This revocation in turn was stricken down by a 1967 U.S. Supreme Court decision declaring Proposition 14 unconstitutional.

Mexican American organizations strongly supported the Rumford Act and equally vociferously opposed Proposition 14.

S

SAL SI PUEDES, literally "get out if you can." Historically, it is a term used to signify the poorest section of a Mexican barrio* and is most commonly associated with the barrio in San José, where César Chávez* lived.

It may also refer to a pessimistic attitude characterized by frustration, loss of hope, and withdrawal, often leading to apathy, and interpreted as laziness or contentment with one's lot. Many Mexican Americans who have lived in extreme poverty develop these symptoms as a defense mechanism against social and psychological battering.

SALAZAR, EULOGIO (?-1968), a long-time Rio Arriba County jailer who had resisted the June 1967 Tierra Amarilla* courthouse raid of Reies López Tijerina's* followers and later testified that he had been wounded by Tijerina in the raid. On January 3, 1968, his battered corpse was found in his car. There was never any evidence to tie Aliancistas* to his murder, and the case remains unsolved.

SALAZAR, RUBÉN (1928-1970), journalist, born on March 3, 1928, in Chihuahua, Mexico. When Ruben was one year old his family migrated to the United States and settled in El Paso, Texas, where he grew up and went to school. Studies at the University of Texas, El Paso, eventually led to a Bachelor of Arts degree and a strong interest in journalism.

In 1949 Rubén Salazar became a naturalized American citizen, and in the following year he entered the United States Army, serving for two years. Upon his release from the army he joined the El Paso *Herald-Post* and began to show the reportorial qualities that were to take him to the top in the news business, and to his death. Deeply interested in investigative reporting, he showed considerable ability in writing stories about drug abuse and poor jail conditions in El Paso. After two years of this work he moved to the *Press Democrat* in Santa Rosa, California, and then in 1957 to the much larger and more prestigious *San Francisco News*. Having served his apprenticeship on these papers, in 1959 he joined the *Los Angeles Times*.

In 1965 he was sent on assignment to Vietnam to cover the fighting there. Following this stint, he was assigned to Mexico City where he became bureau chief for the *Times*. When he returned from Mexico City, Salazar was selected by the *Times* editorial staff for a new special assignment.

At the end of the 1960s, with the rise of Chicano awareness and the beginning militancy of the city's population, the *Times* editorial staff decided that what was needed was a special column to explain Chicano life to the Los Angeles community and asked Rubén Salazar to undertake the job. As a Mexican American, a political moderate, and a reporter of outstanding abilities, he was ideal for the new task.

In his new role as spokesman for La Raza* Salazar pulled no punches and inevitably came into conflict with opposing interests. After one of his columns Los Angeles Police Chief Edward Davis became very angry at what he considered Salazar's inflammatory remarks. At both the *Times* office and at station KMEX-TV, where he also worked, efforts were made to have Salazar tone down controversial phraseology.

In the midst of this came the National Chicano Moratorium.* Over twenty thousand Mexican Americans of all ages from all over the United States gathered in East Los Angeles to march in protest against the Vietnam War. The parade ended at Laguna Park where the marchers and their friends sat down to enjoy the rest of the program. Trouble erupted in a nearby liquor store and within minutes a patrol car was in front of the liquor store, and what soon became a massive confrontation covering twenty-eight blocks began. Rubén Salazar and two coworkers from KMEX were there covering the story. Late in the afternoon Salazar and his friends dropped into the nearby Silver Dollar Cafe for a beer. Soon afterwards sheriff's deputies fired at least two high-velocity tear gas projectiles into the cafe. One of them hit Salazar in the left temple killing him instantly.

Shortly after he died, a park in East Los Angeles was renamed for him, and La Raza honored him with a corrido* that described his life and death.

FURTHER READING: David F. Gómez, "Killing of Ruben Salazar: Nothing Has Changed in the Barrio," *Christian Century* 88 (Jan. 13, 1971): 49-52.

SALINAS, a town and valley that lies on the western edge of the Coast Range east of Monterey Bay. Salinas is the seat of Monterey County, California, with a population of about sixty thousand. The name was derived from the Spanish word for the salt marshes at the mouth of the river to which the Spaniards gave that name. The river is surrounded by fertile farm land planted with lettuce, sugar beets, artichokes, and other vegetables and has become an important center for processing and shipping these farm products. In 1970 it became the scene of an attempt by César Chávez* and his United Farm Workers* to unionize the lettuce industry. *See* LETTUCE STRIKE, SALINAS.

SALINAS, PORFIRIO, JR. (1910-1973), artist. Salinas, who was born near Bastrop, Texas, was third in a Tejano* family of seven children. He specialized in landscapes of his native state, especially in "bluebonnet scenes" and also painted matadors, bulls, and bullfight scenes as a hobby. Growing up in San Antonio, he attended school there and from early youth showed exceptional artistic ability. Although he painted to sell and therefore to please people, he put together a style described as heightened realism, which is notable for the honesty and vividness with which it depicts Texas landscapes. Without formal art training, he developed an eye for typical southwestern scenes and as a result became one of Texas's most popular artists. He was known as President Lyndon B. Johnson's favorite painter and was commissioned by Lady Bird Johnson to paint some of the president's best-loved scenes along the Pedernales River. At one time five of his paintings hung in the White House. He died April 18, 1973.

FURTHER READING: Ruth Goddard, *Porfirio Salinas*, Austin: Rock House Press, 1975; John H. Jenkins, "Porfirio Salinas," *Southwestern Art* 1 (1967).

SALPOINTE, JEAN BAPTISTE (1825-1898), missionary and bishop. French born and educated, Salpointe was recruited by Bishop Jean Baptiste Lamy* for missionary work in the Southwest. He arrived in 1859 and first worked among the Catholics of northern New Mexico. In 1866 he was sent by Lamy to head the work of reorganizing the church in the territory of Arizona and was made bishop of that area. Although he initially had some minor friction with Nuevo Mexicanos* because of cultural differences, he did an outstanding job of organizing parishes and building churches in this sparsely settled region. His resounding success as an administrator led to his being appointed archbishop of Santa Fe in 1885 where he succeeded Lamy. He retired in 1894, returning to Tucson, Arizona.

SALT WAR (1866-1877), a complex political and economic conflict that began in the early 1860s when salt deposits called Guadalupe Lakes, about one hundred miles east of El Paso on the American side, began to be used freely by Mexicans and Mexican Americans of the border region. The first stage of the Salt War began about 1866 when Samuel Maverick, using a land certificate, tried to acquire complete possession of the salt beds. But his claim did not cover the entire deposit, and public use continued.

Toward the end of the following year a group of Anglo Republican politicians formed a company to complete the monopoly of the salt lakes; however, the title proved defective, and the politicians split into two groups referred to as a Salt Ring and an Anti-Salt Ring, moving the dispute into the political arena. In 1869 Albert T. Fountain, head of the Anti-Salt Ring, was elected to the Texas Senate on a platform of securing continued public use of the deposits. At this point two of his former supporters, Louis Cardis and Father Antonio Borajo, both Italian-origin Mexicans who hoped to control the salt beds as they already controlled the Mexican vote, split with Fountain and created a permanent division of the Republican party in the El Paso area. One death resulted from this bitter quarrel.

A second stage in the Salt War began developing in the early 1870s when a recently arrived Missouri Democrat named Charles Howard first joined forces with Cardis and then, splitting with him, tried to end the free use of the salt beds by taking all the salt land not already owned by Maverick. Howard set a fee for taking salt and in September 1877 had two Mexican Americans arrested for trying to get salt at Guadalupe Lakes. Their arrest led to rioting and Howard, after being held by the mob for several days, agreed to relinquish his claim to the salt beds. Holding Cardis responsible for his difficulties, Howard killed him in El Paso on October 10.

At the beginning of December 1877 Howard again tried to prevent free access to the salt lakes and was besieged in the San Elizario ranger station by a mob of about five hundred Mexicans and Mexican Americans. After four days, during which two Anglos were killed by the mob, Howard surrendered and with two fellow Anglos was executed by a firing squad. A good deal of looting and rapine followed in San Elizario and on the outskirts of El Paso. After several days, troops and a posse of Anglos restored order by killing several Mexicans and chasing the leaders of the mob across the border. Some were later indicted, but no one was ever brought to trial. The only result of a subsequent congressional investigation was the restationing of troops at Fort Bliss, which had been abandoned shortly before. Finally, Mexican Americans and Mexicans had to pay for salt from Guadalupe Lakes when ownership of the salt beds was later confirmed to Howard's father-in-law.

FURTHER READING: Charles L. Sonnichsen, *The El Paso Salt War, 1877*, El Paso: C. Hertzog, 1961.

SAMANIEGO, MARIANO G. (1844-1907), political leader and businessman. Becoming an American citizen as a result of the Gadsden Purchase* (1853), Samaniego moved to Tucson a decade later after graduating from the St. Louis University. Here he became a leading rancher, freighter, and public official, serving four terms in the territorial legislature from the mid-1870s to the mid-1890s. Samaniego was a strong advocate of public education at both the primary and university levels. With the founding of the state university in 1891, he became an early member of the board of trustees and for a while was acting treasurer. He took an active role in the Arizona Pioneers Historical Society, serving many years in leadership positions. He also was a founder and president of the Alianza Hispano-Americana,* established to protect Mexican American civil rights and cultural identity while encouraging acculturation.

SAMORA, JULIAN (1920-), sociologist, educator. Samora, one of the leading contemporary Mexican American intellectuals, was born and educated in Colorado. In 1953 he obtained his Ph.D. in Sociology and Anthropology at the University of Wisconsin with a doctoral dissertation on minority leadership in a bicultural community. Since then he has been an extremely active researcher and teacher in the area of Mexican American sociology. Among his most important publications are *La Raza: Forgotten Americans* (Notre Dame, Indiana: University of Notre Dame Press, 1966), *Mexican-Americans in a Midwest Metropolis* (Berkeley: University of California, 1967), and *Los Mojados: The Wetback Story* (Notre Dame, Indiana: University of Notre Dame Press, 1971). Dr. Samora has served on a number of important commissions and boards and has served as visiting professor at several leading universities. Since 1959 he has taught at the University of Notre Dame where he also directs a Mexico Border Studies Project sponsored by the Ford Foundation.

SAN ANTONIO, first settled in 1718 as a way station between the then capital of Texas, Los Adaes, and settlements south of the Rio Grande. The area of the presidio of San Antonio de Bexar and the mission San Antonio de Valero (whose church became known as the Alamo) was given the status of villa in 1731. Soon San Antonio became an important trading and transportation center and in 1773 was made the capital of Texas. After Mexican independence in 1821 it became the headquarters of the lieutenant governor of the state of Coahuila y Tejas and had a population of about twenty-five hundred.

As a regional capital San Antonio became a center of federalism that developed early in the 1830s. The Texas separatist movement defeated the central government's troops there in December 1835, and a group of Texan soldiers early in the following year defended to the death the mission-fortress of the Alamo. After the battle of San Jacinto many Mexicans initially fled the town; however, during the latter half of the nineteenth century the city's Mexican population continued to grow steadily as it became an important trade center and shipping point.

Removed from its political role as capital after 1836, San Antonio developed as a communications and military headquarters, and in the second half of the nineteenth century it came to be a focal point of the range cattle industry. By 1900 San Antonio was the largest city in Texas with a population of 53,321 engaged in commerce, banking, foundries, flour milling, and breweries. As the Mexican Revolution of 1910 developed, it became an important refugee center, and in 1910 Francisco Madero issued his famous Plan de San Luis (Potosí)* from there.

During World War I and in the 1920s there was rapid urban expansion, largely due to the establishment of military bases nearby and postwar federal employment. In this period many Mexican Americans shifted from agricultural work to industry, but a continuing heavy influx of Mexican nationals made the area an important labor reservoir for the entire Rocky Mountain region.

Up to 1920 San Antonio had the largest Mexican-descent population of any city in the United States, and in 1930 its population remained more than 35 percent Spanish-speaking. By 1940 the city had a population of more than a quarter of a million, and a decade later the metropolitan area population had reached nearly half a million. According to the 1970 census this number had risen to 650,188, of whom approximately 50 percent were of Mexican origin.

SAN ANTONIO PECAN SHELLERS' STRIKE. *See* PECAN SHELLERS' STRIKE.

SAN ANTONIO YOUTH ORGANIZATION (SANYO), a War on Poverty organization founded in mid-1965 in San Antonio, Texas. Begun as a youth program, it soon expanded into a more general service agency for the poverty-stricken. By 1968 it had developed fifty neighborhood councils and centers in the San Antonio area. Nearly 80 percent of these councils were predominantly Mexican American. Working with various public and private groups in order to promote health, education, recreation, and community well-being, the association provides information and connections for jobs, scholarships, services, and other opportunities for improvement.

SAN JACINTO, BATTLE OF (April 21, 1836), the decisive battle in the Mexican attempt to suppress the Texas revolt.* Troops under General Sam Houston attacked Mexican forces under General Santa Anna* encamped near the San Jacinto River and in the ensuing debacle killed about six hundred Mexican soldiers and captured four hundred more, including Santa Anna. As a result, Santa Anna agreed to the Treaty of Velasco* providing for Texas independence. Although there were some subsequent attempts by Mexico to invade and conquer Texas, San Jacinto essentially ensured Texas independence.

SAN JOSE, the county seat of Santa Clara County. San Jose is the center of the second largest Mexican American community in California. In numbers and rate of growth, it ranks among the most important urban concentrations of Mexican Americans in the United States.

Founded in 1777 by the Spanish commander of the presidio at San Francisco, Lt. José Joaquín Moraga, as the Pueblo of San José, two hundred years later it is a sprawling metropolis with a large Mexican American minority, the greater part of which lives in the barrios* of the east side.

These Mexican American barrios developed in the 1920s when Mexicans began arriving in large numbers and settled in the Mayfair area, which at the time was isolated from the rest of the city. At that time the major economic attraction of San Jose for Mexicans was the canneries, first established in 1871. By the late 1940s the canneries had a labor force of over thirty-eight thousand, the vast majority being Mexican American.

The period since World War II has strikingly changed the character of San Jose. In 1950 there were ninety-five thousand inhabitants, and the provisional figures of the 1980 census indicated a population of about 636,000 of whom more than 140,000 are Mexican Americans.

Traditionally the Anglo American community in San Jose has tended to view Mexican Americans as a social problem. A history of nonparticipation in city and county government by Mexican Americans contributes to their political and economic isolation today.

SAN JOSÉ INCIDENT (1917). The tiny Mexican village of San José, Coahuila, on the banks of the Rio Grande,* became the center of an international incident when U.S. cavalry and some Texas rangers* crossed the border and attacked it. The Americans were pursuing a bandit gang (common along the border during the chaos of the 1910 Mexican Revolution*) whose trail led them to the village. When they were fired on, the one hundred fifty troops fired back, and between twelve and twenty Mexicans were killed. Mexican authorities were indignant at the American violation of Mexican territory and killing of Mexican villagers.

SAN PASQUAL, BATTLE OF (1846), a skirmish between Californios* and United States forces during the Mexican War* at the Indian village of San Pasqual near San Diego. In the mistaken belief that California was securely in American hands, Colonel Stephen Kearny* had left New Mexico for California with one hundred men. At the beginning of December 1846 his approach was blocked by a force of one hundred Californio horsemen under Andrés Pico. On the morning of December 6 Kearny attacked the Californios at San Pasqual, some thirty miles northeast of San Diego. In a running skirmish the Californios, fighting with muskets and lances, were able to inflict heavy losses on the Americans. Eighteen were killed and about an equal number wounded, including Kearny, while the Californio force suffered one death and a dozen wounded. After the Californios withdrew, Kearny claimed a victory since he remained in possession of the battlefield. However, the Americans continued to be in a difficult position, and only with the help of a two-hundred-man rescue party were they able to reach San Diego.

SÁNCHEZ, GEORGE I. (1906-1972), dean of Mexican American scholars. Sánchez was born on October 4, 1906, in Albuquerque, New Mexico, of Nuevo Mexicano* parents who both came from families with long histories in the territory. His formative years were spent in the mining town of Jerome, Arizona, where his father worked in the copper pits of the then booming copper center of Arizona.

After attending secondary schools in both Arizona and New Mexico, he began teaching at Yrrisarri, located fifty miles east of Albuquerque, while attending the University of New Mexico. He also served as principal and supervisor in Bernalillo County from 1923 through 1930. By 1934 George Sánchez had his Ed.D. in Educational Administration from the University of California at Berkeley after completing his B.A. in Education and Spanish at the University of New Mexico and his M.S. in Educational Psychology and Spanish at the University of Texas.

In 1935 he became a research associate for the Julius Rosenwald Fund in Chicago. Beginning with this position, he established himself during the following thirty-five years as one of the foremost experts on the educational and social needs of Spanish-speaking groups in the United States. He also became an authority and education specialist in Latin American education. Throughout his professional career he lectured, consulted, and directed studies on education, language, and minority affairs for colleges, universities, foundations, and state, federal, and foreign governments. As a pioneer in bilingual,* bicultural* education, his methods and philosophy are being used in many programs today.

George I. Sánchez lived a versatile and productive life and distinguished himself as the author and editor of hundreds of articles, numerous books, films, and reports on the social and educational problems and needs of the Mexican American. With a grant from the Carnegie Foundation, in 1938 he began his research on the people of New Mexico. This study of the economic, social, and political conditions of New Mexicans became the first edition of the classic work, *Forgotten People*, published in 1940 by the University of New Mexico Press. With considerable detail this major work documents the limited educational opportunities available to the Spanish-speaking people of New Mexico during the late 1930s. The author concludes by pointing out that social conditions of his people were not due to a lack of interest in education, but arose from the conditions of an impoverished economy that affected every aspect of their existence.

For over forty-five years Dr. Sánchez served as educator and spokesman for La Raza* and as a champion against social and educational segregation. His contributions as scholar, writer, editor, social philosopher, civil rights leader, international administrator, and consultant on Inter-American affairs, migrant education, and Indian affairs earned him the title, "most distinguished Mexican American scholar of our time." In one of his last commentaries on the status of Mexican Americans, he stated that the new impetus of the Chicano movement* would finally help right the wrong that had been inflicted upon his people and that his hopes and aspirations lay with the youth of La Raza and their renewed determination.

SÁNCHEZ, PHILLIP V. (1929-), politician. Born into a family of seven children of an immigrant Mexican couple in Pinedale, California, at the beginning of the Great Depression, Phil Sánchez joined in the family migrant agricultural work when his father abandoned wife and children. He attended school in his hometown of Pinedale, near Fresno, California, and went on to Coalinga Junior College and to Fresno State College, where he graduated in 1953 as "outstanding male graduate." First hired as an administrative analyst by Fresno County, he became the county's chief administrative officer in 1962. Deeply involved in Mexican American community affairs and a member of several college boards, he was named Fresno's Outstanding Young Man and one of the state's five outstanding young men.

In 1971 Phil Sánchez was named by President Nixon as national director of the Office of Economic Opportunity and two years later was named United States ambassador to Honduras, which position he held till 1976 when he became ambassador to Colombia. He is the author of several articles on public administration.

SÁNCHEZ, ROBERT (1934-), teacher, clergyman, archbishop. Robert Sánchez was born in Socorro in south-central New Mexico and educated for the priesthood in his native state and at the Gregorian University in Rome. Ordained in 1959, he spent the ensuing decade and a half as a teacher and assistant principal in St. Pius X High School in Albuquerque and as pastor of two New Mexican parishes. In 1973 he was elected president of the archdiocesan Priests' Senate, and in the following year was appointed by the Pope to be Archbishop of Santa Fe, becoming the first Mexican American archbishop.

SANDOVAL, SECUNDINO (1933-), artist. Born and raised in New Mexico, Sandoval graduated from college in 1958 and worked as a technical illustrator first, and later as a draftsman and designer. His avocation during these years, painting in oils, acrylics, and most recently watercolors, finally led him to become a full-time painter. His paintings, which have been shown in many galleries and shows and have won numerous awards, are characterized by a simple and spontaneous naturalism.

SANTA ANNA, ANTONIO LÓPEZ DE (1794-1876), politician, general, and president of Mexico. Born at Jalapa in the state of Veracruz, Santa Anna began a military career just months before the outbreak of the Mexican revolt for independence in 1810 and was sent to help put down the revolutionary movement in Texas. When Agustín de Iturbide developed his plan for Mexican independence, Santa Anna joined in that movement and in 1822 was promoted to brigadier general; by the end of the decade he was military commander and governor of Veracruz.

For three decades Santa Anna dominated Mexican history and between 1833 and 1855 was president eleven separate times, four times with dictatorial powers. Like many of his contemporaries, Santa Anna was a person of limited political convictions and switched at times from liberal to conservative and from federalist to centralist. During his first presidency he had the task of putting down the Texas revolt, with disastrous results for Mexico. During his ninth and tenth times as president he led his country in an unsuccessful effort to resist the invasion of Mexico by United States armed forces in the Mexican War,* and during his eleventh and final occupation of the presidential chair he sold the Mesilla Valley to the United States in the Gadsden Purchase Treaty* of 1853.

FURTHER READING: Oakah Jones, *Santa Anna*, New York: Twayne Publishers, 1968; Wilfrid Calcott, *Santa Anna*, Norman, Oklahoma: University of Oklahoma Press, 1936.

SANTA BARBARA, CALIFORNIA. As a Spanish-Mexican town, Santa Barbara was the outgrowth of the presidio and mission* established there in 1782.

Of the three frontier institutions: presidio, mission, and pueblo,* the pueblo had become dominant by the latter years of the Mexican period and contained about six hundred Californios. After the American takeover in 1846 a period of Anglo-Mexican conflict began that persisted into the 1850s, fed by the influx of Anglos and by their demands for complete cultural surrender by Californios, who remained in political control of the town. Floods and a long drought during the 1860s ended the already weakened Mexican-dominated pastoral economy of the area, and a heavy Anglo influx early in the next decade brought an end to Californio domination of local politics. During the 1880s and 1890s Santa Barbara rapidly became Americanized, and its Mexican American population became increasingly dependent economically and isolated socially.

At the beginning of the twentieth century Santa Barbara began to receive an influx of Mexican immigrants, who developed a separate barrio* from that of the Californios, but who shared with the latter the unskilled and low-skill labor market. The Great Depression of the 1930s led to repatriation of from one to two thousand of these additions to Santa Barbara's Mexican-descent population, but enough remained to establish the basis of the city's present Chicano population. Among California cities, Santa Barbara continues to have one of the highest percentages of Mexican Americans.

SANTA DE CABORA, LA. *See* URREA, TERESA.

SANTA FE, capital of New Mexico, founded in 1609 by Don Pedro de Peralta, third governor of the Province of Nuevo México. It developed slowly, but by 1740 Santa Fe had become a trade center for Mexican traders from Chihuahua and French traders from the Mississippi Valley. Later Americans continued this activity over the famous Santa Fe Trail.*

After American occupation in 1846, Santa Fe became a center of political intrigue and disturbances between Anglo Americans and native New Mexicans. In many ways this cultural and political conflict still exists today.

In 1849 a stage line was established over the Santa Fe Trail between Independence, Missouri, and Santa Fe. With the coming of the railroads in the late 1870s, freighters and stagecoaches disappeared and by the 1880s the old Santa Fe Trail was dead.

The railroad's arrival in 1879 brought a period of prosperity to the town, and during the next thirty years the conglomerate of architecture which faces the plaza was built. Today the ancient Palace of the Governors still stands guard over the north side of the plaza while on the other three sides storefronts in brick buildings of the style of the 1890s rub elbows with Spanish-Pueblo buildings. In the 1940s the town became conscious of the unique type of architecture which is its heritage and returned to the authentic Pueblo style.

With statehood in 1912, New Mexico's capital began a new chapter in its history. Federal as well as new state buildings were erected, schools were built, and a permanent population of government employees came to live in the town. Between 1880 and the admission of New Mexico to the Union, the population had been static, hovering between five and six thousand. But by 1920 it had jumped to eight thousand; by 1930 it was twelve thousand; in 1970 forty-two thousand; and today it numbers over fifty thousand.

Today Santa Fe is a city tempered by over three hundred years of Spanish and Mexican traditions. The native Spanish-speaking population represents 60 percent of the people. Expensive homes stand shoulder to shoulder with primitive adobe houses on the same sunny hillsides, following the same simple lines. Since 1900 painters, musicians, and novelists have come to absorb the beauty of the town and its surroundings, and have made it an art and cultural center.

SANTA FE EXPEDITION (1841), an ill-starred invasion of Nuevo México* province by an armed group of merchants sent by Texas President Mirabeau Buonoparte Lamar. The expedition was planned on the assumption that New Mexicans were dissatisfied with Governor Manuel Armijo's* administration and willing to accept Texas rule.

In June 1841 some three hundred Anglo and Mexican Texans, organized into five military companies led by General Hugh McLeod, left for Santa Fe with twenty-one wagons loaded with two hundred thousand dollars worth of trade goods. Encountering hostile Indians, prairie fires, and scorching heat, they also lost their way. The poorly managed expedition then split into two groups, believing that this division would speed their journey. When they finally reached New Mexico, members were suffering intensely and were taken prisoners by Armijo without a shot being fired. At Santa Fe some of the Texans were executed and the remainder were sent by foot on a long march to prison in Mexico City. The survivors were eventually released.

This Texas expedition and the mistreatment of the prisoners served to aggravate ill feelings between Texans and Nuevo Mexicanos.*

SANTA FE RING, an informal association that originated in the early 1870s from the Maxwell Land* Company's need for political power in order to obtain government acceptance of its claim to two million acres rather than ninety-seven thousand acres, the legal maximum under Spanish and Mexican law. It consisted of an Anglo group which largely dominated the territorial government, working closely with about twenty important Nuevo Mexicano* families. The Ring manipulated land sales and, although its membership shifted, it held together sufficiently to dominate the economic exploitation of New Mexico's resources until its control was broken by Bronson Cutting* at the beginning of this century. The most prominent figure in the ring was Thomas B. Catron.*

SANTA FE TRADE, the annual commerce which was opened between Santa Fe, New Mexico, and the Missouri frontier after Mexican independence in 1821. Earlier there had been some trade carried on over this route, but it was discouraged by Spain, and American traders often were imprisoned and lost their goods. In the fall of 1821 William Becknell, trading with Indians in the southwestern plains, learned that Mexican independence now opened the way for trade with New Mexico. He took his pack mules to Santa Fe where he sold his merchandise at an enormous profit. In the following year he returned with three heavily loaded wagons, pioneering a route that was soon to be followed by other traders. By the mid-1820s the yearly trade amounted to about one hundred thousand dollars and attracted Indian attacks, leading to military escorts for a few years.

By 1830 the trade had become well defined, amounting to two hundred fifty thousand dollars yearly. At Santa Fe the traders paid import duties to the New Mexican officials and arranged their trade goods for sale or continued on to Chihuahua City where a larger market that included the states of Chihuahua, Durango, and Aguascalientes awaited them.

In two decades about sixty of the Anglo Santa Fe traders settled down in New Mexico, married Nuevo Mexicanas,* and became Mexican citizens—among them were Kit Carson,* James Magoffin,* and Charles Bent.* Some leading Nuevo Mexicanos also entered the trade and usually were able to avoid payment of customs duties—among them was Governor Manuel Armijo.*

The trade brought New Mexico ample supplies of manufactured goods including textiles, tools, glassware, clothing, and paper and provided a market for mules, woolen blankets, and silver. This economic development was revolutionary in scope and extended into the political area as well, as the Nuevo Mexicano government became heavily dependent on the Santa Fe trade for its regular income. As a result of the trade, New Mexico's isolation from the United States was greatly reduced—but not her isolation from central Mexico. New Mexico was becoming increasingly dependent economically on the United States, and Mexican officials feared the traders were only the vanguard of American manifest destiny.*

After the Mexican War,* trade expanded considerably and at the height of the California gold period amounted to $5 million annually. By 1880 the arrival of the Atchison, Topeka, and Santa Fe* switched the trade route from the Santa Fe Trail to the new railroad.

FURTHER READING: Lewis E. Atherton: "Disorganizing Effects of the Mexican War on the Santa Fe Trade," *Kansas Historical Quarterly* 6 (1937): 115-23; Robert L. Duffus, *The Santa Fe Trail*, Albuquerque: University of New Mexico Press, 1971.

SANTA FE TRAIL. One of the historic trade routes of the West, the Santa Fe Trail, officially initiated by Mexican independence in 1821, began at Franklin (later Independence), Missouri and ran in a fairly direct line to Santa Fe, New Mexico. At a rate of about fifteen miles per day, the wagons first passed over the flat prairie that extended to Council Grove, Kansas.

From Council Grove southwest to the Arkansas River the geography changed as the wagons passed into the dry high plains region, the home of Comanche and Pawnee Indians. After leaving the Arkansas River the wagons faced the arid sixty-mile crossing of the Cimarron Desert of northwestern Oklahoma, and once that barrier had been crossed, began the final approach to Santa Fe. An alternate "mountain branch" of the trail took the wagons along the Arkansas River to Bent's Fort where it then headed more directly south through Raton Pass and rejoined the main trail in northeastern New Mexico.

SANTERO, a carver of wooden statues of the saints and Jesus, usually in a primitive art style. Santeros were especially common in New Mexico in the Spanish, Mexican, and American periods.

SCHENLEY INDUSTRIES, a large, diversified liquor company, a subsidiary of Rapid-American Corporation. Schenley owned grape orchards involved in the 1965 Delano grape strike.* On April 6, 1966, Schenley made agricultural labor history by becoming the first corporate employer to recognize a farm labor organization as bargaining agent for field workers.

SCHOOLS. *See* EDUCATION.

SCOTT, WINFIELD (1786-1866), general. Having risen from captain to commanding general of the United States Army by 1841, Scott developed plans for the invasion of Mexico when the United States-Mexican War* broke out in 1846. Refused a field command for political reasons at first, in 1847 he was placed in command of an army to invade the Mexican heartland. He landed with his forces at Veracruz and by September 14, 1847, was in possession of Mexico City.

SECONDARY BOYCOTT, an act of labor solidarity to exert indirect pressure on an employer through a second party neutral to the basic labor conflict. It often includes such practices as refusal to make purchases from a neutral party who handles or sells the product of the employer and refusal by union members to use or work with the employer's product.

SECRETARIAT FOR THE SPANISH SPEAKING (of the National Conference of Catholic Bishops). Formerly called the Bishops Committee for the Spanish Speaking, it was organized in 1945 by four western Catholic bishops under the leadership of Archbishop Robert E. Lucey* of San Antonio and the sponsorship of the American Board of Catholic Missions. Its purpose was to organize effective programs to improve the physical and spiritual lives of Mexican Americans. The committee developed a wide variety of social services including credit unions, maternity programs, leadership training, and housing cooperatives; it also conducted citizenship and voter registration drives and built clinics and meeting centers.

In 1968 the secretariat became a division of the United States Catholic Conference, and seven years later it was made an agency of the National Conference of Catholic Bishops. It continues to act as an informational and idea center for programs to improve the socioeconomic, health, and religious aspects of Chicano communities. With headquarters in Washington, D.C., the secretariat is involved in employment, education, manpower, leadership training, health, and civil rights, as well as pastoral work. It also sponsors regional and national conferences on these topics. The secretariat has played an active role in the Chicano movement, most notably in the settlement of farm labor disputes such as the one at Delano.*

SEGREGATION, the establishment by law or custom of separate facilities for social or ethnic groups, resulting in discrimination in favor of one group over the others; the separation of ethnic, religious, or racial groups, either by law or by custom; the requirement of the subordinate group to use separate facilities. Segregation also may refer to any type of discrimination or denial of civil rights.

Most segregation practices involving Mexican Americans have not had their basis in law. Yet, it has not been unusual for Mexican Americans to find themselves refused service in certain restaurants, clubs, and other privately owned facilities. They have found also that the sign "We reserve the right to refuse service to anyone" often may mean "No Mexicans," especially in regions close to the border.

In housing, too, segregation has come about as part of the unwritten law that Mexicans and their descendants live in a separate section of town from the Anglos. Even in areas where Mexicans outnumber the Anglo population, discriminatory practices have kept Mexicans in inferior housing.

Segregation in schools has, until recently, been a common practice, justified on the basis of a language barrier. Until 1947 in California segregated schools were provided for and justified under the Education Code for the purpose of providing special education for those who did not speak English.

As early as 1930 Mexican American parents began fighting school-district policies through the courts and since then have won many favorable decisions. In the case of *Independent School District (Texas)* v. *Salvatierra* (1930) the court ruled that segregation can be used only for legitimate purposes of special education. It found that segregation had been used for Mexicans only, without regard for individual ability. In 1945 Mexican American parents in Southern California sued the local board of education for discriminatory practices (*Westminster School District et al.,* v. *Gonzalo*

*Méndez** *et al.*). The court ruled, and the decision was upheld on appeal, that equal protection of the law was not provided for in segregated schools.

SEGUÍN, JUAN N. (1806-1890), Tejano* patriot and politician. Born in San Antonio into a prominent Tejano family of French antecedents, Seguín became politically active by the time he was eighteen, being elected alcalde of San Antonio. His father, Erasmo Seguín, was a close friend of Stephen Austin* and a sympathetic neighbor to the Anglo settlers in Texas. Juan shared his father's attitudes.

When Antonio López de Santa Anna* began his efforts to create a centralized government in the mid-1830s Seguín led the opposition in San Antonio, and when the Texan revolt for federalism and eventually for separation from Mexico occurred, his position was clear. Appointed a captain in the Texan cavalry, he headed a small contingent of Tejanos at the Alamo,* but was sent through the Mexican lines to get help before Santa Anna's final attack. He continued to serve in the remainder of the Texas Revolt and was promoted to lieutenant colonel.

At the end of the war he was put in command of the devastated town of San Antonio—a job made difficult for him not only by repeated Mexican attempts to reconquer the city but also by the swarms of recently arrived Anglo adventurers who were often brutal in their mistreatment of Tejanos. In 1838 he was elected to the Texas senate; when he stepped down from that position two years later, he was elected mayor of San Antonio. His firm defense of fellow Tejanos before the onslaught of disorderly Anglo elements earned him much enmity, and he was unjustly accused of betraying the ill-fated Texas Santa Fe Expedition* of 1841 and of being friendly to invading Mexican forces. Eventually Seguín bowed to Anglo pressures and resigned as mayor in April 1842. Fearing for his family and himself, he moved across the Rio Grande* into Mexico.

At Nuevo Laredo he was jailed by Mexican authorities and then was ordered by Santa Anna to be sent to Mexico City. However, the local commandant suspended Santa Anna's order on condition that Seguín join the Mexican army. Feeling he had no alternative, Seguín accepted Mexican military service and fought on the Mexican side during the U.S.-Mexican War.* After the Treaty of Guadalupe Hidalgo* Seguín reappeared at the Texas border, requesting permission to return to his native Texas. Permission having been granted, he remained quietly in the United States for nearly two decades. Then in 1867 he again crossed over the Rio Grande into Mexico and apparently lived in Nuevo Laredo until his death in his mid-eighties.

SER, the acronymn for Service, Employment, and Redevelopment. SER is a federally funded nonprofit organization formed to make available education, vocational training, and job training and placement to the underemployed and economically disadvantaged. SER was begun in Texas in 1964 through the efforts of the League of United Latin American Citizens* and the G.I. Forum;* it has since spread throughout the Southwest and Midwest. Through contracts with the federal government, it conducts employment preparation programs with special emphasis on local job needs. It also provides English language training, adult education courses, counseling, and a job placement service. At its peak SER guided twenty-three community projects located in all five southwestern states.

SERRA, JUNÍPERO (1713-1784), Franciscan missionary and California pioneer. Born on Majorca in the Mediterranean and educated at the university there, Serra abandoned a promising career as a professor to become a missionary in the New World. After working for nearly a decade among the Indians of the Sierra Madre Oriental in eastern Mexico, he was appointed president of the Franciscan missions in Baja California.

When the Spanish government decided to occupy Alta California,* the first settlement expedition was organized in Baja California and Father Serra was made coleader with its military commander, Gaspar de Portolá. Serra's main task was to establish a string of missions that would help pacify the Indians and hold the region for Spain. Despite his poor health, he was indefatigable in his missionary zeal and by the time of his death had set up nine missions between San Diego and San Francisco. His support of an overland route from central Mexico by which supplies and colonists could reach Alta California was largely responsible for the expeditions of Juan Bautista de Anza.*

More than any other person, Serra was responsible for the early development of orchard and garden agriculture in California.

FURTHER READING: Omer Englebert, *The Last of the Conquistadors: Junípero Serra, 1713-1784,* New York: Harcourt Brace, 1956.

***SERRANO* v. *PRIEST*.** John Serrano, Jr. brought suit against the California State Treasurer in 1968 on the grounds that his son was receiving an inferior education in the barrio* of East Los Angeles because schools were financed by local property taxes, the base of which was low there. In decisions handed down by the California courts in August 1971, April 1974, and December 1977 (California Supreme Court), it was held that financing of schools primarily through local property taxes failed to provide equal protection of the law and therefore had to be changed. Since then state income taxes have been used to reduce disparities in school funding from one district to another.

SHEEP INDUSTRY. *See* LIVESTOCK INDUSTRY.

SILEX, HUMBERTO, union organizer, founder of Local 509 of International Union of Mine, Mill, and Smelter Workers.

Silex entered the United States from Mexico in 1921, and after serving in the United States Army, settled in El Paso, Texas. Employed by the American Smelting and Refining Company, he organized Local 509, largely made up of Mexican Americans, and later became its president. His union activities finally led to his arrest and subsequent deportation proceedings, which he successfully fought and won. He is considered one of the outstanding Mexican labor leaders of his time.

SINARQUISTA MOVEMENT, a Mexican reactionary sociopolitical movement begun in the late 1930s, possibly with some connections to the Spanish Falange and certainly with fascist support. Its purpose was to work for national regeneration and a turning away from selfish materialism to what were seen as Mexico's older moral and ethical values. The term means "without anarchy," and, therefore, implies order. The Sinarquistas opposed Mexico's role in World War II and propagandized about the draft, service outside of Mexico, and treatment of Mexican soldiers. Sinarquismo was never widely accepted in Mexico.

Inevitably there were efforts to extend Sinarquista ideas to the barrios* of the Southwest. In Los Angeles two local leaders, Pedro Villaseñor and Martín Cabrera, were active in publishing *El Sinarquista*, a newspaper which carried various rumors to discourage Mexican Americans from actively participating in the war effort. Sinarquistas advocated return of the Southwest to Mexico, a view which found some support in a Chicano* population that in 1940 was over 30 percent Mexican-born. The movement was taken by both the United States and Mexico with some seriousness. Although the Sinarquistas claimed a large membership in the Southwest, probably not more than two or three thousand joined the organization. Carey McWilliams,* who was on the scene, felt that Sinarquismo was a factor in the Zoot Suit Riots.*

FURTHER READING: Enrique L. Prado, "Sinarquism in the United States," *New Republic* 109 (26 July 1943): 97-102.

SLEEPY LAGOON (1942-1944), a famous court case during World War II. On August 2, 1942, young José Díaz was found on the outskirts of Los Angeles so severely beaten that he died from a fractured skull without regaining consciousness. On the basis of a gang fight the night before at a nearby popular swimming hole (that the press dubbed the Sleepy Lagoon), twenty-three Mexican Americans and one Anglo member of the 38th Street youth gang were arrested. Subsequently they were indicted by the grand jury, and twenty-two were tried en masse on some sixty charges ranging from murder to criminal conspiracy; charges against the other two were dropped after they were granted right to a separate trial.

From Judge Charles W. Fricke on down to the prosecuting attorneys there was much anti-Mexican bias shown during the long trial. The prosecution repeatedly called attention to the Mexican origin of the youths, and they were denied haircuts and changes of clothing. After a trial that lasted several months, on January 13, 1943, the jury found three guilty of first degree murder, nine guilty of second degree murder, five guilty of assault, and five not guilty.

In the fall a Sleepy Lagoon Defense Committee, headed by Carey McWilliams,* opened a national fund campaign to finance an appeal of the court's verdicts. A year later, on October 4, 1944, the District Court of Appeals reversed the lower court, dismissing the case for lack of evidence and criticizing both judge and prosecutor for the conduct of the trial. Following the Sleepy Lagoon case the Los Angeles press and police department strongly stressed Mexican American crime—a development that was to help lead to the so-called Zoot Suit riots* in June 1943.

SLOAT, JOHN D. (1781-1867), naval officer. Stationed off the Mexican coast at Mazatlán in command of the U.S. Pacific Squadron in late 1845, Commodore Sloat, on hearing of hostilities between the United States and Mexico in Texas, sailed to Monterey, California. On July 7, 1846, he took possession of Monterey without meeting resistance, thereby becoming the first American military governor of California. A week later he turned over his command to Commodore Robert F. Stockton* because of ill health and at the end of July left for the East Coast.

SONORANS, inhabitants of the north Mexican state of Sonora, immediately adjacent to Arizona and the southwestern part of New Mexico. The term usually is used to describe the Mexican miners from Sonora who flocked to the California mines in the early years of the gold rush. To a lesser extent it is used to refer to the Mexican immigrants who came to California up to the end of the nineteenth century.

SOUTHWEST, an area whose boundaries are defined differently by various scholars. In its broadest sense it includes the present states of California, Arizona, New Mexico, Texas and parts of Nevada, Utah, Colorado, and Oklahoma. A narrower definition would include only New Mexico, Arizona, and the El Paso region of west Texas. There are, of course, definitions in between these two extremes.

SOUTHWEST COUNCIL OF LA RAZA. *See* NATIONAL COUNCIL OF LA RAZA.

SOUTHWESTERN AGRICULTURAL LABOR. *See* AGRICULTURAL LABOR, SOUTHWESTERN.

SOUTHWESTERN AGRICULTURE. *See* AGRICULTURE, SOUTHWESTERN.

SPANISH AMERICAN, used in the United States when referring to all Spanish-speaking groups resident in the United States, regardless of their origin or ethnicity. Also used, sometimes patronizingly, by Anglo Americans instead of Mexican American or Chicano.*

In New Mexico the term has been used in the twentieth century by Mexican Americans when referring to themselves. Usage of the term often implies a denial of mestizo* and indigenous origins and culture.

SPANISH BACKGROUND. While contemporary Mexican and Chicano* ideology has stressed the important Indian background, it is obvious that a large part of contemporary Mexican American culture is derived from Iberian roots. One need point out only language and religion, not to mention music, institutions, and traditions. The Iberian peninsula itself was a considerable ethnic mix, and although at first emigration was limited to Queen Isabel's citizens in the western half of Spain, soon all peninsular inhabitants were allowed into New Spain, and even some foreigners settled there. By definition the Mexican was a mestizo* and if his mother was Indian, his father was almost certainly a Spaniard of mixed ethnic pedigree.

About 1000 B.C. a Germanic people known as Celts wandered down into the center and west of the Iberian peninsula, mixing with the earlier peoples to form the Celto-Iberians. At about the same time Phoenicians established trading centers along the southwest coast. In the seventh and sixth centuries B.C. they were followed by Greek traders who were active on the east coast, setting up centers like Emporion and Heraclia. Meanwhile in the north another wave of nomadic Celts descended on the peninsula and settled there, and in the south Carthagenians established themselves along the coast, leaving their mark in towns like Cartago Nova (Cartagena).

In 201 B.C. the Romans claimed Spain as a result of the Second Punic War with Carthage and slowly extended their control over the whole peninsula. For the next six hundred years Rome dominated the Iberian peninsula; extensive changes occurred in religion, language, and government and a distinct urban culture developed. The upper classes, especially, became thoroughly Romanized; and important Roman figures like Trajan, Seneca, and Quintilian were of peninsular origin. In the second century A.D. Jewish exiles of the great diaspora arrived, and toward the end of the fifth century the first wave of Vandals and Visigoths began to invade and eventually conquered the peninsula. Then in 711 A.D. Moors crossed over from North Africa and the last important contribution to the mosaic of peninsular culture was begun.

As the result of long and finally successful efforts from 718 to 1492 to drive out the Moors, Spanish nationalism slowly evolved. By the middle of the thirteenth century the Moors had been ousted from the entire peninsula except the southeast province of Granada, and from the many earlier feudal entities four kingdoms had been consolidated: Navarre, Castile, Aragon, and Granada. The marriage of Ferdinand of Aragon and Isabel of Castile in 1469 joined (if scarcely merged) the two largest kingdoms, and soon Navarre and Granada were added by conquest. The fall of Moorish Granada in 1492 freed the sovereigns to expand overseas, and in that year Christopher Columbus initiated discoveries that were to lead to establishing the Viceroyalty of New Spain (Mexico).

In Mexico the Spaniards soon destroyed the Aztec upper class and substituted their own; the formal religion of the Indians, too, was largely extirpated, and Spanish Catholicism replaced it. In short, the more highly organized aspects of Indian culture were replaced with Iberian equivalents, but the ordinary daily aspects of Mexican life went on as they had for centuries. Only slowly and only in the towns did a mestizo culture develop.

FURTHER READING: Julian Bishko, "The Iberian Background of Latin American History: Recent Progress and Continuing Problems," *Hispanic American Historical Review* 36 (1956): 50-80; Ramón Menéndez Pidal, *The Spaniards in Their History*, New York: W. W. Norton and Co., 1966; J. H. Elliot, *Imperial Spain, 1469-1716*, New York: New American Library, 1966; P. Bosch-Gimpera, *La formacíon de los pueblos de España,* México, D.F.: Imprenta Universitaria, 1944; Harold Livermore, *A History of Spain*, New York: Grove Press, Inc., 1960.

SPANISH SURNAME, a term used for persons who have a Spanish last name. In the United States it is often used as a euphemism for Mexican or Mexican American in affirmative action jargon.

Many Spanish surname individuals do not necessarily have ethnic identifications with Latin American or Spanish culture; nor do they speak Spanish or have appreciation for culture other than Anglo American.

SPIC, also spik and spig. Pejorative term for any Latin American. In the United States the term is often applied to Mexican Americans and Puerto Ricans although it is also used for Italians with whom the term originated. It apparently derives from spaghetti, or spaghetti-eater.

STATEHOOD, NEW MEXICO. Under the provisions of the Treaty of Guadalupe Hidalgo* the manner and time of the incorporation of the territory acquired from Mexico as a result of the United States-Mexican War was left to the discretion of the United States Congress. In New Mexico military governors continued to administer the area as they had done before the treaty. Although a constitutional convention held at Santa Fe petitioned Congress for admission as a state in mid-1850, that body ignored the convention and in September established the Territory of New Mexico, which included Arizona and the east area of the upper Rio Grande* claimed also by Texas. A civilian Anglo territorial governor was appointed by Washington.

From 1850 until 1912 the voters of New Mexico struggled in vain for statehood. Efforts to achieve statehood during the four decades following 1850 ended in failure; a serious attempt in 1875 was voted down by southern congressmen and another in 1889 was defeated by Republican fears of a Democratic state. In 1905 an attempt was made to bring in Arizona and New Mexico as the single state of Arizona, but this was rejected by Arizona voters (largely Anglo) who feared political domination by the large majority of Hispanos in New Mexico.

Finally Congress passed an enabling act in 1910 which led to the calling of a constitutional convention. The thirty-three Nuevo Mexicano and sixty-seven Anglo representatives at that convention drew up a document that went far beyond the Treaty of Guadalupe Hidalgo in guaranteeing Mexican American civil and cultural rights. It provided for racial equality, equal recognition of Spanish and English languages, bilingual teachers, and a prohibition against separate schools. Moreover, these parts of the constitution were made virtually unamendable by providing: "This section shall never be amended except upon a vote of the people of this state, in an election at which at least three-fourths of the electors voting in the whole state and at least two-thirds of those voting in each county in the state shall vote for such amendment."

In January 1912 New Mexico became the forty-seventh state when President William H. Taft signed the bill of admission. The long delay in obtaining statehood unquestionably was due to Anglo racial and cultural prejudice.

FURTHER READING: Reuben W. Heflin, "New Mexico Constitutional Convention," *New Mexico Historical Review* 21 (January 1946); Jack E. Holms, *Politics in New Mexico*, Albuquerque: University of New Mexico Press, 1967; Robert W. Larson, *New Mexico's Quest for Statehood, 1846-1912*, Albuquerque: University of New Mexico Press, 1968.

STEREOTYPING, the use of a set of fixed assumptions, often exaggerated, which allow an individual or a society to classify individuals in groups.

These assumptions or beliefs may determine the attitudes of culture groups toward each other.

Even before Anglo Americans came into contact with Mexicans (and later Mexican Americans), a variety of stereotypes began to develop. To most English settlers on the eastern seaboard Mexicans were an ignorant, pope and priest ridden people who lived in the tropics where they miscegenated with local natives, producing an inferior, hybridized progeny and who needed to have "real" christianity brought to them. By the early 1880s, after more widespread contact between Anglos and Mexicans along their common border, modern stereotypes began to develop. Some people saw Mexicans as dirty, lazy, illiterate, deceitful, volatile, unpredictable, romantic, fond of fiesta and dancing, given to gambling, delinquent, addicted to drinking and criminality, fast with the knife, and fond of bright colors and flowers.

These stereotypes were developed and perpetuated by writers in the second half of the nineteenth century, especially by novelists who discovered "romance" in the alienness of southwestern society. In this century stereotypes have been spread much more widely by motion pictures and television; one has only to recall the simple-minded, bumbling, if charming, Mexican sidekick of the Hollywood hero as portrayed in *The Cisco Kid* and the villainous Mexican bandit as portrayed in *Treasure of Sierra Madre*. On television the even more familiar figure of the Frito Bandito, or the Mexican, sombrero pulled down over his face, sleeping against a sun-drenched adobe wall has served to reinforce a negative image.

In general these stereotypes support the assumption that the Mexican is simple, childlike, irresponsible, and untrustworthy, and therefore they have served to justify Anglo discrimination against him. Clearly, these views serve to rationalize and justify exclusion and discrimination; Mexican Americans may be denied their civil liberties, their right to equality in society and before the law.

FURTHER READING: Blaine P. Lamb, "The Convenient Villain: The Early Cinema Views the Mexican-American," *Journal of the West* 14, no. 4 (October 1975): 75-81; Arthur G. Petit, *Images of the Mexican American in Fiction and Film*, College Station: Texas Agricultural and Mechanical University, 1980.

STOCKTON, ROBERT F. (1795-1866), commodore. Beginning his naval career during the War of 1812, Stockton rose to the position of commodore by the time of the outbreak of the United States-Mexican War* in 1846. Arriving at Monterey, California, in mid-1846, he soon succeeded Commodore John D. Sloat* as commander of the United States forces in California. He actively led in the conquest of California and became its second American military governor. After the Cahuenga Treaty* he named John Charles Frémont* to succeed him as governor and left the West Coast for Washington, D.C.

STREET RAILWAY STRIKE, LOS ANGELES. In mid-1910 Mexican and Mexican American employees of the Los Angeles street railway went on strike for higher wages. The strike spread to other branches of industry, including the metal trades, in an atmosphere of bitter labor strife. The dynamiting of the Los Angeles *Times* building in the middle of the strike by individual union officials because of the *Times*' strong antiunion stance caused a strong reaction and helped lead to the failure of the strike.

STRIKES. *See* LABOR ORGANIZATION.

STUDENT MOVEMENTS. The decade of the 1960s was one of increased student political questioning and activity. Among Mexican American high school and college students this led to a movement, allied to other protest activities of the 1960s, for greater ethnic self-determination and self-control—a movement that called itself Chicano.* As a result, in the second half of the sixties numerous student groups were organized all across the Southwest—Mexican American Youth Organization* (MAYO), United Mexican American Students* (UMAS), Movimiento Estudantil Chicano de Aztlán* (MECHA), Mexican American Student Confederation (MASC), Brown Berets,* and many others. Established for different reasons by different people at different times, these organizations covered a broad ideological span, but all took a new and questioning look at American society and the role of Mexican Americans in it.

Beginning largely as protest movements, they moved rather quickly to reconstruct Mexican Americans' self-image and in the process turned toward increasing cultural nationalism. As its heroes these movements tended to take old Mexican revolutionary leaders like Pancho Villa,* Emiliano Zapata,* and Ricardo Flores Magón* as well as new ones like Rodolfo Gonzales,* Reies López Tijerina,* José Angel Gutiérrez,* César Chávez,* and Che Guevara. While most of the organizations went through some ideological change, typically from more radical to middle of the road, all had considerable impact on the lives and especially the education of Mexican Americans. Their greatest success was probably in bringing about the introduction of Chicano courses at all levels of education and in the creation of Chicano programs at both the undergraduate and graduate levels in colleges and universities. Largely as a result of their efforts, more than seventy colleges and universities in the five southwestern states began programs in Mexican American studies between 1967 and 1970.

SURRUMATO, a pejorative term used by Hispanic New Mexicans when referring to Mexicans who have settled in the United States. In Mexico, surrumato is a synonym for stupid or outcast, and also means poorly dressed or raggedy.

SUTTER, JOHN A. (1803-1880), Mexican land grantee and California pioneer. Of German and Swiss origins, Sutter came to San Francisco in 1839 by way of New York, Missouri, New Mexico, Oregon, Hawaii, and Alaska. From Mexican Governor Juan B. Alvarado* he obtained the largest possible land grant—48,400 acres—in the Sacramento Valley. Here he developed a self-sufficient economy with Indian labor and welcomed Anglo settlers to his New Helvetia colony as they began to arrive at the beginning of the 1840s. When the Bear Flaggers* initiated the American conquest of California, Sutter supported them. He was later elected to the 1849 Constitutional Convention.

Meanwhile, discovery of gold on his property led to extensive squatting on his land by miners and others. His economic base was ruined, and Sutter, bankrupt, was unable to recover his lands, although his grant was confirmed by the United States. He died virtually penniless in Washington, D.C.

FURTHER READING: Johann A. Sutter, *New Helvetia Diary: A Record of Events Kept by John A. Sutter and His Clerks at New Helvetia, California from September 9, 1845 to May 25, 1848*, San Francisco: The Grabhorn Press, 1939; James P. Zollinger, *Sutter, the Man and his Empire*, New York: Oxford University Press, 1939.

SWEETHEART CONTRACT, a derisive term referring to an agreement between an employer and a union, as seen by another union. The implication is that the agreement is one imposed by the employer on a kept, or company, union, or that the agreement does not represent the wishes of a majority of union members and is not in their best interest.

T

TAOS REBELLION (1847). After the taking of New Mexico by Colonel Stephen Kearny* and his Missouri volunteers in August 1846, most Nuevo Mexicanos* had apparently acquiesced to American rule. As a result, Kearny left in late September for California, and in December Colonel Alexander Doniphan and his men also departed from Santa Fe for Chihuahua leaving behind only a small American force. Meanwhile antagonism to Americans was on the rise, and a group of leading Nuevo Mexicanos began plotting the overthrow of the Americans on the coming Christmas Eve. Among the rebel leaders were Colonel Diego Archuleta, Tomás Ortiz, his brother the Rev. Juan Felipe Ortiz, and Father Antonio José Martínez.* Their quarrel seems to have been with the expansive land interests of the Americans and their Nuevo Mexicano allies. However, the secret of the plot quickly got out, the revolt was thwarted, and most of the ringleaders (clerics excepted) were arrested. On January 5, 1847, Governor Charles Bent* issued a proclamation condemning the rebel leaders and asking for continued support of the government. He then left to visit his family in Taos.

On January 19 Governor Bent was murdered and scalped by a new set of revolutionaries, made up of Indians and Mexicans of the Taos pueblo and led by a peón,* Pablo Montoya and the Toaseño Indian Tomasito. At the same time the rebels killed Sheriff Luis Lee, young Narciso Beaubien, Cornelio Vigil, and a number of Americans. Colonel Sterling Price, apprised of the attack, organized a force of nearly five hundred men, including some Nuevo Mexicanos, with which he decisively defeated the revolutionaries and seized most of their leaders. The Taos uprising appears to have been spontaneous, and there is no evidence to connect it to the earlier plot or its clerical leaders.

The surviving rebel leaders were then tried in a civilian court for murder and for having tried to overthrow the American government in Mexican New Mexico. Despite some question about the legality of the trial, fifteen men were condemned to death, at least one of them for the crime of treason against a government which he did not acknowledge and which had not yet acknowledged him as one of its citizens.

Some historians have seen the Taos revolt as a symptom of the conflict between the large land grantees and encroachers on pueblo lands on one hand and the poor and landless on the other, rather than between Americans and Nuevo Mexicanos. The destruction by the rebels of many deeds and documents lends some credence to this theory, and it is true that land acquisitions by the Americans and their Nuevo Mexicano friends were set back two decades. The revolt showed that New Mexico was yet to become part of the United States, and it left a long heritage of bitterness and ill-will between Anglo and Mexican Americans in New Mexico.

FURTHER READING: Warren A. Beck, *New Mexico: A History of Four Centuries*, Norman: University of Oklahoma Press, 1962.

TAYLOR GRAZING ACT (1934), Congressional legislation to protect the right of small stock raisers to graze their animals on national forest lands, while protecting the land from overgrazing. Under the Taylor Act each stockman was issued grazing permits for federal lands based on the number of animals he owned. The permits were transferrable, though not saleable. Some large operators were able to acquire additional permits by buying animals from small stock raisers. Others were forced to reduce the size of their herds and flocks with resulting unemployment for their Mexican American workers.

TAYLOR, PAUL S. (1895-), economist, professor, and author. Born in Sioux City, Iowa, and educated in local schools, Paul Taylor entered the University of Wisconsin where he studied under John R. Commons and Richard T. Ely. He graduated in 1917 with a degree in Labor Economics just in time to serve in the Marine Corps in World War I. Severely gassed in France, he returned to the United States and went to the University of California at Berkeley for a year of graduate work. Working with both historians and economists there, he obtained his doctorate in economics in 1922 and then stayed on to teach.

In 1927 Taylor began the study that was to engross the rest of his life—the study of Mexican migration and labor. Out of the data he gathered from Nueces County, Texas, in the southeast to the Imperial Valley in the southwest, and from Bethlehem, Pennsylvania, in the northeast to the Valley of the South Platte in Colorado, he published a series of thirteen volumes on Mexican labor in the United States. In 1933 he investigated the San Joaquin cotton strike* and compiled a history of that confrontation between eight thousand migrants and the valley cotton growers. Temporarily reducing his workload at the university to work for the California State Relief Administration, in 1935 Taylor began collaborating with the documentary photographer Dorothea Lange, whom he later married. A few years later when the LaFollette Civil Liberties Committee* undertook its investigation of California's "factories in the field," Taylor was both an important witness and a source of numerous graphs, statistical tables, and drawings illustrating labor problems. The committee used his study of the 1933 cotton strike as evidence in its report.

Arguing that industrialized agriculture led to an industrialized class of migrant rural poor, Taylor focused his studies on the Reclamation Act of 1902 and especially its 160-acre limitation, so long ignored by the federal Reclamation Service. As a professor at the University of California, Taylor was chairman of the Department of Economics at Berkeley from 1952 to 1956 and also helped to develop the Institute of Industrial Relations there. In addition to his service to the LaFollette Committee he also has acted as advisor to various government agencies and commissions. After his retirement in 1962 he kept his old office at Berkeley and has continued his work of research, writing, and counseling students and countries.

FURTHER READING: Richard Street, "The Economist as Humanist—The Career of Paul S. Taylor," *California History* 58, no. 4 (Winter 1979/80), 350-61.

TAYLOR, ZACHARY (1784-1850), general. In his twenties Taylor began a military career that carried him from lieutenant to general. When the dispute over the boundary of Texas with Mexico arose in 1845, Taylor was sent from New Orleans to the Nueces River area in south-central Texas with a force of fifteen hundred men in a precautionary move by the United

States. Early in 1846, on orders from Washington, he moved his army into the disputed area between the Nueces and the Rio Grande, where it was attacked by Mexican forces. This Mexican action led to a declaration of war by the United States on May 13. *See also* MEXICAN WAR.

TEAMSTERS UNION. *See* INTERNATIONAL BROTHERHOOD OF TEAMSTERS, CHAUFFEURS, WAREHOUSEMEN, AND HELPERS OF AMERICA (IBT).

TEATRO CAMPESINO, the most successful of Chicano* theatres. Teatro Campesino has earned an international reputation and has inspired many other Chicano theatre groups. It was founded by Luis Valdez* in 1965. Initially the theatre had one specific, political goal—the organization of farm workers. For two years the Teatro Campesino was actively involved in the everyday struggles of the farm workers' strike. It joined the strikers on their march to Sacramento, California, publicizing the strike and gathering public support for the farm workers union (National Farm Workers Association*).

The Teatro Campesino broadened its objectives in 1967 when it established El Centro Campesino Cultural in Del Rey, California. (Presently the Centro is located in San Juan Bautista, California.) This cultural center was designed to impart to students a sense of pride about being Chicano through a variety of courses dealing with Chicano culture. To this end the Teatro Campesino was utilized with so much success that it shifted its focus from the farm workers to Chicano culture in all its ramifications. Its most important emphasis, however, remained political. Stated briefly, the farm workers theatre has five principal objectives: (1) to raise the consciousness of the Chicano, (2) to inform the Chicano of negative conditions that exist to oppress him, (3) to politicize the Chicano so he can overcome the existing conditions of oppression, (4) to inform the Chicano of his rich heritage so as to instill in him pride in his culture, and (5) to strengthen the spirit of the Chicano by communicating values such as love, hope, and kindness.

Since the immediate goal of the Teatro Campesino was the organization of the farm workers, the content of its first actos (plays) dealt exclusively with the strike. Plays such as *Las dos Caras del Patroncito* (1965) and *Quinta Temporada* (1966) dramatize the socioeconomic and political plight of the campesinos and their struggles against agribusiness. For the most part these early plays are comedies, characterized by "bittersweet humor."

With the success of El Centro Campesino Cultural and the unionization of the farm workers (NFWA), the Teatro Campesino broadened its repertoire to include everything and anything related to Chicano culture. Thus it has developed and performed plays that deal with a variety of Chicano-related themes: acculturation (*Los Vendidos*, 1967); Chicano militants (*The Militants*, 1969); education (*No Sacó Nada de la Escuela*, 1969); Vietnam (*Vietnam Campesino*, 1970; *Soldado Raso*, 1971); racial prejudice (*Zoot Suit*, 1978); and others. This last play is loosely based on the events surrounding the Sleepy Lagoon* murder of 1942 and the Zoot Suit Riots* of 1943 in Los Angeles.

With the formal opening of *Zoot Suit* on Broadway in 1979, a year after a successful run at the Mark Taper Forum in Los Angeles, the Teatro Campesino took a center stage position in American theatre. *F.J.*

TEJANO, in its broadest sense, a term referring to all Texans of Mexican descent. These are also referred to as Latin Americans as well as Mexican Americans, and in historical materials sometimes as Tex-Mex or simply as Mexicans. In a narrower sense Tejano is used to designate Texans of Mexican descent in or from the period of the 1830s and 1840s.

TELLES, RAYMOND L. JR. (1915-), ambassador, Texas political leader, businessman, and colonel in the Air Force. Raymond Telles was born and grew up in El Paso, Texas, where he attended grade and high school and later the International Business College and the University of Texas. In 1934 he entered government service as an accountant and remained seven years until the outbreak of World War II. He then joined the Air Force, where he became a colonel and was awarded the Bronze Star as well as various decorations by Latin American governments. He returned to El Paso where he was subsequently elected four times to the position of county clerk (1949-1957); he then ran for mayor of El Paso and was elected for two terms.

In 1961 Telles was appointed by President John F. Kennedy as ambassador to Costa Rica, a position he held for six years during which he was influential in bringing that country into the Central American Common Market. At the end of this tour of duty he was appointed by President Lyndon B. Johnson to chair the United States section of the joint United States-Mexico Border Development and Friendship Commission. At the end of his two year term he returned to private business, primarily as a consultant. In 1971 President Richard Nixon appointed him as a commissioner to the Equal Employment Opportunity Commission, where he continued his public service for five more years. Telles has served as military aide to three presidents and also to a number of visiting Latin American dignitaries. He has been the recipient of numerous civic awards.

TENAYUCA (BROOKS), EMMA (1916-). Born and raised in San Antonio, Texas, Emma Tenayuca was a serious student who, by the time she entered high school, had begun to question American society and the Mexican American's inferior position in it. In the early 1930s she began a life of helping La Raza* by speaking out for civil rights and reform. With the onset of the Great Depression, Emma, who had adopted a radical stance, helped organize a 1931 march of unemployed Texans on the state capital in Austin, under the auspices of the Trade Union Unity League.* Three years later she organized the Workers Alliance, the most militant labor organization in San Antonio, which staged sit-down strikes and demonstrations to demand relief and work for the unemployed.

In 1937 Emma married Homer Brooks of Houston, a leader of the Communist party in Texas, but she remained in San Antonio where she became one of the principal leaders in the pecan strike,* which broke out early in the following year. Although Emma and the Workers Alliance dominated the strike initially, Donald Henderson, president of the United Cannery, Agricultural, Packing and Allied Workers of America,* soon took the leadership away from her in a purge of local communists. Claiming a nervous breakdown from overwork, Emma left for New York to study communist methods. A year later she returned briefly to San Antonio to stage a massive party rally, which ended before it began, in a gigantic riot. Emma Tenayuca fled to California where, after a brief effort to enter the Mexican American labor movement, she disappeared into anonymity.

FURTHER READING: Carlos Larralde, *Mexican American Movements and Leaders*, Los Alamitos, Calif.: Hwong Publishing Co., 1976; Emma Tenayuca and Homer Brooks, "The Mexican Question in the Southwest," *The Communist* (March 1939).

TENNEY COMMITTEE. In 1941 the California legislature established a Fact-Finding Committee on Un-American Activities in imitation of the federal model and headed by Assemblyman Jack B. Tenney. The Tenney Committee, as it was known, soon became prosecutor, judge, and jury in what were legislative trials of suspect liberal and radical organizations and individuals. During 1943-1944 the committee subpoenaed several members of the Sleepy Lagoon* Defense Committee and grilled them in an effort to establish Communist connections. This curtailed fund-raising by the committee. During the 1947 strike by the National Farm Labor Union* at Di Giorgio* farms, Tenney summoned witnesses to a hearing in Los Angeles in February. Among those questioned were H. L. Mitchell* and Hank Hasiwar. Tenney's committee found no evidence either of membership in the Communist party by officers of the union or of communist domination of the strike, as charged by many grower opponents of the union. The activities of the Tenney Committee helped lead to the famous University of California loyalty oath controversy in 1949. In June, after accusing fellow members of the state legislature of having communist sympathies, Tenney was forced to resign from the committee, and Senator Hugh M. Burns took over as chairman.

TEXAS. In 1836 when Texas declared its independence from Mexico, there were approximately four thousand Mexican Texans compared to an estimated thirty thousand Anglos. Anti-Mexican feeling generated by the massacre at Goliad* and the Battle of the Alamo* remained alive in the minds of Anglos and influenced their views of persons of Mexican origin and the way they were treated. Thus, Mexican Texans found themselves greatly outnumbered among people who were culturally different and often prejudiced against them.

During the period of the Texas Republic and after Texas achieved statehood, persons with Spanish surnames could vote and hold office. Nevertheless, it was only in a few counties like Starr, Webb, and Duval, where Mexican Americans were in the majority, that they were able to elect members of their ethnic group to office. Even in these areas their political influence was often reduced by being a part of political machines dominated by Anglos who paid little attention to their problems.

Under Spain and Mexico Mexicans had acquired land grants which gave them title to millions of acres of land in Texas. Although the American state of Texas recognized the validity of these grants, pressure for land from the rapidly growing Anglo population resulted in much of this acreage being acquired by Anglo Texans, by either legal or illegal means. However, in counties in the southern part of the state, like Webb, Starr, and Hidalgo, many Mexican Americans were successful in retaining their rancho properties.

As the range cattle industry developed in Texas, many Mexican Americans found employment as vaqueros* on ranches. Most of the sheepherders of Texas were of Mexican origin as were the sheep-shearing crews. Another source of jobs for Mexican Americans in the nineteenth century was the building of railroads in south and west Texas. Some Mexican Americans gravitated to cities like El Paso, Corpus Christi, and San Antonio where they worked as laborers, but census reports show a number of urban Mexican Americans employed as barbers, silversmiths, harnessmakers, drivers of ox-carts, and clerks in stores. A few, like Francisco Yturria of Brownsville, achieved success as merchants and bankers.

The economic development that had the most profound effect on Mexican Americans was the coming of commercial agriculture to the state. The spread of cotton culture across the state created a tremendous demand for labor which was partially met by Mexican Americans and supplemented by workers from Mexico. As early as the 1890s Mexican Americans from south Texas were following the cotton crop across the state on foot, and returning to their homes after four or five months. The state-wide migration of Mexican American farm workers was facilitated by improvements in highways and greater use of automobiles during the 1920s.

The development of citrus and market vegetable industries in south Texas created an additional demand for Mexican American laborers. Winter months were spent in south Texas working in the fruit and vegetable fields or packing sheds, while in the summer and fall laborers picked cotton as it matured throughout the state.

The demand for seasonal farm labor was filled almost entirely by persons of Mexican descent. Workers in Mexico were not slow in responding to the increasing need for labor north of the border. Although wages offered in Texas were low and working conditions were poor by American standards, many Mexicans found this employment more attractive than that available in their own country. As a result, there was a great migration of workers from Mexico to Texas. Mexican immigration, along with the high birth rate of Mexican Americans, brought about a large increase in the size of the Spanish surname population of the state.

Most Mexican Americans made their homes in the counties of south Texas and in the large cities of the state. They formed a reservoir of cheap, mobile labor. Since World War II a majority has found employment in the rapidly expanding industrial economy of Texas, usually as unskilled or semiskilled laborers. In recent years growing numbers of them have become skilled workers and are entering the professions.

Over the years Mexican Americans in Texas have reacted in a variety of ways to an Anglo-controlled society. Some, like Juan Cortina,* resorted to violence to protest injustices. Others have formed organizations like the League of United Latin American Citizens (LULAC)* and the American G.I. Forum* to work for changes beneficial to Mexican Americans. Many have felt the need for a more aggressive policy than was offered by these two organizations and established groups like the Mexican American Youth Organization (MAYO),* the Raza Unida Party,* and the Brown Berets* that have used the politics of confrontation to promote interests of the group.

Mexican Americans in Texas have adjusted to their situation by developing a culture that is a mixture of Mexican and American elements. In the colonias* and barrios* of Texas this culture has found institutional expression in the founding of mutual aid societies, Spanish language newspapers and radio stations, and church groups. It is a dynamic culture that is constantly changing and one in which Mexican Americans take great pride and work with great tenacity to retain.

FURTHER READING: Douglas E. Foley, et al., *From Peones to Politicos: Ethnic Relations in a South Texas Town, 1900-1977*, Austin: University of Texas

Press, 1978; Américo Paredes, *With His Pistol in His Hand: A Border Ballad and Its Hero*, Austin: University of Texas Press; John S. Shockley, *Chicano Revolt in a Texas Town*, Notre Dame: University of Notre Dame Press, 1958, 1974; Paul Schuster Taylor, *American-Mexican Frontier*, Chapel Hill: University of North Carolina Press, 1934; Robert A. Cuellar, *A Social and Political History of the Mexican-American Population of Texas, 1929-1963*, San Francisco: R & E Research Associates, 1974; Rie Jarratt et al., *The Mexican Experience in Texas*, New York: Arno Press, 1976.

G.O.C.

TEXAS COUNCIL ON MIGRANT LABOR, organized in 1957 to improve travel and living conditions of migrant workers. The Council was abolished eight years later and its functions were transferred to the Texas Good Neighbor Commission.*

TEXAS EMIGRANT AGENT LAW. *See* EMIGRANT AGENCY LAW.

TEXAS GOOD NEIGHBOR COMMISSION. *See* GOOD NEIGHBOR COMMISSION.

TEXAS RANGERS, originally a ranging company of mounted militia, first set up in 1823 by Stephen Austin. During the difficulties leading up to the Texas Revolt and independence in the 1830s a ranger paramilitary force was reinstated as protection against Indian activities on the northwestern frontier, and after an independence that Mexico did not accept, rangers were also given the task of protecting the southern border from Mexican incursions and raids. The rangers, like the society they came from, considered Indians and Mexicans as longtime enemies. They were also agents of frontier expansion. During the United States-Mexican War* a ranger unit of about five hundred men fought in Mexico with General Zachary Taylor* and later with Winfield Scott.* Its members quickly developed a reputation as undisciplined troops who seldom brought in Mexican prisoners.

After the war a much reduced ranger force resumed its earlier tasks of keeping the peace on the Indian frontier and of fighting border bandits and rustlers to the south. It was involved in the fight against Juan Cortina* on the eve of the Civil War without notable success. During postwar reconstruction the rangers were more or less replaced by a state police force, but in 1874 a new ranger organization was established by the Texas state government. With the Indian problems of the West nearing their end these new rangers concerned themselves primarily with cattlemen's feuds, rustlers, border brigands, and southwestern badmen. Too often rangers viewed intimidation and violence as a justified means to pacify the frontier. Ranger policy, under Captain L. H. McNally, was to take no prisoners except old men, women, and children. The rangers often acted, in effect, as an Anglo landowner force, and many innocent Mexicans suffered from their shoot-first-and-ask-any-questions-later attitude. Mexican Americans often were the victims of law enforcers as well as of lawbreakers.

In the twentieth century the Texas rangers have suffered from two problems: involvement in politics and their use to hold back the tide of unionism, especially in agriculture where the aspirants to unionization were mostly Mexican Americans and Mexican nationals. During World War I the ranger force was expanded to about one thousand, largely to pay off political debts by making appointments to this Texas state "nobility."

The rangers played a role in the anti-Mexican bloodletting that characterized the Texas border during World War I. In 1919, as a result of charges brought against the rangers by José T. Canales* of the Texas legislature, they were reorganized and reduced to five companies totaling seventy-five men. Under Governor Miriam A. Ferguson in the 1930s the rangers again became deeply embroiled in politics, and in reaction to this involvement, in 1935 Texas created a Department of Public Safety of which the Rangers, eventually divided into six sections with a total complement of sixty-two men, were a part. In the 1970s the total force was expanded to ninety-four men. Since 1935 rangers have been selected and promoted on the basis of recommendations, exams, and performance.

Newly purged and its members trained in the latest technology and skills, in the 1960s the rangers nevertheless continued some older patterns of action. During and after the Crystal City* elections of 1963 a ranger force under Captain Alfred Y. Allee actively harassed the cinco candidatos* mayor and later Juan Cornejo and other Chicano city officials. In the melon strike of 1966-1967 in the lower Rio Grande Valley,* harassment, mass arrests, and verbal abuse and threats were among the techniques used by the rangers. In 1967 the Texas Council of Churches filed suit against the rangers, asking for an injunction to keep them from interfering with the clergy in its work during the strike. In another 1967 case, *Medrano* v. *Allee*,* the United States Supreme Court ruled against the rangers seven years later. Subsequent investigation of the strike resulted in criticism of the rangers, especially for violating the civil rights of strikers and appearing to be on the side of the growers.

Viewed by Tejanos* as a force designed to repress them, the rangers have aggravated ethnic conflict along the border more often than they reduced it.

FURTHER READING: Julian Samora, et al., *Gunpowder Justice: A Reassessment of the Texas Rangers*, Notre Dame: University of Notre Dame Press, 1979; Walter Prescott Webb, *The Texas Rangers, A Century of Frontier Defense*, Boston: Houghton Mifflin Co., 1935.

TEXAS REVOLT (1835-1836), often confused in the popular mind with the

Mexican War* (1846-1848). The Texas Revolt began with Antonio López de Santa Anna's* election to the presidency and his institution of a centralized government in Mexico City by the mid-1830s. It was part of social, economic, and political differences between Anglo and Mexican Texans that earlier had led to rising tensions both within Texas and between the Anglo Texan majority there and the government in Mexico City. Mexican legislation of 1830 severely limiting further Anglo immigration and imposing tariffs between Texas and the United States added to Anglo distrust of the government. When Stephen Austin,* the leading Anglo empresario,* was arrested for fomenting revolution and imprisoned in Mexico City, one of the last voices for legality and moderation was stilled. Upon his return to Texas in July 1835, Austin began to lead the separatist-independence movement, and in the fall, when Santa Anna sent four thousand Mexican troops under General Perfecto de Cos* to enforce collection of customs duties, the Texas Revolt had definitely begun.

When his army was decisively defeated and General Cos was forced to withdraw across the Rio Grande,* Santa Anna personally took command in Mexico City. He quickly recruited and organized a second conscript army to attack the Texans who had meanwhile defeated the garrison at Goliad,* seized its material, and had taken the Alamo* in San Antonio with its military supplies. Leading his ill-trained, six-thousand-man army northward in a remarkable two-month, one-thousand-mile march to San Antonio, Santa Anna announced a no-quarter policy, attacked, and took the Alamo on March 6, 1836. With this major victory, a second one at Goliad* two weeks later, and a no-prisoner policy in both victories, Santa Anna seemed to have the Texan revolutionaries on the run.

With Santa Anna in pursuit, Sam Houston led the Texas forces, stung by the massacres at the Alamo and Goliad, on an eastward retreat. Then, on April 21 he turned and attacked Santa Anna's unprepared army at San Jacinto. The battle was over in eighteen minutes, and Santa Anna was taken prisoner as he tried to flee. The Mexican army retreated to the Rio Grande, and Santa Anna secured his own eventual release by signing the Treaty of Velasco* with the Texans on May 14. Thus the Texas Revolt ended with independence for Texas, although Mexico continued to claim it. Mexico was unable to regain control despite blockading and invasions.

FURTHER READING: Paul Horgan, *Great River: The Rio Grande in North American History*, vol. 2, New York: Rinehart, 1954.

THE EAST LOS ANGELES COMMUNITY UNION (TELACU), founded in 1968 by Esteban Torres with labor union support as an antipoverty program. TELACU has grown into a multi-million dollar community development organization under the leadership of its current president, David Lizarraga. In a highly effective manner it has both provided leadership training for Chicanos* and stimulated positive community change. One of its major successes has been in obtaining appointive political positions for Mexican Americans, especially members of its own staff.

TIERRA AMARILLA, the tiny county seat of Rio Arriba County, New Mexico, made famous by its connection with Reies López Tijerina* and his Alianza Federal de Pueblos Libres.* Tierra Amarilla came to national attention as a result of the June 5, 1967 courthouse raid there by followers of Tijerina.

Tierra Amarilla is also the name of a large New Mexican land grant covering much of present Rio Arriba County.

TIJERINA, REIES LÓPEZ (1926-), Chicano* activist leader; founder and president of the Alianza Federal de Mercedes, now known as the Alianza Federal de Pueblos Libres.* Tijerina was born near San Antonio, Texas, into a large and poor sharecropper family that was forced to become migrant laborers, following the crops to Colorado, Wyoming, and Michigan; as a result he obtained little formal schooling. Around 1940 he joined the Assembly of God church, went to a Texas Bible school, and upon graduation did evangelistic work along the border. After ten years, spent mostly as an itinerant preacher, Tijerina broke with the fundamentalist church. In 1955 he established a short-lived (because of local hostility and harassment) cooperative settlement of seventeen Mexican American families in Arizona, called Valle de la Paz (Valley of Peace). While at Valle de la Paz Tijerina was twice charged with grand theft but never brought to trial.

During the 1950s Tijerina began to develop an interest in Spanish and Mexican land grants and gradually became convinced that all the troubles of Mexican Americans could be traced back to the loss of their lands. In 1958 and 1959 he spent time in Mexico researching the history of southwestern land grants and even tried to interest the Mexican government in the question. In 1960 he moved to Albuquerque where he obtained work as a church janitor and quietly began developing his movement. During the next few years he continued his study and research of the land grant issue, and in February 1963, with his five brothers and a few dozen followers, he organized the Alianza Federal de Mercedes* (Federal Alliance of Grants), with the aim of returning lands to the heirs of the original grantees. Tijerina then began an evangelistic stumping of northwestern New Mexico to win converts to the alianza; he also solicited political recognition and support. By mid-1966 he claimed twenty thousand followers and led a group of them on a sixty-mile march from Santa Fe to the capital where they presented their protests to Governor Jack Campbell. In October he also led a group in a takeover of part of the Kit Carson National Forest, which he declared to be the Republic of Rio Chama. This act led to his arraignment on federal charges. Violence, arson, and vandalism against Anglo residents mounted and, fearing arrest, Tijerina resigned as president of the alianza and disbanded it in mid-1967, only to reorganize it immediately as the Alianza Federal de Pueblos Libres* (Federal Alliance of Free Towns).

The arrest of ten alianza members on June 4 led to a dramatic raid by aliancistas on the Tierra Amarilla courthouse in which the jailer and a policeman were wounded. After a massive manhunt Tijerina was arrested and charged with numerous offenses in connection with the raid. Already under federal indictment for his part in the 1966 Kit Carson National Forest incident, he was found guilty (of assault) in November, but appealed his conviction and two-year sentence.

Now the darling of the radical left, Tijerina branched out from New Mexico in his activities. His attendance at the National Conference for New Politics was followed in mid-1968 by a leading role in the Poor People's* march on Washington, D.C., and then his candidacy for governor of New Mexico. He was disqualified, however, because of his felony conviction.

In mid-December 1968 Tijerina's month-long trial on federal charges stemming from the courthouse raid ended in an acquittal. However, in the following February his earlier conviction was upheld (and again appealed), and in June he had a confrontation with Forest Service officers that led to a three-year federal prison sentence. That fall the U.S. Supreme Court rejected his earlier appeal, and in October Tijerina began serving his federal sentence. His trial on state charges stemming from the courthouse raid was now held and resulted in his receiving two state prison terms of one-to-five and two-to-ten years, to run concurrently.

On July 27, 1971, Tijerina was released from prison on five-year parole with the proviso that he hold no office in the alianza. At the El Paso Raza Unida* convention in September 1972 he acted as a moderating influence and two months later took the same role at a national Chicano Congress on Land and Cultural Reform which he organized. Since the mid-1970s Tijerina, no longer a fiery Chicano leader, has been calling for brotherhood and devoting much of his time to an attempt to interest the president of Mexico in the New Mexican land grant issue. So far his efforts have failed. As the 1980s begin, Tijerina again is directing his attention toward reviving the Rio Chama republic.

Tijerina consistently has held as his main objective the recovery for Nuevo Mexicanos* of grant lands lost since 1848. In his ideas there is also some ethnic separatism, at least in a cultural sense. He has had the support of Chicano activists (until the 1970s) and of rural Nuevo Mexicanos of the Rio Arriba area. Most other Mexican American leaders have been cautious about unqualified endorsement of Tijerina; in the broad La Raza* community opinion is also divided.

FURTHER READING: Richard Gardner, *Grito! Reies Tijerina and the New*

Mexico Land Grant War of 1967, Indianapolis, Ind.: Bobbs-Merrill Co., 1970; Peter Nabokov, *Tijerina and the Courthouse Raid*, Albuquerque: University of New Mexico Press, 1969; Patricia B. Blawis, *Tijerina and the Land Grants: Mexican Americans in Struggle for Their Heritage*, New York: International Publishers Company, 1971.

TÍO TACO, synonymous with coconut and vendido.* Tío Taco is a pejorative term for Mexican Americans who ingratiate themselves with Anglo Americans by denying their ethnicity and culture, and who sycophantically attempt to assimilate into the predominant culture. Militant-activist groups consider Tío Tacos to be enemies of La Raza* and sell-outs.

FURTHER READING: Richard V. Thornton, "Tío Taco is Dead," *Newsweek* 75 (June 29, 1970): 22-28.

TIREMAN, LLOYD S. (1896-), educator. Educated exclusively in his native Iowa, after his undergraduate studies, Tireman obtained both his M.A. and, in 1927 his Ph.D., at the University of Iowa. After serving as superintendent of schools in several Iowa cities while completing his graduate degrees, in 1927 he obtained a position at the University of New Mexico. His area of specialization was children's literature and educational problems of Spanish-speaking children. In this latter area he did some outstanding early work for which he became widely known in the Southwest.

TOLAN COMMITTEE, the popular name for the United States Congress Committee to Investigate the Migration of Destitute Citizens which, just before World War II, became the Select Committee Investigating National Defense Migration, headed by Representative John Harvey Tolan. One of its important actions was the recommendation that a joint United States-Mexican committee be established to ensure that a wartime labor shortage would not occur. The ultimate result of this recommendation was the first Bracero Program;* it was established in 1942 and ended in 1947.

TORRES, FRANCISCO (?-1892), Mexican American laborer, lynched in Santa Ana, California, in August 1892. Working at the Modjeska Ranch, under foreman William McKelvey, Torres refused to accept a tax deduction of $2.50 from his wages and demanded to be paid in full. Torres and McKelvey quarreled and fought over the issue, resulting in McKelvey's death. Torres escaped.

Though no one witnessed the killing, the press accused Torres of the murder. Apprehended and jailed, Torres never made it to trial. A mob of townspeople dragged him out of his cell and lynched him. One of numerous Mexican American lynchings in Western history, Torres's hanging was the last one reported in California history.

TORTILLA CURTAIN INCIDENT (1978-1979), a dispute concerning the construction of a border fence. In late October 1978 a news story concerning a proposed border fence made front pages in both the United States and Mexico. Headlined as the tortilla curtain, the eleven-mile-long fence at El Paso and Tijuana was described as being a twelve-foot-high barrier composed of a five-foot lower section of expanded metal construction, sharp enough to cut off the toes of climbers and a seven-foot upper section of chain-link fencing topped with barbed wire. In Mexico City newspapers a further ingredient was added to the story—an allegation that the United States was sending fourteen thousand armed troops to the border. The result was an angry reaction at national and local levels in both countries despite assurances that the fence was not designed to maim and that troops were not being sent.

On October 24 leaders of various Mexican American organizations protested the fence, and in El Paso a Coalition Against the Fence was organized. Six weeks later a demonstration was scheduled at El Paso, as criticism on both sides of the border continued to build up. A subsequent survey in El Paso and Ciudad Juárez showed that leaders in both cities were overwhelmingly opposed to the fence project. Early in January 1979 Associate Attorney General Michael Egan visited El Paso to inform local leaders of changes in the proposed fence, and in the following month the Southwest Border Region Commission made a recommendation against building the fence. In March feelings of anger and frustration arising out of the tortilla curtain incident flared anew because of a crackdown on illegal commuters. As a result the Cordova Bridge was blockaded for two days by Mexican demonstrators.

Finally, on April 25 the Immigration and Naturalization Service* announced that the fence project had been revised and the fence design changed. The new fence would be lower, the expanded metal part redesigned, and the barbed wire gone. Also the total length would be only eight miles. In addition, an announcement was made that the Mexican government, having been consulted, had no objections to the redesigned fence. This new sensitivity to Mexican feelings helped soothe ruffled border sensibilities, and the tortilla curtain incident faded.

TRADE UNION UNITY LEAGUE, a communist-sponsored, revolutionary labor organization conceived in the late 1920s as the radical answer to the American Federation of Labor. The league was especially successful in marginal industries like mining, agriculture, and textiles—the first two of which employed many Mexican Americans. The TUUL concentrated its organizing efforts among unskilled California agricultural workers, beginning early in 1930 and working particularly with casual and migratory harvest labor. A common technique for TUUL organizers was to move into an unorganized, spontaneous strike and give it organization and leadership sometimes retaining a façade of local leaders. It was this pattern that caused most growers to equate agricultural labor organizations with communism and to accuse organizers of being communists.

The TUUL worked in the fields through an organization called successively The Agricultural Workers Industrial League, the Agricultural Workers Industrial Union, and ultimately the Cannery and Agricultural Workers Industrial Union.* This last organization, after some success, declined and virtually disappeared by the end of 1934. In March of the following year the TUUL and all affiliated organizations were terminated by Communist party directives in line with the new worldwide united front policy.

FURTHER READING: Stuart Jamieson, *Labor Unionism in American Agriculture*, Washington, D.C.: U.S. Government Printing Office, 1945; reprint, New York: Arno Press, 1976.

TREATY OF GUADALUPE HIDALGO. *See* GUADALUPE HIDALGO, TREATY OF.

TREATY OF VELASCO. *See* VELASCO, TREATY OF.

TREVIÑO, LEE (BUCK) (1939-), golfer. Born in Dallas, Texas, Treviño was raised by his mother and grandfather. Living in a home next to a golf course, he began playing golf on his own two-hole course with an old, cut-down club by the time he was six. On completing the seventh grade, Treviño dropped out of school to work full-time at the golf course. At age seventeen he joined the U.S. Marines and served two two-year hitches. While in the Marines Lee first began to take golf seriously and upon his discharge in 1961 got a job as a pro at a small Dallas golf club. Four years later he decided to go on the golf tournament circuit. After an unsure beginning, Lee Treviño found his stride, and in 1968 he earned over $125,000 in prize money. In 1971 he earned $231,000, and in that year became the first golfer to win the United States, Canadian, and British opens in a single year.

A glib, wise-cracking extrovert on the golf course, Lee Treviño is also a warm, generous person who usually gives part of his winnings to a local charity. This generosity and affability has developed for him a large following of both youths and adults known as "Lee's Fleas," and his sportsmanship has gained him wide respect among golfers.

TUCK, RUTH (?-), author, sociologist. A pioneer writer on Mexican American migrants and braceros,* she is widely criticized for her portrayal of Mexican Americans as being weak, lazy, indifferent, and un-American.

In her best known work, *Not With the Fist, Mexican American in a*

Southwest City, (1956), she portrays the acculturation and assimilation problems that Mexican Americans have endured. In the process, however, she also presents a stereotype of Mexican Americans as passive and fatalistic.

TUCSON, originally a Pima Indian village (*schookson*—at the foot of the black mountain) in the vicinity of the modern city which bears this name. Archaeological evidence shows the area to have been occupied by Hohokam Indians—possible ancestors of the Pimas—from at least 800 A.D. Jesuit priest Eusebio Francisco Kino* may have visited the site in November 1694, but it is first mentioned by name in an 1699 entry in the diary of Juan Matheo Mange (Manje), Kino's military escort. San Cosme was the saint's name assigned by Kino to the Indian village.

In 1700 Kino founded a mission at Bac, a slightly larger Pima community about ten miles from Tucson, and in 1752 the Spanish placed a presidio at Tubac, a third Pima town fifty miles to the south. From the latter date until their expulsion in 1767, the Jesuits occasionally stationed missionaries in Tucson, which was called San Agustín. After the expulsion of the Jesuits, Father Francisco Garcés, the first Franciscan priest at San Xavier del Bac, renamed the site San Agustín in 1768, and the name is still used to identify the cathedral of the Tucson diocese.

Captain Juan Bautista de Anza,* the Spanish military commander at Tubac, persuaded the Tucson Indians in 1770 to construct adobe breastworks and a tower—the first European structures in the village. These were followed shortly thereafter by a church.

Colonel Hugo Oconór laid out the site for a new presidio on August 20, 1775, the date today's Tucsonans celebrate the founding of the modern city. During the following ten years the Spanish soliders constructed a high adobe wall around the presidio; and between the mid-1780s and 1821, when the Spanish period ended, Tucson was one of the major military installations anchoring the northern frontier line.

Following Mexican independence the Tucson garrison often found itself without a full complement of men, in spite of the fact that the Mexican national congress in 1826 had authorized its continuation as a military establishment. Apache attacks on Sonoran ranches, farms, and towns greatly increased during the 1830s and 1840s, and during these decades Tucson served as a place of refuge for families from outlying areas.

After the outbreak of the Mexican War,* Colonel Philip St. George Cooke led the Mormon Battalion into the area. Greatly outnumbered and outgunned, the Mexican presidial troops withdrew from the post, and Cooke's troops were warmly received by the local residents who, in their constant fear of the Apaches, were glad to see such a show of military strength. After the conclusion of the United States-Mexican War in 1848, Tucson became a major stopping point for persons traveling the southern route to the California gold fields. With the Gadsden Purchase* in 1853, it became a part of the United States although Mexican troops remained in the town until 1856 to protect the inhabitants against hostile Indians.

Existing censuses from the Spanish and Mexican periods show only a few hundred Tucson residents, and it seems unlikely that the Spanish Mexican population in the entire area of modern Arizona ever exceeded one thousand persons prior to 1855. After 1854 individuals from the neighboring state of Sonora and elsewhere in northern Mexico came to the city. Among the Mexican newcomers who played leadership roles in the early American period were Mariano Samaniego,* Esteban Ochoa,* Leopoldo Carrillo, Carlos Velasco, the Aguirre brothers, Frederick Ronstadt, and Carlos Jácome. Representatives of older southern Arizona families often intermarried with the newcomers, as they did with Anglos. There were few Anglo women in Tucson prior to 1880, and Anglo males commonly chose Mexican wives.

The pattern of Anglo-Mexican intermarriage, begun in the mid-1880s, has been a distinguishing feature of Tucson inter-ethnic relations and continues to the present day. A study done in the late 1950s revealed that more than 25 percent of all Spanish-surnamed persons obtaining marriage licenses were planning to wed individuals with Anglo surnames. The study also showed that these "mixed" marriages involved Mexican males and Anglo females in nearly 50 percent of the cases, as contrasted with the pattern a century earlier when almost all male partners were Anglos and female partners, Mexicans. Another distinct feature of Tucson is the predominantly (nearly 70 percent) Sonoran origin of its Mexican American residents.

In spite of a more cordial relationship between Anglos and Mexican Americans than prevails in some other large southwestern cities, Tucson has known periods of discrimination. One such period came during the last decade of the nineteenth century and prompted Mexican Americans in 1894 to organize the Alianza Hispano-Americana,* apparently the first urban defense association for persons of Mexican descent in the history of the United States.

During the 1970s Tucson Mexican Americans came to occupy many important public positions in the community, including those of postmaster and city manager. In 1979, two of six city councilmen were Mexican Americans, as were two state senators and two state representatives from Tucson's six legislative districts. A Mexican American also headed the board of the city's largest school district. Raúl H. Castro,* a Tucsonan born in Sonora, was elected Arizona's first Mexican American governor in 1974.

At the end of World War II Mexican Americans formed about 25 percent of the total population of Tucson; in the period since that time they have declined to slightly under 20 percent. According to the 1970 census the Spanish-surnamed population of the community was 45,537. However, a tract-by-tract count of persons who identified themselves as being of Mexican origin showed 66,606 within the Tucson city limits. Prominent contemporaries of Mexican descent born in Tucson include rock singer Linda Ronstadt* and singer-composer Lalo Guerrero.

FURTHER READING: Sidney B. Brinckerhoff and Odie B. Faulk, *Lancers for the King*, Phoenix: Arizona Historical Foundation, 1965; Bernice Cosulich, *Tucson,* Tucson: Arizona Silhouettes, 1953; Henry Dobyns, *Spanish Colonial Tucson*, Tucson: University of Arizona Press, 1976; John L. Kessell, *Friars, Soldiers, and Reformers*, Tucson: University of Arizona Press, 1976; James E. Officer, "Historical Factors in Inter-Ethnic Relations in the Community of Tucson," *Arizoniana* (Journal of the Arizona Pioneers' Historical Society), Fall 1960; Jay J. Waggoner, *Early Arizona*, Tucson: University of Arizona Press, 1975. *J.E.O.*

TUUL. *See* TRADE UNION UNITY LEAGUE. *See also* LABOR ORGANIZATION.

U

UFW. *See* UNITED FARM WORKERS.

UFWOC. *See* UNITED FARM WORKERS. *See also* CESAR CHAVEZ; DELANO; LABOR ORGANIZATION.

UGARTE, MANUEL, (1878-1951), journalist, diplomat, politician, and author. Born on February 27, 1878, in Buenos Aires, Argentina, Ugarte completed his education in Buenos Aires and also studied at various universities in France. In 1900 Ugarte visited the United States and became convinced that Latin America was in danger of being absorbed and dominated by the United States. As a result of this observation, he spent the rest of his life writing against the Yankee peril. He also expounded on the themes of the injustices and discriminatory treatment suffered by Mexicans in the United States.

Author of several books, his most outstanding are: *El porvenir de la América Latina*, Valencia: F. Sempere y Cía., 1911; and *El destino de un continente*, Madrid: Mundo Latino, 1923.

UMAS. *See* UNITED MEXICAN AMERICAN STUDENTS.

UNDOCUMENTED, a term used to describe those who enter the United States without proper immigrant papers. This term was established by a resolution passed at the Tenth International Labor Organization (ILO) Regional Conference of American States at Mexico City in 1974. Considered nonpejorative, it is probably the term most widely used today to describe the illegal Mexican immigrant. The term illegal, which is viewed as mildly pejorative because it implies criminality, also is used; the more pejorative wetback, having a long history of use, generally is avoided today. The Mexican terms "espalda mojada" (literally wet back) and "mojado" (wet one) refer to the fact that one way of crossing the border between Mexico and the United States is by swimming or wading the Rio Grande.* Another Mexican term, "alambrista" (from alambre, "wire") refers to the high wire fence marking parts of the northwestern border, especially between California and Baja California Norte. The alambrista has presumably climbed over the fence or gone through a gap or hole.

Border crossing has a long and complex history. Until the early 1900s crossings in both directions took place with little regard for the boundary. In 1904 a federal patrol was established along the Mexican border, principally to prevent illegal entry of Chinese. Immigration stations were not established along the Mexico-United States border until 1907. The period of the Mexican Revolution (1910-1920) led to a dramatic increase in Mexican emigration, and the decade of the twenties saw the flow more than doubled. Much of this immigration wave was greatly encouraged by labor agents from the Southwest. The depression of the early 1920s, however, led to a demand for Mexican exclusion; and in 1924 Congress officially recognized the Border Patrol* and appropriated nearly a million dollars for its greatly expanded role in controlling illegal immigration.

The depression years of the 1930s were a time of little emigration from Mexico, but the outbreak of World War II at the end of that decade followed by the Korean conflict beginning in 1950 and rapid population growth in Mexico led to an outpouring of Mexican nationals. By 1949 more than a quarter of a million undocumented Mexicans were apprehended; in 1951 the figure had jumped to half a million and in 1954 it was one million, partly as a result of Operation Wetback.* The second half of the fifties and first half of the 1960s showed a sharp decline in apprehensions, which averaged only fifty-three thousand per year for the decade. This apparent decline in undocumented workers reversed itself at the end of the Bracero Program* in 1964, and the 1970s witnessed a sharp rise in illegals apprehended and sent back to Mexico. By 1973 the number was over half a million and four years later it had passed the million mark. Estimates made by immigration officials of the total number of undocumented aliens in the United States at the end of the decade varied from three to twelve million, with Los Angeles alone being credited with more than one million. A preliminary study by the 1979 Select Commission on Immigration and Refugee Policy indicated that the number of undocumented aliens was between three and one half and five million, with Mexicans making up no more than three million. Whatever the number, recent estimates are that illegals bring into the Mexican economy about $2 billion annually. *See* *also* IMMIGRATION and IMMIGRATION AND NATURALIZATION SERVICE.

FURTHER READING: Leo Grebler, *Mexican Immigration to the United States: The Record and Its Implication*, Los Angeles: University of California, 1966; Julian Samora, *Los Mojados: The Wetback Story*, Notre Dame: University of Notre Dame Press, 1971; Walter Fogel, *Mexican Illegal Alien Workers in the United States*, Los Angeles: University of California Press, 1978.

See also Appendix F tables: DEPORTABLE ALIENS and DEPORTABLE ALIENS FOUND.

UNIONISM. *See* LABOR ORGANIZATION.

UNITED CANNERY, AGRICULTURAL, PACKING AND ALLIED WORKERS OF AMERICA (UCAPAWA). In mid-1937 the Congress of Industrial Organizations chartered UCAPAWA, an international for agricultural workers, and began organizing efforts in competition with AFL efforts. In 1944 UCAPAWA became the Food, Tobacco, and Agricultural Workers International, which was subsequently ousted from the CIO because of communist domination.

UNITED FARM WORKERS (UFW), originally organized in 1962 by César Chávez* as the Farm Workers Association (FWA) at Delano,* California. The organization has been to some degree more a social movement than a labor union, carefully molded by the ideas of Chávez. Developed by Chávez throughout the San Joaquin Valley according to his theories, its membership was largely made up of Mexican Americans, recruited by home visits and with the principal goal of developing leaders. By 1965 it had some fifty chapters, a membership of more than fifteen hundred, and the name had been changed to the National Farm Workers Association. The NFWA organized a credit union, a cooperative grocery store, a drug store, a gas station, a clinic, and other service agencies. In early May 1965 it engaged in its first strike, that of rose grafters in McFarland, California. The strike was successful. In September of that year the NFWA joined Filipino strikers of the AFL-CIO's Agricultural Workers Organizing Committee* under Larry Itliong* at Delano, despite the union's lack of preparation and financial resources. Chávez led the NFWA in a strict policy of nonviolence, and the growers resorted to the courts and the help of local law enforcement agencies.

In December the union initiated a consumers' boycott of Schenley Industries, one of the Kern County grape growers. In the same month Walter Reuther of the United Automobile Workers visited Delano, giving the union a donation of ten thousand dollars and pledging five thousand dollars monthly from the UAW. To help dramatize the strike and boycott and to ask legislative help from Governor Edmund G. Brown, Chávez and union members began a twenty-five-day march to Sacramento in mid-March 1966. Just before the marchers reached the capital Chávez was able to give them the good news that Schenley had agreed to recognize the NFWA, and on April 6 the NFWA and Schenley signed a contract which included provisions for a NFWA hiring hall and $1.75 per hour wage.

With Schenley signed up, the next obvious target for the NFWA was Di Giorgio* Farms. In the midst of NFWA-Di Giorgio negotiations the International Brotherhood of Teamsters* announced it was in the contest and opened a costly, full-scale campaign with support from Di Giorgio. Needing financial support to fight the Teamsters, Chávez merged the NFWA with the AWOC to form the United Farm Workers Organizing Committee (UFWOC) of the AFL-CIO. In the August 30 elections UFWOC won the field workers by a vote of 530 to 331. By mid-1967, with major wine-grape growers signed up, UFWOC turned to unionize table-grape growers and especially Giumarra Vineyards,* the principal target after August. A year later UFWOC initiated a general grape boycott when it was found that Giumarra was illegally using other growers' labels to escape consequences of the picketing. Because of economic pressures caused by the boycott, some grape growers began serious negotiations in mid-1969 and a year later the major table-grape growers had signed three-year contracts with UFWOC.

With the grape strike ended, UFWOC turned to lettuce growers in California and Arizona and to Florida citrus growers, signing up Minute Maid, the state's largest grower, to a three-year contract. In the lettuce industry the Teamsters again initiated all-out competition, quickly signing contracts with a majority of the Salinas lettuce growers. Despite earlier no-raiding agreements by the Western Conference of Teamsters, locals continued to sign contracts with growers for field workers, and the struggle of the Chávez union went on.

In February 1972 UFWOC became a full-fledged AFL-CIO union, changing its name to the United Farm Workers (UFW). The year 1973 was a difficult one for the UFW. While carrying on discussions with the Teamsters over raiding, it lost a majority of its grape contracts to the Teamsters as these came up for renewal. This reversal was apparently the result of grower preference for the Teamsters and UFW inexperience in implementing its contracts, especially in operating hiring halls. By the end of a year of vicious Teamster attack on the UFW, it retained only twelve contracts and its membership was reduced by 90 percent to about five thousand.

During this period the UFW was able to send some of its organizers elsewhere, particularly to Texas and Arizona, to begin similar unionization in these areas. At home there were some successes in the Salinas lettuce strike, but far more important was the election of Jerry Brown to the governorship in 1974 and his calling a special session to pass a state Agricultural Labor Relations Act* the following year. In field worker elections held under the ALRA, the UFW made a dramatic comeback; by March 1976 it had won two-thirds of the elections held. However, in the November elections, Proposition 14, which would have modified the ALRA in a pro-union direction, was soundly voted down.

The UFW-Teamster struggle for workers via election went on into 1977 when a fifth no-raiding agreement finally seemed to take hold, ending or at least muting the long rivalry. In February 1978 the UFW boycott against lettuce, grapes, and wine was ended. At this time the UFW had about 100 contracts covering some 30,000 agricultural workers, or about 10 percent of California's farm labor. A year later the UFW struck lettuce growers in the Imperial Valley and in February 1979 walked out of eight Salinas fields demanding wage increases. By September the long lettuce strike seemed to be nearing an end, with a number of growers agreeing to a basic $5.00 per hour wage.

FURTHER READING: Dick Meister and Anne Loftis, *A Long Time Coming: The Struggle to Unionize America's Farm Workers*, New York: Macmillan, 1977; Paul Fusco and George D. Horowitz, *La Causa, The California Grape Strike*, New York: Collier Books, 1970; Jacques E. Levy, *César Chávez: Autobiography of La Causa*, New York: W. W. Norton and Co., 1975.

UNITED LATIN AMERICAN COUNCIL, a San Jose, California, umbrella organization, which in the 1960s represented some twenty-plus Mexican American groups.

UNITED MEXICAN AMERICAN STUDENTS (UMAS), a Chicano* youth organization established in May 1967 as the result of a conference held by the Loyola University (Los Angeles) Human Relations Commission. By the end of its first year it had ten chapters in the Los Angeles area, having absorbed other groups. The Mexican American Students Association* at East Los Angeles (Junior) College, with one of the largest area Chicano youth memberships, remained out. UMAS played an important part in the 1968 high school student "blowouts" in Los Angeles. Although UMAS increasingly shifted toward a more political stance, it opposed the Mexican American Political Association's* support of national candidates, preferring to back Chicano candidates in heavily Chicano districts. In late 1969 UMAS changed to Movimiento Estudiantil Chicano de Aztlán* (MECHA).

UNITED STATES BISHOPS COMMISSION ON FARM LABOR DISPUTES. *See* SECRETARIAT FOR THE SPANISH SPEAKING.

UNITY LEAGUES, Chicano* civil rights groups organized in the aftermath of World War II. Among these were the Unity Leagues of the Los Angeles area, formed by Ignacio López, editor of *El Espectador* in nearby San Bernardino, and aided by Fred Ross* of the American Council on Race Relations. The Unity Leagues' goal was to end discrimination against Mexican Americans by whatever means were at hand. Sometimes this meant getting out the vote to elect a Chicano to office; at other times it meant filing suit in the courts. The leagues had some local success in solving barrio* problems through organization and political pressure. In 1947 they became part of civil rights sentiments that led to the development of the Community Service Organizations* which helped elect Edward Roybal* to the Los Angeles city council on his second try in 1949.

URBANISM. Urbanization is a major characteristic of the Mexican saga in the United States. Although many Americans still think of Chicanos* as farm workers, today 90 percent are born, grow up, and die in cities. Yet Chicano urbanism is not a new phenomenon; it is part of a larger historical process.

During the Spanish colonization of what is now the Southwest, community living formed part of the early urban experience. Following the founding of Santa Fe in 1609, the Spaniards established three principal types of communities as part of their northern frontier defenses: pueblos* or towns such as Santa Fe and Los Angeles, presidios or military forts such as San Antonio and San Francisco, and missions* such as those at San Diego and Santa Barbara along the California coast. While these settlements were predominantly pastoral and agricultural, still they formed permanent Spanish enclaves on the frontier.

With Mexican independence in 1821 a new period began both for Mexico and for what then became the Mexican borderlands. The more liberal trade policies pursued by the Mexican government increased the prosperity of the Mexican frontier communities by making some of them into centers of trade. Santa Fe, Taos, San Diego, Santa Barbara, and Monterey exemplified this new prosperity. Ironically, these changes generated by independence eventually helped set the conditions for conquest of the Mexican borderlands by the United States in the Mexican War* (1846-1848). The conquest, in turn, introduced yet another period in the community history of the Southwest.

Following the Mexican War many of these early Mexican communities underwent an Americanization process. Not only did conquest integrate them into the American market system, but as Anglo Americans migrated to the Southwest the very ethnic composition of these towns changed. Towns in California, for example, such as San Diego, Los Angeles, San Francisco, and Santa Barbara mushroomed by the 1880s in population and commercial activities. Yet the Americanization of California and indeed of the Southwest did not mean an end to the Mexican urban experience. Mexicans continued to live in towns and cities, but they did so increasingly in de facto segregated barrios*—the "old towns"—surrounded by new residential and business areas where Yankee migrants lived and worked.

The early twentieth century inaugurated another period in the history of Chicano urbanism. Between 1900 and 1930 over a million Mexicans entered the United States, encouraged by the possibilities of jobs, especially in the Southwest where American capitalists had invested in mining, railroad construction, ranching, agriculture, and trade. The ravages of the Mexican Revolution of 1910, of course, also drove Mexicans out of their homeland and across the border. The phenomenal increase in Mexican immigration, in turn, changed the face of various southwestern communities. In cities such as Los Angeles and San Antonio, Mexican immigration either expanded older barrios or created new ones. The impact of Mexican immigration on major southwestern cities can be seen in the following figures: the Mexican population of Los Angeles went from 29,757 in 1920 to 97,116 in 1930; in San Antonio the increase went from 41,469 to 82,373; and in El Paso it went from 39,571 in 1920 to 58,291 in 1930.

The Great Depression temporarily halted Mexican immigration but did not lessen the movement of Mexicans into cities. As unemployed Anglos replaced Mexican farm workers in the competition for jobs, the flow of Mexican refugees from the rural areas to urban ones increased. It was in the cities where Mexicans scraped a living or resorted to relief until the New Deal public works programs put many to work.

United States involvement in World War II created even greater urban opportunities for Chicanos. By 1940 well over half of the Mexican population already lived in cities, and the war accelerated this demographic process. Due to war production, Chicanos found jobs in the cities and many learned new skills. Hence, World War II not only increased the urbanization of Chicanos but provided a degree of job mobility as well.

The post-World War II era has further stimulated the movement of Mexicans into the cities. By the 1960s Mexicans constituted a predominantly urban population. With over a million Mexicans Los Angeles, for example, represented the urban capital of Chicanos and the third largest congregation of people of Mexican descent next to Mexico City and Guadalajara. In addition, San Antonio, Dallas, Houston, Tucson, Phoenix, San Diego, Santa Barbara, Fresno, San Francisco, and Denver had significant Mexican communities. El Paso was a major southwestern metropolis with a Mexican majority. New Mexico, of course, had numerous Mexican communities. Moreover, midwestern cities since the 1920s had experienced the Mexican presence. Consequently, by the 1960s large numbers of Mexicans resided in Chicago, Gary, Detroit, and Minneapolis. Lesser cities throughout the Southwest also had major concentrations of Mexicans, especially in south Texas and along the border.

Besides a greater concentration of native-born Mexican Americans in cities during the postwar years, the period has also seen a massive flow of undocumented workers from Mexico into major American cities. As a result, the urban Mexican population has mushroomed during the past twenty years. This urban population is characterized by its diversity and heterogeneity. It is both native-born and immigrant. It is documented and undocumented. It is working-class and middle-class. It is English-speaking and Spanish-speaking.

The 1980s undoubtedly will see a continuation of urban life for most Mexican Americans. With a high birth rate both for native-born Mexican Americans and among recent immigrants, the inner cities of the Southwest by the end of the century will unquestionably be Mexican. In California, for example, according to the 1970 census, the average size of Spanish-surnamed families was 4.54, while for all families it was only 3.65. This "Mexicanization" of southwestern cities will create many opportunities for Chicanos as well as problems. How these will be addressed will determine the future status of Chicanos in the United States. What cannot be doubted, however, is that Chicanos, descendants of a population centuries old in the Southwest, are now emerging as the urban core of the Southwest. The future of the city in the Southwest may be largely in their hands.

FURTHER READING: Tomás A. Arciniega, *The Urban Mexican American*, Las Cruces: (ERIC) New Mexico State University, 1971; Albert M. Camarillo, "Chicano Urban History: A Study of Compton's Barrio, 1936-1970," *Aztlán* 2 (Fall 1971): 79-106; Oscar J. Martínez, "Chicanos and the Border Cities: An Interpretive Essay," *Pacific Historical Review* 46 (February 1977): 85-106; Ricardo Romo, "The Urbanization of the Southwestern Chicanos in the Early Twentieth Century," *New Scholar* 6 (1977): 183-207; Lyle W. Shannon and Magdaline Shannon, *Minority Migrants in the Urban Community: Mexican-American and Negro Adjustment to Industrial Society*, Beverly Hills, Calif.: Sage Publications, 1973.

M.T.G.

URREA, TERESA (1873-1906), curandera* and mystic who was forced to leave Mexico in May 1892 because the Porfirio Díaz government feared her influence over the Yaqui and Mayo Indians of Sonora. She lived with her father first at Nogales and then at El Paso, but continued harassment from the Mexican government, which blamed her for border attacks by revolutionaries who called themselves Teresistas, forced the family to move away from the border city to Clifton, Arizona.

Known already in Mexico as "la santa de Cabora" (Cabora was the name of one of her father's ranches) because of her cures, in the United States she became, as she had earlier in Mexico, the center of a cult, the members of which believed she had preternatural powers to cure both physical and mental illnesses. Her fame led to her being persuaded in 1900 to become part of a medical company through which her talents would be made available to people all over the United States. By 1904, disillusioned with the commercialism of the medical company, Teresa dissolved her contract and returned to Clifton, where she continued her help to the sick and distressed until her death two years later.

FURTHER READING: Frank B. Putnam, "Teresa Urrea, 'the Saint of Cabora,'" *Southern California Quarterly* 45 (September 1963): 245-64; Richard Rodríguez and Gloria C. Rodríguez, "Teresa Urrea: Her Life as it Affected the Mexican-U.S. Frontier," *El Grito: Journal of Contemporary Mexican American Thought* 5 (Summer 1972): 48-68.

V

VALDEZ, LUIS (1940-), dramatist and political activist. Born in Delano,* California, into a family of migrant farm workers, Valdez attended schools throughout the San Joaquin Valley and graduated from James Lick High School in San Jose, where his family finally settled. Enrolling at San Jose State College, he majored in Mathematics and English, completing his B.A. in 1964. The San Jose State Drama Department produced his first full-length play entitled *The Shrunken Head of Pancho Villa*.

After college Valdez worked with the San Francisco Mime Troupe for several months and in October of 1965 joined César Chávez* in Delano where he created El Teatro Campesino,* the farm-workers' theater. The Teatro served to educate the campesino* and dramatized the plight of the struggling farm workers throughout the country. In the summer of 1967 El Teatro performed before the Senate Subcommittee on Agricultural Labor in Washington, D.C.

After two years with the union and a national fund raising tour, Valdez moved the Teatro to Del Rey, California. In 1969 he again moved the Teatro (and cultural center) to Fresno, opening its doors to a greater number of people. In Fresno the Teatro produced a film entitled *I am Joaquín,* which won several awards, published a new work, *Actos*, by Luis Valdez, and created a national organization of Chicano theater groups throughout the Southwest called Tenaz. During this same time Valdez also taught at Fresno State College, helping to shape the newly created La Raza* Studies from 1968 to 1970. He also taught at the University of California at Berkeley and at Santa Cruz from 1971 to 1974.

In 1971 Valdez went to the Philippines as one of three United States representatives to the first Third World Theater Conference. In the same year, the Teatro made its final move—to San Juan Bautista, California, a mission town ninety miles south of San Francisco where it purchased forty acres of land. Under Valdez's direction El Centro Campesino Cultural,* established here, has turned into a professional production company, creating popular theater and concerts, and distributing cultural materials.

In the summer of 1973, Valdez's* work with El Teatro attracted European director Peter Brook who later brought his International Center Group for Theater Research to San Juan Bautista for a two-month workshop. Valdez was also appointed to the advisory boards of the International Theater Institute in New York and the Public Broadcasting System's Visions Project at KCET in Los Angeles.

VALDEZ, PHIL ISADORE (1946?-1967). A native of Española, New Mexico, Phil Valdez joined the navy in 1965. After training as a hospital corpsman, he was sent to Vietnam where he was killed on January 29, 1967, as he went to aid two wounded marines caught in the enemy line of fire. Valdez was posthumously awarded the Navy Cross. In July 1974 the navy named a 4,200-ton antisubmarine escort ship U.S.S. *Valdez* in his honor.

VALLEJO, MARIANO G. (1808-1890), Californio* leader and military commandant. Born in Monterey, the capital of Mexican Alta California, Mariano Vallejo grew up in an upper-class Californio family. As a youngster his interest in the world outside of California was awakened by the privateering raid of the French-Argentine Hypolite Bouchard in 1818 and by his clerking in the store of William Hartnell, an English trader. At fifteen he became a cadet at the Monterey presidio; by the time he reached twenty-one he commanded a force that put down an Indian rebellion at Mission San José. Meanwhile he had been elected to the territorial legislature, thereby joining the two careers he was to pursue the rest of his life—the military and politics.

While still in his mid-twenties, Vallejo became an outstanding northern California leader and was appointed military commander of the entire northern part of the territory and also named administrator of Mission San Francisco Solano during secularization of the missions. In these various capacities he acquired several land grants. During the entire Mexican period (1821-1846) Vallejo trod carefully in the shifting sands of California politics and gradually split with his nephew Juan Bautista Alvarado* when the latter seemed to him to be neglecting his job as governor in the early 1840s. More and more he came to the conclusion that an American takeover would be best for California.

When the Bear Flag Revolt* broke out, Vallejo was seized and jailed at Sutter's Fort for two months. Under American rule he was named to the legislative council and later was appointed by Colonel Stephen Kearny* as northern Indian agent. In 1849 he was one of eight Californios elected to the constitutional convention and then was elected to the new state's first senate. In the early 1850s he was one of the first Californios to file for validation of his land grants. His joy at confirmation in 1855 was shortlived when squatters and speculators appealed this favorable decision all the way to the U.S. Supreme Court, which invalidated his title to the large Soscol land grant. The expenses involved in defense of his property caused the family fortunes to slump severely.

In the 1870s Vallejo devoted himself to writing a history of California while he continued his economic and civic interests. When he died quietly in January 1890, he owned only 280 acres of his once large landholdings.

FURTHER READING: Myrtle M. McKittrick, *Vallejo, Son of California*, Portland: Binford & Mort, 1944.

VAQUERO, cowboy. The vaquero provided the cowboy of the Western plains with most of the accouterments, techniques, and terminology of the range-cattle industry. Early Anglo and black cowboys of the West borrowed clothing, western saddles, other equipment, roping and roundup techniques, and Spanish vocabulary (rodeo, bronco, mustang, chaps, lariat, hackamore, dally, hoosgow, McCarthy), all from the Mexican vaquero.

VASCONCELOS, JOSÉ. *See* MESTIZAJE.

VÁSQUEZ, TIBURCIO (1835-1875), Californio* bandit. Vásquez was one of six children born into a respected middle-class family at Monterey, California, in the middle of the Mexican era. Little is known of his early years except that he obtained an above average education for the time and place and that he was fluent in both Spanish and English.

In 1852 he and some companions were attending a dance in Monterey at which a fight occurred and a local Anglo constable was killed. To avoid the fate of a friend who was seized—lynching—Vásquez fled to the mountains where he began the life of an outlaw. In a period when Anglo culture was making heavy inroads in Californio society Vásquez was seen by many Mexican Americans as an avenger of their wrongs, and they often provided him with shelter, information, and support.

Arrested in 1857 for horse stealing, Vásquez was sentenced to five years in San Quentin prison; however, during a prison break two years later he escaped. After a few months he was recaptured and returned to serve his full sentence. Upon release from prison he seems to have worked as a professional gambler at New Almaden, California, but in 1867 he was arrested on cattle rustling charges and served three more years in San Quentin. When he got out of prison Vásquez organized a small band and began a series of daring payroll holdups and stage robberies. In mid-1873 the governor offered a one-thousand-dollar reward for Vásquez, dead or alive.

Vásquez's capture came about, however, not because of the reward, but because of his personal life and betrayal by one of his own men, Abdón

Leiva. Leiva caught Vásquez with his wife and informed the sheriff of his hideouts. By early 1874 the reward had been raised to $6,000 dead or $8,000 alive—an incentive for one of the most intensive manhunts in California history. Vásquez was finally captured near Los Angeles and transferred to San José for trial. In jail Vásquez continued to be a bandit-hero. He had many visitors, mostly women, posed for photographs, and talked to newsmen, justifying his life of crime as a defense of Mexican American rights against Anglo injustice.

His trial, which began January 5, 1875, lasted only four days. Both Abdón Leiva and his wife, whom Vásquez had abandoned, testified against him; he was found guilty of murder, and Governor Romualdo Pacheco* refused to intervene in the case. On March 19 Vásquez was hanged at the San Jose courthouse and buried the next day at the Santa Clara Catholic Cemetery.

FURTHER READING: Ben C. Truman, *Life, Adventures and Capture of Tiburcio Vásquez, the Great California Bandit and Murderer,* Los Angeles: Los Angeles Star Office, 1874; Ernest May, "Tiburcio Vásquez," *Historical Society of Southern California Quarterly* 29 (1947): 123-34; Robert Greenwood, *The California Outlaw: Tiburcio Vásquez,* New York: Arno Press, 1960.

VELASCO, TREATY OF, (May 1836). As a result of General Antonio López de Santa Anna's* capture in the battle of San Jacinto (April 21, 1836), the Treaty of Velasco, ending hostilities between the Texans and Mexico, was signed by Santa Anna and Texas President David G. Burnet on May 14, 1836. It provided that Texas would be independent and that Mexican troops would be withdrawn to south of the Rio Grande.* A secret agreement implied that the Rio Grande was to be the boundary of Texas, but no definite delineation was agreed on. Later Santa Anna repudiated this favorable interpretation and, of course, the Mexican congress declared any agreements made by Santa Anna while prisoner were null and void.

At the beginning of the 1840s the Velasco Treaty was an important argument used by Texans as a basis for their claim to half of New Mexico east of the Rio Grande and as justification for the ill-fated Santa Fe Expedition.* After the Treaty of Guadalupe Hidalgo* it led to a similar claim that was settled by the federal government paying Texas $10 million in the Compromise of 1850.

VENCEREMOS BRIGADE, a radical organization begun in 1964 by Chicano* students. At the end of the 1960s some members of the group went to Cuba to demonstrate their solidarity with the Cuban revolutionaries and their support of the social revolution. In 1969 and 1970 they worked in the cane fields helping Cuba in its efforts to achieve a sugar harvest goal of ten million tons.

VENDIDO, a sell-out; a term of contempt, synonymous with coconut* and Tío Taco.* This epithet is used by Chicanos* to describe Mexican Americans who allow themselves to be used by the Anglo American establishment, or whose behavior toward Anglos is regarded as fawning and servile.

LA VIDA NUEVA, a student newspaper begun in early 1969 by students at East Los Angeles College belonging to a group with the same name, organized in the preceding December. It represented a strongly ethnic and activist viewpoint.

VIGIL, DONACIANO (1802-1877), governor, soldier. Born in Santa Fe, New Mexico, into an old Nuevo Mexicano* family dating back to the Reconquista* at the end of the seventeenth century, he grew up in the provincial capital. Although he lacked formal schooling, he was taught by his father and continued to expand his education all his life. In 1823 he began a military career by joining the Santa Fe presidial company and participated in several campaigns against the Navaho Indians. Allied with Governor Manuel Armijo,* he began his political career in 1838 with his election to the Nuevo México legislature and was appointed the governor's civil-military secretary in the following year.

As war between Mexico and the United States appeared imminent, Vigil directed much of the preparation. With Armijo's last-minute withdrawal, Vigil and the other military leaders decided not to resist the advancing American forces. General Stephen Kearny* and his army took over Santa Fe in August 1846 and set up an American government. Because of wide Hispanic support and his pro-American stance Vigil was named territorial secretary. Upon Governor Charles Bent's* assassination in January 1847, he became acting governor. After the territorial convention of 1848 he stepped down from the governorship but was reappointed territorial secretary. When New Mexico formally became a territory by the Compromise of 1850* he continued to serve in both the legislative assembly and the territorial council. In his late sixties his last governmental position was that of San Miguel County school director. Vigil died in Santa Fe at age 75 respected by all, Anglos and Hispanos alike. That New Mexico's transition from Mexican to American territory was accomplished with minimal difficulty owed much to his wise leadership.

FURTHER READING: Stanley Francis Crocchiola, *Giant in Lilliput: The Story of Donaciano Vigil*, Pampa, Texas: Pampa Print Shop, 1963.

VIGILANTISM, the practice of taking over the function of the judicial system through some type of extra-legal organization, usually a committee or posse. In the American West vigilante activity was widespread in the second half of the nineteenth century and ranged from the vigilance committees of the California gold rush era to the White Caps* of New Mexico. In the first instance the vigilantees were Anglos and in the second, Nuevo Mexicanos. Because of Anglo racial bias and their own minority status, Mexican Americans and Mexicans frequently suffered from vigilante excesses, especially in mining areas where vigilantism often became simply a form of lynch law. While Western vigilantism, in theory, was invoked to bring about law and order in situations where the judicial system was nonexistent, incapable of action, or corrupt, sometimes it merely reflected local anti-Mexican bias.

FURTHER READING: W. Eugene Hollon, *Frontier Violence*, New York: Oxford University Press, Inc., 1974; John W. Caughey, *Their Majesties the Mob*, Chicago: University of Chicago Press, 1960; Robert W. Blew, "Vigilantism in Los Angeles, 1835-1874," *Southern California Quarterly* 54, no. 1 (Spring 1972): 11-30.

VILLA, FRANCISCO (PANCHO) (1878-1923), north Mexican revolutionary leader. Born of a peón* family on a hacienda* about 100 kilometers north of Durango as Doroteo Arrango, Villa's early life was one of hard ranch work in the course of which he became an outstanding horseman. According to history-legend, he was forced to flee to the mountains after wounding a landowner while defending his sister, and became a fugitive and cattle rustler under the name of Pancho Villa.

In 1910 Villa joined Francisco Madero in the revolt against Porfirio Díaz. After Madero's assassination, he fought with Venustiano Carranza's forces against the usurper Victoriano Huerta, but split with the former after Huerta's defeat and exile. His rupture with Carranza led to a series of battles, including two devastating defeats at Celaya in 1915 that ended Villa's importance in the 1910 revolution. He retired to Chihuahua from which state he maintained a precarious control over the local area. During this period he antagonized the United States by several attacks culminating in the 1916 raid on Columbus, New Mexico, which led to the unsuccessful Pershing punitive expedition into Mexico.

After Carranza's murder in 1920 the federal government bought off Villa with a hacienda in Durango and other perquisites. Three years later Villa's assassination by gunmen near Parral, Chihuahua, created a tremendous stir because most Mexicans believed persons high in government were involved in the killing.

Like Zapata,* Villa was a symbolic leader of the poorest elements in Mexican society, and it was therefore quite natural that in the late 1960s he became, with Zapata, a symbol for many Chicano militants.

FURTHER READING: Robert E. Quirk, *The Mexican Revolution, 1914-1915*, New York: W. W. Norton & Co., 1960; Martín Luis Guzmán, *Memoirs of Pancho Villa*, Austin: University of Texas Press, 1965; Clarence C. Clendenen, *The United*

States and Pancho Villa: A Study in Unconventional Diplomacy, Ithaca, N.Y.: Cornell University Press, 1961.

VILLARREAL, JOSÉ ANTONIO (1924-), novelist. Villarreal was born in Los Angeles, California. When he was three months old his family moved to Santa Clara where Villarreal received his elementary and secondary education. He earned his B.A. in English from the University of California at Berkeley in 1950.

Villarreal has been an assistant professor of English at the University of Colorado, a visiting assistant professor at the University of Texas at El Paso, a visiting lecturer at the University of Santa Clara, a technical editor and writer for aerospace industries, and an editor and translator for Stanford Research Institute. Currently he and his wife live in Mexico City where he teaches at an American high school and does free-lance writing.

Although Villarreal has written several short stories and essays, he is best known for his two novels: *Pocho* and *The Fifth Horseman*. *Pocho* was first published in 1959 by Doubleday, long before the Chicano* literary renaissance of the 1970s. In this respect, Villarreal's first novel is of particular historical significance since it was probably the first Chicano novel to be published in the United States by a major American publishing company. Partly autobiographical, *Pocho* is based on Villarreal's own youth in Santa Clara in the 1940s.

In 1974 *The Fifth Horseman*, Villarreal's second novel, was also published by Doubleday. This historical novel, a broad epic on humanity set in the 1910 Mexican Revolution,* ends at the point where *Pocho* begins—with the death of Pancho Villa. Besides following each other sequentially, *Pocho* and *The Fifth Horseman* share the same theme: in both works the author affirms life. Villarreal depicts man's hopes and frustrations in his incessant struggle to live life to its fullest extent—to exercise his will and express and develop his individuality. *F.J.*

VIRGIN OF GUADALUPE. *See* GUADALUPE, VIRGIN OF.

VIVA KENNEDY CLUBS. During the 1960 elections Mexican American supporters of the Democratic presidential candidate, John F. Kennedy, saw him as sympathetic to their political and economic aspirations. Under the leadership of Dr. Hector García* and Carlos McCormick of the American G.I. Forum,* an organization called Viva Kennedy was formed to elicit Chicano* support for the Democratic candidate. These clubs captured the imagination of Mexican Americans all over the Southwest and led to their enthusiastic participation in the electoral process for the first time. Not only were the Viva Kennedy clubs helpful to Kennedy's victory, but the movement's success also gave much needed confidence to its Mexican American leaders. As one result, after the election they founded in Texas a more permanent organization at first called Mexican Americans for Political Action (Texas MAPA, not to be confused with California MAPA, Mexican American Political Association*) and then Political Association of Spanish-speaking Organizations* (PASO).

VIZZARD, JAMES L. (1916-), economist, agricultural labor expert. Born and educated in San Francisco, Father Vizzard earned his B.A. and M.A. at Gonzaga University in Spokane, Washington. As a Jesuit novitiate he taught at the University of Santa Clara from 1940 to 1942 and then continued his religious education, being ordained a priest in 1946. An admirer and disciple of Paul Taylor,* he did graduate studies in Economics at the University of Chicago, Georgetown University, and the Department of Agriculture Graduate School from 1949 to 1954. In the following year he went to work for the National Catholic Rural Life Conference, beginning an association that was to last for nearly a quarter century. During this time he became a close friend of César Chávez,* and in the 1960s was vice chairman and chairman of the National Council on Agricultural Life and Labor.

In 1970 Father Vizzard was appointed director of the social apostolate for the California province of the Society of Jesus, a role he filled until 1973 when, at the insistence of César Chávez, he accepted the position of legislative representative for the United Farm Workers* in Washington. Poor health caused him to resign from that post in 1978.

From the 1950s onward Father Vizzard was a frequent expert witness on agricultural economics before congressional committees; during this same time he was a corresponding editor of *America* and the author of numerous articles on agricultural problems, especially agricultural labor, and on foreign aid and trade.

VOLUNTARIOS, LOS, a group founded by Rodolfo "Corky" Gonzales* in 1963 at Denver, Colorado, in order to achieve greater economic and social equality for Mexican Americans. The organizing of Los Voluntarios was in many ways the beginning of the Crusade For Justice.* The group monitored police activities and protested brutality in the arresting of Chicanos.* In an April 1966 speech to Los Voluntarios Corky asserted that a new crusade for justice had been born and soon established the Crusade as the instrument of his goals.

W

WASP, acronym for white Anglo-Saxon Protestant; today a mildly pejorative term widely used for Anglo American. The term implies a polite racism, devotion to capitalist values, and a Puritan ethic. WASPs are seen as imposing these as the predominant values and mores of American life. Since Mexican Americans have their own epithets, such as gringo* and gabacho,* when referring to Anglo Americans, WASP has only limited usage among them.

WESTERN FEDERATION OF MINERS, a radically oriented labor union founded in 1893. It played a leading role in founding the more radical Industrial Workers of the World* (IWW) in the next decade. Many Mexican American and Mexican miners joined the federation and learned organizing skills in its numerous strikes, especially between 1893 and the 1920s. *See also* LABOR ORGANIZATION.

WESTMINSTER CASE (1947). See *MÉNDEZ ET AL.* v. *WESTMINSTER SCHOOL DISTRICT ET AL.*

WETBACK. *See* UNDOCUMENTED.

WHEATLAND RIOT (1913), an important agricultural strike incident. Ralph Durst, owner of a Yuba County hop ranch near Wheatland, California, and a large employer of migrant labor, advertised in the summer of 1913 for workers to pick his hops. The 2,800 workers who showed up, many of them Mexican Americans, were offered low pay and lived in subhuman housing and sanitation conditions on the Durst ranch where temperatures at times ranged over 100° F. in the shade. Led by IWW* organizers Richard (Blackie) Ford and Herman Suhr, the workers elected a committee headed by Ford to demand better working and living conditions.

While Ford was addressing a meeting of the workers in August 1913 a sheriff's posse arrived to arrest him, and a deputy fired a warning shot into the air. In the ensuing riot four people were killed and many others were injured. Four companies of the national guard ended the melee, arresting about one hundred of the workers. In the following year Ford and Suhr were convicted of second degree murder and sentenced to life imprisonment.

The incident led to a general awareness of the plight of migratory workers and to inspection of farm labor camps by the new state Commission of Immigration and Housing. The Wheatland Riot is usually seen as a landmark in early history of farm labor unionism, particulary in California.

FURTHER READING: Stuart Jamieson, *Labor Unionism in American Agriculture*, Washington, D.C.: U.S. Department of Labor, 1945; reprint, New York: Arno Press, 1976.

WHITE CAPS (LAS GORRAS BLANCAS), a secret organization formed in northeastern New Mexico in the late 1880s to defend the old Hispanic-Mexican economic way of life against the inroads made by Anglo land speculators, homesteaders, railroads, and cattle and lumber companies. With the advent of cheap barbed wire, these groups began fencing in the lands they claimed, thus forcing out small landowners who grazed their animals on these lands.

Called Las Gorras Blancas by the Nuevo Mexicano* poor because its members wore white hoods, the White Caps were closely related to the Caballeros de Labor,* and many men were important leaders in both organizations, particulary Juan José Herrera. Like the Caballeros de Labor the White Caps was an organization that began in the Midwest and spread over the United States, and like the Caballeros de Labor it had a different motivation and history among Mexican Americans in the Southwest. The White Caps began their work in April 1889 with the total destruction of four miles of barbed wire fence near Las Vegas, New Mexico, and continued for a year and a half during which time thousands of Atchison, Topeka and Santa Fe Railroad ties were cut, crops were destroyed, houses and bridges burned, and people were threatened and shot. Powerless against Anglo and Nuevo Mexicano rico* control and fencing of the land, and especially village common lands, poor Nuevo Mexicanos responded with violence which was supported by a majority of local people.

Out of the White Caps there developed in 1890 a new political organization, El Partido del Pueblo,* which fought for the objectives of the White Caps. By mid-1890 White Cap tactics had achieved considerable success, and El Partido del Pueblo held promise of further political solutions. However, the turn to politics failed, and although occasional White Cap violence occurred subsequently, it remained local and ineffective. The White Caps were immediately and temporarily successful, but ultimately failed to stem the onslaught against their old way of life.

FURTHER READING: Andrew B. Schlesinger, "Las Gorras Blancas, 1889-1891," *Journal of Mexican American History* 1, no. 2 (Spring 1971): 87-143; Robert J. Rosenbaum, "Las Gorras Blancas of San Miguel County, 1889-1890," in *Chicano: The Evolution of a People*, Renato Rosaldo et al., eds., Minneapolis: Winston Press, 1973, pp. 128-33.

WHITECARDER, a foreigner having Form I-186 documentation, which allows him or her into the United States for a maximum of three days for business or recreation. Whitecarders must remain within twenty-five miles of the border. Despite the fact that employment makes them illegal aliens, most are employed in the United States border region, commuting regularly. In 1968 the U.S. Commission on Civil Rights estimated that there were about 1,250,000 I-186 cards in use.

WORLD WAR I (1914-1918) had a considerable impact on Mexican Americans. As a result of the wartime economy many were able for the first time to advance to higher-skilled, better-paying jobs; some moved from agricultural work and unskilled, hazardous occupations into construction, mining, and midwestern industry.

As more and more Mexican Americans moved out of the Southwest, St. Louis and Kansas City became stopovers and distribution centers. As a result, by the end of the war the Chicago area had a population of about four thousand and Detroit had twice that many. Most worked in steel, automobile manufacturing, railroading, and meat packing. Meanwhile the demand for agricultural, mining, and railroad workers in the Southwest and the push factor of the Mexican Revolution caused about one hundred fifty thousand Mexican nationals to enter the United States during the war years, either legally on a temporary war-time basis or without documentation. This large number of workers had a domino effect on Mexican American workers in the Southwest, pushing them northward to midwestern industrial centers and to new economic opportunities. Wartime economic developments brought Mexican Americans widespread employment and relatively good wages.

On the negative side, the World War I years saw a rise in revolutionary border banditry and in its suppression by the United States Army and Texas Rangers, in the course of which some innocent Mexican Americans suffered. Feelings ran high between Anglos and Mexican Americans along the border partly as the result of the United States invasion and seizure of Veracruz (1914), the Plan de San Diego* (1915), Francisco Villa's* raid on Columbus, New Mexico (1916), and the Zimmerman telegram* (1917). Many longtime Mexican residents returned to Mexico because of rumors that they would be drafted under the 1917 Selective Service Act. In south Texas especially, Mexican American loyalty to the United States was called into question and often they were identified with "the enemy." Despite these difficulties and urgings of radical leaders like Ricardo Flores Magón* not to fight for the United States, Mexican American volunteering for service in the armed forces was proportionately greater than that of any other ethnic group. Thousands served in the United States military forces and many civilians supported the war effort.

The World War I experiences of Mexican Americans did leave behind some residue of mistrust and alienation. The most important positive results of wartime experiences were the broadening of cultural horizons, raising of levels of expectations, and weakening of traditional and long-standing patterns of southwestern isolation.

WORLD WAR II (1939-1945). A major turning point for Chicanos, this war provided a variety of opportunities for improving their economic and social position. Manpower needs forced American industry to open its doors wider to Mexican American employees during the war years, and job areas previously closed to them by unions now welcomed their skills. As a result the 1940s saw a greater dispersion of Mexican Americans from the Southwest to the booming war industry centers of the Midwest and the West Coast.

During World War II more than three hundred thousand Mexican Americans served in the various branches of the Armed Forces, and a high percentage served in the more hazardous branches, such as the marines and paratroops. They took part in most campaigns of the war, from North Africa to the Pacific islands, and in the process became the country's most decorated ethnic minority.

World War II experiences generally were very valuable for Mexican Americans; the war gave many their first exposure to life outside the barrio,* and they returned home with new aspirations. The G.I. Bill of Rights provided some with job training, higher education, and home and business loans. Out of wartime skills and a sense of self-confidence came a number of important social, political, and service organizations like MAPA,* CSO,* and the American G.I. Forum,* as well as new, more assertive leadership like that of Dr. Hector García* and César Chávez.*

However, not all war-related experiences were positive. Despite the fact that the war was being fought in the name of the "four freedoms" enunciated by President Franklin D. Roosevelt, Chicanos continued to suffer discrimination. During the war years there were racist episodes like the Sleepy Lagoon* affair and the Zoot Suit* riots and afterwards there was the Felix Longoria* case. Mexican Americans still encountered signs reading "No Mexicans Served" and found themselves barred from public swimming pools and segregated in theaters and bathrooms. Perhaps most importantly Mexican Americans continued to be held back by inferior education and lack of educational opportunity. In the postwar era Mexican Americans used their new-found confidence, skills, leaders, and organizations to tackle these problems.

FURTHER READING: Raul Morín, *Among the Valiant*, Los Angeles: Borden Publishing Co., 1963; Charles P. Loomis, "Wartime Migration from the Rural Spanish-Speaking Villages of New Mexico," *Rural Sociology* 7 (December 1942): 384-95; Charles P. Loomis and Nellie H. Loomis, *Skilled Spanish-American War-Industry Workers from New Mexico*, Washington, D.C.: United States Department of Agriculture, Bureau of Agricultural Economics, November 24, 1942.

X

XIMENES, VICENTE TREVIÑO (1919-), research economist, politician. Ximenes was born in Floresville, Texas and became affiliated with the United States government in 1939 when he worked as company clerk for the Civilian Conservation Corps. During World War II Ximenes flew some fifty missions as a bombardier with the United States Air Force, earning the Distinguished Flying Cross and the Air Medal. He was discharged with the rank of major. After teaching for a year in a Wilson County, Texas elementary school, Ximenes entered college and received his B.A. and M.A.

from the University of New Mexico in 1950 and 1951 respectively. During this time he also was active in establishing a branch of the American G.I. Forum* in New Mexico. He was then appointed a research economist at the University of New Mexico. In 1964 he accepted a position with the State Department.

On June 9, 1967, President Johnson announced the creation of The Inter-Agency Committee on Mexican American Affairs, and appointed Vicente Ximenes to chair the new agency. The task of the Ximenes Committee was to search for solutions to Mexican American problems. Although the committee had little authority and no enforcement powers, its creation at least recognized the importance of Mexican Americans.

Ximenes has been the recipient of various honors including the G.I. Forum leadership award in 1960 and the United Nations Human Rights award in the same year.

Y

YOUTH LIBERATION CONFERENCE (1969), the first of a series of conferences held by young Chicano* activists to promote solidarity and to exchange ideas. These conferences helped lead later to the formation of La Raza Unida Party.*

Z

ZAPATA, CARMEN, actress, director. For the past decade Carmen Zapata has been a television, film, and stage actress and has received numerous acting awards and honors. She is also the founder and director of the Bilingual Foundation of the Arts, which provides Spanish-language drama to the large Hispanic audience of the greater Los Angeles area. She is perhaps most widely known for her work in the Public Broadcast System's show, Villa Alegre; but she is also active in a number of Chicano* organizations and teaches drama at East Los Angeles College.

ZAPATA, EMILIANO (1879-1919), leader and symbol of the agrarian revolt in Mexico. Born in a small town in the Mexican state of Morelos and raised in a mestizo* culture, Zapata overcame very humble circumstances by hard work and a basic education. When Morelos sugar landowners began expanding their holdings at the expense of small landowners and of village common lands at the end of the nineteenth century, Zapata became a local resistance leader, and when the 1910 Mexican Revolution* broke out he became an important leader in his home state. President Francisco Madero's failure to return lost lands to the peasants caused Zapata to rise in revolt with his agrarian reform platform of the Plan de Ayala in late 1911.

After Madero's overthrow by Victoriano Huerta, Zapata continued as a rebel and finally was successful in having the Plan de Ayala incorporated into the revolutionary goals by the Aguascalientes Convention of 1914. In a somewhat uneasy alliance with Francisco Villa,* Zapata continued the struggle for agrarian reform against Venustiano Carranza and his supporters. The defeat of Villa at Celaya in 1915 caused Zapata to withdraw to the mountains of Morelos where his forces continued a tenacious guerrilla action, isolated from the national movement. In 1919 Zapata was treacherously murdered by federal troops under Colonel Jesús Guajardo, who were supposedly defecting to the agrarian reform cause.

Always a symbol of the revolt of the poor agrarian masses against both the landowners and the government in Mexico City, Zapata was naturally taken by Chicano militants in the late 1960s as a symbol for their cause. He signified not only the rising up of the powerless but also the nationalism that many militants then espoused.

FURTHER READING: Michael C. Meyer and William L. Sherman, *The Course of Mexican History*, New York: Oxford University Press, 1979; John Womack, Jr., *Zapata and the Mexican Revolution*, New York: Alfred A. Knopf, Inc., 1969.

ZARAGOZA, IGNACIO (1829-1862), general. A Tejano* by birth and related to the Seguín* family, he was educated in Monterrey, Nuevo León (Mexico) and entered a military career. Fighting on the liberal side in the Mexican liberal-conservative civil war of the 1850s and 1860s, he was quickly promoted and by 1861 was minister of war. In the fighting against invading French forces he achieved the climax of his military career by repelling the French army at Puebla in the state of Puebla (Mexico) on May 5, 1862. Because May 5 (Cinco de Mayo*) has become an important Mexican American cultural holiday, Zaragoza is a minor cultural hero.

ZAVALA, ADINA EMILIA DE (1861-1955), civil leader and historian. The granddaughter of Lorenzo de Zavala,* Adina was born near Houston and grew up in Galveston and San Antonio. After completing her education she taught school near Dallas and at San Antonio. She became deeply interested in the preservation of historical sites and in about 1890 organized a women's group (associated with the Daughters of the Republic of Texas) for this purpose. Her most important achievement was the prevention of the razing of part of the Alamo* early in the 1900s. In 1912 Miss Zavala founded the Texas Historical and Landmarks Association and soon thereafter became a charter member of the Texas State Historical Association. Because of her deep historical interests, in 1923 she was appointed by the governor to the Texas Historical Board and later also served on the Texas Centennial Committee. Until her death she remained active in various Texas historical and civic organizations. She was the author of a number of historical works including *History and Legends of the Alamo*, San Antonio, Texas: (N.P.), 1917.

FURTHER READING: L. Robert Ables, "The Second Battle for the Alamo," *Southwestern Historical Quarterly* 70 (1966-1967).

ZAVALA, LORENZO DE (1788-1836), political leader. Born in Yucatan, Zavala had become an ardent liberal while still in his teens. As the result of his excellent education in preparation for the priesthood, he was able to become a leading political figure, serving as Yucatecan representative to the Spanish parliament, as a member of the Mexican Constituent Congress and later of the Senate, as governor of the state of México, and national treasury minister. In 1829 he became one of the few Mexicans to receive an empresario* grant in Texas. Three years later he was reelected governor and then became in rapid succession a national deputy and minister to France.

Concerned about Santa Anna's* centralism, he returned to Texas in 1835 to take a leading role in the Texas movement for federal separatism and then independence. In March 1836 he was elected vice president of the new republic, an office from which he resigned in October because of ill health. He died less than a month later. He was the author of several books on early Mexican political history including *Ensayo histórico de las revoluciones de México, desde 1808 hasta 1830,* Paris, 1831.

ZIMMERMAN TELEGRAM (1917), a proposal from the German government, not yet at war with the United States, to President Venustiano Carranza of Mexico, offering to return to Mexico the southwestern part of the United States lost during the Mexican War* (1846-1848) in return for an alliance with Germany. This dispatch of January 16, 1917, was intercepted and revealed to the American government. The potential threat of a Mexican-German alliance contributed to further mistrust of Mexicans and Mexican Americans in the United States during World War I.

ZOOT-SUITER, a term used primarily by Anglos to describe a Chicano youth who affected a certain dress and lifestyle common in the 1940s. A zoot-suiter usually wore baggy, pegged trousers, a long draped jacket heavily padded at the shoulders, a low-crowned, wide-brimmed hat, and a long key chain.

ZOOT-SUIT RIOTS, (1943), Los Angeles disturbances also known as the Pachuco Riots. During World War II, many Mexican Americans experienced a certain measure of affluence for the first time. With this affluence came a new sense of racial pride and a new awareness of discrimination and prejudice. Youth gangs were formed, especially in the barrio* of Los Angeles, to protect residents against servicemen and the police, and the fashionable zoot suit was widely viewed as a symbol of unity and membership.

The so-called Zoot-Suit Riots achieved national prominence and began on June 3, 1943, when sailors went on a rampage, assaulting Chicanos and stripping them of their clothing. The Los Angeles police and Los Angeles County sheriff's deputies reacted with unwarranted, large-scale arrests of Chicanos and with general overpolicing of Mexican American neighborhoods.

Growing in intensity, these assaults continued through June 7, until the conflict became so extreme that the State Department intervened and declared Los Angeles off-limits to all military personnel.

Although local authorities denied any racial overtones to the riots, and official versions of the violence absolved military and police personnel of any blame, a citizens' committee headed by Bishop Joseph T. McGucken of Los Angeles found that they were caused primarily by racial prejudice, stimulated by police practices and by inflammatory newspaper reporting.

Apart from the obvious physical effects, the Zoot-Suit Riots of 1943 had a deep impact on the Mexican American community and resulted in multiplying discriminatory practices against Mexican Americans. This overt, outrageous assault contributed to increased anger and bitterness among Mexican Americans, which is still prevalent today.

FURTHER READING: Robert M. Fogelson, *The Los Angeles Riots*, New York: New York Times, 1969; Ismael Dieppa, *The Zoot-Suit Riots Revisited: The Role of Private Philanthropy in Youth Problems of Mexican-Americans*, Los Angeles: University of Southern California Press, 1973; California, Governor, *Citizens Committee Report on the Zoot Suit Riots*, Sacramento: Printing Office, 1943.

APPENDIX **A**
BIBLIOGRAPHY OF GENERAL WORKS

This briefly annotated bibliography includes documentary collections, readers, and some sociology, political science, and human geography surveys which can be of value in understanding the historical experience of La Raza. It also lists some state histories of California, Texas, New Mexico, Arizona, and Colorado. For works on specific historical personages, issues, and events, see the further reading suggestions at the end of essays in the *Dictionary*.

Abbott, Carl. *Colorado, A History of the Centennial State*. Boulder, Colorado: Colorado Association, 1976.

Acuña, Rodolfo. *Occupied America: A History of Chicanos*, 2d ed. New York: Harper & Row, 1981.

______. *Occupied America: The Chicano's Struggle Toward Liberation*. New York: Harper & Row, 1972. Chicanos as a third-world people; the theme is one of internal colonialism.

______. *The Story of the Mexican Americans: The Men and the Land*. New York: American Book Company, 1969.

Alford, Harold J. *The Proud Peoples*. New York: David McKay Co., 1972. Popular history; good on migrant workers.

Anderson, George B., ed. *History of New Mexico, Its Resources and People*, 2 vols. New York: Pacific States Publishing Co., 1907. Volume one has complete list of land court decisions, pp. 204-8.

Ashworth, May Herley, ed. *Spanish-Speaking Americans in the U.S.A.* New York: Friendship Press, 1953. A collection of articles.

Bakker, Elna. *The Great Southwest*. Palo Alto, Calif.: American West Publishing Co., 1972. A general work, not much on Chicanos.

Bean, Walton. *California: An Interpretive History*. New York: McGraw-Hill, 1968. A useful state history with some reference to Mexican Americans.

Beck, Warren A. *New Mexico, A History of Four Centuries*. Norman: University of Oklahoma Press, 1962. A good general survey with some Mexican American material; good on cultural conflict.

Brown, Gertrude, and Guerra, Manuel. *Our Mexican Heritage*. Lexington, Mass.: Ginn & Co., 1972. A grade school text; emphasis on Mexican background.

Burma, John H., ed. *Mexican-Americans in the United States: A Reader*. Cambridge, Mass.: Schenkman Publishing Co., 1970. Sociological essays; some have been attacked for bias.

Carter, Thomas P. *Mexican Americans in School: A History of Educational Neglect*. New York: College Entrance Examinations Board, 1970. An excellent discussion of the Chicano and public education.

Castro, Tony. *Chicano Power: The Emergence of Mexican America*. New York: Saturday Review Press, 1974. A topical approach to history in the 1960s with emphasis on the Movimiento.

Caughey, John W. *California: A Remarkable State's Life History*, 3d ed. Englewood Cliffs, N.J.: Prentice Hall, Inc., 1970. Updated to include material on Chicano history.

Connor, Seymour U. *Texas: A History*. New York: Thomas Y. Crowell Co., 1971. A useful survey.

Cotera, Martha P. *Profile of the Mexican American Woman*. Austin, Texas: National Educational Laboratory, 1976. A study of the Chicana from prehistory to the present.

______., and Hufford, Larry, eds. *Bridging Two Cultures: Multidisciplinary Readings in Bilingual Bicultural Education*. Austin: National Educational Laboratory, 1980. A series of excellent readings in the Mexican American heritage.

Coy, Harold. *Chicano Roots Go Deep*. New York: Dodd, Mead & Co., 1975.

Cruz, Frank H. *Latin Americans: Past and Present*. Boston: Houghton-Mifflin Co., 1972.

De La Garza, Rudolph; Kruszewski, Z. Anthony; and Arciniega, Tomás A., comps. *Chicanos and Native Americans: The Territorial Minorities*. Englewood Cliffs, N.J.: Prentice-Hall Inc., 1973. A collection of articles on political science experience resulting from a workshop on Southwest Ethnic Groups at University of Texas at El Paso, 1972.

Dunn, Lynn P. *Chicanos: A Study Guide and Source Book*. San Francisco: R & E Research Associates, 1975. A useful tool for teachers.

Durán, Livie, and Russell, Bernard, eds. *Introduction to Chicano Studies: A Reader*. New York: Macmillan Co., 1973. Historical background, cultural problems, and adjustments—topically arranged articles.

Faulk, Odie B. *Land of Many Frontiers: A History of the American Southwest*. New York: Oxford University Press, 1968. Some information on Mexican Americans placed in a general survey.

Fergusson, Erna. *New Mexico: A Pagent of Three Peoples*, 2d ed. New York: Alfred Knopf, 1964. Good popular history, but little on the twentieth-century Mexican American.

Forbes, Jack D., ed. *Aztecas del norte: The Chicanos of Aztlán*. Greenwich, Conn.: Fawcett Publications, Inc., 1973. A topical collection of fairly short historical articles; many are contemporary.

______. *Mexican-Americans: A Handbook for Educators*. Berkeley, Calif.: Far West Laboratory for Educational Research and Development, 1967. An excellent early brief guide to Mexican American history.

Galarza, Ernesto; Gallegos, Herman; and Samora, Julian. *Mexican-Americans in the Southwest*. Santa Barbara, Calif.: McNally & Loftin, 1970. A concise overview with a sociological emphasis.

García, F. Chris, and de la Garza, Rudolph O. *The Chicano Political Experience: Three Perspectives*. North Scituate, Mass.: Duxbury Press, 1977. A socio-political study of Chicano organizing.

García, Richard A. *The Chicanos in America 1540-1974: A Chronology and Fact Book*. Dobbs Ferry, New York: Oceana Publications, 1977. A useful tool for teachers.

Garrison, George P. *Texas: A Contest of Civilizations*. Boston: Houghton-Mifflin Co., 1903.

Gómez, David F. *Somos chicanos: Strangers In Our Own Land*. Boston: Beacon Press, 1973. Life in the barrio; social history.

Gómez, Rudolph, ed. *The Changing Mexican-American: A Reader*. Boulder, Colorado: Pruett Publishing Co., 1972. A collection of general articles on the Chicano.

González, Nancie L. *Spanish-Americans of New Mexico: A Heritage of Pride*. Albuquerque: University of New Mexico Press, 1969. A largely cultural history of Nuevo Mexicanos, plus recent political events.

Grebler, Leo; Moore, Joan W.; and Guzmán, Ralph C. *The Mexican-American People: The Nation's Second Largest Minority*. New York: The Free Press, 1970. A massive social science resource book; includes an excellent bibliography.

Haddox, John H. *Los Chicanos: An Awakening People*. El Paso: The University of Texas Press, 1970. A brief essay on the contemporary Chicano scene.

Hafen, LeRoy R. *Colorado and its People*, 4 vols. New York: Lewis Historical Publishing Co., 1948. Detailed Colorado history by an outstanding western historian.

Hammond, George P., and Donnelly, Thomas C. *The Story of New Mexico: Its History and Government*. Albuquerque: University of New Mexico Press, 1936. A broad survey with some emphasis on the Nuevo Mexicano.

Heizer, Robert F., and Almquist, Alan J. *The Other Californians: Prejudice and Discrimination Under Spain, Mexico and the United States to 1920*. Berkeley and Los Angeles: University of California Press, 1971. Describes racial and other prejudice under three flags.

Helm, June, ed. *Spanish Speaking People in the United States*. Seattle: University of Washington Press, 1969. An ethnological study.

Hernández, Luis F. *Aztlan: The Southwest and Its People*. Rochelle Park, N.J.: Hayden Book Co., 1976.

Hogan, William R. *The Texas Republic: A Social and Economic History*. Norman: University of Oklahoma Press, 1946.

Hollon, W. Eugene. *The Southwest: Old and New*. New York: Alfred Knopf, 1961. A useful general survey from the sixteenth to twentieth centuries.

Horgan, Paul F. *Great River: The Rio Grande in North American History*, 2 vols. New York: Holt, Rinehart & Winston, 1954. A lyric panoramic view of New Mexican history.

______. *The Heroic Triad*. New York: World Publishing Co., 1971. Essays in

Mexican, Indian, and Anglo cultural interaction.

Howard, John R., ed. *Awakening Minorities: American Indians, Mexican Americans, Puerto Ricans*. Chicago: Aldine Publishing Co., 1970.

Hundley, Norris, Jr., ed. *The Chicanos*. Santa Barbara, Calif.: American Bibliographical Center—Clio Press, 1975. A collection of nine articles from *The Pacific Historical Review*.

Lamb, Ruth S. *Mexican Americans: Sons of the Southwest*. Claremont, Calif.: Ocelot Press, 1970. Thin on modern era except for civil rights movement.

Lamar, Howard R. *The Far Southwest, 1846-1912: A Territorial History*. New York: W. W. Norton & Co., 1970. Purely political history; good for New Mexico, especially for admission to statehood and the Santa Fe ring.

Landes, Ruth. *Latin Americans of the Southwest*. St. Louis: McGraw-Hill Book Co., 1965. Brief survey, heavily anthropological.

Larralde, Carlos. *Mexican American Movements and Leaders*. Los Alamitos, Calif.: Hwong Publishing Co., 1976. A series of biographical essays on various leaders of Chicano movements, 1848 to 1976.

Lavendar, David. *The Southwest*. New York: Harper & Row, 1980. Popular general history of the Southwest, little emphasis on the Mexican American.

León, Nephtalí de. *Chicanos: Our Background and Our Pride*. Lubbock, Texas: Trucha Publications, 1972. An activist's personal interpretation of the Chicano experience.

López y Rivas, Gilberto. *The Chicanos: Life and Struggles of the Mexican Minority in the United States*. New York: Monthly Review Press, 1973. Translation of a Mexican work published in 1971, with some added readings.

______. *Los chicanos: una minoria nacional explotada*, 2d ed. México, D.F.: Editorial Nuestro Tiempo, 1973. Emphasis on Mexican immigration to the United States.

______. *Conquest and Resistance: The Origins of the Chicano National Minority*. San Francisco: R & E Research Associates, Inc., 1979.

Ludwig, Edward W., and Santibáñez, James, eds. *The Chicanos: Mexican American Voices*. New York: Penguin Books, Inc., 1971. A collection of writings, topically arranged; many historical in nature.

McWilliams, Carey. *The Mexicans in America: A Student's Guide to Localized History*. New York: Teacher's College Press, Columbia University, 1968. A brief handbook in a series on local history.

______. *North From Mexico*. New York: Greenwood Press, 1968. Reprint of 1949 edition. Pioneering work by a journalist who was involved.

Machado, Manuel A., Jr. *Listen Chicano! An Informal History of the Mexican American*. Chicago: Nelson-Hall Inc., 1978. A conservative interpretation of the Chicano experience.

Maciel, David R., ed. *La otra cara de México: el pueblo chicano*. México, D.F.: Ediciones "El Caballito," 1977. A collection of documents: history, economics, social education, culture.

Maciel, David R., and Bueno, Patricia, comps. *Aztlán: historia del pueblo chicano (1848-1910)*. México, D.F.: Sepsetentas, 1975. A collection of nine articles by various historians, Anglo, Chicano, and Mexican.

Mangold, Margaret M., ed. *La causa chicana: The Movement Toward Justice*. New York: Family Service Association of America, 1972. A collection of articles on the Mexican American search for social justice.

Martínez, Al. *Rising Voices: Profiles of Hispano-American Lives*. New York: New American Library, 1974. A collection of short biographies of fifty-two outstanding Spanish-speaking Americans with photos; also in Spanish, *Voces que surgen*.

Martínez, Elizabeth Sutherland, and Longeaux y Vásquez, Enriqueta. *Viva La Raza! The Struggle of the Mexican-American People*. Garden City, New York: Doubleday, 1974. Heavy emphasis on political activities of the late sixties and early seventies by two activists.

Martínez, Gilbert T., and Edwards, Jane. *The Mexican American: His Life Across Four Centuries*. Boston: Houghton Mifflin Co., 1973. A grade school survey, heavy on the pre-Mexican War era.

Martínez, Orlando. *Viva Chicano! The Story of Mexicans in America*. New York: Gordon Cremonesi, 1979.

Meier, Matt S., and Rivera, Feliciano. *The Chicanos: A History of Mexican Americans*. New York: Hill & Wang, 1972. A wide-ranging survey with emphasis on immigration.

______. *Los chicanos, una historia de los mexicano-americanos*. Mexico, D.F.: Editorial Diana, 1976. A Spanish language version of *The Chicanos*.

______, eds. *Readings on La Raza*. New York: Hill & Wang, 1974. Readings from c. 1900 to 1974; heavy on immigration.

Meinig, D. W. *Southwest: Three Peoples in Geographic Change, 1600-1970*. New York: Oxford University Press, 1971. An insightful study in historical geography and relations of Mexicans, Indians, and Anglos.

Mirandé, Alfredo, and Enríquez, Evangelina. *La chicana: the Mexican-American Woman*. Chicago: University of Chicago Press, 1979. A sociohistorical study of the Chicana and her changing social role.

Moore, Joan W. *Los mexicanos de Los Estados Unidos y el movimiento chicano*. Mexico, D.F.: Fondo de Cultura Economica, 1972. Spanish language version of *Mexican Americans*.

Moore, Joan W., with Alfredo Cuellar. *Mexican Americans*. Englewood Cliffs, New Jersey: Prentice Hall, 1970. A socioeconomic survey, with a chapter on Chicano politics by Cuellar.

Moore, Joan W., with Harry Pachon. *Mexican Americans*, 2d ed. Englewood Cliffs, New Jersey: Prentice Hall, 1976. A revision and updating of Moore's earlier work.

Moquin, Wayne, and Van Doren, Charles, eds. *A Documentary History of the Mexican Americans*. New York: Praeger, 1971. Comprehensive collection of articles, mostly contemporary to the events.

Nava, Julian. *Mexican Americans: A Brief Look at Their History*. New York: Anti-Defamation League of the B'nai B'rith, 1970. A fifty-page pamphlet.

______. *Mexican Americans: Past, Present and Future*. New York: The American Book Company, 1969. A high school text, heavy on historical background, especially Mexican.

______, ed. *Viva la raza: Readings on Mexican Americans.* New York: Van Nostrand-Reinhold, 1973. A collection of sixty-eight selections, many extremely brief.

Nostrand, Richard L. *Los chicanos: geografía histórica regional.* México, D.F.: Sepsetentas, 1976. A study in historical geography, with valuable maps and tables.

Perrigo, Lynn I. *The American Southwest: Its People and Cultures.* New York: Holt, Rinehart and Winston, 1971. Fairly detailed revision of 1968 survey with some Chicano materials.

______. *Texas and Our Spanish Southwest.* Dallas, Texas: Banks Upshaw & Co., 1968. Survey of southwestern history with emphasis on Mexican contributions.

Pinchot, Jane. *Mexicans in America.* Minneapolis: Lerner Publications, 1973.

Prago, Albert. *Strangers in Their Own Land: A History of Mexican Americans.* New York: Four Winds Press, 1973. A brief, rather simplistic historical survey.

Quintanilla, Guadalupe. *Espiritu siempre eterno del méxico americano.* Washington, D.C.: University Press of America, 1977.

Rendón, Armando B. *Chicano Manifesto: The History and Aspirations of the Second Largest Minority in America.* New York: Macmillan Co., 1971. A passionate leftist interpretation.

Richardson, Rupert N. *Texas, the Lone Star State*, 2d ed. Englewood Cliffs, New Jersey: Prentice Hall, 1958. Good coverage of general Texas history.

______. and Rister, Carl C. *The Greater Southwest: The Economic, Social and Cultural Development of Kansas, Oklahoma, Texas, Utah, Colorado, Nevada, New Mexico, Arizona and California from the Spanish Conquest to the Twentieth Century.* Glendale, Calif.: Arthur H. Clark, Co., 1934.

Rivera, Feliciano. *A Mexican American Source Book.* Menlo Park, Calif.: Educational Consulting Associates, 1970. A useful early source book for social study teachers.

Rosaldo, Renato; Calvert, Robert; and Seligmann, Gustav. *Chicano: The Evolution of a People.* Minneapolis, Minn.: Winston Press, 1973. A book of readings, heavily historical and some sociological.

Samora, Julian, ed. *La Raza: Forgotten Americans.* Notre Dame, Indiana: University of Notre Dame Press, 1966. A collection of seven essays on the sociology of Mexican Americans by authorities in the various areas.

Samora, Julian, and Simon, Patricia Vandel. *A History of the Mexican-American People.* Notre Dame, Indiana: University of Notre Dame Press, 1977. A broad survey, apparently designed as a high school text.

Servín, Manuel P., ed. *An Awakened Minority: The Mexican-Americans*, 2d ed. Beverly Hills: Glencoe Press, 1974. Extensively revised second edition, broader in coverage than the first edition.

______, ed. *The Mexican-Americans: An Awakening Minority.* Beverly Hills, Calif.: Glencoe Press, 1970. Sixteen modern historical essays on Chicano topics, heavily twentieth century.

Simmen, Edward, ed. *Pain and Promise: The Chicano Today*. New York: New American Library, 1972. A collection of historical and sociological articles covering 1900 to 1970.

Simmons, Marc. *New Mexico: A Bicentennial History*. New York: W. W. Norton & Co., 1977.

Smith, Michael M. *The Mexicans in Oklahoma*. Norman: University of Oklahoma Press, 1980.

Stoddard, Ellwyn R. *Mexican Americans*. New York: Random House, 1973. A basic sociopolitical and historical study with twentieth century emphasis.

Tebbel, John, and Ruiz, Ramón E. *South by Southwest: The Mexican-American and His Heritage*. Garden City, New York: Doubleday & Co., 1969. A brief grade school survey, mostly about Mexico.

Trejo, Arnulfo D., ed. *The Chicanos: As We See Ourselves*. Tucson: University of Arizona Press, 1979. A collection of essays by Chicano experts in a variety of disciplines.

University of Arizona Faculty. *Arizona, Its People and Resources*. Tucson: University of Arizona Press, 1972. A collection of essays by University of Arizona faculty members.

Valdez, Luis, and Steiner, Stan, eds. *Aztlán: An Anthology of Mexican American Literature*. New York: Alfred A. Knopf, 1972. A collection of readings, historical rather than literary.

Waltrip, Rufus, and Waltrip, Lela. *Mexican American Story*. Boulder, Colorado: Shields Publishing Co., 1973.

Weber, David J., ed. *Foreigners in Their Native Land: Historical Roots of the Mexican Americans*. Albuquerque: University of New Mexico Press, 1973. Good combination of essays and readings, mostly 1800 to 1912.

Woofter, T. J., Jr. *Races and Ethnic Groups in American Life*. New York: McGraw-Hill Book Co., 1933. Includes some information on Mexicans in Chicago.

Wright, Kathleen. *The Other Americans: Minorities in American History*, 3d ed. Los Angeles: Lawrence Publishing Co., 1969.

Wyllys, Rufus K. *Arizona: The History of a Frontier State*. Phoenix, Arizona: Hobson & Herr, 1950. A good summary textbook.

APPENDIX B CHRONOLOGY OF MEXICAN AMERICAN HISTORY

Origin and Background of the Mexican People

50,000 (?)-10,000 B.C.	Migrators from Asia began moving into North and South America.
7,000-2,000 B.C.	A maize economy developed.
2,000-1,000 B.C.	A village culture developed.
1,500 B.C.-1000 A.D.	Mayan civilization flourished in Guatemala and Yucatan.
350-850 A.D.	Teotihuacano civilization flourished on the great central plateau of Mexico. The impact of this Central Mexican culture spread south into Central America and also north into southwestern United States.
700-900 A.D.	Toltecs, a Nahua people, dominated the central plateau of Mexico.
ca. 1300-1521 A.D.	Aztecs (Mexicas) built upon the civilization of the Toltecs.

Origin and Background of the Spanish People

ca. 20,000 B.C.	Late Paleolithic Cromagnon man made Altamira cave drawings. Iberian culture developed.
ca. 1,000 B.C.	Celts moved into central Spain. Phoenicians established trading posts on southeastern coast of Spain.
ca. 700 B.C.	Greek traders on the east coast founded Emporion and Heraclia.
ca. 550 B.C.	Celtic tribes infiltrated northern Spain.
ca. 500 B.C.	Carthagenians established themselves on southeast coast and founded Cartago Nova (Cartagena).
200 B.C.	Romanization of the Iberian peninsula began; Latin language, government, religion, and culture were established.
ca. 100 A.D.	Many Jews came to Spain in the diaspora.
ca. 500 A.D.	Vandals and Goths invaded and conquered Hispania.

711 A.D.	Moors invaded Spain from North Africa and conquered it in a few years.
718-1492	Spanish war of reconquest took place.
ca. 1000	Castile emerged as a separate kingdom.
1230	Castile and León were definitively united.
1469	The marriage of Ferdinand and Isabel marked the beginning of a united Spain.

Spaniards in the New World

1492	Columbus discovered a new world.
1519	Hernán Cortés landed in Mexico. He was helped by Malinche, a Nahua chieftain's daughter.
1521	With the help of Indian allies, Cortés conquered the Aztecs and their capital of Tenochtitlán.
1521-1550	Spaniards explored outward from Tenochtitlán-Mexico City.
1528-1536	Alvar Núñez Cabeza de Vaca, Estevan el Negro and their companions wandered from Florida through the Southwest to the west coast of Mexico.
1539	As a result of Cabeza de Vaca's report, Fray Marcos de Niza led a preliminary expedition to seek Cíbola.
1539-1543	Hernando de Soto explored across the gulf coast from Florida to eastern Texas.
1540-1542	Francisco Vásquez de Coronado led a large expedition into the northern borderlands, exploring the areas of what is now northern Mexico, the states of New Mexico, Arizona, and parts of Kansas, Nebraska, Wyoming, Colorado, and Oklahoma.
1598	Juan de Oñate began colonization, founding a settlement which he named San Gabriel.
1609	Santa Fe (de San Francisco) was founded.
1680	Pueblo Indians revolted, led by medicine man Popé, chasing all Spaniards out of New Mexico.
1692-1696	Diego de Vargas reestablished settlements in New Mexico.
1706	Albuquerque was founded to assure the reconquest.
1740s	French trappers and traders began to penetrate New Mexico.
1780s	Apache raiding was curbed by a long military campaign.
1800	New Mexico had about twenty thousand settlers in fourteen towns.

Texas, a Defensive Expansion

1682	Sieur de La Salle's trip down the Mississippi River aroused concern about the northeast border of New Spain.
1707	Chihuahua was established as a mining center.
1718	San Antonio de Bexar was founded.
1750s	Texas missions among the Apaches failed.
1763	Treaty of Paris ended Franco-Spanish rivalry in the Southwest; Louisiana became Spanish.
1800	Texas had about four thousand settlers, mostly in four settlements.

California, the Last Borderland

1542-1543	Juan Rodríguez Cabrillo explored the west coast north from Mexico.
1769	Spain decided to colonize California because of fear of Russian intrusion.
	Junípero Serra and Gaspar de Portolá led the expedition from Baja California to San Diego.
1775	Juan Bautista de Anza led a colony overland from Sonora to Alta California.
1777	The Pueblo San José was begun.
1781	Pueblo Nuestra Señora de Los Angeles de la Portiúncula was founded.
1800	California had about twelve hundred settlers. Twenty-one missions, three pueblos, and four presidios were eventually established.

Creation of Mexican Culture

1519-1821	The creation of Mexican culture was a gradual process that took place during three centuries of the colonial period.
	The fusion of Spanish and Indian blood produced the mestizo, dominant in Mexico today.
	The Spanish language incorporated many Indian words, such as tomate, coyote, chile, chocolate, guajalote, and others.
	As the state religion Roman Catholicism became an integral part of Mexican culture.
1810	Father Miguel Hidalgo y Costilla gave the Grito de Dolores, which called for independence from Spain, September 16.
1811-1815	Father José María Morelos y Pavón continued the revolutionary leadership.
1815-1820	Revolution declined as royalists won.
1821	Agustín de Iturbide obtained Mexican independence in a conservative counter-revolution with the Plan de Iguala.
	The northern frontier reflected newly gained freedoms after the 1810 revolution.
	Legislatures and local governing councils were established in New Mexico and California.
	Full citizenship of Indians and mestizos was emphasized.
1822	Iturbide was crowned emperor of Mexico.
1824	Iturbide's brief reign was overthrown and replaced by a federal republic.
	A bitter struggle between federalists and centralists developed in Mexico.

The War Between the United States and Mexico (1846-1848)

After the establishment of the Mexican Republic, Stephen Austin and others obtained empresario colony grants in Texas.

1829	There were approximately thirty thousand Anglo-Saxons and seven thousand Mexicans in Texas. Friction developed between Anglo settlers and the Mexican government. The Mexican government began to regret admitting Anglo-Saxon colonists into Texas.
1829	President Vicente Guerrero issued a decree abolishing slavery (which scarcely existed in Mexico outside of Texas).
1830	It was further decreed that custom duties should be collected and the flood of immigrants reduced. The Law of 1830 was not enforced, and Anglos continued to pour into the Texas area despite it.
1830-1836	Anglo-Texan relations with the Mexican government deteriorated.
1834	The first newspaper west of the Mississippi, *El Crepúsculo de la Libertad*, was printed briefly at Santa Fe.
1836	As president, General Antonio López de Santa Anna replaced the 1824 federalist constitution with a centralist document. Texans, Anglo and Mexican, demanded a return to federalism. Santa Anna tried to suppress their insubordination. Approximately 180 Anglos and Mexicans in the Alamo, led by William B. Travis, refused to surrender to the Mexican army led by Santa Anna. Santa Anna was taken prisoner at San Jacinto and forced to sign the Treaty of Velasco, which recognized Texas independence.
1837-1840	The United States, Great Britain, and France recognized the Republic of Texas.
1836-1846	Mexican-U.S. relations deteriorated as cultural, racial, and economic conflict continued along the Texas border.
1841	A militarized Texas expedition entered New Mexico but was defeated by Governor Manuel Armijo and its members were sent to prison in central Mexico.
1846	U.S. President James Polk ordered General Zachary Taylor to move from the Nueces River to the north bank of the Rio Grande. The United States declared war on Mexico on May 13. New Mexico was invaded and taken by Stephen Kearny. John Charles Frémont commanded the Americans at Sonoma, California, where the Bear Flag Republic was proclaimed. Conquest of California took place under commodores John Sloat and Robert Stockton. On July 7 United States annexation of California was proclaimed at Monterey. General Zachary Taylor invaded northern Mexico and fought Santa Anna at Buena Vista.
1847	General Winfield Scott carried the war successfully into central Mexico. Mexico City surrendered on September 14, 1847. Cahuenga Capitulation "treaty" in California.

1848	The Treaty of Guadalupe Hidalgo ended the war on February 2. Mexico lost half of its territory to the U.S., including California, Utah, Nevada, New Mexico, Arizona, and, of course, Texas. The boundary between the U.S. and Mexico was set along the Rio Grande and Gila rivers. The treaty guaranteed former Mexicans their property, civil rights, and freedom of religion.
1853	Santa Anna agreed to sell a strip of land south of the Gila River to the U.S. for $10 million. This La Mesilla Valley land was the Gadsden Purchase—forty-four thousand acres in southern Arizona and New Mexico.

California

1849	California's first constitutional convention was held in September. Eight of its forty-eight members were Californios.
1849	The gold rush brought great numbers of prospectors to northern California.
1850	By 1850, one hundred thousand newcomers had arrived: eighty thousand Anglo-Americans, eight thousand Mexicans, and five thousand South Americans.
	Mexicans and other Latin Americans began to be violently persecuted by Anglo American and European miners.
	Tensions between Latin American and Anglo American miners climaxed in the Foreign Miners Tax law of 1850.
	The law caused fifteen thousand miners, mostly Chileans, Peruvians, and Sonorans to leave the gold fields.
	The California miners adopted the main principles of Spanish and Mexican mining laws as being best suited to their needs.
	Spaniard José Sadoc Alemany was appointed first bishop of Monterey; he later became the first archbishop of San Francisco.
1851	The Land Act established a three-man commission known as the Board of Land Commissioners to pass on all California land claims.
	In California land ownership changed drastically by 1856 through purchase, financial manipulation, legislation, litigation, violence, and other tactics.
1855-1959	*El Clamor Público*, published by Francisco Ramírez in Los Angeles, defended Californio civil rights.
1875	Romualdo Pacheco became the first and only Mexican American (Californio) governor of California.
	Statewide, Californio political influence virtually ended.

The New Mexico Territory after 1848

1846	Stephen Kearny named trader Charles Bent of Taos as territorial governor.
1847	The Taos revolt led to the death of Governor Bent and others.

Mexican Americans, because of their isolation, stressed retention of culture, language, and traditions.

Nuevo Mexicanos were able to continue in positions of political power from the 1850s onward and remained there even until the 1930s.

1851 Jean Baptiste Lamy arrived in Santa Fe as first bishop of New Mexico, Arizona, and Colorado.

1853 The Gadsden Purchase Treaty added the Mesilla Valley to New Mexico and Arizona.

1878-1891 Extensive railroad development occurred in New Mexico, changing its economic base.

1880s White Caps (Gorras Blancas) became active in New Mexico.

Caballeros de Labor were briefly established in the Southwest.

1894 The Spanish-American Alliance was founded in Arizona.

1897-1907 Miguel Antonio Otero II was governor of the New Mexican territory.

Texas and the Border

The meeting of Anglo and Mexican in the Southwest created a climate of cultural conflict.

Border banditry and hostility continued between Mexicans and Anglos—especially on the Texas border.

1857 The Cart War in Texas furnished continuing evidence of Anglo-Mexican antagonisms.

1861-1865 The Civil War found Tejanos, like other Americans, divided.

1866 There were early Galveston, Texas, labor organizing activities by Mexican Americans.

The border between the United States and Mexico continued to be a political border rather than a cultural or economic one.

1878 The El Paso Salt "War" renewed old antagonisms.

Migration—North From Mexico

Mexican immigrants helped build the economic empire which exists in the Southwest today.

1880 The census indicated a Mexican-descent population of about two hundred thirty thousand in the U.S.

1880s Mexican workers migrated to Texas as braceros in cotton.

1900 After 1900 immigration brought rapidly increasing numbers of Mexicans to the Southwest as railroads were completed in northern Mexico.

Mexican American and Mexican labor made up a majority of workers on eighteen western railroads.

1900-1950 Mexican and Mexican American labor constituted 60 percent of the labor in southwestern mines.

Southwestern agriculture was based directly on the use of Mexican and Mexican American labor.

1903	Mexican Americans played important roles in organizing copper miners in the Clifton-Morenci strike.
1912	Arizona and New Mexico became states.

World War I

1914-1918	During World War I Mexican laborers began to appear in midwestern industrial areas as railroad, steel mill, and packing plant workers.
1916	Ezequiel Cabeza de Vaca was elected first Mexican American governor of the state of New Mexico.
1917	The 1917 Immigration Act included a head tax. However, it was waived for Mexican immigrants during the war.
	Many Mexican Americans served in the armed forces of the United States during World War I.
	Other Mexican Americans, in increasing numbers, continued to provide labor for railroads, agriculture, and industry.
1920	The census showed four hundred eighty-six thousand Mexican-born persons and two hundred fifty-two thousand native-born persons of Mexican-born parentage in the U.S.
1920-1929	Immigration from Mexico on permanent visas exceeded five hundred thousand.
	In this same period undocumented immigration reached large numbers.
1920s	First intensive debate occurred on limiting Mexican immigration by including hemisphere countries in the quota system.
1925	The Border Patrol was created by U.S. Congress.
1929-1939	The Great Depression resulted in a drastic decline in new immigration from Mexico; it also produced a massive return of Mexicans to Mexico.
1930	The census showed an estimated 1,509,000 Mexican-descent population in the U.S.
	Approximately half a million Mexicans returned to Mexico, or were forced to return.
1940	The census showed a 1,571,000 Mexican-descent population in the U.S.

Mexican American Organizations

	Mexican immigrants were pioneers of the trade union movement in the West.
1903	Mexican sugar beet workers went on strike at Ventura, California.
1910	Mexican workers struck the street railway in Los Angeles.
1921	La Ordén de Hijos de America was founded in San Antonio.
1927	Confederación de Uniones Obreras Mexicanas (CUOM) was formed in southern California.
1929	League of United Latin American Citizens (LULAC) was founded in Texas.

1933	The El Monte (California) Berry Strike led to the formation of the Confederación de Uniones de Campesinos y Obreros Mexicanos (CUCOM).
1934	Liga Obrera de Habla Española was organized in Gallup, New Mexico.
1936	Rev. Mariano S. Garriga became the first Mexican American bishop (coadjutor) of the Corpus Christi diocese.
1938	The pecan shellers of San Antonio, Texas, went on strike.

World War II

1940-1946	Demands for foreign labor increased because World War II drew domestic farm workers into industry and military service.
1941-1946	During World War II great numbers of Mexican Americans enlisted in the armed forces.
	Seventeen Mexican Americans were awarded the Congressional Medal of Honor.
1942	The Sleepy Lagoon murder took place and the Sleepy Lagoon Committee was formed in Los Angeles.
1943	"Zoot-Suit" race riots occurred in Los Angeles, San Diego, and Oakland; other large American cities also had similar race riots.
	The Bracero Program began bringing Mexican workers to the United States under bilateral government agreements.
	Public Law 45 regulated the World War II Bracero Program.
1945	The Bishops Committee for the Spanish-Speaking was created.
	An exodus of Mexican Americans from rural to urban areas began.

Post World War II and the Mexican American

1947	The United States terminated the wartime Bracero Program. Less formal arrangements continued.
1948	American G.I. Forum was founded in Corpus Christi, Texas, by Mexican American veterans under the leadership of Dr. Hector García.
	The Community Service Organization (CSO) was developed in Los Angeles.
1950	The census showed about a 2,282,000 Mexican-descent population in the U.S.
1950-1953	Mexican Americans served during the Korean War.
1951	Public Law 78 implemented the reorganized Bracero Program.
1952	The McCarran-Walter Act modified the 1921 and 1924 immigration acts. Passed over President Harry Truman's veto, it was used later to deport Mexican immigrants active in labor organizing.
1954	"Operation Wetback"—a massive repatriation effort—began in June 1954. More than one million "returned" to Mexico in the succeeding twelve months.

Feelings of alienation from American society and mistrust of the government were again strengthened.

1956 Legal immigration from Mexico reached a peak of sixty-five thousand and averaged over forty-two thousand per year through 1966.

1959 In California the Mexican American Political Association (MAPA) began its activities.

1960 The census indicated a Mexican American population of about 3,465,000.

Viva Kennedy clubs were organized in the Southwest.

The Political Association of Spanish-Speaking Organizations (PASO) was founded in Texas.

1961 Joseph J. Jova was appointed U.S. ambassador to Honduras.

1963 César Chávez began his farm labor movement in the Central Valley of California.

Reies López Tijerina founded the Alianza Federal de Mercedes in New Mexico.

1964 Mexican Americans served during the Vietnam War.

Raúl Héctor Castro was appointed ambassador to El Salvador.

The Bracero Program was terminated at the close of the calendar year, twenty-two years after its inception. Commuters now became an important source of cheap labor.

1965 Joseph M. Montoya was elected to the U.S. Senate from New Mexico.

Mexican Americans became more involved in the political arena; they began to assert themselves, especially in student and youth groups like MAYO, MASC, UMAS, the Brown Berets, and MECHA.

The Delano grape strike began under the leadership of César Chávez.

1966 Led by César Chávez, United Farm Workers marched from Delano to Sacramento.

Rodolfo "Corky" Gonzales organized the Crusade for Justice in Denver, Colorado.

Starr County (Texas) melon strike took place.

Mexican American participants in an Albuquerque Equal Employment Opportunity Commission meeting walked out in protest of the fact that there was not a single Mexican American on the EEOC staff.

1967 *El Grito*, a journal of contemporary Chicano thought, began publication in Berkeley, California.

The Tierra Amarilla courthouse raid took place.

José Angel Gutiérrez founded the Mexican American Youth Organization (MAYO) in San Antonio, Texas.

David Sánchez organized the Brown Berets in Los Angeles.

The Mexican American Legal Defense Education Fund (MALDEF) was incorporated in Texas.

A grape boycott began and soon spread all over the United States.

1968	Demonstrations, sitins, school walkouts, and boycotts—all reflected the civil rights movement and the new stance of Chicanos.
	El Plan de Santa Bárbara emerged from a Chicano conference in that city.
1969	"Corky" Gonzales founded La Raza Unida Party in Colorado.
	First Chicano Youth Conference in Denver led to the Plan de Aztlán.
	A Chicano anti-Vietnam rally was held in Los Angeles.
	El Movimiento Estudantil Chicano de Aztlán (MECHA) was founded.
1970	The census showed a Mexican American population of approximately 6,186,000.
	United Farm Workers successfully ended the table grape strike.
	César Chávez then turned to unionize the Salinas lettuce fields.
	Rev. Patrick Flores became the second Mexican American bishop.
	A Chicano moratorium was organized in Los Angeles; Rubén Salazar was killed by a tear gas projectile.
	José Angel Gutiérrez formed the Raza Unida Party in Texas out of MAYO.
1971	At Crystal City, Texas, the Raza Unida Party won city elections.
	Reies López Tijerina was freed from prison on parole after serving three years.
	The first Chicana Conference in Houston, Texas, discussed the role of Chicanas in the Movimiento.
1972	Mrs. Ramona Acosta Bañuelos became the first Mexican American treasurer of the United States.
1972-1974	The Farah strike at El Paso finally ended in success.
1973	Philip V. Sánchez was appointed ambassador to Honduras.
	The United Farm Workers lost a majority of its 1970 three-year contracts with California grape growers to the Teamsters Union.
1974	Rev. Robert F. Sánchez became the first Mexican American archbishop of the Santa Fe diocese.
	Raúl H. Castro was the first Mexican American to be elected governor of Arizona.
	Jerry Apodaca was elected governor of the state of New Mexico, the first Mexican American since the 1918 election of Octaviano Larrazolo.
1975	The California Labor Relations Act was passed by the California state legislature.
1976	In the presidential election 4.9 million Hispanics were eligible to vote, of whom 55 percent (2.7 million) registered to vote and of whom 37 percent (1.8 million) voted.
1977	The United Farm Workers-Teamsters feud was finally brought to an end.
	César Chávez led a twelve-mile march through the Coachella Valley.

1978	The United Farm Workers' boycott against lettuce growers, table grape growers, and Gallo winery was ended by César Chávez.
	The United States Supreme Court upheld the Alan Bakke decision of the lower courts.
1979	The United Farm Workers' strike against Imperial Valley and Salinas lettuce growers was renewed.
	César Chávez led a San Francisco-Salinas march to publicize the lettuce strike.
	Secretary of Agriculture Robert Bergland announced the end of federal funding for labor-saving agricultural machinery research.
	The issue of free public education for children of undocumented workers became widely discussed.
1980	The "Decade of the Hispanics" began.
	Professor Julian Nava was appointed the first Mexican American ambassador to Mexico.
1980	A preliminary census count showed approximately nine million Mexican-descent Americans.

APPENDIX C

THE COMPLETE TEXT OF THE TREATY OF GUADALUPE HIDALGO AND THE PROTOCOL OF QUERÉTARO

MEXICO: FEBRUARY 2, 1848

Treaty of Guadalupe Hidalgo. Treaty of Peace, Friendship, Limits, and Settlement (with additional and secret article which was not ratified), with Map of the United Mexican States and with Plan of the Port of San Diego, signed at Guadalupe Hidalgo February 2, 1848. Originals of the treaty and additional and secret article in English and Spanish.*

Treaty and additional and secret article submitted to the Senate February 23, 1848. Ratified by the United States March 16, 1848. Ratified by Mexico May 30, 1848. Ratifications exchanged at Querétaro May 30, 1848. Proclaimed July 4, 1848.

In the name of Almighty God:

The United States of America, and the United Mexican States, animated by a sincere desire to put an end to the calamities of the war which unhappily exists between the two Republics, and to establish upon a solid basis relations of peace and friendship, which shall confer reciprocal bene-

En el nombre de Dios Todo-Poderoso.

Los Estados-Unidos mexicanos y los Estados-Unidos de América, animados de un sincero deseo de poner término á las calamidades de la guerra que desgraciadamente existe entre ambas Repúblicas, y de establecer sobre báses sólidas relaciones de paz y buena amistad, que procuren recíprocas ventajas

*These six words are from the title ascribed to the map in the English version of the treaty, Article 5; the title of the map is "Mapa de los Estados Unidos de Méjico."

SOURCE: From Hunter Miller, ed., *Treaties and Other International Acts of the United States of America*, vol. 5 (Washington, D.C.: U.S. Government Printing Office, 1937).

fits upon the citizens of both, and assure the concord, harmony and mutual confidence, wherein the two peoples should live, as good neighbours, have for that purpose appointed their respective Plenipotentiaries: that is to say, the President of the United States has appointed Nicholas P. Trist, a citizen of the United States, and the President of the Mexican Republic has appointed Don Luis Gonzaga Cuevas, Don Bernardo Couto, and Don Miguel Atristain, citizens of the said Republic; who, after a reciprocal communication of their respective full powers, have, under the protection of Almighty God, the author of Peace, arranged, agreed upon, and signed the following

Treaty of Peace, Friendship, Limits and Settlement between the United States of America and the Mexican Republic.

á los Ciudadanos de uno y otro pays, y afianzen la concordia, armonia y mútua seguridad en que deben vivir, como buenos vecinos, los dos pueblos; han nombrado á este efecto sus respectivos Plenipotenciarios; á saber, el Presidente de la República mexicana á Don Bernardo Couto, Don Miguel Atristain y Don Luis Gonzaga Cuevas, ciudadanos de la misma República; y el Presidente de los Estados-Unidos de América á Don Nicolas P. Trist, ciudadano de dichos Estados; quienes despues de haberse comunicado sus plenos poderes, bajo la proteccion del Señor Dios Todo-poderoso, autor de la paz, han ajustado, convenido y firmado el siguiente

Tratado de Paz, Amistad, Límites y Arreglo definitivo entre la República mexicana y los Estados-Unidos de América.

ARTICLE I.

There shall be firm and universal peace between the United States of America and the Mexican Republic, and between their respective countries, territories, cities, towns and people, without exception of places or persons.

ARTÍCULO I.

Habrá paz firme y universal entre la República mexicana y los Estados-Unidos de América y entre sus respectivos paises, territorios, ciudades, villas y pueblos, sin escepcion de lugares ó personas.

ARTICLE II.

Immediately upon the signature of this Treaty, a convention shall be entered into between a Commissioner or Commissioners appointed by the General in Chief

ARTÍCULO II.

Luego que se firme el presente Tratado habrá un convenio entre el comisionado ú comisionados del Gobierno mexicano, y el ó los que nombre el General en Gefe de

of the forces of the United States, and such as may be appointed by the Mexican Government, to the end that a provisional suspension of hostilities shall take place, and that, in the places occupied by the said forces, constitutional order may be reestablised, as regards the political, administrative, and judicial branches, so far as this shall be permitted by the circumstances of military occupation.

las fuerzas de los Estados-Unidos, para que cesen provisionalmente las hostilidades, y se restablezca en los lugares ocupados por las mismas fuerzas el órden constitucional en lo político, administrativo y judicial, en cuanto lo permitan las circunstancias de ocupacion militar.

Article III.

Immediately upon the ratification of the present treaty by the Government of the United States, orders shall be transmitted to the Commanders of their land and naval forces, requiring the latter, (provided this treaty shall then have been ratified by the Government of the Mexican Republic and the ratifications exchanged) immediately to desist from blockading any Mexican ports; and requiring the former (under the same condition) to commence, at the earliest moment practicable, withdrawing all troops of the United States then in the interior of the Mexican Republic, to points, that shall be selected by common agreement, at a distance from the sea-ports, not exceeding thirty leagues; and such evacuation of the interior of the Republic shall be completed with the least possible delay; the Mexican Government hereby binding itself to afford every facility in it's power for

Artículo III.

Luego que este Tratado sea ratificado por el Gobierno de los Estados-Unidos, se expedirán órdenes á sus comandantes de tierra y mar previniendo á estos segundos (siempre que el Tratado haya sido ya ratificado por el Gobierno de la República mexicana y cangeadas las ratificaciones) que inmediatamente alcen el bloqueo de todos los puertos mexicanos, y mandando á los primeros (bajo la misma condicion) que á la mayor posible brevedad comiencen á retirar todas las tropas de los Estados-Unidos que se halláren entonces en el interior de la República mexicana, á puntos que se elegirán de comun acuerdo, y que no distarán de los puertos mas de treinta leguas: esta evacuacion del interior de la República se consumará con la menor dilacion posible, comprometiéndose á la vez el Gobierno mexicano á facilitar, cuanto quepa en su arbitrio, la evacuacion de las tropas ameri-

rendering the same convenient to the troops, on their march and in their new positions, and for promoting a good understanding between them and the inhabitants. In like manner, orders shall be despatched to the persons in charge of the Custom Houses at all ports occupied by the forces of the United States, requiring them (under the same condition) immediately to deliver possession of the same to the persons authorized by the Mexican Government to receive it, together with all bonds and evidences of debt for duties on importations and on exportations, not yet fallen due. Moreover, a faithful and exact account shall be made out, showing the entire amount of all duties on imports and on exports, collected at such Custom Houses, or elsewhere in Mexico, by authority of the United States, from and after the day of ratification of this treaty by the Government of the Mexican Republic; and also an account of the cost of collection; and such entire amount, deducting only the cost of collection, shall be delivered to the Mexican Government, at the City of Mexico, within three months after the exchange of ratifications.

canas; á hacer cómodas su marcha y su permanencia en los nuevos puntos que se elijan; y á promover una buena inteligencia entre ellas y los habitantes. Igualmente se librarán órdenes á las personas encargadas de las Aduanas marítimas en todos los puertos ocupados por las fuerzas de los Estados-Unidos, previniéndoles (bajo la misma condicion) que pongan inmediatamente en posesion de dichas Aduanas á las personas autorizadas por el Gobierno mexicano para recibirlas, entregándoles al mismo tiempo todas las obligaciones y constancias de deudas pendientes por derechos de importacion y exportacion, cuyos plazos no estén vencidos. Ademas se formará una cuenta fiel y exacta que manifieste el total monto de los derechos de importacion y exportacion recaudados en las mismas Aduanas marítimas ó en cualquiera otro lugar de México por autoridad de los Estados-Unidos desde el dia de la ratificacion de este Tratado por el Gobierno de la República mexicana; y tambien una cuenta de los gastos de recaudacion: y la total suma de los derechos cobrados, deducidos solamente los gastos de recaudacion, se entregará al Gobierno mexicano en la ciudad de México á los tres meses del cange de las ratificaciones.

The evacuation of the Capital of the Mexican Republic by the troops of the United States, in virtue of the above stipulation, shall be completed in one month

La evacuacion de la capital de la República mexicana por las tropas de los Estados-Unidos, en consequencia de lo que queda estipulado, se completará al mes de

after the orders there stipulated for shall have been received by the commander of said troops, or sooner if possible.

Article IV.

Immediately after the exchange of ratifications of the present treaty, all castles, forts, territories, places and possessions, which have been taken or occupied by the forces of the United States during the present war, within the limits of the Mexican Republic, as about to be established by the following Article, shall be definitively restored to the said Republic, together with all the artillery, arms, apparatus of war, munitions and other public property, which were in the said castles and forts when captured, and which shall remain there at the time when this treaty shall be duly ratified by the Government of the Mexican Republic. To this end, immediately upon the signature of this treaty, orders shall be despatched to the American officers commanding such castles and forts, securing against the removal or destruction of any such artillery, arms, apparatus of war, munitions or other public property. The City of Mexico, within the inner line of intrenchments surrounding the said City, is comprehended in the above stipulations, as regards the restoration of artillery, apparatus of war, &c.

recibirse por el comandante de dichas tropas las órdenes convenidas en el presente artículo, ó antes si fuere posible.

Artículo IV.

Luego que se verifique el cange de las ratificaciones del presente Tratado, todos los castillos, fortalezas, territorios, lugares y posesiones que hayan tomado ú ocupado las fuerzas de los Estados-Unidos, en la presente guerra, dentro de los límites que por el siguiente artículo van á fijarse á la República mexicana, se devolverán definitivamente á la misma República, con toda la artilleria, armas, aparejos de guerra, municiones, y cualquiera otra propiedad pública existente en dichos castillos y fortalezas cuando fueron tomados, y que se conserve en ellos al tiempo de ratificarse por el Gobierno de la República mexicana el presente Tratado. A este efecto inmediatamente despues que se firme, se expedirán órdenes á los oficiales americanos que mandan dichos castillos y fortalezas para asegurar toda la artilleria, armas, aparejos de guerra, municiones, y cualquiera otra propiedad pública, la cual no podrá en adelante removerse de donde se halla, ni destruirse. La ciudad de Mexico dentro de la linea interior de atrincheramientos que la circundan queda comprendida en la precedente estipulacion en lo que toca á la devolucion de artilleria, aparejos de guerra ect[a]

The final evacuation of the territory of the Mexican Republic, by the forces of the United States, shall be completed in three months from the said exchange of ratifications, or sooner, if possible: the Mexican Government hereby engaging, as in the foregoing Article, to use all means in it's power for facilitating such evacuation, and rendering it convenient to the troops, and for promoting a good understanding between them and the inhabitants.

If, however, the ratification of this treaty by both parties should not take place in time to allow the embarcation of the troops of the United States to be completed before the commencement of the sickly season, at the Mexican Ports on the Gulf of Mexico; in such case a friendly arrangement shall be entered into between the General in Chief of the said troops and the Mexican Government, whereby healthy and otherwise suitable places at a distance from the ports not exceeding thirty leagues shall be designated for the residence of such troops as may not yet have embarked, until the return of the healthy season. And the space of time here referred to, as comprehending the sickly season, shall be understood to extend from the first day of May to the first day of November.

La final evacuacion del territorio de la República mexicana por las fuerzas de los Estados-Unidos quedará consumada á los tres meses del cange de las ratificaciones, ó antes si fuére posible, comprometiendose á la vez el Gobierno mexicano, como en el artículo anterior, á usar de todos los medios que estén en su poder para facílitar la tal evacuacion, hacerla cómoda á las tropas americanas, y promover entre ellas y los habitantes una buena inteligencia.

Sin embargo si la ratificacion del presente Tratado por ambas partes no tuviére efecto en tiempo que permita que el embarque de las tropas de los Estados-Unidos se complete, antes de qui comience la estacion malsana en los puertos mexicanos del golfo de México; en tal caso se hará un arreglo amistoso entre el gobierno mexicano y el General en gefe de dichas tropas, y por medio de este arreglo se señalarán lugares salubres y convenientes (que no disten de los puertos mas de treinta leguas) para que residan en ellos hasta la vuelta de la estacion sana las tropas que aun no se hayan embarcado. Y queda entendido que el espacio de tiempo de que aquí se habla, como comprensivo de la estacion malsana, se extiende desde el dia primero de Mayo hasta el dia primero de Noviembre.

All prisoners of war taken on either side, on land or on sea, shall be restored as soon as practicable after the exchange of ratifications of this treaty. It is also agreed that if any Mexicans should now be held as captives by any savage tribe within the limits of the United States, as about to be established by the following Article, the Government of the said United States will exact the release of such captives, and cause them to be restored to their country.

Todos los prisioneros de guerra tomados en mar ó tierra por ambas partes se restituirán á la mayor brevedad posible despues del cange de las ratificaciones del presente Tratado. Queda tambien convenido que si algunos mexicanos estuviéren ahora cautivos en poder de alguna tríbu salvage dentro de los límites que por el siguiente artículo van á fijarse á los Estados-Unidos, el Gobierno de los mismos Estados-Unidos exigirá su libertad y los hará restituir á su pays.

Article V.

The Boundary line between the two Republics shall commence in the Gulf of Mexico, three leagues from land, opposite the mouth of the Rio Grande, otherwise called Rio Bravo del Norte, or opposite the mouth of it's deepest branch, if it should have more than one branch emptying directly into the sea; from thence, up the middle of that river, following the deepest channel, where it has more than one, to the point where it strikes the southern boundary of New Mexico; thence, westwardly, along the whole southern boundary of New Mexico (which runs north of the town called *Paso*) to it's western termination; thence, northward, along the western line of New Mexico, until it intersects the first branch of the river Gila; (or if it should not intersect any branch of that river, then, to the

Artículo V.

La línea divisoria entre las dos Repúblicas comenzará en el golfo de México tres leguas fuera de tierra frente á la desembocadura del rio Grande, llamado por otro nombre rio Bravo del Norte, ó del mas profundo de sus brazos, si en la desembocadura tuviére varios brazos: correrá por mitad de dicho rio, siguiendo el canal mas profundo, donde tenga mas de un canal, hasta el punto en que dicho rio corta el lindero meridional de Nuevo-México; continuará luego hácia occidente por todo este lindero meridional (que corre al Norte del pueblo llamado *Paso*) hasta su término por el lado de occidente: desde allí subirá la linea divisoria hácia el Norte por el lindero occidental de Nuevo-México, hasta donde este lindero esté cortado por el primer brazo del rio Gila; (y si no está cortado

point on the said line nearest to such branch, and thence in a direct line to the same;) thence down the middle of the said branch and of the said river, until it empties into the Rio Colorado; thence, across the Rio Colorado, following the division line between Upper and Lower California, to the Pacific Ocean.

por ningun brazo del rio Gila, entonces hasta el punto del mismo lindero occidental mas cercano al tal brazo, y de allí en una línea recta al mismo brazo): continuará despues por mitad de este brazo y del rio Gila hasta su confluencia con el rio Colorado; y desde la confluencia de ambos rios la línea divisoria, cortando el Colorado, seguirá el límite que separa la Alta de la Baja California hasta el mar Pacífico.

The southern and western limits of New Mexico, mentioned in this Article, are those laid down in the Map, entitled "*Map of the United Mexican States, as organized and defined by various acts of the Congress of said Republic, and constructed according to the best Authorities. Revised Edition. Published at New York in 1847 by J. Disturnell:*" of which Map a Copy is added to this treaty, bearing the signatures and seals of the Undersigned Plenipotentiaries. And, in order to preclude all difficulty in tracing upon the ground the limit separating Upper from Lower California, it is agreed that the said limit shall consist of a straight line, drawn from the middle of the Rio Gila, where it unites with the Colorado, to a point on the coast of the Pacific Ocean, distant one marine league due south of the southernmost point of the Port of San Diego, according to the plan of said port, made in the year 1782 by Don Juan Pantoja, second sailing mas-

Los linderos meridional y occidental de Nuevo-México, de que habla este artículo, son los que se marcan en la Carta titulada: *Mapa de los Estados-Unidos de México, segun lo organizado y definido por las varias Actas del Congreso de dicha República y construido por las mejores autoridades: Edicion revisada que publicó en Nueva-York en 1847 J. Disturnell*, de la cual se agrega un ejemplar al presente Tratado, firmado y sellado por los Plenipotenciarios infrascriptos. Y para evitar toda dificultad al trazar sobre la tierra el límite que separa la Alta de la Baja California, queda convenido que dicho límite consistirá en una linea recta tirada desde la mitad del rio Gila en el punto donde se une con el Colorado, hasta un punto en la costa del mar Pacífico, distante una legua marina al Sur del punto mas meridional del puerto de San Diego, segun este Puerto está dibujado en el plano que levantó el año de 1782 el segundo

ter of the Spanish fleet, and published at Madrid in the year 1802, in the Atlas to the voyage of the schooners *Sutil* and *Mexicana:* of which plan a copy is hereunto added, signed and sealed by the respective plenipotentiaries.

In order to designate the Boundary line with due precision, upon authoritative maps, and to establish upon the ground landmarks which shall show the limits of both Republics, as described in the present Article, the two Governments shall each appoint a Commissioner and a Surveyor, who, before the expiration of one year from the date of the exchange of ratifications of this treaty, shall meet at the Port of San Diego, and proceed to run and mark the said boundary in it's whole course, to the Mouth of the Rio Bravo del Norte. They shall keep journals and make out plans of their operations; and the result, agreed upon by them, shall be deemed a part of this Treaty, and shall have the same force as if it were inserted therein. The two Governments will amicably agree regarding what may be necessary to these persons, and also as to their respective escorts, should such be necessary.

The Boundary line established by this Article shall be religiously respected by each of the two Republics, and no change shall ever be made therein, except by the express and free consent of both

Piloto de la Armada española Don Juan Pantoja, y se publicó en Madrid el de 1802 en el átlas para el viage de las goletas Sutil y Mexicana; del cual Plano se agrega copia firmada y sellada por los Plenipotenciarios respectivos.

Para consignar la linea divisoria con la precision debida en mapas fehacientes, y para establecer sobre la tierra mojones que pongan á la vista los límites de ambas Repúblicas, segun quedan descritos en el presente artículo, nombrará cada uno de los dos Gobiernos un comisario y un agrimensor que se juntarán antes del término de un año contado desde la fecha del cange de las ratificaciones de este Tratado, en el Puerto de San Diego, y procederán á señalar y demarcar la expresada linea divisoria en todo su curso hasta la desembocadura del rio Bravo del Norte. Llevarán diarios y levantarán planos de sus operaciones: y el resultado convenido por ellos se tendrá por parte de este Tratado, y tendrá la misma fuerza que si estuviése inserto en él; debiendo convenir amistosamente los dos Gobiernos en el arreglo de cuanto necesiten estos individuos, y en la escolta respectiva que deban llevar, siempre que se crea necesario.

La linea divisoria que se establece por este artículo será religiosamente respetada por cada una de las dos Repúblicas, y ninguna variacion se hará jamás en ella, sino de expreso y libre consenti-

nations, lawfully given by the General Government of each, in conformity with it's own constitution.

miento de ambas naciones, otorgado legalmente por el Gobierno general de cada una de ellas, con arreglo á su propia constitucion.

Article VI.

The Vessels and citizens of the United States shall, in all time, have a free and uninterrupted passage by the Gulf of California, and by the River Colorado below it's confluence with the Gila, to and from their possessions situated north of the Boundary line defined in the preceding Article: it being understood, that this passage is to be by navigating the Gulf of California and the River Colorado, and not by land, without the express consent of the Mexican Government.

If, by the examinations which may be made, it should be ascertained to be practicable and advantageous to construct a road, canal or railway, which should, in whole or in part, run upon the river Gila, or upon it's right or it's left bank, within the space of one marine league from either margin of the river, the Governments of both Republics will form an agreement regarding it's construction, in order that it may serve equally for the use and advantage of both countries.

Artículo VI.

Los buques y ciudadanos de los Estados-Unidos tendrán en todo tiempo un libre y no interrumpido tránsito por el golfo de California y por el rio Colorado desde su confluencia con el Gila para sus posesiones y desde sus posesiones sitas al Norte de la linea divisoria que queda marcada en el artículo precedente; entendiéndose que este tránsito se ha de hacer navegando por el golfo de California y por el rio Colorado, y no por tierra sin expreso consentimiento del Gobierno mexicano.

Si por reconocimientos que se practiquen se comprobáre la posibilidad y conveniencia de construir un camino, canal ó ferrocarril que en todo ó en parte corra sobre el rio Gila ó sobre alguna de sus márgenes derecha ó izquierda en la latitud de una legua marina de uno ó de otro lado del rio, los Gobiernos de ambas Repúblicas se pondrán de acuerdo sobre su construccion á fin de que sirva igualmente para el uso y provecho de ambos paises.

Article VII.

The river Gila, and the part of the Rio Bravo del Norte lying below the southern boundary of

Artículo VII.

Como el rio Gila y la parte del rio Bravo del Norte que corre bajo el lindero meridional de

New Mexico, being, agreeably to the fifth Article, divided in the middle between the two Republics, the navigation of the Gila and of the Bravo below said boundary shall be free and common to the vessels and citizens of both countries; and neither shall, without the consent of the other, construct any work that may impede or interrupt, in whole or in part, the exercise of this right: not even for the purpose of favouring new methods of navigation. Nor shall any tax or contribution, under any denomination or title, be levied upon vessels or persons navigating the same, or upon merchandise or effects transported thereon, except in the case of landing upon one of their shores. If, for the purpose of making the said rivers navigable, or for maintaining them in such state, it should be necessary or advantageous to establish any tax or contribution, this shall not be done without the consent of both Governments.

The stipulations contained in the present Article shall not impair the territorial rights of either Republic, within it's established limits.

Nuevo-Mexico se dividen por mitad entre las dos Repúblicas, segun lo establecido en el artículo quinto, la navegacion en el Gila y en la parte que queda indicada del Bravo será libre y comun á los buques y ciudadanos de ambos paises, sin que por alguno de ellos pueda hacerse (sin consentimiento del otro) ninguna obra que impida ó interrumpa en todo ó en parte el ejercicio de este derecho, ni aun con motivo de favorecer nuevos métodos de navegacion. Tampoco se podrá cobrar (sino en el caso de desembarco en alguna de sus riberas) ningun impuesto ó contribucion bajo ninguna denominacion ó título á los buques, efectos, mercancias ó personas que naveguen en dichos rios. Si para hacerlos ó mantenerlos navegables fuere necesario ó conveniente establecer alguna contribucion ó impuesto, no podrá esto hacerse sin el consentimiento de los dos Gobiernos.

Las estipulaciones contenidas en el presente artículo dejan ilesos los derechos territoriales de una y otra República dentro de los límites que les quedan marcados.

Article VIII.

Mexicans now established in territories previously belonging to Mexico, and which remain for the future within the limits of the United States, as defined by the present treaty, shall be free to

Artículo VIII.

Los mexicanos establecidos hoy en territorios pertenecientes antes á México y que quedan para lo futuro dentro de los límites señalados por el presente Tratado á los Estados-Unidos, podrán perma-

continue where they now reside, or to remove at any time to the Mexican Republic, retaining the property which they possess in the said territories, or disposing thereof, and removing the proceeds wherever they please; without their being subjected, on this account, to any contribution, tax or charge whatever.

Those who shall prefer to remain in the said territories, may either retain the title and rights of Mexican citizens, or acquire those of citizens of the United States. But they shall be under the obligation to make their election within one year from the date of the exchange of ratifications of this treaty: and those who shall remain in the said territories, after the expiration of that year, without having declared their intention to retain the character of Mexicans, shall be considered to have elected to become citizens of the United States.

In the said territories, property of every kind, now belonging to Mexicans, not established there, shall be inviolably respected. The present owners, the heirs of these, and all Mexicans who may hereafter acquire said property by contract, shall enjoy with respect to it, guaranties equally ample as if the same belonged to citizens of the United States.

necer en donde ahora habitan, ó trasladarse en cualquier tiempo á la República mexicana, conservando en los indicados territorios los bienes que poseen, ó enagenándolos y pasando su valor á donde les convenga, sin que por esto pueda exigírseles ningun género de contribucion, gravámen ó impuesto.

Los que prefieran permanecer en los indicados territorios, podrán conservar el título y derechos de ciudadanos mexicanos, ó adquirir el título y derechos de ciudadanos de los Estados-Unidos. Mas la eleccion entre una y otra ciudadania deberán hacerla dentro de un año contado desde la fecha del cange de las ratificaciones de este Tratado. Y los que permaneciéren en los indicados territorios despues de transcurrido el año, sin haber declarado su intencion de retener el carácter de mexicanos, se considerará que han elegido ser ciudadanos de los Estados-Unidos.

Las propiedades de todo género existentes en los expresados territorios, y que pertenecen ahora á mexicanos no establecidos en ellos, serán respetadas inviolablemente. Sus actuales dueños, los herederos de estos, y los mexicanos que en lo venidero puedan adquirir por contrato las indicadas propiedades, disfrutarán respecto de ellas tan amplia garantia, como si perteneciesen á ciudadanos de los Estados-Unidos.

ARTICLE IX.

The Mexicans who, in the territories aforesaid, shall not preserve the character of citizens of the Mexican Republic, conformably with what is stipulated in the preceding article, shall be incorporated into the Union of the United States and be admitted, at the proper time (to be judged of by the Congress of the United States) to the enjoyment of all the rights of citizens of the United States according to the principles of the Constitution; and in the mean time shall be maintained and protected in the free enjoyment of their liberty and property, and secured in the free exercise of their religion without restriction.

ARTÍCULO IX.

Los Mexicanos que, en los territorios antedichos, no conserven el caracter de ciudadanos de la República Mexicana, segun lo estipulado en el artículo precedente, serán incorporados en la Union de los Estados Unidos, y se admitirán en tiempo oportuno (á juicio del Congreso de los Estados Unidos) al goce de todos los derechos de ciudadanos de los Estados Unidos conforme á los principios de la constitucion; y entretanto serán mantenidos y protejidos en el goce de su libertad y propiedad, y asegurados en el libre ejercicio de su religion sin restriccion alguna.

[One of the amendments of the Senate struck out Article 10.]

ARTICLE XI.

Considering that a great part of the territories which, by the present Treaty, are to be comprehended for the future within the limits of the United States, is now occupied by savage tribes, who will hereafter be under the exclusive controul of the Government of the United States, and whose incursions within the territory of Mexico would be prejudicial in the extreme; it is solemnly agreed that all such incursions shall be forcibly restrained by the Government of the United States, whensoever this may be necessary; and

ARTÍCULO XI.

En atencion á que una gran parte de los territorios que por el presente Tratado van á quedar para lo futuro dentro de los límites de los Estados-Unidos se halla actualmente ocupada por tríbus salvages, que han de estar en adelante bajo la exclusiva autoridad del Gobierno de los Estados-Unidos, y cuyas incursiones sobre los distritos mexicanos serian en extremo perjudiciales; está solemnemente convenido que el mismo Gobierno de los Estados-Unidos contendrá las indicadas incursiones por medio de la fuerza

that when they cannot be prevented, they shall be punished by the said Government, and satisfaction for the same shall be exacted: all in the same way, and with equal diligence and energy, as if the same incursions were meditated or committed within it's own territory against it's own citizens.

siempre que así sea necesario; y cuando no pudiére prevenirlas, castigará y escarmentará á los invasores, exigiéndoles ademas la debida reparacion: todo del mismo modo y con la misma diligencia y energia con que obraria, si las incursiones se hubiesen meditado ó ejecutado sobre territorios suyos ó contra sus propios ciudadanos.

It shall not be lawful, under any pretext whatever, for any inhabitant of the United States, to purchase or acquire any Mexican or any foreigner residing in Mexico, who may have been captured by Indians inhabiting the territory of either of the two Republics, nor to purchase or acquire horses, mules, cattle or property of any kind, stolen within Mexican territory by such Indians.

A ningun habitante de los Estados-Unidos será lícito bajo ningun pretesto comprar ó adquirir cautivo alguno, mexicano ó extrangero residente en México, apresado por los indios habitantes en territorio de cualquiera de las dos Repúblicas, ni los caballos, mulas, ganados, ó cualquiera otro género de cosas que hayan robado dentro del territorio mexicano.

And, in the event of any person or persons, captured within Mexican Territory by Indians, being carried into the territory of the United States, the Government of the latter engages and binds itself in the most solemn manner, so soon as it shall know of such captives being within it's territory, and shall be able so to do, through the faithful exercise of it's influence and power, to rescue them and return them to their country, or deliver them to the agent or representative of the Mexican Government. The Mexican Authorities will, as far as practicable,

Y en caso de que cualquier persona ó personas cautivadas por los indios dentro del territorio mexicano sean llevadas al territorio de los Estados-Unidos, el Gobierno de dichos Estados-Unidos se compromete y liga de la manera mas solemne, en cuanto le sea posible, á rescatarlas, y á restituirlas á su pays ó entregarlas al agente ó representante del Gobierno mexicano, haciendo todo esto, tan luego como sepa que los dichos cautivos se hallan dentro de su territorio, y empleando al efecto el leal ejercicio de su influencia y poder. Las autoridades

give to the Government of the United States notice of such captures; and it's agent shall pay the expenses incurred in the maintenance and transmission of the rescued captives; who, in the mean time, shall be treated with the utmost hospitality by the American authorities at the place where they may be. But if the Government of the United States, before receiving such notice from Mexico, should obtain intelligence through any other channel, of the existence of Mexican captives within it's territory, it will proceed forthwith to effect their release and delivery to the Mexican agent, as above stipulated.

For the purpose of giving to these stipulations the fullest possible efficacy, thereby affording the security and redress demanded by their true spirit and intent, the Government of the United States will now and hereafter pass, without unnecessary delay, and always vigilantly enforce, such laws as the nature of the subject may require. And finally, the sacredness of this obligation shall never be lost sight of by the said Government, when providing for the removal of the Indians from any portion of the said territories, or for it's being settled by citizens of the United States; but on the contrary special care shall then be taken not to place it's Indian occupants under the neces-

mexicanas darán á las de los Estados-Unidos, segun sea practicable, una noticia de tales cautivos; y el agente mexicano pagará los gastos erogados en el mantenimiento y remision de los que se rescaten, los cuales entre tanto serán tratados con la mayor hospitalidad por las autoridades Americanas del lugar en que se encuentren. Mas si el Gobierno de los Estados-Unidos antes de recibir aviso de México, tuviére noticia por cualquiera otro conducto de existir en su territorio cautivos mexicanos, procederá desde luego á verificar su rescate y entrega al agente mexicano, segun queda convenido.

Con el objeto de dar á estas estipulaciones la mayor fuerza posible, y afianzar al mismo tiempo la seguridad y las reparaciones que exige el verdadero espíritu é intencion con que se han ajustado, el Gobierno de los Estados-Unidos dictará sin inútiles dilaciones, ahora y en lo de adelante las leyes que requiera la naturaleza del asunto, y vigilará siempre sobre su ejecucion. Finalmente el Gobierno de los mismos Estados-Unidos tendrá muy presente la santidad de esta obligacion siempre que tenga que desalojar á los indios de cualquier punto de los indicados territorios, ó que establecer en él á ciudadanos suyos; y cuidará muy especialmente de que no se ponga á los indios que

sity of seeking new homes, by committing those invasions which the United States have solemnly obliged themselves to restrain.

ocupaban antes aquel punto, en necesidad de buscar nuevos hogares por medio de las incursiones sobre los distritos mexicanos, que el Gobierno de los Estados-Unidos se ha comprometido solemnemente á reprimir.

ARTICLE XII.

In consideration of the extension acquired by the boundaries of the United States, as defined in the fifth Article of the present Treaty, the Government of the United States engages to pay to that of the Mexican Republic the sum of fifteen Millions of Dollars.

Immediately after this treaty shall have been duly ratified by the Government of the Mexican Republic, the sum of three millions of dollars shall be paid to the said Government by that of the United States at the city of Mexico, in the gold or silver coin of Mexico. The remaining twelve millions of dollars shall be paid at the same place and in the same coin, in annual instalments of three millions of dollars each, together with interest on the same at the rate of six per centum per annum. This interest shall begin to run upon the whole sum of twelve millions, from the day of the ratification of the present treaty by the Mexican Government, and the first of the instalments shall be paid at the expiration of one year from the same

ARTÍCULO XII.

En consideracion á la estension que adquieren los límites de los Estados-Unidos, segun quedan descritos en el artículo quinto del presente Tratado, el Gobierno de los mismos Estados-Unidos se compromete á pagar al de la Republica mexicana la suma de quince millones de pesos.

Inmediatamente despues que este Tratado haya sido ratificado por el Gobierno de là República mexicana, se entregará al mismo Gobierno por el de los Estados-Unidos, en la ciudad de Mexico, y en moneda de plata ú oro del cuño mexicano, la suma de tres millones de pesos. Los doce millones de pesos restantes se pagarán en México, en moneda de plata ú oro del cuño mexicano, en abonos de tres millones de pesos cada año, con un rédito de seis por ciento anual: este rédito comienza á correr para toda la suma de los doce millones el dia de la ratificacion del presente Tratado por el Gobierno mexicano, y con cada abono anual de capital se pagará el rédito que corresponda á la suma abonada. Los plazos para los abonos de capital corren desde

day. Together with each annual instalment, as it falls due, the whole interest accruing on such instalment from the beginning shall also be paid.

el mismo dia que empiezan á causarse los réditos.

Article XIII.

The United States engage moreover, to assume and pay to the claimants all the amounts now due them, and those hereafter to become due, by reason of the claims already liquidated and decided against the Mexican Republic, under the conventions[1] between the two Republics severally concluded on the eleventh day of April eighteen hundred and thirty-nine, and on the thirtieth day of January eighteen hundred and forty three: so that the Mexican Republic shall be absolutely exempt for the future, from all expense whatever on account of the said claims.

Artículo XIII.

Se obliga ademas el Gobierno de los Estados-Unidos á tomar sobre sí, y satisfacer cumplidamente á los reclamantes, todas las cantidades que hasta aquí se les deben y cuantas se venzan en adelante por razon de las reclamaciones ya liquidadas y sentenciadas contra la República mexicana conforme á los convenios[1] ajustados entre ambas Repúblicas el once de Abril de mil ochocientos treinta y nueve, y el treinta de Enero de mil ochocientos cuarenta y tres; de manera que la República mexicana nada absolutamente tendrá que lastar en lo venidero, por razon de los indicados reclamos.

Article XIV.

The United States do furthermore discharge the Mexican Republic from all claims of citizens of the United States, not heretofore decided against the Mexican Government, which may have arisen previously to the date of the signature of this treaty: which discharge shall be final and perpetual, whether the said claims be rejected or be allowed by the Board of Commissioners provided

Artículo XIV.

Tambien exoneran los Estados-Unidos á la República mexicana de todas las reclamaciones de ciudadanos de los Estados-Unidos no decididas aun contra el Gobierno mexicano, y que puedan haberse originado antes de la fecha de la firma del presente Tratado. Esta exoneracion es definitiva y perpetua, bien sea que las dichas reclamaciones se admitan, bien sea que se desechen por el tribunal

for in the following Article, and whatever shall be the total amount of those allowed.

de Comisarios de que habla el artículo siguiente, y cualquiera que pueda ser el monto total de las que queden admitidas.

ARTICLE XV.

The United States, exonerating Mexico from all demands on account of the claims of their citizens mentioned in the preceding Article, and considering them entirely and forever cancelled, whatever their amount may be, undertake to make satisfaction for the same, to an amount not exceeding three and one quarter millions of Dollars. To ascertain the validity and amount of those claims, a Board of Commissioners shall be established by the Government of the United States, whose awards shall be final and conclusive: provided that in deciding upon the validity of each claim, the board shall be guided and governed by the principles and rules of decision prescribed by the first and fifth Articles [1] of the unratified convention, concluded at the City of Mexico on the twentieth day of November, one thousand eight hundred and forty-three; and in no case shall an award be made in favour of any claim not embraced by these principles and rules.

If, in the opinion of the said Board of Commissioners, or of the claimants, any books, records or

ARTÍCULO XV.

Los Estados-Unidos exonerando á México de toda responsabilidad por las reclamaciones de sus ciudadanos mencionadas en el artículo precedente, y considerándolas completamente chanceladas para siempre, sea cual fuére su monto, toman á su cargo satisfacerlas hasta una cantidad que no exceda de tres millones doscientos cincuenta mil pesos. Para fijar el monto y validez de estas reclamaciones, se establecerá por el Gobierno de los Estados-Unidos un Tribunal de Comisarios, cuyos fallos serán definitivos y concluyentes, con tal que al decidir sobre la validez de dichas reclamaciones, el tribunal se haya guiado y gobernado por los principios y reglas de decision establecidos en los artículos [1] primero y quinto de la convencion, no ratificada, que se ajustó en la ciudad de México el veinte de Noviembre de mil ochocientos cuarenta y tres: y en ningun caso se dará fallo en favor de ninguna reclamacion que no esté comprendida en las reglas y principios indicados.

Si en juicio del dicho tribunal de Comisarios, ó en el de los reclamantes se necesitáre para la

[1] For the text of those articles, see the editorial notes.

documents in the possession or power of the Government of the Mexican Republic, shall be deemed necessary to the just decision of any claim, the Commissioners or the claimants, through them, shall, within such period as Congress may designate, make an application in writing for the same, addressed to the Mexican Minister for Foreign Affairs, to be transmitted by the Secretary of State of the United States; and the Mexican Government engages, at the earliest possible moment after the receipt of such demand, to cause any of the books, records or documents, so specified, which shall be in their possession or power, (or authenticated Copies or extracts of the same) to be transmitted to the said Secretary of State, who shall immediately deliver them over to the said Board of Commissioners: provided that no such application shall be made, by, or at the instance of, any claimant, until the facts which it is expected to prove by such books, records or documents, shall have been stated under oath or affirmation.

justa decision de cualquier reclamacion algunos libros, papeles de archivo ó documentos que posea el Gobierno mexicano, ó que estén en su poder; los Comisarios, ó los reclamantes por conducto de ellos, los pedirán por escrito (dentro del plazo que designe el Congreso) dirigiéndose al Ministro mexicano de Relaciones exteriores, á quien transmitirá las peticiones de esta clase el Secretario de Estado de los Estados-Unidos: y el Gobierno mexicano se compromete á entregar á la mayor brevedad posible, despues de recibida cada demanda, los libros, papeles de archivo ó documentos, así especificados, que posea ó estén en su poder, ó copias ó extractos auténticos de los mismos, con el objeto de que sean transmitidos al Secretario de Estado, quien los pasará inmediatamente al expresado Tribunal de Comisarios. Y no se hará peticion alguna de los enunciados libros, papeles ó documentos, por ó á instancia de ningun reclamante, sin que antes se haya aseverado bajo juramento ó con afirmacion solemne la verdad de los hechos que con ellos se pretende probar.

Article XVI.

Each of the contracting parties reserves to itself the entire right to fortify whatever point within it's territory, it may judge proper so to fortify, for it's security.

Artículo XVI.

Cada una de las dos Repúblicas se reserva la completa facultad de fortificar todos los puntos que para su seguridad estime convenientes en su propio territorio.

ARTICLE XVII.

The Treaty of Amity, Commerce and Navigation, concluded at the city of Mexico on the fifth day of April A.D. 1831, between the United States of America and the United Mexican States, except the additional Article, and except so far as the stipulations of the said treaty may be incompatible with any stipulation contained in the present treaty, is hereby revived for the period of eight years from the day of the exchange of ratifications of this treaty, with the same force and virtue as if incorporated therein; it being understood that each of the contracting parties reserves to itself the right, at any time after the said period of eight years shall have expired, to terminate the same by giving one year's notice of such intention to the other party.

ARTÍCULO XVII.

El Tratado[1] de Amistad, Comercio y Navegacion concluido en la ciudad de Mexico el cinco de Abril del año del Señor 1831, entre la República mexicana y los Estados-Unidos de América, esceptuandose el artículo adicional y cuanto pueda haber en sus estipulaciones incompatible con alguna de las contenidas en el presente Tratado, queda restablecido por el periodo de ocho años desde el dia del cange de las ratificaciones del mismo presente Tratado, con igual fuerza y valor que si estuviese inserto en él; debiendo entenderse que cada una de las partes contratantes se reserva el derecho de poner término al dicho Tratado de Comercio y Navegacion en cualquier tiempo luego que haya expirado el periodo de los ocho años, comunicando su intencion á la otra parte con un año de anticipacion.

ARTICLE XVIII.

All supplies whatever for troops of the United States in Mexico, arriving at ports in the occupation of such troops, previous to the final evacuation thereof, although subsequently to the restoration of the Custom Houses at such ports, shall be entirely exempt from duties and charges of any kind: the Government of the United States hereby engaging and pledging it's faith to establish, and

ARTÍCULO XVIII.

No se exigirán derechos ni gravámen de ninguna clase á los artículos todos que lleguen para las tropas de los Estados-Unidos á los puertos mexicanos ócupados por ellas, antes de la evacuacion final de los mismos puertos y despues de la devolucion á México de las Aduanas situadas en ellos. El Gobierno de los Estados-Unidos se compromete á la vez, y sobre esto empeña su fé, á

vigilantly to enforce, all possible guards for securing the revenue of Mexico, by preventing the importation, under cover of this stipulation, of any articles, other than such, both in kind and in quantity, as shall really be wanted for the use and consumption of the forces of the United States during the time they may remain in Mexico. To this end, it shall be the duty of all officers and agents of the United States to denounce to the Mexican Authorities at the respective ports, any attempts at a fraudulent abuse of this stipulation, which they may know of or may have reason to suspect, and to give to such authorities all the aid in their power with regard thereto: and every such attempt, when duly proved and established by sentence of a competent tribunal, shall be punished by the confiscation of the property so attempted to be fraudulently introduced.

establecer y mantener con vigilancia quantos guardas sean posibles para asegurar las rentas de México, precaviendo la importacion, á la sombra de esta estipulacion, de cualesquiera artículos que realmente no sean necesarios, ó que excedan en cantidad de los que se necesiten para el uso y consumo de las fuerzas de los Estados-Unidos mientras ellas permanezcan en México. A este efecto todos los oficiales y agentes de los Estados-Unidos tendrán obligacion de denunciar á las autoridades mexicanas en los mismos puertos qualquier conato de fraudulento abuso de esta estipulacion que pudiéren conocer ó tuvieren motivo de sospechar; así como de impartir á las mismas autoridades todo el auxilio que pudiéren con este objeto. Y cualquier conato de esa clase, que fuére legalmente probado, y declarado por sentencia de tribunal competente, será castigado con el comiso de la cosa que se haya intentado introducir fraudulentamente.

Article XIX.

With respect to all merchandise, effects and property whatsoever, imported into ports of Mexico whilst in the occupation of the forces of the United States, whether by citizens of either republic, or by citizens or subjects of any neutral nation, the following rules shall be observed:

Artículo XIX.

Respecto de los efectos, mercancias y propiedades importados en los puertos mexicanos durante el tiempo que han estado ocupados por las fuerzas de los Estados-Unidos, sea por ciudadanos de cualquiera de las dos Repúblicas, sea por ciudadanos ó subditos de alguna nacion neutral, se observarán las reglas siguientes:

I. All such merchandise, effects and property, if imported previously to the restoration of the Custom Houses to the Mexican Authorities, as stipulated for in the third Article of this treaty, shall be exempt from confiscation, although the importation of the same be prohibited by the Mexican tariff.

II. The same perfect exemption shall be enjoyed by all such merchandise, effects and property, imported subsequently to the restoration of the Custom Houses, and previously to the sixty days fixed in the following Article for the coming into force of the Mexican tariff at such ports respectively: the said merchandise, effects and property being, however, at the time of their importation, subject to the payment of duties, as provided for in the said following Article.

III. All merchandise, effects and property described in the two rules foregoing, shall, during their continuance at the place of importation, or upon their leaving such place for the interior, be exempt from all duty, tax or impost of every kind, under whatsoever title or denomination. Nor shall they be there subjected to any charge whatsoever upon the sale thereof.

IV. All merchandise, effects and property, described in the first and second rules, which shall have been removed to any place in the

I. Los dichos efectos, mercancias y propiedades siempre que se hayan importado antes de la devolucion de las Aduanas á las autoridades mexicanas conforme á lo estipulado en el artículo tercero de este Tratado, quedarán libres de la pena de comiso aun cuando sean de los prohibidos en el arancel mexicano.

II. La misma exencion gozarán los efectos, mercancias y propiedades que lleguen á los puertos mexicanos, despues de la devolucion á México de las Aduanas marítimas y antes de que expiren los sesenta dias que van á fijarse en el artículo siguiente para que empieze á regir el arancél mexicano en los puertos; debiendo al tiempo de su importacion sujetarse los tales efectos, mercancias y propiedades, en cuanto al pago de derechos, á lo que en el indicado siguiente artículo se establece.

III. Los efectos, mercancias y propiedades designados en las dos reglas anteriores quedarán exentos de todo derecho, alcabála ó impuesto, sea bajo el título de internacion, sea bajo cualquiera otro, mientras permanezcan en los puntos donde se hayan importado, y á su salida para el interior; y en los mismos puntos no podrá jamás exigirse impuesto alguno sobre su venta.

IV. Los efectos, mercancias y propiedades designados en las reglas primera y segunda que hayan sido internados á cualquier

interior, whilst such place was in the occupation of the forces of the United States, shall, during their continuance therein, be exempt from all tax upon the sale or consumption thereof, and from every kind of impost or contribution, under whatsoever title or denomination.

V. But if any merchandise, effects or property, described in the first and second rules, shall be removed to any place not occupied at the time by the forces of the United States, they shall, upon their introduction into such place, or upon their sale or consumption there, be subject to the same duties, which, under the Mexican laws, they would be required to pay in such cases, if they had been imported in time of peace through the Maritime Custom Houses, and had there paid the duties conformably with the Mexican tariff.

VI. The owners of all merchandise, effects or property, described in the first and second rules, and existing in any port of Mexico, shall have the right to reship the same, exempt from all tax, impost or contribution whatever.

With respect to the metals, or other property exported from any Mexican port, whilst in the occupation of the forces of the United States, and previously to the restoration of the Custom House at such port, no person shall be required by the Mexican Authorities,

lugar ocupado por fuerzas de los Estados-Unidos, quedarán exentos de todo derecho sobre su venta ó consumo, y de todo impuesto ó contribucion bajo cualquier título ó denominacion, mientras permanezcan en el mismo lugar.

V. Mas si algunos efectos, mercancias ó propiedades de los designados en las reglas primera y segunda se trasladáren á algun lugar no ocupado á la sazon por las fuerzas de los Estados-Unidos; al introducirse á tal lugar, ó al venderse ó consumirse en él, quedarán sujetos á los mismos derechos que bajo las leyes mexicanas deberian pagar en tales casos si se hubiéran importado en tiempo de paz por las Aduanas marítimas, y hubiesen pagado en ellas los derechos que establece el arancél mexicano.

VI. Los dueños de efectos, mercancias y propiedades designados en las reglas primera y segunda, y existentes en algun puerto de México, tienen derecho de reembarcarlos, sin que pueda exigírseles ninguna clase de impuesto, alcabála ó contribucion.

Respecto de los metales y de toda otra propiedad exportados por cualquier puerto mexicano durante su ocupacion por las fuerzas Americanas y antes de la devolucion de su Aduana al Gobierno mexicano, no se exigirá á ninguna persona por las autoridades

whether General or State, to pay any tax, duty or contribution upon any such exportation, or in any manner to account for the same to the said Authorities.

de Mexico, ya dependan del Gobierno general, ya de algun Estado que pague ningun impuesto, alcabála ó derecho por la indicada exportacion, ni sobre ella podrá exigírsele por las dichas autoridades cuenta alguna.

ARTICLE XX.

Through consideration for the interests of commerce generally, it is agreed, that if less than sixty days should elapse between the date of the signature of this treaty and the restoration of the Custom Houses, conformably with the stipulation in the third Article, in such case, all merchandise, effects and property whatsoever, arriving at the Mexican ports after the restoration of the said Custom Houses, and previously to the expiration of sixty days after the day of the signature of this treaty, shall be admitted to entry; and no other duties shall be levied thereon than the duties established by the tariff found in force at such Custom Houses, at the time of the restoration of the same. And to all such merchandise, effects and property, the rules established by the preceding Article shall apply.

ARTÍCULO XX.

Por consideracion á los intereses del comercio de todas las naciones queda convenido que si pasáren menos de sesenta dias desde la fecha de la firma de este Tratado hasta que se haga la devolucion de las Aduanas marítimas, segun lo estipulado en el artículo tercero; todos los efectos, mercancias y propiedades que lleguen á los puertos mexicanos desde el dia en que se verifique la devolucion de las dichas Aduanas hasta que se completen sesenta dias contados desde la fecha de la firma del presente Tratado, se admitirán no pagando otros derechos que los establecidos en la tarifa que esté vigente en las expresadas Aduanas al tiempo de su devolucion, y se extenderán á dichos efectos, mercancias y propiedades las mismas reglas establecidas en el artículo anterior.

ARTICLE XXI.

If unhappily any disagreement should hereafter arise between the Governments of the two Republics, whether with respect to the interpretation of any stipulation in this treaty, or with respect to

ARTÍCULO XXI.

Si desgraciadamente en el tiempo futuro se suscitáre algun punto de desacuerdo entre los Gobiernos de las dos Repúblicas, bien sea sobre la inteligencia de alguna estipulacion de este Tratado, bien

any other particular concerning the political or commercial relations of the two Nations, the said Governments, in the name of those Nations, do promise to each other, that they will endeavour in the most sincere and earnest manner, to settle the differences so arising, and to preserve the state of peace and friendship, in which the two countries are now placing themselves: using, for this end, mutual representations and pacific negotiations. And, if by these means, they should not be enabled to come to an agreement, a resort shall not, on this account, be had to reprisals, aggression or hostility of any kind, by the one Republic against the other, until the Government of that which deems itself aggrieved, shall have maturely considered, in the spirit of peace and good neighbourship, whether it would not be better that such difference should be settled by the arbitration of Commissioners appointed on each side, or by that of a friendly nation. And should such course be proposed by either party, it shall be acceded to by the other, unless deemed by it altogether incompatible with the nature of the difference, or the circumstances of the case.

sobre cualquiera otra materia de las relaciones políticas ó comerciales de las dos Naciones, los mismos Gobiernos á nombre de ellas se comprometen á procurar de la manera mas sincera y empeñosa allanar las diferencias que se presenten y conservar el estado de paz y amistad en que ahora se ponen los dos payses, usando al efecto de representaciones mútuas y de negociaciones pacíficas. Y si por estos medios no se lográre todavia ponerse de acuerdo, no por eso se apelará á represalia, agresion ni hostilidad de ningun género de una República contra otra hasta que el Gobierno de la que se crea agraviada haya considerado maduramente y en espíritu de paz y buena vecindad si no seria mejor que la diferencia se terminára por un arbitramento de Comisarios nombrados por ambas partes, ó de una nacion amiga. Y si tal medio fuére propuesto por cualquiera de las dos partes, la otra accederá á él, á no ser que lo juzgue absolutamente incompatible con la naturaleza y circunstancias del caso.

Article XXII.

If (which is not to be expected, and which God forbid!) war should unhappily break out between the two Republics, they do

Artículo XXII.

Si (lo que no es de esperarse, y Dios no permita) desgraciadamente se suscitáre guerra entre las dos Republicas, estas para el

now, with a view to such calamity, solemnly pledge themselves to each other and to the world, to observe the following rules: absolutely, where the nature of the subject permits, and as closely as possible in all cases where such absolute observance shall be impossible.

I. The merchants of either Republic, then residing in the other, shall be allowed to remain twelve months (for those dwelling in the interior) and six months (for those dwelling at the sea-ports) to collect their debts and settle their affairs; during which periods, they shall enjoy the same protection, and be on the same footing, in all respects, as the citizens or subjects of the most friendly nations; and, at the expiration thereof, or at any time before, they shall have full liberty to depart, carrying off all their effects, without molestation or hindrance: conforming therein to the same laws, which the citizens or subjects of the most friendly nations are required to conform to. Upon the entrance of the armies of either nation into the territories of the other, women and children, ecclesiastics, scholars of every faculty, cultivators of the earth, merchants, artizans, manufacturers and fishermen, unarmed and inhabiting unfortified towns, villages or places, and in general all persons whose occupations are

caso de tal calamidad se comprometen ahora solemnemente, ante sí mismas y ante el mundo á observar las reglas siguientes de una manera absoluta si la naturaleza del objeto á que se contraen, lo permite; y tan extrictamente como sea dable en todos los casos en que la absoluta observancia de ellas fuére imposible.

I. Los comerciantes de cada una de las dos Repúblicas que á la sazon residan en territorio de la otra, podrán permanecer doce meses los que residan en el interior, y seis meses los que residan en los puertos para recoger sus deudas y arreglar sus negocios; durante estos plazos disfrutarán la misma proteccion y estarán sobre el mismo pié en todos respectos, que los ciudadanos ó súbditos de las naciones mas amigas; y al expirar el término, ó antes de él, tendrán completa libertad para salir y llevar todos sus efectos sin molestia ó embarazo, sujetándose en este particular á las misma leyes á que estén sujetos y deban arreglarse los ciudadanos ó súbditos de las naciones mas amigas. Cuando los ejércitos de una de las dos naciones entren en territorios de la otra, las mujeres y niños, los eclesiásticos, los estudiantes de cualquier facultad, los labradores, comerciantes, artesanos, manufactureros, y pescadores que estén desarmados y residan en ciudades, pueblos ó lugares no fortificados, y en general todas

for the common subsistence and benefit of mankind, shall be allowed to continue their respective employments, unmolested in their persons. Nor shall their houses or goods be burnt or otherwise destroyed: nor their cattle taken, nor, their fields wasted, by the armed force, into whose power, by the events of war, they may happen to fall; but if the necessity arise to take any thing from them for the use of such armed force, the same shall be paid for at an equitable price. All churches, hospitals, schools, colleges, libraries and other establishments for charitable and beneficent purposes, shall be respected, and all persons connected with the same protected in the discharge of their duties and the pursuit of their vocations.

las personas cuya ocupacion sirva para la comun subsistencia y beneficio del género humano, podrán continuar en sus ejercicios sin que sus personas sean molestadas. No serán incendiadas sus casas ó bienes, ó destruidos de otra manera; ni serán tomados sus ganados, ni devastados sus campos por la fuerza armada en cuyo poder puedan venir á caer por los acontecimientos de la guerra; pero si hubiére necesidad de tomarlos alguna cosa para el uso de la misma fuerza armada, se les pagará lo tomado á un precio justo. Todas las iglesias, hospitales, escuelas, colegios, librerias y demas establecimientos de caridad y beneficencia serán respetados; y todas las personas que dependan de los mismos, serán protegidas en el desempeño de sus deberes y en la continuacion de sus profesiones.

II. In order that the fate of prisoners of war may be alleviated, all such practices as those of sending them into distant, inclement or unwholesome districts, or crowding them into close and noxious places, shall be studiously avoided. They shall not be confined in dungeons, prison-ships or prisons; nor be put in irons, or bound, or otherwise restrained in the use of their limbs. The officers shall enjoy liberty on their paroles, within convenient districts, and have comfortable quarters; and the common soldiers

II. Para aliviar la suerte de los prisioneros de guerra, se evitarán ciudadosamente las prácticas de enviarlos á distritos distantes, inclementes ó malsanos, ó de aglomerarlos en lugares estrechos y enfirmizos. No se confinarán en calabozos, prisiones ni pontones; no se les aherrojará, ni se les atará, ni se les impedirá de ningun otro modo el uso de sus miembros. Los oficiales quedarán en libertad bajo su palabra de honor, dentro de distritos convenientes, y tendrán alojamientos cómodos; y los soldados rasos se colocarán en

shall be disposed in cantonments, open and extensive enough for air and exercise, and lodged in barracks as roomy and good as are provided by the party in whose power they are for it's own troops. But if any officer shall break his parole by leaving the district so assigned him, or any other prisoner shall escape from the limits of his cantonment, after they shall have been designated to him, such individual, officer, or other prisoner shall forfeit so much of the benefit of this Article as provides for his liberty on parole or in cantonment. And if an officer so breaking his parole, or any common soldier so escaping from the limits assigned him, shall afterwards be found in arms, previously to his being regularly exchanged, the person so offending shall be dealt with according to the established laws of war. The officers shall be daily furnished by the party in whose power they are, with as many rations, and of the same articles as are allowed either in kind or by commutation, to officers of equal rank in it's own army; and all others shall be daily furnished with such ration as is allowed to a common soldier in it's own service: the value of all which supplies shall, at the close of the war, or at periods to be agreed upon between the respective commanders, be paid by the other party, on a mutual adjustment of accounts for the subsistence of prisoners; and such ac-

acantonamientos bastante despejados y extensos para la ventilacion y el ejercicio, y se alojarán en cuarteles tan ámplios y cómodos como los que use para sus propias tropas la parte que los tenga en su poder. Pero si algun oficial faltare á su palabra saliendo del distrito que se le ha señalado; ó algun otro prisionero se fugáre de los límites de su acantonamiento despues que estos se les hayan fijado, tal oficial ó prisionero perderá el beneficio del presente artículo por lo que mira á su libertad bajo su palabra ó en acantonamiento. Y si algun oficial faltando así á su palabra, ó algun soldado raso saliendo de los límites que se le han asignado fuére encontrado despues con las armas en la mano antes de ser debidamente cangeado, tal persona en esta actitud ofensiva será tratada conforme á las leyes comunes de la guerra. A los oficiales se proveerá diariamente por la parte en cuyo poder estén, de tantas raciones compuestas de los mismos artículos como las que gozan en especie ó en equivalente los oficiales de la misma graduacion en su propio ejército: á todos los demas prisioneros se proveerá diariamente de una racion semejante á la que se ministra al soldado raso en su propio servicio: el valor de todas estas suministraciones se pagará por la otra parte al concluirse la guerra, ó en los periodos que se convengan entre sus respectivos comandantes, precediendo

counts shall not be mingled with or set off against any others, nor the balance due on them be withheld, as a compensation or reprisal for any cause whatever, real or pretended. Each party shall be allowed to keep a Commissary of prisoners, appointed by itself, with every cantonment of prisoners, in possession of the other; which Commissary shall see the prisoners as often as he pleases; shall be allowed to receive, exempt from all duties or taxes, and to distribute whatever comforts may be sent to them by their friends; and shall be free to transmit his reports in open letters to the party by whom he is employed.

una mútua liquidacion de las cuentas que se lleven del mantenimiento de prisioneros: tales cuentas no se mezclarán ni compensarán con otras; ni el saldo que resulte de ellas, se reusará bajo pretesto de compensacion ó represalia por cualquiera causa real ó figurada. Cada una de las partes podrá mantener un Comisario de prisioneros nombrado por ella misma en cada acantonamiento de los prisioneros que esten en poder de la otra parte: este Comisario visitará á los prisioneros siempre que quiera; tendrá facultad de recibir, libres de todo derecho ó impuesto, y de distribuir todos los auxilios que pueden enviarles sus amigos, y libremente transmitir sus partes en cartas abiertas á la autoridad por la cual está empleado.

And it is declared that neither the pretence that war dissolves all treaties, nor any other whatever, shall be considered as annulling or suspending the solemn covenant contained in this Article. On the contrary the state of war is precisely that for which it is provided; and during which it's stipulations are to be as sacredly observed as the most acknowledged obligations under the law of nature or nations.

Y se declara que ni el pretesto de que la guerra destruye los tratados, ni otro alguno, sea el que fuére, se considerará que anula ó suspende el pacto solemne contenido en este artículo. Por el contrario el estado de guerra es cabalmente el que se ha tenido presente al ajustarlo, y durante el cual sus estipulaciones se han de observar tan santamente como las obligaciones mas reconocidas de la ley natural ó de gentes.

Article XXIII.

This Treaty shall be ratified by the President of the United States of America, by and with the advice and consent of the Senate

Artículo XXIII.

Este Tratado será ratificado por el Presidente de la República mexicana, previa la aprobacion de su Congreso General; y por el Pre-

thereof; and by the President of the Mexican Republic, with the previous approbation of it's General Congress: and the ratifications shall be exchanged in the city of Washington or at the seat of government of Mexico, in four months from the date of the signature hereof, or sooner if practicable.

In faith whereof, we, the respective Plenipotentiaries, have signed this Treaty of Peace, Friendship, Limits and Settlement, and have hereunto affixed our seals respectively. Done in Quintuplicate at the city of Guadalupe Hidalgo on the second day of February in the Year of Our Lord one thousand eight hundred and forty-eight.

N. P. Trist. [Seal]
Luis G. Cuevas [Seal]
Bernardo Couto [Seal]
Migl Atristain [Seal]

sidente de los Estados-Unidos de América con el consejo y consentimiento del Senado; y las ratificaciones se cangearán en la ciudad de Washington ó donde estuviere el gobierno Mexicano á los cuatro meses de la fecha de la firma del mismo Tratado, ó antes si fuere posible.

En fé de lo cual, nosotros los respectivos Plenipotenciarios hemos firmado y sellado por quintuplicado este Tratado de Paz, Amistad, Límites y Arreglo definitivo; en la ciudad de Guadalupe Hidalgo el dia dos de Febrero del año de Nuestro Señor mil ochocientos cuarenta y ocho.

Bernardo Couto [Seal]
Migl Atristain [Seal]
Luis G. Cuevas [Seal]
N. P. Trist. [Seal]

NOTES

The Treaty of Guadalupe Hidalgo, as signed, comprised four papers; these are the treaty proper, the additional and secret article, the authenticated Disturnell Map, and the authenticated Plano del Puerto de S. Diego (see Article 5 of the treaty). The additional and secret article was not ratified on either part and did not go into force.

• • •

Following the headnote is printed the text of the treaty proper, in English and Spanish; the text so printed is not, however, as to five of the twenty-two articles which remained [1] in the treaty, the text as signed, but the text as amended. The changes made pursuant to the Senate resolution of advice and consent are set forth in the respective instruments of ratification and are incorporated in the printed text. Accordingly, while the print here has been collated primarily with one of the two signed originals in the treaty file, the collating has, of necessity, taken into account the changes made in Articles 3, 9, 11, 12, and 23, which are described in detail below, under the heading "The Senate Amendments".

• • •

The Senate Amendments

By the amendments of the Senate resolution of advice and consent of March 10, 1848 (Executive Journal, VII, 337–38, 340), the articles of the treaty proper as signed were proposed to be altered in various respects; the text so amended was that which went into force, as the Senate amendments were accepted by the Government of Mexico; it is that definitive text which follows the headnote.

In the opening lines of Article 3 there were inserted in the first parenthesis the words "and the ratifications exchanged" ("y cangeadas las ratificaciones") following "Mexican Republic" ("República mexicana"). The effect of the amendment was to make the exchange of ratifications (and not merely ratification by the two Governments) a condition precedent to the giving of orders for the raising of the blockade and the commencement of evacuation; in the event, both the ratification on the part of Mexico and the exchange took place on the same day, May 30, 1848.

For Article 9, the Senate amendment was a new text, adapted from Article 3 of the Treaty for the Cession of Louisiana (Document 28), which, indeed, was the basis of the first paragraph of the article as originally written; as signed, Article 9 read thus (collated with the first original):

Article IX.

The Mexicans who, in the territories aforesaid, shall not preserve the character of citizens of the Mexican Republic, conformably with what is stipulated in the preceding Article, shall be incorporated into the Union of the United States, and admitted as soon as possible, according to the principles of the Federal Constitution, to the enjoyment of all the rights of citizens of the United States. In the mean time, they shall be maintained and protected in the enjoyment of their liberty, their property, and the civil rights now vested in them according to the Mexican laws. With respect to political rights, their condition shall be on an equality with that of the inhabitants of the other territories of the United States; and at least equally good as that of the inhabitants of Louisiana and the Floridas, when these provinces, by transfer from the French Republic and the Crown of Spain, became territories of the United States.

The same most ample guaranty shall be enjoyed by all ecclesiastics and religious corporations or communities, as well in the discharge of the offices of their ministry, as in the enjoyment of their property of every kind, whether individual or corporate. This guaranty

Artículo IX.

Los mexicanos que en los territorios antedichos no conserven el carácter de ciudadanos de la República mexicana segun lo estipulado en el precedente artículo, serán incorporados en la Union de los Estados-Unidos y se admitirán lo mas pronto posible conforme á los principios de su constitucion federál al goze de la plenitud de derechos de ciudadanos de dichos Estados-Unidos. En el entretanto serán mantenidos y protegidos en el goze de su libertad, de su propiedad y de los derechos civiles que hoy tienen segun las leyes mexicanas. En lo respectivo á derechos políticos su condicion será igual á la de los habitantes de los otros territorios de los Estados-Unidos, y tan buena á lo menos, como la de los habitantes de la Luisiana y las Floridas, cuando estas Provincias por las cesiones que de ellas hicieron la República francesa y la Corona de España pasaron á ser territorios de la Union Norte-Americana.

Disfrutarán igualmente la mas amplia garantia todos los eclesiásticos, corporaciones y comunidades religiosas tanto en el desempeño de las funciones de su ministerio, como en el goze de su propiedad de todo género, bien pertenezca esta á las personas en particu-

125186°—37——18

shall embrace all temples, houses and edifices dedicated to the Roman Catholic worship; as well as all property destined to it's support, or to that of schools, hospitals and other foundations for charitable or beneficent purposes. No property of this nature shall be considered as having become the property of the American Government, or as subject to be, by it, disposed of or diverted to other uses.

Finally, the relations and communication between the Catholics living in the territories aforesaid, and their respective ecclesiastical authorities, shall be open, free and exempt from all hindrance whatever, even although such authorities should reside within the limits of the Mexican Republic, as defined by this treaty; and this freedom shall continue, so long as a new demarcation of ecclesiastical districts shall not have been made, conformably with the laws of the Roman Catholic Church.

lar, bien á las corporaciones. La dicha garantia se extenderá á todos los templos, casas y edificios dedicados al culto católico-ro-romano, así como á los bienes destinados á su mantenimiento y al de las escuelas, hospitales y demás fundaciones de caridad y beneficencia. Ninguna propiedad de esta clase se considerará que ha pasado á ser propiedad del Gobierno Americano ó que puede este disponer de ella ó destinarla á otros usos.

Finalmente las relaciones y comunicacion de los católicos existentes en los predichos territorios, con sus respectivas autoridades eclesiásticas serán francas, libres y sin embarazo alguno, aun cuando las dichas autoridades tengan su residencia dentro de los límites que quedan señalados por el presente Tratado á la República mexicana, mientras no se haga una nueva demarcacion de distritos eclesiásticos, con arreglo á las leyes de la Iglesia católica-romana.

Article 10, as signed, was wholly stricken from the treaty, without substitution of new matter; it read as follows (collated with the first original):

ARTICLE X.

All grants of land made by the Mexican Government or by the competent authorities, in territories previously appertaining to Mexico, and remaining for the future within the limits of the United States, shall be respected as valid, to the same extent that the same grants would be valid, if the said territories had remained within the limits of Mexico. But the grantees of lands in Texas, put in possession thereof, who, by reason of the circumstances of the country since the beginning of the troubles between Texas and the Mexican Government, may have been prevented from fulfilling all the conditions of their grants, shall be under the obligation to fulfill the said conditions within the periods limited in the same respectively; such periods to be now counted from the date of the exchange of ratifications of this treaty: in default of which the said grants shall not be obligatory upon the State of Texas, in virtue of the stipulations contained in this Article.

ARTÍCULO X.

Todas las concesiones de tierra hechas por el Gobierno mexicano, ó por las autoridades competentes en territorios que pertenecieron antes á Mexico y quedan para lo futuro dentro de los límites de los Estados-Unidos, serán respetadas como válidas, con la misma extension con que lo serian si los indicados territorios permaneciéran dentro de los límites de México. Pero los concesionarios de tierras en Tejas, que hubieren tomado posesion de ellas, y que por razon de las circunstancias del pays desde que comenzaron las desavenencias entre el Gobierno mexicano y Tejas, hayan estado impedidos de llenar todas las condiciones de sus concesiones, tendrán la obligacion de cumplir las mismas condiciones, dentro de los plazos señalados en aquellas respectivamente, pero contados ahora desde la fecha del cange de las ratificaciones de este Tratado; por falta de lo qual las mismas concesiones no serán obligatorias para el Estado de Tejas en virtud de las estipulaciones contenidas en este artículo.

The foregoing stipulation in regard to grantees of land in Texas, is extended to all grantees of land in the territories aforesaid, elsewhere than in Texas, put in possession under such grants; and, in default of the fulfilment of the conditions of any such grant, within the new period, which, as is above stipulated, begins with the day of the exchange of ratifications of this treaty, the same shall be null and void.

La anterior estipulacion respecto de los concesionarios de tierras en Tejas, se extiende á todos los concesionarios de tierras en los indicados territorios fuera de Tejas, que hubieren tomado posesion de dichas concesiones: y por falta de cumplimiento de las condiciones de alguna de aquellas dentro del nuevo plazo que empieza á correr el dia del cange de las ratificaciones del presente Tratado, segun lo estipulado arriba, serán las mismas concesiones nulas y de ningun valor.

The Mexican Government declares that no grant whatever of lands in Texas has been made since the second day of March one thousand eight hundred and thirty six; and that no grant whatever of lands in any of the territories aforesaid has been made since the thirteenth day of May one thousand eight hundred and forty-six.

El Gobierno mexicano declara que no se ha hecho ninguna concesion de tierras en Tejas desde el dia dos de Marzo de mil ochocientos treinta y seis; y que tampoco se ha hecho ninguna en los otros territorios mencionados despues del trece de Mayo de mil ochocientos cuarenta y seis.

From the second paragraph of Article 11, these concluding words (which followed a semicolon) were stricken: "nor to provide such Indians with fire-arms or ammunition by sale or otherwise" (in the Spanish version, "ni en fin venderles ó ministrarles bajo cualquier título armas de fuego ó municiones").

The deletions from Article 12 by the Senate amendments will be seen from the following text, which is that of the article as signed, with the stricken clauses in italics and bracketed (collated with the first original):

ARTICLE XII.

In consideration of the extension acquired by the boundaries of the United States, as defined in the fifth Article of the present Treaty, the Government of the United States engages to pay to that of the Mexican Republic the sum of fifteen Millions of Dollars[, *in the one or the other of the two modes below specified. The Mexican Government shall, at the time of ratifying this treaty, declare which of these two modes of payment it prefers; and the mode so elected by it shall be conformed to by that of the United States*].

[*First mode of payment: Immediately after this treaty shall have been duly ratified by the Government of the Mexican Republic, the sum of three Millions of Dollars shall be paid to the said Government by that of the United States at the city of Mexico, in the gold or silver coin of Mexico. For the remaining twelve millions of dollars, the United States shall create a stock, bearing an interest*

ARTÍCULO XII.

En consideracion á la estension que adquieren los límites de los Estados-Unidos, segun quedan descritos en el artículo quinto del presente Tratado, el Gobierno de los mismos Estados-Unidos se compromete á pagar al de la Republica mexicana la suma de quince millones de pesos[, *de una de las dos maneras que van á explicarse: El Gobierno mexicano al tiempo de ratificar este Tratado declarará cual de las dos maneras de pago prefiere; y á la que así elija, se arreglará el Gobierno de los Estados-Unidos al verificar el pago*].

[*Primera manera de pago.—Inmediatamente despues que este Tratado haya sido ratificado por el Gobierno de la Republica mexicana, se entregará al mismo Gobierno por el de los Estados-Unidos en la ciudad de Mexico, y en moneda de plata ú oro del cuño mexicano, la suma de tres millones de pesos. Por los doce millones de pesos restantes los Estados Unidos crearán un fondo*

of six per centum per annum, commencing on the day of the ratification of this Treaty by the Government of the Mexican Republic, and payable annually at the city of Washington: the principal of said stock to be redeemable there, at the pleasure of the Government of the United States, at any time after two years from the exchange of ratifications of this treaty; six months public notice of the intention to redeem the same being previously given. Certificates of such stock, in proper form, for such sums as shall be specified by the Mexican Government, and transferable by the said Government, shall be delivered to the same by that of the United States.

público que gozará redito de seis por ciento al año, el cual rédito ha de comenzar á correr el dia que se ratifique el presente Tratado por el Gobierno de la Republica mexicana, y se pagará anualmente en la ciudad de Washington. El capital de[1] dicho fondo público será redimible en la misma ciudad de Washington en cualquiera época que lo disponga el Gobierno de los Estados-Unidos, con tal que hayan pasado dos años contados desde el cange de las ratificaciones del presente Tratado, y dándose aviso al público con anticipacion de seis meses. Al Gobierno mexicano se entregarán por el de los Estados-Unidos los Bonos correspondientes á dicho fondo, extendidos en debida forma, divididos en las cantidades que señale el expresado Gobierno mexicano, y enagenables por este.

Second mode of payment:] Immediately after this treaty shall have been duly ratified by the Government of the Mexican Republic, the sum of three millions of dollars shall be paid to the said Government by that of the United States at the city of Mexico, in the gold or silver coin of Mexico. The remaining twelve millions of dollars shall be paid at the same place and in the same coin, in annual instalments of three millions of dollars each, together with interest on the same at the rate of six per centum per annum. This interest shall begin to run upon the whole sum of twelve millions, from the day of the ratification of the present treaty by the Mexican Government, and the first of the instalments shall be paid at the expiration of one year from the same day. Together with each annual instalment, as it falls due, the whole interest accruing on such instalment from the beginning shall also be paid. [*Certificates in proper form, for the said instalments respectively, in such sums as shall be desired by the Mexican Government, and transferable by it, shall be delivered to the said Government by that of the United States.*]

Segunda manera de pago—]Inmediatamente despues que este Tratado haya sido ratificado por el Gobierno de la República mexicana, se entregará al mismo Gobierno por el de los Estados-Unidos, en la ciudad de Mexico, y en moneda de plata ú oro del cuño mexicano, la suma de tres millones de pesos. Los doce millones de pesos restantes se pagarán en México, en moneda de plata ú oro del cuño mexicano, en abonos de tres millones de pesos cada año, con un rédito de seis por ciento anual: este rédito comienza á correr para toda la suma de los doce millones el dia de la ratificacíon del presente Tratado por el Gobierno mexicano, y con cada abono anual de capital se pagará el rédito que corresponda á la suma abonada. Los plazos para los abonos de capital corren desde el mismo dia que empiezan á causarse los réditos. [*El Gobierno de los Estados-Unidos entregará al de la República mexicana pagarés extendidos en debida forma, correspondientes á cada abono anual, divididos en las cantidades que senale el dicho Gobierno mexicano, y enagenables por este.*]

The Senate amendment to Article 23, which provided for the exchange of ratifications "in the city of Washington", inserted after the quoted words "or at the seat of government of Mexico" (in the Spanish, "ó donde estuviere el gobierno Mexicano").

The Senate resolution of advice and consent made no specific reference to the Spanish version of the treaty; but in respect of the

[1] The second original has "del".

amended articles no textual question of importance arises; no Spanish version of the amended text appears in any of the formal instruments except the Mexican ratification; with that instrument the Spanish version of the text here printed following the headnote has, to the limited extent necessary, been collated; in respect of two articles (11 and 12) the Senate amendments were partial deletions, requiring merely the omission of equivalent words of the Spanish; Article 10 was wholly stricken; the new matter inserted in two articles (3 and 23) was but a few words; for Article 9 a new text was written in English in the Senate resolution and in Spanish in the Mexican ratification; for the English of Article 9 the source is the attested Senate resolution in the treaty file. It might almost equally well be the duplicate United States instrument of ratification, for in this regard the two are precisely the same except that the latter has brackets in lieu of parentheses.

The Additional and Secret Article

The additional and secret article of the Treaty of Guadalupe Hidalgo is one of few instances of a secret article of a treaty signed on behalf of the United States (see Documents 7 and 69). The additional and secret article was stricken out pursuant to the resolution of the Senate, was not ratified on either part, and did not go into force; it provided for a more extended term for the exchange of ratifications than that written in Article 23 of the treaty proper (eight months instead of four); less than four months elapsed between signature and exchange (February 2 and May 30, 1848); this became possible because of the amendment to Article 23, which permitted the exchange to take place "at the seat of government of Mexico".

The text of the additional and secret article is as follows, collated with the first of the two originals in the treaty file; it is to be said that there are no variances between those two papers except in matters of capitalization, accents, and one quite immaterial comma in the English version:

Additional and Secret Article

Of the Treaty of Peace, Friendship, Limits and Settlement between the United States of America and the Mexican Republic, signed this day by their respective Plenipotentiaries.

In view of the possibility that the exchange of the ratifications of this treaty may, by the circumstances in which the Mexican Republic is placed, be delayed longer than the term of four months fixed by it's twenty-third Article for the exchange of ratifications of the same; it is hereby agreed that such delay shall not, in any manner, affect the force and validity of this Treaty, unless it should exceed the term of eight months, counted from the date of the signature thereof.

Artículo adicional y secreto

Del Tratado de Paz, Amistad, Límites y arreglo definitivo entre la Republica mexicana y los Estados-Unidos de América firmado hoy por sus respectivos Plenipotenciarios.

En atencion á la posibilidad de que el cange de las ratificaciones de este Tratado se demore mas del término de cuatro meses fijados en su artículo veinte y tres; por las circunstancias en que se encuentra la Republica mexicana, queda convenido que tal demora no afectará de ningun modo la fuerza y validez del mismo Tratado, si no excediére de ocho meses contados desde la fecha de su firma.

This Article is to have the same force and virtue as if inserted in the treaty to which it is an Addition.

In faith whereof, we, the respective Plenipotentiaries have signed this Additional and Secret Article, and have hereunto affixed our seals respectively. Done in Quintuplicate at the City of Guadalupe Hidalgo on the second day of February, in the year of Our Lord one thousand eight hundred and forty-eight.

N. P. Trist. [Seal]
Luis G. Cuevas [Seal]
Bernardo Couto [Seal]
Migl Atristain [Seal]

Este artículo tendrá la misma fuerza y valor que si estuviese inserto en el Tratado de que es parte adicional.

En fé de lo cual, nosotros los respectivos Plenipotenciarios hemos firmado y sellado este artículo adicional y secreto. Hecho por quintuplicado en la Ciudad de Guadalupe Hidalgo el dia dos de Febrero del año de Nuestro Señor mil ochocientos cuarenta y ocho.

Bernardo Couto [Seal]
Migl Atristain [Seal]
Luis G. Cuevas [Seal]
N. P. Trist. [Seal]

• • •

PROTOCOL OF QUERÉTARO MAY 26, 1848

On the day following ratification of the Treaty of Guadalupe Hidalgo by the Mexican senate (May 25) U.S. commissioners Nathan Clifford and Ambrose Sevier gave Mexican officials oral explanations of the United States Senate amendments to the treaty. At the suggestion of Minister of Relations Luis de la Rosa they later put these explanations into written form subsequently known as the Protocol of Querétaro from the town in which they were written.

Protocol

In the city of Queretaro on the twenty sixth of the month of May eighteen hundred and forty-eight at a conference between Their Excellencies Nathan Clifford and Ambrose H. Sevier Commissioners of the United States of America, with full powers from their Government to make to the Mexican Republic suitable explanations in regard to the amendments which the Senate and Government of the said United States have made in the treaty of peace, friendship, limits and definitive settlement between the two Republics, signed in Guadalupe Hidalgo, on the second day of February of the present year, and His Excellency Don Luis de la Rosa, Minister of Foreign Affairs of the Republic of Mexico, it was agreed, after adequate conversation respecting the changes alluded to, to record in the present protocol the following explanations which Their aforesaid Excellencies the Commissioners gave in the name of their Government and in

En la Ciudad de Queretaro á los veinte y seis dias del mes de Mayo del año de mil ochocientos cuarenta y ocho reunidos el Escelentisimo Señor Dⁿ Luis de la Rosa, Ministro de Relaciones de la Republica Mexicana y los Escelentisimos Señores Nathan Clifford y Ambrosio H. Sevier, comisionados con Plenos Poderes del Gobierno de los Estados unidos de America para hacer al de la Republica Mexicana las esplicaciones convenientes sobre las modificaciones que el Senado y Gobierno de dichos Estados unidos han hecho al Tratado de paz, amistad, limites y arreglo definitivo entre ambas Republicas, firmado en la Ciudad de Guadalupe Hidalgo el dia dos de Febrero del presente año; despues de haber conferenciado detenidamente sobre las indicadas variaciones, han acordado consignar en el presente protocolo las siguientes esplicaciones, que los espresados Escelentisimos Señores co-

fulfillment of the Commission conferred upon them near the Mexican Republic.

misionados han dado en nombre de su Gobierno y desempeñando la comision que este les confirió cerca del de la Republica Mexicana.

FIRST.

The american Government by suppressing the IXth article of the Treaty of Guadalupe and substituting the III. article of the Treaty of Louisiana [1] did not intend to diminish in any way what was agreed upon by the aforesaid article IXth in favor of the inhabitants of the territories ceded by Mexico. Its understanding that all of that agreement is contained in the III[d] article of the Treaty of Louisiana. In consequence, all the privileges and guarantees, civil, political and religious, which would have been possessed by the inhabitants of the ceded territories, if the IXth article of the Treaty had been retained, will be enjoyed by them without any difference under the article which has been substituted.

PRIMERA.

El Gobierno americano suprimiendo el articulo IX del Tratado de Guadalupe, y substituyendo á él el articulo III del de la Luisiana,[1] no ha pretendido disminuir en nada lo que estaba pactado por el citado articulo IX en favor de los habitantes de los territorios cedidos por Mexico. Entiende que todo eso está contenido en el articulo III del Tratado de la Luisiana. En consecuencia todos los gozes y garantias que en el orden civil, en el politico y religioso tendrian los dichos habitantes de los territorios cedidos, si hubiese subsistido el articulo IX del Tratado, esos mismos sin diferencia alguna tendrán bajo el articulo q. se ha substituido.

SECOND.

The American Government by suppressing the Xth article of the Treaty of Guadalupe did not in any way intend to annul the grants of lands made by Mexico in the ceded territories. These grants, notwithstanding the suppression of the article of the Treaty, preserve the legal value which they may possess; and the grantees may cause their legitimate titles to be acknowledged before the american tribunals.

Conformably to the law of the United-States, legitimate titles to every description of property personal and real, existing in the ceded territories, are those which were legitimate titles under the Mexican law in California and New-Mexico up to the 13th of May 1.846, and in Texas up to the 2[d] March 1.836.

SEGUNDA.

El Gobierno americano suprimiendo el articulo X del Tratado de Guadalupe, no ha intentado de ninguna manera anular las conceciones de tierras hechas por Mexico en los territorios cedidos. Esas conceciones, aun suprimido el articulo del Tratado, conservan el valor legal que tengan; y los concesionarios pueden hacer valer sus titulos legitimos ante los Tribunales americanos.

Conforme á la ley de los Estados unidos son titulos legitimos en favor de toda propiedad mueble ó raiz ecsistente en los territorios cedidos, los mismos que hayan sido titulos legitimos bajo la ley mexicana hasta el dia 13. de Mayo de 1.846. en California y en Nuevo Mexico y hasta el dia 2. de Marzo de 1.836. en Tejas.

THIRD.

The Government of the United States by suppressing the concluding paragraph of article XIIth of the Treaty, did not intend to deprive the Mexican Republic of the free and unrestrained faculty of ceding, conveying or transferring at any time (as it may judge best) the sum of the twelfe millions of dollars which the same Government of the United-States

TERCERA.

El Gobierno de los Estados unidos suprimiendo el parrafo con que concluye el articulo XII del Tratado, no ha entendido privar á la Republica Mexicana de la libre y expedita facultad de ceder, traspasar ó enagenar en cualquier tiempo (como mejor le parezca) la suma de los doce millones de pesos que el mismo Gobierno de los

[1] Document 28.

is to deliver in the places designated by the amended article.

And these explanations having been accepted by the Minister of Foreign Affairs of the Mexican Republic, he declared in name of his Government that with the understanding conveyed by them, the same Government would proceed to ratify the Treaty of Guadalupe as modified by the Senate and Government of the United States. In testimony of which their Excellencies the aforesaid Commissioners and the Minister have signed and sealed in quintuplicate the present protocol.

[Seal] A. H. Sevier.
[Seal] Nathan Clifford
[Seal] Luis de la Rosa

Estados unidos debe entregar en los plazos que expresa el articulo XII modificado.

Y habiendo aceptado estas explicaciones el Ministro de Relaciones de la Republica Mexicana, declaró en nombre de su Gobierno que bajo los conceptos que ellas importan, vá á proceder el mismo Gobierno á ratificar el Trado de Guadalupe segun ha sido modificado por el Senado y Gobierno de los Estados unidos. En fé de lo cual firmaron y sellaron por quintuplicado el presente protocolo los Escelentisimos Señores Ministro y comisionados ante-dichos.

[Seal] Luis de la Rosa
[Seal] A. H. Sevier.
[Seal] Nathan Clifford

APPENDIX D
GLOSSARY OF CHICANO TERMS

alambrista, from alambre, "wire"; a person who crosses the border illegally by (figuratively) climbing a fence

aleluya, a protestant

aliancista, a member of the Alianza Federal de Mercedes, Reies López Tijerina's organization

Anglo, short for Anglo American; in the Southwest sometimes designating all non-Mexican-descent Americans

Aztlán, mythical homeland of the Aztec or Mexica Indians

barrio, district; in the United States, the Mexican American quarter of town

blowout, school walkout; a tumult or riot

bolillo, Tejano word of uncertain origin for an Anglo

caballero, literally a horseman, therefore a gentleman

cacique, originally a native chief of the Caribbean; today a political boss

Califas, a caló term for California

caló, a Chicano dialect of Spanish, spoken in the barrio

carnal, brother (Chicano)

carnalismo, brotherhood

caudillo, strong man; leader, often military

Causa, La, The Cause, the Chicano struggle for the economic, political, and social rights of American citizenship

chavalo, Chicano slang for youth; a "kid"

chingada, la, a term with many shades of meaning; a woman who passively allows herself to be violated, the violated "mother"; a woman who sells out La Raza, a traitor; Malinche is seen as the very personification of la chingada. Hijo de la chingada, an S.O.B.

cofradía, brotherhood, an association of people with common goals, a gang

compadre, title parents use for their child's godfather, buddy

con safos, a colloquial expression meaning the same back to you

curandero, healer, herb doctor
enganchista, literally a recruiter; one who recruits farm labor
gabacho, pejorative term for white; originally meaning French and foreign
gachupín(es), colonial term of derogation used to identify a Spaniard
gringo, pejorative term for foreigner, originally from griego "Greek" and therefore foreign
Grito de Dolores, famous cry of Father Miguel Hidalgo which initiated the Mexican Revolution of 1810
hacienda, a large agricultural holding
hermandad, brotherhood, sisterhood
hermano (a), brother (sister)
Hispano, New Mexican of Hispanic-Mexican origins
huelguista, striker
jefa, jefita, literally chief, little chief (female); mother
jefe, literally chief, therefore father
jefitos, parents
lambiscón (lambión), apple polisher, boot-licker
Latin American, often used in Texas to mean Mexican because of the frequent pejorative use of the latter term
machismo, term used to connote virile manliness; from macho, "male"
macho, male, masculine
maestro, teacher, master; often used in referring to a skilled craftsman
malinchismo, selling-out La Raza, from Malinche, Cortés's Indian mistress
manito, truncated form of hermanito, "little brother"; slightly pejorative term for Spanish-speaking New Mexican
mapista, a member or supporter of the Mexican American Political Association (MAPA)
mexicano, properly a person from Mexico; also (inaccurately) a person of Mexican descent in the United States Southwest
migra, la, immigration officer(s) and the Immigration and Naturalization Service
mojado, literally "wet"; one who enters the United States illegally, theoretically by swimming the Rio Grande
norteño, a person from northern Mexico
nuevo mexicano, Hispanic-Mexican inhabitant of area of New Mexico
pachuco (also chuco), pejorative term for a Chicano follower of a "hip" life-style, especially in the late 1940s
pachuquismo, pejorative term for a "hip" life-style within the barrio, usually followed by the young
patrón, boss, protector, patron; often a landowner or politician
pelado, literally plucked, a penniless, downtrodden social outcast
peón(es), worker, usually tied to the land; used pejoratively to denote low class
pinta, jail, prison, penitentiary
pinto, barrio term for a prison inmate
pocho, pejorative word for an Americanized Mexican; Mexican term for a California Chicano
pollo, a green inexperienced person

presidio, military fort or garrison
ranchero, owner of a ranch; or related to ranching
rancho, a rural property, often one on which cattle are raised; a correctional institution
raza, la, ethnic term for Spanish-speaking people, connoting a spirit of kinship and a sense of common destiny
real, a Spanish coin worth twelve and one-half centavos; used today in expressions like dos reales (two bits)
repatriados, Mexicans who returned to Mexico, especially in the 1930s.
rinche, ranger, a member of the Texas Rangers
sinarquismo, a right-wing radical political philosophy originating in Mexico with the Union Nacional Sinarquista
soplón, labor informer, squealer, stool pigeon
surrumato, pejorative term, especially used in New Mexico, for Mexican; a foolish person
tecato, drug addict
tejano, Hispanic-Mexican inhabitant of Texas area
tertulia, a social gathering for conversation or entertainment
tío taco, Chicano pejorative version of an Uncle Tom
vato (bato), guy, dude, a barrio term
vato loco, a crazy dude, a pachuco
vendido, sellout, one who betrays La Raza
vieja, a term of endearment for wife or mother; literally old woman
viejo, father; also husband; literally old man
wetback, a Mexican who crosses the border into the United States illegally

APPENDIX E
MEXICAN AMERICAN JOURNALS

The following is a list of the more important Mexican American periodicals, with some very brief descriptions. The annotation bilingual on some is a description of policy and does not mean to say that others do not publish some materials in both Spanish and English. While a majority emphasize literature, these journals vary considerably in purpose and outlook, as well as in literary quality and physical appearance. Some appear irregularly and some no longer appear. All have served to define the Chicano, his culture, and his goals.

Agenda: A Journal of Hispanic Issues
National Council of La Raza
1725 I Street, N.W.
Washington, D.C., bimonthly

Agenda concerns itself with matters of interest to the nationwide Hispanic population. These include legal matters, education, the arts, culture, and history.

Atisbos: Journal of Chicano Research
Chicano Graduate Students Association
Stanford University
Stanford, Calif., irregular, bilingual

A forum for research on and by Mexican Americans, *Atisbos* aims to provide Chicano scholars with a clearing-house and a calendar of events.

Aztlán: International Journal of Chicano Studies and Research
Chicano Studies Center
University of California
Los Angeles, Calif., quarterly

Highly scholarly in its focus, *Aztlán* publishes articles on language, literature, and art, but especially works in the social sciences.

The Bilingual Review/La Revista Bilingüe
Department of Romance Languages
City College of New York
New York, N.Y., three times a year, bilingual

The *Review* aims to serve basically as a bibliographic and research resource for scholars and as a literary journal. Its audience is the larger Latino community.

Bronce Magazine
1560 34th Avenue
Oakland, Calif.

A monthly dealing with the social sciences as they affect the Chicano.

Caracol: La Revista De La Raza
Texas Institute for Educational Development
1511 Alebra St.
San Antonio, Texas, monthly, bilingual

Caracol stresses the arts and literature; it publishes short articles, interviews, and reviews.

Carta Abierta. Keeping an Eye on the Chicano Literary World
University of California
3408 Dwinelle Hall
Berkeley, California, three times a year.

As its title indicates, *Carta Abierta* stresses Chicano literature and literary criticism.

Chicano Law Review
Chicano Law Student Association
School of Law, University of California
Los Angeles, Calif., annual

The *Review* limits itself to legal issues, presented in a popular style, as they affect the Chicano.

Chismearte
Concilio de Arte Popular
5605½ Figueroa Street
Los Angeles, Calif., quarterly

Chismearte features literature, poetry, and art, especially as they relate to the Chicano's social struggle.

Comexas News Monitoring Service
Comité de México y Aztlán
P.O. Box 12062
Oakland, Calif., monthly

A well-indexed news-monitoring service based on clippings from seven large southwestern newspapers.

Con Safos: Reflections of Life in the Barrio
P.O. Box 31085
Los Angeles, Calif., irregular, bilingual

During its four-year life (1968-1971) *Con Safos* emphasized short stories, poetry, political and historical articles.

La Cucaracha
P.O. Box 5034
Pueblo, Colorado, irregular

La Cucaracha features Colorado Chicano news and issues.

De Colores: Journal of Chicano Expression and Thought
Pajarito Publications
2633 Granite Ave., N.W.
Albuquerque, New Mexico, quarterly, bilingual

Community oriented, *De Colores* publishes literary works, criticism, historical essays, and interviews.

Entrelíneas
Ethnic Awareness Center
University of Missouri
Kansas City, Mo., irregular

Entrelíneas publishes a wide variety of popular articles on literature, art, and current events, as well as book reviews.

Escolios, Revista de Literatura. Creación-Teoría-Crítica
California State University
University Publications School of Letters and Sciences
Los Angeles, Calif., semiannual, bilingual

Escolios publishes creative literary pieces and literary criticism.

Fuego de Aztlán
University of California
3408 Dwinelle Hall
Berkeley, Calif., irregular

Fuego de Aztlán publishes both prose and poetry work of young Chicano writers.

El Grito: A Journal of Contemporary Mexican American Thought
Quinto Sol Publications
P.O. Box 9275
Berkeley, Calif., quarterly, bilingual

El Grito was a journal of quality that published writers, artists, poets, and politicos of the barrio.

El Grito del Sol: A Chicano Quarterly
Tonatiuh International
2150 Shattuck Avenue
Berkeley, Calif., quarterly, bilingual

A high-quality journal similar to *El Grito*, and to an extent its successor.

Journal of Comparative Cultures
National Bilingual Education Association
9332 Vista Bonita
Cypress, Calif., annual

Formerly named the *Journal of Mexican American Studies*, it now includes other minorities, but stresses the Mexican American. It is concerned with the social issues, and its emphasis is on education.

Journal of Mexican American History
University of California
P.O. Box 13861
Santa Barbara, Calif., irregular

An excellent historical journal publishing a variety of articles of concern to Chicano historians.

La Luz
La Luz Publications
8000 East Girard Ave.
Denver, Colo., monthly

A slick national magazine, *La Luz* publishes a variety of popular articles of interest to the wider Latino audience, but emphasizes lo Chicano.

Magazín
311 North Zarzamora Ave.
San Antonio, Texas, irregular, bilingual

Magazín features news, essays on literature, history, and folklore.

Maize: Notebooks of Xicano Art and Literature
Centro Cultural de la Raza Publications
P.O. Box 8251
San Diego, Calif., quarterly

Maize is a journal of creative literature, poetry, and art edited by the poet Alurista.

Mango
329 South Willard Ave.
San José, Calif., irregular, bilingual

A publication emphasizing creative literature, poetry, and the arts.

Mizquiztli: Un Cuaderno de Arte, Poesía, Cuento y Canto
Chicano Fellows
Stanford University
Stanford, Calif., irregular, English

A literary journal, it published short stories and poetry.

El Nahuatzen
310 Calvin Hall
University of Iowa
Iowa City, Iowa, semiannual

Founded in 1978, *El Nahuatzen* is a literary journal which emphasizes poetry.

Nuestro: The Magazine for Latinos
Nuestro Publications
1140 Avenue of the Americas
New York, N.Y., monthly, bilingual

A popular national magazine aimed at the wider Hispanic audience, it covers cultural and political developments across the United States.

La Palabra, Revista de Literatura Chicana
Arizona State University
Department of Foreign Languages
Tempe, Arizona, semiannual, Spanish

La Palabra is strictly a literary review.

Papeles de la Frontera
P.O. Box 422
El Centro, Calif., monthly, bilingual

Papeles de la Frontera features reviews and literary news as well as creative literature.

Rayas. Newsletter of Chicano Arts and Literature
Pajarito Publications
2633 Granite Ave., N.W.
Albuquerque, New Mexico, bimonthly, bilingual

Newspaper in format, *Rayas* concerns itself with cultural events, creative literature, poetry, and recent Chicano publications.

La Raza: News and Political Thought of the Chicano Struggle
3518 City Terrace Drive
P.O. Box 31004
Los Angeles, Calif., irregular, bilingual

La Raza is basically a news essay magazine which emphasizes the political; it also publishes some literary materials, including poetry.

Regeneracíon
P.O. Box 4157 T.A.
Los Angeles, Calif., irregular

Basically a news essay journal, *Regeneracíon* also publishes some literary materials and graphics.

Revista Chicano-Riqueña
Indiana University Northwest
3400 Broadway
Gary, Indiana, quarterly, bilingual

Revista Chicano-Riqueña is a high-quality journal devoted to Chicano and Puerto Rican literature and literary criticism, and promoting cultural pluralism in the process.

Somos
Los Padrinos of Southern California
P.O. Box 5697
San Bernardino, Calif., monthly

Somos combines news and essays with special emphasis on California.

El Tecolote
P.O. Box 40027
San Francisco, Calif., monthly

El Tecolote presents a radical view of Chicano and Latin American political and social problems.

Tejidos: A Bilingual Journal for the Stimulation of Chicano Creativity and Criticism
P.O. Box 7383
Austin, Texas, quarterly, bilingual

Tejidos publishes essays and creative literary selections on a wide variety of Chicano topics.

Xalman
601 Montecito Street
Santa Barbara, Calif., semiannual, bilingual

Xalman features criticism, poetry, drama, music, and art.

APPENDIX F

TABLES OF CENSUS, EDUCATION, EMPLOYMENT, AND IMMIGRATION STATISTICS

Table 1.

Hispanic American Population, By Various Identifiers (April 1970)

Identifier	United States	Southwestern States[1]	Remainder of United States	Middle Atlantic States[2]	Florida
NUMBER					
Spanish origin[3]	9,072,602	5,008,556	4,064,046	1,749,363	405,036
Spanish surname[4]	(X)	4,667,975	(X)	(X)	(X)
Spanish language[5]	9,589,216	5,662,700	3,926,516	1,873,051	451,382
Spanish heritage[6]	9,294,509	6,188,362	3,106,147	1,052,682	451,382
Spanish language or surname[7]	10,114,878	6,188,362	3,926,516	1,873,051	451,382
Spanish birth or parentage[8]	5,241,892	2,321,642	2,920,250	1,738,802	336,961
PERCENT OF SPANISH ORIGIN[9]					
Spanish origin	100.0	100.0	100.0	100.0	100.0
Spanish surname	(X)	93.2	(X)	(X)	(X)
Spanish language[5]	105.7	113.1	96.6	107.1	111.4
Spanish heritage[6]	102.4	123.6	76.4	60.2	111.4
Spanish language or surname	111.5	123.6	96.6	107.1	111.4
Spanish birth or parentage	57.8	46.4	71.9	99.4	83.2

X Not applicable.

NOTES

[1]Arizona, California, Colorado, New Mexico, and Texas.

[2]New York, New Jersey, and Pennsylvania.

[3]U.S. Bureau of the Census, Census of Population: 1970, Subject Reports, PC(2)-1C, Persons of Spanish Origin, 1973, table 1.

[4]U.S. Bureau of the Census, Census of Population: 1970, Subject Reports, PC(2)-1D, Persons of Spanish Surname, 1973, table 1.

[5]This group consists of all persons of Spanish mother tongue and all other persons in families in which the head or wife reported Spanish as his or her mother tongue. U.S. Bureau of the Census, Census of Population: 1970, Supplementary Report, PC(S1)-30, Persons of Spanish Ancestry, 1973, table 3.

[6]This group consists of persons of Spanish language or surname in the 5 Southwestern States, persons of Puerto Rican birth or parentage in the 3 Middle Atlantic States, and persons of Spanish language in the remaining 42 States and the District of Columbia. U.S. Bureau of the Census, Census of Population: 1970, General Social and Economic Characteristics, PC(1)-C, 1972, table 85 (United States) and table 49 (States).

[7]*Ibid.*, table 86 (United States) and table 49 (States).

[8]*Op.cit.*, PC(S1)-30, table 5.

[9]**Figures represent ratio of specified population to Spanish-origin population** (per 100).

SOURCE: Bureau of the Census, Current Population Reports, Population Characteristics. Persons of Spanish Origin in the United States: March 1976, Table 1, Page 9.

TABLE 2
Total U.S. and Spanish Origin Population by Age Brackets (March 1976)

Sex and age	Total persons	Spanish origin						Not Spanish origin	Do not know or not reported
		Total	Mexican	Puerto Rican	Cuban	Central or South American	Other Spanish		
BOTH SEXES									
Total........thousands..	211,140	11,117	6,590	1,753	687	752	1,335	195,214	4,809
Percent........	100.0	100.0	100.0	100.0	100.0	100.0	100.0	100.0	100.0
Under 5 years........	7.4	12.8	13.3	12.5	5.6	14.1	13.7	7.1	7.2
5 and 6 years........	3.3	5.3	5.4	6.1	2.5	5.0	5.4	3.2	2.8
7 to 9 years........	4.9	7.2	7.4	7.3	3.5	6.0	8.7	4.7	4.8
10 to 13 years........	7.4	10.0	9.9	11.3	8.0	7.1	11.3	7.3	7.0
14 and 15 years........	4.0	4.6	4.7	5.0	4.4	3.7	4.3	4.0	3.3
16 and 17 years........	3.9	4.4	4.4	4.9	4.0	3.6	4.3	3.9	2.6
18 and 19 years........	3.8	4.0	4.2	3.7	4.1	2.5	4.1	3.9	3.0
20 and 21 years........	3.7	3.7	3.9	3.9	3.3	3.0	3.2	3.7	3.3
22 to 24 years........	5.2	5.2	5.8	5.1	3.6	3.9	4.2	5.2	5.8
25 to 29 years........	8.2	8.2	8.6	7.6	4.3	12.5	6.8	8.1	10.8
30 to 34 years........	6.6	6.5	6.3	6.8	3.7	10.6	5.8	6.6	8.2
35 to 44 years........	10.8	11.4	10.5	12.3	16.6	15.5	9.4	10.8	11.8
45 to 54 years........	11.1	8.1	7.8	6.6	16.9	6.8	7.5	11.3	9.7
55 to 64 years........	9.4	4.9	4.3	4.5	10.0	3.7	6.3	9.6	9.3
65 to 74 years........	6.5	2.7	2.5	1.9	7.1	1.3	3.0	6.7	7.1
75 years and over........	3.8	1.1	1.0	0.5	2.5	0.7	1.9	3.9	3.2
18 years and over........	69.0	55.7	54.9	53.0	72.0	60.6	52.2	69.7	72.2
21 years and over........	63.3	49.6	48.4	46.9	66.5	56.9	46.4	64.0	67.7
Median age........years..	28.9	20.9	20.3	19.6	36.8	25.5	19.1	29.3	29.7

MALE									
Total..........thousands..	102,344	5,439	3,285	849	315	355	636	94,548	2,358
Percent..........	100.0	100.0	100.0	100.0	100.0	100.0	100.0	100.0	100.0
Under 5 years..........	7.8	13.6	13.9	13.8	7.5	14.6	14.2	7.4	7.1
5 and 6 years..........	3.5	5.8	5.8	7.3	2.3	5.5	6.1	3.4	3.4
7 to 9 years..........	5.1	7.6	7.8	6.8	3.5	8.7	9.0	5.0	5.0
10 to 13 years..........	7.8	10.2	9.6	12.9	7.0	9.9	11.2	7.7	7.4
14 and 15 years..........	4.2	4.9	4.7	5.8	4.5	2.6	5.8	4.2	3.1
16 and 17 years..........	4.1	5.0	4.6	6.2	4.4	4.0	5.9	4.1	2.3
18 and 19 years..........	3.9	3.9	4.0	3.5	4.5	2.1	4.4	3.9	2.7
20 and 21 years..........	3.8	3.6	4.1	3.3	3.2	1.7	2.4	3.8	2.9
22 to 24 years..........	5.2	5.1	5.6	4.9	3.8	3.3	4.3	5.2	6.1
25 to 29 years..........	8.3	7.9	8.6	6.1	4.3	11.8	5.9	8.2	11.0
30 to 34 years..........	6.6	5.8	5.4	5.9	3.1	11.2	6.0	6.6	9.0
35 to 44 years..........	10.9	10.7	10.3	10.5	14.4	14.8	8.6	10.8	13.4
45 to 54 years..........	11.0	8.2	8.1	6.7	20.5	6.5	5.6	11.2	10.2
55 to 64 years..........	9.1	4.6	4.4	4.0	8.9	1.9	5.9	9.4	8.7
65 to 74 years..........	5.8	2.4	2.3	1.6	6.4	1.2	2.8	6.0	5.3
75 years and over..........	2.9	0.9	0.8	0.7	1.6	0.2	1.8	3.0	2.4
18 years and over..........	67.5	53.0	53.6	47.2	70.8	54.7	47.7	68.2	71.7
21 years and over..........	61.7	47.2	47.3	42.3	65.1	51.8	42.4	62.4	67.5
Median age..........years..	27.8	19.5	19.8	17.1	36.3	22.8	17.2	28.2	29.5

SOURCE: U.S. Bureau of the Census. "Persons of Spanish Origin in the United States: March 1976." *Current Population Reports*, Series P-20, no. 310, 1977. Table 3.

TABLE 2 (continued)

Total U.S. and Spanish Origin Population by Age Brackets (March 1976)

Sex and age	Total persons	Spanish origin						Not Spanish origin	Do not know or not reported
		Total	Mexican	Puerto Rican	Cuban	Central or South American	Other Spanish		
FEMALE									
Total..........thousands..	108,795	5,678	3,305	904	372	398	700	100,666	2,451
Percent..........	100.0	100.0	100.0	100.0	100.0	100.0	100.0	100.0	100.0
Under 5 years..........	7.0	12.1	12.8	11.2	4.0	13.6	13.1	6.7	7.3
5 and 6 years..........	3.2	4.8	5.0	5.0	2.6	4.6	4.8	3.1	2.3
7 to 9 years..........	4.6	6.8	7.0	7.7	3.5	3.6	8.5	4.5	4.7
10 to 13 years..........	7.1	9.8	10.2	9.8	8.8	4.5	11.4	6.9	6.6
14 and 15 years..........	3.8	4.3	4.6	4.2	4.3	4.7	3.0	3.8	3.6
16 and 17 years..........	3.8	3.9	4.2	3.7	3.8	3.1	2.9	3.8	2.9
18 and 19 years..........	3.8	4.1	4.5	3.9	3.8	2.8	3.8	3.8	3.4
20 and 21 years..........	3.7	3.8	3.6	4.5	3.4	4.1	3.9	3.7	3.6
22 to 24 years..........	5.2	5.4	6.0	5.2	3.5	4.4	4.2	5.1	5.6
25 to 29 years..........	8.0	8.5	8.5	8.9	4.3	13.2	7.6	8.0	10.6
30 to 34 years..........	6.6	7.1	7.2	7.7	4.2	10.0	5.7	6.5	7.4
35 to 44 years..........	10.8	12.0	10.7	14.0	18.4	16.2	10.1	10.7	10.3
45 to 54 years..........	11.2	7.9	7.5	6.6	13.7	7.1	9.2	11.4	9.3
55 to 64 years..........	9.6	5.2	4.3	5.0	10.9	5.4	6.6	9.8	9.8
65 to 74 years..........	7.1	3.0	2.7	2.2	7.7	1.4	3.3	7.3	8.8
75 years and over..........	4.6	1.3	1.1	0.4	3.3	1.2	2.0	4.8	4.0
18 years and over..........	70.5	58.3	56.1	58.4	73.1	65.8	56.4	71.2	72.7
21 years and over..........	64.8	51.9	49.6	51.3	67.7	61.4	50.0	65.5	68.0
Median age..........years..	29.9	22.2	20.9	22.0	37.1	26.7	21.3	30.4	29.8

TABLE 3
Total and Spanish Origin Population for the Five Southwestern States by age (1976)

Sex and age	Total population	Total Spanish origin	Mexican origin	Other Spanish origin[1]
BOTH SEXES				
Total .... thousands..	39,186	6,414	5,490	924
Percent	100.0	100.0	100.0	100.0
Under 5 years	7.7	13.0	12.9	13.3
5 and 6 years	3.4	5.2	5.3	4.7
7 to 9 years	5.0	7.5	7.4	7.8
10 to 13 years	7.2	9.8	9.8	9.7
14 and 15 years	3.8	4.5	4.6	3.9
16 and 17 years	4.0	4.5	4.5	4.9
18 and 19 years	3.9	4.1	4.1	4.0
20 and 21 years	3.7	3.7	3.9	2.7
22 to 24 years	5.4	5.5	5.8	3.6
25 to 29 years	8.7	8.4	8.6	7.0
30 to 34 years	7.0	6.4	6.2	8.1
35 to 44 years	11.2	10.5	10.5	10.3
45 to 54 years	10.8	8.2	8.1	8.8
55 to 64 years	8.9	4.8	4.6	5.9
65 to 74 years	6.0	2.7	2.7	3.0
75 years and over	3.4	1.3	1.1	2.4
18 years and over	68.9	55.5	55.5	55.6
21 years and over	63.2	49.4	49.3	50.3
Median age .... years..	28.5	20.8	20.7	21.2

SOURCE: U.S. Bureau of the Census, "Persons of Spanish Origin in the United States: March 1976." *Current Population Reports*, Series P-20, no. 310, 1977. Table 4.

TABLE 3 (continued)
Total and Spanish Origin Population for the Five Southwestern States by age (1976)

Sex and age	Total population	Total Spanish origin	Mexican origin	Other Spanish origin[1]
MALE				
Total....thousands..	19,201	3,176	2,741	432
Percent....	100.0	100.0	100.0	100.0
Under 5 years....	7.8	13.6	13.4	14.7
5 and 6 years....	3.6	5.6	5.7	5.1
7 to 9 years....	5.2	7.6	7.6	7.7
10 to 13 years....	7.5	9.8	9.5	11.3
14 and 15 years....	4.1	4.8	4.8	4.4
16 and 17 years....	4.2	4.7	4.4	6.6
18 and 19 years....	4.0	3.9	3.8	4.4
20 and 21 years....	3.7	3.9	4.3	1.3
22 to 24 years....	5.3	5.4	5.7	3.6
25 to 29 years....	8.7	8.6	8.9	6.3
30 to 34 years....	6.8	5.6	5.2	7.7
35 to 44 years....	11.2	10.2	10.4	9.5
45 to 54 years....	10.8	8.3	8.2	8.4
55 to 64 years....	8.8	4.6	4.7	3.8
65 to 74 years....	5.5	2.5	2.4	2.9
75 years and over....	2.6	1.0	0.9	2.0
18 years and over....	67.6	53.9	54.5	50.0
21 years and over....	61.6	47.8	48.2	45.5
Median age....years..	27.6	20.0	20.3	18.0

FEMALE				
Total....thousands..	19,985	3,238	2,749	489
Percent....	100.0	100.0	100.0	100.0
Under 5 years....	7.5	12.4	12.4	12.0
5 and 6 years....	3.2	4.8	4.8	4.3
7 to 9 years....	4.9	7.3	7.2	7.9
10 to 13 years....	6.9	9.8	10.0	8.3
14 and 15 years....	3.4	4.3	4.5	3.5
16 and 17 years....	3.8	4.3	4.5	3.4
18 and 19 years....	3.8	4.3	4.4	3.6
20 and 21 years....	3.7	3.6	3.5	4.0
22 to 24 years....	5.5	5.5	5.9	3.5
25 to 29 years....	8.6	8.2	8.3	7.5
30 to 34 years....	7.2	7.3	7.1	8.4
35 to 44 years....	11.1	10.7	10.6	10.9
45 to 54 years....	10.8	8.2	8.0	9.1
55 to 64 years....	9.0	5.0	4.5	7.8
65 to 74 years....	6.4	3.0	3.0	3.0
75 years and over....	4.2	1.5	1.3	2.7
18 years and over....	70.2	57.2	56.6	60.5
21 years and over....	64.7	51.0	50.4	54.6
Median age....years..	29.3	21.6	21.2	24.6

TABLE 4
Education: Years of School Completed (Percent Age of Total and Spanish Origin Population Twenty-five Years Old and Over, March 1976)

Sex, years of school completed, and age	Total persons	Spanish origin		
		Total	Mexican	Other Spanish[1]
MALE				
Percent Completed Less Than 5 Years of School				
Total, 25 years and over	4.2	17.7	23.0	10.0
25 to 29 years	0.9	4.9	5.7	3.5
30 to 34 years	0.8	7.7	12.0	2.1
35 to 44 years	2.5	13.5	18.7	6.2
45 to 64 years	4.5	26.1	33.0	16.2
65 years and over	11.7	47.0	63.8	25.2
Percent Completed 4 Years of High School or More				
Total, 25 years and over	64.7	41.4	34.6	51.3
25 to 29 years	86.0	57.7	53.9	65.1
30 to 34 years	81.8	58.9	48.6	72.1
35 to 44 years	72.9	42.1	34.5	52.7
45 to 64 years	58.7	30.1	22.9	40.6
65 years and over	34.7	13.5	5.0	24.6
Percent Completed 4 Years of College or More				
Total, 25 years and over	18.6	8.6	5.9	12.6

FEMALE				
Percent Completed Less Than 5 Years of School				
Total, 25 years and over	3.6	19.6	25.2	12.7
25 to 29 years	0.7	5.7	6.2	4.9
30 to 34 years	0.7	9.0	12.1	4.5
35 to 44 years	1.7	15.8	20.6	10.8
45 to 64 years	3.3	26.4	36.5	15.5
65 years and over	9.2	54.2	70.3	35.8
Percent Completed 4 Years of High School or More				
Total, 25 years and over	63.5	37.3	30.5	45.6
25 to 29 years	83.5	58.4	53.5	65.4
30 to 34 years	78.9	43.4	38.7	50.2
35 to 44 years	72.0	38.8	30.0	48.3
45 to 64 years	60.8	26.5	18.0	35.8
65 years and over	38.3	14.1	3.9	25.8
Percent Completed 4 Years of College or More				
Total, 25 years and over	11.3	4.0	2.1	6.1

SOURCE: U.S. Bureau of the Census. "Persons of Spanish Origin in the United States: March 1976." *Current Population Reports*, Series P-20, no. 310, 1977. Table 7.

[1]Includes Puerto Rican, Cuban, Central or South American, and other Spanish origin.

TABLE 5
Employment Status

Employment status of the population 16 years and over by sex, race, and Hispanic origin, quarterly averages, not seasonally adjusted

(Numbers in thousands)

Employment status	Total		Black[1]		Hispanic origin[2]		White	
	I 1979	I 1980	I 1979	I 1980	I 1979	I 1980	I 1979	I 1980
TOTAL								
Civilian noninstitutional population	160,570	163,216	16,884	17,270	7,642	8,183	140,857	142,957
Civilian labor force	101,260	103,265	10,199	10,321	4,848	5,215	89,254	91,061
Percent of population	63.1	63.3	60.4	59.8	63.4	63.7	63.4	63.7
Employment	94,901	96,318	8,891	8,983	4,443	4,715	84,319	85,602
Percent of population	59.1	59.0	52.7	52.0	58.1	57.6	59.9	59.9
Unemployment	6,360	6,947	1,308	1,338	404	500	4,934	5,460
Unemployment rate	6.3	6.7	12.8	13.0	8.3	9.6	5.5	6.0
Median duration, in weeks[3]	6.5	6.4	7.7	7.2	6.3	5.8	6.2	6.2
Not in labor force	59,310	59,950	6,685	6,949	2,795	2,968	51,603	51,896
Discouraged workers	724	967	188	219	49	60	540	709
Men								
Civilian noninstitutional population	75,981	77,264	7,574	7,740	3,639	3,959	67,116	68,161
Civilian labor force	58,576	59,269	5,319	5,346	2,940	3,212	52,284	52,929

Percent of population	77.1	76.7	70.2	69.1	80.8	81.1	77.9	77.7
Employment	55,146	55,352	4,643	4,630	2,723	2,945	49,588	49,799
Percent of population	72.6	71.6	61.3	59.8	74.8	74.4	73.9	73.1
Unemployment	3,430	3,917	676	716	217	267	2,696	3,129
Unemployment rate	5.9	6.6	12.7	13.4	7.4	8.3	5.2	5.9
Median duration, in weeks[3]	7.3	7.3	9.0	8.1	6.3	6.4	6.9	7.1
Not in labor force	17,405	17,996	2,255	2,393	699	747	14,832	15,232
Discouraged workers	286	364	69	96	14	20	216	263
Women								
Civilian noninstitutional population	84,589	85,951	9,310	9,531	4,004	4,224	73,741	74,796
Civilian labor force	42,684	43,997	4,880	4,975	1,908	2,003	36,970	38,132
Percent of population	50.5	51.2	52.4	52.2	47.7	47.4	50.1	51.0
Employment	39,755	40,967	4,248	4,353	1,720	1,770	34,732	35,802
Percent of population	47.0	47.7	45.6	45.7	43.0	41.9	47.1	47.9
Unemployment	2,929	3,030	632	622	188	233	2,238	2,330
Unemployment rate	6.9	6.9	12.9	12.5	9.8	11.6	6.1	6.1
Median duration, in weeks[3]	5.4	5.1	6.4	6.2	6.5	4.9	5.1	4.9
Not in labor force	41,905	41,955	4,430	4,556	2,096	2,221	36,772	36,664
Discouraged workers	438	603	114	123	35	40	324	446

SOURCE: U.S. Department of Labor, Bureau of Labor Statistics, February 1980. Report 584, Table 1.

[1] Data relate to black workers only, except as noted. According to the 1970 census, black workers constituted 89 percent of the "black and other" population group.

[2] Data on persons of Hispanic origin are tabulated without regard to race, which means that they are also included in the data for white and black workers. At the time of the 1970 census, approximately 96 percent of the Hispanic-origin population was white.

[3] Data for black workers pertain to the "black and other" population group.

TABLE 6
Income of Persons of Mexican Origin Fourteen Years Old and Older (1975)

Type of Spanish origin, sex, and income	Total	In metropolitan areas			Outside metropolitan areas
		Total	In central cities	Outside central cities	
MEXICAN ORIGIN--Continued					
Male					
Number of persons............thousands..	2,067	1,571	868	703	496
Number of persons with income thousands..	1,817	1,375	765	610	442
Percent..........................	100.0	100.0	100.0	100.0	100.0
$1 to $999 or loss.....................	8.8	7.9	8.0	7.9	11.4
$1,000 to $1,499......................	4.4	4.1	4.4	3.8	5.1
$1,500 to $1,999......................	3.5	3.4	3.5	3.3	3.7
$2,000 to $2,499......................	4.2	3.9	4.6	3.2	4.9
$2,500 to $2,999......................	3.2	2.7	3.2	2.1	4.6
$3,000 to $3,499......................	4.3	3.9	3.3	4.7	5.6
$3,500 to $3,999......................	3.6	3.1	2.6	3.8	4.9
$4,000 to $4,999......................	7.0	6.8	6.2	7.6	7.4
$5,000 to $5,999......................	8.0	7.4	6.9	7.9	10.0
$6,000 to $6,999......................	6.9	6.8	7.7	5.6	7.3
$7,000 to $7,999......................	7.2	7.4	7.4	7.3	6.6
$8,000 to $8,999......................	5.7	5.8	5.3	6.4	5.3
$9,000 to $9,999......................	6.3	6.5	6.4	6.6	5.8
$10,000 to $11,999....................	9.0	9.8	10.0	9.6	6.5
$12,000 to $14,999....................	8.7	9.5	9.5	9.5	6.2
$15,000 to $19,999....................	6.6	7.5	7.9	7.1	3.9
$20,000 to $24,999....................	1.6	2.0	1.7	2.3	0.4
$25,000 to $49,999....................	0.9	1.1	1.0	1.2	0.2
$50,000 and over......................	0.3	0.3	0.5	0.1	0.2

Median income..................dollars..	6,450	6,970	6,945	7,011	5,237
Mean income....................dollars..	7,355	7,805	7,846	7,753	5,959
Female					
Number of persons............thousands..	2,147	1,645	907	738	502
Number of persons with income thousands..	1,326	1,033	580	453	293
Percent..........................	100.0	100.0	100.0	100.0	100.0
$1 to $999 or loss......................	20.5	17.7	16.7	19.0	30.3
$1,000 to $1,499.........................	10.8	10.4	10.5	10.1	12.3
$1,500 to $1,999.........................	8.7	8.4	9.0	7.7	9.6
$2,000 to $2,499.........................	7.0	7.0	6.8	7.2	7.3
$2,500 to $2,999.........................	5.9	6.2	5.9	6.5	5.0
$3,000 to $3,499.........................	7.0	7.5	8.2	6.6	5.1
$3,500 to $3,999.........................	5.9	5.9	6.1	5.6	5.9
$4,000 to $4,999.........................	9.4	9.7	9.8	9.5	8.3
$5,000 to $5,999.........................	7.7	7.8	7.5	8.3	7.1
$6,000 to $6,999.........................	5.1	5.5	6.3	4.5	3.9
$7,000 to $7,999.........................	3.5	4.1	4.6	3.3	1.4
$8,000 to $8,999.........................	3.2	3.7	4.4	2.8	1.4
$9,000 to $9,999.........................	1.7	2.1	1.6	2.8	0.3
$10,000 to $11,999.......................	1.7	1.8	1.2	2.7	1.1
$12,000 to $14,999.......................	1.4	1.6	1.0	2.3	0.8
$15,000 to $19,999.......................	0.5	0.5	0.4	0.7	0.3
$20,000 to $24,999.......................	-	-	-	-	-
$25,000 to $49,999.......................	0.1	0.1	-	0.2	-
$50,000 and over.........................	-	-	-	-	-
Median income..................dollars..	2,750	3,019	3,057	2,959	1,885
Mean income....................dollars..	3,414	3,629	3,565	3,710	2,655

SOURCE: U.S. Bureau of the Census. "Persons of Spanish Origin in the United States: March 1976." Current Population Reports, Series P-20, no. 310, 1977. Table 13.

TABLE 7
Mexican Immigrants to the United States (1900-1977)

YEAR	NUMBER	YEAR	NUMBER	YEAR	NUMBER
1900	237	1927	67,721	1953	17,183
1901	347	1928	59,016	1954	30,645
1902	709	1929	40,154	1955	43,702
1903	528	1930	12,703	1956	61,320
1904	1,009	1931	3,333	1957	49,321
1905	2,637	1932	2,171	1958	26,791
1906	1,997	1933	1,936	1959	22,909
1907	1,406	1934	1,801	1960	32,708
1908	6,067	1935	1,560	1961	41,476
1909	16,251	1936	1,716	1962	55,805
1910	18,691	1937	2,347	1963	55,986
1911	19,889	1938	2,502	1964	34,448
1912	23,238	1939	2,640	1965	37,969
1913	11,926	1940	2,313	1966	45,163
1914	14,614	1941	2,824	1967	42,371
1915	12,340	1942	2,378	1968	43,563
1916	18,425	1943	4,172	1969	44,623
1917	17,869	1944	6,598	1970	44,469
1918	18,524	1945	6,702	1971	50,103
1919	29,818	1946	7,146	1972	64,040
1920	52,361	1947	7,558	1973	70,141
1921	30,758	1948	8,384	1974	71,586
1922	19,551	1949	8,083	1975	62,205
1923	63,768	1950	6,744	1976	57,863
1924	89,336	1951	6,153	1977	44,079
1925	32,964	1952	9,079		
1926	43,316				

SOURCE: The statistics from 1900 to 1964 are from Bureau of the Census, *Historical Statistics of the United States*, Washington, D.C., 1976. The statistics from 1965 to 1977 are from the Immigration and Naturalization Service, *Annual Report* for those years. Immigration data to 1907 refer only to seaport arrivals.

TABLE 8
Deportable Aliens Found

YEAR	MEXICAN	OTHER	TOTAL
1968	151,705	60,352	212,057
1969	201,636	81,921	283,557
1970	277,377	67,976	345,353
1971	348,178	71,948	420,126
1972	430,213	75,736	505,949
1973	576,823	79,145	655,968
1974	709,959	78,186	788,145
1975	680,392	86,208	766,600
1976	781,474	94,441	875,915
1977	954,778	87,437	1,042,215
1978	976,667	81,310	1,057,977
1979	998,830	77,588	1,076,418

SOURCE: *Annual Reports*, U.S. Immigration and Naturalization Service.

APPENDIX G
FIGURES

FIGURE 1.
Distribution of Workers by Type of Work, 1976

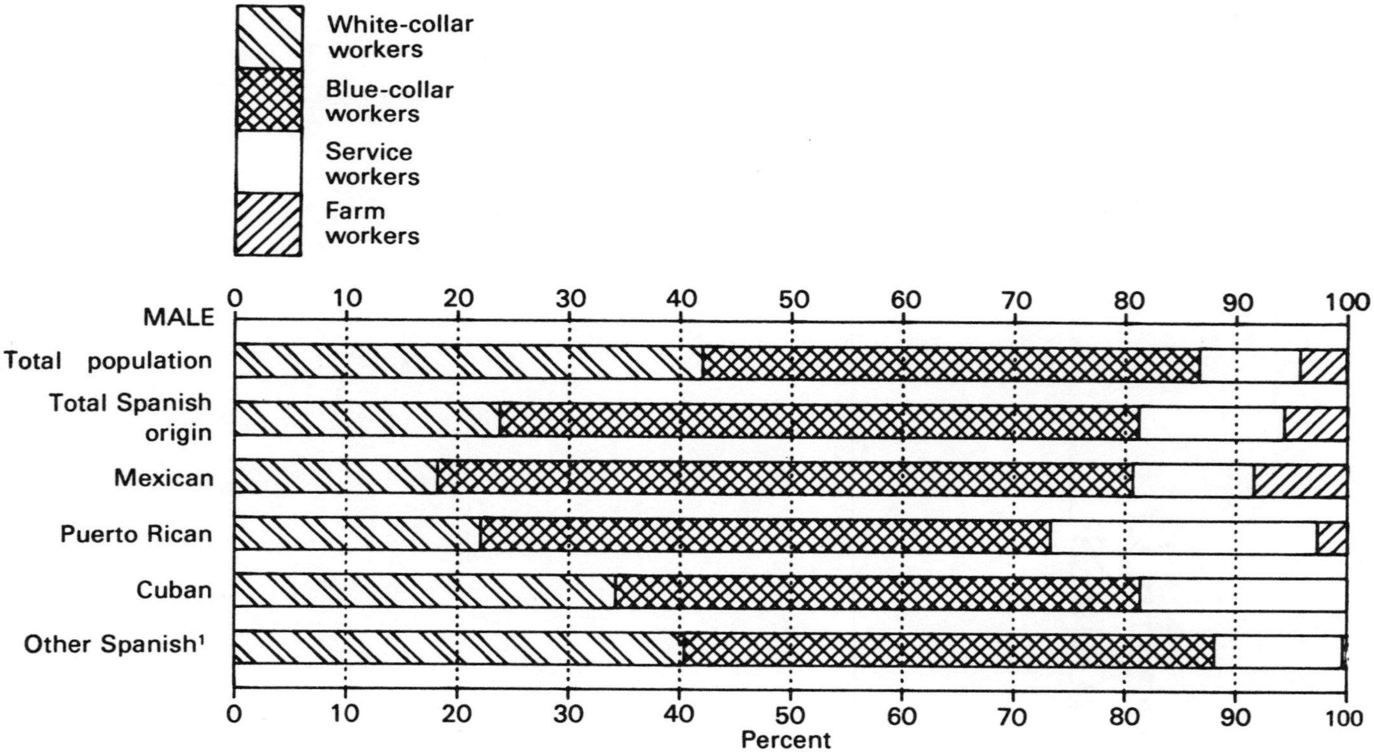

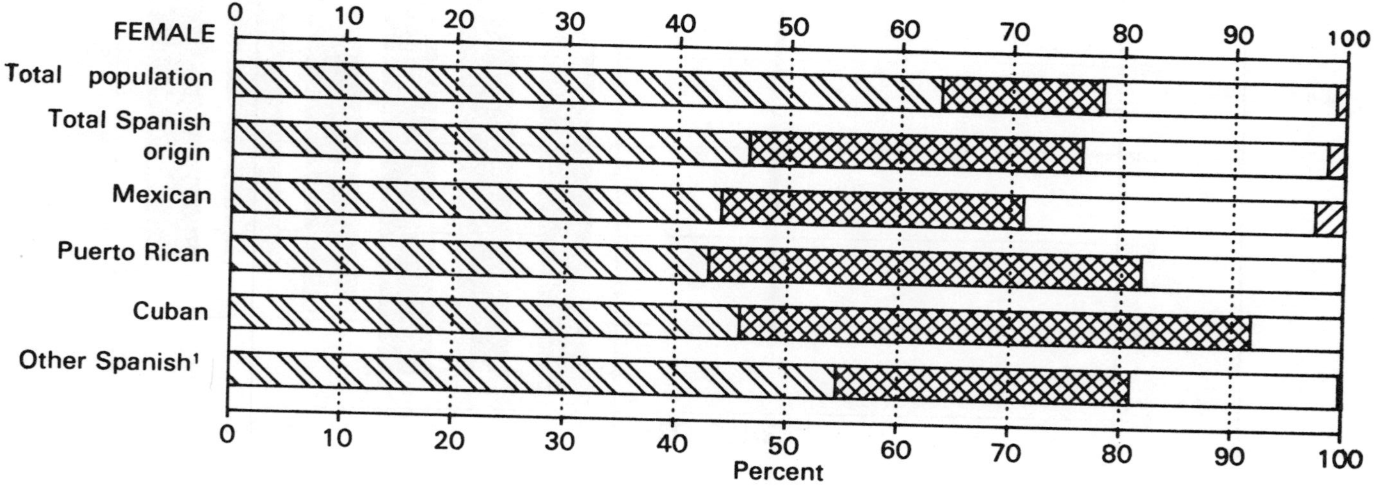

SOURCE: U.S. Bureau of the Census. "Persons of Spanish Origin in the United States: March 1976." *Current Population Reports*, Series P-20, no. 310, 1977. Figure 6.

FIGURE 2
Deportable Aliens

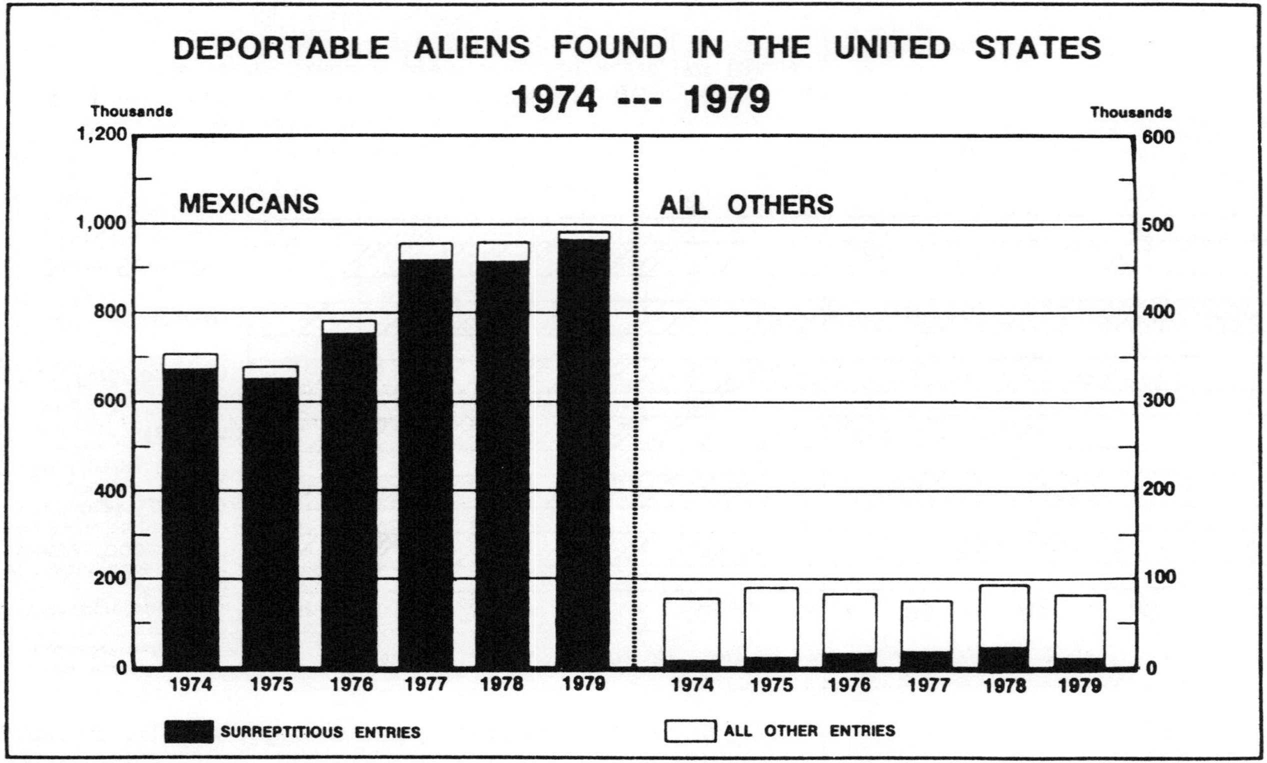

SOURCE: Immigration and Naturalization Service, *1979 Annual Report*, p. 3.

FIGURE 3
Principal Activities of Immigration Border Patrol Years (1970-1979*)

Activities and accomplishments	1970	1971	1972	1973	1974	1975	1976	TQ 1976	1977	1978	1979
Persons apprehended.	233,862	305,902	373,896	503,936	640,913	602,249	701,558	176,579	820,412	870,640	896,929
Deportable aliens located	231,116	302,517	369,495	498,123	634,777	596,796	696,039	175,150	812,541	862,217	888,729
Mexican aliens.	219,254	290,152	355,099	480,588	616,630	579,448	678,356	169,774	792,613	841,525	866,761
Working in agriculture	53,674	74,423	84,084	101,220	111,289	116,250	116,197	24,063	103,300	96,297	102,817
Working in trades, crafts, and industry	13,625	15,895	21,217	24,996	26,555	24,413	24,043	4,958	24,393	30,989	30,879
Others.	151,955	199,834	249,798	354,372	478,786	438,785	538,116	140,753	664,920	714,239	733,065
Canadian aliens. . . .	7,786	7,512	8,245	8,669	7,392	7,253	5,929	2,161	5,759	6,534	5,722
All others	4,076	4,853	6,151	8,866	10,755	10,095	11,754	3,215	14,169	14,158	16,246
Smugglers of aliens located	3,298	3,814	4,564	6,355	8,074	6,860	9,600	2,478	12,405	13,306	15,280
Aliens smuggled into the United States. . .	18,747	19,765	24,918	41,589	83,114	90,385	82,910	22,577	138,805	159,191	172,688
Aliens located who were previously expelled	67,440	90,402	115,758	152,441	182,351	184,610	186,861	42,925	241,108	266,808	259,147

SOURCE: U.S. Department of Justice, *1979 Annual Report of the Immigration and Naturalization Service*, Table 1, p. 15.

*1970-1976 years end June 30.
1977-1979 years end September 30.

FIGURE 3 (continued)
Principal Activities of Immigration Border Patrol Years (1970-1979*)

Activities and accomplishments	1970	1971	1972	1973	1974	1975	1976	TQ 1976	1977	1978	1979
Aliens with previous criminal records located	3,764	4,220	4,379	11,190	10,902	10,308	13,110	2,755	12,333	11,907	12,449
Conveyances examined	1,791,932	2,024,382	2,473,433	2,665,728	2,905,091	3,469,895	3,277,302	1,020,437	3,676,959	3,657,760	4,029,717
Trains	30,533	39,124	45,146	50,696	46,984	37,783	41,322	11,453	44,657	49,707	56,139
Automobiles	1,311,173	1,507,857	1,892,757	2,020,228	2,230,318	2,663,239	2,440,005	771,291	2,647,337	2,569,925	2,790,760
Buses	172,911	173,132	167,522	173,731	156,712	133,524	128,130	32,384	126,498	119,525	126,256
Boats	15,576	13,768	12,550	11,958	9,887	8,212	7,179	3,358	5,547	8,272	8,076
Other conveyances	261,739	290,501	355,458	409,115	461,190	627,137	660,666	201,951	851,920	910,331	1,048,486
Persons questioned	6,805,260	7,663,759	9,023,631	9,506,719	10,201,915	11,265,421	10,782,761	3,278,056	11,605,507	11,343,451	11,899,583
On trains	44,688	66,519	76,246	89,243	89,711	71,544	218,729	20,106	89,313	118,923	103,405
In automobiles	3,415,921	4,029,243	4,855,487	5,134,971	5,590,959	6,887,865	6,144,505	1,989,685	6,844,121	6,642,924	6,841,247
In buses	997,324	1,070,739	1,208,486	1,137,808	1,164,537	1,040,427	907,859	272,870	928,303	921,421	988,686
On boats	34,109	33,979	30,414	29,906	25,965	22,710	19,803	9,375	15,842	22,435	20,894
On other conveyances	652,651	711,211	871,073	969,526	1,087,626	1,187,192	1,198,548	404,715	1,395,325	1,451,439	1,631,841
Pedestrians	1,660,567	1,752,068	1,981,925	2,145,265	2,243,117	2,055,688	2,293,317	581,305	2,332,603	2,186,309	2,313,510
Seizures:											
Automobiles and trucks	263	410	699	1,228	1,014	880	672	193	698	535	399
Airplanes	7	5	—	2	6	2	—	—	2	1	—
Other conveyances	50	8	10	20	21	35	29	4	36	28	22
Value of seizures	$4,547,371	$6,153,227	$12,961,440	$25,953,970	$47,210,261	$28,654,414	$18,019,213	$5,311,621	$19,557,845	$8,348,181	$9,967,197
Narcotics	3,864,903	5,379,189	11,708,554	23,464,030	45,056,331	26,301,857	16,035,162	4,727,826	17,071,475	6,251,346	8,448,233
Other	682,468	774,038	1,252,886	2,489,940	2,153,930	2,352,557	1,984,051	583,795	2,486,370	2,096,835	1,518,964

APPENDIX H
MAPS

MAP 1: Northern Mexico and Adjacent United States, 1824-1836

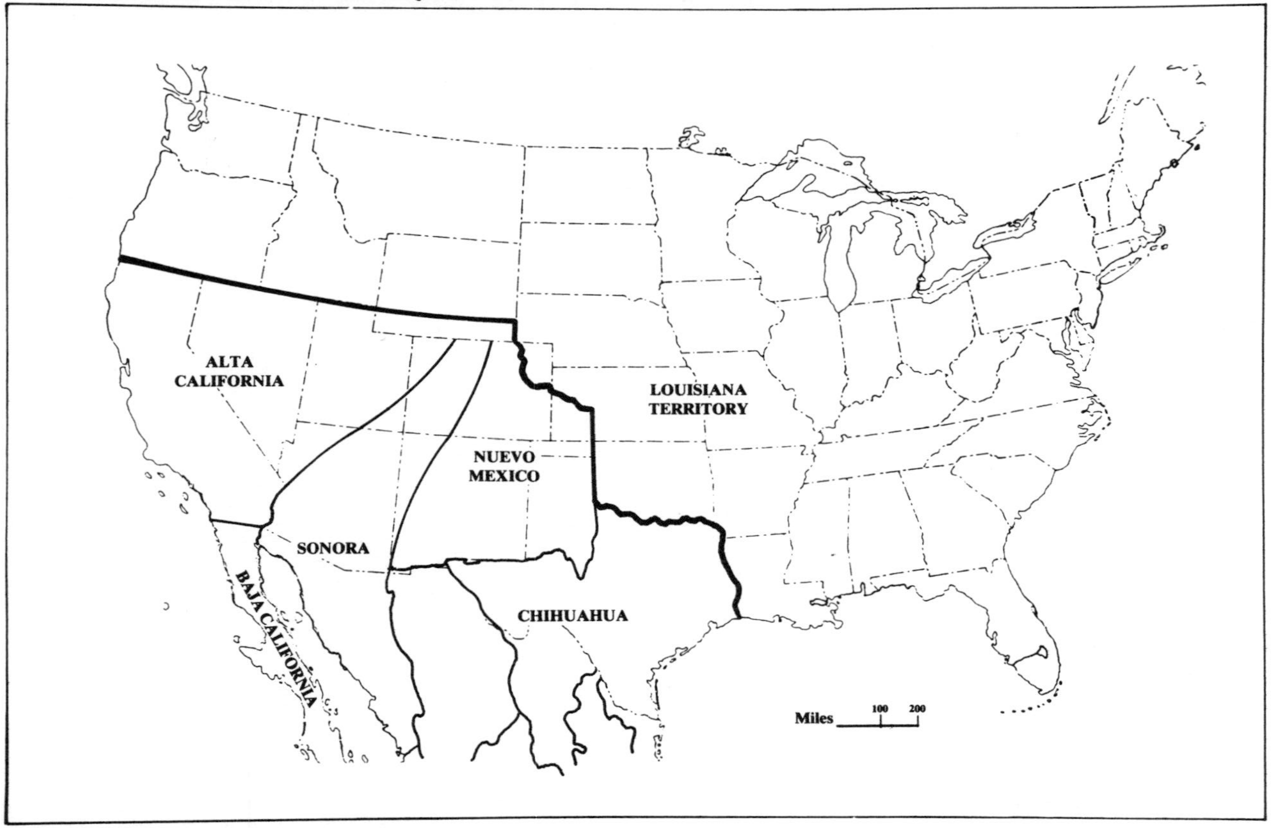

MAP 2: Texas Claims and Mexican War Results

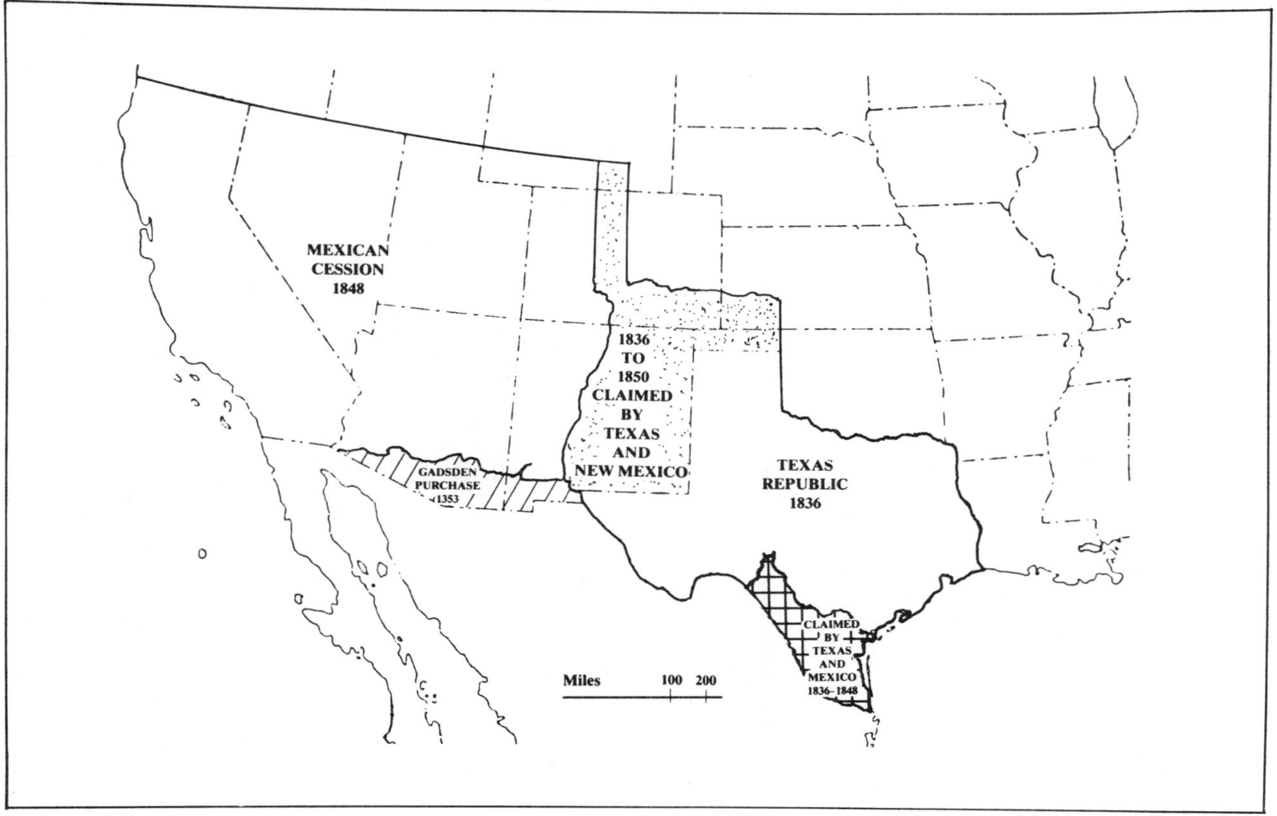

MAP 3: States and Territories formed Partly or Entirely from the Mexican Cession

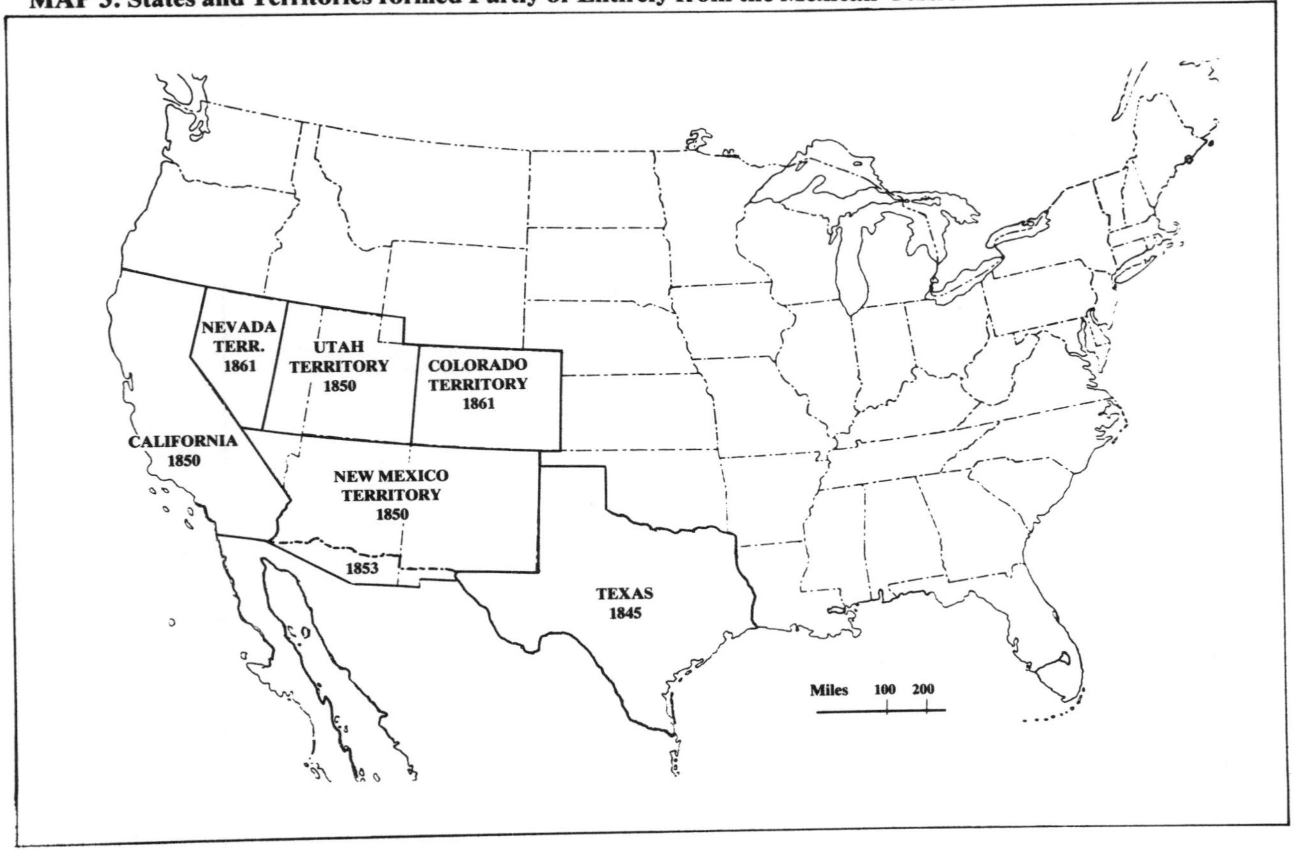

MAP 4: Distribution of Spanish-Speaking Americans, 1970 in about 1983

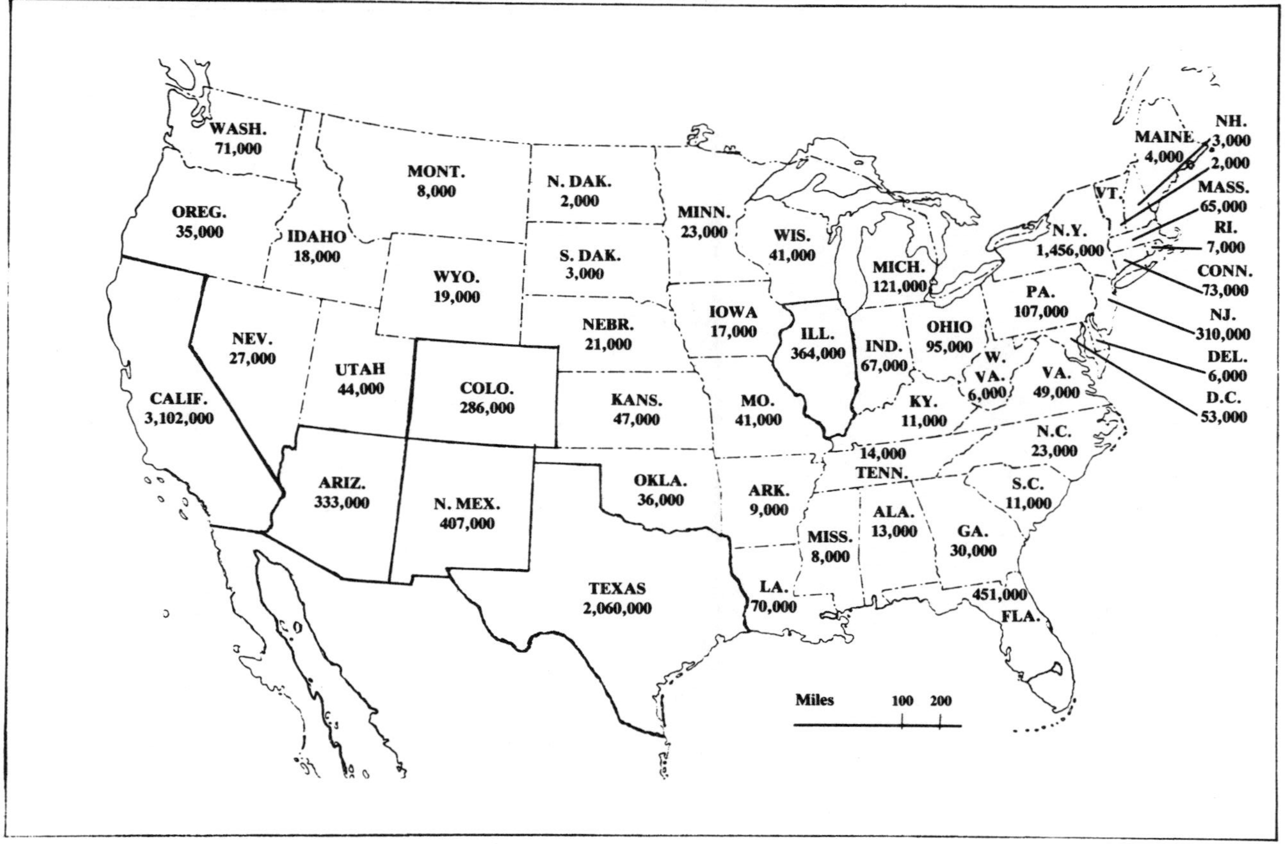

MAP 5: Spanish Origin Population, 1980 Provisional

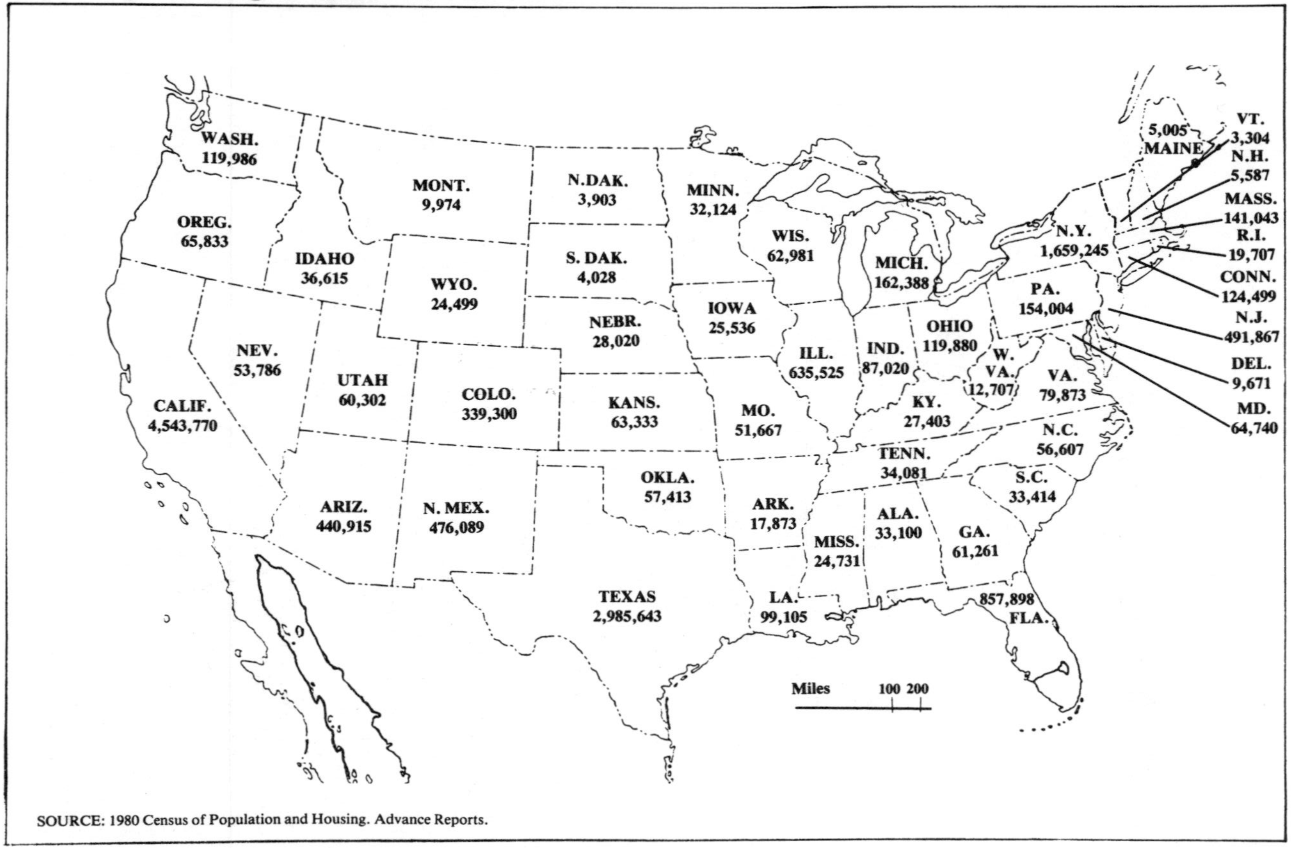

SOURCE: 1980 Census of Population and Housing. Advance Reports.

INDEX

Page numbers set in **bold face** indicate the location of the main entry.

X